W9-BMJ-585

MASTER
VISUALLY®

by Tom Bunzel

Visual®

Microsoft®
Office 2007

Wiley Publishing, Inc.

Master VISUALLY® Microsoft® Office 2007

Published by
Wiley Publishing, Inc.
111 River Street
Hoboken, NJ 07030-5774

Published simultaneously in Canada

Library of Congress Control Number: 2007933270

ISBN: 978-0-470-13547-1

Manufactured in the United States of America

10 9 8 7 6 5 4 3 2 1

FOR PURPOSES OF ILLUSTRATING THE CONCEPTS AND TECHNIQUES DESCRIBED IN THIS BOOK, THE AUTHOR HAS CREATED VARIOUS NAMES, COMPANY NAMES, MAILING, E-MAIL AND INTERNET ADDRESSES, PHONE AND FAX NUMBERS AND SIMILAR INFORMATION, ALL OF WHICH ARE FICTITIOUS. ANY RESEMBLANCE OF THESE FICTITIOUS NAMES, ADDRESSES, PHONE AND FAX NUMBERS AND SIMILAR INFORMATION TO ANY ACTUAL PERSON, COMPANY AND/OR ORGANIZATION IS UNINTENTIONAL AND PURELY COINCIDENTAL.

Contact Us

For general information on our other products and services, please contact our Customer Care Department within the U.S. at 800-762-2974, outside the U.S. at 317-572-3993, or fax 317-572-4002.

For technical support, please visit www.wiley.com/techsupport.

Trademark Acknowledgments

BICENTENNIAL
1807
WILEY
2007
BICENTENNIAL

Wiley Publishing, Inc.

U.S. Sales

Contact Wiley
at (800) 762-2974 or
fax (317) 572-4002.

Praise for Visual Books...

"If you have to see it to believe it, this is the book for you!"

—PC World

"A master tutorial/reference — from the leaders in visual learning!"

—Infoworld

"A publishing concept whose time has come!"

—The Globe and Mail

"Just wanted to say THANK YOU to your company for providing books which make learning fast, easy, and exciting! I learn visually so your books have helped me greatly — from Windows instruction to Web development. Best wishes for continued success."

—Angela J. Barker (Springfield, MO)

"I have over the last 10–15 years purchased thousands of dollars worth of computer books but find your books the most easily read, best set out, and most helpful and easily understood books on software and computers I have ever read. Please keep up the good work."

—John Gatt (Adamstown Heights, Australia)

"You're marvelous! I am greatly in your debt."

—Patrick Baird (Lacey, WA)

"I am an avid fan of your Visual books. If I need to learn anything, I just buy one of your books and learn the topic in no time. Wonders! I have even trained my friends to give me Visual books as gifts."

—Illona Bergstrom (Aventura, FL)

"I have quite a few of your Visual books and have been very pleased with all of them. I love the way the lessons are presented!"

—Mary Jane Newman (Yorba Linda, CA)

"Like a lot of other people, I understand things best when I see them visually. Your books really make learning easy and life more fun."

—John T. Frey (Cadillac, MI)

"Your Visual books have been a great help to me. I now have a number of your books and they are all great. My friends always ask to borrow my Visual books — trouble is, I always have to ask for them back!"

—John Robson
(Brampton, Ontario, Canada)

"I write to extend my thanks and appreciation for your books. They are clear, easy to follow, and straight to the point. Keep up the good work! I bought several of your books and they are just right! No regrets! I will always buy your books because they are the best."

—Seward Kollie (Dakar, Senegal)

"What fantastic teaching books you have produced! Congratulations to you and your staff."

—Bruno Tonon (Melbourne, Australia)

"Thank you for the wonderful books you produce. It wasn't until I was an adult that I discovered how I learn — visually. Although a few publishers claim to present the materially visually, nothing compares to Visual books. I love the simple layout. Everything is easy to follow. I can just grab a book and use it at my computer, lesson by lesson. And I understand the material! You really know the way I think and learn. Thanks so much!"

—Stacey Han (Avondale, AZ)

"The Greatest. This whole series is the best computer-learning tool of any kind I've ever seen."

—Joe Orr (Brooklyn, NY)

Credits

Project Editor
Sarah Hellert

Acquisitions Editor
Jody Lefevere

Copy Editor
Marylouise Wiack

Technical Editor
Diane Koers

Editorial Manager
Robyn Siesky

Business Manager
Amy Knies

Sr. Marketing Manager
Sandy Smith

Editorial Assistant
Laura Sinise

Special Help
Barbara Moore

Manufacturing
Allan Conley
Linda Cook
Paul Gilchrist
Jennifer Guynn

Book Design
Kathie Rickard

Project Coordinator
Erin Smith

Layout and Graphics
Carrie Foster
Cheryl Grubbs
Joyce Haughey
Jennifer Mayberry
Melanee Prendergast
Amanda Spagnuolo

Screen Artist
Jill A. Proll

Proofreader
Toni Settle

Quality Control
Todd Lothery

Indexer
Broccoli Information Management

Wiley Bicentennial Logo
Richard J. Pacifico

Vice President and Executive Group Publisher
Richard Swadley

Vice President and Publisher
Barry Pruett

Composition Director
Debbie Stailey

About the Author

Tom Bunzel specializes in knowing how to make technology work. He has appeared on Tech TV's *Call for Help* and has been a featured speaker at InfoComm and PowerPoint LIVE, as well as working as a technology coach for corporations including Iomega and the Neuroscience Education Institute. He has taught West Los Angeles College Extension classes as well as privately around Southern California, and he does presentation and video consulting in Southern California.

Tom Bunzel has written a number of books on digital media and PowerPoint. He was a contributing editor to *Presentations* magazine and writes a weekly column for the Microsoft Office Reference Guide at InformIT.com.

He can be reached through his Web site, www.professorppt.com.

Author's Acknowledgments

This book is dedicated to my mother and father.

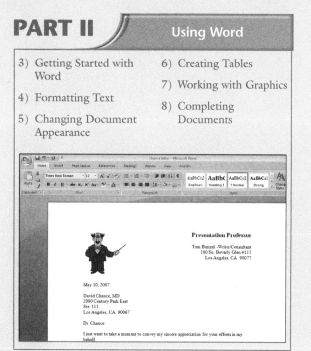
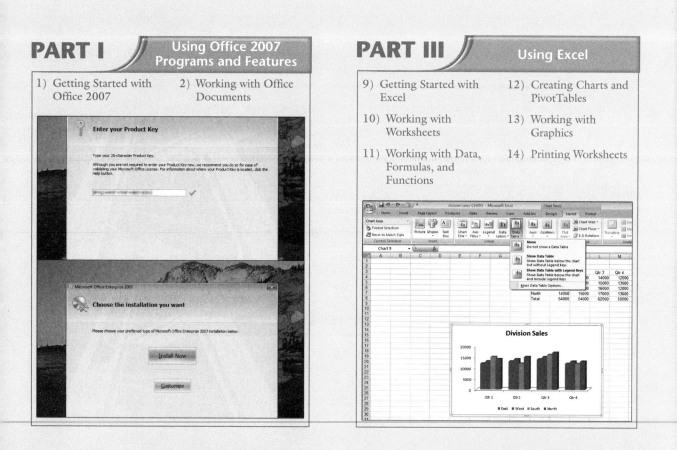
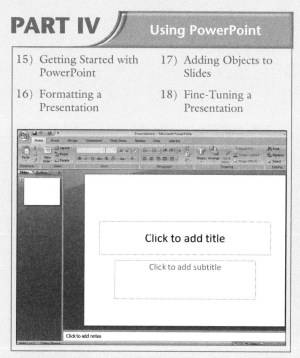

WHAT'S INSIDE

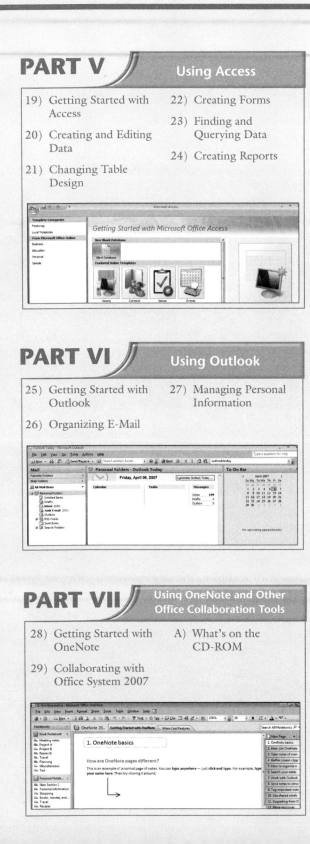

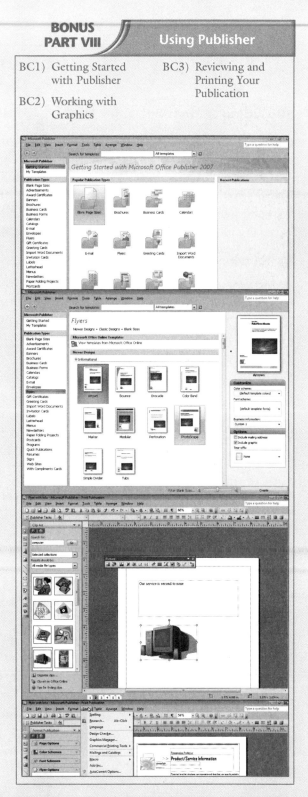

PART I

Using Office 2007 Programs and Features

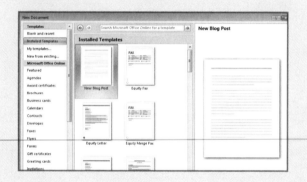

PART II

Using Word

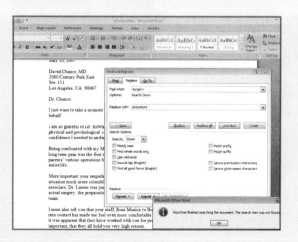

TABLE OF CONTENTS

4 Formatting Text

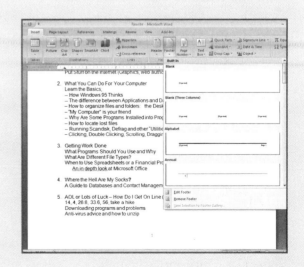

5 Changing Document Appearance

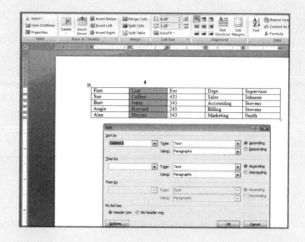

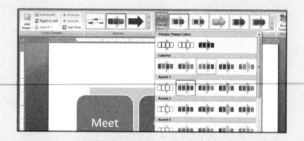

TABLE OF CONTENTS

PART III   Using Excel

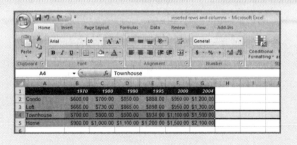

11 Working with Data, Formulas, and Functions

12 Creating Charts and PivotTables

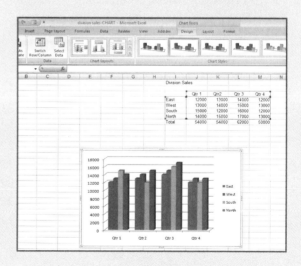

TABLE OF CONTENTS

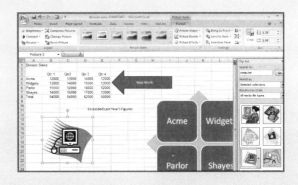

PART IV — Using PowerPoint

16 Formatting a Presentation

17 Adding Objects to Slides

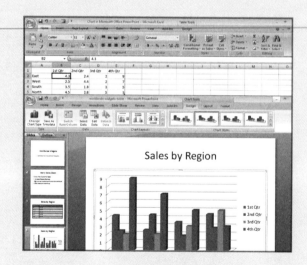

18 Fine-Tuning a Presentation

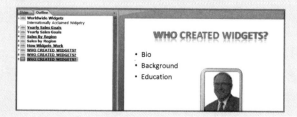

TABLE OF CONTENTS

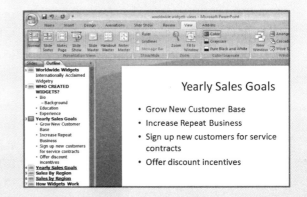

PART V — Using Access

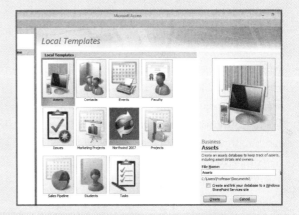

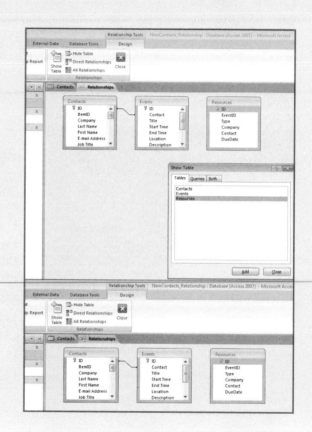

21 Changing Table Design

22 Creating Forms

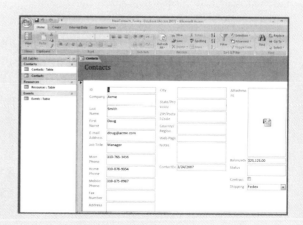

TABLE OF CONTENTS

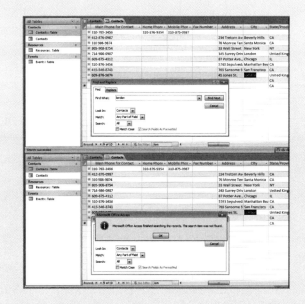

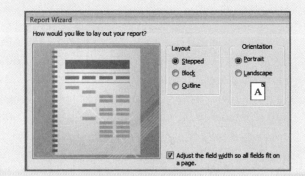

PART VI   Using Outlook

PART VII Using OneNote and Other Office Collaboration Tools

TABLE OF CONTENTS

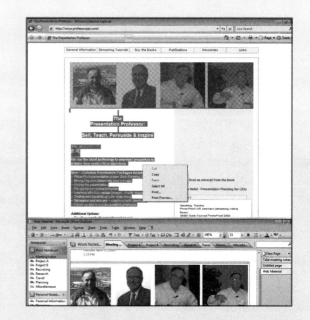

29 Collaborating with Office System 2007

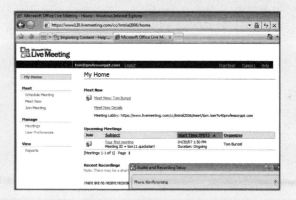

A What's on the CD-ROM

BONUS PART VIII

Using Publisher

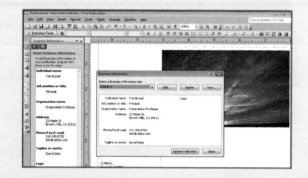

TABLE OF CONTENTS

How to Use this Master VISUALLY Book

Do you look at the pictures in a book or newspaper before anything else on a page? Would you rather see an image than read how to do something? Search no further. This book is for you. Opening *Master VISUALLY Microsoft Office 2007* allows you to read less and learn more about the Office 2007 suite of programs.

Who Needs This Book

This book is for a reader who has never used this particular technology or software application. It is also for more computer-literate individuals who want to expand their knowledge of the different features that the Office 2007 suite offers.

Book Organization

Master VISUALLY Microsoft Office 2007 has 29 chapters and is divided into seven parts.

Part I, "Using Office 2007 Programs and Features," covers the installation and diagnostics of the Office 2007 suite. This part also deals with the common features of the various programs in terms of working with documents and templates, and saving in different versions. It also covers the search features of the Vista operating system.

Part II, "Using Word," covers the basics of the suite's word-processing program, Microsoft Word. You will learn about entering and formatting text, creating tables, including graphics, diagrams, and pictures, and using the other features of the Ribbon. Part II also covers the features related to completing documents, working with reviewers, comparing multiple versions, creating a document with mail merge, and printing your document.

Part III, "Using Excel," covers the basics of working with a spreadsheet and data list in Excel. You will learn how to format and revise your worksheets, add and move columns and rows, and make the spreadsheet print correctly. You will also work with data, formulas, and functions to perform calculations in your worksheet and refer to cells in your formulas and functions. You will use Excel's charting tools to create charts and PivotTable charts, and enhance their appearance with the Excel galleries and effects features.

Part IV, "Using PowerPoint," covers the presentation program of the Office suite. You will learn how to create a slide show from a template or blank presentation, and add titles, bullets, and layouts to your slides. You will also learn how to format and design your slides by adding clip art, pictures, SmartArt graphics, and WordArt styles. You will see how to animate the

entrance, exit, and emphasis of slide objects. The main elements of fine-tuning and presenting a slide show will be covered, including printing your slides, handouts, and notes pages for distribution.

Part V, "Using Access," covers the creation, revision, and management of a database file in Microsoft Office. You will learn how to create a database from a blank file or a template, and how to add the essential elements: tables to hold your data; forms for data entry; queries to filter, sort, and locate data; and reports that can be printed or distributed electronically. You will also learn how to alternate between design and display mode, and how to add fields and records as well as format the various elements of your database objects.

Part VI, "Using Outlook," covers the communications features of the Office suite. You will learn how to manage, send, and receive e-mail, as well as organize e-mail into various folders. The essentials of handling spam and subscribing to RSS feeds are also covered. The Calendar feature of Outlook is covered, as well as maintaining a contact list, working with tasks, and keeping sticky notes.

Part VII, "Using OneNote and Other Office Collaboration Tools," covers the essentials of keeping notes in an organized notebook, noting Web pages, and using tags and other organizational tools in OneNote. The essentials of a shared notes session are covered, along with other collaboration tools, including Live Meeting, using a SharePoint workspace, and an introduction to Microsoft Groove and Vista Meeting Space, all of which are methods for collaborating on and sharing your Office documents.

The CD-ROM that accompanies this book includes a bonus part, "Using Publisher." This part covers the creation of publications from the various Publisher templates, along with moving through a document and making revisions. Publications include graphics, and so this section shows you how to insert clip art and pictures and wrap text around them. It also covers the Design Gallery, Content Library, and Design Checker, as well as features that help you review and print your publications.

Chapter Organization

This book consists of tasks, all of which are listed in the book's table of contents. A *task* is a set of steps that show you how to complete a specific computer task.

Each task usually appears on two facing pages. It has an introduction to the topic, a set of full-color screen shots and steps that guide you through the task, and a tips section. This format allows you to quickly look at a topic of interest and learn it instantly.

Chapters group together three or more tasks with a common theme. A chapter may also contain pages that give you the background information needed to understand the tasks in the chapter.

What You Need to Use This Book

To use this book, you will need at least the basic version of the Microsoft Office 2007 suite. The hardware and software requirements for the suite are as follows:

- Computer and processor: 500 megahertz (MHz) processor or higher
- Memory: 256 megabytes (MB) RAM or higher
- Hard drive: 1.5 gigabytes (GB); a portion of this drive space will be freed after installation if you remove the original download package from the hard drive.
- Drive: CD-ROM or DVD drive
- Display: 1024×768 or higher resolution monitor
- Operating System: Microsoft Windows Vista; Microsoft Windows XP with Service Pack (SP) 2, Windows Server 2003 with SP1; or later operating system.

Using the mouse

This book uses the following conventions to describe the actions you perform when using the mouse:

Click

Press your left mouse button once. You generally click your mouse on something to select it on the computer screen.

Double-click

Press your left mouse button twice. Double-clicking something on the computer screen generally opens whatever item you have double-clicked.

Right-click

Press your right mouse button. When you right-click anything on the computer screen, the program displays a shortcut menu containing commands that are specific to the selected item.

Click and drag, and release the mouse

Move your mouse pointer and hover it over an item on the computer screen. Press and hold down the left mouse button. Now, move the mouse to where you want to place the item and then release the button. You use this method to move an item from one area of the computer screen to another.

The Conventions in this Book

A number of typographic and layout styles have been used throughout *Master VISUALLY Microsoft Office 2007* to distinguish different types of information.

Bold

Bold type represents the names of commands and options that you interact with. Bold type also indicates text and numbers that you must type into a dialog box or window.

Italics

Italic words introduce a new term and are followed by a definition.

Numbered Steps

You must perform the instructions in numbered steps in order to successfully complete a task and achieve the final results.

Bulleted Steps

These steps point out various optional features. You do not have to perform these steps; they simply give additional information about a feature.

Indented Text

Indented text tells you what the program does in response to your following a numbered step. For example, if you click a certain menu command, a dialog box may appear, or a window may open. Indented text may also tell you what the final result is when you follow a set of numbered steps.

Notes

Notes give additional information. They may describe special conditions that may occur during an operation. They may warn you of a situation that you want to avoid, such as the loss of data. A note may also cross-reference a related area of the book. A cross-reference may guide you to another chapter, or another section within the current chapter.

Icons and Buttons

Icons and buttons are graphical representations within the text. They show you exactly what you need to click to perform a step.

 You can easily identify the tips in any section by looking for the Master It icon. Master It sections offer additional information, including tips, hints, and tricks. You can use the Master It information to go beyond what you have learn learned in the steps.

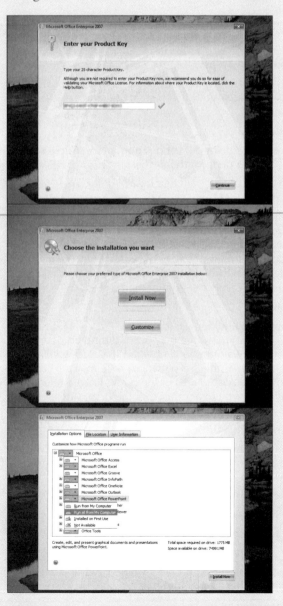

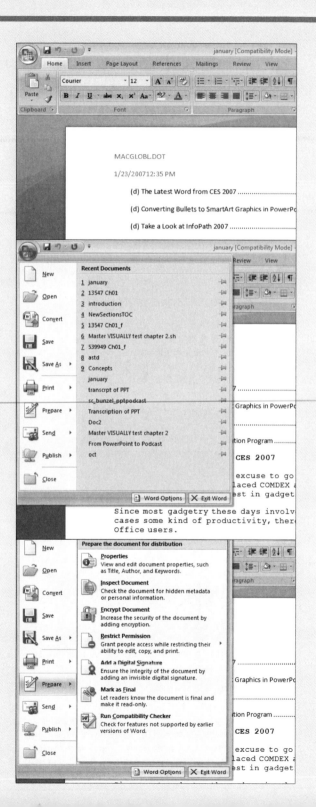

2 Working with Office Documents

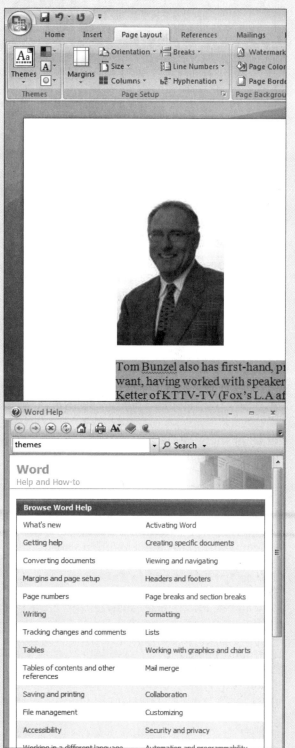

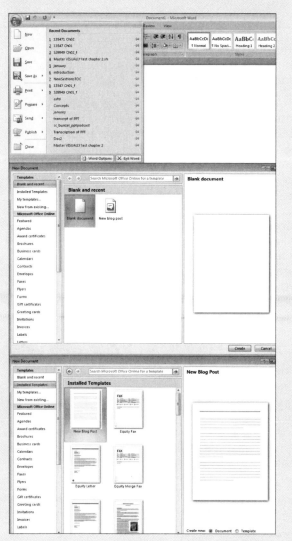

An Introduction to Microsoft Office 2007

Microsoft Office 2007 is a software suite, or collection of programs. Purchasing a software suite is less expensive than buying each program individually. Different Office 2007 versions contain various combinations of programs; some of the programs in this book may not be available in your suite.

Office 2007 is available at computer and electronic superstores. The programs come on a set of discs, and so you need a DVD drive to install them, unless you purchase a license and download the files from Microsoft. If you already have a version of Office, but want to upgrade, you can do so. Some new computers come with Office 2007 as part of the computer package. If you work in a large company, some or all of the programs may already be on your computer.

The main Office 2007 programs share a common appearance and work in a similar way; the revised interface makes these programs simpler to use. Part I covers features and aspects that are common to all Office 2007 programs.

Create Documents in Word

Microsoft Word is a word-processing program that lets you create documents such as letters, reports, manuals, and newsletters. You can edit text, rearrange paragraphs, and check for spelling errors. Word also has many formatting features that allow you to change the appearance of a document. For example, you can apply various fonts, align text, and add page numbers. You can also enhance a document by adding a graphic or creating a table.

For all of these formatting options, you can take advantage of galleries that preview how formatting will look before you apply it. If you want, you can also take advantage of reference features that enable you to generate a table of contents, index, footnotes, endnotes, and citations, as well as to apply various style guides. You can learn more about Word in Part II.

Create Spreadsheets in Excel

Microsoft Excel is a spreadsheet program that you can use to organize, analyze, and attractively present calculations and data, such as a budget or sales report. It allows you to enter and edit information efficiently in a worksheet. You can enhance the appearance of a worksheet by formatting numbers, changing the color of cells, and adding graphics. You can use formulas and functions to calculate and analyze the data, including specialized functions for engineering and statistical analysis.

Conditional formats allow you to analyze data visually so that important information stands out and trends can be instantly spotted. Excel's chart tools provide a means to represent data in many different ways, from standard bar and pie charts to more exotic scatter and area charts. You can learn more about Excel in Part III.

Create Presentations in PowerPoint

Microsoft PowerPoint is a program that helps you plan, organize, and design professional presentations. You can use the features in PowerPoint to edit and organize text, and to add objects to the slides, including shapes, pictures, charts, and tables. You can use your computer screen, 35mm slides, or overhead transparencies to deliver a presentation.

PowerPoint comes with many pre-set templates that can make your presentation look more professional, with coordinated colors, fonts, and graphics. In addition, PowerPoint themes and special effects enable you to create diagrams and other visuals that would otherwise require third-party graphics programs.

PowerPoint animation features let you present your information in stages, so that it is easier for an audience to absorb more complex ideas. You can learn more about PowerPoint in Part IV.

Create Databases in Access
Microsoft Access is a database program that allows you to store and manage large collections of information. You can use a database to store your personal information, such as addresses, music collections, and recipes. Companies often use a database to store information such as client orders, expenses, inventory, and payroll.

An Access database consists of several components that provide different ways to work with the data; these include tables, forms, queries, and reports. Access comes with a collection of pre-set database templates that you can use to learn more about the program and later revise for your own applications.

Besides just storing important information in a systematic way, Access uses queries that allow you to analyze your information according to your own needs or to connect to external data sources. Forms created in Access enable you to enter data into tables quickly, and even post forms and tables online to let others view or work with large amounts of information. You can learn about Access in Part V.

Manage Information in Outlook
Microsoft Outlook is a program that helps you manage your e-mail messages, appointments, contacts, tasks, and notes. You can send, receive, print, save, and handle e-mail messages, as well as attach and send files to other recipients. In addition to e-mail, Outlook includes a Calendar for keeping track of your appointments, Contacts for storing information about the people who you communicate with, Tasks for keeping a To-Do List, and Notes to create on-screen reminders, similar to paper sticky notes.

You can plan your workday, week, month, or year by entering appointments and longer events into the Calendar and seeing all of your time-sensitive items in an organized page called Outlook Today, or the To-Do Bar.

Outlook's many options let you configure and view your most important information in a variety of ways. You can also view subscription Web pages in an RSS panel in the Mail area; this allows you to import information into Outlook instead of going online with your Web browser.

Contacts can be organized into various categories and views to allow you to keep in touch with clients, prospects, or other people, as well as to keep track of their important information. You can learn more about Outlook in Part VI.

Collaborate with OneNote and Other Tools
The Office system can help you stay organized and collaborate with others. OneNote is an electronic loose-leaf notebook with tabs and intuitive search tools that lets you save and retrieve important information, including text, graphics, and Web links.

OneNote's integration with Outlook and Internet Explorer allows you to keep track of online information and to send it directly to your colleagues or associates. The pre-set tabs for sections and pages allow you to begin organizing your notebook as soon as you open OneNote. You can learn more about OneNote in Part VII.

Besides OneNote, other Office-related products, such as SharePoint Services, Groove, Live Meeting, and Vista's Meeting Space can enable you to share documents with others and to conduct online meetings to be more productive. You can learn more about collaboration features in Part VII.

Create Graphical Documents with Publisher (Bonus Chapters)
Microsoft Publisher is a desktop publishing program that designs and creates newsletters, birthday or holiday cards, or anything that requires a pleasing combination of text and art. If you have more complex layout needs, then Publisher is a better program than Word for building professional-looking documents. Publisher is discussed on the book's CD-ROM.

Install
Office 2007

Because the Microsoft Office Suite has various components depending upon the version that you purchase or license, installing the product can be time consuming. Office also requires a large amount of hard drive space. You should spend some time in advance thinking about which Office 2007 programs and which specific features you want to install, based on the type of work that you generally do.

If you install a *default* installation using the Install Now option without customizing your options, there is also the possibility that certain features or programs will remain uninstalled, requiring you to add them later on, if necessary.

You can avoid this by doing the following: installing the full version through the Customize option; opening the specific program option boxes to check the various individual program features; and choosing the Run All from My Computer option for each Office program.

If you use the Install Now option, you may conserve drive space on a hard drive. However, in the future, some Office features, such as file converters, may be uninstalled by the default installation, and you will need your Office disc to add those items.

Install Office 2007

Using Install Now

1 Insert your Office disc to begin installation.

2 Enter your product key.

  ● A check mark appears to confirm the key.

3 Click Continue.

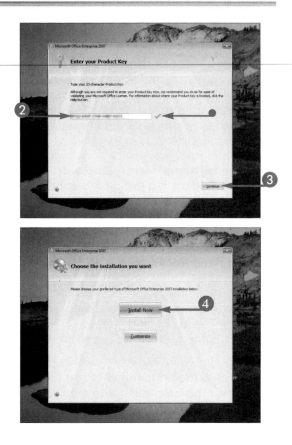

The installation screen appears.

4 Click Install Now for the default installation.

Note: *The default installation may omit some features and require you to reinsert the Office disc again later on if you need the uninstalled features; however, it will use less storage space than customizing and installing all programs and features on your computer.*

Customize your Office installation

① Repeat Steps 1 to 3. In the installation screen that appears, click Customize.

  ● The Installation Options tab uses white boxes to indicate which programs will be fully installed.

  ● Gray boxes indicate programs with partially installed features.

② Click the down arrow to expand a gray box program ([⬛ ▾]).

③ Click Run all from my Computer to install the entire program.

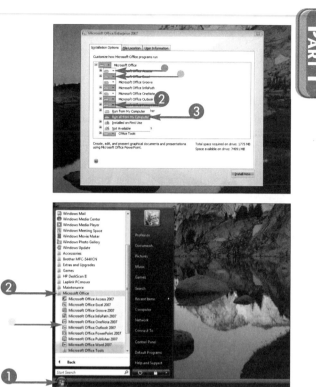

Open the Start menu to locate Office

① Click Start.

② Click Microsoft Office.

  ● The programs that you installed are available to use.

How do I make sure that all of the Office programs completely install?

▼ To install everything, you need to choose the Customize option. At the very top of the Installation Options panel, click the down arrow to expand the main Microsoft Office gray box ([⬛ ▾]) and choose Run All from My Computer for all of Microsoft Office.

How do I use the least amount of drive space when I install Office?

▼ When you open the Installation Options tab, choose any programs that you do not want to install and select Not Available to prevent them from being installed. If you only need the basic features of a program, click the plus sign ([⊞]) to the left of the program name and select only those features that you need. If you are not sure about how much of the program you may want to use when you first install Office, choose Installed on First Use but be prepared to insert your Office disc the first time you use that program.

How do I install Office to a secondary hard drive or other partition?

▼ In the Installation window, choose the File Location tab and browse to the other drive. Before installing to another location, right-click the drive window and create a new Program or Office folder that you can point to when you begin the Office installation. Creating secondary hard drives and partitions is beyond the scope of this book. You can learn more about these features in *Master VISUALLY Windows Vista* (Wiley, 2007).

Add or Remove Office 2007 Features

I f you chose the Install Now option instead of the Customize option when you installed the Microsoft Office Suite, then some features, and even some programs, may not have been installed.

You may also have forgotten to install some features or programs, or chosen not to in order to conserve drive space.

You can always use your Office program disc again to fine-tune or append your installation. When you reinsert your disc, you are given a choice to Repair Office, Remove Office, or Add or Remove Features.

The Repair Office option can help you to solve a few issues that may arise if an Office program is not working properly.

The Remove Office option can allow you to change your license in order to move your programs to another computer.

The Add or Remove Features option enables you to add programs or features that you may have omitted previously, or to conserve drive space by getting rid of Office programs that you never use.

Add or Remove Office 2007 Features

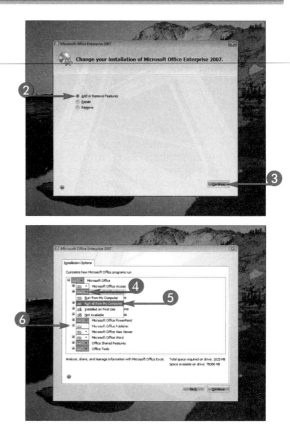

1 Reinsert your Office installation disc.

2 Make sure that the Add or Remove Features option is selected (◎ changes to ◉).

3 Click Continue.

4 Click the down arrow to expand a gray box program ( ) whose features you want to add.

5 Click Run all from My Computer to make sure that those features will be installed.

6 Click the plus sign (⊞) next to any installed programs.

● The program list expands to show additional features, with uninstalled features appearing as gray boxes.

⑦ Click the down arrow to expand an uninstalled feature ( ) that you want to install.

⑧ Click Continue.

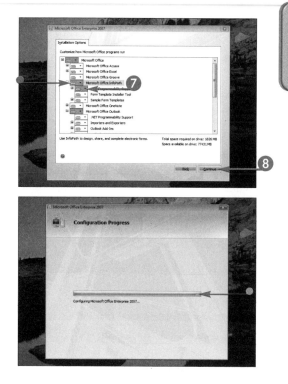

● Your Office installation changes to reflect the additional programs and features that you chose to run from your computer.

Why would Microsoft not enable all features of all of the Office programs to install automatically when I click Install Now?

▼ There are different versions of Office, each with a different set of programs, and some programs come with features that very few users may need. Some users may want to conserve storage space and install only those programs and features that they need. Unfortunately, this means that sometimes a default installation is not sufficient to give a user all of the program features that he expects.

How do I know how much space a program or feature will require, and how much space I have available?

▼ As you modify your installation options, the total amount of drive space required for that installation, and the space available on that drive, appear directly above the Back and Continue buttons.

Why would I need to repair or remove Office?

▼ You would need to repair Office if you notice screens freezing or error messages appearing. The Repair option may fix many of these problems. You would need to remove Office if you want to install your Office programs on another computer. This is because you can only install a single version of Office on one laptop and one desktop.

9

Run Office Diagnostics

Y ou can run Microsoft Office Diagnostics in Microsoft Office 2007 to help you to discover why your computer is *crashing*, or closing abnormally. The diagnostic tests can solve some problems directly and may identify ways that you can solve other problems.

Office Diagnostics gathers and compiles important information from your computer, and stores it on your computer. When Office Diagnostics determines that the data may be useful to help diagnose and fix a

problem, the system asks whether you want to send the information to Microsoft.

After it completes the tests, Office Diagnostics prompts you to visit a Web page to get customized advice, based on the results of the tests. Any information that you share with Microsoft is completely anonymous, and absolutely no information is personally identifiable as being yours. To learn more about information confidentiality, see the help files in a Microsoft Office program.

Run Office Diagnostics

1 Click Start.

2 Click Microsoft Office.

3 Click Microsoft Office Tools.

4 Click Microsoft Office Diagnostics.

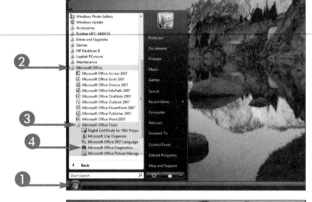

The Microsoft Office Diagnostics Introductory screen opens.

5 Click Continue.

The Start Diagnostics screen appears.

6 Click Run Diagnostics.

● Office Diagnostics runs, fixing problems and pointing you to other solutions.

What do the diagnostic tests do?

▼ Memory Diagnostic checks your computer's random access memory (RAM). Compatibility Diagnostic looks for conflicts in the versions of Office programs installed. Disk Diagnostic checks for problems with your hard drive. Setup Diagnostic seeks out corruption in the files and registry settings. You can also run Update Diagnostics to check whether your computer is up to date with installed free service packs from Microsoft. To enable Update Diagnostics, click the Office button, and then click to open the options for the Office specific program. In the Trust Center, click Advanced Trust Center Settings, and then click Privacy Options. Select the checkbox for Download a file periodically that helps determine system problems. (☐ changes to ☑). Wait about a week to allow the file to be downloaded, and then run Microsoft Office Diagnostics again.

How can Office Diagnostics fix my installation?

▼ In addition to fixing or deleting corrupt files, Office Diagnostics connects to a server and checks for additional fixes and patches that can help your Office installation perform better.

What else can I do to make sure that my installation is up to date and working properly?

▼ Click the Office button in any program that is experiencing problems, and select its specific program options. Click the Resources buttons for other options, such as receiving updates, running diagnostics, or connecting to Microsoft Office Online for additional help and information. For specific error messages and problems, consult the Microsoft Knowledge Base.

Start and Exit a Program

Office allows you to start a program in several ways. You can either start a program using the Start menu or using a shortcut icon. What happens after you start a program depends on which program you select. When you use a program frequently it will also have a shortcut in the Favorites menu, or you can add a program shortcut to the desktop.

In Word, Excel, and PowerPoint, a blank document displays so that you can start creating a document, workbook, or presentation, respectively. In Access, the Getting Started window opens, with options for creating a new database.

When you open Outlook for the first time, you need to set up your e-mail connection. Outlook then opens to Outlook Today and your Personal folders. You can open Outlook from the main Office programs or click the E-mail link in the Favorites panel of the Start menu.

In Publisher, you see a blank area and the task pane. You can select whether to create a new blank database or Web template, open an existing database or Web template, or create or open an existing Publisher document. OneNote opens with a set of tabbed sections with ideas and tips on how to use the program.

Although this task illustrates how to start an Excel document, you can use these steps to start any Office application. For more information on getting started with Word, Excel, PowerPoint, Access, Outlook, and OneNote, see their respective parts. For Publisher, see the book's CD-ROM.

When you finish working in the program, you must save your documents and then exit the program. This frees up system resources.

Start and Exit a Program

① Click Start.

② Click All Programs.

③ Click Microsoft Office.

④ Click the program that you want to start.

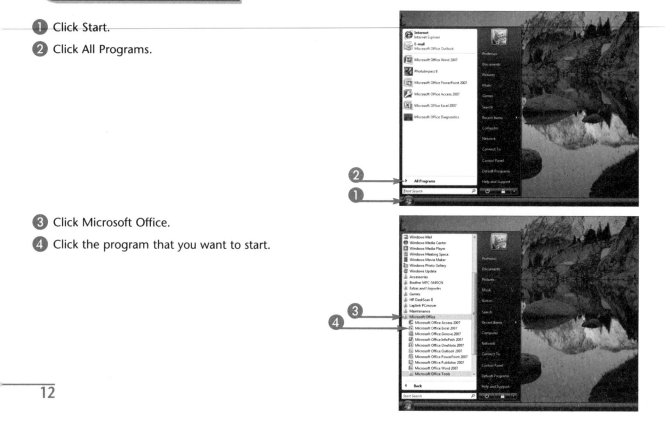

The program window appears, displaying a blank document.

⑤ Click the Office button.

The Office button menu opens.

⑥ Click Close.

● You can also click the Close button (☒) for the program window. If its contents have changed, you are prompted to save the file.

The program closes.

Note: *In Access and Publisher, you have a choice of using a preset template or a blank document. See the task "Create a New Document" in Chapter 2.*

I do not see my programs listed on the All Programs menu. Why not?

▼ If the All Programs menu does not list your programs, then you may not have installed Office, or you may have installed only a few of the Office programs instead of the full suite. See the task "Add or Remove Office 2007 Features" for more information on installing Microsoft Office.

How do I delete a shortcut icon?

▼ To delete a shortcut icon, right-click the icon, select Delete, and then confirm the deletion by clicking Yes. Deleting a shortcut does not delete the program or the document to which the shortcut applies.

Can I speed up the process of opening a program or document?

▼ Yes. The easiest way is to create a shortcut icon by dragging the program name from the Start menu to the desktop. Click Start and then click All Programs. You see a list of all of the Office programs. Click and drag the desired program from the menu to the desktop; Windows automatically creates a shortcut. You can also save documents to the desktop or drag shortcuts from any saved documents to the desktop. When you double-click the document icon or its shortcut, it opens in the appropriate program.

Using the Office Button

Each Microsoft Office program has an Office button in the upper-left corner of the screen that assists you with many common functions.

Using the Office button is the fastest way to save a document under another name, to another location, or in another format. It also provides quick access to print and print preview functions, as well as other tasks that are relevant to the program that you are using.

The Office button also opens a list of the most recent documents that you have created and saved in the program, allowing you to quickly open one or more of these documents without locating them on your computer.

You can use the Office button to convert documents created in older versions of Office to the Office 2007 format, in order to take advantage of the new features of Office 2007. The Office button also lets you finalize or prepare a final version, publish a document online, or send it by e-mail.

① Click the Office button.

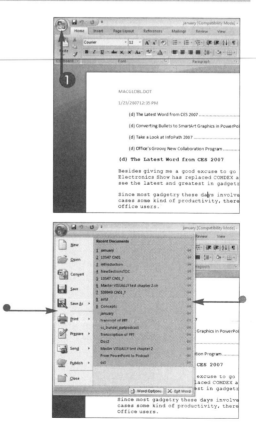

● The program displays options in the left panel.

● The most recent Word documents display in the right panel.

② Move your mouse over the Office buttons that
have right arrow pointers (▶).

● The option expands to reveal other tasks
that you can perform.

● You can move your mouse to reveal other
options.

③ Click within your document to exit the Office
button options and return to your document.

MASTER IT

Why would I need to use Convert?

▼ If you open a document that was created
with a previous version of an Office
program, it is opened in *Compatibility
Mode*, which keeps it in its original version.
To use the features of Office 2007, you
must convert it to the new format. See
the task "Save in Different Versions" in
Chapter 2 for more information.

How do I use the Publish feature?

▼ You can publish to a server used for
document management or SharePoint
services. See Chapter 29 for more
information on these options. For a blog
item, you would need to set up a hosted
blog Web site and enter the username
and password information.

What can I do with the Prepare feature?

▼ The Prepare feature involves routing a
document through a series of reviewers
and finalizing it. In the final format of a
document, you want to remove any
reviewer comments and revise or remove
metadata for Web searches, which you can
do under the Prepare feature. The
metadata also indexes the document so
that it can be located more easily using the
search features of Windows Vista.

How do I use the Document Workspace?

▼ Document Workspaces are part of the
collaboration features of Windows
SharePoint services. SharePoint lets you set
up an online location for meetings and for
working with clients and associates in
other locations, or as part of a team. See
Chapter 29 for more information.

Create a New Document

Microsoft Office allows you to create a new document with the Office button.

Each document is like a separate piece of paper. Creating a new document is similar to placing a new piece of paper on your screen.

When you start most programs, Office displays a blank document based on the default template. A *template* is a pre-designed document, which may include text, formatting, and even content. The default template defines generic page margins, default fonts, and other settings that are appropriate for a typical document. You simply type text to create your new document.

You can also create documents based on other templates by selecting from several common document types. Some templates are installed on your computer as part of Office 2007, while many others are available online. All of them are available through the Office button.

The Office button includes several options for creating new documents. These options vary from program to program. To learn more about the Office button, see Chapter 1.

Create a New Document

Using the default template

1 Click the Office button.

2 Click New.

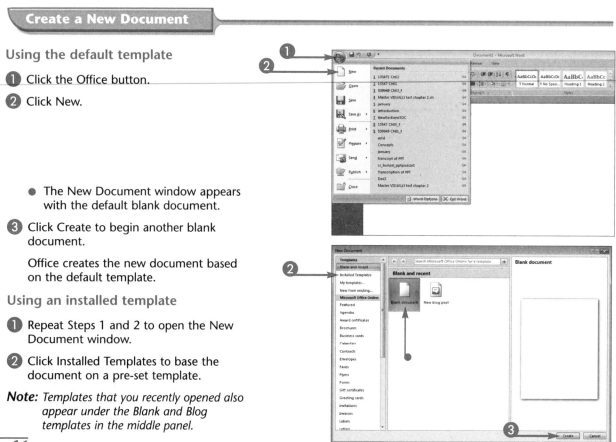

● The New Document window appears with the default blank document.

3 Click Create to begin another blank document.

Office creates the new document based on the default template.

Using an installed template

1 Repeat Steps 1 and 2 to open the New Document window.

2 Click Installed Templates to base the document on a pre-set template.

Note: *Templates that you recently opened also appear under the Blank and Blog templates in the middle panel.*

● Installed templates appear in the middle panel.

③ Select another template on which to base your new document.

● A preview of the document template appears in the right panel.

④ Click Create.

Office creates the new document based on the template that you selected.

Do I have to close a document before I can create a new one?

▼ No. You can have several documents open at the same time, except for Microsoft Access, which can only open one database at a time. But closing a document when you finish working on it frees up system resources.

What is New from Existing?

▼ When you open a document, revise it, and save it, the old version disappears. When you create a new document with New from Existing, the original document is left alone and unchanged. A new document based on it is opened with a generic document name such as Document3. This prevents you from overwriting a file that you may need in the future.

What are My Templates?

▼ My Templates are templates that you have already created and saved as templates. To save your own template, create a document with all of the text and formatting that you want to include. Click the Office button and then click Save As. The Save As dialog box opens. Type a template name, click the Save as type down arrow (▼), and then click Template as the file type. Note that the name of the actual template file type varies, depending on the program. When you save the document as a template, you make this template available in the My Templates folder.

Open a Document

You can open a previously saved document to review and make changes to it. To open a document, you need to know its location — the drive and folder where Office stores the document.

Keep in mind that, by default, documents are stored in your Documents (Vista) or My Documents (Windows XP) folder, unless you choose another location.

Using the Office button, you can access a particular drive and folder in Windows XP, or search by file types and other parameters in Vista. See the task "Using Vista Search Features," later in this chapter.

If a document is in a subfolder, click the main folder to reveal its contents and locate the file that you want. You can create new folders on the desktop for existing projects. Using these desktop folders, you can easily locate files to open for editing, before moving the desktop folders to your main Documents or My Documents folder when the project is complete.

You can open documents in other file formats if you have the proper file converter installed. You simply select the file, and the program converts automatically. If the document does not convert, and a file converter is available but not installed, Office prompts you to insert your Office discs. Follow the on-screen instructions and try opening the file again.

Open a Document

① Click the Office button.

② Click Open.

The Open dialog box appears.

③ Click the Folders up arrow (⌃).

● Your file folders are opened and available.

④ Click the Document folder under your username.

⑤ Click the name of the document that you want to open.

⑥ Click Open.

You can also double-click the filename to open the document.

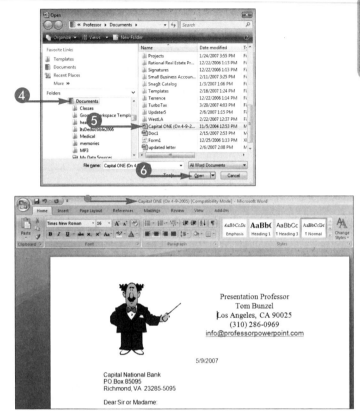

Office displays your document on-screen. You can now review and make changes to the document.

● The name of the document appears at the top of the screen.

Can I quickly open a document with which I recently worked?

▼ Yes. Most Office programs remember the names of the last documents with which you worked. To quickly open one of these documents, click the Office button and then select the name of the document that you want to open from the right panel. If you are using Microsoft Vista, you can also double-click any document in a search folder to open it.

Can I sort the icons displayed in the Open dialog box other than by name?

▼ Yes. Sorting icons can help you find the document that you want to open more easily. Click the Views down arrow (▾) in the Open dialog box and then click Details. You can then click an option to sort the icons by file type, file size, or by the date the files were last modified.

Work with Multiple Windows

Because you can have more than one document open at a time, you can also view more than one document on the screen in various positions.

Opening documents in multiple windows allows you to refer to information in one document as a reference and use it in another.

You can open one or more additional documents using the Office button, and then move or copy text or other material from them to the current document. You can also use the New Window feature to open a second window for the current document in Word, Excel and PowerPoint, by using the View tab of the

Ribbon. This is helpful with a long document where you need to refer to text in another section or to move the text around more efficiently.

Remember that when multiple windows are open for the same program, each window has its own set of options and features. This allows you to use the scroll bar and Ribbon in any document or window, to navigate or locate parts of the document that you need.

You can also use the Switch Windows feature on the View tab to toggle between Office documents in the same program and keep all of them at full screen view.

1 Click the View tab on the Ribbon.

● The View tab options appear.

2 Click Arrange All.

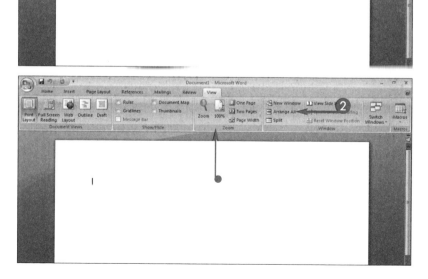

● The open documents appear in separate windows, one above the other.

③ Click to activate the other document.

④ Scroll through the document to locate items that you may need.

⑤ Click the Maximize (☐) or Restore (❐) button on your original document.

The maximized document returns to full screen view.

● You can also click the Close button (☒) in an active document to close the document window.

How does the View Side by Side command work?

▼ The View Side by Side command creates a configuration where the documents are not stacked, but instead scroll beside each other. When you select View Side by Side, the Compare Side by Side dialog box lets you select which of the open documents you want to compare next to one another.

When would I use the New Window or Split commands?

▼ Clicking New Window gives you another full screen view of the same document. Using the Split feature lets you view a part of the document in a window of its own. When the document is split, a Remove Split option appears on the Ribbon. Both features give you access to different parts of the same document at one time.

Is there another way to access open documents or even other files quickly?

▼ Yes. Holding down the Alt and Tab keys at the same time opens a window on top of your screen that shows all of your open programs and files. By holding down the Alt key and pressing the Tab key, you can toggle through the open files and see the selected filename at the top of the window. When you release the Tab key, the selected file opens in full screen view. Repeat the process to return to the original document.

Save and Close a Document

You can save your document to store it for future use. To avoid losing your work, remember to save your changes regularly.

When you create a new document, Office gives it a generic name depending upon the program that you use, such as Document1, Workbook1, and so on.

The first time you save a document, you should assign it a meaningful name and note its location. You can also save your document to the default location, which is My Documents in Windows XP or Documents

in Windows Vista. After that, you can simply use the Save button to save the document as you work.

For filenames, you can type up to 255 characters, including spaces. You cannot use characters such as pipes (|), carets (^), asterisks (*), colons (:), or question marks (?). The program automatically assigns a file extension, which indicates the type of file.

When you finish working with your document, you can close the document to remove it from your screen. You can continue working with other documents until you exit the program.

Save and Close a Document

Save a document

1 Click the Office button.

2 Click Save As.

3 Click a document type.

This example saves the file as a PowerPoint file.

The Save As dialog box appears.

4 Click Folders and then select a location.

The default location is your Documents folder.

● The current name of the document appears here.

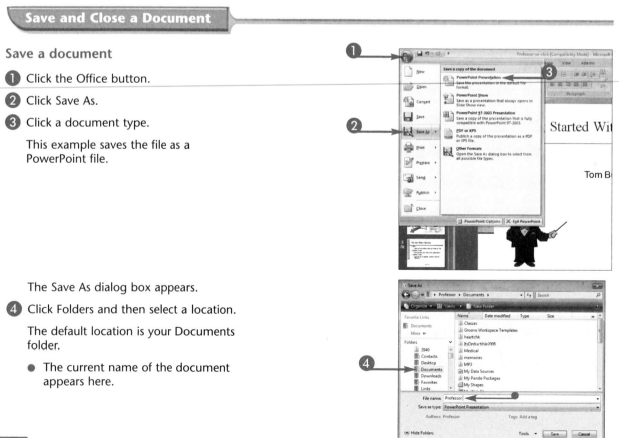

5 Type a new name for a revised document to keep the original the same.

6 Click Save.

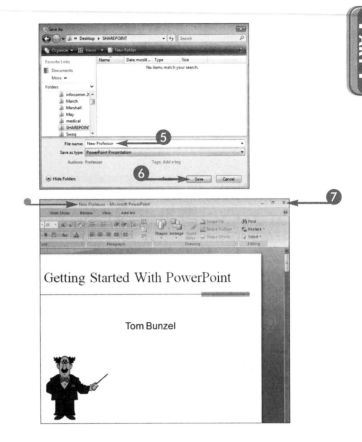

• The document is saved in PowerPoint 2007 format and is no longer in Compatibility Mode.

Note: See the next task, "Save in Different Versions."

Close a document

1 Click the Close button (⊠) for the document window.

The document closes.

How do I share my document with someone who does not have Office 2007?

▼ You can save most documents in a variety of formats. For example, you can save a Word document as plain or rich text, or as other program types and versions. In the Save As dialog box, click the Save As Type down arrow (▾), click the format, and then click Save. Office may prompt you to install the appropriate filter. To do so, insert the Office CD-ROM and follow the on-screen instructions.

What happens if I do not assign a meaningful name to a document?

▼ Your work will still be saved, but it will be harder to locate, because you will have numerous files named Document1, Document2, and so on in your Documents or My Documents folder.

How do I change the default folder location?

▼ Click the Office button and then click the program's Options button at the bottom of the panel. In the program's Options dialog box, click the Save tab. You will see options for saving documents in certain formats, and also the default locations for saving documents or files.

Save in Different Versions

When you save an Office 2007 document, it is saved by default in one of the new Office 2007 file formats. This means that you can use many of the new features of Office 2007, and its file system will conform to an XML standard. These new versions of Office applications have an "x" appended to the file type suffix, so that a Word document saved in 2007 format will be Document.docx.

However, a document saved in an Office 2007 format cannot be opened or revised by previous versions of Office. To maintain backward compatibility so that users with previous versions of Office can open the document, you can save it in Office 97-2003 format.

If you open a document that was created with a previous version of Office, it opens in Compatibility Mode, allowing you to revise it and continue saving it in either the old version or Compatibility Mode. You can also use Save As to update it to Office 2007 in order to use all of the Office 2007 features with the open document.

Save in Different Versions

Save in Office 97-2003 format

1 Click the Office button.

2 Click Save As.

3 Click the application's Office 97-2003 Document format.

This example uses Word.

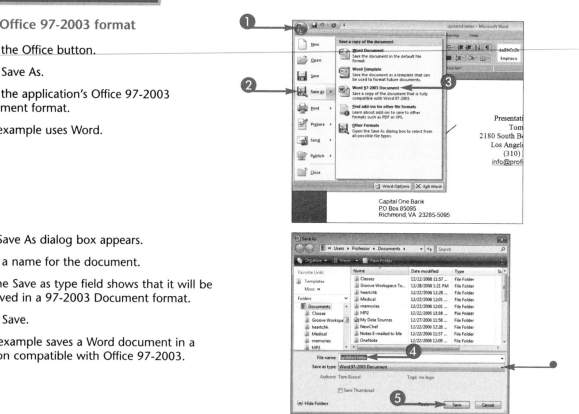

The Save As dialog box appears.

4 Type a name for the document.

- The Save as type field shows that it will be saved in a 97-2003 Document format.

5 Click Save.

This example saves a Word document in a version compatible with Office 97-2003.

Save in Office 2007 format

① Click the Office button.

② Click Save As.

③ Click the application's Document format.

This example uses Word.

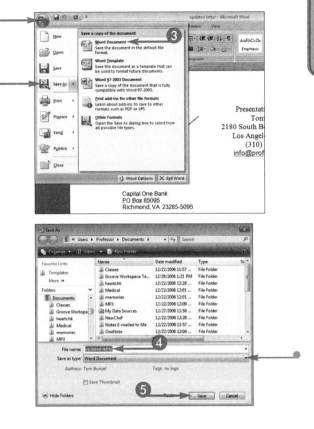

The Save As dialog box appears.

④ Type a name for the document.

● The Save as type field shows the document type.

This example selects the Word Document type.

⑤ Click Save.

Office saves the document in the format you selected.

What happens when I want to save a document that I opened in a previous version?

▼ When you click the Office button and then click Save As in a document from a previous version, there are two options that you can choose. You can continue to save it as an Office 97-2003 document, or, if you select the Office 2007 Document format, there will be a check box in the Save As dialog box that lets you maintain compatibility with the older version. However, this may mean that certain features of Office 2007 will remain unavailable while the document remains in Compatibility Mode.

How do I know whether I am working with an Office 97-2003 document or an Office 2007 document?

▼ When you are still in Compatibility Mode and have not updated a file to 2007 format, the words 'Compatibility Mode' appear in the document filename at the top of the program window.

What if I change the version of my document and need to get the older version back?

▼ Until you are comfortable with the different versions, you can save them with names that refer to their versions; for example, "2003 version.ppt." You can also right-click any Office 2007 document in Windows Vista and select Restore Previous Versions.

Using Vista
Search Features

When you use Windows Vista, you may notice that the Save As dialog box has both a Folders and a Favorite Links panel on the left. The Favorite Links are categories that organize your files so that they are catalogued by Vista Explorers.

Vista Explorers are windows that quickly open to allow a much more robust search capability. Besides searching actual filenames and the contents of files, Explorers use the properties of your Office documents and files with searchable data in the form of keywords, comments, or other information. These keywords can be added as *metatags* to a document when it is saved, allowing Vista to index the file more precisely. The new desktop search capability of Vista, using the new Explorers, enables you to locate, sort, organize, and work with your Office documents as never before.

Vista Explorers create virtual folders that contain references to files that meet your search criteria. Depending upon your search parameters, Vista Explorers either populate an existing virtual folder, or create a new one with the items that meet your specifications.

Using Vista Search Features

Add a metatag search parameter to a document

1 Open the document that you want to save with Vista search parameters.

2 Click the Office button.

3 Click Save As.

4 Click the document type.

This example selects the Word Document type.

● The Save As dialog box appears, with the document type selected in the Save as type field.

5 In the Tags or Add a Tag field, type a category or search parameter.

6 Click Save.

Windows Vista saves the file with a searchable metatag that you chose.

Perform a metatag search

1 Click the Start button.

2 Type your search term into the Start Search field.

● Vista locates all documents that have the term as text or as a metatag.

3 Click See all results.

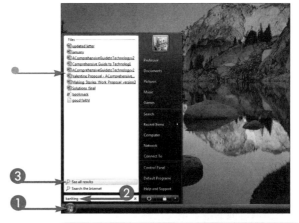

A Vista Explorer window opens.

● Documents meeting your search criteria appear here.

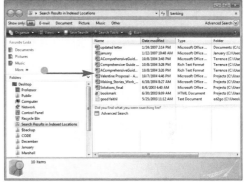

What do you mean that Vista Explorers are virtual folders?

▼ Unlike the actual physical folders that you may be used to, and that are still available at the bottom of the Vista Explorer left panel, the Explorers organize all of your files by type, such as E-mail, Document, Picture, Music, and Other. As you continue to create files in these file types, they are automatically appended to these virtual search folders although they remain physically present wherever you saved them.

Can I save a set of files that I have located using the Vista Explorer?

▼ Yes. Click Save Search in the Vista Explorer window to save and name your search. This allows you to run the same search with the same parameters by just opening the newly named and saved search folder. Any additional files that you have created or saved that meet the search criteria will also be referenced in the search folder.

Can I modify the search options in the Vista Explorer window?

▼ Yes. There are two main ways to change how Vista searches or to run a more comprehensive search. To change how searches are performed, click the Search Tools down arrow (▼) and select Search Options. To refine an individual search, click Advanced Search in the top right. A new set of fields opens in which you can provide more specific information for the Vista Explorer to narrow the search for the files you want.

Explore the Contextual Ribbon

Each of the main Office 2007 programs — Word, Excel, PowerPoint, Access, and in some instances, Outlook — include a contextual Ribbon to let users find formatting options more easily. By using the eight Ribbon tabs, you can open a complete set of coordinated formatting options with a single mouse click.

For example, the Word 2007 Ribbon has seven main components or tabs, each of which enables the user to perform specific tasks in order to produce professional-looking documents.

Clicking one of the tabs brings up a different set of related options for that part of the overall task.

Clicking the Alt key reveals pop-up keyboard shortcuts for the Ribbon, Office button, and other key features. Selecting an object in the document or file may also bring up contextual features and options.

All of the four main Office 2007 programs have a Home tab with similar formatting options and other options that are specific to the application. The other Ribbon tabs enable functions and features that support the main features of that specific program. Proceeding through the Ribbon generally follows the main tasks of producing a completed document, and comprises a typical workflow.

Word

You can use Word's Home tab to change the look of selected parts of your document. As the main formatting area of Word 2007, the default Home tab of the Ribbon enables you to paste from the Clipboard, change fonts, format paragraphs, and apply styles. Format Painter and Search and Replace features are also part of Word's Home tab. See the next task for more information about applying styles from the Word Home tab.

You can use Word's other Ribbon tabs to insert material, change the page layout, create professional references and mailings, review a document among colleagues, or change the view of your document.

Excel

The Home tab in Excel has basic formatting features for changing font styles and colors, along with copy-and-paste functions. The Home tab also contains features that let you quickly change the format for different data types, such as percentage, currency, and so on. You can also quickly insert or delete rows or columns of cells, and sort and locate data. A wide variety of conditional formats also let you display values by color or icons.

The other Excel tabs let you insert material, change the page layout or look of your worksheet, work with formulas, and reference and connect to other types of data. You can also review a workbook among colleagues, or change the view of your worksheet.

PowerPoint

The Home tab in PowerPoint has standard formatting tools for fonts and paragraphs, along with copy-and-paste functions, the Format Painter, and editing tools such as search, replace, and select.

The Home tab in PowerPoint 2007 lets you quickly insert a new or duplicate slide, change its layout, or delete slides from your presentation.

To make your slides more visually exciting, PowerPoint's Home tab lets you add and arrange shapes, and apply quick styles and effects to selected shapes. In typical Ribbon fashion, selected objects bring up other contextual menus, such as the drawing tools.

Other PowerPoint Ribbon tabs let you further refine the design of your slide or entire presentation, add animation or movement to selected slide elements, and refine the playback of your slide show. You can also review a presentation among colleagues or change the view of your current slide show.

Access

The Access Home tab gives you basic formatting options to change the look of text in a table, form, report, or other object, along with Rich Text Format (RTF) editing to make these items look more professional.

As a database program based on tables, the Access Home tab also lets you quickly add or delete records, sum totals in a table, check spelling, and more.

The Table tools become active contextually in the Home tab if a table is open, and change accordingly for other database-related items such as forms, queries, or reports.

The other Access Ribbon tabs let you quickly and easily create other tables, forms, reports, and queries, or connect to external data from other databases or data sources.

The Access Ribbon's database tools let you work with macros, establish relationships, analyze tables, and create and manage switchboards. The Datasheet tab lets you further refine the properties of your table by changing the data type, or by formatting or adding fields, columns, or relationships.

Keep in mind that you may not see all of the tabs or features if you are running in Compatibility Mode (Office 97-2003).

Preview Galleries and Themes

When you work with the Ribbon tabs in the Office 2007 programs, you may notice some conventions that are common to all of the Office programs. As you create or select a part of your document, such as a block of text or a graphic, the appropriate formatting options, and sometimes a gallery, will pop up on the Ribbon.

In many cases you can implement major formatting changes and alter the look of blocks of text or graphics by using galleries of pre-set styles.

There are also sets of color-coordinated themes that you can use to change the look of the graphics in your

document. Themes affect the background, chart, diagrams, text, or other elements of your document in ways that you can predict before you apply them.

Office 2007 provides a *live preview* of these galleries or themes as you scroll through them, and only applies the formatting when you actually click one of the choices.

You can also create your own selections for any of these galleries or themes by formatting text or graphics the way you want and then saving a selected portion as a gallery item or theme.

Preview Galleries and Themes

Apply a style from a gallery

① Click and drag through a block of text to select it.

② Click the Home tab.

③ Click the Quick Styles down arrow (▼).

Other Quick Styles appear.

④ Hover your mouse over selections in the Quick Styles gallery.

The live preview shows you the results in the selected text.

⑤ Click a style to apply it to the selected text.

● The style is applied.

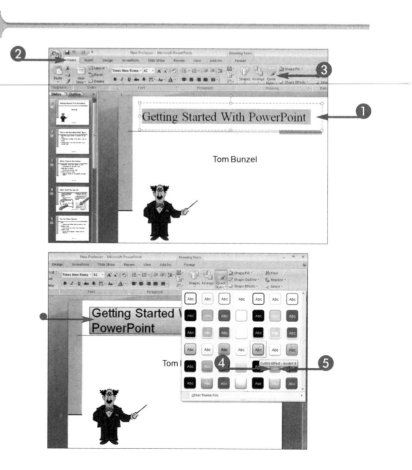

Apply a theme from a gallery

1. Click the Design tab.

2. In the Themes group, click the Colors down arrow (▼).

3. Select a theme.

   The theme changes the look of the graphics in the document.

4. Click the Themes group More button.

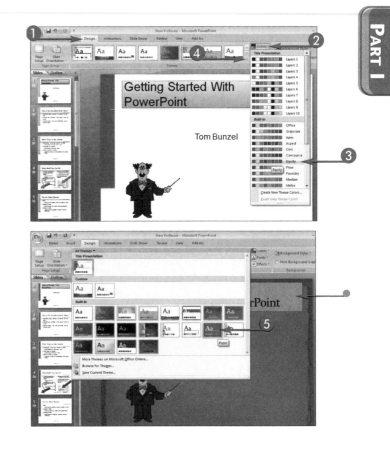

   Complete theme sets appear in a gallery.

5. Click a theme.

   ● Office applies graphic colors, text colors, and effects to your document.

Are themes and galleries the same in all Office programs?

▼ Not exactly. Each program uses a different set of galleries to show formatting options in a live preview display that you can apply to selected elements. Themes with graphic colors, text colors, and effects are also available but are applied differently in the various Office programs.

How do I add a formatting decision to a gallery or theme?

▼ Make whatever changes you want to text, graphics, or other elements with the gallery for that option open. You can use other formatting features in the Ribbon or just the items in the current gallery. Then use the Save feature at the bottom of the gallery to save the changes that you made to the gallery to apply in other sections or documents.

Can I use styles that came with older Office documents?

▼ Yes. The Style gallery in this task consists of Quick Styles in PowerPoint. In Word, you can locate and apply other formats and styles that came with an older Word document in Compatibility Mode by clicking the Change Styles down arrow (▼) in the Styles group on the Home tab.

Get Help

O ffice 2007 combines a local help directory with Microsoft online. You can access Microsoft Office Help online if you have an active Internet connection when you open the Help window.

You can access both local and online help areas by pressing the F1 key. You can locate help topics by browsing through the general topics, typing a term in the search field at the top of the Help window, or

opening the Table of Contents and going through the various help topics.

Articles pertaining to your help topic display with a ? icon. If you are connected to Microsoft Office Help online, you may also see documents related to the help parameters that you typed, along with animated or video demos that guide you through the process relating to your question or issue.

Get Help

1 With a document open, press F1.

The Help window opens.

2 Type in a term relating to your question.

3 Click Search.

Topics appear that relate to your question.

④ Click the Table of Contents button (■).

- ● You can also click the topic of interest to display that help page.

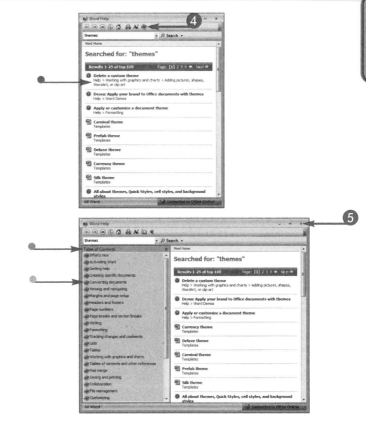

- ● The Table of Contents panel appears.

- ● You can click a book icon to expand a topic.

⑤ Click the Close button (☒) to close the Help window.

What happened to the index?

▼ In previous versions of Office, there was a help index that you could browse to find topics of interest. Office 2007 uses more intelligent search algorithms, and so you can find answers by typing questions in English, rather than guessing what the correct term should be. For example, you can type "How do I change file formats?" to get more information on that feature.

What is the purpose of the toolbar buttons in the Help window?

▼ You can use the toolbar buttons in the Help window to navigate backward and forward among previous topics. You can also print a topic, as well as maximize and restore the Help window.

What other Help commands are available?

▼ You can click the Help toolbar buttons to change font sizes (🅰) or to keep the Help window on top (📌).

What happened to the Office Assistant?

▼ In previous versions of Office, the Office Assistant was an on-screen character that appeared by default when you started an Office application. The on-screen character has been replaced with the Type a Question text box in the menu bar of the main Office Help window.

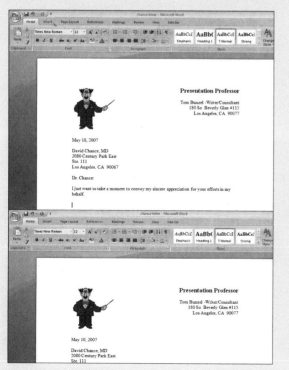

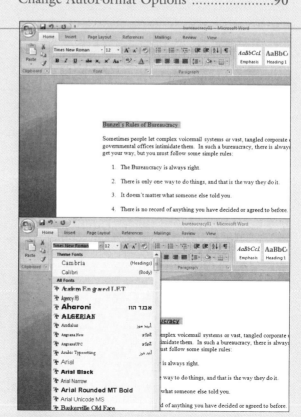

PART II
USING WORD

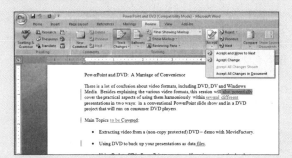

An Introduction to Word

Microsoft Word 2007 can be used for a lot more than just ordinary documents. Word lets you create brochures, flyers, Web pages, and even blogs, using professional-looking graphics.

Enter and Edit Text

Word includes many features, such as templates, building blocks, and themes, to help you create documents. You can save time by saving and reusing common types of documents, such as letters, memos, and reports. You can also outline, change, and update any document. You can move and reassemble blocks of text and graphics, as well as check for spelling and grammar mistakes.

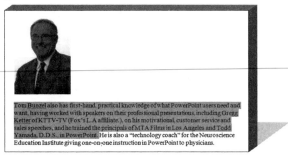

Tom Bunzel also has first-hand, practical knowledge of what PowerPoint users need and want, having worked with speakers on their professional presentations, including Gregg Ketter of KTTV-TV (Fox's L.A affiliate.), on his motivational, customer service and sales speeches, and he trained the principals of MTA Films in Los Angeles and Todd Yamada, D.D.S., in PowerPoint. He is also a "technology coach" for the Neuroscience Education Institute giving one-on-one instruction in PowerPoint to physicians.

To learn more about entering text, see the task "Type and Select Text," later in this chapter. You can learn more about templates, themes, and building blocks in Chapter 5.

Format Text

Word allows you to enhance the appearance of text by using formatting options found on tabs in the Word Ribbon. Formatting options include changing font sizes, styles, and colors to help make your document look professional. Page layout options include changing the amount of space between lines of text or aligning text in different ways. Formatting text can help you organize a document with a table of contents, index, or other references.

To speed up formatting, you can use one of Word's existing styles or create your own styles so that you apply consistent formatting to your text. You can learn how to format text and use styles in Chapter 4.

Format Documents

In addition to formatting the text, you can also make changes to the document's overall appearance. You can add page numbers, headers, or footers to the top or bottom of a page, display text in newspaper-style columns, or add a page border.

Features such as footnotes or endnotes allow you to provide additional information about text in a document. You can change the margins for a document, center text on a page, or specify whether you want to print a document in the portrait or landscape orientation. To learn more about formatting your document, see Chapter 4.

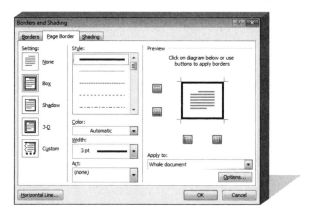

View and Print Documents

You can display your document in one of several views, each appropriate for a particular task. The Draft view focuses on the text rather than the formatting of the document. If you are creating an outline, then you can change to Outline view. The Print Layout view shows the effects of page formatting, such as page breaks and columns. There is also a Full Screen Reading view for reading documents on screen and a Web Layout view to simulate how a document will look in a Web browser when saved in HTML format. Before printing your document, Word allows you to preview the printer output to see how it looks on the page.

You can also use Word to automate complex tasks such as mail merge and envelope printing. To learn more about page views, see Chapter 5. To learn more about printing, see Chapter 8.

Insert Tables

Tables help you organize and display information in a document. Word lets you insert a table on the screen similar to drawing a table with a pen and paper. You can enhance the appearance of a table by changing the cell borders, adding shading to cells, and aligning the position of text in cells. For more information on creating and formatting tables, see Chapter 6.

Insert Graphics

Word comes with many types of graphics that you can use to enhance the appearance of a document. Graphics such as text effects, Shapes, SmartArt, and professionally designed clip art can help to make a document more interesting or to draw attention to important information.

After adding a graphic to a document, you can further enhance the document by wrapping text around the graphic. To learn more about using graphics in a Word document, see Chapter 7.

For more information on Word, you can visit the following Web site: http://office.microsoft.com/en-us/word/FX100487981033.aspx.

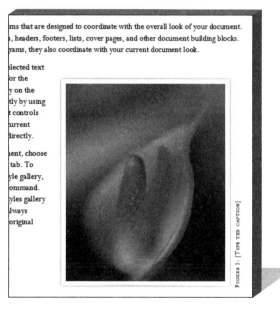

ms that are designed to coordinate with the overall look of your document.
s, headers, footers, lists, cover pages, and other document building blocks.
rams, they also coordinate with your current document look.

lected text
or the
y on the
tly by using
t controls
urrent
directly.

ent, choose
tab. To
yle gallery,
ommand.
yles gallery
lways
original

FIGURE 1: [TYPE THE CAPTION]

Explore the Contextual Ribbon

The Word 2007 Ribbon has seven main components, each of which enables the user to perform specific tasks for producing professional documents.

You can click one of the tabs to bring up a different set of related options for a particular task. You can also select a portion of a document to bring up more contextual options.

With the Ribbon, you can work with parts of a document or the entire document to make formatting changes, reorganize sections, add references, and go through a final review to make sure that your final document is polished and professional.

Home
You can use the Home tab to change the fonts, paragraph, or styles of selected parts of your document.

The Home tab also has features that copy and paste to and from the Clipboard and apply formats from one selection to another. The Find and Replace Text feature in the Home tab lets you quickly change one word or phrase to another.

Insert
The Insert tab lets you place important elements in your document to supplement the text. For example, tables can help you organize data.

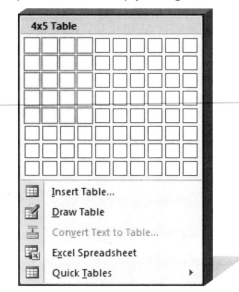

You can also insert pictures, clip art, shapes, SmartArt, and charts. You can quickly manage hyperlinks, bookmarks, headers and footers, or symbols, and use the Quick Parts feature to organize building blocks. The Insert tab also lets you put symbols, equations, and other objects into your document.

Page Layout

The Page Layout tab lets you set options for margins, line breaks, columns, indents, and line spacing.

	Normal		
	Top: 1"	Bottom: 1"	
	Left: 1"	Right: 1"	
	Narrow		
	Top: 0.5"	Bottom: 0.5"	
	Left: 0.5"	Right: 0.5"	
	Moderate		
	Top: 1"	Bottom: 1"	
	Left: 0.75"	Right: 0.75"	
	Wide		
	Top: 1"	Bottom: 1"	
	Left: 2"	Right: 2"	
	Mirrored		
	Top: 1"	Bottom: 1"	
	Inside: 1.25"	Outside:1"	
	Office 2003 Default		
	Top: 1"	Bottom: 1"	
	Left: 1.25"	Right: 1.25"	

Custom Margins...

In Page Layout you can also quickly revise the overall look of a page or an entire document by applying a theme, background color, or page border. The Page Layout tab enables you to align, group, and manage the layers of inserted objects and graphics, moving them in front of or behind one another.

References

The References tab lets you create professional documents with organized sections, tables of contents, or an index.

Mark Index Entry

Index

Main entry: The Challenge for Presenters

Subentry:

Options

○ Cross-reference: See

◉ Current page

○ Page range

Bookmark:

Page number format

☐ Bold

☐ Italic

This dialog box stays open so that you can mark multiple index entries.

Mark   Mark All   Cancel

You can also manage sources, citations, and a bibliography. If you use images in a document, the References tab lets you manage them efficiently with a table of figures and captions. You can also add footnotes and endnotes to formal documents.

Mailings

The Mailings tab lets you quickly and easily create documents, labels, and envelopes by merging with a data source such as an address book or database. In addition, before you commit a mailing to print, you can preview, filter, and sort the merged documents. You can also add, update, and revise fields in the Mailings tab.

Review

The Review tab lets you run spelling and grammar checks and perform a number of research functions. Markups by multiple reviewers are handled in the Review tab; Document Compare lets you compare different versions of a document and combine them into a final version.

View

You can enable the main five document Views in the View tab, along with Rulers, Gridlines, a Document Map, and Thumbnails. Switching between windows of open documents or viewing them on the same screen lets you work with more than one document at a time.

Add-Ins

The Add-Ins tab is mainly for additional features that were created by developers and third-party programmers. If add-ins are installed, the tab will be present. If you need to load or de-activate pre-programmed code, templates, or other programs that work with Microsoft Word, you can use the Add-Ins tab.

Keep in mind that you may not see all of the tabs or features within any tab if you are running in Compatibility Mode (Office 97-2003).

Type and Select Text

You can type text into your document quickly and easily and let Word help you with its built-in features. Simply press the keys on the keyboard, and as you type, the characters appear on-screen, and the insertion point moves to the right.

Word has a word wrap feature, which automatically moves your text to the next line when it reaches the end of a line. You press Enter only when you want to start a new line or paragraph. You should not press Enter at the end of each line. This creates *hard returns*, which make it difficult to add or delete text because the returns do not adjust automatically at the end of each line.

As you type, Word automatically checks your document for spelling and grammar errors, underlining any errors that it finds. Word also corrects hundreds of common typing, spelling, and grammar errors for you. For example, Word automatically replaces "istead" with "instead" as you type. For more information about the AutoCorrect feature, see the task "Using AutoCorrect," later in this chapter.

Selecting text is necessary in order to change its appearance by reformatting or altering its font or style. You can select text by dragging your cursor over it or by using various keyboard shortcuts.

Type and Select Text

Type your text and review errors

1 Type the text for your document.

2 Press Enter when you want to start a new paragraph.

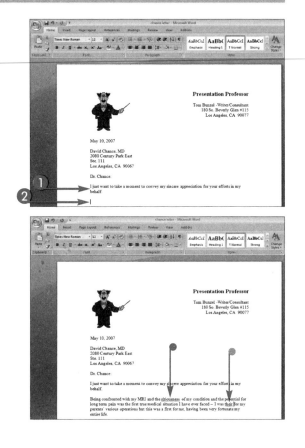

● Word underlines misspelled or unrecognized words in red. The red, wavy underline does not appear when you print the document.

● A blue underline indicates grammatical mistakes.

Note: *You can find more information on spelling and grammar checks later in this chapter.*

Select text

① Click at the start of the text that you want to select.

② Drag your mouse pointer across the text to select it.

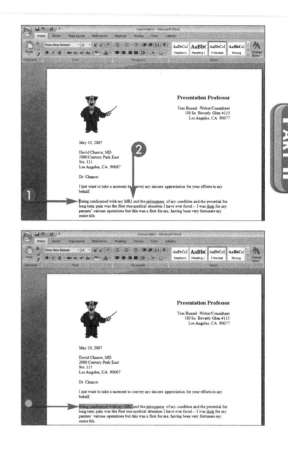

PART II

● Word selects the text.

MASTER IT

Are there shortcuts for selecting text?

▼ Yes, Word includes several shortcuts for selecting text:

- To select a word, double-click the word.

- To select a sentence, hold down the Ctrl key and click within the sentence that you want to select.

- To select a paragraph, triple-click within the paragraph.

- To select an entire line of text, click in the area to the left of the line.

How do I select all of the text in my document?

▼ The easiest way to select all of the text in the document is to use the keyboard shortcut, Ctrl+A. You can also click the Select down arrow (▼) in the Editing group on the Home tab and choose Select All.

How do I deselect text?

▼ To deselect text, click outside the selected area.

I accidentally deleted text that I had selected. What happened?

▼ If you select text, and you type anything, even a single character, then Word replaces the text with the new text that you type. If this happens, simply click the Undo button (⟲) on the Quick Access toolbar to undo the deletion. You can also press Ctrl+Z.

Insert and Delete Text

You can insert and delete text in your document. The capability to add and remove text in a document makes it possible to revise different parts of a document at different times, instead of working from the beginning directly to the end.

When you add new text to your document, the existing text moves to make room for the added text. You can also add a blank line to your document with a hard return to make room for additional text.

You can remove text or blank lines that you no longer need from your document. You can also select any amount of text that you want to remove from your document, such as a few characters, a sentence, or an entire paragraph. When you remove text from your document, the remaining text moves to fill any empty spaces.

Insert text

① Click where you want to insert the new text.

You can press the up-, down-, right-, or left-arrow key to move the insertion point in any direction.

② Type the text that you want to insert.

You can insert a blank line by pressing Enter.

● The text that you type appears where the insertion point flashes on the screen. Word adjusts existing text to make room.

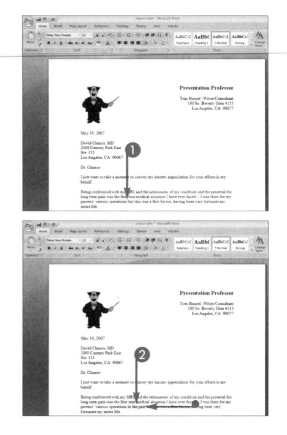

Delete text

1 Select the text that you want to delete.

Press Delete to remove the text.

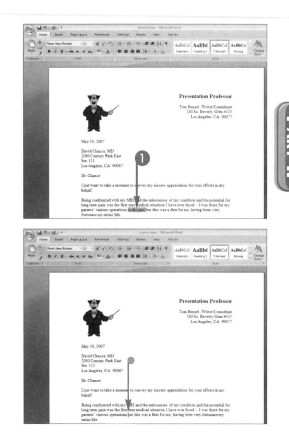

● Word deletes the selected text and adjusts the existing text accordingly.

Can I recover text that I accidentally deleted?

▼ Yes. You can click the Undo button ( ) on the Quick Access toolbar to recover your text. For more information on the Undo feature, see the task "Undo Changes."

How can I get rid of text or hard returns without going through the selection process?

▼ You can put your cursor at the end of the text or hard returns that you want to delete, and press the Backspace key to remove the unwanted items.

Can I delete characters as I type?

▼ Yes. If you make a mistake, you can press the Backspace key to delete characters to the left of the insertion point. You can also delete characters to the right of the insertion point by pressing the Delete key.

Can I quickly change the text that I inserted to uppercase letters?

▼ Yes. Word offers five case styles that you can use to change the appearance of text in your document — Sentence case, lowercase, UPPERCASE, Title Case, and tOGGLE cASE. Select the text that you want to change. Click the Change Case down arrow ( ) on the Font group on the Home tab.

Move or
Copy Text

Y ou can reorganize your document by moving text from one location to another. Moving text can help you find the most effective structure for your document. For example, you may want to reorder the paragraphs in a document so that they flow better.

When you move text, the text disappears from its original location in your document and moves to the new location.

In addition to moving text, you can also copy text to a different location in your document. This is helpful

when you want to use the same information, such as an address, in several locations in your document. When you copy text, the text appears in both the original and new locations.

When you move or copy text to a new location in your document, Word shifts the existing text to make room for the text that you move or copy.

For both tasks, Word uses the metaphor of cutting, copying, and pasting. You use the Cut and Paste buttons to move text, and the Copy and Paste buttons to copy text.

Move or Copy Text

Move text

1 Click the Home tab.

2 Select the text that you want to move.

3 Click the Cut button ( ).

4 Click where you want to place the cut text.

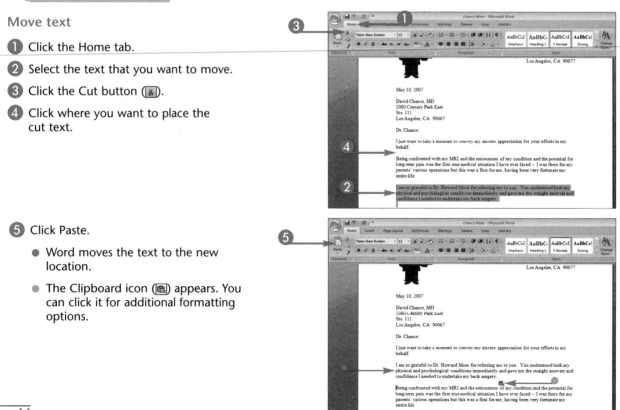

5 Click Paste.

● Word moves the text to the new location.

● The Clipboard icon ( ) appears. You can click it for additional formatting options.

Copy text

1. Click the Home tab.

2. Select the text that you want to copy.

3. Click the Copy button (⊞).

   Word makes a copy of your text and places it on the Clipboard.

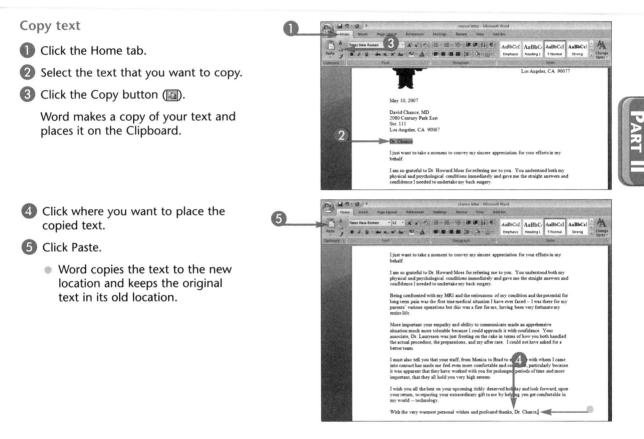

4. Click where you want to place the copied text.

5. Click Paste.

   ● Word copies the text to the new location and keeps the original text in its old location.

Is there another method to cut or copy text?	While working with selected text, I often drag and drop the text by accident. Is there a way to turn off this feature?	When does the Clipboard icon (⊞) appear?
▼ Yes. You can also drag and drop text. To move text, select it, place your mouse pointer over the text, and then press the left-mouse button. Drag the text to the new location and release the left-mouse button to place it where you want it to be. To copy, follow the same procedure, but hold down the Ctrl key as you drag.	▼ Yes. Click the Office button and select the Word Options button at the bottom of the pane. The Word Options dialog box opens. Click Advanced. Under Editing Options, uncheck the option to allow text to be dragged and dropped (☑ changes to ☐).	▼ The Clipboard icon may appear when you cut or copy text. Click this icon to display an options menu. Instead of the text automatically conforming to the format of the area where it was pasted, you can click Keep Source Formatting (◎ changes to ◉). Other options on this menu allow you to keep text formatting or use the default paste options.

Move through a Document

Word allows you to move quickly through a document, saving you time when you type and edit. When you want to edit or select text, you need to place your insertion point at the location in the document where you want to make a change. You can use either the mouse or the keyboard to move to the insertion point.

In longer documents, you can also display the other pages of a document. You can move through the

document screen by screen or page by page. Word also provides shortcuts for moving quickly to the top of the document and to the end of the document.

You can also use scroll bars to scroll up and down or left and right. The location of the scroll box on the scroll bar indicates which area of the document you are viewing. When you drag the scroll box, Word displays a box containing the page number.

Move through a Document

① Click to move the cursor to the spot where you want to move.

② Click the scroll bar.

● The scroll bar up and down arrows are highlighted.

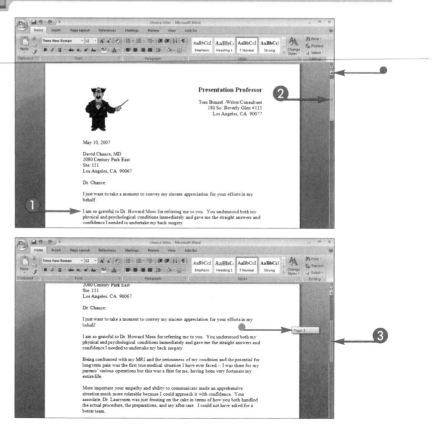

③ Drag the scroll box through the document.

● The page numbers pop up as you move through the document.

Release the mouse on the page that you want to revise.

Display previous and next pages

1 Click one of the following buttons:

Previous Page (⬆) displays the previous page.

Next Page (⬇) displays the next page.

Word scrolls in the indicated direction.

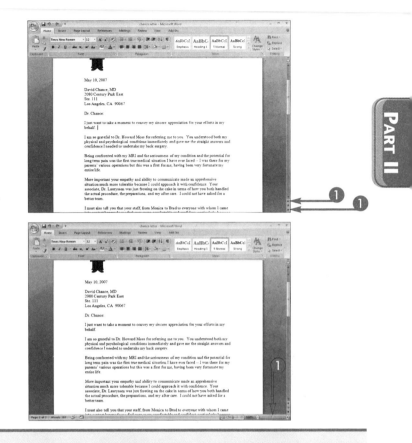

Zoom in and out of a document

1 Click the Zoom Slider (⬜), and it is highlighted

When you drag the slider toward the minus sign, the document zooms in.

When you drag the slider toward the plus sign, the document zooms out.

How do I use the keyboard to move through a document?

▼ You can use any of the following keys and key combinations to move through a document:

Press	To move
Left Arrow	Left one character
Right Arrow	Right one character
Up Arrow	Up one line
Down Arrow	Down one line
Home	To the beginning of the line
End	To the end of the line
Ctrl+Right Arrow	Right one word
Ctrl+Left Arrow	Left one word
Ctrl+Home	To the top of the document
Ctrl+End	To the end of the document

I have a mouse with a special wheel between the left- and right-mouse buttons. Can I use this wheel to scroll through my document?

▼ Yes. Moving this wheel lets you quickly scroll through a document. A mouse like this is helpful when you want a finer control when scrolling through a large document.

How can I quickly move to another page?

▼ If you know the page number, you can use the Go To command. Click the Home tab, click the Find down arrow (▼), and then click Go To. Or, in the Find and Replace dialog box, click the Go To tab and click Page in the Go to what section. Type the page number in the Enter page number field, and then click Go To.

Undo Changes

Word remembers the last changes that you made to your document. If you change your mind, you can cancel them by using the Undo feature.

The Undo feature can cancel your last editing and formatting changes. For example, you can cancel editing changes such as deleting a paragraph or typing a sentence. You can also cancel formatting changes such as underlining a word or increasing the size of text.

You can use the Undo feature to cancel one change at a time or many changes at once. Word stores a list of changes that you make to your document. When you select the change that you want to cancel from the list, Word cancels the change, and all of the changes that you have made since that change.

You can also "undo" the undo. That is, you can cancel the undo changes by clicking the Redo button.

Undo Changes

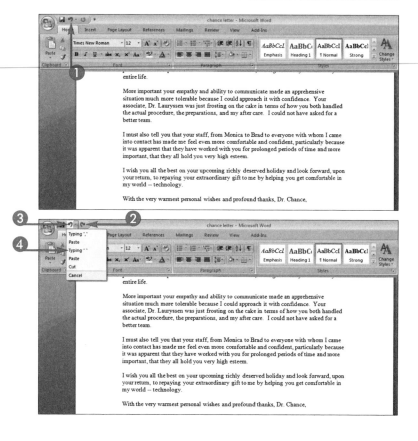

Undo one change

① Click the Undo button (🔄).

Word cancels the last change that you made.

Undo multiple changes

② Click the Redo button (🔄).

Word cancels the last change you made, by reversing the results of using the Undo feature.

③ To choose which change you want to undo, click the Undo button down arrow (🔄).

④ Click the change that you want to undo.

Word cancels the change that you selected, and all of the changes above it in the list.

Insert a Page Break

If you want to start a new page at a specific place in your document, you can insert a page break. Word automatically determines the length of the pages by the paper size and margin settings that you set, and inserts a page break when you enter text past the bottom of a page.

When you insert a break in Print Layout view, you see the actual pages. To learn about the various views in Word, see Chapter 5.

MASTER IT

Is there a faster way to insert page breaks in my document?

▼ Yes. You can quickly insert a page break in your document by holding down the Ctrl key and pressing Enter. A page break appears at the insert point in your document.

How do I remove a page break?

▼ To remove the page break, switch to Print Layout view, click the dotted line labeled Page Break, and press Delete. You can also go past the page break and press the Backspace key.

PART II

Insert a Page Break

1 Click the Insert tab.

2 Click where you want to start a new page.

3 Click Page Break.

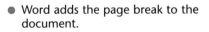

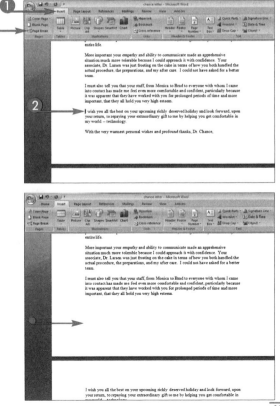

● Word adds the page break to the document.

Find
Text

You can locate instances of a specific word or phrase in a document by using the Find feature.

By default, when you search for text in your document, Word finds the text, even if it is part of a larger word. For example, if you search for "place," Word also finds "places," "placement," and "commonplace."

The word or phrase that you want to find may appear in several locations in your document. After you start the search, Word finds and highlights the first instance

of the word or phrase. You can continue the search to find the next instance of the word or phrase, or cancel the search at any time.

The More button allows you to narrow your search by matching the case, finding whole words, or using wildcards. You can also use the Reading Highlight feature to make all instances of your search parameter visible at the same time.

To learn how to replace the words that you find, see the next task, "Replace Text."

Find Text

① Click the Home tab.

② Click Find.

● The Find and Replace dialog box appears.

③ Type the text that you want to find.

④ Click Find Next.

Using the Reading Highlight

● The next instance of the search term is highlighted.

⑤ Click Reading Highlight.

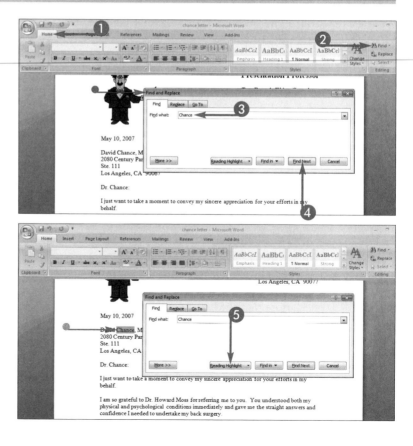

6 Click Highlight All.

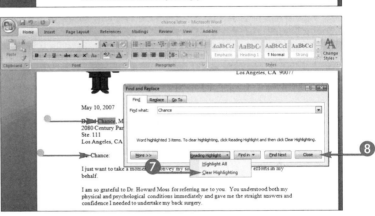

- All instances of the search term are highlighted in the document.

7 Click Reading Highlight and then Clear Highlighting.

The reading highlights disappear.

8 Click Close to complete the search.

How do I move the Find and Replace dialog box so that I can view my document?

▼ Position the mouse pointer over the title bar of the Find and Replace dialog box, and then click and drag the dialog box to a new location.

Are there advanced search features?

▼ Yes. If you click the More button in the Find and Replace dialog box, then you will find more detailed search options. (See the next task to view these additional options.) For example, you can click Match case (☐ changes to ☑) to find words that exactly match uppercase and lowercase letters. With this option selected, a search for "Letter" would not find "letter" or "LETTER."

What does the Find whole word option do?

▼ You can click Find whole words only (☐ changes to ☑), a More button option, to search for words that are not part of a larger word. For example, with this option, a search for "work" would not find "homework" or "coworker."

What does the Use wildcards option do?

▼ You can click Use wildcards (☐ changes to ☑), a More button option, to insert wildcard characters in your search. The ? wildcard represents any single character. For example, "h?t" would find "hit" and "hut." The * wildcard can represent many characters. For example, "h*t" would find "heat" and "haunt."

Replace Text

The Replace feature can locate and replace every occurrence of a word or phrase in your entire document, or in only part of the document.

This is useful if you need to replace a name throughout a document. For example, if you have a letter to ABC Inc. and you want to send the same letter to XYZ Corp., Word can replace ABC Inc. with XYZ Corp. throughout the document.

The Replace feature is also useful if you repeatedly misspell a name in your document. For example, you can quickly change all occurrences of McDonald to Macdonald.

Word locates and highlights each occurrence of the word or phrase in your document. You can replace the found word or phrase, or ignore the match. If you are sure of the replacements, you can also replace all of the occurrences of the word or phrase in your document at once.

The More button allows you to narrow your search by finding specific formatting. To learn more about the matching case, finding whole words only, and wildcard options for this button, see the previous task, "Find Text."

Replace Text

① Click the Home tab.

② Click Replace.

● The Find and Replace dialog box appears.

③ Type the text that you want to replace.

You can press Tab to move to the Replace with field.

④ Type the new text.

⑤ Click Find Next to start the search.

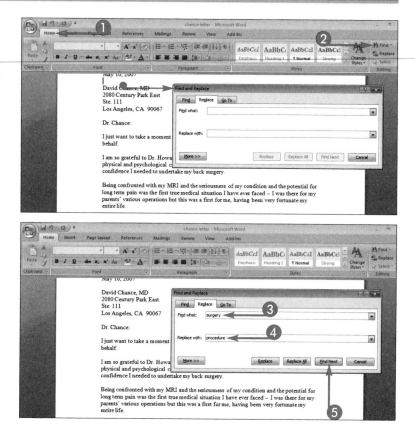

● Word highlights the first matching word it finds.

6 Click one of these options.

Replace: Replaces the word.

Replace All: Replaces all occurrences of the word.

Find Next: Ignores the word and continues the search.

7 Click More to choose additional search options.

● You can click Less to close the additional search options.

8 Continue confirming or ignoring replacements.

● When the search is complete, a dialog box appears.

9 Click OK to close the dialog box.

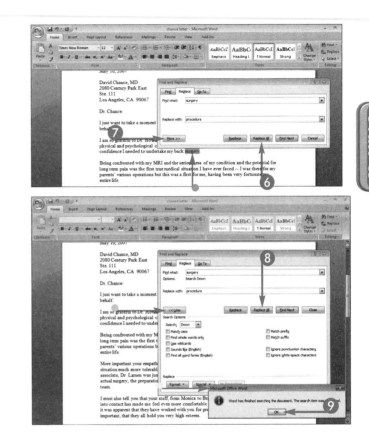

Can I use the Replace feature to change the formatting of text in my document?

▼ Yes. In the Find and Replace dialog box, remove any text from the Find what and Replace with fields, and click the More button. Click the Find what field, click Format, and select a format property, such as Font, Paragraph, or Style. If a dialog box appears, select the property that you want to replace, and then click OK. Click the Replace with field and repeat the process to specify your new formatting.

How do I stop the formatting search?

▼ Click the Find what field and click No Formatting. Then click the Replace with field and click No Formatting again.

When I clicked Replace All, Word made changes that I did not want. What can I do?

▼ You can always click the Undo button (↩ ▾) to reverse your replacements. To prevent undesirable replacements, try clicking Replace a few times to see whether the change is what you want. For example, if you replace *man* with *person*, you can end up with *personager* instead of *manager*. In most cases, it is a good idea to use the More button options with Replace all to narrow your search.

Using AutoCorrect

W ord automatically corrects hundreds of typing, spelling, and grammatical errors as you type. The AutoCorrect feature uses its list of common errors and Word's dictionary to correct errors in your document. You can add your own words and phrases to the AutoCorrect dictionary.

The AutoCorrect feature replaces common errors such as "aboutthe," "includ," and "may of been" with the correct word or phrase.

The feature capitalizes the first letter of new sentences and the names of days. It also inserts symbols into

your document when you type certain characters. For example, when you type (c), the © symbol automatically appears in your document. This is useful when you want to quickly insert symbols into your document that do not appear on your keyboard.

You can review a list of AutoCorrect entries and add new entries. For example, suppose that you consistently misspell or mistype *cabinet*. You can add an AutoCorrect entry for the incorrect spelling with its correct spelling so that Word automatically corrects it.

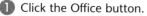

Using AutoCorrect

Type an AutoCorrect entry

① Type an incorrect spelling of a word.

After you add a space or a tab, Word automatically replaces the incorrect word with the correct one.

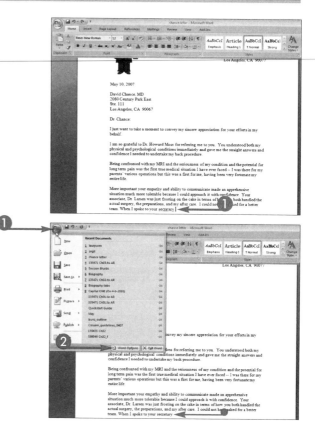

● In this example, AutoCorrect replaced the misspelled word *secratary* with *secretary,* but you can use the AutoCorrect feature with any misspelled word that is in the AutoCorrect dictionary.

Change AutoCorrect options

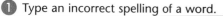

① Click the Office button.

② Click Word Options.

The Word Options dialog box appears.

3 Click Proofing.

4 Click AutoCorrect Options.

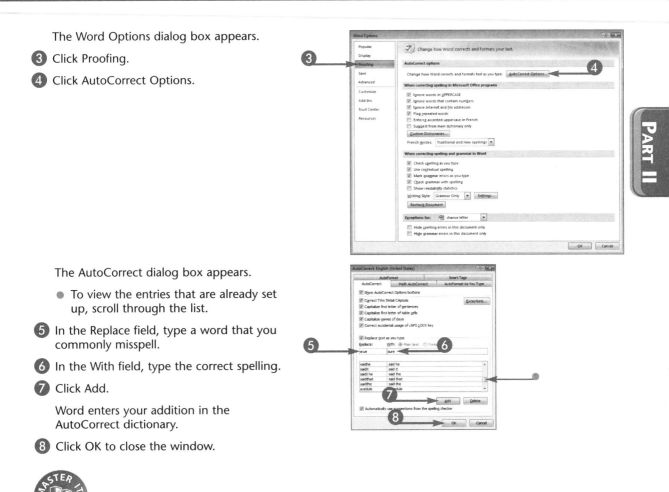

The AutoCorrect dialog box appears.

● To view the entries that are already set up, scroll through the list.

5 In the Replace field, type a word that you commonly misspell.

6 In the With field, type the correct spelling.

7 Click Add.

Word enters your addition in the AutoCorrect dictionary.

8 Click OK to close the window.

What other types of errors does the AutoCorrect feature correct?

▼ When you type two consecutive uppercase letters, the AutoCorrect feature converts the second letter to lowercase. This feature also corrects accidental usage of the Caps Lock key.

Can I change my AutoCorrect options?

▼ Yes. Uncheck any options that are enabled by default in the AutoCorrect window of the Word Options dialog box. Alternatively, in the AutoCorrect dialog box, scroll through the entries that are already set up, select the entry that you want to delete, and then click the Delete button.

The AutoCorrect feature did not replace a spelling error in my document. Why?

▼ The AutoCorrect feature automatically replaces a spelling error when there is only one suggestion to correct the error. To have the AutoCorrect feature always correct a spelling error, right-click the misspelled word. Click AutoCorrect and then click the word that you want to always replace the misspelled word.

Using Contextual Spell Check

Word checks your document for spelling as you type. You can correct the errors that Word finds to make sure that your document is professional and accurate. A misspelled word can mar an otherwise perfect document, creating an impression of sloppy work or carelessness.

Word automatically corrects common spelling errors, such as "adn" and "recieve," as you type. For information on the AutoCorrect feature, see the previous task, "Using AutoCorrect."

You can run a complete spelling and grammar check from the Review tab, by using the Spelling and

Grammar feature. You can also press the F7 key to begin a spelling and grammar check.

Word can check spelling and locate important errors *contextually*, and even correct the use of apostrophes in contractions.

For example, the correct spelling of "their" or "there" depends upon context, or how it is used in a particular sentence or paragraph. Word evaluates the context and suggests changes based on its perception of the possible misuse of words.

Using Contextual Spell Check

View errors as you type

- Word underlines a possible error in blue.

① Right-click the error.

- A menu appears with suggestions to correct the error.

② Click one of the suggestions.

- You can ignore the error by clicking Ignore.

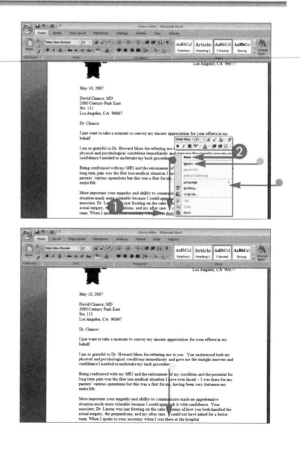

Depending on what you select, Word either ignores the error or corrects it.

Check the entire document

1 Click the Review tab.

2 Click Spelling & Grammar.

● The Spelling and Grammar dialog box appears, displaying the first misspelled word and suggestions for corrections.

3 Click a suggestion.

4 Click Change to correct only this error.

You can also click Change All to correct the flagged word throughout the entire document.

If the word is correct, you can click Ignore Once to skip this occurrence or Ignore All to skip all occurrences.

If you use a word in a special way, you can click Add to Dictionary. For example, if the name of a store included "Kurtains."

5 Continue making changes through the document.

A dialog box appears, indicating that the spell check is complete.

Does a spell check ensure that the document does not have any mistakes?

▼ No. You still must proofread your document. Word only recognizes spelling errors, not usage errors. For example, *to*, *two*, and *too* all have different meanings and uses. If they are spelled correctly, Word does not flag them, even if you use them incorrectly.

Can I prevent Word from underlining spelling errors?

▼ Yes. If the underlining that Word uses to indicate spelling errors distracts you, you can hide it. In the Spelling and Grammar dialog box, click the Options button. In the next dialog box, you can make various changes, including disabling the underlining feature.

How can I stop Word from flagging words that are spelled correctly?

▼ Word flags any words that do not exist in its dictionary as misspelled. You can add a word to the dictionary so that Word recognizes it during future spell checks. Right-click the word that you want to add to the dictionary and then select Add.

If you want to have Word automatically correct the word, open the Spelling and Grammar dialog box and click AutoCorrect.

Check Grammar

By default, Word checks grammar along with the spell check unless you turn off that feature by deselecting its option in the Spelling and Grammar dialog box.

The grammar check feature finds errors such as capitalization problems, punctuation mistakes, misused words, and common mistakes such as passive voice or misuse of a pronoun.

For some mistakes, Word makes suggested corrections. You can use one of these suggestions. In addition, you can ignore the flagged error, edit the sentence, or view an explanation of the error.

Word uses a certain writing style with set rules by default. You can change to a different writing style and select which settings Word checks for you.

Keep in mind that you still need to proofread your work because the grammar checker is not perfect, and it may not find all of the mistakes in a document.

Check Grammar

① Click the Review tab.

② Click Spelling & Grammar.

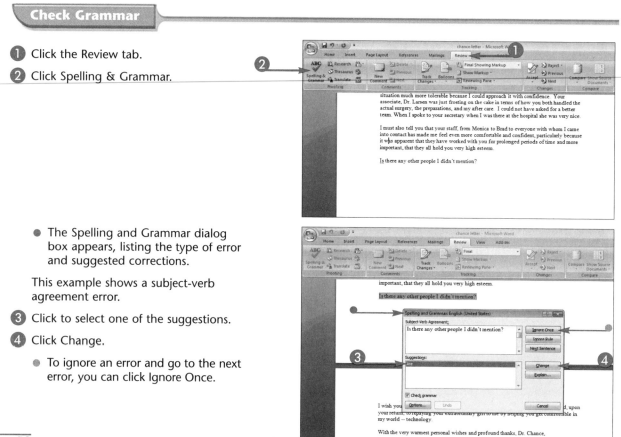

● The Spelling and Grammar dialog box appears, listing the type of error and suggested corrections.

This example shows a subject-verb agreement error.

③ Click to select one of the suggestions.

④ Click Change.

● To ignore an error and go to the next error, you can click Ignore Once.

This example shows a sentence that should be a question.

5 Continue correcting or editing the spelling and grammar changes.

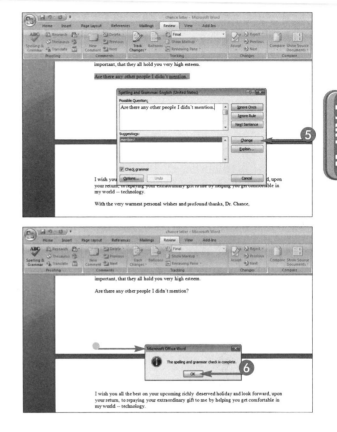

• Word completes the spell and grammar check.

6 Click OK to close the dialog box.

How can I view the rules that Word uses to check for spelling and grammar mistakes?

▼ Click the Options button in the Spelling and Grammar dialog box to open the Spelling and Grammar Options dialog box. You can also view the settings for the selected writing style by clicking the Settings button in the options dialog box.

In the options dialog box, by default Grammar is checked, but Style is not. You can enable Style options including cliches, colloquialism and jargon, contractions, fragments, gender specific words, hyphenated and compound words, particular numerical styles, passive sentences, possessive and plurals, and other potential style issues that may be relevant to conform to your office or association guidelines.

Can I change the options that Word uses to check grammar?

▼ Yes. Click the Office button and click the Word Options button. The Word Options dialog box opens. Under Proofing, you will find various options that Word uses to check grammar. There is also a Settings button that allows you to make further modifications to the Grammar Check feature and to determine which items to check for and which to ignore.

Although Word may not have the precise corrections in all cases, it will at least call attention to these issues and allow the user to adjust the language to meet guidelines set by an editor or manager. For all of these options, click the check boxes (▢ changes to ☑) to enable them.

Using the Thesaurus

You can use a thesaurus to replace a word in your document with a synonym that shares the same meaning but is more suitable. Using the thesaurus included with Word is faster and more convenient than searching through a printed thesaurus.

If the word that you want to replace has more than one meaning, you can select the correct meaning, and Word displays the synonyms for that meaning.

If you do not see a word that fits your situation, you can use the Look Up button in the Thesaurus dialog box to view synonyms for any of the listed words.

If the thesaurus does not offer a suitable replacement for the word, you do not have to make a replacement. You can simply cancel out of the thesaurus.

What if Word cannot find the word that I select?

▼ If Word cannot find your selection in the thesaurus, it displays the closest match. You can also use the down arrow (▼) near the top of the task pane to use another thesaurus or go online for more reference options.

Using the Thesaurus

① Click or select the word that you want to check.

② Click the Review tab.

③ Click Thesaurus.

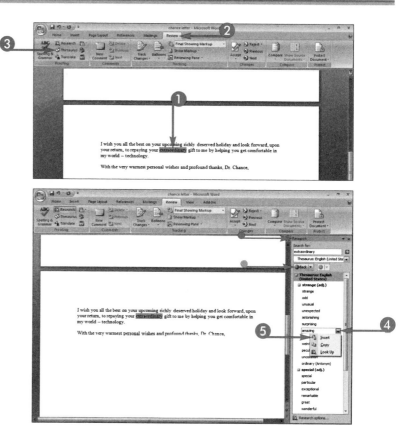

● The Thesaurus task pane appears.

④ Click the down arrow (▼) for the desired alternative word.

⑤ Click Insert.

Your selection replaces the word in the document.

● To return to the original choices, you can click the Back button.

Count Words

You can quickly determine the number of words in your document as well as other document statistics, such as the number of pages, characters, paragraphs, and lines.

Counting words in a document is useful if your document must contain a specific number of words. For example, most newspapers and magazines require that submitted pieces contain a certain number of words.

You can count the words in your entire document or just a specific section of selected text. When you count the words in an entire document, you can choose to include the words in any footnotes and endnotes in the document by selecting the Include Footnotes and Endnotes option.

How do I include textboxes, footnotes, and endnotes in the word count?

▼ When you click the Word Count button (📖) in the Proofing group, you can enable a check box that lets you include textboxes, footnotes, and endnotes.

Count Words

● Word keeps a running total of the words in your document on the status bar.

① Select a block of text in which you want to count the words.

● Word changes the status bar to include the selected block along with the total number of words in the document.

② Click the Review tab.

③ Click the Word Count button (📖) in the Proofing group.

● The Word Count dialog box opens. This dialog box provides more information on the number of characters, paragraphs, and lines, and allows you to include textboxes, footnotes, and endnotes.

Create and Insert
a Quick Parts Entry

You can use the Quick Parts feature to store text that you use frequently. Blocks of formatted text and styles can be reused in other documents. This lets you avoid typing the same text over and over again.

You can insert a built-in or created Quick Parts entry into your document quickly and easily.

Quick Parts is part of the Building Blocks in Word 2007. You will also find a Building Blocks Organizer in the

Quick Parts panel, which you can use to change Quick Parts properties or to delete any Quick Parts that you no longer use.

As you work with Quick Parts in Word, when you exit a document, Word prompts you whether you want to save the Building Block modified from the Quick Parts creation.

See Chapter 5 for more about the Building Blocks feature and organizer.

Create and Insert a Quick Parts Entry

Create a Quick Parts entry

1 Select the text that you want to set up as a Quick Parts entry.

2 Click the Insert tab.

3 Click Quick Parts.

4 Click Save Selection to Quick Part Gallery.

● The Create New Building Block dialog box appears.

5 Type a name for your Quick Parts.

6 Click OK.

Word stores your Quick Parts entry.

Insert a Quick Parts entry

1. Click where you want the Quick Parts entry to appear.

2. Click the Insert tab.

3. Click Quick Parts.

4. Click the Quick Parts entry that you want to insert.

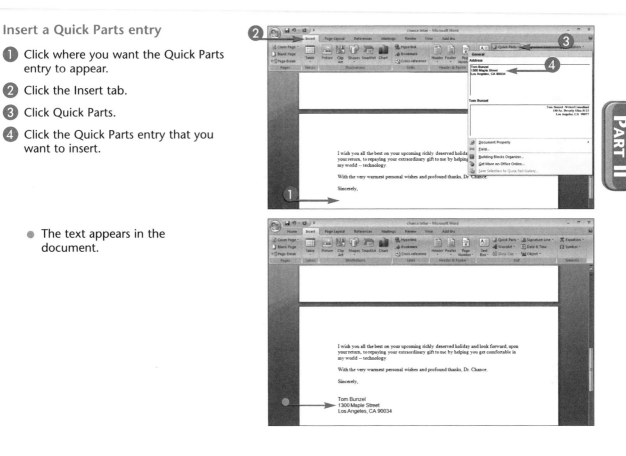

- The text appears in the document.

MASTER IT

Why do you give the Quick Parts entry a name?

▼ If you want to use the Building Blocks Organizer to locate the Quick Parts entry, giving it a name makes it a lot easier to find. If you do not give your Quick Parts entry a name, a name will be extrapolated from the block of text that you select.

Can I delete a Quick Parts entry?

▼ Yes. To delete an entry, click Quick Parts and then click Building Blocks Organizer. Locate the Quick Part by name or category and select it. Click the Delete button at the bottom of the panel. The Quick Part is deleted.

How do Quick Parts and Building Blocks relate to one another?

▼ Quick Parts is a *gallery* of stored objects that appear under the Quick Parts option in the Insert tab. All of the galleries are considered *building blocks* and can be organized, added, and deleted by using the Building Blocks Organizer.

Insert Date and Time

W ord provides a quick method to insert the date and time that you can include in documents, such as letters or invoices that require a time stamp.

You can select from several date formats, such as 2/13/2008, Tuesday, February 13, 2008, and others. You can also select from several time formats, including standard time or military time. Some formats include both the date and time.

By default, Word inserts the date and time simply as text, which you can modify and delete like other text.

What if I want to update the date and time every time I open my document?

▼ You can insert a field code that Word updates by clicking the Update Automatically option (☐ changes to ☑). *Field codes* are containers of information that can change; they are not actual text but instead coded information about what should go in that part of a document. Field codes are how mail merges are done. For more on mail merges, see Chapter 8.

For example, you may use this option in a template that you use repeatedly to ensure that Word inserts the current date rather than a set date. Field codes appear as regular text in your document. You can update a field code by selecting it and pressing the F9 key.

Insert Date and Time

1 Click where you want to insert the date or time.

2 Click the Insert tab.

3 Click Date and Time.

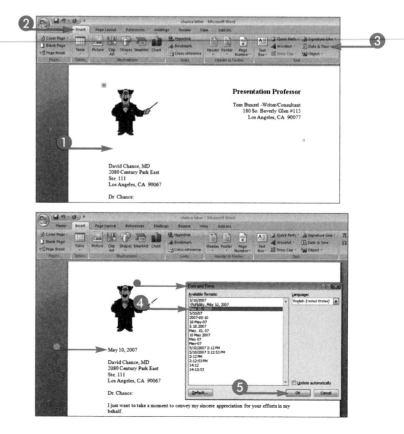

● The Date and Time dialog box appears.

4 Click a format.

5 Click OK.

● Word inserts the date and/or time in your document.

Insert Symbols or Special Characters

In some documents, you may want to insert special typographical symbols such as a trademark or copyright symbol.

You can also select from a list of special characters, such as an em dash or en dash, and insert them quickly into a document. You can insert them using the listed shortcut key.

Word's AutoCorrect feature can also help you to quickly insert some symbols into your document as you type. For more information on the AutoCorrect feature, see the task "Using AutoCorrect."

How do I use the Equation feature?

▼ The Equation feature has two parts. Built-in equations can be inserted by clicking the Equation down arrow (▾) in the Symbols group. If you click Equation itself, you get a placeholder for adding an equation manually by typing it in. In addition, a *contextual Ribbon* appears with a full set of Equation Tools in a separate tab, letting you design and save your own equations. A more complete gallery of mathematical symbols is also available in the Equation Tools. For more information on equations, consult online help. You can press the F1 key to access online help.

Insert Symbols or Special Characters

1 Click where you want to insert the character.

2 Click the Insert tab.

3 Click Symbol.

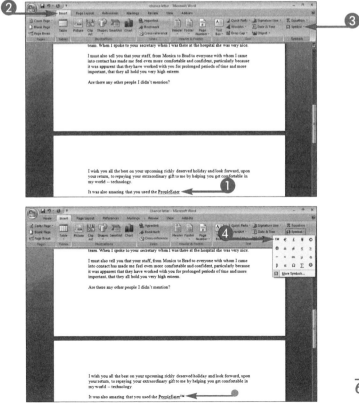

The Symbol menu appears.

4 Click a symbol or click More Symbols (Ω).

● Word inserts the character in your document.

Bold, Italicize, and Underline Text

You can use the Bold, Italic, and Underline features to change the style of text in your document. You use these features more than other formatting options to help you emphasize information and enhance the appearance of your document.

You can use one feature at a time or any combination of the three features to change the style of text.

The *Bold* feature makes text appear darker and thicker than other text. You can bold headings and titles to make them stand out from the rest of the text in your document.

The *Italic* feature slants text to the right. You may want to italicize quotations and references in your document.

The *Underline* feature adds a line underneath text, which is useful for emphasizing important text, such as key words in your document. Keep in mind that it may confuse Web visitors if you use underlining in a Word document that you include on a Web site, because Web building programs use this formatting for hyperlinks.

Bold, Italicize, and Underline Text

① Click the Home tab.

② Select the text that you want to change.

Note: To learn how to select text, see Chapter 3.

③ Click one or more of the following buttons:

Bold (**B**)

Italic (*I*)

Underline (U)

This example uses bold, italic, and underline.

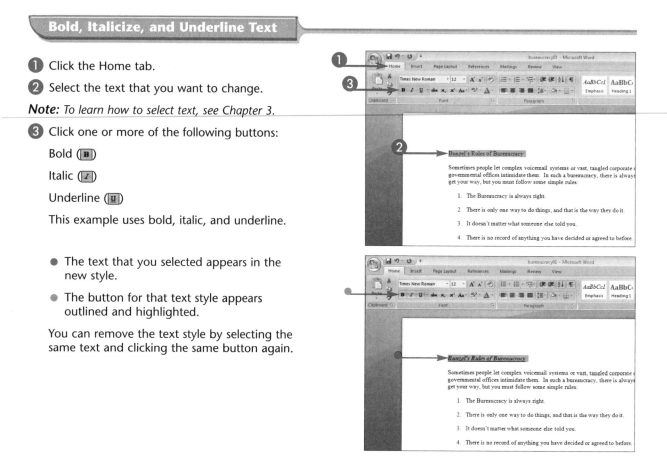

● The text that you selected appears in the new style.

● The button for that text style appears outlined and highlighted.

You can remove the text style by selecting the same text and clicking the same button again.

Change the Font Style

You can enhance the appearance of your document by changing the design, or font, of the text.

You can quickly change the font using the Font drop-down list. Word lists the available fonts from which you can choose, with the most recently applied fonts appearing at the top of the list. This allows you to quickly select fonts that you use often.

The other fonts in the list appear in alphabetical order. Because fonts appear in the list as they appear in your document, you can preview a font before you select it.

The fonts that you have available depend on your printer and your particular computer setup. These fonts have been added either with your application programs, or separately.

You can install additional fonts on your computer to use in all of your programs, including Word. You can obtain fonts from computer stores and on the Internet. Consult the Windows help system to learn how to add fonts to your computer.

Change the Font Style

① Click the Home tab.

② Select the text that you want to change.

Note: To learn how to select text, see Chapter 3.

③ Click the Font down arrow (▼) to display a list of the available fonts.

The Theme Fonts menu opens.

④ Move your mouse over the font styles to see live previews of how they will look.

⑤ Click the font that you want to use.

● The text that you selected changes to the new font.

Change the Font Size

You can increase or decrease the size of text to fit the needs of your document. Generally, you use larger text to draw attention to specific sections, or to make your text easier to read. By contrast, smaller text allows you to fit more information on a page, making it ideal for figure captions or for standardized contract language such as disclaimers.

By default, Word applies the Calibri font and a text size of 11 points. Word measures the size of text in points, with 72 points equaling one inch. You can change just the font size of specific text or the default setting itself. Word automatically adjusts the line spacing when you change the font size.

How can I change font size or the default font size?

▼ You can either change your font size using the Font Size drop-down list, which offers a range of sizes, or by using the Font dialog box. You can change the default font by typing some text in that font in your document, selecting it, and then clicking the dialog box launcher on the Font group of the Home tab. In the Font dialog box, click the Default button. Word asks you to confirm that you want to make the currently selected font and size the default. Click Yes.

Change the Font Size

1 Click the Home tab.

2 Select the text that you want to change.

Note: To learn how to select text, see Chapter 3.

3 Click the Font Size down arrow (▼).

The Font Size drop-down list opens.

4 Move your mouse over the font sizes to see live previews of how they will look.

5 Click the size that you want to use.

● The text that you selected changes to the new size.

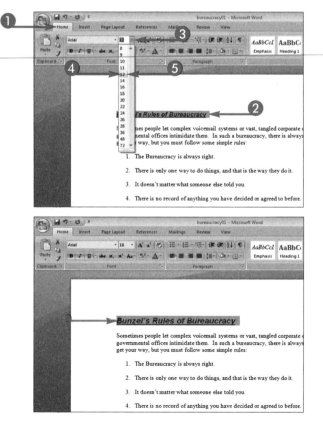

Highlight Text

Y ou can use the Highlight feature in your document to mark text that you want to review later, or text that you want your reader to notice. When you highlight text, Word changes the background color of the text, making it stand out from the rest of the text in your document.

When you print a document that contains colored or highlighted text using a black-and-white printer, the text appears in shades of gray. For best printing results, consider applying the highlight option only when you have a color printer. For black-and-white printers, consider using a light highlight color, such as yellow, which prints on paper as a light gray.

You can also use black highlighting or shading with white text for titles or headlines.

MASTER IT

How do I remove highlights from my text?

▼ To remove highlights, select the highlighted text. Click the Highlight button (🖊️▼) and then click No Color. Word removes the highlight. You can also use the Clear Formatting button (📃) to clear the highlight and all other formatting from your selection.

Is there a way to quickly highlight lots of text?

▼ Yes. When the Highlight button has a color selected, you can click it without any text selected (🖑 changes to 🖊️). You can then highlight text by dragging through it. To turn your highlighter (🖊️) back to a pointer (🖑), press Esc on your keyboard.

Highlight Text

1 Click the Home tab.

2 Select the text that you want to highlight.

Note: To learn how to select text, see Chapter 3.

3 Click the Highlight button down arrow (🖊️▼).

4 Move your mouse over any color for a live preview of how the selected text will look.

5 Click the highlight color that you want to use.

● Word highlights the text in the color that you selected.

Note: You can also click the Highlight button (🖊️▼) to accept a preselected highlight color.

Align
Text

Y ou can use the alignment buttons in the Paragraph group of the Home tab to change the alignment of text in your document. By default, Word aligns text along the left margin.

In addition to left alignment, Word allows you to center text between the left and right margins, as well as align text along the right margin. You use the Center Align option to make headings and titles in your document stand out from left-aligned text. You apply the Right Align option to align lists, numbers, or for special graphic effects in your documents.

You can also justify text to align your document along both the left and right margins, which makes your text fit neatly on a line. You can apply this option to text that appears in columns, such as in a newsletter. The Justify option can sometimes leave unusually large spaces between words.

You can also use Word's Click and Type feature to align text that you enter in a document. Available only in the Print Layout and Web Layout views, the Click and Type feature lets you quickly left-align, center-align, or right-align new text.

Align Text

Using the Ribbon

1 Click the Home tab.

2 Select the text that you want to align.

Note: *To learn how to select text, see Chapter 3.*

3 Click one of the following buttons:

Align Left (≡)

Center (≡)

Align Right (≡)

Justify (≡)

● The text displays the new alignment.

Using Click and Type

1 Click the Print Layout View button () to display the document in Print Layout view.

2 Click to the left of the page (⬚ changes to an insertion point, |).

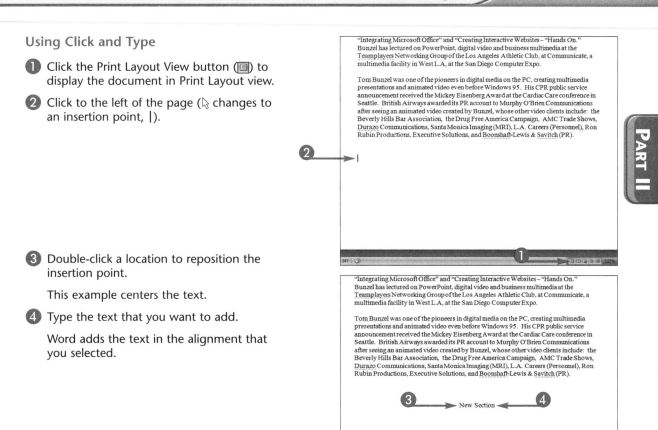

3 Double-click a location to reposition the insertion point.

This example centers the text.

4 Type the text that you want to add.

Word adds the text in the alignment that you selected.

PART II

How do I undo an alignment?

▼ To undo an alignment, click the Undo button (◄), or select another alignment.

How do I justify the last line of my paragraph?

▼ By default, Word does not justify the last line of a paragraph. To do so, click the end of the line and then press Shift+Enter.

Are there more ways to change alignment?

▼ Yes. You can also use the dialog box launcher (◻) for the Paragraph group. In the Indents and Spacing tab of the Paragraph dialog box, click the alignment that you want from the Alignment drop-down list and then click OK.

Can I apply different alignments within a single line of text?

▼ Yes. For example, you can left-align your name and right-align the date on the same line. In Print Layout or Web Layout view, click to the right of a left-aligned word or phrase, and click to establish an insertion point (|). Move to another part of the line, double-click to establish another insertion point, and type your text. The text will align to the second insertion point, but there will be less room between the text and the margin.

Indent Paragraphs

You can use the Indent feature to make paragraphs in your document stand out.

Word allows you to indent the left edge of a paragraph in several ways. For example, you can indent the first line of a paragraph. This saves you from having to press Tab at the beginning of new paragraphs.

You can also indent all but the first line of a paragraph to create a *hanging indent*. You can use hanging indents when you are creating a resume, glossary, or bibliography. Hanging indents are also useful for numbered lists.

You can indent all of the lines in a paragraph. This is useful when you want to set quotations apart from the rest of the text in your document.

You can also indent the right edge of all of the lines in a paragraph, when you want to emphasize a block of information in your document. Right-indenting is best used in combination with left-indenting, and not on its own.

To apply a simple left indent, you can use the buttons in the Paragraph group on the Ribbon. You can apply other indents using the Paragraph dialog box.

Indent Paragraphs

Using the Ribbon

① Click the Home tab.

② Select the paragraphs that you want to indent.

Note: To learn how to select text, see Chapter 3.

③ Click one of the following buttons:

   Increase indent (🔲)

   Decrease indent (🔲)

   Word indents the paragraph.

Using the dialog box

① Click the Home tab.

② Select the paragraphs that you want to indent.

③ Click the dialog box launcher (🔲) for the Paragraph group.

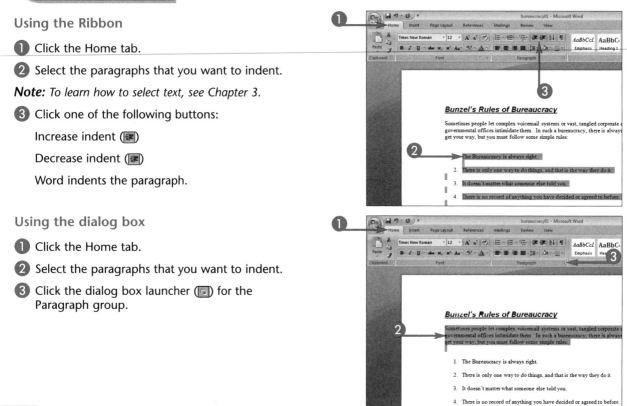

The Paragraph dialog box appears, displaying the Indents and Spacing tab.

4 Type a value in the Left and Right indent fields.

● To set a first line or hanging indent, you can click the Special down arrow () and then click to select the indent type; you can type the amount to indent in the By box.

5 Click OK.

● Word indents the paragraph with the options that you selected.

Bunzel's Rules of Bureaucracy

Sometimes people let complex voicemail systems or vast, tangled corporate or governmental offices intimidate them. In such a bureaucracy, there is always a way to get your way, but you must follow some simple rules:

1. The Bureaucracy is always right.
2. There is only one way to do things, and that is the way they do it.
3. It doesn't matter what someone else told you.
4. There is no record of anything you have decided or agreed to before.
5. Repeat everything you are told three times, ask that it be verified, then repeat it again.
6. Write down the person you are talking to, and the time you called. Always get a confirmation number.
7. You can get angry and try to intimidate but you should be prepared to hear, "if you want to dial a number, please hang up and dial again." Never use obscene language.

Can I set the indents using the Ruler?

▼ Yes. If the Ruler is not displayed, click the View tab on the Ribbon and then click to select the Ruler check box (☐ changes to ☑). Then drag the appropriate indent marker on the Ruler:

Drag 🔳 to set a first-line indent.

Drag 🔳 to set a left indent.

Drag 🔳 to set a hanging indent after selecting only the lines to indent.

Can I set indents for more than one paragraph?

▼ Yes. To set indents for several paragraphs, select the paragraphs that you want to format and set the indent. If you want to set the indent for just one paragraph, you can just click within that paragraph and set the indent.

What other options can I set using the Paragraph dialog box?

▼ You can set the alignment using the Alignment drop-down list. You can also set line and paragraph spacing. For more information, see the task "Change Line and Paragraph Spacing."

Set
Tabs

You can use tabs to line up columns of information at specific positions in your document. Word automatically places a tab every 0.5 inches across a page. You can either use this default setting by pressing the Tab key, or set your own tabs.

You should use tabs instead of spaces to line up information. If you use spaces, the information may not line up properly when you print your document.

Word offers several types of tabs from which to choose. The tab that you add depends on how you

want to line up your information. When you choose the Left tab, Word lines up the left side of your text with the tab. The Center tab lines up the center of your text with the tab. When you choose the Right tab, Word lines up the right side of your text with the tab. You can use the Decimal tab to line up the decimal points in numbers. The Bar tab inserts a vertical line at the tab stop. You can set a hanging indent; the first line of the paragraph is not indented, but the lines that follow are indented. If you set a first-line indent, the first line of the paragraph is indented, but the lines that follow are not.

Set Tabs

① Select the text that you want to contain the new tab settings.

Note: *To learn how to select text, see Chapter 3.*

● If the Ruler is not displayed, click to display the View tab in the Ribbon, and then select the Ruler options check box (☐ changes to ☑).

② Click the tab selector at the left end of the Ruler until it displays the type of tab that you want, and then click the Ruler at the location you want.

Left Tab (⬛)

Center Tab (⬛)

Right Tab (⬛)

Decimal Tab (⬛)

Bar Tab (⬛)

Hanging Indent (⬛)

First Line Indent (⬛)

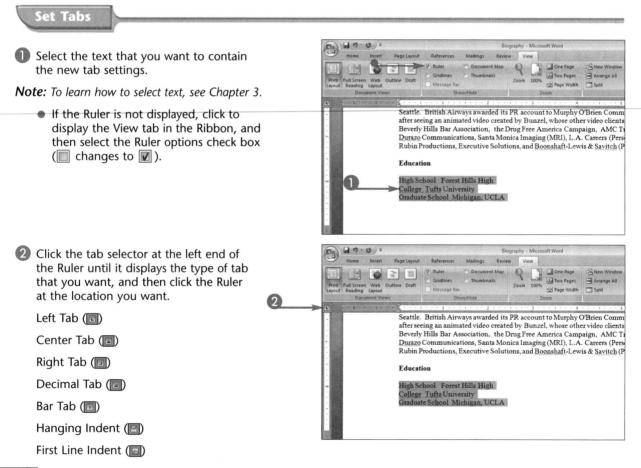

③ Click the location on the Ruler where you want to add the tab.

● The new tab stop appears on the Ruler.

④ Click next to the text that you want to move and press the tab key.

The paragraph aligns to the new tab setting.

● If necessary, you can insert more tabs.

You can delete a tab by selecting the text containing the tab and dragging the tab downward off the Ruler.

PART II

How can I move a tab?

▼ To move a tab, select the paragraphs containing the tab. The tab setting for the selected paragraphs appears on the Ruler. Drag the tab to a new location on the Ruler to change the tab setting.

Is there another method to align columns of information?

▼ Yes. For detailed columns, you can create a table to align data. Tables give you a lot more flexibility in formatting your information. See Chapter 6 for more information on creating tables.

Is there a dialog box available to set tabs?

▼ Yes. You can display the Tabs dialog box by clicking the dialog box launcher (▣) for the Paragraph group of the Home tab. Click the Tabs button in the lower-left section of the Paragraph dialog box. This method enables you to set a tab at a certain inch-mark, select a tab type, and also use leader characters, such as a row of dots, before a tab. Leader characters make information, such as a table of contents, easier to read.

Change Line and Paragraph Spacing

You can change the amount of space between the lines of text and the paragraphs in your document. *Line spacing* is the distance between two lines of text, while *paragraph spacing* is the distance between two paragraphs.

You can choose a line spacing option such as single, 1.5 lines, or double. By default, each new document uses 1.15 line spacing. Word uses the text size to determine line spacing size, which it measures in points. For example, if you select single-line spacing for text using a 10-point font size, the line spacing is

approximately 10 points. You can also add space above or below a paragraph. Using paragraph spacing is better than adding an extra hard return between paragraphs because you have more control over the exact amount of space between the paragraphs.

For paragraph spacing, you can select the amount of points to add. (Keep in mind that there are 72 points to an inch.) You can set spacing either before or after a paragraph, or both. For example, you may want to add space just after document headings so that the headings are not too close to the body text.

Change Line and Paragraph Spacing

Change paragraph spacing

1. Click the Home tab.

2. Select the paragraphs that you want to change.

Note: *To learn how to select text, see Chapter 3.*

3. Click the Line Spacing down arrow (⬛) in the Paragraph group.

   The Line Spacing menu appears.

4. Click a different Line Spacing option.

   ● The line spacing for the selected text changes to reflect your choice.

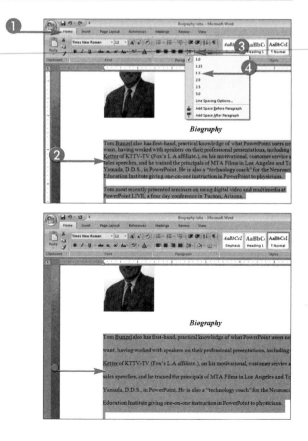

Change indents and spacing options

1 Click the Home tab.

2 Click the Line Spacing down arrow (📑) in the Paragraph group.

3 Click Line Spacing Options.

● The Paragraph dialog box appears, displaying the Indents and Spacing tab.

4 You can use the Line Spacing down arrow (▼) to choose different spacing options.

5 Click OK.

● The line spacing for the selected text changes to reflect your choice.

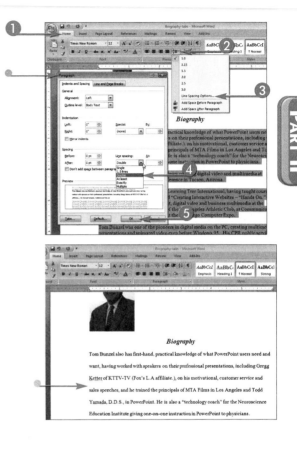

Can I use the keyboard to change line spacing?

▼ Yes. Select the text that you want to change. Press Ctrl+1 to apply single-line spacing, Ctrl+5 to apply 1.5-line spacing, and Ctrl+2 to apply double-line spacing.

How can I add space before or after paragraphs?

▼ With your paragraphs selected, click the Line Spacing down arrow (📑) in the Paragraph group. In the menu that appears, you can select options such as Add Space Before Paragraph and Add Space After Paragraph.

Is there a Live Preview option that I can use to see how paragraph spacing will look?

▼ No, but there is a preview pane in the Indents and Spacing tab of the Paragraph dialog box. Click the Line Spacing down arrow (📑) in the Paragraph group and click Line Spacing Options. In the dialog box that appears, there is a preview window where you can see how the line spacing will look before you apply it.

Add Bullets

You can begin each item in a list with a bullet. Bullets can help to make the list easier to read. You use bullets for items that are not in a particular order, such as a shopping list, agenda, and key points in a document.

You can format a document with bullets in one of two ways. First, you can quickly insert bullets through the Paragraph group in the Home tab. The default bullet is a round button. Word applies the last style that you used if it was different from the default.

If you want a bullet style other than the default, you can select a style that suits your document using the Bullet Library menu. For example, you may want to use round or square bullets in a formal business letter, and arrow or check-mark bullets in more informal documents.

When you add bullets, Word automatically formats the paragraphs as hanging indents.

Add Bullets

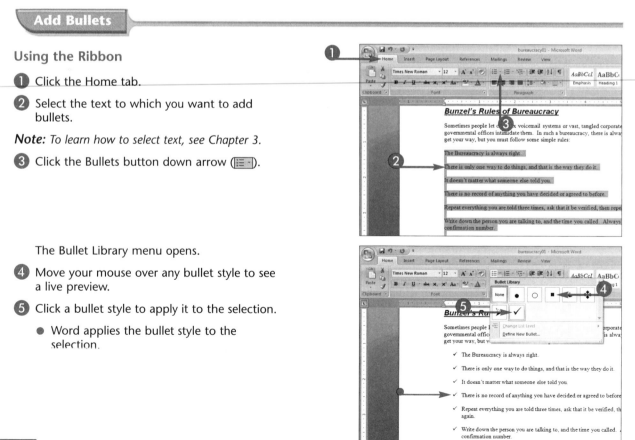

Using the Ribbon

1 Click the Home tab.

2 Select the text to which you want to add bullets.

Note: *To learn how to select text, see Chapter 3.*

3 Click the Bullets button down arrow (⊟▾).

The Bullet Library menu opens.

4 Move your mouse over any bullet style to see a live preview.

5 Click a bullet style to apply it to the selection.

● Word applies the bullet style to the selection.

Change bullets

 Click the Home tab.

② Select the text to which you want to apply a new bullet style.

③ Click the Bullets button down arrow (⊞▾).

The Bullet Library menu opens.

④ Click a bullet style.

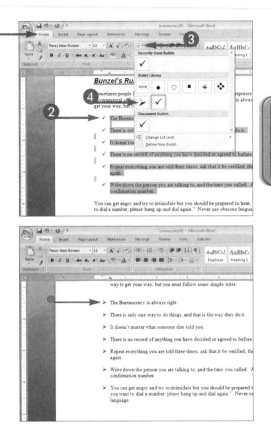

● Word applies the bullet style to the selection.

How can I remove bullets?

▼ Just select the bullet list and click the Bullets button down arrow (⊞▾) in the Paragraph group. When the Bullet Library menu opens, select None. You can also use the Clear Formatting button (⟐) to remove the bullets as long as there is no other special formatting applied to the selection.

Do I have to use the Bullet Library?

▼ No. If you just want to use the default bullet style (⊙), you can just select the range of text, and click directly on the Bullets button (⊞▾). Word applies the default bullet style to your list.

Create a Numbered List

Y ou can begin each item in a list with a number to make your document easier to read. You use numbers for items that must appear in a specific order, such as directions or steps.

The Numbered List feature has two advantages over typing a list manually. First, you do not have to worry about incorrectly numbering your text. Second, when you add or delete an item to or from a numbered list, Word automatically renumbers the entire list for you.

You have two methods available for inserting a numbered list. You can use the numbered list button in the Paragraph group of the Home tab to quickly select the default numbering style, or you can use the Numbering Library menu to select from a set of styles. Word offers a variety of number styles to suit your needs, including numbers, letters, and Roman numerals.

When you create a numbered list, Word automatically formats the paragraphs as hanging indents.

Create a Numbered List

Using the Ribbon

1 Click the Home tab.

2 Select the text that you want to make a numbered list.

Note: To learn how to select text, see Chapter 3.

3 Click the Numbers button down arrow (▾).

The Numbering Library menu opens.

4 Move your mouse over any number style to see a live preview.

5 Click a number style.

● Word applies the number style to the selection.

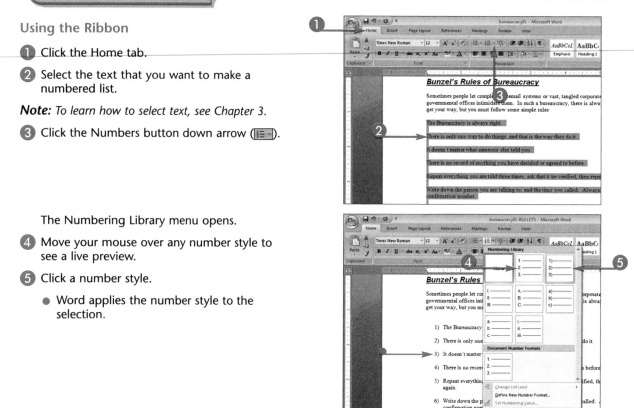

Change number style

1 Click the Home tab.

2 Select the text to which you want to apply a new number style.

3 Click the Numbers button down arrow (▦).

The Numbering Library menu opens.

4 Click a number style.

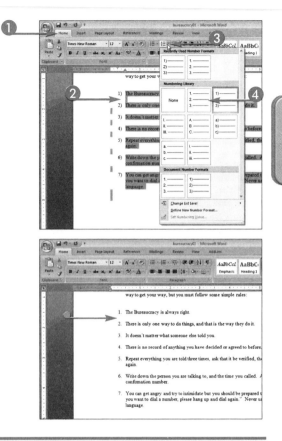

● Word applies the number style to the selection.

How can I create a numbered list as I type?

▼ Type **1.**, insert a space or a tab, and then type the first item in the list. Press Enter; Word automatically starts the next item with the next number. To end the numbered list, press Enter twice or press Backspace. You must click the Automatic Numbered Lists option (▢ changes to ☑) in the Proofing Options dialog box for this feature to work. See the task "Change AutoFormat Options" to learn more about this feature.

Can I change the number that Word uses to start my list?

▼ Yes. Select the first numbered item and click the Numbers button down arrow (▦). The Numbering Library menu opens. Click Set Numbering Value to change the beginning value of the list.

What other options do I have for lists?

▼ You can also create outlines and custom lists. You can use the Outline view button (▣) to create a multi-level outline and define your levels. You can also use the Multi Level List button (▦) to define a custom list with different types of levels. For more information on these features, consult Word's online help.

Apply a Quick Style

You can quickly format the text in your document by applying a Quick Style to it. Quick Styles can save you time when you want to apply the same formatting to many different areas in a document. Quick Styles also help you keep the appearance of text in a document consistent.

For example, if you manually format all of your document headings, you may accidentally use different formatting for each heading, which can confuse your reader. Applying a Quick Style ensures that all of the document headings contain the same formatting.

Word includes several Quick Styles that you can apply to text in your document. You can also create a Quick Style and apply it. To create a Quick Style, see the task "Create a Quick Style."

To apply a Quick Style, you need to select the text to which you want to apply it and open the Quick Style gallery. As you move your mouse over the Quick Styles in the gallery, you will see a live preview of how the selection would look if you applied that Quick Style.

Apply a Quick Style

1 Click the Home tab.

2 Select the text to which you want to apply a style.

Note: *To learn how to select text, see Chapter 3.*

3 Click the Quick Style gallery More button.

The Quick Style gallery opens.

● As your mouse moves over a Quick Style, a live preview shows you how it will look.

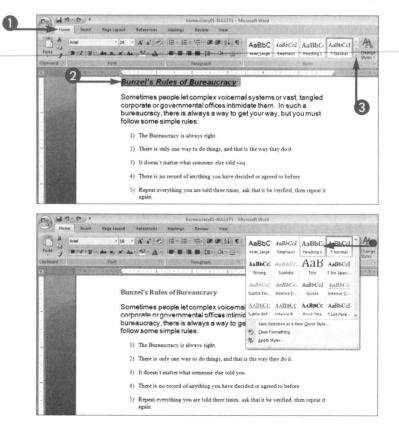

④ Click the Quick Style that you want to apply.

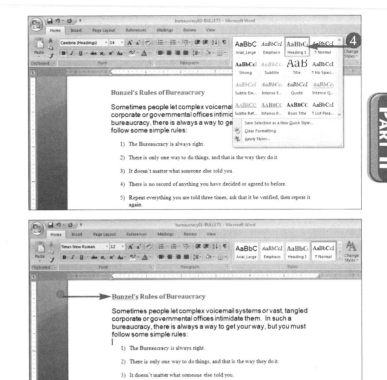

● In the document, Word applies the Quick Style to your selected text.

Can I apply Quick Styles with a keyboard command?

▼ Yes. Select a block of text and press Ctrl+Shift+S. The Apply Styles dialog box appears, where you can type in the name of a Quick Style, or select one from the drop-down list, and quickly apply it to the selection.

Why is the style that I created yesterday not in my Quick Styles gallery?

▼ You are probably working in a different document based on a different template. Open the document with the style that you created yesterday and copy and paste a block of the text into your new document. Word adds the Quick Style to the gallery for the new document. If you want to change the style's name, right-click it and select Modify. For more information, see the task "Modify a Quick Style."

Can I get rid of a style that I applied but do not like?

▼ Yes. To remove the last Quick Style that you applied, click the Undo button (🔄), click the Clear Formatting button (🖌), or just select another Quick Style such as Normal. To remove a Quick Style from the gallery, right-click the style and click Remove from Quick Style Gallery. For more information, see the task "Modify a Quick Style."

Create a Quick Style

You can create and save a *Quick Style* that allows you to apply multiple formatting changes to text in one step.

You can store your new style in the Quick Styles gallery so that you can apply it to text in new documents that you create.

You can also save your Quick Style as a *building block* that you can reapply to a document. If you do not store the style in a saved template, you can apply the style to text in the current document only. For more information on templates and building blocks, see the tasks "Create New Documents from Templates," and "Using the Building Blocks Organizer" in Chapter 5.

For information on applying one of Word's built-in Quick Styles or a style that you have created, see the task "Apply a Quick Style."

Create a Quick Style

1 Click the Home tab.

2 Select the text that displays the formatting that you want to save.

Note: *To learn how to select text, see Chapter 3.*

3 Click the More button.

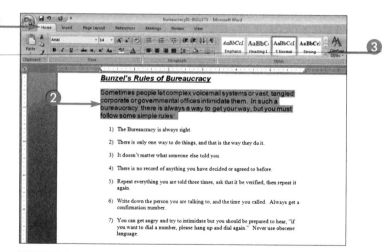

The Quick Styles gallery opens.

4 Click Save Selection as a New Quick Style.

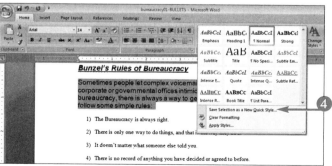

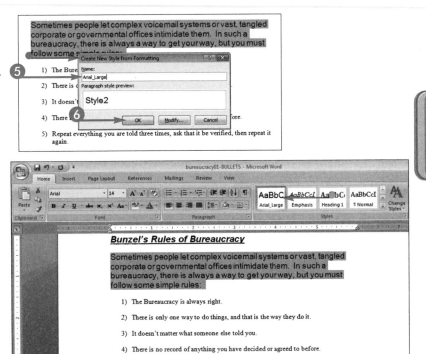

- The Create New Style from Formatting dialog box appears.

5 Type a name for the new style.

6 Click OK.

- Word adds your newly created Quick Style to the Quick Styles gallery.

How can I quickly apply a new style to a new document?

▼ To the right of the Quick Styles gallery is Change Styles. You can click its down arrow (⊡) to see a submenu of style sets, colors, or fonts. Click Style Set to find a list of pre-formatted Quick Style sets. Try applying one of these Quick Style sets to a new blank document, or to a document that is already formatted, to give it a distinctively different look, with all of the elements coordinated. The gallery of Quick Styles changes to reflect the Quick Style set that you clicked. You can then use all of the styles in the gallery to build your document.

If I find a Quick Style set that I like, can I make it the default set for all documents?

▼ Yes. You can click the Change Styles down arrow (⊡) and instead of applying a style set, you can click Set as Default to make the current style set the default set for any new documents. You should probably save the current default style set before you do this to make sure that you can reapply it In the future.

When I select text for a new Quick Style and I open the Quick Styles gallery, the selected text keeps changing its appearance. What is happening?

▼ When you move your mouse through any gallery, such as the Quick Styles gallery, Word's Live Preview feature shows you what it would look like if the style were selected and applied. When you move your mouse outside the gallery, the feature will stop.

Modify a Quick Style

You can change a Quick Style that you have created. When you do so, Word automatically changes all of the text that is formatted using that Quick Style. This helps you to quickly update the appearance of the document. Modifying the Quick Style allows you to experiment with several formats until the document appears the way you want.

Modifying a Quick Style also ensures consistency in a document's formatting. Rather than worry about changing all of the headings in a document, you can apply a heading Quick Style to the text. When you

need to modify that Quick Style, you only need to modify it once; Word updates all paragraphs formatted with that Quick Style, saving you time and ensuring consistency.

You can modify a Quick Style in one of two ways. First, you can select new formatting options in the Modify Style dialog box. Second, you can modify text formatted with the Quick Style that you want to change and then update the Quick Style with the Update to Match Selection command.

Modify a Quick Style

1. Click the Home tab.

2. Select the Quick Style that you want to change.

3. Right-click the Quick Style.

4. Click Modify.

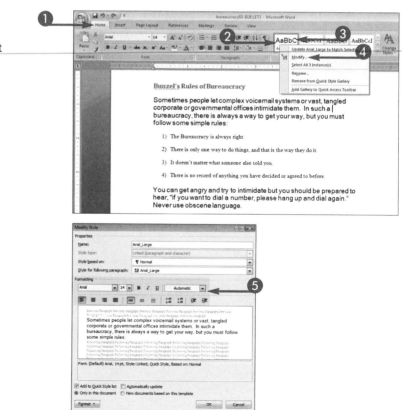

The Modify Style dialog box opens.

5. Click a formatting option.

● In this example, click the font size down arrow (▾) and choose a new font size.

You can make any other changes that you want to the Quick Style.

6 Click OK.

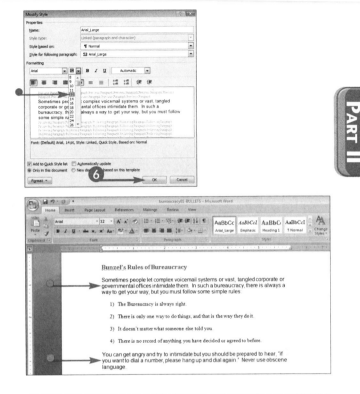

● All of the text that uses the modified style displays your changes.

PART II

MASTER IT

What types of formatting changes can I make to a style?

▼ Using the buttons in the Modify Style dialog box, you can change the font type, size, style, and color. You can also change alignment, paragraph and line spacing, and indents. In addition, you can click the Format button in the lower-left corner of the dialog box to set tabs, add borders or frames, assign a shortcut key, or add numbering.

How do I add a style from a Word 2003 document to the Quick Styles gallery?

▼ When you open a Word 2003 document in Compatibility Mode, its original styles are available through the Styles group More button. You can select text that is formatted with this style and make it a Quick Style as described in the task "Create a Quick Style."

How do I use the Update to Match Selection command to modify a style?

▼ Make formatting changes to any of the text that you want to modify and then select the text. In the Quick Styles gallery, right-click the style that is selected and then click Update (Name of Style) to Match Selection from the menu that appears.

Can I select all text that has a certain style applied to it?

▼ Yes. To do so, right-click the Quick Style in the Quick Style gallery and then click Select All (Number of) Instances. Word selects all text that is formatted with this style in your document.

Copy Formatting

I f you need to use the same formatting only once or twice, and you do not want to go to the trouble of creating a style, you can make one section of text in your document look exactly like another by copying the formatting. For more information on creating and applying styles, see the tasks "Create a Quick Style" and "Apply a Quick Style."

If you copy the formatting of text that contains more than one type of the same formatting, such as multiple fonts, then Word copies only the first type of formatting. For example, if you select a paragraph that contains the Times New Roman font followed by the Arial font, then Word copies only the Times New Roman font format.

Copy Formatting

1 Click the Home tab.

2 Select the text that has the formatting that you want to copy.

3 Click the Format Painter button (🖌).

Your mouse pointer (🖎) turns into a paintbrush (🖌).

4 Drag through the text that you want to change.

5 Release the mouse button.

● Word copies the formatting to the selected text.

Show or Hide Formatting

Y ou can display paragraph and other formatting marks in your document. Formatting marks can help you to edit your document and check for errors such as extra spaces between words.

Word displays several formatting marks. For example, the paragraph mark (¶) indicates where you pressed the Enter key to start a new paragraph in the document. A small arrow (→) indicates where you pressed the Tab key to indent text. The space mark (▪)

shows where you pressed the spacebar to leave a blank space.

When you display formatting marks, Word also displays hidden text in your document. Word underlines text with a dotted line (.....) to indicate hidden text. Formatting marks appear only on your screen; they do not appear in your printed documents.

When you finish reviewing your document with formatting marks, you can hide them again.

PART II

Show or Hide Formatting

1 Click the Home tab.

2 Click the Show/Hide button (¶).

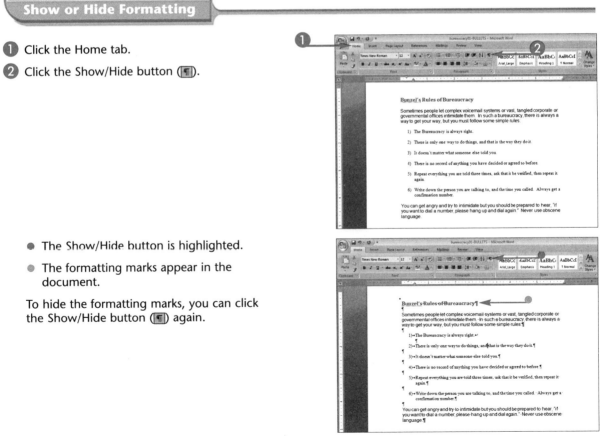

● The Show/Hide button is highlighted.

● The formatting marks appear in the document.

To hide the formatting marks, you can click the Show/Hide button (¶) again.

Change AutoFormat Options

Y ou can change the default formatting that Word automatically applies to your text as you type. You can review all of the automatic changes that Word makes and deactivate some or all of the options.

By default, if you type two hyphens, Word replaces them with an em dash (—). Word also replaces certain fractions with fractional characters; for example, Word replaces 1/2 with ½. Word also replaces ordinals (1st)

with superscript characters (1st). In some cases, Word applies some styles and formatting. For example, if you type an asterisk (*), press Tab, type text, and press Enter, Word formats the paragraph as a bulleted list item.

You can review and change these and many other options in the AutoFormat As You Type and AutoFormat tabs of the AutoCorrect dialog box.

Change AutoFormat Options

① Click the Office button.

② Click Word Options.

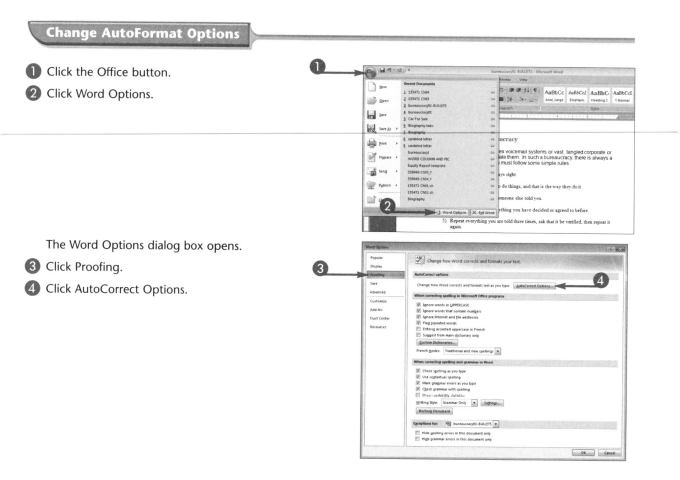

The Word Options dialog box opens.

③ Click Proofing.

④ Click AutoCorrect Options.

The AutoCorrect dialog box opens.

⑤ Click the AutoFormat tab.

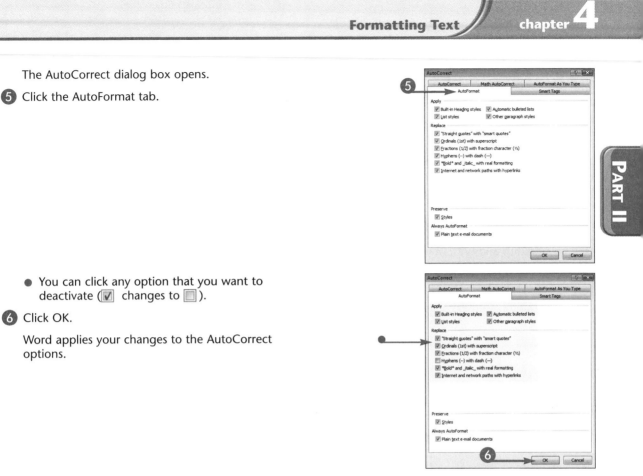

● You can click any option that you want to deactivate (☑ changes to ☐).

⑥ Click OK.

Word applies your changes to the AutoCorrect options.

MASTER IT

There are still some features that Word uses automatically that I want to turn off. How can I do that?

▼ Besides the AutoFormat tab in the AutoCorrect dialog box, you should also take a close look at the AutoFormat As You Type tab, where other features are turned on (or off) by default. You can deselect the check boxes (☑ changes to ☐) to turn off the automated bullets or numbered lists as you type, along with a number of other suggested features.

There are still some symbols that are replaced without my wanting them to. What else can I do?

▼ You can click the AutoCorrect tab in the AutoCorrect dialog box and see whether you have any symbols in the list that are set to replace certain keystrokes that you prefer not to use, such as copyright or registered trademark. For more information, see the task "Using AutoCorrect" in Chapter 3.

Change the Document View

Word offers several ways to display your document. You can choose the view that best suits your needs by clicking the appropriate icon in the lower-right section of your screen.

The Print Layout view is the default view and displays your document, as it would appear on a printed page. It includes top and bottom margins, headers, footers, and page numbers. This view is most appropriate when making formatting changes to the entire document, as shown in this chapter. Print Layout view is a quick and easy alternative to Print Preview.

Full Screen Reading view is for reviewing a long document and not making any changes. It is particularly useful for reading on a notebook.

Web Layout view displays your document as it would appear in a Web browser. If you plan to save your document as a Web page, then you can refer to the Web Layout view to preview how it will look online.

Outline view presents your document in outline format so that you can organize your ideas more easily. For more information on the Outline view, see the task "Using Outline View."

Draft view is best for editing longer documents and lets you see important formatting such as section breaks.

Change the Document View

Print Layout view

① Click the Print Layout View button (⊞) on the status bar.

● This view simplifies the document so that you can quickly enter, edit, and format text, and it displays the document as it would appear on a printed page.

Full Screen Reading view

① Click the Full Screen Reading view button (⊞) on the status bar.

● This view lets you read your document on the computer, especially a notebook, without making changes. It is best for longer documents.

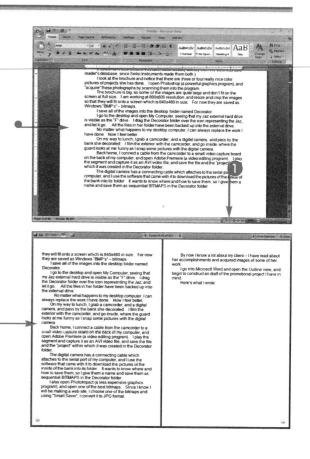

PART II

Web Layout view

1️⃣ Click the Web Layout View button () on the status bar.

● This view lets you see how your document would appear online if you saved it as a Web page.

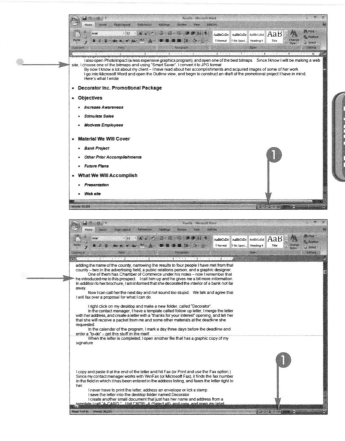

Draft view

1️⃣ Click the Draft View button () on the status bar.

● This view lets you see a larger screen for your document without a ruler.

MASTER IT

What is the difference between Draft view and Print Layout view?

▼ Draft view provides more screen space by removing the Ruler from the left side of the screen, and providing a larger view of the page. It also reveals section breaks but does not show margins. Print Layout view is meant to show you the closest representation of how the document will look when it is output by your printer. It also shows your headers, footers, margins, and page numbers.

When would I use Print Preview instead of Print Layout view?

▼ Even though Print Layout view simulates your print output, it cannot show you a full-page view of the document unless you zoom out. For more information about zooming in or out, see the task "Move through a Document" in Chapter 3. The Print Preview, which appears under the Print options when you click the Office button, lets you fine-tune your print options and see your entire document at once, including multiple-page spreads.

Using Outline View

Outline view is used to view your documents in a hierarchical structure, with smaller topics nested under larger topics. It is a convenient way to view the overall flow of topics within your document and to adjust the main points for each topic so that they flow smoothly from one to another.

When using the default template, Word uses Heading 1, Heading 2, and Heading 3 styles for assigning three different heading levels within your document. Depending on the complexity of your document, you can create additional heading levels.

You can change to Outline view so that you see only the highest-level headings, all of the first- and second-level headings, or all of the headings in your document. This allows you to evaluate each topic level to make sure that it fits appropriately with the document flow. For example, in a document about animals, you would probably include a topic called "Tigers" under a topic called "Big Cats," rather than on the same level or higher in the outline.

When you switch to Outline view, an Outlining tab also appears on the Ribbon, giving you additional outline features.

Using Outline View

Show a document outline

1 Click the Outline View button (▤).

The document changes to Outline view.

● The Outlining tab appears on the Word Ribbon.

● You can click Close Outline View to return to the document.

● You can click (▤) to change back to Print Layout view, or (▤) for Draft view.

Show specific heading levels

① Click the Show Level down arrow (▼).

② Click the heading level that you want to view.

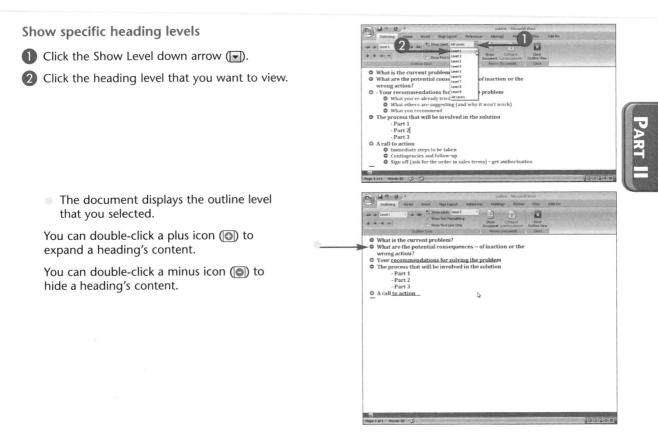

● The document displays the outline level that you selected.

You can double-click a plus icon (⊕) to expand a heading's content.

You can double-click a minus icon (⊖) to hide a heading's content.

What does the Outlining tab in the Ribbon do?

▼ The Outlining tab in the Ribbon loads by default, and contains tools that let you move topics up and down, as well as promote or demote topics, without using the Cut-and-Paste feature.

How do I move my topics in the Outlining tab in the Ribbon?

▼ You can change your topic order within the document, or promote or demote topics, using the following tools in the Outlining tab in the Ribbon. Select the topic and then click one of the following keys:

Move Topic Up (▲)
Move Topic Down (▼)
Promote Topic (◄)
Demote Topic (►)
Promote to Heading 1 (◄◄)
Demote to Body Text (►►)

You can also use the Tab key to demote, and Shift+Tab to promote, a selected topic.

Change Margins

Y ou can change the margins to suit your needs. A margin is the amount of space between the text in your document and the edge of your paper.

Every page has a margin at the top, bottom, left, and right edges. By default, Word automatically sets margins of 1" on all sides.

Increasing the size of margins increases the white space on your page. This can help to make your document easier to read. However, reducing the size of margins lets you fit more information on a page.

Keep in mind that most printers cannot print right to the edge of a page and typically require that you use a margin of at least 0.25 inches on all sides. You can check the manual that came with your printer for more information about its exact settings.

A change to the margins affects either all of the pages in your document, or only the text that you select. To change the margins for only specific pages in your document, you must divide your document into sections, using the Breaks feature of the Page Setup group in the Page Layout tab on the Ribbon. For more about section breaks, refer to *Teach Yourself VISUALLY Word 2007* (Wiley, 2007).

Change Margins

① Click the Page Layout tab.

② Click the Margins down arrow ([▼]).

The Margin Options menu opens.

③ Click Custom Margins.

● You can also select a margin pre-set to apply it to the document.

The Page Setup dialog box appears, where you can specify margin values.

④ Change a margin setting.

This examples decreases the left and right margins.

⑤ Click OK.

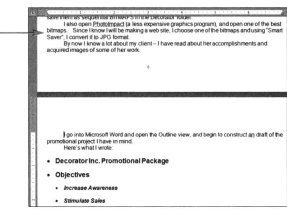

● Word changes the margins of your document.

PART II

Can I change the left and right margins for only part of my document?

▼ Yes. Click the Breaks down arrow (▼) to insert either a Continuous or Next Page section break in the document. Then use the Margin options in the Page Setup group in the Page Layout tab on the Ribbon to adjust the margins within the section that you want to change.

What other method can I use to change my margins?

▼ Make the Ruler visible by clicking the View Ruler button (▣) on the right scroll bar. Place your cursor over the right or left margin (➥ changes to ⟷) and drag the margin in or out. You can also visually drag the margin marker in the Print Preview window to change the page margins. See Chapter 8 for more information on using print preview.

I would like to have a guide in the document to show me the margins. Can I do that?

▼ Yes. Click the Office button and choose Word Options; the Word Options dialog box opens. Click Advanced options in the left panel and scroll down to the Show Document Content section. Click to select the Show Text Boundaries option (☐ changes to ☑).

Align Text on a Page

You can vertically align text on each page of your document to fit your needs. You can choose to align the text to the top, center, or bottom of the page, or to justify the text.

By default, Word vertically aligns document text to the top of the page. When you select the center-align option, Word aligns the text between the top and bottom margins of the page. When you select bottom alignment, your text aligns to the bottom of the page. The justified option spaces your text evenly on the page. You can center-align text to create title pages and short memos. For more information on margins, see the task "Change Margins." You must switch to Print Layout view or Print Preview to see any changes in the margins. See the task "Change the Document View," as well as Chapter 8, to learn about previewing a document.

MASTER IT

What if I want to remove the vertical alignment from my document?

▼ To remove the alignment, perform Steps 1 to 6 in this task. In Step 6, click Top and then click OK. This returns you to the default alignment. Alternatively, right after you make the changes, click the Undo button (⟲).

Align Text on a Page

1 Click anywhere in the document or section that you want to vertically align.

2 Click the Page Layout tab.

3 Click the Page Setup group dialog box launcher (▣).

4 In the Page Setup dialog box, click the Layout tab.

5 Click the Vertical alignment down arrow (▼) and click a vertical alignment option.

● You can click the Section start down arrow (▼) to align only a certain section of your document.

6 Click OK.

● Word vertically aligns the text on the page.

● You can click the Zoom Slider (▣) to view more of the page.

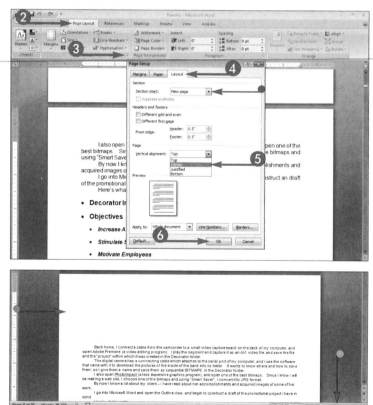

98

Change Page Orientation

You can change the orientation of pages in your document to fit your page content. Orientation refers to the way that Word prints information on a page.

Portrait is the standard page orientation, and you can use it to print most documents, such as letters, reports, and brochures. Portrait orientation prints information across the short side of a page. Landscape orientation prints information across the long side of a page. Certificates and tables are often printed using landscape orientation. You can change the page orientation for only specific pages in your document. For example, in a report, you can print a page displaying a table in landscape orientation and print the rest of the pages in portrait orientation.

MASTER IT

How do I apply a different orientation for only part of a document?

▼ To change the orientation for part of a document, in the Page Layout tab, click the Breaks down arrow (▼) to insert a Next Page section break in the document. Then use the steps in this task to apply a different orientation to the page.

PART II

Change Page Orientation

1 Click the Page Layout tab.

2 Click the Orientation down arrow (▼) in the Page Setup group.

The Orientation menu appears.

3 Click the Orientation option that you want to apply.

Word changes the orientation of the page.

● You can click the Zoom Slider (▣) to view more of the page.

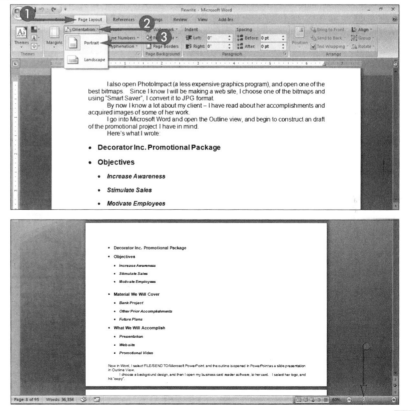

Add Page Numbers

You can have Word number the pages in your document. Numbering pages can help to make a long document easier to organize so that your reader can keep the pages in order.

Word can display page numbers at the top or bottom of the pages in your document. When you add page numbers, Word sets up headers or footers for the document. When you add, remove, or rearrange text in your document, Word automatically adjusts the page numbers for you. You can also hide the page number on the first page of the document, which is useful when your first page is a title page.

You can choose to align your page numbers to the left, right, or center. You can also use the inside or outside alignment options if you plan to bind your document.

You can preview the position and alignment settings that you choose for the page numbers. Page numbers display on your screen only in the Print Layout view or in Print Preview. For more information about using Print Preview, see the task "Change the Document View," as well as Chapter 8.

Add Page Numbers

1 Click the Insert tab.

2 Click the Page Number down arrow (⬇).

The Page Number menu appears.

3 Select a placement option.

This example uses Bottom of Page.

A submenu appears.

4 Click one of the page number options.

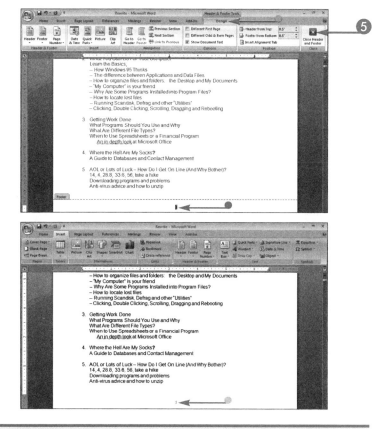

- Word applies the page number choice that you selected as a preview.

This example shows a page number in the footer.

- The Header and Footer Tools Design tab opens.

⑤ Click Close Header and Footer to accept the page number options.

- Word adds the page numbers to your document.

You may have to scroll to the bottom or top of the page to view the page numbers.

Can I specify a format for my page numbers, such as letters or Roman numerals?

▼ Yes. To do this, click the Page Numbers down arrow (▼) and select Format Page Numbers. In the Page Number Format dialog box, click the Number Format down arrow (▼) and select the Number format that you want to use for the page numbers. Then click OK.

What are headers and footers?

▼ *Headers* and *footers* are placeholders that appear at the top and bottom of your document, respectively, to hold information such as page number, date, or other relevant repetitive data. When you add page numbers, Word creates a header or footer, depending on the position that you select. You can also include other document information in a header or footer. For more, see the task "Add a Header or Footer."

How do I remove page numbers?

▼ To remove page numbers, you must delete the page numbers from the documents header or footer. To display headers and footers, select the Insert tab and then click either Header or Footer in the Header and Footer group of the Insert tab on the Ribbon. Click Remove Footer or Edit Footer (or Remove Header or Edit Header) to modify or delete only the page number.

Add a Header
or Footer

You can add a header and footer to every page in your document to give it a more professional look. A *header* appears at the top of the page, while a *footer* appears at the bottom.

A header or footer can contain information such as a company name, the author's name, or the chapter title. You can edit and format this text as you would any other text in your document. See Chapter 4 for more information on formatting text.

You can use the Header and Footer options on the Insert tab on the Ribbon to insert special information. For example, you can insert the page number and the

total number of document pages into a header or footer. If you add, remove, or rearrange text, Word automatically adjusts the page numbers for you.

You can also quickly insert the date and time into a header or footer. Word updates the date and time automatically every time you open or print your document if you click the Update Automatically option checkbox in the Insert Date and Time dialog box.

Word displays the headers and footers in a document only in the Print Layout view and Print Preview. For more information about Print Preview, see the task "Change the Document View," as well as Chapter 8.

Add a Header or Footer

① Click the Insert tab.

② Click either the Header or Footer down arrow (⏷).

Word displays the Header or Footer options menu.

③ Click an option.

This example selects Blank footer from the Built-In options menu.

● The Header and Footer Tools Design tab opens.

④ Type and format the text you want.

● You can add a page number to the footer. See the task "Add Page Numbers" for more information.

Note: For more information on formatting text, see Chapter 4.

⑤ Click Close Header and Footer when you have finished creating the header or footer.

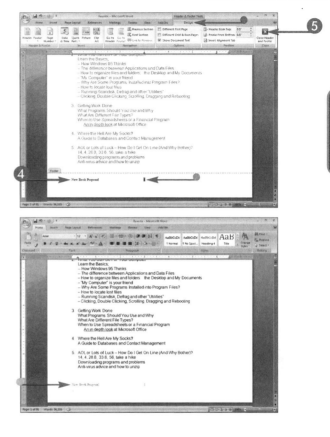

● Word inserts the header or footer information.

You may have to scroll up or down to view the top or bottom of the page.

This example shows the footer on the page.

How do I delete a header or footer?

▼ Click either the Header or Footer down arrow (▼) and then click either Edit Header or Edit Footer. Select all of the information in the header or footer area and then press Delete.

What other information can I quickly insert into a header or footer?

▼ The Header and Footer Tools Design tab contains an Insert panel with Date and Time, Quick Parts, Picture, and Clip Art options. For more information about inserting the date and time, or how to create and insert a Quick Parts entry, see Chapter 3.

What formatting options do a header and footer automatically include?

▼ A header and footer include some predefined tabs, such as a center tab and a right-aligned tab. This formatting sets up three areas for information: one at the left margin, one centered on the page, and one at the right margin. You can press Tab to move and type text in the center or right side of the header or footer.

Add Footnotes or Endnotes

You can add a footnote or endnote to your document to provide additional information about specific text. Footnotes and endnotes can contain information such as an explanation, comment, or reference to the text. Footnotes appear at the bottom of a page, while endnotes appear at the end of a document. Word displays the footnote or endnote area of your document in the Print Layout view.

Word numbers the footnotes or endnotes that you add, beginning with the number 1 or the Roman numeral i. You can enter any amount of text for a footnote or endnote.

After you insert your footnote or endnote, you can see it in any view except Draft or Outline view. When you move the mouse pointer over the footnote or endnote number, Word displays the footnote or endnote text.

If you add or remove footnotes or endnotes, Word automatically adjusts the numbers of the footnotes or endnotes in your document. Word also ensures that the text that you type for a footnote always begins on the same page as the footnote number.

Add Footnotes or Endnotes

① Click the References tab.

② Click where you want the number of the footnote or endnote to appear.

③ Click a footnote option.

This example uses Insert Footnote.

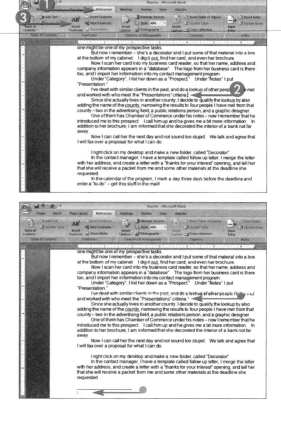

● Word inserts a footnote or endnote with the first automatic number in the document.

● Word creates a footnote or endnote entry at the bottom of the page for you to enter information.

④ Type the text for the footnote or endnote.

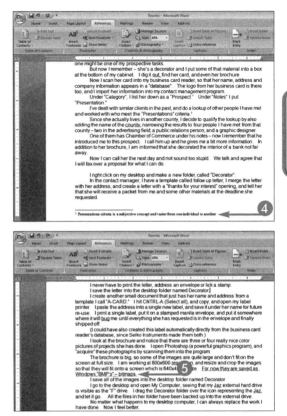

⑤ Continue to the next place where you want to insert a footnote, and repeat these steps.

MASTER IT

How do I edit an existing footnote or endnote?

▼ You can edit a footnote or endnote as you would edit any text in your document. Just move to the page that contains the footnote or endnote, and click within its area to edit your text normally. You can find your footnotes or endnotes in succession by clicking Next Footnote, or by clicking the Next Footnote down arrow (▼) to move to the next or previous footnote or endnote.

How do endnotes work?

▼ Endnotes are similar to footnotes, except that the referenced information appears at the end of the document, rather than at the bottom of the page that contains the reference number.

Can I delete a footnote or endnote?

▼ Yes. You can delete a footnote or endnote that you no longer need by selecting the footnote or endnote number in your document, and then pressing Delete.

Can I change the formatting of footnotes or endnotes?

▼ Yes. Click the dialog box launcher (▣) in the Footnotes group of the References tab. In the Footnote and Endnote dialog box, select the options that you want to change. For example, you can select a number format, a custom mark, the starting number, and the type of numbering. Although the default setting is Continuous, you can also restart numbering in each section.

Add and View Comments

omments are notes that you make in a document that can be used as reminders, questions, or discussion points. They are typically used in a document that is being routed to different people in an organization for review, but you can also use them for your own writing. Word comments duplicate the effect of writing notes in the margins, attaching yellow adhesive notes to a page, or other means of editing a document by hand.

People can add other comments, or modify comments that are already added to the document. This helps to make the reviewing process flow smoothly. Also, by using comments, you can route a document using e-mail to a remote reviewer, so that the reviewing process can take place quickly.

In Normal view, you can add comments in the review pane at the bottom of the window. In Print Layout view, the comments appear in the page margins, with callout lines leading back to the text to which the comment applies.

Add and View Comments

Add a comment in Print Layout view

1 Place your cursor in the document where you want to insert a comment, or select an appropriate block of text.

Note: *To learn more about selecting text, see Chapter 3.*

2 Click the Review tab.

3 Click New Comment.

- The selected text is automatically highlighted.

- A comment balloon appears in the margin, with a callout line leading back to the highlighted text.

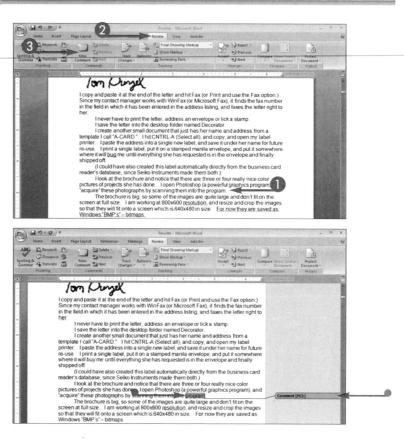

④ Type your comment after the colon (:) in the comment balloon.

⑤ Click the Draft View button (■).

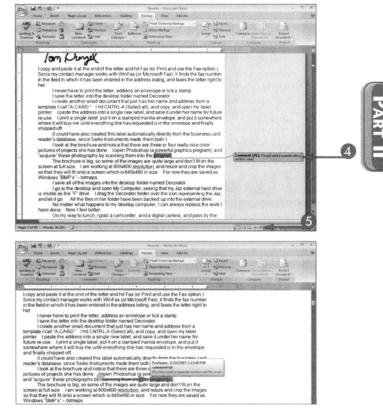

● In Draft view, the comment text only appears when you move the cursor over the highlighted comment.

How do I delete a comment?

▼ You can delete a comment after you have inserted it into your document. Locate the comment by using the Previous or Next comment button in the Comments group of the Review tab. Then click anywhere in the comment and click Delete in the Comments group of the Review tab.

Can any of the comments be formatted?

▼ Yes. Comments can be formatted just like any other text in Word. You can use bold, italics, or different fonts for your comments. See Chapter 4 for more information on formatting text in Word.

Is there a way to print comments?

▼ By default, Word will not print comments. To enable comment printing, click the Office button and then click Print. In the Print dialog box, click the Print What down arrow (▼). Select the Document showing markup option and click OK. Your document will print with comments. For more information on printing Word documents, see Chapter 8.

Do I have to enter comments in each view?

▼ No. You can switch between Draft view and Print Layout view, and your comments are visible, regardless of the view in which you entered them.

Create Columns

You can display text in columns similar to those that you find in a newspaper. This format is useful for creating documents such as newsletters and brochures, and can make your document easier to read.

You can create one, two, or three columns of equal size, or up to 45 columns if you like. You can also create two columns and have one column wider than the other. Using one wide column can add an interesting visual effect to your document.

Regardless of the number of columns that you create, Word fills one column with text before starting a new column. You can control where Word places text by inserting column breaks. You can also have Word display a vertical line between the columns.

In the Print Layout view, Word displays columns side-by-side. For more information, see the task "Change the Document View." The columns appear when you print your document, whether or not you display them on your screen.

Create Columns

1 Click the Page Layout tab.

2 Select the text that you want to format into columns.

3 Click the Columns down arrow (⏷).

The Columns menu appears.

4 Click the column format that you want to use.

● The text layout changes to the column configuration that you chose.

5 Click the Columns down arrow (⏷).

6 Click More Columns.

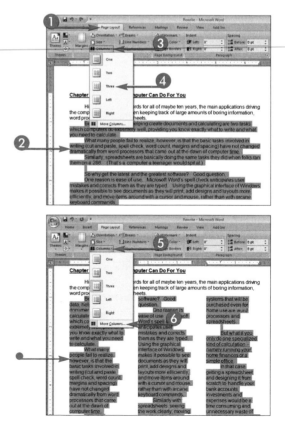

The Columns dialog box opens, where you can change the pre-set configuration manually.

⑦ Click a column format.

⑧ Click OK.

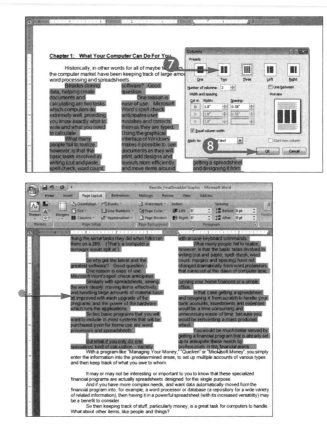

● The text layout changes to the column configuration that you chose.

Can I quickly create columns for an entire document?

▼ Yes. Press Ctrl+A to select the entire document. Then follow the steps in this task to create columns for the entire document.

How do I move text from one column to the top of the next column?

▼ Just copy and paste (or drag and drop) the selected text from one column to another. The columns will adjust to the new placement of the text. You can also click the Breaks down arrow (▼) and select a column break to indicate that the text following the break should begin in the next column.

Do I need to use the Columns dialog box to change the width of the columns?

▼ No. You can place your cursor over any column edge in the ruler for that column until ▷ changes to ◁═▷. You can then drag the column edge to the left or right to manually adjust the width of the columns.

How would I make one part of my document a certain number of columns and place a different number of columns immediately after it?

▼ Return to your columns and select the second portion again, and repeat the steps in the task, choosing the options you want. The newly selected text conforms to the new configuration.

Create New Documents from Templates

Rather than selecting a lot of individual formatting options, you may want to start with a document that includes some formatting (and even text) that is already set up for you. To do so, you can use Microsoft Office installed templates. These templates save you time when creating common types of documents, such as letters, faxes, memos, and reports. Templates provide the layout and formatting so that you can concentrate on the content of your document.

When you select a template, a document immediately appears on your screen with areas for you to fill in your personalized information. For example, the letter templates provide areas for the name of the person to whom you are sending the letter, the date, and the salutation of the letter. You can replace the sample text in the template with the text that you want to use.

Other templates provide other layouts and appropriate text for the document type. The templates that install with Word 2007 also have some themed layouts for different types of documents for the same organization. More templates are available for download directly through the Templates panel.

Create New Documents from Templates

1 Click the Office button.

2 Click New.

The New Document dialog box appears, displaying the Templates panel.

3 Click Installed Templates.

4 Scroll down to locate the template that you want.

- Previews of selected templates appear in the right pane.

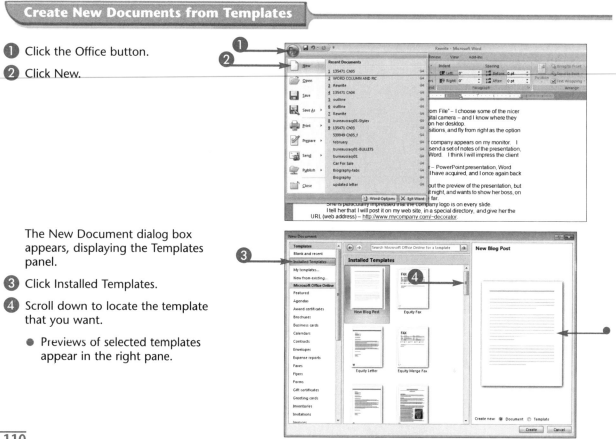

⑤ Click the document template that you want to use.

⑥ Click Create.

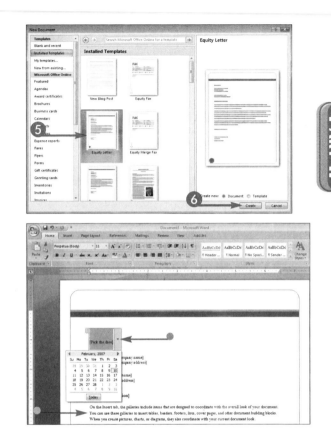

The document appears on your screen.

● You can revise the built-in features of the template.

In this example, you can click the down arrow (▼) next to the date to select a date from the pop-up calendar.

● You can now enter information where required to complete the document.

Can I create my own templates?

▼ Yes. Open the document that you want to use as the basis for the template. Click the Office button, click the Save As down arrow (▼), and choose Word Template. Type a name for the template and then click Save. Make sure that you designate the Templates folder in which you want to save it. The next time you create a new document, follow these steps to find a saved template. Click the Office button and click New. In the New Document window, click My templates for Word 2007.

How does the New Blog Post feature work?

▼ Blogs are online bulletin boards that need to be hosted on a Web site. When you select a New Blog Post template, Word asks you where the blog is hosted, so that when you save the entry, it can be posted directly online. In order to use this feature, you need to have an online blog site and be able to enter the location, username, and password.

Apply a Theme to a Document

A theme lets you create documents that look like they have been professionally designed for printing, e-mail, reading in Word, or distribution online.

With the application of a complete theme, you can make sure that your fonts, colors, and any special effects that you use in your document are properly coordinated.

Themes are available in the Themes group of the Page Layout tab on the Ribbon. You can use the drop-down menu for the main themes to apply a complete theme, or use the Color, Font, and Effects subsections to fine-tune the current theme.

If you make changes to the current theme, and you like the combination of colors, fonts, and effects that you have created, you can save the revised theme as a new theme that you can reuse later on in other projects.

Besides the themes that are built in to Office 2007, you can also find more themes online at the Microsoft Office 2007 Web site.

1 Click the Page Layout tab.

2 Click the Themes down arrow (⏷).

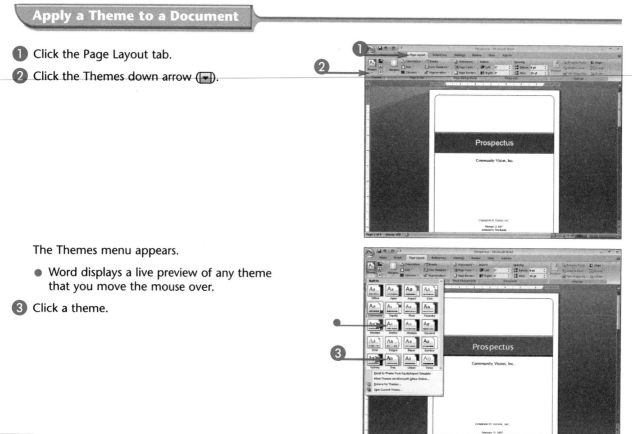

The Themes menu appears.

● Word displays a live preview of any theme that you move the mouse over.

3 Click a theme.

- The document changes to resemble the elements of the theme.

Note: *Because themes generally affect mainly the colors of graphic objects, their subtle results may not be clearly visible in black and white.*

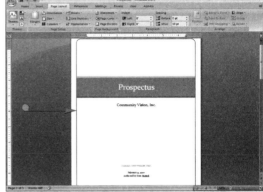

- You can revise the theme manually if you like. For example, you can choose a different set of colors, fonts, or effects from those specific options in the Theme group.

4 Click the Themes down arrow (⏷).

5 Click Save Current Theme.

Word saves the theme so that you can reuse the combination of colors, fonts, and effects that you created.

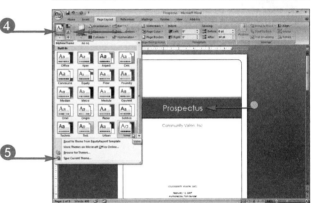

Can I create documents in Word that resemble the themes of other files, like Excel spreadsheets or PowerPoint slide shows?

▼ Yes. Note the name of the theme that you applied in the other program, or that you created and saved. In Word, click the Themes down arrow (⏷) and then click Browse for Themes. Locate the theme by name to load and apply it.

Why is my Themes group unavailable?

▼ You have opened a document that was created in a previous version of Word, and it is still in Compatibility Mode. You will need to save it as a Word 2007 document to use the Themes feature. For more information on updating files to Office 2007 format, see the task "Save in Different Versions" in Chapter 2.

When I try to browse for themes in Vista, a Vista Explorer appears, but I cannot seem to locate them. How can I locate them?

▼ In Vista, use the regular Folders area in the lower-left of the Explorer window to click Computer. Then go from the main C: drive to Program Files, Microsoft Office and Document Themes. You will find the installed and saved themes in that folder.

Using the Building Blocks Organizer

Word allows you to save blocks of text and formatting, in different files and templates, to reuse later.

Building Blocks are saved units of text and formatting that Word stores in the various galleries so that you can use them in other documents.

The most basic Building Blocks are the Quick Parts, which are covered in Chapter 3. You can easily insert them using the Insert tab of the Ribbon. Other galleries that use Building Blocks include Headers, Footers, Cover Pages, AutoText, Text Boxes, Page Numbers, and Tables.

The best way to learn more about Building Blocks and to apply different Building Blocks to your document is to use the Building Blocks Organizer.

The Building Blocks Organizer lets you see and change the name of any gallery element or Building Block, its category, the gallery in which it is stored, and the template to which it is attached.

You can then use the Building Blocks Organizer to see a preview of any Building Block, insert any Building Block into your document, or edit its properties to change its gallery, name, category, or template.

Using the Building Blocks Organizer

1 Click the Insert tab.

2 Click the Quick Parts down arrow (▼).

The Quick Parts menu appears.

3 Click Building Blocks Organizer.

The Building Blocks Organizer dialog box appears.

4 Click the gallery heading.

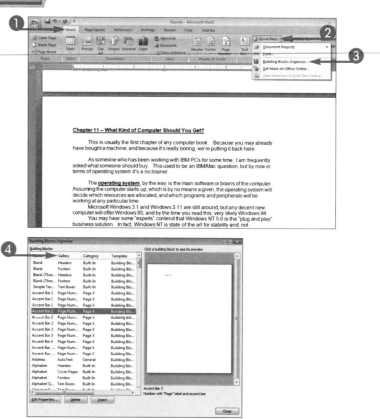

- Word sorts the Building Blocks by gallery names by default.

5 Click a Building Block.

This example uses Cover Page.

- A preview appears in the right pane.

6 Click Insert.

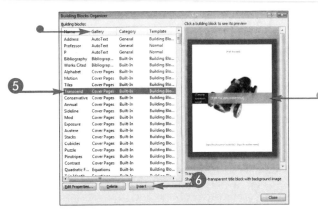

Word inserts the Building Block into the document.

MASTER IT

I created a Building Block in Quick Parts, but when I inserted it, the formatting did not work. Why?	**Can I use my Building Blocks in other Word documents?**	**I have a favorite cover page that I would rather use as a Quick Part. How can I do this?**
▼ When you select a unit of text for a Building Block, make sure that you also select the Paragraph mark (¶) in the selection. If you do not also select the Paragraph mark, the Building Block may not work the way you intend. Use the Show/Hide Formatting (¶) button on the Home tab to display the Paragraph marks so that they are easier to select.	▼ Yes. After inserting your Building Blocks, save the document as a template. When you create a new document based on the template that you saved, your Building Blocks will be available in all documents that are based on that template. For more information, see the task "Create New Documents from Templates."	▼ By using the Building Block Organizer, you can change the gallery to which a Building Block belongs. By editing its gallery property, you can make a cover page (or text box or table style) available as a Quick Part. For more information see the next page for remaining steps of this task.

continued

Using the Building Blocks Organizer *(Continued)*

By using the Building Blocks Organizer, you can create and modify a set of Quick Parts and organize them into galleries to use in other documents.

By creating Quick Parts entries that are stored as Building Blocks, you can maintain consistency of language and style, so that each time you insert a block of text or combination of text and graphics into a new document, it is the same.

The Building Block Organizer maintains your saved Building Blocks, along with those that come with Word 2007, in a database. They can be sorted by name, gallery, category, or template.

To make locating a particular Building Block easier, you can modify its properties so that it is stored in a gallery, and under a category that makes sense to you.

When you edit a Building Block property in the Building Block Organizer, you can assign a built-in category, put the edited Building Block in the general category, or create a new category. For example, you could store a set of Building Blocks in either the AutoText or Quick Parts gallery, but further modify their properties with a New Category for a specific client.

Using the Building Blocks Organizer *(continued)*

Modify a Building Block

1. Repeat Steps 1 to 3 from the previous page to open the Building Blocks Organizer dialog box.

2. Click a Building Block.

   This example uses an AutoText Building Block.

3. Click Edit Properties.

- The Modify Building Block dialog box appears.

4. Click the Gallery down arrow (⬇).

5. Click Quick Parts.

- A prompt asks if you want to redefine the Building Block entry.

6 Click Yes.

7 Click OK in the Modify Building Block dialog box.

8 Click Close in the Building Blocks Organizer.

PART II

9 Click the Quick Parts down arrow (▾).

- Your Building Block is now a Quick Parts entry.

When you exit Word, you are prompted to save the Building Block.

What are the Normal and Building Block templates?

▼ Normal is the standard blank document template for Microsoft Word. It also stores any AutoText Building Blocks. There is also a main Building Blocks template in Microsoft Office 2007 that stores the information for the Building Blocks in the other galleries.

Why would I want to create my own category in the Building Blocks Organizer?

▼ If you use a lot of different Building Blocks for different purposes — perhaps for different clients or projects — then assigning your custom Building Blocks to specific categories will make them easier to find in the Organizer. Creating your own category is especially useful once you have accumulated many different Building Blocks in various galleries.

I have created some Building Blocks that I no longer need. How do I delete them?

▼ Open the template that contains the Building Block that you want to delete. On the Insert tab, in the Text section, click Quick Parts, and then click Building Blocks Organizer. If you know the name of the Building Block, click Name to sort by name. Otherwise, you can locate it in the appropriate gallery for that Building Block. Select the entry, and then click Delete. When you close the template, click Yes when you are prompted to save it. The Building Block that you deleted is no longer available in any galleries, although the original content on which it was based may still appear in the template.

Create a Table

Y ou can create a table to neatly display information, such as columns of numbers, in your document. Word lets you draw a table as you would draw it with a pencil and paper, or create a table using the default style.

A *table* consists of rows, columns, and cells. A *row* is a horizontal line of cells, a *column* is a vertical line of cells, and a *cell* is the area where a row and column intersect. You enter text into individual cells. For more information on entering text, see the task "Type Text in a Table."

Drawing a table gives you a great deal of flexibility because you can select the style for each line in the table. You can also draw each column and row to the size you want.

When you create a table with the default style, you can select the number of rows and columns to include. The default table style makes the columns all the same size, but you can format the table to fit your needs.

Create a Table

① Click the Insert tab.

② Click the Table down arrow (▼).

③ Select the table configuration that you want by clicking and dragging through the grid.

④ Click to apply the table configuration.

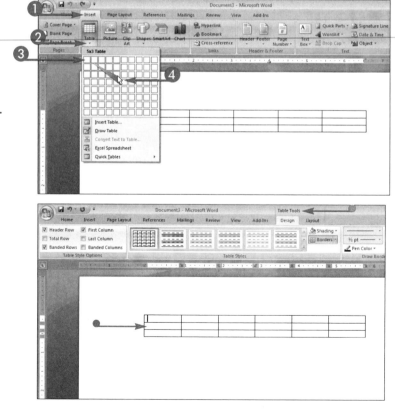

● Word creates a new table with the configuration that you chose.

● The Table Tools open on the contextual Ribbon, with the Design tab active. A Layout tab also appears.

Draw table lines

1. Click the Insert tab.

2. Click the Table down arrow (▼).

3. Click Draw Table.

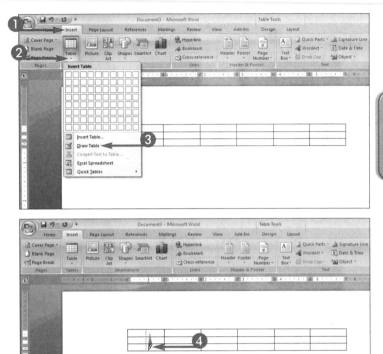

The pointer cursor (↳) turns into a pencil cursor (✎).

4. Draw a straight line vertically or horizontally within the table.

Word adds a border to the table.

You can click Draw Table in the Draw Borders group again to turn off the table draw function.

Can I create a table with a design applied?

▼ Yes. After clicking the Table down arrow (▼) in the Insert tab, select Quick Tables. This opens a gallery of table styles as Building Blocks that you can insert into a document and revise to your own specifications. For more information on Quick Tables, see the last task in this chapter, "Using Quick Tables."

How do I make the columns even?

▼ Drag through all of the columns in the table to select them, or just the ones that you want to be evenly sized. Click the Layout tab of the Table Tools, and then click the Distribute columns button (▤) in the Cell Size group. Your column widths will be evenly sized. You can do the same thing for rows using the Distribute rows button (▤).

Can I change the line styles in my table?

▼ Yes. You can apply a different style or thickness. To change the line style, click the Line Style down arrow (▼) in the Design tab of the Table Tools, and click a style. To change the thickness of the line, click the Line Weight down arrow (▼) and click a thickness. In the table, your pointer cursor (↳) turns into a pencil cursor (✎), letting you click to apply a new line thickness and style over an existing border.

Type Text in a Table

Y ou can enter data quickly and easily into an existing table. Like typing in a document, Word wraps text to the next line within a cell table and adjusts the row height. You can insert a paragraph break to create two paragraphs within the cell. To learn how to draw or insert a default table, see the task "Create a Table."

You can edit and format text in a table as you would edit and format any text in your document. To learn more about formatting text, see Chapter 4.

MASTER IT

Can I add blank lines within the cells of my table?

▼ Yes. You can press Enter if you want to end a paragraph, insert a blank line, or insert a paragraph break within a cell.

My text appears stacked, even though the text direction is correct. Why?

▼ You may have inadvertently added some indentation to the text that you typed. Select the text and remove any indents. For more information, see the task "Indent Paragraphs" in Chapter 4.

Type Text in a Table

① Click the cell where you want to type text.

② Type the text.

③ Press Tab to move to the next cell.

You can press Shift+Tab to move back one cell.

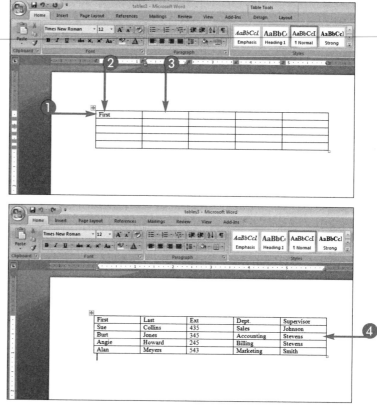

④ Repeat Steps 1 and 2 until you type all of the text.

You can also make formatting changes to the entries.

Note: *To learn more about how to format text, see Chapter 4.*

This example shows a completed table.

Sort Text

You can alphabetize the entries in a table, selecting any of the columns to use as the sort column. The Layout tab of the Table Tools displays a Sort button. This button opens a dialog box where you can choose among sorting options such as Sort Ascending and Sort Descending. The options sort text as well as numeric entries.

Although these commands appear in the Table Tools, you can use them to sort any text in a document. That is, you can sort any paragraphs in a document, even if the text does not appear in table form.

How can I undo a sort?

▼ If you sort a table and do not like the results, you can click the Undo button (🔄). If you frequently sort a table and want to have the option of returning it to its original order, consider adding a column to number your rows. You can then use this column to sort and return the table to its original order. To learn how to enter text or numbers, see the task "Type Text in a Table."

Sort Text

1 Click to select the cells in the column that you want to sort.

2 Click the Layout tab of the Table Tools.

3 Click Sort.

● The Sort dialog box opens, showing the column you selected in the Sort by field.

You can use the sort options to fine-tune how you want to sort items.

● You can click to select either an ascending or descending order (◎ changes to ◉).

4 If your table has a header row, you can click to select the Header Row option (◎ changes to ◉).

5 Click OK.

● Word applies the sort to the table.

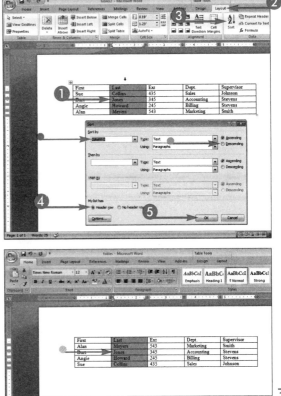

Change Column Width

After you create a table, you can change the width of its columns. You can do so to make more room for the entries. If the entries are short, you can also make the column narrower to reduce the amount of white space, or to fit your table onto one page.

You cannot change the width or height of a single cell. When you make changes to the column width, all of the cells in the column are affected.

When you begin to change the width of a column, Word displays a dotted line on your screen to indicate the new width until you click to put it into place.

MASTER IT

Can I also change the row height?

▼ Yes. Word automatically adjusts the size of the row, depending on the size of the font. For information on changing the font size, see Chapter 4. You can also adjust the row height in the same way that you adjust the column width: by dragging the row border. Most often, you do not need to adjust the row height because the default size is usually just right.

Change Column Width

① Position your cursor over the right border of the column that you want to change (⤢ changes to ⊩).

② Drag the column border to a new position.

A dashed line shows the new position.

③ Release the mouse to apply the change.

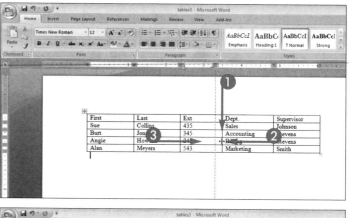

● Word repositions the column border where you placed it.

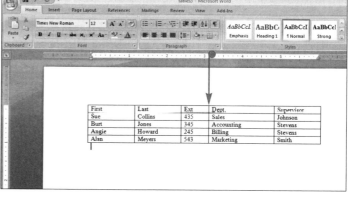

Erase Lines

You can easily erase the interior and exterior lines of a table when you no longer need them. For example, you can erase the interior lines between two or more small cells to create one large cell to display a title at the top of your table. You can also create a title cell when you create the table by not drawing the columns in this row. You might erase the exterior lines of a table as a special effect when you structure the layout of a page. When you erase the lines that make up the outside of your table, remember that the table does not have a solid border when you print it. For more information on printing a document, see Chapter 8.

Word highlights the lines that you select to erase. If you erase a line between two cells that contain text, the text appears in the new, larger cell. If you have two cells with different text formats, you must change the format of all of the text in the new, larger cell. For information on formatting text, see Chapter 4.

Erase Lines

① Click in the table to activate the Table Tools.

② Click the Design tab.

③ Click Eraser (𝕜 changes to ⊘).

④ Click the line that you want to erase.

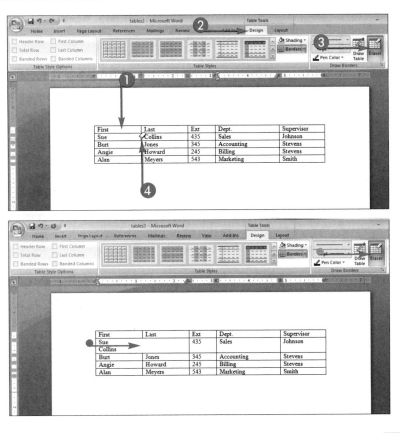

● The line disappears. If you erase a column border line, the two columns combine.

⑤ Continue clicking to trace down the entire border in order to erase it.

● You can click Eraser to change your cursor back to a pointer. (⊘ changes to 𝕜).

Add or Delete a Row or Column

I f you want to insert additional information into an already existing table, you can add a row or column. To learn how to create a table, see the task "Create a Table."

When you add a new row or column, you start by selecting where you want to place that row or column. You can place the new row above or below the current row. You can insert the new column to the left or right of the current column. You can access

these four commands through the menu or through buttons on the Table Tools on the Ribbon.

You can delete a row or column that you no longer need. When you delete a row or column from your table, you also delete all of the information in the cells in that row or column. If you accidentally delete a row or column, you can use the Undo feature to restore the lost information.

Add a row or column

1 Click within the row or column that is next to where you want to insert the new row or column.

- The Table Tools tabs become activated.

2 Click the Layout tab.

- In the Rows and Columns group, you can click one of the following buttons:

Click (⊞) to insert a row below.

Click (⊞) to insert a column to the left.

Click (⊞) to insert a column to the right.

- If you add a row, Word adds it either above or below the insertion point. If you add a column, Word adds it either to the left or to the right of the insertion point.

This example adds a column to the right.

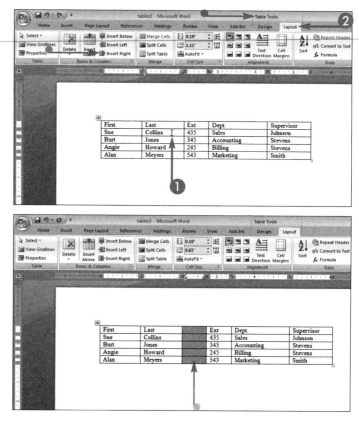

Delete a row or column

① Click within the row or column that you want to delete.

  ○ The Table Tools tabs become activated.

② Click the Layout tab.

③ Click the Delete down arrow (🔽).

④ Click Delete Rows or Delete Columns.

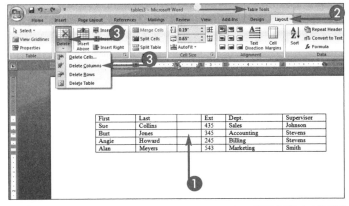

  ● Word removes the row or column and all of its contents from the table.

This example deletes a column.

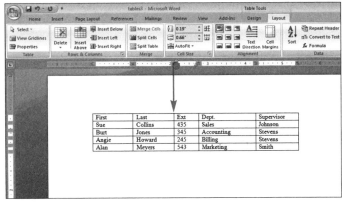

Is there a button that I can use to change my table with specific options?

▼ Yes. With the table active and Table Tools open, in the Layout tab, click Properties in the Table group. The Table Properties dialog box appears, and allows you to set more precise options for a cell, row, column, or the entire table.

How do I delete text?

▼ Select the text by dragging the mouse pointer across it, and then press the Delete key. Word deletes the text, but the table cell remains. You can also select the Delete Cells command in the Delete menu; when prompted, you can shift your remaining cells accordingly.

Can I add several rows or columns at once?

▼ Yes. To do so, select the same number of rows or columns that you want to add to your existing table. Then use the Insert command for rows or columns. The existing rows or columns shift, and Word inserts the new rows or columns into your table.

How can I delete an entire table?

▼ If you select a table and press Delete, Word deletes the text, but the table structure remains. To delete the entire table, click within the table. With Table Tools activated, click the Layout tab. Click the Delete down arrow (🔽) and click Delete Table.

Move or Resize a Table

Word allows you to move or resize your table, giving you greater flexibility in document layout. You generally move or resize a table to accommodate data deletions or additions. For more information on creating a table, see the task "Create a Table."

You can move a table from one location in your document to another. When you position the mouse pointer over a table, the table move handle appears at the top-left corner of the table, allowing you to move the table to a new location.

You can change the size of a table within your document. Resizing a table does not change the size of the entries in the table. When you position the mouse pointer over a table, the table resize handle appears at the bottom-right corner of the table.

Keep in mind that Word can only display the move and resize handles in the Print Layout view. See Chapter 5 to learn more about using the various views in Word.

Move a table

① Click Print Layout View (▤).

Word changes to Print Layout view.

Note: *To learn more about changing views, see Chapter 5.*

② Click to select the table.

③ Position the mouse pointer over the upper-left corner of the table that you want to move.

The mouse pointer (⟍) changes to the table move handle (✛).

④ Drag the table move handle to move the table to a new location.

● A dashed outline indicates the new location.

⑤ Release the mouse.

The table appears in the location where you released the mouse.

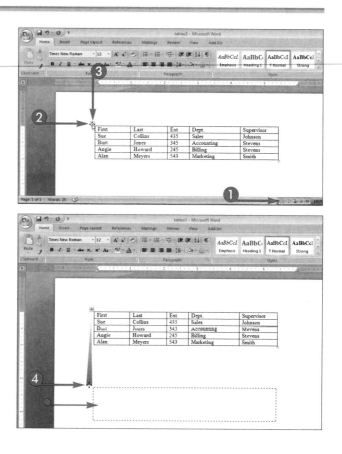

Resize a table

① Click 📖 to change to Print Layout view.

Note: *To learn more about changing views, see Chapter 5.*

② Click to select the table.

③ Position the mouse pointer over the lower right of the table

The mouse pointer (👆) changes to the table resize handle (👆).

④ Drag the table resize handle (👆) until the table is the size that you want.

A dashed outline indicates the new size.

⑤ Release the mouse.

● Word resizes the table.

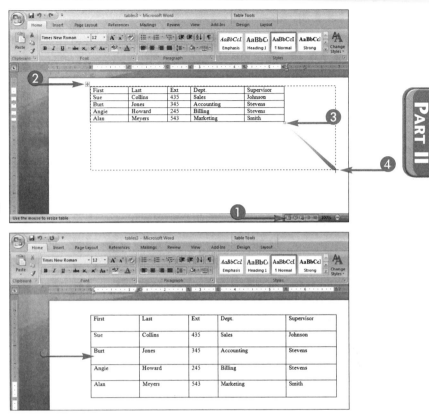

Can I change the alignment of my table?

▼ Yes. You can use the Alignment group of the Layout tab of the Table Tools to choose from nine different alignment styles. Drag through the columns, rows, or cells that you want to align to select them, and then choose the type of alignment that you want by clicking the appropriate buttons in the Alignment group.

I see a mouse pointer with vertical lines and two arrows. What does this mean?

▼ If you see this mouse pointer, you have positioned the pointer on the border of a column. You can use this pointer (◄||►) to resize the column width. For more information, see the task "Change Column Width."

How do I undo a change?

▼ If you move or resize a table by accident, you can undo the change by clicking the Undo button (🔄).

Change Table Borders

Y<span></span>ou can enhance the appearance of your table by changing the borders. By default, Word uses a solid, thin, black line for the borders of your table and cells.

You can change the border for a cell, a range of cells, or your entire table. Changing the border for specific cells in your table can help you separate data or emphasize important information.

Word offers several line styles from which you can choose. You can also select a line thickness and color

for the border. Word uses the line style, thickness, and color that you select for the border for all of the new tables that you create until you exit the program.

After you select the various border options, you must specify to which sides of the table you want to apply the border. For example, you can apply a border option to the outside, inside, right, or left border. Changing only some of the borders for the cells that you select can give your table an interesting visual effect.

Change Table Borders

Change the line style

1. Click to select the table.

   ● The Table Tools tabs become active.

2. Click the Design tab.

3. Click the Line Styles down arrow (⬇).

   The Line Styles menu options appear.

4. Click the line style that you want to use.

Change the line weight

5. Click the Line Weight down arrow (⬇).

   The Line Weight menu options appear.

6. Click the line thickness that you want to use.

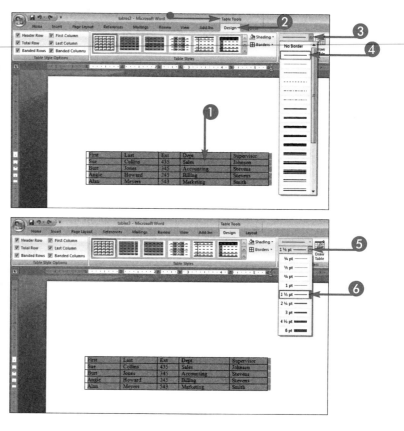

Change the border color

7 Click the Pen Color down arrow ().

The Pen Colors menu options appear.

8 Click the line color that you want to use.

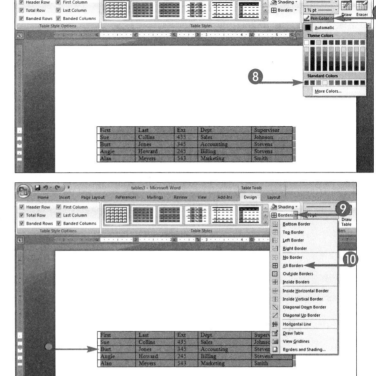

Apply formatting

9 Click the Borders down arrow ().

The Borders menu options appear.

10 Select the borders to which you want to apply the selected line color and format.

You can select All Borders or another configuration.

● Word formats the borders with the options that you selected.

Does Word 2007 have an AutoFormat option for tables?

▼ Yes. You can use the Quick Tables Building Blocks under the Table menu on the Insert tab, or apply a table gallery from the Design tab of the Table Tools. For more information, see the tasks "Using Table Styles with Galleries" and "Using Quick Tables."

Can I remove a border from my table?

▼ Yes. You generally remove a border when you use a table to organize the placement of information in your document and do not want the border to appear when you print your table. Click No Border from the Line Style drop-down list, and then click the border that you want to remove.

I removed a border from my table, but a faint border still displays on my screen. How do I remove the faint border?

▼ Word displays faint borders, called gridlines, for each table that you create. To remove all of the gridlines from a table, click Table and then click Hide Gridlines. To once again display the gridlines, click Table and then click Show Gridlines. Gridlines appear only on-screen, and not in the printed document.

Add Shading
or Color to Cells

You can draw attention to an area of your table by adding shading or color to cells, both of which change the background of the cells.

Word offers several shades of gray that you can add to the cells in your table. The available shades of gray range from light gray to black. Word also offers several colors that you can use, including blue, yellow, and violet.

If you use a black-and-white printer, any color that you add to cells appears as a shade of gray when you

print your table. If you have a color printer or if you display the document on-screen rather than print it, the table appears in color.

Make sure that the shading or color that you want to add to cells works well with the color of your text. For example, readers may find black text on a violet background difficult to read.

If you no longer want cells in your table to display shading or color, you can easily remove the shading or color from the cells by using the No Color option.

Add Shading or Color to Cells

1 Click and drag the mouse pointer through the cells to select them.

● The Table Tools tabs become active.

2 Click the Design tab.

3 Click the Shading down arrow (▼) in the Table Styles group.

4 Move the mouse over any color for a live preview.

5 Click to apply the shading color.

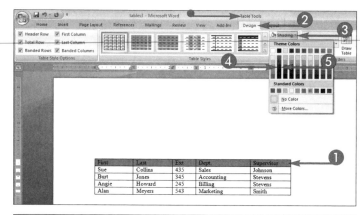

● The cells display the shading color.

To remove shading or color from cells, you can repeat these steps, and then click No Color in Step 5.

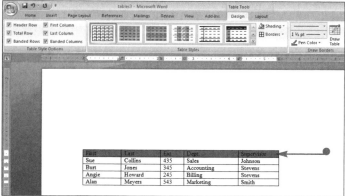

Change Text Position in Cells

You can enhance the appearance of your table by changing the position of text in cells. Changing the position of text can help you lay out the text in your table to suit your needs, or make long lists of information easier to read. For example, you can align names to the top and left of cells, and align related items, such as salaries, to the top and right of the adjacent cells.

By default, Word aligns text to the top and left of a cell. However, Word provides nine options that combine the left, right, center, top, and bottom alignment positions. For example, you can center headings and titles horizontally and vertically in cells to make the text stand out.

When you change the position of text that fills an entire cell, you may need to increase the column width or row height to see the change. To change the column width or row height, see the task "Change Column Width."

Change Text Position in Cells

① Click and drag the mouse pointer through the cells to select them.

● The Table Tools tabs become active.

② Click the Layout tab.

③ Click one of the nine alignment options in the Alignment group.

● The selected text displays the new alignment.

This example centers the text.

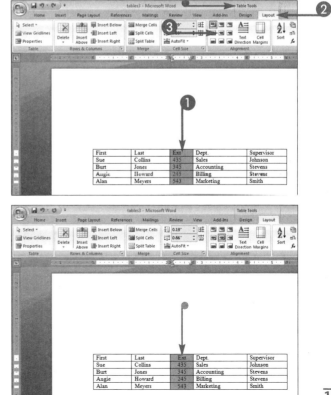

Using Table Styles with Galleries

Word offers many ready-to-use table styles, which you can apply to give your table a new appearance or to help make the information in your table easier to read. Table Styles galleries allow you to apply several table properties at once, saving you time and effort.

Some of the types of table styles include Simple, Classic, Colorful, and 3-D Effects. The Simple designs use only basic formatting. The Classic styles use simple borders and conservative colors. The Colorful styles use color combinations that make your table stand out. The 3-D Effects styles give your table the appearance of depth.

A table style includes formatting options such as borders, fonts, shading, and color. You can specify which formatting options you want Word to apply to your table. You can also have Word apply special formatting, such as italics, to the heading rows in your table. You can choose to apply special formatting to the last row, first column, and last column.

You can use the Live Preview feature to preview a table style in order to determine whether the style suits your table or document. When you apply an AutoFormat, Word replaces any previous formatting changes with the new options.

Using Table Styles with Galleries

① Click anywhere in the table that you want to change.

● The Table Tools tabs become active.

② Click the Design tab.

③ Click the More button to open the Table Styles gallery.

The Table Styles gallery appears and displays the available pre-set table designs.

④ Move your mouse over any table style.

● You can see a live preview of the style applied to the table.

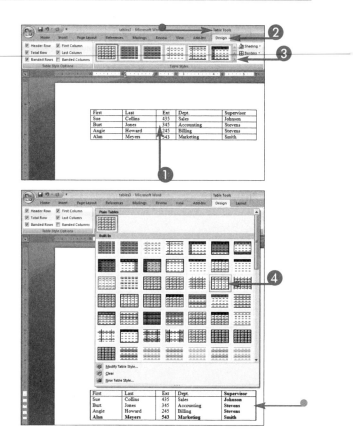

5 Scroll through the gallery until you see a table style that you want to apply.

6 Click to apply the table style.

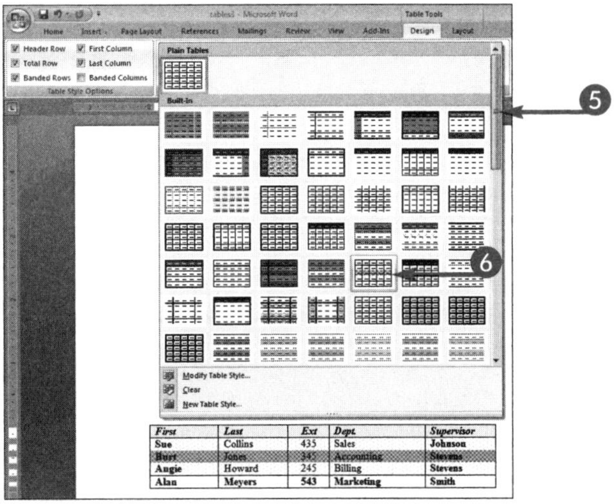

- Word displays the table with the new design, replacing any previously made formatting changes.

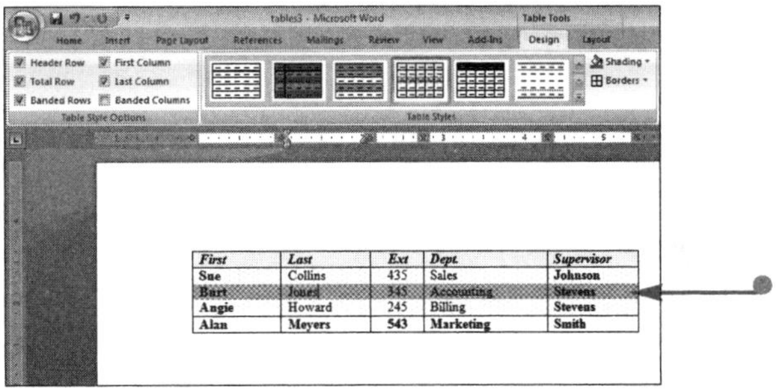

MASTER IT

Is there an easy way to get back to the original table design?

▼ Yes. If you have only applied a few designs, then you can use the Undo button (↶) to undo the last few formats. You can also reopen the Table Design gallery; at the top, you will find a plain table that you can apply.

Can I apply a table design to only part of my table?

▼ No. Word applies the design to the entire table. To change only part of your table, you must select the cells that you want to change and then format those cells. For more information, see the tasks "Change Table Borders" and "Add Shading or Color to Cells."

Is there a way to tone down some of the table styles?

▼ Yes. When you open the Design tab in Table Tools, look at the Table Style Options group. You can click an option to deselect it (☑ changes to ☐). This reduces the corresponding effect in the table styles as you apply them.

Using Quick Tables

Word also offers many ready-to-use designs that you can select for your table before you enter any information.

These Quick Tables have generic information already added to their contents, and so you can get an idea of which types of table would be most appropriate to use as a Quick Table.

You can also save any table that you create using the features in this chapter, as a Quick Table that you can insert into other documents using the same template.

Quick Tables are a gallery of Building Blocks. For more information about using and organizing your Building Blocks, see the task "Using the Building Blocks Organizer" in Chapter 5.

Using Quick Tables

1. Click the Insert tab.
2. Click the Table down arrow (⏷).
3. Click Quick Tables.

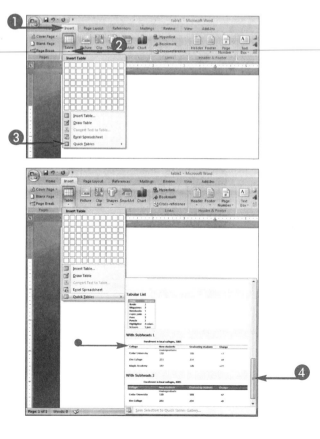

- The Quick Tables gallery appears and displays a set of completed tables with information.

4. Scroll down to find a table style that you like.

5 Click a Quick Table.

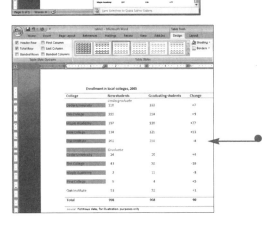

● Word inserts the Quick Table into your document.

You can revise and make formatting changes to the table.

What is the difference between Quick Tables and the Table Styles gallery?

▼ Quick Tables have information already in the cells for you to change for your own purposes. The Table Styles gallery only applies its formatting to an existing table. When you save your own Quick Table to the Quick Tables gallery by using the Save Selection command, you also save the contents of the table. When you save a table style to the Table Styles gallery, you save only the formatting that is applied to the table.

Can you apply a table style to a Quick Table?

▼ Theoretically, yes. However, you may get some unexpected results when you combine the effects of the two galleries. You are probably better off creating your own table style and applying it to a plain table with content, and using the Quick Tables for specific tasks similar to the ones shown in the Quick Tables gallery.

What is the purpose of the AutoFit command?

▼ The AutoFit command in the Layout tab of the Table Tools changes the size of your table, based on the amount of text in the table. This ensures that the text fits neatly in your table. You can resize the table to fit the contents, the window, or a fixed column width. You can also choose to distribute the rows or columns evenly so that they are all the same size.

Insert a Picture

Word allows you to insert pictures into your documents. For example, you can insert a digital photograph or a scanned image, as well as most types of graphic files. When you acquire your images from a digital camera or scanner, you should make a note of where you save them. You will need their folder location to put them into your document.

By default, when you insert a picture, Word displays the pictures in the My Pictures folder in Windows XP, or the Pictures folder in Windows Vista.

You can switch to another drive or folder to find the picture that you want to insert. You can also preview your files before you select a picture to insert.

After you insert a picture, you can move and resize the image. You can also delete a picture that you no longer need. For information on moving, resizing, or deleting a picture or other graphic, see the task "Move, Copy, or Resize a Graphic."

To see your pictures, clip art, or shapes in your documents, you can use Print Layout view.

Insert a Picture

1 Click the location where you want to add a picture.

2 Click the Insert tab.

3 Click Picture.

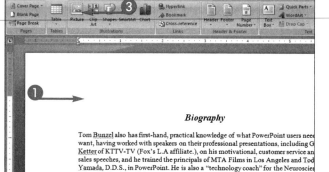

The Insert Picture dialog box appears.

4 Click the image that you want to insert.

You can select another drive or folder to locate the picture you want.

5 Click Insert.

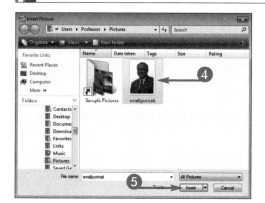

- The Picture Tools open on the Ribbon.

- Word places the picture in the document, with selection handles for resizing, rotating, and moving.

You can click elsewhere in the document to remove the selection handles.

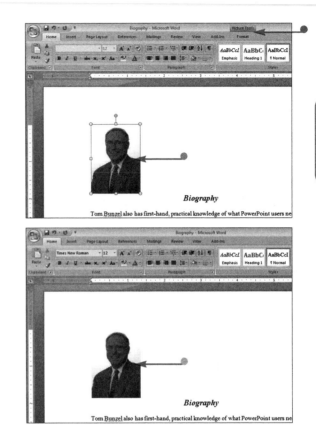

- Word sets the picture inside your document.

How can I view other file types?

▼ By default, Word shows all picture file types in the Insert Picture dialog box. To limit the list to a particular file type, click the Files of type down arrow (▾) for Windows XP, or the Pictures down arrow (▾) for Windows Vista, and then click the type of file.

How do I insert a picture from a digital camera or scanner?

▼ You can use either a bundled utility program or a flash memory card to transfer images from a digital camera or scanner to a folder on your computer, such as your Pictures (Windows Vista) or My Pictures (Windows XP) folder. If your camera or scanner has a flash memory card or a USB connector, it will probably show up as a hard drive in Windows to make image downloading easier.

How do I locate images more easily in a folder?

▼ You can preview an image by clicking the Views down arrow (▾) and selecting an option. In Windows XP you have thumbnail options, while in Windows Vista you have various icon sizes. You can also locate pictures using the Details option by file size, filename, and other parameters.

Add a Clip Art Image

Word includes professionally designed clip art images that you can add to your document. These clip art images can help to make your document more interesting and entertaining.

The first time you open the Clip Organizer, Office prompts you to search for and categorize the images in the Clip Organizer. You can follow the on-screen prompts to guide you through this process.

If you begin to use some of the more specialized features in the Clip Organizer into the Clip Organizer, you can make sure that Office categorizes all of your images, so that you can type a keyword and then search for matching images. You can categorize your image and media files automatically — which takes some time — or add individual folders to the Clip Organizer.

If you use Windows Vista, you can also use the Vista Explorers to locate different kinds of images and media files. For more information, see the task "Using Vista Search Features" in Chapter 2.

After you add a clip art image, you can move and resize it. You can also delete a clip art image that you no longer need. For more information, see the task "Move, Copy, or Resize a Graphic."

Add a Clip Art Image

① Click the location where you want to add a clip art image.

② Click the Insert tab.

③ Click Clip Art.

● The Clip Art task pane appears.

④ Type a search term for the image that you want to insert.

⑤ Click Go.

Word displays the clip art images that match your search criteria.

You can scroll through the list to display other matching images.

6 Click the down arrow (▼) next to the image that you want to insert.

A menu appears.

7 Click Insert.

Alternatively you can also click the image to insert it.

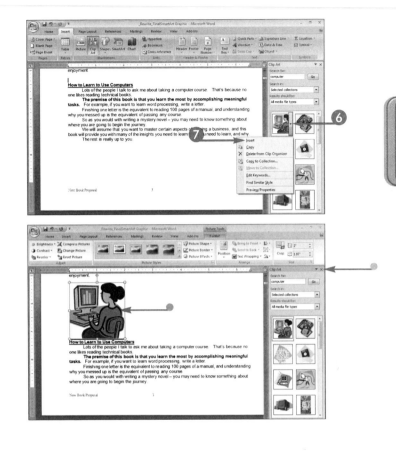

● The clip art image appears in the document.

To deselect the clip art image, click outside of it in the document.

● The Clip Art task pane remains open. To close the task pane, you can click Close (✕).

How can I limit my search?

▼ You can limit the search to a particular folder or drive. To do so, click the Search in down arrow (▼) in the Clip Art pane. In the submenu, you can deselect the Collections in which to search (☑ changes to ☐). To limit the search to a particular media file type, click the Results should be down arrow (▼) and deselect a media type (☑ changes to ☐).

Can I edit a clip art image?

▼ Yes. To do so, click the clip art image. The Drawing Tools open on the Ribbon. You can use the features of the Format tab of the Drawing Tools to add shape styles and effects, or to reposition the graphic in front of or behind other objects.

Where can I find more clip art images?

▼ If you are connected to the Internet, you can visit the Media Gallery Online Web site, to find additional clip art images. In the Clip Art pane, click the Clip Art on Office Online link, and then follow the instructions on your screen.

Add
Shapes

Word provides many ready-made shapes that you can add to enhance the appearance of your document or draw attention to important information.

You can only display shapes in the Print Layout and Web Layout views. Word offers several categories of shapes, including Lines, Basic Shapes, Block Arrows, Callouts, and Stars and Banners. To learn more about the Print Layout or Web Layout views, see Chapter 5.

Each category contains individual shapes. When you select a shape, Word creates it, selects it in the

document, and opens the Drawing Tools on the Ribbon. You can later move and resize the shape to better suit your needs. You can also delete a shape that you no longer need. For more information, see the task "Move, Copy, or Resize a Graphic."

As you draw, your object covers the background text in the document. You can change the placement of the text and graphics. For more information, see the task "Change the Position of a Graphic."

Add Shapes

① Click the Print Layout View button (▦).

Note: *To learn more about the different views in Word, see Chapter 5.*

② Click the Insert tab.

③ Click the Shapes down arrow (▾).

The Shapes menu appears.

④ Click the shape that you want to add.

⑤ Position your cursor where you want to place the shape (↳ changes to ✛).

⑥ Click and drag the mouse until the shape is the size that you want.

⑦ Release the mouse.

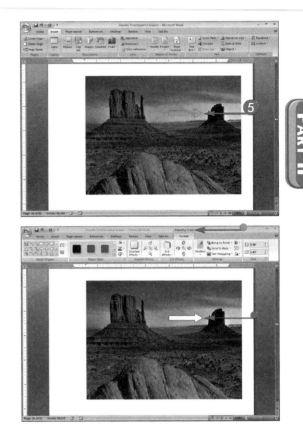

● The shape appears in the document with selection handles.

● The Drawing Tools tab opens on the Ribbon.

How can I quickly copy a shape?

▼ You can copy any shape or group of shapes. To do so, select it, press the Ctrl key, and drag to create a copy, or "clone," of the selected shape. To select multiple shapes, press the Shift key as you click, or trace a rectangle around, the shapes.

How do I draw a square or circle?

▼ In the Shapes menu, click the rectangle or oval icon to draw a square or a circle, respectively. Then hold down the Shift key as you draw the shape so that the rectangle is drawn as a square, or the oval is drawn as a circle.

Can I add text to a shape?

▼ Yes. Right-click the shape that you want to change. Click Add Text and then type the text that you want the shape to display. When you finish typing, click outside the shape.

Can I draw my own shape?

▼ Yes. In the Insert tab, click the Shapes down arrow (▼) and select the Lines category. Click the Freeform tool (✎). When you finish drawing your shape, double-click to stop drawing.

Add a SmartArt Graphic

Word allows you to insert fairly sophisticated diagrams into your documents. For example, you can include an organizational chart of your company, or you can include flow charts of common tasks or procedures.

You can select from a gallery of pre-designed diagrams. You can then add or replace the text placeholders with text for your particular diagram contents.

When you insert a SmartArt graphic or diagram, the SmartArt Tools appear on the Ribbon. You can use the SmartArt Tools to select different formatting options. For example, you can change the colors or text, and add effects. You can also use Themes to change the look of SmartArt diagrams. See the task "Apply a Theme to a Document" in Chapter 5.

After you add a SmartArt graphic, you can move and resize it in your document. You can also delete a diagram that you no longer need. For more information, see the task "Move, Copy, or Resize a Graphic."

Add a SmartArt Graphic

① Click the location where you want to add the graphic.

② Click the Insert tab.

③ Click SmartArt.

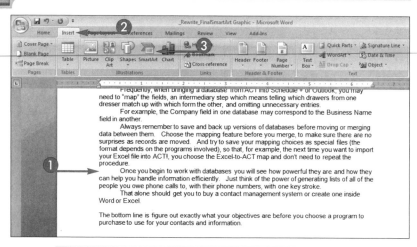

The Choose a SmartArt Graphic dialog box appears, displaying All categories.

④ Select the type of graphic that you want to insert.

⑤ Select a SmartArt graphic.

⑥ Click OK.

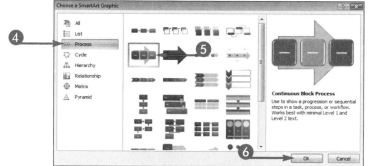

Word adds the diagram to your document.

- The SmartArt Tools appear on the Ribbon.
- Text placeholders appear where you can add text.

7 Type your text into the Type your text here panel.

Note: *Pressing the Enter key creates another SmartArt Shape and text placeholder. To move between text entries in the Type your text here panel, use your mouse to select each item or the down or up arrows on the keyboard.*

- You can click the Close button (☒) to close the Type your text here panel. With the Type your text here panel closed, you can click the arrow pointing away from the selected SmartArt graphic to reopen it and revise the text.

8 Click outside the diagram box to return to the document.

Word places the completed SmartArt graphic.

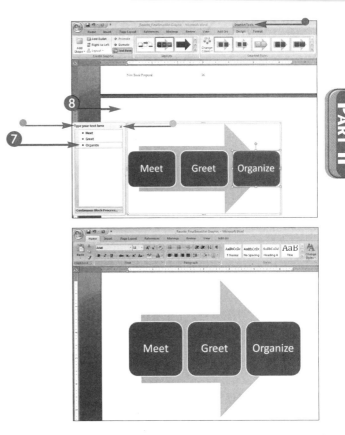

MASTER IT

How can I view a description of the various SmartArt graphics?

▼ When you click a SmartArt graphic in the Choose a SmartArt Graphic dialog box, Word displays the appropriate usage of the selected graphic in a panel in the right panel of the gallery. You can use this information to determine whether you want to insert a particular SmartArt graphic.

Why do I see a basic diagram gallery instead of the SmartArt graphics?

▼ This is because you are working with an older version of a Word document in Compatibility Mode. To see the full range of SmartArt graphics, save it as a Word 2007 file. For more information, see the task "Save in Different Versions" in Chapter 2.

How do I edit text in a SmartArt graphic?

▼ Use the Type your text here panel to change the text. To edit the formatting of text that you have included as part of the SmartArt graphic, click within the SmartArt graphic and then within the particular text that you want to change. You should see the flashing insertion point. You can make any formatting changes to the text.

Move, Copy, or Resize a Graphic

Y ou can move or copy a graphic from one location in your document to another. When you move a graphic, the graphic disappears from its original location in your document. When you copy a graphic, the graphic appears in both the original and new locations.

You can change the size of a graphic within your document. The resizing handles that appear when you select a graphic allow you to change the height and width of the graphic. For example, you use the top

and bottom handles to change the height of the graphic, the side handles to change the width of the graphic, and the corner handles to change the height and width of the graphic at the same time.

To make any of these changes, you must first select the graphic. Keep in mind that when you select the graphic, not only do the selection handles appear, but the Picture Tools also appear automatically on the Ribbon.

Move, Copy, or Resize a Graphic

Move a graphic

1 Click to select the graphic that you want to move (⬚ changes to ✛).

2 Drag the graphic to a new location.

As you drag, the cursor (⬚) represents the graphic.

3 Drop the graphic where you want it.

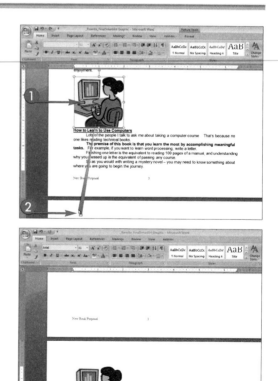

● The graphic appears in the new location.

You can copy a graphic by holding down the Ctrl key as you perform Step 2.

Resize a graphic

1 Click the graphic that you want to resize.

Selection handles appear around the graphic.

2 Position the cursor over one of the resizing handles on a corner (⬚ changes to ⬚).

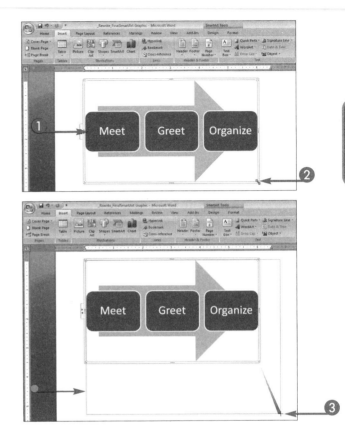

3 Drag the handle until the graphic is the size that you want.

● An outline appears for the new size.

4 Release the handle.

The graphic appears in the new size.

What can I do if I have trouble moving a clip art image?

▼ Many clip art images are comprised of smaller shapes, and if you try to grab them from the inside, you may move one of the inside shapes instead of the whole clip art image. Try selecting the image as a whole. You can also drag a rectangle around the image to select it entirely, so that a ⌐ appears at the corner. Then grab the edge of the clip art image to move it in its entirety.

How do I align graphics in my document?

▼ You can align graphics in the same way that you would with text. Select the graphic by clicking it or, for clip art, drag through it to select it. In the Home tab of the Ribbon, use the paragraph alignment tools to reposition the graphic. For more information, see the task "Align Text on a Page" in Chapter 5.

How can I delete a graphic?

▼ Click the graphic and press the Delete key. This removes the graphic and any elements within the graphic, including the text.

Change the Position of a Graphic

After you add a graphic to your document, you can wrap text around the graphic or change its position to enhance the appearance of the document.

Word offers several ways that you can wrap text around a graphic. For example, you can have Word wrap text to form a square around a graphic, or fit text tightly around the edges of a graphic. Word also lets you place a graphic behind or in front of text. You can choose the In Line with Text option to have Word position the graphic within the text of the document.

You can choose how you want to align a graphic with the text in your document. This lets you specify which sides of the graphic that you want the text to wrap around. Word can align the graphic to the left, center, or right of the text.

The Ribbon options vary slightly, depending upon the type of graphic that you want to position. For example, you may need to find the Position or Text Wrapping features under an Arrange option for a SmartArt graphic.

Change the Position of a Graphic

1 Click the graphic that you want to wrap text around.

● Tools open on the Ribbon for the type of graphic that you selected, such as Shape, Picture, or WordArt.

2 Click to display the Format tab, if necessary.

3 Click the Position down arrow ([▼]).

The In Line with Text and With Text Wrapping galleries appear.

You can move your mouse over any of the options for a live preview of how it will look with the text.

4 Click an option to set it for the graphic and the surrounding text.

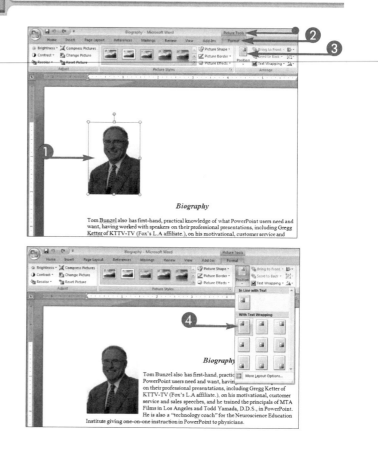

PART II

● Word applies the option that you chose, and leaves the graphic selected.

5 Click the Position down arrow (▼) to reopen the In Line with Text and With Text Wrapping galleries.

6 Click More Layout Options.

● The Advanced Layout options dialog box opens.

7 Click the Picture Position tab.

8 Use the options in the dialog box to change the position of the graphic.

This example changes the alignment of the graphic from left to right.

● Word applies the option that you chose.

Change Graphic Colors and Add Effects

When you add a graphic to your document, you can do a number of things to make it stand out on the page and give it greater impact.

Depending upon the type of graphic that you add to a page, Word opens a Tools group on the Ribbon to allow you to change its appearance in many different ways.

In the case of simple shapes, you can select them individually or in groups to apply the different formatting options. SmartArt graphics have their own distinct style gallery. You can also select individual elements within SmartArt graphics to add distinctive visual effects that make one or more parts of a SmartArt graphic stand out.

Depending upon the graphics that you select, you can add effects such as 3D, color, fills, and outline, alone or in combination. You can also use the Arrange feature to align multiple shapes or to position them on the page in front of or behind other shapes.

You can use the Position or Text Wrapping feature to move the shapes in relation to the text. For more information, see the previous task, "Change the Position of a Graphic."

Change Graphic Colors and Add Effects

① Click the graphic to which you want to add effects.

- Tools open on the Ribbon for the type of graphic that you selected, such as a SmartArt, Shape, or WordArt graphic.

② Click to display the Design tab, if necessary.

③ Click the Change Colors down arrow (▾).

A Color options menu appears.

You can move your mouse over any color combination for a live preview.

④ Click a color combination to apply it to the graphic.

Word applies the options that you chose, and the graphic remains selected.

⑤ Click the SmartArt Styles More button.

The Best Match for Document gallery opens.

You can move your mouse over any style to see a live preview.

6 Click a style.

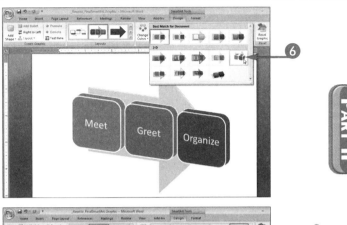

Word applies the style that you selected to the graphic.

● You can click Reset Graphic to return it to its original design.

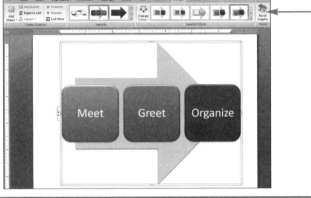

Can I change one SmartArt graphic into another while I am applying effects?

▼ Yes. In the Design tab of the SmartArt Tools on the Ribbon, you will find a Layouts gallery similar to the one that you used to insert the original graphic. By clicking the Layouts More button, you can change the layout of the SmartArt graphic to any other configuration. You can also access the Layout options by right-clicking the edge of the SmartArt graphic.

Can I add more elements to my SmartArt graphic?

▼ Yes. Select any individual shape in the graphic and then click the Add Shape down arrow (▼). A drop-down menu of options appears. You can decide whether to add a new shape before or after the selected shape, or above or below it.

When would I add an Assistant?

▼ An Assistant is a special shape in an organizational chart that is directly connected to only one other shape. The organizational chart is the first SmartArt graphic under the Hierarchy section, and is the only SmartArt diagram that has the Assistant as a feature.

continued

Change Graphic Colors
and Add Effects *(Continued)*

Once you have inserted a SmartArt graphic, you can use Format tab of the SmartArt Tools on the Ribbon to give the graphic a more professional look and feel.

You can select one or more of the shapes in the SmartArt diagram, and, in the Format tab of the SmartArt Tools, you can choose from an entire gallery of shape styles. The Shape Styles gallery has a variety of pre-set designs to change the appearance of the shapes in the SmartArt diagram.

Next to the Shape Styles gallery you can also open galleries for shape fills, shape outlines, and shape effects.

Depending upon the SmartArt graphic you inserted, you can apply a variety of different effects to the shape in the Shape Effects gallery. You can add or adjust a shadow, use a reflection, insert a glow, add a soft edge, or rotate the shape in 3D. For many shapes a bevel effect gives them a distinctive edge or sense of depth.

You can also use the WordArt styles in the Format tab of the SmartArt Tools to enhance the appearance of your text with WordArt. Select the text in your graphic and then use either the WordArt styles or individual galleries for text fill, text outline, or text effects.

Change Graphic Colors and Add Effects *(continued)*

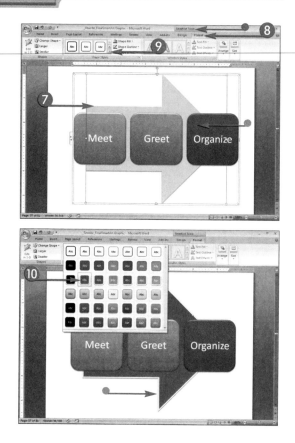

⑦ Click to select one or more shapes in the graphic to which you want to add effects.

You can press the Shift key to select more than one shape.

● Tools open on the Ribbon for the type of graphic that you selected, such as SmartArt, Shape, or WordArt.

⑧ Click the Format tab.

⑨ Click the Shape Styles More button.

The Shape Styles gallery appears.

You can move your mouse over any style for a live preview.

⑩ Click a shape style to apply it to the selected shapes.

● Word applies the options that you chose, and the shapes remain selected.

⑪ Click the Shape Effects down arrow (⏷).

The Shape Effects menu opens.

⑫ Click any effect to open its gallery.

You can move your mouse over any effect for a live preview.

⑬ Click a Shape Effect.

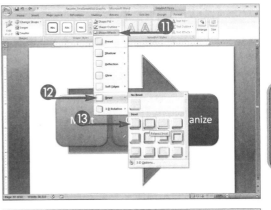

● Word applies the effect to the graphic.

You can click anywhere outside the graphic to set it in the page.

Can I apply a gradient effect to a shape?

▼ Yes. Click the Shape Fill down arrow (⏷) in the Format tab of the SmartArt Graphic Tools. In the drop-down options, select Gradient, and apply a light or dark gradient, based on the current fill color of the selected shape. To change the gradient colors, first change the fill color of the shape. The gradient options change to reflect the new fill color.

Can I add effects to the text in a shape or SmartArt graphic?

▼ Yes. Click the WordArt Styles More button or the Text Fill, Text Outline, or Text Effects down arrow (⏷). Word displays menus of effects that you can select to alter the appearance of the text in your graphics or shapes.

Instead of resetting the graphic, I want to go back to a previous look. How do I do that?

▼ To the right of the Office button, click the Undo button down arrow (⏷). Then go back sequentially to the step where you had the graphic the way you wanted it. If you plan ahead, you can save various versions of the document with the Save As command under the Office button. This allows you to save different stages of your graphic until you get the look you want.

Work with Reviewers

You can use the Review tab on the Word Ribbon to enter comments into a document and show revisions in balloons — a callout to the Review Panel that details the change that was made. In this way you can track changes among a series of associates or colleagues whose comments and edits need to be integrated into the document.

You can distribute a document for review by e-mail or over a network, or using some of the collaboration features in Chapter 29.

When you work with reviewers and turn on the Track Changes feature, each reviewer's edits appear in the document in a different color, enabling the author to clearly see whose edits need to be reflected in the final version.

Once the reviewers have made their edits and comments in a document, the author can use the Review tab of the Ribbon to navigate easily to the next or previous edit, and then either accept or reject the edit. The author can also revise the document according to the suggested edits.

You can then save the final document, incorporating one or more of the changes, with or without the markup edits, or in its original form.

You can also use the Review tab of the Ribbon to run a spell or grammar check, access research services, protect your document from unauthorized access, and compare one or more documents. For more information on comparing documents, see the next task, "Compare Multiple Versions."

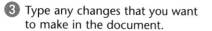

Work with Reviewers

Review a document

① Click the Review tab.

② Click Track Changes.

③ Type any changes that you want to make in the document.

● Word underlines and enters the changes that were made by another person in a different color.

Changes made by the current user are also shown underlined and in a different color.

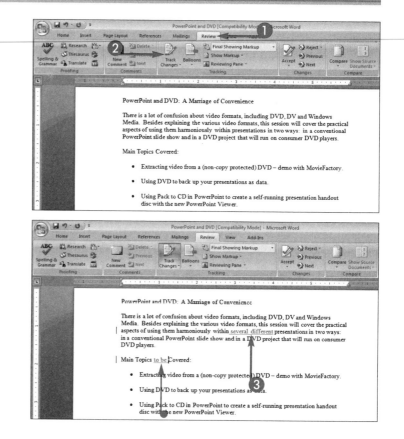

Accept or reject changes

① Click the Review tab.

② Click Track Changes.

③ Click Next.

● Word moves to the next edit.

④ Click Accept to accept the change and move to the next edit.

Alternatively, you can click Reject to reject the change and move to the next edit.

You can click the Accept or Reject down arrow (▾) for more options.

● With changes accepted or rejected, the text assumes a normal font color.

● Word continues to move to the subsequent edits within the document.

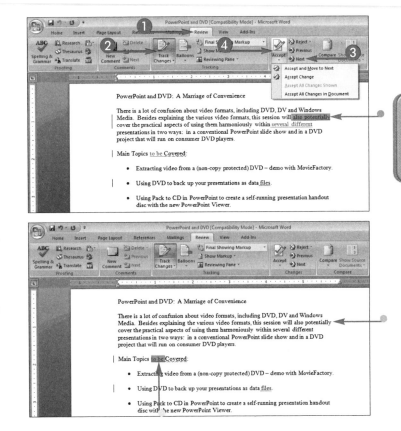

How do I use balloons?

▼ By default, balloons are used for comments and formatting changes. The balloons display the change in a colored bubble in the margin. You can click the Balloons down arrow (▾) to revise these options and also to show all changes within the document in balloons if you prefer.

What is the Reviewing pane?

▼ This feature gives you more room for detailed comments or reasons for edits, as well as for tabulating the number of edits. To access the Reviewing pane, you can click the Reviewing Pane down arrow (▾) in the Tracking group of the Review tab. This opens a window, either below the document as a horizontal reviewing pane, or next to the document for a vertical reviewing pane.

How do I change the font color for reviewers, or set other options for tracked changes?

▼ You can click the Track Changes down arrow (▾) and then click Change Tracking Options. A dialog box appears, with different settings for reviewers to differentiate their edits.

Compare Multiple Versions

You can save a lot of time when many people have made changes to the same document, either as reviewers or just by editing the file.

Instead of having to open both documents in separate windows to compare them and then decide how the final edits should go, the Compare feature of the Review tab of the Ribbon lets you open them in separate windows along with a final compared version of the document.

This allows you to select and finalize different versions of the same document by one author, or to combine multiple reviewed versions by associates or colleagues.

In either case, a series of windows opens, with a final version available where you can decide which parts of the compared documents you want to accept for the completed file.

You can also choose the legal blackline option, which compares two documents and displays only what is changed between them. The documents that are being compared are not changed. The legal blackline comparison is displayed by default in a new third document.

If you want to compare changes from a number of reviewers, you should not select the legal blackline option. Instead, you should click the Combine option.

Compare Multiple Versions

1 Click the Review tab.

2 Click Compare.

3 In the menu that appears, click either the Compare or Combine option.

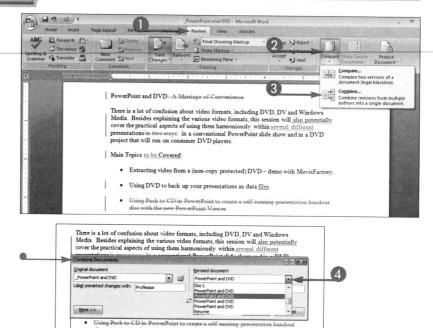

● The Combine Documents or Compare Documents dialog box appears.

This example uses the Combine Documents dialog box.

4 Click the Revised document down arrow (▼) to open the original and revised documents that you want to compare or combine.

5 Click OK to close the dialog box.

6️⃣ Click Show Source Documents.

7️⃣ Click Show Both.

● Your combined or compared document appears in the central panel.

● Your source documents appear in the right panel.

● You can use the Changes group to accept or reject the various edits in the central panel.

Note: *For more information on reviewing and tracking changes, see the previous task.*

You can save the combined or compared document under a new name.

Can I compare more than two versions of a document?

▼ No, not at this time. To work with multiple versions, you may need to open multiple windows to edit your files down to two versions that you can compare or combine. For more information, see the task "Work with Multiple Windows" in Chapter 2.

Why do I have multiple compared documents open in Vista or Windows XP?

▼ You may have clicked the Compare or Combine feature and opened your source files without clicking the Show Source Documents button. This results in a hidden combined document. To avoid confusion, close all of your open unsaved files. Begin again with two documents and show the source documents with the combined document. When you are finished making comparisons, save your final combined document.

Can I determine which parts of a document I want to compare, and omit some parts from the comparison?

▼ Yes. In either the Compare Documents or Combine Documents dialog box, click the More button to open an options panel that lets you fine-tune the parts of the document that you want to compare or combine. Select or deselect the check boxes to enable or disable the various options.

Using the Document Inspector

The Word Document Inspector lets you prepare a final version of your document that is stripped of information that you do not want recipients to see or know about.

When you complete a document, you probably want to remove all signs of tracked changes, comments, and any other unnecessary components.

While you can either merge these changes or accept or reject them, the traces of the various editing features remain in the document.

There may be saved metatags, or information for search indexes, watermarks, or other extraneous or unwanted material in a document that needs to be finalized and distributed outside of your company.

Word documents can also contain information that is formatted as hidden text. If you do not know whether your document has hidden text, you can use the Document Inspector to search for it.

Documents that you save in Word 2007 format can also contain custom XML data that is not visible within the document. Examples of XML data include the underlying code for features such as tracked changes. The Document Inspector can find and remove this XML data.

Alternatively, you can use the Final setting in the Tracking group of the Review tab to make absolutely sure that there is nothing in your document that you do not want distributed.

Using the Document Inspector

① Click the Office button.

② Click Prepare.

③ Click Inspect Document.

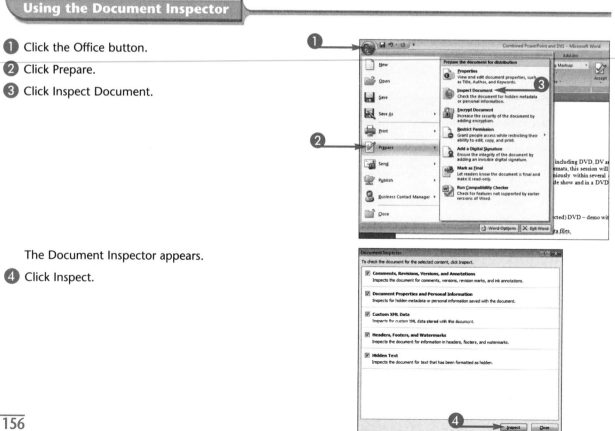

The Document Inspector appears.

④ Click Inspect.

PART II

- Word inspects the document for remaining unwanted data.

The Document Inspector reports the inspection results.

5 Click Remove All to remove all extraneous data from the document.

6 Click Close to exit the Document Inspector.

You can now save the inspected document as a final version.

How does an inspected document differ from one marked as final?

▼ When you apply the Mark as Final command to a document in the Prepare submenu of the Office button, Word makes it a read-only document, so that no further changes can be made or saved with the document. An inspected document can be revised and resaved, although that would probably mean that it should be inspected again.

What if I want certain information to remain with the final document?

▼ When you open the Document Inspector, look at the various categories of content that it will examine. To prevent a parameter from being inspected, click to deselect its check box (☑ changes to ☐).

Can I see some of the information before the Document Inspector removes it from my document?

▼ Yes. You can check some of the metadata and other document properties that will be removed by the Document Inspector by clicking the Office button, then clicking Prepare, and then selecting Properties. You can see and revise certain document properties such as author, title, and keywords. For more information about how metatags and keywords are used in Windows Vista, see the task "Using Vista Search Features" in Chapter 2.

Preview a Document

Y ou can use the Print Preview feature to see how your document will look when you print it.

The Print Preview feature allows you to view the layout of a page in your document. If your document contains more than one page, you can use the scroll bar to view the other pages.

You can magnify an area of a page in your document. This allows you to view the area in more detail.

You can have Word display several pages in the Print Preview window at once, which allows you to view the overall style of a long document.

Depending on the setup of your computer, Word can display up to 32 pages in the Print Preview window.

When you finish using Print Preview, you can close the Print Preview window to return to your document.

Although you cannot edit your document in Print Preview, you can visually adjust the margins of your document without having to doing so manually in the Page Setup dialog box. To learn more about margins, see Chapter 5.

Preview a Document

Using Print Preview

① Click the Office button.

② Move your mouse over Print or click the arrow (▶).

③ Click Print Preview.

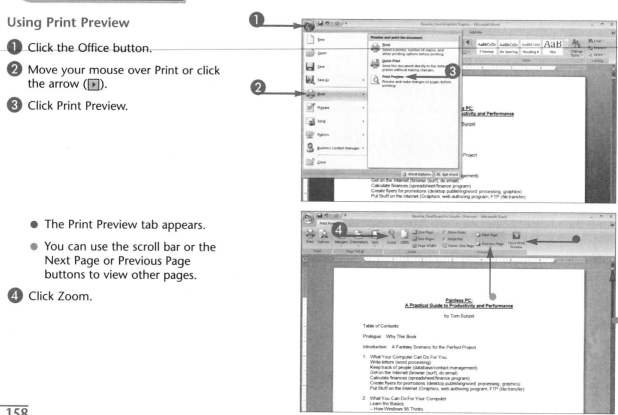

● The Print Preview tab appears.

● You can use the scroll bar or the Next Page or Previous Page buttons to view other pages.

④ Click Zoom.

Display multiple pages

The Zoom dialog box opens.

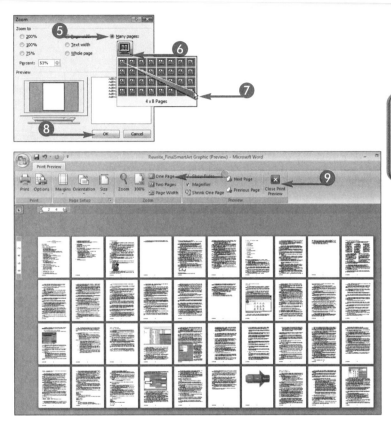

5 Click to select the Many Pages option (⊙ changes to ⦿).

6 Click the Many Pages button down arrow (▾).

7 Drag to create a preview of the pages to display.

8 Click OK.

Multiple pages of the document appear.

● To display one page again, you can click One Page.

9 Click Close Print Preview.

Windows exits Print Preview.

PART II

Print a Document

Y ou can print a paper copy of any document. Before you print your document, make sure that the printer is on and contains an adequate supply of paper. Check your printer manual if you have any questions on operating the printer.

If you have more than one printer, Word allows you to select the printer that you want to use. This is useful if you want to use different printers to print different types of information. For example, you may want to

use a black-and-white printer to print a draft of your document, and a color printer to print the final version.

You can print multiple copies of your document, such as when you are printing a brochure or handouts for a presentation. You can also specify the part of your document that you want to print. You can print the entire document, a range of pages, or just the selected text.

Print a Document

1 Click the Office button.

2 Move your mouse over Print or click the arrow (▶).

3 Click Print.

You can send the entire document directly to the default printer by selecting Quick Print.

Alternatively, you can select Print Preview. For more information on Print Preview, see the task "Preview a Document."

The Print dialog box appears.

● You can click the down arrow (▼) and choose a different printer.

- To print only a range of pages, you can click to select the Pages option (◎ changes to ◉); you can then enter an individual page number or a range of pages separated by a dash (–).

- You can use the Number of Copies spinner button (⬍) to change the number of copies that you want to print.

  You can click OK to print with the options that you set.

④ Click Options.

⑤ In the Word Options dialog box, click to select any print options that you want to use (☐ changes to ☑).

⑥ Click OK to return to the main Print dialog box.

⑦ Click OK again in the Print dialog box to print, or click Cancel to exit the Print dialog box.

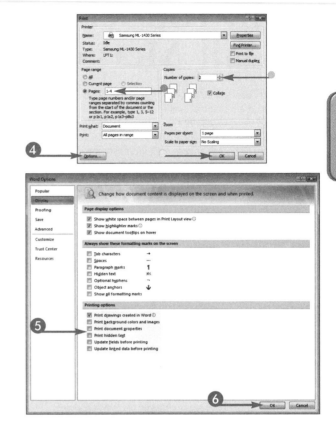

How do I change my default printer?

▼ In Windows XP, open your Control Panel and click Printers and Faxes. In Windows Vista, open the Control Panel and click Printers. Right-click the printer that you want to make the default, and select it as the default printer.

How can I preview my document before I print it?

▼ To preview a document, click the Office button, click Print, and then click Print Preview. The Print Preview feature gives you an idea of how the document will appear on the printed page. You can then make any necessary changes before you print. For more information, see the previous task, "Preview a Document."

How do I stop a print job?

▼ You can cancel a print job in the print queue. If the document is short, you may not have time to stop it. If it is a long document, or if you are printing several documents, you should have enough time to display the queue and stop the print job.

Office displays the Printer icon in the taskbar while you print a document; double-click this icon to display the print queue. Click the print job that you want to cancel, click Document, and then click Cancel Printing.

An Introduction to Mail Merge

You can use the Mail Merge feature to quickly produce a personalized letter for each individual on your mailing list. Mail Merge is useful for when you often send the same document, such as a letter, announcement, notification, or advertisement, to many people. This feature saves you from having to type information such as the name and address of a person on each letter.

You can also use the Mail Merge feature to print a mailing label for each person on your mailing list so that you do not have to type individual labels. You can then use these labels on envelopes or other mailing packages.

Whether you use the Mail Merge feature to produce personalized letters or to print mailing labels, the Mail Merge Wizard guides you through the steps of performing a mail merge.

Create a Main Document

The first step in performing a mail merge is to create a main document. A *main document* is a letter that you want to send to each person on your mailing list. You start with this main document so that Word makes the connection between this document and its type (such as form letters or labels), and the data source.

Keep in mind that letters and mailing labels are not the only uses for a merged document. You can also mail merge other document types. For example, you can do a mail merge to create name badges for a convention or to create cards for your Rolodex. When you use the main document to create award certificates, you can print them on paper that is specifically for this purpose.

As a first step, you select the document type, create or retrieve the data source, and complete the final letter with additional field references.

You can also use the existing open or current document for your mail merge by going directly to Step 2 of the wizard.

Create and Save the Data Source

After you create a main document, you must create or select a data source. A *data source* contains the information that changes in each letter, such as the name and address of each person on your mailing list. A data source consists of *fields*, which are specific categories of information. Each field has a name, such as Last Name or City. When you complete all of the

fields for a specific person, you have created a *record*, which contains all of the information for one person on your mailing list.

The most common data source is your Outlook Address Book, which is comprised of your Contact List. See Chapters 25 to 27 for more information about how Outlook works as a contact manager.

Make sure that you plan ahead and determine the information that you want your data source to include. Word and Outlook contain some predefined fields. You can select from a set of predesigned fields in an address list, or you can customize the address list, by adding and deleting fields.

You only need to create or select a data source once. After your initial work, you can use the data source for future mail merges where you require the same list of names and addresses. To use a previously created data source, you must open the data source after creating the main document.

Complete the Main Document

With the main document set up with the fields and information you want, you can connect to the appropriate data in the data source, and merge your data. To complete the main document, you type the text of the letter that you want to send. You also insert special instructions into the main document. These instructions, called *mail merge field codes*, tell Word where to place the personalized information from the data source. For example, when you insert the mail merge field code for Last Name in the document, Word pulls the specific information from each record and inserts the last name in the document. Word helps you in this step by providing some pre-designed blocks of information, including an address block and a greeting line.

In addition to the mail merge codes, you can type the text of the document, using any of the editing and formatting features of Word. For example, you can make text bold, change the font, use different page margins, and so on. Also, just because you include a mail merge code in the data source, this does not mean that you have to use it in the main document. You may use some merge fields from the data source more than once, and you may not use other merge fields at all.

```
2/17/2007

«AddressBlock»

«GreetingLine»

Let me use this opportunity to
have done on my behalf in the

Thank you.
```

Merge the Main Document and Data Source

After you complete the main document, you can combine, or *merge*, the main document and the data source to create a personalized letter for each person on your mailing list. Word replaces the mail merge codes in the main document with the personalized information from the data source.

```
2/17/2007

Jeff Smith
Largo Inc.
234 Tretorn Ave.
Beverly Hills, CA 90211

Dear Jeff,

Let me use this opportunity to
have done on my behalf in the

Thank you.
```

After the mail merge is completed, the Mailings tab on the Ribbon has additional options to allow you to revise the fields or the content of your mail merge project.

You can use the Write & Insert Fields group to highlight the current fields to make them easier to find and revise, change the options for your address block or greeting line, and insert new Merge Fields into your document.

The Match Fields option can be used if the field names of your data source have been mismatched or erroneously connected to the fields in the current document.

You can edit the recipient list to change the final output of the project, or use Preview Result to see exactly how the final project will look with the data merged into it.

You can also use Merge & Finish in the Mail Merge tab on the Ribbon to generate mail merge e-mail messages with Outlook 2007. For more information on using Outlook for e-mail, see Chapter 26.

Create a Letter with Mail Merge

Y ou can use the Mail Merge feature to quickly create a personalized letter for each individual on your mailing list. To do so, you must start by creating a main document, which contains the text that remains the same in each letter that you send to the people on your mailing list. You can create your main document from a new or existing document.

You can use the Office button to begin a new blank document or select a template. You can also use the Office button to open an existing document and base your mail merge document on it. In either case, you

must ensure that there is space for the field codes that will bring your merged data into the main document.

Word offers different types of main documents, including form letters, mailing labels, catalogs, or envelopes; this task shows you how to create a form letter. For information on mailing labels, see the task "Print Mailing Labels." You can also apply what you learn in that task to printing envelopes; again, you can get a general idea of the process from the task "Print Mailing Labels."

Create a main document

1 Open or create your main document.

Note: *See Chapter 2 for more information on opening or creating a new Office document.*

Word displays the new document on-screen.

2 Click the Mailings tab.

3 Click the Start Mail Merge down arrow ([▼]).

4 Click Step by Step Mail Merge Wizard.

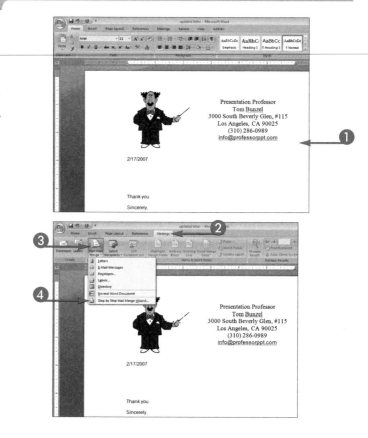

- The Mail Merge task pane appears.

5 Click to select the Letters option (◎ changes to ◉).

6 Click the Next: Starting document link.

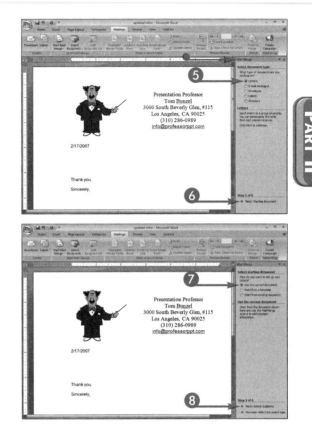

The next pane of the wizard appears.

7 In the Select Starting Document section, click to select an option for how you want to set up your letters (◎ changes to ◉).

Note: *To use one of Word's templates to create a letter for the main document, see Chapter 5.*

This example uses the current document.

8 Click the Next: Select recipients link.

Can I have Word automatically insert the current date and time into a main document?

▼ Yes. After you insert a date or time, Word automatically updates the information each time you open or print the document. Click where you want the date and time to appear. Click the Insert tab on the Ribbon and click Date & Time in the Text group. In the Date & Time dialog box, click the format you want to use. Click the Update automatically option (☐ changes to ☑) and then click OK.

How do I use the main document with a different data source?

▼ You can use the same main document with a different data source to create letters using the data in that data source. To do so, open the main document. Word automatically displays the Mail Merge task pane, listing the current associated data source. You can select a different list by clicking the Select a different list link in Step 3 of the wizard, and then clicking the list that you want to use.

continued

Create a Letter with
Mail Merge *(Continued)*

The next step in performing a mail merge is to create or select a data source, which contains the personalized information that changes in each letter, such as the name and address of each person on your mailing list.

A data source contains fields and records. A field is a specific category of information in the data source. For example, a field can contain the first names of all of the people on your mailing list. A record is a collection of information about one person in a data source. For example, a record can contain the name, address,

telephone number, and account information for one person. Make sure that you take time to plan and properly set up the data source to determine the fields that you need.

Word provides an address list with common field names for form letters. A *field name* is a name, such as Last Name or City, that is assigned to each field. If you do not want to include a particular field, do not add it to the merge document, or you can press Delete on your keyboard to remove it. You can also delete the field by customizing the options for the Address Block.

Create a Letter with Mail Merge *(continued)*

Create or select a data source

The next pane of the wizard appears, where you can select the recipients for the letters.

⑨ In the Select Recipients section, click the Select from Outlook Contacts option (◎ changes to ◉).

⑩ Click the Choose Contacts Folder link.

The Select Contacts dialog box appears.

If you have more than one Outlook user, you may be prompted to choose a user's profile.

⑪ Click to select the personal folder with your main Outlook contacts.

If Business Contact Manager is part of your Office Suite, then you can also use its contact list.

⑫ Click OK.

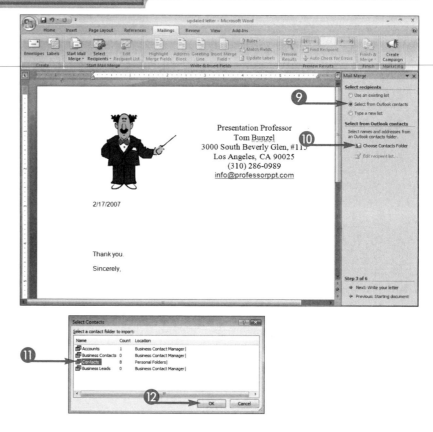

The Mail Merge Recipients dialog box appears.

● You can deselect any recipients to exclude them (☑ changes to ☐).

⑬ Click OK.

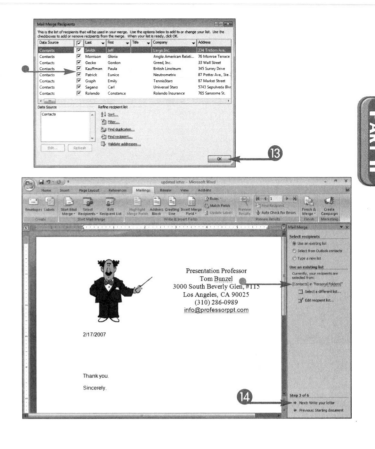

● Word adds the data source to the task pane.

⑭ Click the Next: Write Your Letter link.

What is Business Contact Manager, and can I use it in a merge file?

▼ Business Contact Manager is an add-in to Outlook 2007. It comes with some configurations of the Office suite, but is not included in others. If you have Business Contact Manager, it will show up as a potential data source when you select to merge data from your Outlook contacts. If you have used Business Contact Manager and have contact data, then you can use it as a merge source. If you do not have it or do not want to use it for the merge source, then select the Contacts folder from the Personal Folders location.

Can I use other sources of data?

▼ Yes. You can create a simple database directly in Word or in an Excel worksheet, or import data from another database such as Access.

How do I use an existing list?

▼ To use an existing list, click the Use an existing list option from the Select Recipients section in the wizard. In the Select Data Source dialog box that appears, select the data source file that you want to use and then click Open.

continued

Create a Letter with Mail Merge *(Continued)*

To complete the main document, you type the text that you want to include in the letter. You must insert special instructions into the document to tell Word where to place the personalized information from the address list.

The instructions that you insert into the main document are called merge fields. A *merge field* is a specific category of information in a data source, such as First Name, City, or State. The available merge fields match the fields in the address list that you completed for each person.

Word helps you by allowing you to use links to insert common information, such as an address block and a greeting.

You can also insert as many merge fields as you need in any other location. The location of a merge field in the main document indicates where the corresponding information from the data source appears when you print the letters. In the main document, a merge field begins and ends with braces.

After you complete the main document, you can merge the main document and the data source to create your letters.

Create a Letter with Mail Merge *(continued)*

Complete the main document

The next pane of the wizard appears, where you can add recipient information.

⑮ Type any text that you want to include.

⑯ To insert an address block for the letter, click the Address Block link.

The Insert Address Block dialog box appears.

⑰ Click to select the address elements that you want to include (☐ changes to ☑).

● You can click a postal address option (◎ changes to ◉).

● The Preview window displays your choices.

⑱ Click OK.

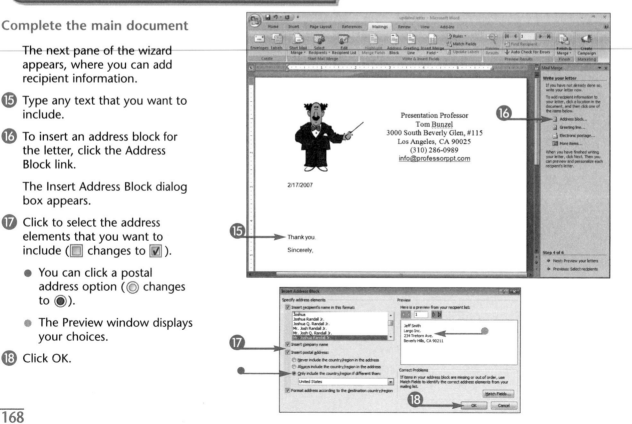

● Word adds the address block field code.

⑲ To insert a greeting, click the Greeting Line link.

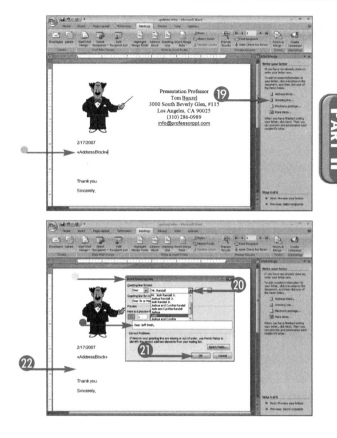

● The Insert Greeting Line dialog box appears.

⑳ Click the down arrows (⊡) to select a greeting, name format, and punctuation symbol.

● The preview displays how the greeting line will appear.

㉑ Click OK.

㉒ Type the rest of the letter.

When the letter is complete, you can save it.

Note: *For more information, see the task "Save and Close a Document" in Chapter 2.*

How do I insert a merge field into the body of a letter?

▼ The links enable you to insert blocks of information in common formats. You may also want to include a merge field in the body of the letter. To do so, click the More items link. In the Insert Merge Field dialog box that appears, click the field that you want to insert and then click Insert. When you finish inserting fields, click Close.

How do I delete a merge field that I have added by mistake?

▼ To delete a merge field, click the field to select it, and press the Delete key.

Can I manually add a merge field by typing the name of the merge field in braces?

▼ No. You must use the Insert Merge Field dialog box to insert the merge field into the letter.

Can I format a merge field?

▼ Yes. You can format a merge field as you would format text in any document. When you merge the main document with the data source, the personalized information in each letter displays the formatting that you apply to the merge field.

continued

Create a Letter with
Mail Merge *(Continued)*

After you complete the main document, you can preview how your letters will look when you merge the main document and the data source. Previewing lets you temporarily replace the merge fields in the main document with the information for a person on your mailing list.

You can preview the merged letters to make sure that they look the way you want. This can help you to find and correct any errors before you waste time and money printing the letters for every person on your mailing list.

After you preview the letters to ensure that there are no errors, you can combine the main document and

the data source to create a personalized letter for each person on your mailing list.

To conserve hard drive space, you should not save the merged document. You can easily re-create the merged document at any time by merging the main document and the data source again.

You can print the personalized letters in the merged document as you would print any Word document. For more information on printing a document, see the task "Print a Document."

Merge the documents

Your letter now contains the merge fields and your typed text.

㉓ Click the Next: Preview your letters link.

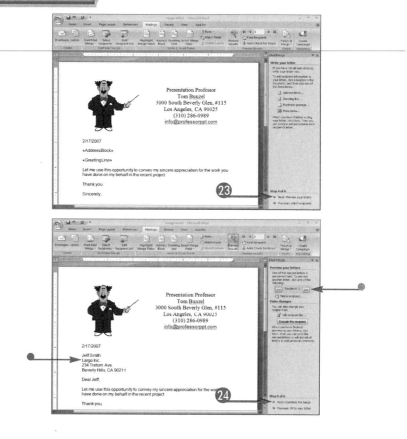

● The main document displays the information for the first record from the data source.

● To preview the information for other records, you can click the Next or Previous buttons (`>>` or `<<`).

㉔ When you finish previewing the information, click the Next: Complete the merge link.

25 Click Print.

● The Merge to Printer dialog box appears.

26 Click to select the records that you want to print (⊙ changes to ⊙).

27 Click OK.

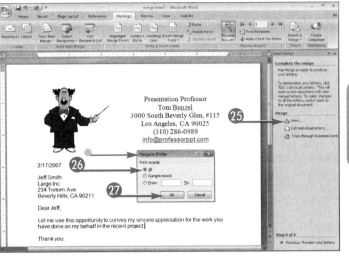

The Print dialog box appears.

28 Click OK.

Word prints the letters.

When previewing merged documents, how can I quickly display the information for a record of interest?

▼ You can scroll through the recipient list using the scroll buttons in the Mail Merge task pane, as shown after Step 23. If you have many recipients, then you can search for an individual recipient by clicking the Find a recipient link to open the Find Entry dialog box. Type the entry that you want to find, select whether to look in all fields or a particular field by clicking the appropriate option, and then click Find Next. Click Cancel to close the Find Entry dialog box.

Can I go back in the merge process to change something?

▼ Yes. You can use the Previous link in the Mail Merge task pane to go back a step. This allows you to go back and make changes to any of the previous steps.

Do I have to include all of the recipients?

▼ No. You can exclude a particular recipient by clicking the Exclude this recipient link when previewing letters after Step 23. You can also select whether to print a letter for just the current record or for a range of records when you merge to the printer.

Print Mailing Labels

You can use the Mail Merge feature to print a label for every person on your mailing list. You can use labels for addressing envelopes and packages, labeling file folders, and creating name tags.

You merge the information from an existing data source to print labels. A data source contains the personalized information that changes on each label, such as the name and address of each person on your mailing list. Be sure to update the information in the data source. Although you will typically use the data source that you used to create the letters, you can also

create a new data source. To create a data source, see Step 3 of the Step by Step Mail Merge Wizard and select the Type a New List option.

Word can print on many popular label products and label types. You can check your label packaging to determine which label product and type of label you are using.

Before you begin, make sure that you consult your printer's manual to determine whether the printer can print labels and which label products your printer supports.

Print Mailing Labels

1 Click the Office button to open or create a new document.

Note: *See Chapter 2 for more information on opening an existing document or creating a new document.*

2 Click the Mailings tab.

3 Click the Start Mail Merge down arrow (▼).

4 Click Step by Step Mail Merge Wizard.

● The Mail Merge task pane appears.

5 Click the Labels option (◉ changes to ◉).

6 Click the Next: Starting document link.

7 Click the Label Options link.

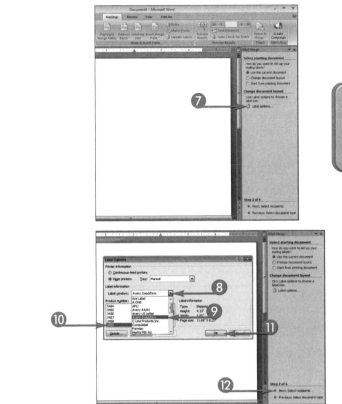

The Label Options dialog box appears.

8 Click the Label vendors down arrow (▼) and select a different label product.

9 Click the type of label that you want to use.

10 Select a product number.

11 Click OK.

12 Click the Next: Select recipients link.

Should I specify the kind of printer that I am using?

▼ Yes. You should specify the kind of printer that you are using so that Word can display the appropriate label products and label types. In the Label Options dialog box, click to select either the Continuous-feed printers or Page printers option (◎ changes to ◉).

Can I create my own labels without using the Mail Merge feature?

▼ Yes. To do so, click Labels in the Create group of the Mailings tab. You can then select the type of label and label address, and print the labels.

Can I specify in which tray I want Word to look for labels in my printer?

▼ If you are using a laser or ink jet printer, you can specify where you want Word to look for the labels. This is useful if you want to feed the labels into your printer manually or if your printer has more than one tray. In the Label Options dialog box, click the Tray down arrow (▼) to specify where you want Word to look for the labels.

continued

Print Mailing
Labels *(Continued)*

You will most often use an existing data source when you are creating mailing labels. You can also create a new one. For information on setting up a data source, see Steps 9 to 14 in the task "Create a Letter with Mail Merge."

When you select a data source, you see all of the people in that address list. By default, Word selects all people in the list. You can also select or deselect which people you want to include. The list conveniently provides buttons for selecting and clearing selections.

After you select the data source, you set up the mailing label format. Word helps you set up a mailing label by providing a link for an address block. This address block contains a predefined address and includes the common format of name, address, city, state, and ZIP code.

Print Mailing Labels *(continued)*

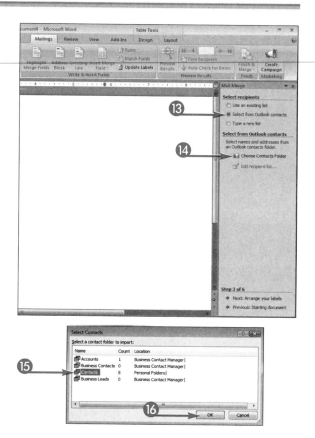

⑬ Click the Select from Outlook Contacts option (◎ changes to ◉).

⑭ Click the Choose Contacts Folder link.

The Select Contacts dialog box appears.

⑮ Click to select the Contacts folder from your Personal folders location.

⑯ Click OK.

- The Mail Merge Recipients dialog box appears.

By default, all of the recipients in the list are selected for inclusion in the mail merge.

⑰ You can click to deselect any recipients that you want to exclude from the mail merge (☑ changes to ☐).

⑱ Click OK.

⑲ Click the Next: Arrange your labels link.

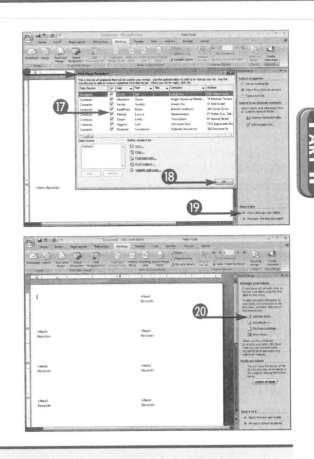

The Arrange your labels section of the wizard appears.

⑳ Click the Address block link.

MASTER IT

Can I edit information in the list?	Can I add entries to the address list?	Can I search for a particular record?
▼ Yes. To do so, click the Edit recipient list link in the Mail Merge task pane. In the Mail Merge Recipients dialog box, you can then edit any of the existing records to update the information. Select the record that you want to update and click Edit.	▼ If you are using your Outlook Contact List, add new contacts to your Outlook Address Book before beginning a mail merge, whether for a letter or label. Also see the note in the task "Create a Letter with Mail Merge" about Business Contact Manager, which is a contact management program included in the Small Business, Professional, and Enterprise versions of Outlook in Office 2007.	▼ Yes. In the Mail Merge Recipients dialog box, click Find Recipient. In the Find Entry dialog box, type the text that you want to find and which fields you want to search. You can either look in all fields or select a specific field. Click Find Next until you find the record that you want. Click Cancel to close the Find Entry dialog box.

continued ▶

Print Mailing Labels *(Continued)*

Y ou can select a format for the name in the address block. You can also select which items to include in the address. For example, you can select whether to include the company name or the country and region.

When you set up the address block, you do so for one label. You can then copy your setup for all of the labels in the document.

Keep in mind that your document may look different than the labels that appear in this task. The number of columns and the size of the labels depend on your selections when you set up the label options.

When you complete the merge and print, you can select which records to print. By default, Word prints all records, but you can also select the current record or a range of records.

Before you merge, you should save the label document. Doing so allows you to use this document for other address lists. Due to its large size, you do not need to save the label document after you merge. You can always merge the main document with the data source at any time.

Print Mailing Labels *(continued)*

The Insert Address Block dialog box appears.

㉑ Click to include the address elements that you want (▣ changes to ✓).

㉒ Click to select a format for the name or a postal address option.

● The Preview window displays your choices.

㉓ Click OK.

Word applies the format to the current label.

㉔ Click Update all labels.

● Word updates the labels to include the address block information.

㉕ Click the Next: Preview your labels link.

● Word displays a preview of the current labels.

㉖ Click the Next: Complete the merge link.

㉗ You can now either edit the individual labels or print by clicking the appropriate link.

Why do the labels contain the text, "Next Record"?

▼ The Next Record code is a specific code that tells Word to pull information from the next record for that label. You do not need to worry about including this field code; Word includes it automatically.

How do I print the labels?

▼ Insert the paper into the printer. (Check your printer documentation for proper label insertion.) To print, click the Print link in the Mail Merge task pane. In the Merge to Printer dialog box, select which records you want to print, and click OK. In the Print dialog box, click OK to print the labels.

What if the preview is not what I want?

▼ If the preview of the labels does not look correct, you can back up through the steps and make any appropriate changes. To do so, click the Previous step link and then make the change. You can also click the Edit individual labels link after completing the merge. This enables you to directly check and edit the merged labels, including font and font size.

Print an Envelope

You can use Word to print an address on an envelope. Printing an address directly on an envelope saves you from creating and attaching a label, or using a typewriter to address the envelope.

Before you begin, make sure that your printer allows you to print envelopes. You can consult the manual that came with your printer to confirm this.

Word scans your document to find a delivery address for the envelope. You can use the address that Word finds or enter another address.

You can specify a return address for the envelope, or, if you do not want a return address, you can omit it. You generally omit the return address if your company uses custom envelopes that already display a return address. When you specify a return address, Word allows you to save it, and uses it as the return address every time you print an envelope. This saves you from having to type the same return address repeatedly.

Print an Envelope

1 Open or create your main document.

Note: *See Chapter 2 for more information on opening or creating a new Office document.*

2 Click the Mailings tab.

3 Click Envelopes.

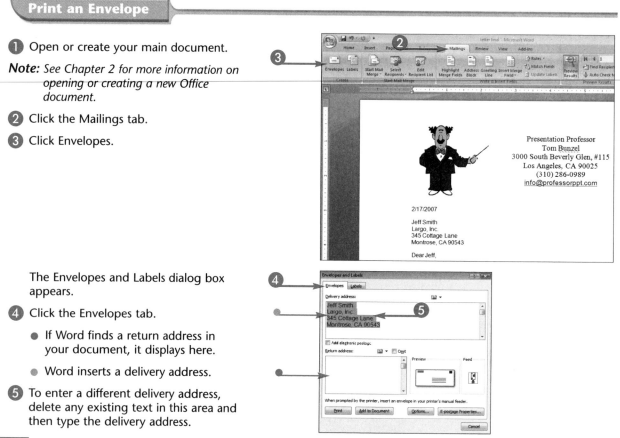

The Envelopes and Labels dialog box appears.

4 Click the Envelopes tab.

● If Word finds a return address in your document, it displays here.

● Word inserts a delivery address.

5 To enter a different delivery address, delete any existing text in this area and then type the delivery address.

178

6 Click this area and type the return address.

● You can click to deselect the Omit check box if you do not want to print a return address (☑ changes to ☐).

○ You can preview the envelope here.

7 Click Print.

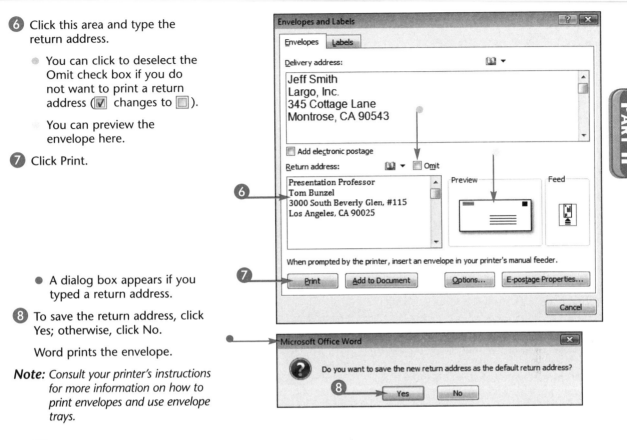

● A dialog box appears if you typed a return address.

8 To save the return address, click Yes; otherwise, click No.

Word prints the envelope.

Note: *Consult your printer's instructions for more information on how to print envelopes and use envelope trays.*

How do I specify the size of the envelope that I want to print?

▼ In the Envelopes and Labels dialog box, click the Options button. In the Envelopes dialog box, click the Envelope size area and then click the envelope size that you want to use. You can select from the most common envelope sizes. After you select the size, click OK.

Can I copy my return address from the letter?

▼ Yes. If want to use a return address that you have added to the document, drag through it to select it, and use the Copy button (🖳) from the Home tab on the Ribbon. You can then paste it into the Return Address area of the Envelopes and Labels dialog box. For more information, see the task "Move or Copy Text" in Chapter 3.

How do I change the font for my delivery or return address?

▼ In the Envelopes and Labels dialog box, click the Options button. In the Envelopes dialog box, click the Font button for the address that you want to change. In the dialog box that appears, select the font options that you want to apply and click OK. Be sure that your changes do not make the text too big to fit on the envelope.

Output to PDF and XPS Formats

Office 2007 enables you to output a number of its programs — including Word — in either PDF or XPS format.

Portable Document Format (PDF) and XML Paper Specification (XPS) are fixed-layout electronic file formats that preserve document formatting and enable file sharing. Both formats ensure that when the file is viewed online or printed, it retains exactly the format that you intended, and that data in the file cannot be easily changed. Both formats are also useful for documents that will be reproduced by using commercial printing methods.

PDF was originally created by Adobe while XPS is a competing distribution format favored by Microsoft. The difference between PDF and XML is that

information in XML is much more easily revised than PDF. XML allows for a central database of information; when changes need to be made to the data the changes have to be made in one place only.

The PDF or XPS add-in is not part of the suite itself and so you must download and install it separately. You can find it at http://office.microsoft.com/en-us/word/HA101675271033.aspx. You can go directly to the download site by clicking the Office button, pausing over Save As, and then clicking Find add-ins for other file formats, which launches the Microsoft Download Center.

Once you install the add-in, the PDF or XPS feature is available under the Save As command when you click the Office button.

Output to PDF and XPS formats

1. Open the document that you want to output to PDF or XPS format.
2. Click the Office button.
3. Click Save As.
4. Click PDF or XPS.

The Publish as PDF or XPS dialog box appears.

5. Click the Save as file type down arrow (▼) to select either XPS or PDF format.

   This example uses PDF format.

6. Click Options.

- The Options dialog box opens.

- You can click to select the Page(s) option if you want to print selected pages (◎ changes to ◉).

7 Click OK.

The default setting is to open the file in your default PDF or XPS reader application.

8 Click Publish.

- Word converts the file to the specified format, and the file opens in the default application.

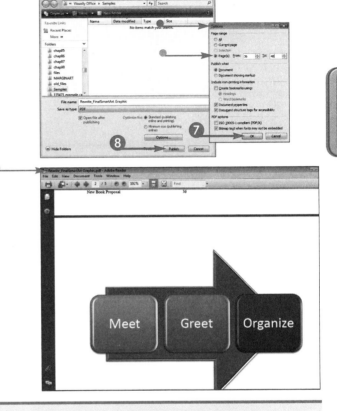

Can I edit the file once it has been converted?

▼ It depends on whether you have a program that edits PDF or XPS files. Adobe Acrobat Reader is the most popular program for reading PDF files, and Internet Explorer can open the XPS files; however, neither is an editor. PDF editors are available from Adobe and other software developers. However, you can always edit the file in Word and then output it again in the format that you want.

How will the minimum size option affect the output?

▼ The Minimum Size option appears under the Optimize For section in the Publish As PDF or XPS dialog box. Although this option compresses any graphics in the document, thus making it smaller to e-mail or download online, it significantly reduces

the print quality. If you need to print as well as e-mail or post your file online, then you may want to output it twice with either option enabled.

Which other Office programs support PDF or XPS output?

▼ This feature works with the following Office programs:

- Microsoft Office Access 2007
- Microsoft Office Excel 2007
- Microsoft Office InfoPath 2007
- Microsoft Office OneNote 2007
- Microsoft Office PowerPoint 2007
- Microsoft Office Publisher 2007
- Microsoft Office Visio 2007
- Microsoft Office Word 2007

PART III
USING EXCEL

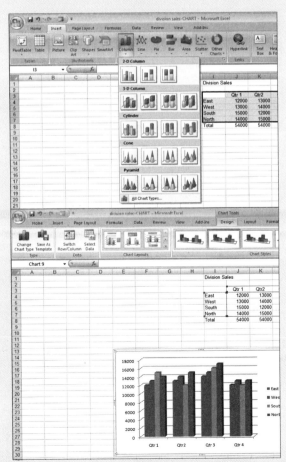

An Introduction to Excel

Excel is a spreadsheet program that you can use to work with and manipulate numerical data. With Excel, you can perform calculations, analyze data, and present information. Excel can help you manage your business and personal finances, and calculate what-ifs and scenarios.

An Excel file, or *workbook*, contains a collection of worksheets that store and keep related data together. The *worksheet* is a grid of columns and rows, and you type data into a *cell* — the intersection of a column and row.

For more information on Excel, you can visit www.microsoft.com/excel.

Type and Edit Data

Excel has many automated features that let you efficiently type and edit data in a worksheet, thus saving you time and effort. For example, Excel automatically fills a series of numbers or text for you. Likewise, with the AutoComplete feature, Excel finishes data or text as you begin to type.

	A	B
1	Sales Quarter	Units Sold
2	1	15
3	2	20
4	3	30
5		100
6		300
7		600

After you enter data into a worksheet, you can add new data, delete data, or move data to a new location, as well as check the text in the worksheet for spelling errors. Excel remembers the last changes that you made to a worksheet, so that you can undo changes that you do not want.

Formulas and Functions

Formulas and functions help you to perform calculations and analyze data in a worksheet. In Excel, a *formula* is an equation that contains mathematical operations, and that references cells within your worksheet or in another worksheet. For example, you might build a multiplication formula to calculate the sales tax on a purchase amount. *Functions* are ready-to-use, built-in formulas that let you perform specialized calculations on your data. The most common function is AutoSum, which you can use to sum a range of numbers.

After you create a formula or insert a function, you can copy it to other cells in a worksheet. Excel automatically changes the cell references in the new formulas or functions for you. If you change a number that you use in a formula or function, Excel automatically recalculates and displays the new result. See Chapter 11 for more information on formulas and functions.

Managing Data in a List

Excel provides powerful tools that allow you to manage and analyze a large collection of data, such as a mailing or product list. After you organize data into a list, you can sort the data in different orders or filter the data to display only the data that meets certain criteria. You can also add subtotals to the list to help summarize the data.

You can also apply a form to an Excel list to make it easier to add or revise your data. Using an Excel list for personal information also lets you use it as a data source for a mail merge in Word or Outlook. For more information on mail merge in Word, see Chapter 8.

Formatting Worksheets

Excel's formatting features can also help you add emphasis to important data in a worksheet. For example, you can use bold, italic, and underline styles to call attention to important data. You can also make data in a worksheet easier to read by changing the font and size, or by changing the appearance of numbers using formats such as currency or percent.

Excel also includes many formatting features that can help you change the appearance of a worksheet. For example, you can change the width of columns and the height of rows to better fit the data in a worksheet, or add borders or color to cells. You can find more information on formatting text and changing borders and colors later in this chapter; see Chapter 10 for more information about changing the column width and row height.

Excel's PivotTables and PivotTable charts let you rearrange your data in different orders to filter or sort information and to make presentations. Using a PivotTable allows you to see your data from a different perspective; for example, you can easily determine who sold the most product or which territory was the most successful in a sales data worksheet where the data may be scattered through several different rows and columns.

Graphics

Excel includes many graphics, such as text boxes, text effects, and AutoShapes, which you can use to illustrate and call attention to information in worksheets and charts. AutoShapes include simple shapes, such as ovals and rectangles, and more complex shapes, such as stars and arrows. You might use a graphic, such as an arrow, to point out an important part of the worksheet.

Excel 2007 has some graphics tools that let you enhance charts and diagrams with special effects, like glow, bevel, shadow, and 3D.

Graphics are also part of the conditional format feature of Excel; you can use data bars, color scales, and icon sets to discern patterns and understand the meaning of your data.

Charts

Excel helps you to create colorful charts to better illustrate the data in a worksheet. For example, a chart may show sales over time so that your audience can visualize the sales trend. You can choose from many chart types, such as bar, line, area, and pie charts. If you change the data in the worksheet, Excel automatically updates the chart to display the changes. You can then move and resize a chart on a worksheet to suit your needs.

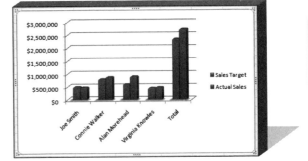

Printing

Excel has several features to help you preview and print a worksheet to your specifications. You can add a header or footer to print additional information, such as your name or the date, at the top or bottom of each page. You can also specify how you want your data to print on a page, adjust the margins for the worksheet, or change the size of the printed data so that it fits on a specific number of pages. Excel's Page Break Preview lets you see how a worksheet looks on paper before you print it.

Start Excel

Excel is a spreadsheet program that helps you organize, analyze, and attractively present data, typically numerical. You can use Excel to present data such as sales projections, budgets, profit and loss statements, and expenses.

When you start Excel, a blank worksheet appears on your screen. A *worksheet* is a grid of rows and columns, and the intersection of a row and column is a *cell*. Cells store the data, such as text and numbers, which you enter into a worksheet.

After you enter your data, you can change the appearance of the worksheet, perform calculations on the data, and produce a paper copy of the worksheet.

When you first start Excel, you may see the task pane. You can use this task pane to perform common tasks.

Start Excel

1️⃣ Click Start.

2️⃣ Click All Programs.

3️⃣ Click Microsoft Office.

4️⃣ Click Microsoft Office Excel 2007.

The Excel window appears, displaying a blank worksheet.

Parts of the Excel Screen

The Excel screen displays several items that help you to perform tasks efficiently. The Excel Ribbon and its tabs, groups, and dialog box launchers can handle most of your formatting requirements.

Some features on your screen may look different, depending on your monitor settings and how you set up your system.

Ⓐ Title Bar

Displays the name of the program and the workbook. If you open a new, unsaved workbook, the default workbook name is Book1.

Ⓒ Ribbon Tabs

Selecting a Ribbon tab opens up a different set of features and options.

Ⓑ Contextual Ribbon

Contains buttons to help you select common commands, such as Save and Print.

Ⓓ Name Box

Displays the cell reference for the active cell.

Ⓔ Active Cell

The cell into which you are currently typing data. It displays a thick border.

Ⓕ Cell

The area where a row and column intersect.

Ⓖ Worksheet Tabs

You click worksheet tabs to switch among the worksheets in your workbook in order to view and compare your data. Excel indicates the currently displayed worksheet with a white tab. The other worksheets in the workbook, which Excel hides from view, have gray tabs.

Ⓗ Tab Scroll Buttons

You can click a scroll button to browse through the numerous tabs in your workbook. Click 🔘 to display the first tab, 🔘 to display the tab to the left of the current tab, 🔘 to display the tab to the right of the current tab, and 🔘 to display the last tab.

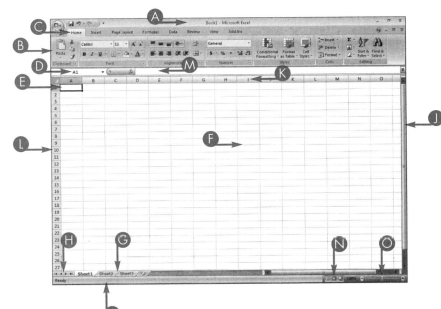

Ⓘ Status Bar

Displays information about the task that you are performing.

Ⓙ Scroll Bars

Allow you to move through the worksheet.

Ⓚ Column

A vertical line of cells, which Excel identifies with a letter.

Ⓛ Row

A horizontal line of cells, which Excel identifies with a number.

Ⓜ Formula Bar

Displays the contents of the active cell.

Ⓝ Views Buttons

Three buttons that let you alternate between Normal view, Page Layout view, and Page Break Preview.

Ⓞ Zoom Slider

Lets you zoom out of your workbook to see more cells, or zoom in for more detail.

PART III

187

Explore the Excel Ribbon

The Excel 2007 Ribbon has seven main components, each of which enables the user to perform specific tasks for producing professional workbooks.

Clicking one of the tabs brings up a different set of related options for a particular task, and selecting a portion of a workbook brings up more contextual options.

With the Ribbon, you can work with parts of a workbook or the entire workbook to make formatting changes, reorganize sections, add references, and go through a final review process to make sure that your workbook is polished and professional.

Home

You can use the Home tab to change the fonts, paragraph alignment, or styles of selected parts of your workbook. The Home tab also displays command buttons that allow you to copy and paste to and from the Clipboard, and apply formats from one selection to another. Find & Select on the Home tab let you quickly replace one word or phrase with another.

The Home tab also has features that allow you to fit text in cells into columns and ensures that the text is visible and not replaced by the #### symbol. Conditional formats and other formatting and style options help you to analyze data and make your worksheets look professional. Editing features let you quickly calculate sums and averages, AutoFill cells, erase, sort, and filter data, and find and select ranges of cells.

Insert

The Insert tab lets you place important elements in your workbook to supplement the text and figures. Tables can help you to organize data, and PivotTables let you reorganize a worksheet and see data in different positions. Pictures, clip art, shapes, SmartArt, and charts can also be inserted to create professional-looking worksheets.

The Insert tab has a powerful Charting section that lets you create many different kinds of charts to visualize data more effectively. You can also quickly manage hyperlinks, bookmarks, headers and footers, or symbols, and use the Quick Parts feature to organize Building Blocks. The Insert tab also lets you put symbols, equations, and other objects into your workbook.

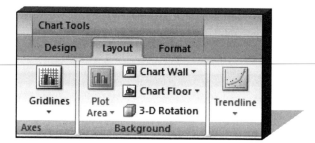

Page Layout

The Page Layout tab lets you set options for margins, orientation, page size, print area, breaks, and background, as well as letting you print titles.

To make sure that you print accurately, the Scale to Fit group lets you adjust the height and width of your columns, rows, and cells. In Page Layout you can also quickly revise the overall look of a page or an entire workbook by applying a theme, background color, or page border. You can also specify whether to show or print gridlines and headings. The Page Layout tab is where you can use Arrange features to align, group, and manage the layers of inserted objects and graphics, moving them in front of, or behind, one another.

Formulas

The Formulas tab lets you create and manage simple and complex functions and formulas in the Function Library group. There are features that allow you to look up and reference functions and formulas, access mathematical and trigonometric functions, and add more specific functions for areas such as statistical analysis and engineering.

In the Formulas tab, the Defined Names group lets you assign names to ranges of cells, and then refer to these names in the current workbook or workbooks, based on the current template. The Formula Auditing group lets you evaluate, trace precedents and dependents within formulas, and perform error checking. A Watch Window provides instant tabulation of formula or function values, and the Calculation group lets you determine when the worksheet recalculates the formulas and functions within the cells.

Data

In the Data tab, you can use a spreadsheet as a database and import and analyze data from Microsoft Access, the Web, text data files, or other sources. In both the Get External Data and Connections group, you can manage various existing database connections. With a data list in your worksheet, you can use the Sort & Filter group to reorganize the data and view only those fields and records that you need for a particular task. The Data Tools group lets you parse data and remove duplicate records, and perform data validation and what-if analysis. The Outline group lets you redefine portions of your worksheet to perform subtotals, and to group and ungroup ranges and cells for various functions and tasks.

Review

The Review tab lets you run spelling and grammar checks and perform a number of research functions, including translation and accessing a thesaurus. Markups by multiple reviewers are handled in the Review tab, as well as protecting and sharing a workbook and tracking changes, all in order to collaborate and edit a workbook into a final version.

View

You can enable the main workbook views in the View tab, as well as show or hide the ruler, gridlines, the formula bar, and headings. Switching between windows of open workbooks, or viewing them on the same screen, lets you work with more than one workbook at a time. You can also freeze, split, or hide windows, save your workspace to return to the same configuration, and alternate among full-screen windows. The View tab also lets you manage and record macros.

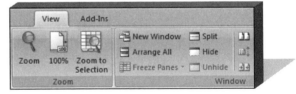

Add-Ins

The Add-Ins tab is mainly for additional features that were created by developers and third parties. If you need to load pre-programmed code, templates, or other programs that work with Excel, or to de-activate them, you can use the Add-Ins tab to do so.

Keep in mind that you may not see all of the tabs or features within any tab if you are running in Compatibility Mode (Office 97-2003) or if you have not installed any add-ins.

PART III

Type Text

Y ou can type text into your worksheet quickly and easily. By default, Excel automatically left-aligns text, which appears in the active cell and in the formula bar at the top of your worksheet. If you make a typing mistake, you simply press Backspace to remove the incorrect data, and then retype the correct data.

Due to the size of a cell, Excel may not display all of the text that you type. If the cell next to the active cell does not contain data, the data spills over into that cell, although the entry is really contained only in the current active cell. If the cell next to the active cell contains data, then Excel truncates the entry. To view all of the text in a truncated cell, you can change the column width, as described in Chapter 10.

How do I save my work?

▼ To save a workbook, click the Office button and then click Save As. Excel saves all worksheets in the workbook. There are three formats for Excel 2007 workbooks: a basic Excel workbook, a macro-enabled version, and a binary version. The examples in this book use the first version, Excel workbook. See Chapter 2 for more information on saving Office documents.

Type Text

① Click the cell where you want to type text.

② Type the text.

- The text that you type appears in the active cell and the formula bar.

- You can click the X (⊠) to cancel the entry, or the check mark (✓) to accept the entry.

③ Press Enter to enter the data and move down one cell.

To enter the data and move one cell in any direction, you can press the up-, down-, right-, or left-arrow keys.

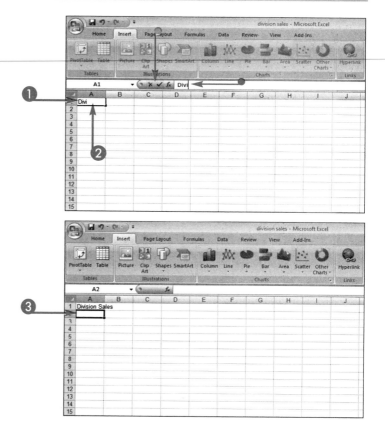

Type Numbers

Y ou can type numbers into your worksheet quickly and easily. By default, Excel automatically right-aligns numbers in the active cell, and they appear in the formula bar at the top of your worksheet.

To enter numerical data, you can use the keys on the top row of the keyboard or the numeric keypad, which is usually at the far right of the keyboard.

Excel displays large numbers either in scientific notation, or as a series of # signs. To see the whole number, you can widen the column. For information on viewing data in a certain format, see the tasks "Format Numbers" and "Change Data Alignment." For more information on changing column width, see Chapter 10.

MASTER IT

How does Excel differentiate between numbers such as ZIP codes and actual values?

▼ Excel cannot tell the difference between numbers that function more as text, such as phone numbers, ZIP codes, and social security numbers, and actual values. To have Excel treat a numeric entry as text, type an apostrophe (') before the number.

How do I enter numbers using the numeric keypad?

▼ To activate the numeric keypad, press the Num Lock key. NUM displays in the status bar to indicate that the keypad is active.

Type Numbers

① Click the cell where you want to type numbers.

② Type the number.

For a negative number, type a minus sign (–) before the entry or type the entry in parentheses.

③ Press Enter to enter the number and move down one cell.

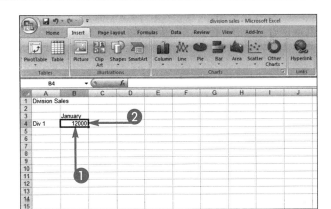

Edit or Delete Data

Excel allows you to edit, correct, and update the data in your worksheet. The flashing insertion point in the cell indicates where Excel will remove or add data. You can move the insertion point to another location in the cell.

When you remove data using the Backspace key, Excel removes the characters to the left of the insertion point. When you remove data using the Delete key, Excel removes characters to the right of the insertion point. When you add data, Excel inserts the characters that you type at the location of the insertion point.

You can delete data that you no longer need from a single cell or a group of cells in your worksheet. This editing technique differs from deleting characters within a cell in that you delete the entire contents of the selected cell or cells.

Edit or Delete Data

Edit data

1 Double-click the cell that you want to edit.

A flashing insertion point appears in the cell.

You can press the left- or right-arrow key to move the insertion point.

You can press Backspace to remove characters to the left of the insertion point, or press Delete to remove characters to the right of the insertion point.

2 Type the new data.

3 Press Enter.

● Excel updates the entry, and the cell below is selected.

Delete data

1. Select the cell or cells containing the data that you want to delete.

Note: To learn how to select a range of cells, see Chapter 11.

2. Press Delete.

● Excel deletes the data in the cells that you selected.

● Excel updates any formulas that reference the deleted cells.

I want to edit or enter data in a large worksheet. Can I display my worksheet headings while I do this?

▼ Yes. You can freeze the row and column headings so that they remain on-screen. Select a cell below and to the right of where you want to freeze. Click the View tab on the Ribbon and then click Freeze Panes. Any rows above, and any columns to the left of, the active cell remain on-screen when you scroll through the worksheet. To undo the freeze, click the View tab on the Ribbon and then click Unfreeze Panes.

What if I want to replace data in the cell?

▼ Click the cell containing the data that you want to replace. Type the new data and press Enter.

Can I edit data using the formula bar?

▼ Yes. Click the cell containing the data that you want to edit. The data in the cell appears in the formula bar. Click in the formula bar and then perform Steps 2 to 3 to edit the data.

Can I undo a change?

▼ Yes. Click the Undo button (⟲). If you change your mind before typing the change, press Esc to exit the cell without making the change.

Move or Copy Data

You can reorganize your worksheet by moving data from one location to another. Moving data can help you find the most effective structure for a worksheet. When you move data, the data disappears from its original location in your worksheet.

You can place a copy of data in a different location in your worksheet. This saves you time because you do not have to retype the data. When you copy data, the data appears in both the original and new location.

To move or copy data, you first cut or copy the selected cells and then paste them. You can do this by using the Cut, Copy, and Paste buttons in the Clipboard group on the Home tab. When you select a cell to which you want to move or copy your data, the new cell becomes the top-left cell of the new block of data.

If the cells that you move or copy contain a formula, Excel may change the cell references in the formula so that the formula still uses the correct cells. For more information on formulas, see Chapter 11.

Move or Copy Data

Move data

1 Click the Home tab.

2 Select the cells that you want to move.

Note: To learn how to select a range of cells, see Chapter 11.

3 Click the Cut button (✂).

You can also press Ctrl+X to cut data.

4 Click where you want to place the data.

5 Click Paste in the Clipboard group.

You can also press Ctrl+V to paste data.

● Excel moves the selected cell or cells to the new location.

6 Click outside the selected range to deselect it.

Copy data

1. Select the cells that you want to copy.

2. Click the Copy button (⬚).

   You can also press Ctrl+C to copy data.

   ● A dashed line appears around your selection to indicate what has been placed on the clipboard.

3. Click the cell where you want to place the data.

4. Click Paste in the Clipboard group.

   You can also press Ctrl+V to paste data.

   ● Excel copies the selected cells and places them in the new location.

Why does Excel ask if I want to replace the contents of the destination cells?

▼ This message appears when you try to paste data to a location that already contains data. To replace the existing data with the selected data, click OK. To cancel the paste, click Cancel.

How can I move or copy data to a different worksheet?

▼ Perform Steps 1 and 2 in either section in this task. Then click the tab of the worksheet where you want to place the data, and perform Steps 3 and 4.

Why does the Clipboard toolbar appear when I move or copy data using the toolbar buttons?

▼ The Clipboard toolbar may appear when you cut or copy two pieces of data in a row, copy the same data twice, or place copied data in a new location and then immediately copy other data.

You also see a Clipboard button (⬚) when you cut or copy data. You can click the down arrow (▼) next to this button to select what you want to paste.

Bold, Italicize, or Underline Text

You can use the Bold, Italic, and Underline features to emphasize and enhance the style of data in your worksheet. You can apply one or all of these features quickly using the appropriate buttons in the Font group of the Home tab on the Ribbon.

The Bold feature makes the selected data appear darker and thicker than other data in your worksheet. You can use the Bold feature to emphasize row and column headings or other important information.

The Italic feature slants the selected data to the right. You may want to italicize notes or explanations that you add to your worksheet.

The Underline feature adds a line underneath the selected data. You can underline data to emphasize it in your worksheet, such as subtotals and totals.

You can also use the Format Cells dialog box to apply these styles, as well as other text effects. For more information, see the task "Apply Special Font Effects." In addition to changing the font style using bold, italic, or underline formatting, you can also select a different font or font size. For more information, see the task "Change Font or Font Size."

Bold, Italicize, or Underline Text

① Click the Home tab.

② Select the cells containing the data that you want to change.

Note: For information about selecting a range of cells, see Chapter 11.

③ Click one or more of the following buttons:

Bold (**B**)

Italic (*I*)

Underline (U)

● The data displays in the style that you selected.

This example uses bold.

You can remove a style by repeating Steps 2 and 3.

Apply a Number Style to Cells

You can quickly change the appearance of numbers in your worksheet to make it easier for other people to understand what the values in your worksheet represent. Excel gives you various numbering style options, including: Number, Comma, Currency, Accounting, Fraction, Percentage, Scientific, Short Date, Long Date, Time, Increase Decimal, and Decrease Decimal. When you change the format of numbers, you do not change the value of the numbers.

You use Currency format, which adds a dollar sign ($) and two decimal places to a number, when you want to display a number as a monetary value.

The Percent format changes a decimal number, such as 0.05, into a percentage format, such as 5%.

The Comma format makes a long number easier to read by adding commas and two decimal places to the number.

You can increase or decrease the number of decimal places that a number displays. If you want to select other number formats, change the look of these styles, or customize each style, see the task "Format Numbers," which covers using the Format Cells dialog box to apply a style.

Apply a Number Style to Cells

1 Click the Home tab.

2 Select the cells containing the numbers that you want to format.

Note: To select a range of cells, see Chapter 11.

3 Click one of the following buttons:

Accounting ($)

Percent (%)

Comma ( )

● Excel displays the numbers in the selected format and adjusts the column width, if necessary.

This example uses the Accounting number style.

● You can click the Increase Decimal button ( ) or the Decrease Decimal button ( ) to change the number of decimal places. You can have up to 15 decimal places.

Format Numbers

Y ou can display the numbers in your worksheet in many different ways. For example, you can display the number 11500 as $11,500.00 to express total sales, or display the number .075 as 7.5% to express the percentage of a project that is completed.

When you change the format of a number, the value of the number does not change.

Excel offers several number format categories including Accounting, Date, Time, Percentage, and Scientific. The category that you choose determines the available options. For example, the Accounting category allows

you to select options such as the number of decimal places and how you want negative numbers to appear.

The Format Cells dialog box displays a sample of the formatting options that you select. This allows you to see how numbers in your worksheet appear in the new format.

When you format a column of numbers, number signs (#) may appear in each cell of the column, indicating that the new format is too wide for the column. For information on changing the column width, see Chapter 10.

Format Numbers

1 Click the Home tab on the Ribbon.

2 Select the cells containing the numbers that you want to format.

Note: To select a range of cells, see Chapter 11.

3 Click the Number Format down arrow (⏷).

The menu displays common formats that you can select.

4 Click More Number Formats.

The Format Cells dialog box appears.

5 Click the Number tab.

6 Click the category that you want.

Depending on the selected category, different options appear.

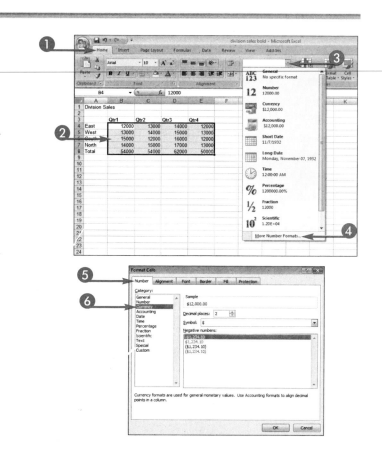

⑦ Click the options that you want to apply.

● You can click the spinner button (⬍) to increase or decrease the number of decimal places.

● You can click an available style for the way that you want negative numbers to appear.

⑧ Click OK.

● Excel displays data in the selected number formatting.

This example formats numbers in the accounting style.

What is a faster method for changing the number format?

▼ You can select from three common number formats — accounting, percent, and comma — by using their buttons in the Number group of the Home tab on the Ribbon. Use this method when you do not need to view the complete list of styles. You can also apply a set of common number styles directly from the Number Format drop-down menu. For more information, see the task "Apply a Number Style to Cells."

How do I remove a number format that I added to my data?

▼ Select the cells containing the data from which you want to remove a number format. Click Number format down arrow (⏷) in the Number group and select General.

Can I create a custom number format?

▼ Yes. You can base your custom number format on an existing number format. In the Format Cells dialog box, click the category for the type of number format that you want to create, and click any options that you want to use. Then click Custom in the Category list. The Type area displays a code for your custom number format. You can modify the code to further customize the number format.

Change Font or Font Size

You can enhance the appearance of your worksheet by changing the font of the data. By default, Excel uses the Calibri font, but you can apply another font to draw attention to headings or to emphasize important data in your worksheet. You can also change the default font. Excel fonts display in the list as they appear in your worksheet so that you can preview a font before you select it. For more information, see the task "Apply Special Font Effects."

Most fonts in the list display either the TT symbol or a printer icon. The TT symbol indicates that the font is

a TrueType font, which means that the font prints exactly as it appears on your screen. The printer symbol indicates a printer font, which may print differently than it appears on your screen.

In addition to changing the font, you can also increase or decrease the size of data in your worksheet. By default, Excel uses a data size of 11 points, with 72 points making an inch. Larger data is easier to read, but smaller data allows you to fit more information on your screen and on a printed worksheet.

Change the font

1 Click the Home tab.

2 Select the cells containing the data that you want to change to a new font.

Note: To select a range of cells, see Chapter 11.

3 Click the Font down arrow (⏷).

Scrolling through the Font drop-down menu provides a live preview of how it will look.

4 Click the font that you want to use. Keep in mind that fonts on your system may vary from those in the figure.

● Excel displays the data in the selected font.

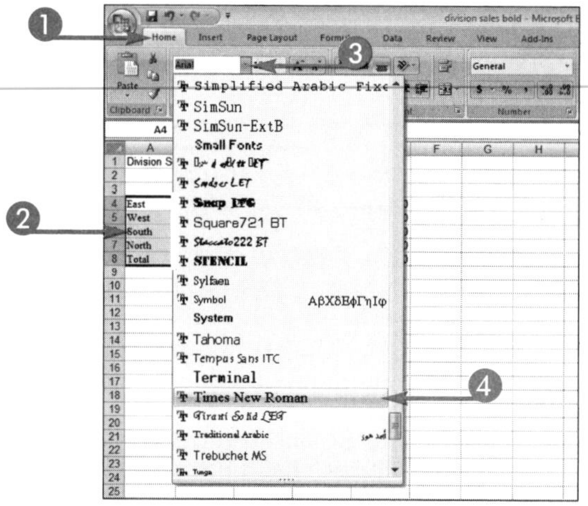

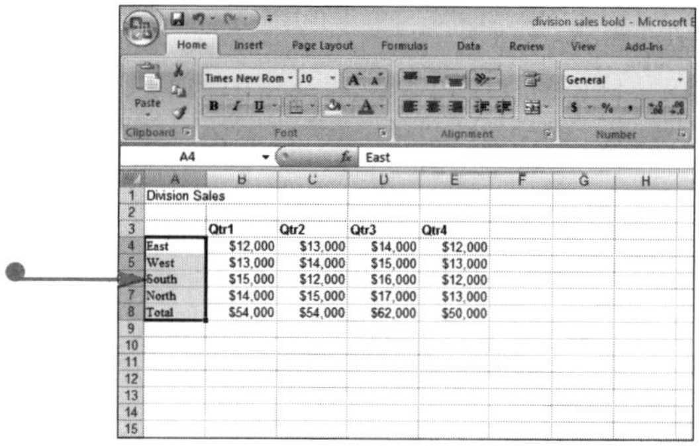

Change font size

1 Click the Home tab.

2 Select the cells containing the data that you want to change to a new size.

Note: *To select a range of cells, see Chapter 11.*

3 Click the Font Size down arrow (▾).

4 Click the size that you want to use.

Scrolling through the Font drop-down menu provides a live preview of how it will look.

You can also type a font size in the text box.

● Excel displays the data in the selected size.

How do I change the font or size of only some of the data in a cell?

▼ Double-click the cell containing the data that you want to change. Drag over the data. Then select the new font or font size using the drop-down menus.

Can I just quickly increase or decrease the font size?

▼ Yes. Select the cell containing the font size that you want to adjust. In the Home tab of the Ribbon, click the Increase Font Size button (A⌃) to increase font size or the Decrease Font Size (A⌄) to decrease font size.

Can I decrease the size of data that displays on my screen without affecting the data's appearance on a printed worksheet?

▼ You can use the Zoom feature to decrease the size of data on your screen without affecting the appearance of the data when you print your worksheet. Click the slider (⊡) in the Zoom group of the View tab, drag in either direction, and watch the corresponding zoom percentage. The smaller the number, the smaller the data appears on-screen.

Change Font or Fill Color

You can add variety and enhance the appearance of your worksheet by changing the font or fill color.

You can change the color of data in a cell to draw attention to titles or other important data in your worksheet. You can also change the background, or *fill color*, of cells. Changing the fill color helps you to distinguish between different areas in your worksheet. For example, in a worksheet that contains monthly

sales figures, you can use a different background color for each month.

When adding color to your worksheet, make sure that you choose background cell colors and data colors that work well together. For example, red data on a blue background is difficult to read.

To learn how to apply multiple formatting features, including color, to your worksheet, see the task "Apply Cell Styles."

Change Font or Fill Color

Change font color

1 Click the Home tab.

2 Select the cells containing the data that you want to change.

Note: To select a range of cells, see Chapter 11.

3 Click the Font Color button down arrow (![A]).

Scrolling through the color menu provides a live preview of how it will look.

4 Click the color that you want to use.

● The data changes to the new color.

This example changes the font color to white.

To reset a color from data, you can perform Steps 1 to 3, and then click Automatic in Step 4.

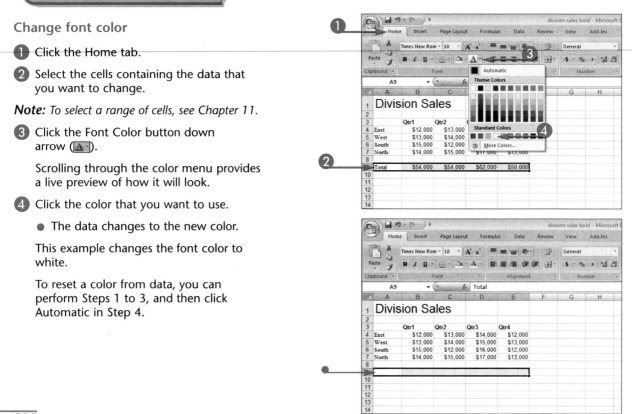

Change fill color

1 Click the Home tab.

2 Select the cells that you want to change to a different color.

Note: *To select a range of cells, see Chapter 11.*

3 Click the Fill Color button down arrow ().

4 Click the cell color that you want to use.

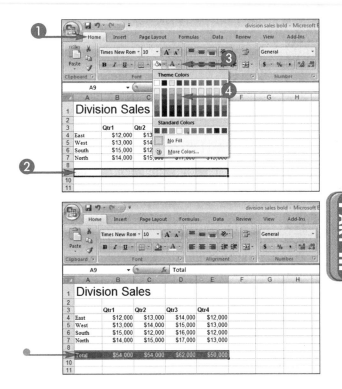

● The cells change to the new color.

To remove a color from cells, you can perform Steps 1 to 3, and then click No Fill in Step 4.

What effects can I apply to change the background of cells when I have a black-and-white printer?

▼ You can add a pattern to the background of cells. Select the cells that you want to display a pattern. Click the dialog box launcher (🔲) in the Font group on the Home tab to open the Format Cells dialog box, and then click the Fill tab. Click the Pattern down arrow (▼) and click the pattern that you want to use. You can also click a color. However, if you are using a black-and-white printer, the color will print as a shade of gray. Click OK to apply the pattern.

Can I have negative numbers automatically appear in red?

▼ Yes. Select the cells to which you want to apply this change. Click the dialog box launcher (🔲) in the Number group to open the Format Cells dialog box, and then click the Number tab. In the Category area, click Number or Currency. In the Negative numbers area, click the negative number format you prefer and then click OK.

How can I quickly change the color of data in my worksheet?

▼ The Font Color button (A) of the Font group on the Home tab displays the last selected data color. To quickly apply this color, click the cells containing the data that you want to change, and then click the Font Color button (A). You can also use the technique in the task "Copy Formatting" to apply the font color of one set of cells to another.

Apply Special Font Effects

Excel includes three font effects that you can apply to data. The *Strikethrough* effect displays a line through the middle of the data and is used for making revision marks. The *Superscript* and *Subscript* effects are useful for mathematical and chemistry equations. They decrease the size of the data and move it either slightly above or slightly below the line of regular-sized data.

In addition, Excel offers several underline styles that you can use to help you draw attention to important data such as totals.

You can use the Format Cells dialog box to add these special font effects, as well as to change the design, style, and size of data in your worksheet. These effects are useful when you want to quickly enhance your worksheet's appearance by changing several formatting options at once. The Format Cells dialog box also lets you make formatting changes that are not available through the Font group in the Home tab on the Ribbon. See the tasks "Change Font or Font Size" and "Bold, Italicize, or Underline Text," for more information on using the Font group in the Home tab on the Ribbon.

Apply Special Font Effects

Open the Format Cells dialog box

1. Click the Home tab.

2. Select the cells containing the data that you want to change.

Note: *To select a range of cells, see Chapter 11.*

3. Click the Font group dialog box launcher ▣.

Select a font effect

The Format Cells dialog box appears.

4. Click the Font tab.

5. Click to select each effect that you want to use (☐ changes to ☑).

Select an underline or font style

6 Click the Underline down arrow (▼), and click the underline style that you want to use.

- You can also change the font by clicking the font, font style, and size that you want to use.

- Your changes appear in the Preview box.

7 Click OK.

- Excel changes the appearance of the selected cells.

This example changes the font to Arial and adds a double underline.

What determines which fonts are available in Excel?

▼ The available fonts depend on the fonts that are installed on your computer and printer. Excel includes several fonts, but other programs on your computer and the built-in fonts on your printer may provide additional fonts.

Can I change the color of data in the cells depending upon its value?

▼ Yes. This feature is called Conditional Formatting and is found in the Styles group on the Home tab. This feature allows you to set rules for how data is formatted and also to apply simple graphics to data to make it stand out. See Chapter 13 for more about Conditional Formatting.

Can I change the default font setting that Excel uses for all of my new workbooks?

▼ Yes. Click the Office button, click Excel Options, and then click the Popular tab. In the When creating new workbooks font area, click the font and size that you want Excel to use for the default font setting and click OK. You must exit and restart Excel to apply the change.

What are the options for underlining data?

▼ You can select single, double, single accounting, or double accounting. The accounting underline styles add a little bit of space between the data and the underline.

PART III

Change Data Alignment

Y ou can change the way that Excel aligns data
within cells in your worksheet. This can
enhance the appearance of your data, making
column headings align with numeric entries.

The Align Text Left option is the default for text
entries; it lines up data with the left edge of a cell. The
Align Text Right option is the default for numeric
entries; it lines up data with the right edge of a cell.
The Center option aligns data between the left and
right edges of a cell.

You can also center a title across a worksheet. When
you use this alignment option, Excel merges the
selected cells into one cell and then centers the entry
within the cell.

In addition to changing the alignment, you can apply
indenting to move data away from the left edge of a
cell. When you indent data, make sure that the cell
width can accommodate all of the data without hiding
part of it. For more information about changing the
column width, see Chapter 10.

Align data

① Click the Home tab.

② Select the cells containing the data that you
want to align.

Note: *To select a range of cells, see Chapter 11.*

③ Click an alignment option:

Align Text Left (⊞)

Center Align (⊞)

Align Text Right (⊞)

● Excel makes the selected change to the cell
alignment.

This example centers the data.

Indent data

① Select the cells containing the data that you
want to indent.

② Click an indent option:

Increase Indent (⊞)

Decrease Indent (⊞)

● Excel indents the entries.

This example increases the indent from the
left margin.

Center data across columns

1 Select the cells that you want to center the data across.

Note: *The first cell should contain the data that you want to center.*

2 Click the Merge & Center button (▦▾).

● Excel centers the data across the cells that you selected.

PART III

How do I align data vertically in cells?

▼ Select the cells containing the data that you want to align vertically. In the Alignment group, click top (▤), middle (▤), or bottom (▤) alignment. For more control, you can click the dialog box launcher (▣) in the Alignment group to open the Format Cells dialog box, and then click the Alignment tab. Click the Vertical down arrow (▾) and click the alignment option that you want to use. Then click OK.

How can I rotate data in cells?

▼ Select the cells containing the data that you want to rotate. In the Alignment group, click the Orientation button (≫▾) and select an orientation option. For more precise control, click the dialog box launcher (▣) in the Alignment group to open the Format Cells dialog box, and then click the Alignment tab. Click the Orientation area and move the text angle manually. You can also use the Degrees spinner button (▣) to adjust the angle of the text, or type in a number of degrees. Then click OK.

Can I display long lines of text in a cell?

▼ Yes. You can display long lines of text in a cell by wrapping the text. Select the cell containing the text that you want to wrap. Then click the Wrap Text button (▤) in the Alignment group on the Home tab.

Add
Borders

You can add borders to enhance the appearance of your worksheet and divide your worksheet into sections. Adding borders can help make important data in your worksheet stand out. For example, in a financial worksheet, you may want to add borders to the cells containing subtotals and totals.

Excel offers a variety of pre-set borders, and you can also create a custom border to suit your needs. Several line styles are available, including broken, bold, and double lines. Although the default border color is black, you can select a color that better suits your worksheet.

You can specify which types of borders you want to add to the selected cells. For example, you can add a top, bottom, left, or right border to cells. You can also add diagonal borders to cells when you want to indicate that data in the cells is no longer valid.

You can preview the borders before you add them to your worksheet to determine whether you like the change before applying it.

Add Borders

1 Click the Home tab.

2 Select the cells that you want to display borders.

Note: To select a range of cells, see Chapter 11.

3 Click the Borders button down arrow (▦ ▾).

The Borders menu appears.

You can click a border style to apply.

4 Click More Borders.

The Format Cells dialog box opens.

5 Click the Border tab.

- You can click the Color down arrow (▼) and choose a color for the border that you want to add.

- You can select a pre-set border style.

  This area displays a preview.

6 Repeat Steps 4 and 5 for each border that you want to add to the selected text.

7 Click OK.

- The cells display the border that you selected.

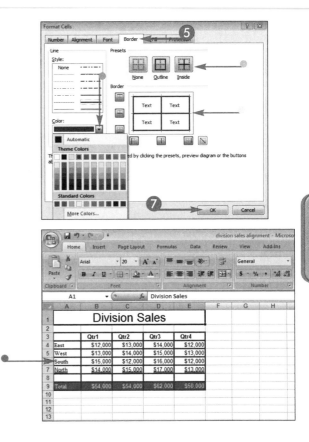

How can I manually add borders to my worksheet?

▼ Select the cells that you want to display borders. Click the Borders button down arrow (▦▼) on the Home tab. You can use the Draw Border option to manually add or erase a border or change the line color of your borders. You can also use the Cell Style gallery to change the borders; for more information, see the task "Apply Cell Styles."

How do I remove borders that I have added to my worksheet?

▼ Perform Steps 1 to 3 in this task, and then click No Border. Excel removes the borders.

Can I print the gridlines displayed on my screen instead of adding borders?

▼ Yes. Click the Page Layout tab on the Ribbon. Under Gridlines in the Sheet Options group, click to select the Print check box (☐ changes to ☑). Excel prints the worksheet gridlines when you print the worksheet.

Can I turn off the gridlines on my screen so that I can more clearly see the borders that I have added?

▼ Yes. Click the Page Layout tab on the Ribbon. Under Gridlines in the Sheet Options group, click to deselect the View check box (☑ changes to ☐). Now you can see your custom borders more clearly.

Copy Formatting

After you format one cell to suit your needs, you can use the Format Painter feature to copy the formatting to other cells in your worksheet.

You can copy formatting to make all of the headings in your worksheet look the same, giving your worksheet a consistent appearance. You can also copy number formatting, such as accounting, date, or percentage, and text formatting, such as font, size, or alignment. Excel also allows you to copy cell formatting, such as cell color or borders.

The only formatting that Excel does not copy is the row height or column width of the cells. To learn how to change the height or width of a cell, see Chapter 10.

MASTER IT

Can I copy formatting to several areas in my worksheet at once?

▼ Yes. To do so, perform the steps in this task, except double-click the Format Painter button (⬚) in Step 3. When you finish selecting all of the cells that you want to display the formatting, press Esc. Excel stops copying the formatting.

Copy Formatting

① Click the Home tab.

② Select the text that has the formatting that you want to copy.

③ Click the Format Painter button (⬚).

The Format Painter button is highlighted.

Your mouse pointer changes to a paintbrush (⬚ changes to ⬚).

④ Select the cells that you want to display the same formatting.

⑤ Release the mouse button.

● Excel copies the formatting to the selected cells.

Clear Formatting

You can remove all of the formatting from cells in your worksheet. When you clear formatting from cells, the data has any special fonts, colors, effects, or styles removed. For example, if you clear the formatting from cells containing dates, the dates change to numbers. If this is not what you intended, you can reapply a different cell style; for more information, see the task "Apply Cell Styles."

You can clear many different types of formatting from cells, including accounting, percentage,

alignment, font, and color. Clearing formatting does not reverse any changes that you made to the row height or column width.

You may need to clear formatting after you remove data from a cell. If you do not clear the formatting, Excel applies the formatting to any new data that you enter in the cell.

If two or more words or numbers in a cell display different formatting, Excel clears the formatting from only the first word or number.

Clear Formatting

1 Click the Home tab.

2 Select the cells containing the formatting that you want to remove.

Note: *To select a range of cells, see Chapter 11.*

3 Click the Clear Formatting button down arrow (⊘▾).

4 Click Clear Formats.

● Excel clears the formatting from the cells that you selected.

Apply Cell Styles

Y ou can give your worksheet a new appearance by applying *cell styles*, which are a series of ready-to-use designs that Excel offers for your convenience. A cell style provides the formatting so that you can concentrate on the content of your worksheet.

Some of the types of cell styles include Good, Bad, and Neutral, Data and Model, Titles and Headings, Themed Cell Styles, and Number Format, which can also format numbers as currency. The colorful cell styles emphasize data by changing the color of the cells that you select.

Excel shows a preview of each available cell style; this allows you to determine which cell style suits the content, purpose, and intended audience of your worksheet.

You can specify which formatting options you want Excel to apply to the selected cells. For example, you may not want to use the font or border options of a particular cell style.

Cell styles are an Office gallery, which means that you see a live preview before applying a style, and you can save your own cell style to the gallery if you have applied formatting manually.

Apply Cell Styles

1 Click the Home tab.

2 Select the cells to which you want to apply a cell style.

This example uses heading cells.

Note: To select a range of cells, see Chapter 11.

3 Click the Cell Styles down arrow (▼).

The Cell Style gallery appears.

You can move your mouse over any heading cell style for a live preview.

4 Click a cell style to apply it to the header cells.

This example applies a heading style.

● The heading cells are reformatted with the selected cell style.

5 Select the remaining cells in the worksheet.

6 Click the Cell Styles down arrow (▾).

You can move your mouse over any themed cell style for a live preview.

7 Click a themed cell style to apply it to the selected cells.

● Excel applies the cell style to the cells.

Note: *To remove any cell style, see the task "Clear Formatting."*

What does the Format as Table command do?

▼ The Format as Table command is useful when you are using the data table features of Excel to maintain a simple database. Turning a worksheet into a table places sort handles into the headers and lets you sort and filter the data. When a worksheet is set up as a table, you can use the Format as Table feature. For more information, see the task "Using a Data Table" in Chapter 11.

Can I use cell styles from other workbooks?

▼ Yes. Open another workbook and return to the current workbook. Open the Cell Styles gallery by clicking the Cell Styles down arrow (▾), and click Merge Styles. Select the workbook from which you want to merge styles and click OK.

How do I create and save my own cell style in the gallery?

▼ Use the features in this chapter to format a range of cells exactly the way you want them, with borders, cell background colors, font colors, and font styles. Then open the Cell Styles gallery by clicking the Cell Styles down arrow (▾), and click New Cell Style. You will be prompted for a name for the style, and you can change the options for all formats that you want the new cell style to apply (☐ changes to ☑). Click OK to save the newly named style.

Check Spelling

You can quickly find and correct spelling errors in your worksheet.

Excel allows you to check the spelling of words in an entire worksheet or only specific cells. When you check the spelling of an entire worksheet, Excel also automatically checks any charts in the worksheet for spelling errors. To check the spelling of only specific cells, you must select the cells before you begin.

Excel checks every word in your worksheet and considers every word that is not in its dictionary to be misspelled. For example, Excel may flag company

names or certain terminology, which you know are not misspelled, but which do not exist in the dictionary.

When Excel flags a word, it selects that cell in the worksheet and lists the flagged word in the Spelling dialog box. Excel provides a list of suggestions for correcting any spelling errors. You can replace the word with a suggestion, or you can ignore the error and continue checking your worksheet.

Excel automatically corrects common spelling errors as you type. For example, Excel automatically replaces "frmo" with "from" and "omre" with "more."

Check Spelling

① Click cell A1 to start the spell check at the beginning of the worksheet.

You can also select an individual cell to check.

② Click the Review tab.

③ Click the Spelling button to start the spell check.

The Spelling dialog box appears.

● This area displays the first misspelled word.

● This area displays suggestions for correcting the word.

④ To correct a spelling error, click a suggestion.

5 Click Change to correct the word in the worksheet.

You can click Change All to change all instances of the word.

You can click Ignore Once to continue the check without changing the word.

You can click Ignore All to skip all occurrences of the word in the worksheet.

You can also type the correct word in the Not in Dictionary text field and click Add to Dictionary.

● Excel corrects the misspellings.

6 Continue to correct or ignore misspelled words.

A dialog box appears, telling you that the spell check is complete.

7 Click OK to close the dialog box.

Can I add a word to Excel's dictionary?

▼ Yes. Excel uses the same dictionary as all Office applications. Because the dictionary does not contain many names and technical terms, your technical or company workbook may contain "misspellings." You can add a word to the Office dictionary so that Excel recognizes it during future spell checks. When Excel displays the word in the Spelling dialog box, click the Add to Dictionary button to add the word to the dictionary.

Can I have Excel automatically correct a spelling error that I often make?

▼ Yes. When Excel displays the misspelled word in the Spelling dialog box, select the correct spelling of the word. Then click the AutoCorrect button. The next time you make the same error, Excel automatically corrects the error.

How can I check the spelling of several worksheets at once?

▼ Press the Ctrl key as you click the tab of each worksheet that you want to check to group the worksheets. Then perform the steps in this task. To later ungroup the worksheets, hold down the Ctrl key as you click each worksheet tab again.

Share a Workbook

Y ou can use the Review tab of the Excel Ribbon to enter comments into a workbook, show revisions in balloons, or track changes among associates or colleagues whose comments and suggestions need to be integrated into the workbook.

You can distribute a workbook by e-mail, over a network, or by using some of the collaboration features in Chapter 29.

When you work with reviewers and turn on the Track Changes feature, each reviewer's comments appear as a border around the cell and a pop-up comment, enabling the author to clearly see whose edits need to be reflected in the final version.

After the reviewers have made their edits and comments in a workbook, the author can use the Review tab on the Ribbon to navigate easily to the next or previous edit, and then either accept or reject that edit. The author can also revise the workbook according to the suggested edits.

A final workbook can then be saved, either incorporating one or more of the changes, with or without the markup edits, or in its original form.

You can also use the Review tab of the Ribbon to run a spelling check, access research services, protect your workbook from unauthorized access, and compare one or more workbooks.

Share a Workbook

Review a workbook

1. Click the Review tab on the Ribbon.

2. Click the Track Changes down arrow (⏷).

3. Click Highlight Changes.

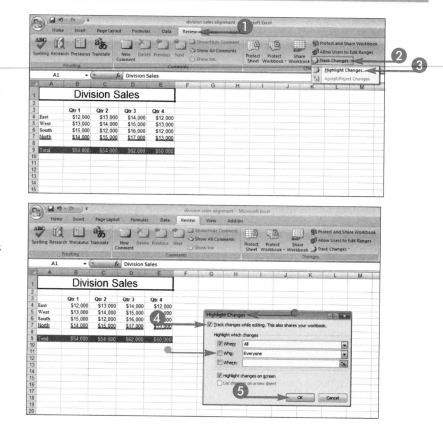

● The Highlight Changes dialog box opens.

4. Click to turn on Track changes while editing (☐ changes to ☑).

● You can click these options to choose when, by whom, or where changes will be made (☐ changes to ☑). Use the down arrows (⏷) to choose which changes to highlight.

5. Click OK.

● Excel saves the workbook and marks it as Shared in the title bar.

Track changes

6 Type in any changes that you want to make in the workbook.

● Excel adds a colored border around the cell or cells for the specific reviewer, and a triangle in the upper-left corner of the cell.

7 Move your mouse over the cell for a detailed look at the comment.

Share your workbook

8 Click Share Workbook.

● The Share Workbook dialog box opens.

● Over a network, you can see who has the workbook open presently. You can prevent changes by more than one user by deselecting the Allow Changes by More Than One User at a Time option (☑ changes to ☐).

9 Click OK to close the dialog box.

How do I distribute a shared workbook?

▼ You can send copies of the shared workbook to various recipients through e-mail; if you have enabled multiple reviewers, then each reviewer can make changes. When you get the workbook back, you can merge the changes or accept or reject them one by one. You can also share workbooks using some of the features in Chapter 29.

How do I prevent others from altering my work?

▼ You should always keep a backup of your workbook. The Review tab of the Ribbon contains buttons for the Protect Workbook and Share Workbook commands. You can use the Advanced tab of the Share Workbook dialog box to set options for how to deal with conflicts, when to update changes, and for how long to track changes.

What is the Information Rights Management Service?

▼ The Information Rights Management Service enables you to verify the identity of any potential user of your workbook. You can click the Protect Workbook down arrow (☐) and select Restricted Access. This opens a window that lets you subscribe to the Information Rights Management Service from Microsoft.

Insert a Row or Column

When you want to insert additional data into your worksheet, you can add a row or column to the worksheet.

When you insert a row, the selected row and the rows that follow shift downward. When you insert a column, the selected column and the columns that follow shift to the right. Excel automatically adjusts the row numbers and column letters in your worksheet for you.

The row that you insert is the same height as the row above it. The column that you insert is the same width as the column to its left.

When you insert a row or column, Excel automatically updates any formulas or cell references that are affected by the insertion. For information on formulas, see Chapter 11.

After Excel inserts the new row or column, you can type data into this row or column. For more information on entering data, see Chapter 9.

Insert a Row or Column

Insert a row

1 Click the Home tab.

2 To select a row, click the row number.

3 Click Insert.

• The new row appears, and all of the rows that follow shift downward.

• You can click the Insert Options icon ([🖉]) to select an option to format your row.

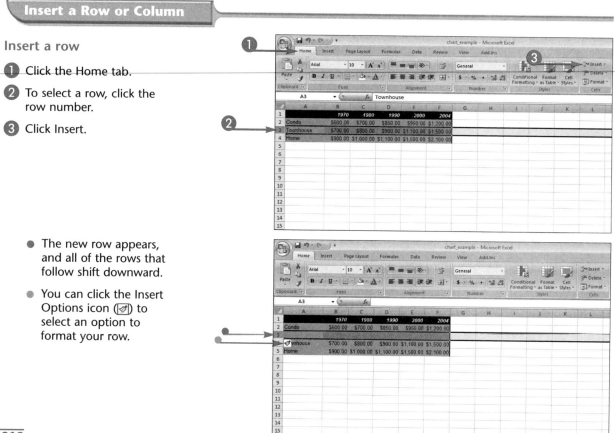

Insert a column

① Click the Home tab.

② To select a column, click the column letter.

③ Click Insert.

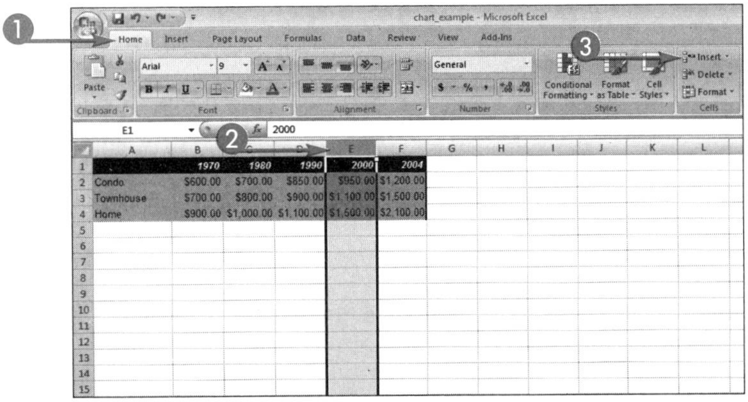

• The new column appears, and all of the columns that follow shift to the right.

You can click the Insert Options icon (⚿) to select an option to format your row.

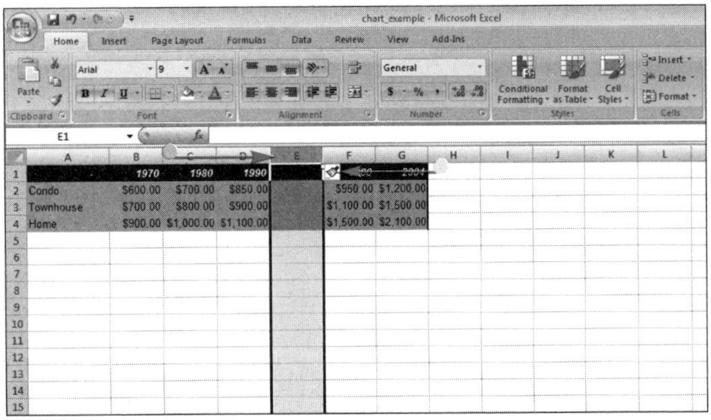

How do I insert several rows or columns at once?

▼ Excel inserts as many rows or columns as you select. For example, to insert three columns, select three columns to the right of where you want the new columns to appear. Click the cursor over the letter of the first column that you want to select, and then drag to highlight the three columns. Make sure that you are in the Home tab of the Ribbon, and click Insert. Excel inserts three columns into your worksheet.

Can I insert a group of cells instead of an entire row or column?

▼ Yes. Select the cells where you want the new cells to appear. Make sure that you are in the Home tab of the Ribbon, and click Insert. Then click an option to specify whether you want to shift the existing cells down or to the right.

Can I select the formatting for the new row or column?

▼ Yes. When you insert a row or column, the Insert Options icon (⚿) appears next to the new row or column. Click the cursor and click to apply the formatting, or no formatting, to the appropriate column or row. The Insert Options icon disappears once you enter data into another cell.

Delete a Row or Column

Y ou can delete a row or column from your worksheet to remove data that you no longer need. When you delete a row or column, Excel deletes all of the data in the row or column.

To delete a row or column, you must first select the row or column that you want to delete. The numbers along the left side of your worksheet identify each row. The letters along the top of your worksheet identify each column.

When you delete a row, the remaining rows in your worksheet shift upward. When you delete a column, the remaining columns shift to the left. Excel automatically adjusts the row numbers and column letters in your worksheet for you.

If you do not want to delete a row or column, you can use the Undo command to immediately return the row or column to your worksheet. For information on using the Undo command to restore deleted data, see Chapter 9.

Delete a Row or Column

Delete a row

1 Click the Home tab.

2 To select the row that you want to delete, click the row number.

3 Click Delete.

● Excel deletes the row and all of the following rows shift upward.

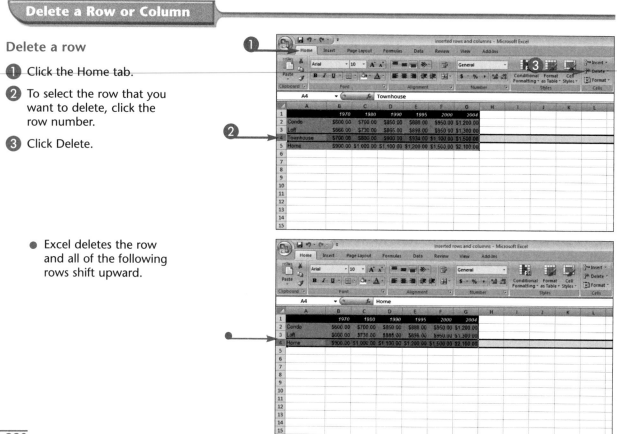

Delete a column

1 Click the Home tab.

2 To select the column that you want to delete, click the column letter.

3 Click Delete.

● Excel deletes the column, and all of the following columns shift to the left.

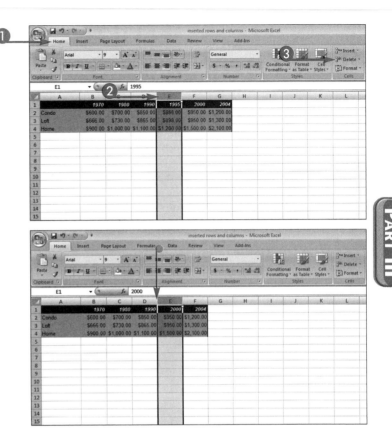

How do I delete several rows or columns at once?

▼ Click the row number or column letter of the first row or column that you want to delete. For example, to select columns that are not adjacent to each other, press the Ctrl key as you click the letters of columns that you want to delete. To select columns that are contiguous, press the Shift key and click the last column or row. Make sure that you are in the Home tab of the Ribbon, and then click Delete.

Can I delete a group of cells instead of an entire row or column?

▼ Yes. Select the cells that you want to delete. Make sure that you are in the Home tab of the Ribbon, and then click Delete. Click an option to specify how you want to shift the remaining cells.

Why does #REF! appear in a cell after I delete a row or column?

▼ If #REF! appears in a cell in your worksheet, then you may have deleted data that Excel needs to calculate a formula. Before you delete a cell, make sure that it does not contain data that Excel uses in a formula. For information on formulas, see Chapter 11.

Hide or Unhide a Column

I f you do not want other people to view confidential data in your worksheet, or if you want to reduce the amount of data that displays on your screen, you can hide the columns that contain the data. Hiding data helps you to work with specific data and can make your worksheet easier to read.

Hiding columns does not affect the formulas and functions in a worksheet, which continue to work when you hide them. You can also use the data from cells in hidden columns when entering formulas and functions in your worksheet.

Hidden columns do not appear in the worksheet, as shown by the letter numbering of the columns, or when you print your worksheet. This allows you to produce a printed copy of your worksheet without including confidential data.

You can redisplay hidden columns at any time to view the data in the columns.

Hide a column

1 Click the Home tab.

2 Select the columns that you want to hide.

Note: To learn how to select a range of cells, see Chapter 11.

3 Click the Format down arrow (▼).

The Format menu appears.

4 Click Hide & Unhide.

5 Click Hide Columns.

● Excel hides the column that you selected.

Unhide a column

1. Click the Home tab.

2. Select the columns on both sides of the column that you want to reveal.

Note: *To learn how to select a range of cells, see Chapter 11.*

3. Click the Format down arrow (▼).

   The Format menu appears.

4. Click Hide & Unhide.

5. Click Unhide Columns.

   ● Excel displays the hidden column.

Can I hide rows in a worksheet?

▼ Yes. Select the rows that you want to hide. From the Format menu on the Home tab, select Hide & Unhide and click Hide Rows. To redisplay the rows, select the rows directly above and below the hidden rows. From the Format menu, select Hide & Unhide and then click Unhide Rows.

If I hide column A, how do I redisplay the column?

▼ Because you cannot access the hidden column, use the Find & Select command. On the Home tab, in the Editing group, click Find & Select, and then click Go To. In the Reference text filed, type **A1** and then press the Enter key. From the Format menu on the Home tab, select Hide & Unhide and then click Unhide Columns.

Can I hide an entire worksheet in my workbook?

▼ Yes. From the Format menu in the Home tab, select Hide & Unhide and then click Hide Sheet. To redisplay the worksheet, from the Format menu, select Hide & Unhide Sheet and click Unhide Sheet. Click the name of the worksheet that you want to redisplay and then click OK.

Does hiding data protect the worksheet?

▼ No, because someone else could unhide the columns. If you want to protect the worksheet, you can assign a password to it, which prevents others from unhiding and changing your data. For more information, see the task "Protect Cells" in Chapter 11.

Change Column Width
or Row Height

Y ou can improve the appearance of your worksheet and display hidden data by changing column width and row height.

If cell text is too long for the cell, it spills over onto the cell to the right. If the cell to the right contains any data, then Excel truncates the text entry. Truncated numeric entries display as #### in the cell. You can change the column width to display all of the text in a cell. As you change the column width, Excel displays a small box containing the average number

of characters that fit in the cell. You can choose to have Excel automatically adjust the column width to fit the longest item in the column.

You can change the height of rows to add space between the rows of data in your worksheet. As you change the row height, Excel displays a small box containing the size of the row in points (one inch equals 72 points). As with column height, you can have Excel automatically adjust the row height to fit the tallest item in the row.

Change Column Width or Row Height

Change column width

① Move your cursor over the right edge of the column heading (⊕ changes to ↔).

② Drag the column edge until the dotted line displays the column width that you want.

● Excel displays a box showing the width of the cell.

③ Release the mouse button.

● The column displays in the new width.

Change row height

1. Move your cursor over the bottom edge of the row heading (⊕ changes to +).

2. Drag the row edge until the dotted line displays the row height that you want.

   ● Excel displays a box showing the width of the cell.

3. Release the mouse button.

   ● The row displays in the new height.

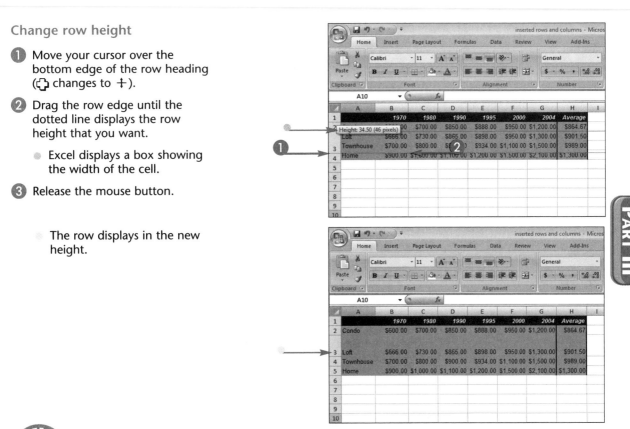

Can I change the width of several columns or the height of several rows at once?

▼ Yes. Click and drag the cursor (↓) over the headings of the columns or the headings of the rows that you want to change. Then drag the right edge of any column heading or the bottom edge of any row heading.

How do I specify an exact row height?

▼ In the Home tab, click the heading of the row that you want to change. Click Format, and then click Row Height. Type the height that you want to use, and click OK.

How do I set Excel to automatically adjust all of the column widths in the worksheet?

▼ Select the entire worksheet by clicking the worksheet selector button above the row number and to the left of the column letters. Then double-click the column divider between columns A and B. Excel adjusts all of the worksheet columns to fit the contents of each column. You can also click Format and then click AutoFit Column Width.

How do I specify an exact column width?

▼ Click the heading of the column that you want to change. Click Format in the Cells group of the Home tab, and then click Column Width. In the Column Width dialog box, type the width that you want to use and click OK.

Add or Delete a Worksheet

The worksheet that you display on your screen is one of several worksheets in your workbook. You can insert a new worksheet to add related information to your workbook.

By default, workbooks contain three worksheets, but you can insert as many new worksheets as you need. Inserting a new worksheet can help you to better organize the information in your workbook. For example, you can store information for each division of a large company on separate worksheets in one workbook.

When you no longer need a worksheet, you can delete the worksheet from your workbook. After you delete a worksheet, Excel permanently deletes the worksheet and all of its data from your workbook. Be sure that you really want to delete the worksheet, because you cannot restore your data after you delete it.

To change the default name on the worksheet tab, see the task "Rename a Worksheet." To learn more about moving between worksheets and the parts of an Excel screen, see Chapter 9.

Add or Delete a Worksheet

Add a worksheet

1. Click the Home tab.

2. Click the tab of the worksheet that you want to appear after the new worksheet.

3. Click the Insert down arrow (▼).

4. Click Insert Sheet.

- Excel adds the new worksheet and displays a tab for it.

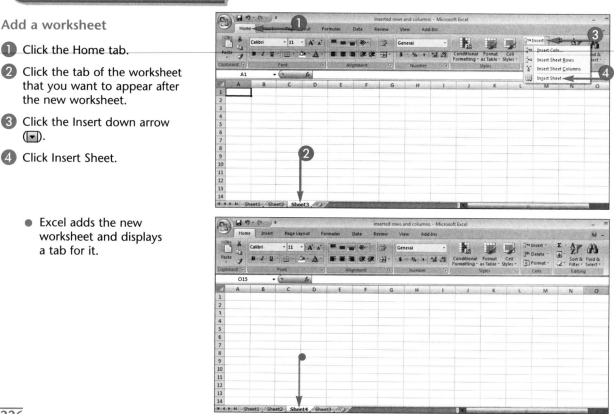

Delete a worksheet

1 Right-click the tab of the worksheet that you want to delete.

2 Click Delete.

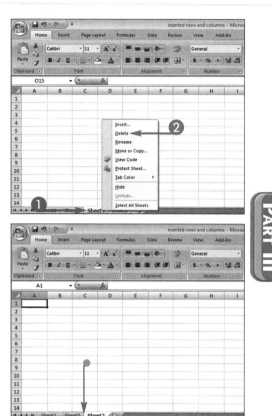

● Excel deletes the worksheet tab and all of the data on that worksheet.

MASTER IT

Can I change the order of the worksheets?

▼ Yes. You can change the order of the worksheets within the workbook. For more information, see the task "Move or Copy a Worksheet."

I deleted a worksheet by mistake. Is there any way to get my data back?

▼ No. When you delete a worksheet, you also permanently delete the data. Be careful when deleting worksheets because you cannot undo this task.

Can I apply a color code to the worksheets?

▼ Yes. You might use color-coding to identify similar worksheets within a workbook. To apply a color code to a tab, right-click the worksheet tab and click Tab Color. Click the color that you want to use from the palette of colors, and then click OK. Excel applies the color.

To remove the color, follow the same steps, but click No Color from the palette of colors.

Rename a Worksheet

Excel automatically provides a name, such as Sheet1, for each worksheet in a workbook. You can give each worksheet in your workbook a new name that better describes its contents. This helps you and other users to more easily identify and find worksheets of interest.

Excel allows you to use up to 31 characters, including spaces, to name a worksheet. You cannot use the following characters in a worksheet name: \ / : ? * [ ]. Each worksheet in a workbook must have a unique name. Generally, short worksheet names are better than long worksheet names because they allow you to display more worksheet tabs on your screen at once.

After you rename a worksheet, you cannot use the Undo feature to return the worksheet to its original name. However, you can rename the worksheet again, using the original name.

When I type a name for a worksheet, I receive an error message. Why does this happen?

▼ If you type the same name as an existing worksheet, then Excel displays an error message. Click OK and type a new name.

Rename a Worksheet

① Double-click the tab of the worksheet that you want to rename.

Excel highlights the current name.

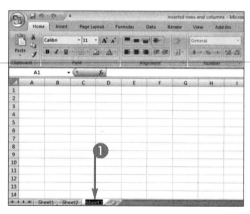

② Type a new name.

③ Press Enter.

Excel renames the worksheet.

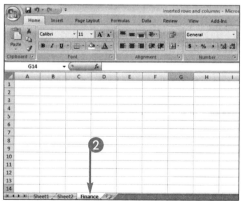

Move or Copy a Worksheet

You can move a worksheet to a new location so that you can reorganize the data in a workbook. For example, you can arrange your workbook so that frequently used worksheets are beside each other. You can also copy a worksheet when you plan to make major changes and you want to have a copy of the worksheet without the changes.

You move and copy worksheets using the Move or Copy dialog box. The only difference between the two operations is that you must select the Create a Copy option to copy a worksheet instead of moving it.

Moving worksheets may cause calculations or charts based on the transferred data to recalculate incorrectly. If this happens, you can edit the formulas so that they refer to the moved sheet. For more information on formulas, see Chapter 11.

After you move a worksheet, you cannot use the Undo feature to return the worksheet to its original location in the workbook. However, you can use the same procedure to move the worksheet back to its original location.

Move or Copy a Worksheet

① Right-click the worksheet tab of the worksheet that you want to move or copy.

② Click Move or Copy.

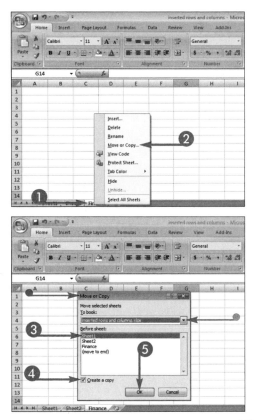

● The Move or Copy dialog box appears.

③ Click where you want to place the new sheet.

④ Click here to create a copy (☐ changes to ☑).

● To move or copy a worksheet to another workbook, you can click the To book down arrow (▾) and then click the workbook.

⑤ Click OK.

Excel moves or copies the worksheet to the new location and adds a (2) to the name.

You can also click and drag worksheet tabs to a new location in the current workbook.

Find Data

Y ou can use the Find feature to quickly locate a word, phrase, or number in your worksheet.

You can have Excel search your entire worksheet or only specific cells. To have Excel search only specific cells, you must select the cells before starting the search.

By default, Excel finds the data that you specify, even if it is part of a larger word or number. For example, searching for the number 105 locates cells that contain the numbers 105, 2105, and 1056.

After you start the search, Excel finds and selects the cell containing the first instance of the word or number, which may appear in several locations in your worksheet. You can continue the search to find the next instance of the word or number, or end the search at any time.

If Excel cannot find the word or number for which you are searching, a dialog box appears, directing you to check the data that you specified.

Find Data

① Click the Home tab.

② Click Find & Select.

The Find and Select menu opens.

③ Click Find.

● The Find and Replace dialog box appears.

④ Type the word or number that you want to find.

⑤ Click Find Next to start the search.

● Excel highlights the first cell containing the word or number.

⑥ Click Find Next to find the next matching word or number.

The dialog box remains open and continues to cycle through the worksheet when you click Find Next.

Note: *You do not see a message stating that the search is complete when the entire worksheet is searched.*

⑦ Click Close when you are finished searching.

The Find and Replace dialog box closes.

Can I have Excel find a word only when it is capitalized?

▼ Yes. You can have Excel find words with exactly matching uppercase and lowercase letters. In the Find and Replace dialog box, click the Options button and then click the Match case option (☐ changes to ☑).

Can I search for the exact contents of a cell?

▼ Yes. You can find cells that contain only an exact match for the data that you specify. In the Find and Replace dialog box, first click the Options button. Then click the Find entire cells only option (☐ changes to ☑).

Can I search for an entry and replace it with another entry?

▼ Yes. Click Edit and then click Replace. In the Replace tab of the Find and Replace dialog box, type both the entry that you want to find and your replacement text or number. Click Find Next to start the search. To replace the word or number with the new data, click Replace. To replace all occurrences of the word or number in your worksheet with the new data, click Replace All. To ignore the word or number and continue with the search, click Find Next.

PART III

Fill a Series

Excel can save you time by completing a text or number series for you. A *series* is a sequence of data that changes, such as a range of consecutive numbers. You can complete a series in a row or column.

Excel completes a text series based on the text in the first cell. Excel can complete a text series such as the days of the week or the months of the year, which you can then use to create column labels. If Excel cannot

determine the text series that you want to complete, it copies the text in the first cell to the cells that you select.

Excel completes a number series based on the numbers in the first two cells. These numbers tell Excel what increment to use for the series. For example, you can create a series of even numbers by typing 2 in the first cell and 4 in the second cell.

Fill a Series

Fill a text series

1 Type the text that you want to start the series.

2 Click the cell containing the text.

3 Click the bottom-right corner (■) of the cell (⬚ changes to +).

4 Drag your cursor over the cells that you want to include in the series.

5 Release the mouse.

- The cells display the series.

- If you want to select a different action, you can click the Insert Options icon that appears (⊞▾) and select an action from the menu. For example, you can fill formatting, fill a series, fill months, or copy cells (◉ changes to ◉).

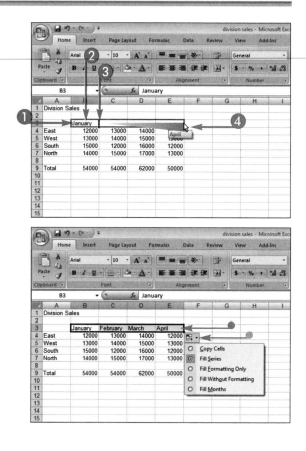

Fill a number series

1 Type the first two numbers that you want to start the series.

2 Select the cells containing the numbers that you entered.

3 Click the bottom-right corner (■) of the cell (⊕ changes to ✚).

4 Drag the cursor over the cells that you want to include in the series.

5 Release the mouse.

● The cells display the series.

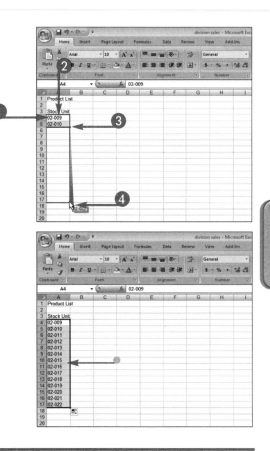

MASTER IT

How can I complete a series for the days of the week without including Saturday and Sunday?

▼ Click the cell containing the day of the week that you want to start the series. Press the right-mouse button as you drag the cursor over the cells that you want to include in the series. Then select Fill Weekdays from the menu that appears.

When I try to fill a series, Excel fills it with the same entries. Why does this happen?

▼ If Excel cannot determine the text series to fill, it simply copies the entry. Also, if you select only one numeric entry, Excel copies that entry. You have to select the first two entries so that Excel knows the pattern to use in the series.

Can I create my own custom series?

▼ Yes. On the worksheet, select the list of items that you want to use in the fill series. Click the Microsoft Office button, and then click Excel Options. In the Excel Options dialog box, click Popular, and then under Top options for working with Excel, click Edit Custom Lists. The Custom Lists Options dialog box opens. Verify that the cell reference of the list of items that you selected displays in the Import list from cells field, and then click Import. Click OK in the dialog box telling you some cells will be ignored. The items in the list that you selected are added to the Custom lists. Click OK to close and exit the Custom Lists Options dialog box.

Enter Dates and Times

A s you create a worksheet, you may want to enter dates and times. For example, you can use dates in invoices and other billing worksheets. You can use times for speed testing or time-stamping the completion of a task.

Excel uses the format for the date and time that matches how you entered the date and time. To format numeric entries differently, see Chapter 9.

Although the date and time look like regular dates and times, they are actually numeric entries. Excel stores dates as serial numbers so that you can use the dates in calculations. For example, you can subtract one date from another to figure the days past due for an account. Also, because Excel stores times as a fractional value of 24 hours, you can use times in calculations.

MASTER IT

How do I quickly enter today's date?

▼ Press Ctrl+; (semicolon).

What formats can I use to type a date?

▼ You can type the following formats: 3/17, 3/17/08, 17-Mar, 17-Mar-08, Mar-08, or Mar-17.

What formats can I use to type a time?

▼ You can type 1:30, 1:30 PM, or 13:30.

Enter Dates and Times

Enter a date

1. Type a date.

2. Press Enter.

   Excel enters the date.

Enter a time

1. Type a time.

2. Press Enter.

   Excel enters the time.

Using AutoComplete

E xcel compares the text that you type to text in other cells in the column. If the first few letters that you type match the text in another cell in the column, Excel can complete the text for you. This feature, called *AutoComplete*, can save you time when you need to type the same text into many cells in a column.

Keep in mind that AutoComplete works only on text entries. It does not work on numeric, date, or time entries.

MASTER IT

What if I do not want to use the AutoComplete entry?

▼ You do not have to use the AutoComplete entry. To enter different text, you can continue typing.

Sometimes I type an entry and Excel changes it. Why does this happen?

▼ A related feature to AutoComplete is *AutoCorrect*, which automatically corrects common spelling errors. You can view the various changes that this feature makes by clicking the Office button, selecting Excel Options, clicking Proofing, and clicking the AutoCorrect button. For more information on spell checking, see Chapter 9.

PART III

Using AutoComplete

1 Type an entry.

2 Start typing the next entry.

Excel displays the matching entry.

3 To enter the text that Excel provides, press Enter or Tab.

● Excel adds the entry to that cell.

Using Cell and Range Names

Y ou can assign a name to a cell or range of cells. Assigning a name to a section of data makes it easier to find the data, or to use that cell or range in a formula.

You can use up to 255 characters for a cell name. The name must begin with a letter or an underscore character (_). You can use any other character, including letters, numbers, and punctuation marks, in the name, but you cannot include spaces. You also

cannot use a cell reference as a name. For example, you cannot name a cell D4.

After you assign a name, you can go to that cell or range using the Reference box.

You can also type the name in a formula. Doing so makes a formula much easier to understand. For example, you can create a formula such as =Income-Expenses, rather than =C4-D4, to track which section of data you use in a calculation.

Using Cell and Range Names

Assign a name

① Click the Formulas tab.

② Select the cells that you want to name.

Note: To select cells, see the task "Select a Range of Cells."

③ Click Define Name.

   ● The New Name dialog box opens with a possible name entered in the Name text field.

④ Accept the suggested name or type a name.

⑤ Click OK.

   ● Excel names the cells and displays the name in the Reference box.

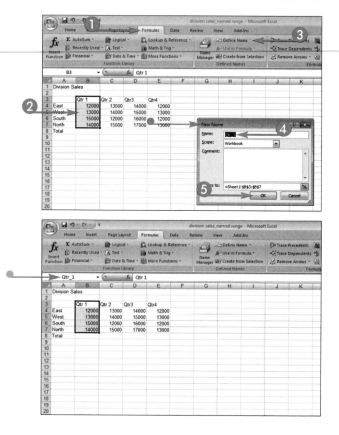

Go to named cells

① Click the Reference box down arrow (▾).

② Click the name that you want to select.

  ● Excel highlights the named cell or range.

Using a name in a formula

① Select the cell where you want the formula.

This example selects cell B8.

② Type a formula with the named cell or cells.

Note: *To create formulas, see the task "Enter and Edit Formulas."*

③ Press Enter to apply the formula.

  ● The result of the calculation appears in the cell.

Why did Excel add an underscore to the suggested name?

▼ Excel has very specific rules for naming ranges, and the suggested name follows the rules. If you type in your own name with a format that is against the rules, Excel displays a dialog box explaining the rules more fully and that you need to change the name accordingly.

How do I delete an assigned name?

▼ Click the Name Manager button in the Formulas tab on the Ribbon. In the Name Manager dialog box, click to select the name that you want to delete, and then click Delete. Click OK and then click Close.

Is there a quick way to assign names?

▼ Yes. In any Ribbon tab, you can select the range of cells that you want to name and then click in the Reference box. Type the name for the range and press Enter. Excel applies the name that you typed to the range, and adds it to the Names list in the Formulas tab on the Ribbon.

Select a Range of Cells

Before performing many tasks in Excel, you must select the cells with which you want to work. For example, if you want to change the appearance of entries by making them bold or changing the font, you must select the cells containing data that you want to change. Similarly, if you want to copy a group of cells or move cells to another location, you start by selecting the cells that you want to move.

Selected cells appear highlighted on your screen. This makes the selected cells stand out from the rest of the cells in your worksheet.

Excel calls a group of cells a *range* and identifies them with a range reference. The range reference consists of the upper-leftmost cell, followed by a colon, and then the lower-rightmost cell. For example, the range A1:C4 contains A1, A2, A3, A4, B1, B2, B3, B4, C1, C2, C3, and C4.

Excel also lets you quickly select all of the cells in a row or column.

Select a Range of Cells

Select a range

1 Click the cursor over the first cell that you want to select.

2 Drag the cursor to highlight all of the cells that you want to select.

● Excel selects the cells in that range.

Select a row

1 Click the number of the row that you want to select (⊕ changes to →).

To select multiple rows, click the number of the first row and drag the cursor to select all of the rows that you want.

● Excel selects the row.

Select a column

1 Click the letter of the column that you want to select (⊕ changes to ↓).

To select multiple columns, click the letter of the first column and drag the cursor to select all of the columns that you want.

● Excel selects the column.

How do I select all of the cells in my worksheet?

▼ To select all of the cells in your worksheet, click the worksheet selector, the blank area to the left of the heading for column A and above the heading for row 1. You can also press Ctrl+A to select all of the cells in your worksheet.

How can I select rows or columns that are not beside each other?

▼ To select rows or columns that are not beside each other in your worksheet, press the Ctrl key as you click the numbers of the rows or letters of the columns that you want to select.

Can I quickly select a large group of cells?

▼ Yes. Click the first cell in the group that you want to select and then scroll to the end of the group. Press Shift as you click the last cell in the group. Excel selects all of the cells between the first and last cell that you select.

How do I deselect a cell?

▼ After you finish working with a selected cell, you can click any other cell in the worksheet to deselect it.

Protect
Cells

Y ou can protect cells in a worksheet to prevent you or others from accidentally changing them. This can help you when you have complicated formulas and key data that you do not want others to change on a shared worksheet.

By default, Excel locks and protects all cells, but it does not activate this feature until you turn on worksheet protection. If you want to leave some cells editable while protecting others, you must unlock the cells to which you want others to have access and then turn on the protection feature to lock all other cells.

When you protect a worksheet, you can also specify what a user can and cannot do. You can prevent them from selecting locked or unlocked cells, formatting cells, inserting or deleting columns and rows, and making other changes.

If a user tries to edit or make unauthorized changes to the worksheet, an error message appears.

To further protect your worksheet, you can also assign a password. When you do so, no one can unprotect the cells without typing the password.

Protect Cells

Unlock cells

1 Click the Home tab.

2 Select the cells to which you want to allow changes.

Note: *To select cells, see the task "Select a Range of Cells."*

3 Click Format.

The Format menu opens.

4 Click Format Cells.

● Alternatively, you can click Lock Cell in Step 4 to lock cells.

The Custom Lists dialog box appears.

5 Click the Protection tab.

6 Click the Locked option (☑ changes to ☐).

7 Click OK.

Excel unlocks the cells that you can change after you turn on the protection feature.

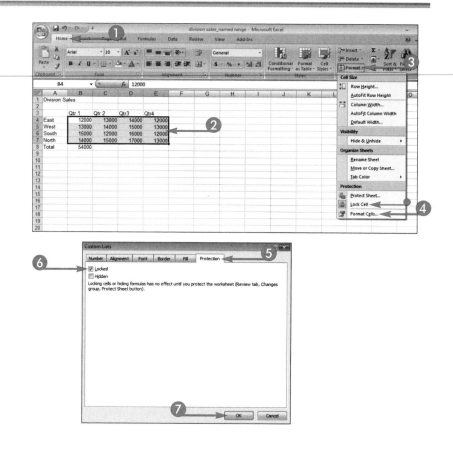

240

Turn on worksheet protection

1 Click the Home tab.

2 Click the Format button.

The Format menu opens.

3 Click Protect Sheet.

● The Protect Sheet dialog box opens.

4 Type a password.

5 Click the options that you want to allow users to perform (☐ changes to ☑).

6 Click OK.

Excel activates the worksheet protection feature. Users cannot change any locked cells.

● A user who attempts to receive a prompt.

Excel asks for the password you specified in Step 4.

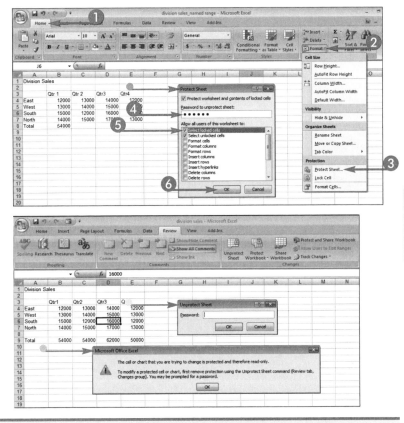

How else can I set a password?

▼ Click the Office button, and then click Save As. In the Save As dialog box, click the Tools down arrow (▼), and then click General Options. If you want reviewers to enter a password before they can view the workbook, type a password in the Password to open text field of the General Options dialog box. If you want reviewers to enter a password before they can save changes to the workbook, type a password in the Password to modify text field of the General Options dialog box. You will be prompted to re-enter the password to set it. Click OK to confirm password and click OK again to set password protection for the saved worksheet.

Can I protect the structure of the entire workbook?

▼ Yes. You can assign a password in the Protect Workbook window of the Review tab to protect your structure and your windows.

I protected my worksheet, but now I cannot make changes to any cells. What is wrong?

▼ By default, Excel locks all cells. Therefore, if you turned on protection, neither you nor any other user can make changes to any of the cells. You must unlock the cells before you protect the worksheet. If you forgot to do so, turn off worksheet protection, unlock the cells, and then turn on worksheet protection. You can turn off worksheet protection in the Review tab on the Ribbon. Click Unprotect Sheet, type your password, and then click OK.

Using a Data Table

E xcel provides powerful tools for organizing and analyzing a large collection of data in a table.

Common tables include mailing tables, price tables, sales tables, phone directories, product tables, library book catalogs, and music collections.

The first row in a table contains column labels, which describe the data in each column.

Each row in a table contains one record. A *record* is a group of related data, such as the name and address of one person on a mailing table. Generally in a table, a row represents a record, and a column represents a *field*, or category of information.

You can create and store a table of data in a worksheet. You can enter data in a table by typing the data directly in the worksheet. You can also use a data form to type data in a table. A data form allows you to focus on one record at a time.

You should generally create only one table in a worksheet. If you need to use the same worksheet for other data or calculations, consider leaving at least one blank column and row between the table and the other data to prevent unwanted data from appearing in the data form.

To take advantage of the form data entry feature of a data table, you need to add the Form button to the Quick Access toolbar, which supplements the features of the Excel Ribbon.

Using a Data Table

Create a data table

1. Type the column labels that describe the data that you plan to type into each column.

   You should format the column labels to ensure that Excel recognizes the text as column labels.

   Note: *See Chapter 9 for more information on formatting data.*

2. Type the information for each record.

   Note: *Do not leave any blank rows within the table. Doing so could cause problems when sorting and filtering.*

3. Save the workbook.

   Note: *For information on saving a document, see Chapter 2.*

Add the data form feature to the Quick Access toolbar

1. Click the Quick Access toolbar More button.

   The Customize Quick Access Toolbar menu appears.

2. Click More Commands.

The Excel Options dialog box opens to the Customize category.

③ Choose Commands Not in the Ribbon.

④ Click Form.

⑤ Click Add.

● Excel adds Form to the customize options.

⑥ Click OK.

Excel adds the Data Form button to the Quick Access toolbar.

Using a data form

① Click any cell in the table.

② Click the Data Form button (📋).

③ In the data form, click New.

④ Type the data for each field in the record.

Note: *Do not press Enter until you have filled all of the fields.*

Repeat Steps 3 and 4 for each record that you want to add.

⑤ Click Close.

Excel adds the new record or records to the data table.

How do I delete a record using a data form?

▼ You can click the Delete button in the data form dialog box to delete the currently displayed record. Excel permanently deletes the record and cannot restore it.

How do I search for a specific record using a data form?

▼ Click the Criteria button in the data form dialog box. Click the area beside the label of the column that you want to use to find the record. Then type the data that you want to find. Click Find Prev or Find Next to display the previous or next matching record.

Can I edit a record in a data form?

▼ Yes. Display the record that you want to edit in the data form dialog box. You can use the Find Next or Find Prev buttons to move from record to record until the one that you want appears. Then click the field containing the data that you want to change and edit the data. If you want to undo changes that you make to a record, you can click the Restore button to undo the changes. You must click the Restore button before you move to another record. Click Close to exit the data form.

PART III

Sort Data in a Table

Y ou can organize a table by changing the order of the records.

To take advantage of table features such as sorting and filtering, which are covered in this and the next task, you will first need to convert your worksheet to a table. To do this, you must select a cell in the worksheet and click the Table button in the Insert tab on the Ribbon. Confirm the range of cells that are contained in your table; Excel places sort handles in the table headers.

You also can sort the data in a table by up to three columns by using the Sort button in the Data tab on the Ribbon. You can sort the data in a table by letter, number, or date. An ascending sort arranges data from lowest to highest, such as 0 to 9, A to Z, or Jan-03 to Dec-03. A descending sort does the opposite.

You should save your workbook before sorting data in case you do not like the results. To save a document, see Chapter 2.

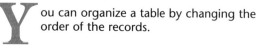

Sort Data in a Table

Create an Excel data table

1 Click any cell in the table.

2 Click the Insert tab.

3 Click Table.

You can also press Ctrl+T or Ctrl+L.

- The Create Table dialog box appears, showing the cell range of the table.

- A dashed line shows the border of the prospective table.

- If your table has a header row, make sure that the My table has headers option is selected (☐ changes to ☑).

4 Click OK to accept the table borders.

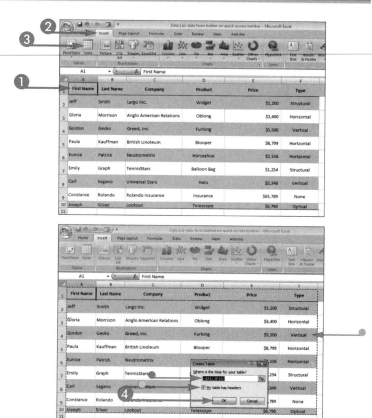

Sort your data form

Excel turns your worksheet into a table with sort and filter arrows (□▾) available in the header row.

Note: *When converted to a table, your data may have a banded style applied.*

● The Design tab of Table Tools opens.

⑤ Click the Data tab.

⑥ Click the filter arrow (□▾) in the column that you want to sort.

⑦ Click to Sort A to Z.

Note: *If the selected column is not text, such as numbers or dates, you will not see the Sort A to Z option.*

● Alternatively, you can choose any cell and click the Sort buttons (⬆↓ or ⬇↑) to do a quick sort.

⑧ Click OK.

● The table appears in the new order. The sort arrow indicates that the column has been sorted.

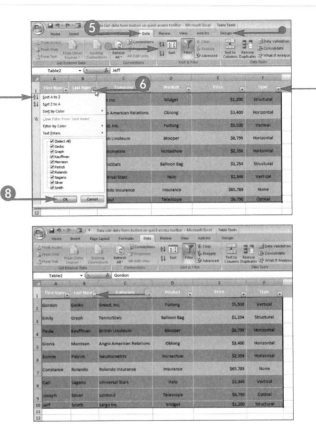

Can I sort multiple columns?

▼ Yes. Click the Data tab on the Ribbon and then click Sort in the Sort & Filter group. In the Sort dialog box, set your first sort options, and then click Add Level to continue to add sort parameters. When you click OK, Excel sorts the entire table with the criteria that you input into the Sort dialog box.

What is Sort by Color?

▼ The Sort by Color command uses the colors of the Conditional Formats that you can apply to a worksheet or table. See Chapter 13 for more information on Conditional Formats.

Can I perform a case-sensitive sort?

▼ Yes. A case-sensitive sort sorts data by capitalization. For example, a case-sensitive ascending sort would place "ann" before "Ann." Click Options in the Sort dialog box. The Sort Options dialog box opens and you can check the Case sensitive check box (☐ changes to ☑). Click OK to exit the Sort Options dialog box and OK again to perform the sort.

How do I undo a sort or remove the Sort and Filter options?

▼ To immediately reverse the results of a sort, click the Undo button (↺▾). Click Filter in the Data tab to remove the Sort and Filter arrows.

Filter Data in a Table

Y ou can filter a table to display only the records containing the data that you want to review.

The Filter feature allows you to analyze data by placing related records together and hiding the records that you do not want to see.

You can select the column containing the data that you want to use to filter the table. You can also specify the data that you want Excel to compare to each record in the table, as well as how Excel should

compare the data to each record. Telling Excel how to compare the data allows you to display records containing data within a specific range. For example, in a table containing customer names and purchase amounts, you can display only customers whose purchases were greater than $1,000.

After you filter a table, Excel displays the row numbers of the records that match the condition that you specified. Excel also hides the non-matching records. Excel does not delete them; they are simply not displayed in the filtered table.

Filter Data in a Table

Before you begin, you must ensure that your worksheet is a table.

Note: For more information, see the task "Sort Data in a Table."

1 Click the Data tab.

2 Click any cell in the table.

3 Click the Filter button to enable the Sort and Filter arrows.

4 Click the filter arrow (▾) in the column that you want to filter.

A menu of Sort and Filter options appears for that column.

● You can click to select (☑) or deselect (☐) any items that you want to exclude.

This example uses number filters. Choices available depend on the data type of the columns.

5 Click Number Filters.

6 Click a comparison criterion, such as Greater Than.

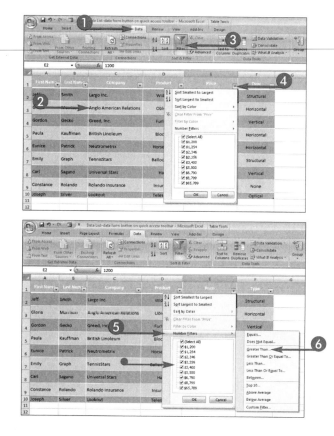

● The Custom AutoFilter dialog box appears.

7 Click the down arrow (▼) to select the comparison that you want to use as the filter.

8 Type the value that you want to compare in this text box.

9 Click OK.

● The table displays only the records matching the data that you specify. The filter down arrow indicates that the column has been filtered.

Excel temporarily hides the other records.

You can turn off the AutoFilter feature and redisplay the entire table by performing Steps 2 to 4 and clicking the Select All option (☐ changes to ☑) after Step 4.

PART III

How can I quickly filter data in a table?	How do I display the top 10 records in a table?	Can I filter with more than one criterion?
▼ Click the filter arrow (▼) in the column and then select the data that you want to use to filter the table. The table displays only the records containing the data that you selected.	▼ Click the filter arrow (▼) in the column that you want to use to filter the table, click Number Filters, and then click Top 10. In the Top 10 AutoFilter dialog box, click the Items area. To display the top 10 records, click Items. To display the top 10 percent of the records, click Percent.	▼ Yes. Perform Steps 1 to 5 in this task and click Custom Filter to open the Custom AutoFilter dialog box. Click the And option if you want both conditions to be met. Click the Or option if you want either condition to be met (◉ changes to ◉).

Add Subtotals to a Range

Y ou can quickly summarize data by adding subtotals to a range that was once a table.

Before you add subtotals to a table, you must sort the column that you want to use to group the records. (To sort data, see the task "Sort Data in a Table.") Then you will need to convert the table to a range.

You can use subtotals to help you analyze the data in a range and quickly create summary reports for the data. For example, in a range containing employee names and sales figures, you can use subtotals to find the total sales made by each employee and the grand total of all sales.

You can use the Subtotals feature to perform several types of calculations, such as calculating the sum of values, counting the number of values, calculating the average value, or finding the maximum or minimum value.

After adding subtotals to a table, you can display just the grand total, the subtotals and the grand total, or all of the data. By default, Excel displays subtotals below each group of data in a column.

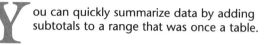

Add Subtotals to a Range

1 Sort the column that you want to use to group the records.

2 Click a cell in the table.

3 Click the Design tab.

4 Click Convert to Range.

5 Click Yes to the prompt. The data table is now a range.

6 Click the Data tab.

7 Click any cell in the range.

8 Click Subtotal.

9 In the Subtotal dialog box, click here and select the column that you want to use to group the records.

Note: The column that you select must match the column that you sorted in Step 1.

10 Click here and select a function.

11 Click the column that contains the values that you want to calculate (▢ changes to ☑).

● You can click an option to replace current subtotals, add a page break, or add a summary (▢ changes to ☑).

12 Click OK.

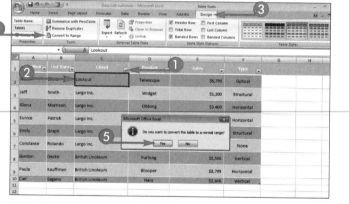

248

The table displays the subtotals or a grand total. You can scroll through the table to see the other totals.

⑬ Click an option to hide or display data.

You can click subtotal 1 (⬚1) to display only the grand total.

You can click subtotal 2 (⬚2) to display only subtotals and the grand total.

You can click subtotal 3 (⬚3) to display all data.

● The table displays the totals that you selected.

This example shows the subtotals and grand totals.

Can I create a chart based on the subtotals in my table?

▼ Yes. Click subtotal 2 (⬚2) at the top of the groupings column to display only the subtotals and grand total. Select the cells containing the subtotals and row labels that you want to display in the chart. Then create the chart. If you later hide or display data in the table, Excel automatically hides or displays the data in the chart. For more information on creating charts, see Chapter 12.

How do I remove subtotals from my table?

▼ Perform Steps 6 to 8 in this task and then click the Remove All button in the Subtotal dialog box.

How do I display subtotals above each group of data in a column?

▼ Perform Steps 6 to 11 in this task and then uncheck the Summary below data option (☑ changes to ⬚) in the Subtotal dialog box.

Can I hide the data that I use in a subtotal?

▼ Yes. Minus signs appear to the left of your subtotaled table. Click the minus sign (⊟) to hide the data that you use in a subtotal. Click the plus sign (⊞) to redisplay the data.

An Introduction to Formulas and Functions

With Excel, you can perform many different calculations with the data that is entered into a worksheet. Formulas allow you to calculate results based on various operations that you can perform with references to specific cells in your worksheet. Functions are predefined formulas used for specific purposes; a simple function would be to find the average of a selected range of values.

As values in certain cells change, the end results or calculations in the formulas and functions are updated. In addition, values in other cells in the current worksheet, or even in other worksheets or workbooks, can change to reflect the results of formulas, functions, or the cells on which their results are based.

The result of a formula can depend upon a function; for example, PI (π) is a function that can be used to calculate a formula, the area of a circle.

References are the cells on which the final result is calculated; for example, a formula calculating the sum of monthly sales will have references to all cells on which the sum is based, or to all of the monthly totals, which could in turn be formula results of weekly totals in the current worksheet, or of weekly totals in another workbook.

There may also be a constant in use in a formula; for example, dividing a total by 12 could create monthly values from another cell that has totals for a year.

Operators are processes like division, multiplication, addition, subtraction or exponential powers. If you wanted to calculate a yearly total based on equal monthly values, for example, you could multiply the monthly value by 12, using the operator *.

Formulas

Excel allows you to use formulas to calculate and analyze data in your worksheet. A formula always begins with an equal sign (=), and includes cell references and some type of mathematical operator. For example, the formula =C4+C5 takes the value in C4 and adds it to C5.

In a formula, it is better to use cell references rather than typing the value directly because this uses Excel's ability to recalculate a formula when you change any data in the referenced cells. If you change the value of C4 in the preceding example, the results automatically update. However, if you type a value, you must manually edit the formula.

You can use arithmetic operators in formulas to perform mathematical calculations. Arithmetic operators include the addition (+), subtraction (–), multiplication (*), division (/), percent (%), and exponent (^) symbols.

You can use comparison operators, which return values of TRUE or FALSE, in formulas to compare two values. Comparison operators include the greater than (>), less than (<), equal to (=), greater than or equal to (>=), less than or equal to (<=), and not equal to (<>) symbols.

Excel performs calculations in a specific order. It calculates percentages first and then exponents, followed by multiplication and division. Excel then calculates addition and subtraction, followed by comparison operators. You can use parentheses ( ) to change the order in which Excel performs calculations. It calculates the data inside the parentheses first. For example, in the formula =10*(1+2), Excel performs the addition before the multiplication. Without parentheses, the multiplication would be performed first, and then the addition.

	A	B	C	D	E
				SUM	▾ X ✓ f_x =SUM(B4:B7)
1	Division Sales				
2					
3		January	February	March	April
4	East	12000	13000	14000	12000
5	West	13000	14000	15000	13000
6	South	15000	12000	16000	12000
7	North	14000	15000	17000	13000
8	Total	=SUM(B4:B7)			
9					

Functions

Excel offers over 200 functions to help you analyze data, including financial, mathematics and trigonometry, date and time, and statistical functions. A *function* is a ready-to-use formula that you can use to perform a calculation on the data in your worksheet. Excel's functions allow you to perform calculations without having to type long, complex formulas.

	A	B	C	D
	Payment	Rate	Term (mos.)	Principal
2	$1,473.35	6.80%	360	$226,000.00
3	$1,500.00	6.12%	360	$247,000.09
4	$173.33			
5	$1,673.33			
6				

A2 =PMT(B2/12,C2,-D2)

A function always begins with an equal sign (=). Excel encloses the data that it uses to calculate a function in parentheses ( ). Each cell or number that Excel uses in a function is called an *argument*. Most functions require at least one argument; you must include it as part of your function. An example of functions with no arguments would be =now() or =rand(). Now would insert the current time based on the system clock. Rand is a special function to insert a random value.

Some functions include optional arguments. When you create a formula, Excel helps you by prompting you for which arguments you want to enter.

Using Formulas and Functions

Formulas and functions are accessed through the Formulas tab on the Excel Ribbon. In the Function Library group, you have access to the most common functions, such as AutoSum, which has a drop-down menu for common functions: Sum, Average, Count, Max(imum), and Min(imum).

The Function Library group also has an option for financial functions. While its options may not be meaningful for users in other fields, financial professionals will recognize these functions and be able to apply them to perform calculations in their data.

Other Function categories in the group include Logical, Text, Date & Time, Lookup & Reference, and Math & Trig.

Errors in Formulas

An error message appears when Excel cannot properly calculate a formula. Errors in formulas are often the result of typing mistakes. You can correct an error by editing the data in the cell containing the error.

indicates that the column is too narrow to display the result of the calculation.

#DIV/0! indicates that the formula divides a number by zero (0). Excel considers a blank cell to contain a value of zero.

#NAME? indicates that the formula contains a function name or cell reference that Excel does not recognize.

#REF! indicates that the formula refers to a cell that is not valid. For example, a cell used in the formula may have been deleted.

#VALUE! indicates that the formula contains a cell reference for a cell that Excel cannot use in a calculation. For example, the formula may refer to a cell containing text.

#N/A indicates that the formula refers to a value that is not available.

#NULL! indicates that the formula refers to an intersection of cells that do not intersect. This may occur when there is a space between two cell references instead of a comma (,) or colon (:).

A *circular reference* occurs when a formula refers to the cell containing the formula. Excel cannot calculate a formula that contains a circular reference, and displays a warning message on your screen when it finds this type of error.

When an error message appears in a cell, you see an Error button. You can click the down arrow and select from available commands to get help, ignore the error, or use the Formula Auditing group in the Formulas tab of the Ribbon. Excel includes auditing tools to check the formulas and functions in a worksheet.

The Formulas tab of the Excel Ribbon also includes a Name Manager so that you can define the names of a range of cells and refer to them more easily in your formulas or functions.

You can use the Watch Window to keep track of the results of formulas and functions without having to navigate directly to the cells that contain their values.

The Calculation options allow you to change the way that values in the cells are refreshed or updated from the default, which is automatically as values are added or revised, to manual when you are ready to recalculate the values based on the data in the worksheet.

PART III

Sum Numbers

The most common calculation in a worksheet is to sum a group of numbers. You can quickly calculate the sum of a table of numbers in your worksheet using the AutoSum feature.

You can use AutoSum to quickly add numbers in rows or columns. When you use AutoSum, you can select a cell below or to the right of the cells containing the numbers that you want to add. The AutoSum feature automatically inserts the SUM function in the cell that you select.

Excel outlines the cells that it uses in the AutoSum calculation with a dotted line. The program guesses which cells you are likely to want to sum by looking at the entries above or to the left of the current cell. If Excel outlines the wrong cells, you can select the cells that you want to use in the calculation.

You can use the status bar calculation to display the sum of numbers without entering a formula in your worksheet. When you select two or more cells, the sum of the selected cells in the bottom-right corner of your screen, along with two other functions, Count and Average.

Sum Numbers

Using AutoSum

1 Click the Home tab.

2 Click the cell below or to the right of the cells containing the numbers that you want to add.

3 Click the AutoSum button (Σ ▾).

● Excel outlines the cells that it will use in the calculation with a dotted line.

If Excel does not outline the correct cells, you can select the cells containing the numbers that you want to add.

Note: *To learn how to select cells, see the task "Select a Range of Cells."*

4 Press Enter to perform the calculation, or click the check mark (✓).

- The result of the calculation appears.

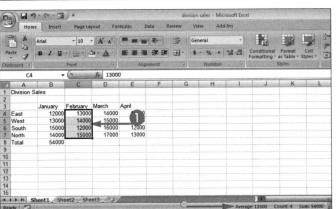

Using status bar calculation

1. Select the cells that you want to include in the calculation.

- This area displays the sum, average, and count of the cells that you selected.

Can I have AutoSum perform other calculations?

▼ Yes. Select the cells that you want to calculate and then click the AutoSum button down arrow (Σ ▾). Select the function that you want to include.

How can I check my formulas?

▼ Excel includes several auditing tools for checking formulas. Click the Formulas tab on the Ribbon. Click Show Formulas. The formulas in your worksheet appear in their cells. You also can use the commands in this menu to trace formulas. For more information, see the task "Audit Formulas."

Can I select other calculations for status bar calculation?

▼ Yes. Select the cells and then right-click the area in the bottom-right corner of your screen that displays the results in the status bar. From the menu that appears, select the calculation that you want to perform. *Average* calculates the average value of a selected group of cells of numbers. *Count* calculates the number of items in a selected group of cells, including text. *Count Nums* calculates the number of values in a selected group of cells containing data. *Max* finds the largest value in a selected group of cells. *Min* finds the smallest value in a selected group of cells.

Enter and Edit Formulas

You can enter a formula into any cell in your worksheet. A formula helps you calculate and analyze data in your worksheet. A formula always begins with an equal sign (=).

When entering formulas, you should use cell references instead of actual data whenever possible. For example, you should type the formula =A1+A2 instead of =10+30. When you use cell references and you change a number in one of those referenced cells, Excel automatically recalculates the formulas for you. For example, if you base your sales commissions on a value

of 10% and then change the value to 12%, all of the commissions in your worksheet automatically change.

A cell displays the result of a formula, while the formula bar displays the actual formula.

You should always be careful to enter the correct cell references and mathematical symbols in a formula. Errors in formulas are often the result of typing mistakes. You can edit a formula to correct an error or change the formula. When you edit a formula, Excel outlines each cell that you use in the formula with a different color.

Enter a formula

1 Click the cell where you want to enter a formula.

2 Type an equal sign (=) to begin the formula.

3 Type the formula.

4 Press Enter.

Note: *To learn more about formulas, see the task "An Introduction to Formulas and Functions."*

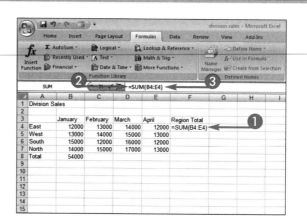

- The result of the calculation appears in the cell. To view the formula that you entered, you can click the cell containing the formula.

- The formula for the cell appears in the formula bar.

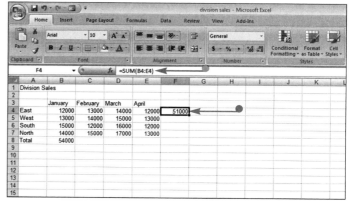

Edit a formula

1 Double-click the cell containing the formula that you want to change.

● The formula appears in the cell.

Excel uses different colors to outline each cell that it uses in the formula.

2 Edit the formula.

Note: To edit data in a cell, see Chapter 9.

3 Press Enter when you finish making changes to the formula.

Excel updates the formula and displays the new results.

Can I reference a cell in another worksheet?

▼ Yes. To do so, type the worksheet name, followed by an exclamation mark and the cell reference. For example, Sheet1!A1. You can also simply go to that worksheet and click the cell that you want to include as you are building the formula.

Can I reference a cell in another workbook?

▼ Yes. To do so, type the workbook name in square brackets and then type the worksheet name, followed by an exclamation mark and the cell reference. For example, [Budget.xlsx]Sheet1!A1.

What is the drop-down list that appears when I begin to type "=SUM"?

▼ This is Excel's contextual help, which helps you to locate and complete functions and formulas. For example, when the menu for SUM appears, click Sum in the list and press Tab; Excel completes the name of the function for you.

PART III

Copy a Formula

I f you want to use the same formula several times in your worksheet, you can save time by copying the formula.

Excel automatically adjusts any cell references so that you avoid manually re-creating each formula.

There are two types of cell references that you can use in a formula — relative and absolute.

A *relative* reference changes when you copy a formula. If you copy a formula to other cells, Excel automatically changes the cell references in the new formulas. For

example, when you copy the formula =A1+A2 from cell A3 to cell B3, the formula changes to =B1+B2.

If you do not want Excel to change a cell reference when you copy a formula, you can use an *absolute* reference, which always refers to the same cell. You make a cell reference absolute by typing a dollar sign ($) before both the column letter and row number. If you copy the formula to other cells, Excel does not change the reference in the new formulas. For example, when you copy the formula =$A$7*B2 from cell B4 to cell C4, the formula changes to =$A$7*C2.

Copy a Formula

Using a relative reference

1 Click the Home tab.

2 Select the formula that you want to copy to other cells.

3 Click the Copy button (image).

4 Select the cell or cells where you want to place the copied formula.

5 Click Paste.

- The results of the formulas appear.

- You can see one of the new formulas, which appears in the formula bar with a new reference, by clicking a copied cell.

Using an absolute reference

1. Type the formula, using dollar signs before the row and column that you want to make absolute.

   You can also press F4 until the reference that you want displays.

2. Press Enter.

3. Select the formula.

4. Click the Copy button ().

5. Select the cell or cells where you want to copy the formula.

6. Click Paste.

   ● The results of the formulas appear.

   When you copy a formula containing an absolute reference, the absolute reference does not change.

MASTER IT

What is another method for copying formulas?

▼ You can also drag a formula to copy it. Select the cell, hold down Ctrl, and drag it to its new location. You can also fill the formula, which is the same as copying. To fill a formula, select it and then drag the fill handle. For more information, see the task "Fill a Series."

What is the best way to revise a formula?

▼ Click to select the cell with the formula and the formula will appear in the formula bar. Click in the formula in the formula bar and use the arrow keys on the keyboard to move the insertion point to the part of the formula you want to revise. Press the Backspace or Delete keys to delete the unwanted portion of the formula and type in the new data. When the formula has been revised, click the checkmark (☑) to set the new formula in the cell.

Excel automatically copied a formula. How did this happen?

▼ Excel can pick up a pattern of worksheet entries and may automatically copy a formula from the cell above it. If this is what you want, you can simply continue entering the row entries and let Excel complete the formula cells. If not, you can type a new entry in the cell.

Enter a Function

A *function* is a ready-to-use formula that you can use to perform a calculation in your worksheet.

Excel offers many functions, and groups the functions into categories according to their use. If you do not know which category contains the function that you want to use, you can choose the All category to display a list of all of the functions.

You can specify the cells containing the numbers that you want to use in a function. Each cell or number in a function is called an *argument*. A function may require one or more arguments.

The arguments in a function are enclosed in parentheses and separated by commas (,) or a colon (:). When commas separate arguments, Excel uses each argument to perform the calculation. For example, =SUM(A1,A2,A3) is the same as the formula =A1+A2+A3. When a colon separates arguments, Excel uses the specified arguments and all arguments between them to perform the calculation. For example, =SUM(B1:B3) is the same as the formula =B1+B2+B3.

Enter a Function

1 Click the cell where you want to enter a function.

2 Type =.

● Excel displays a list of functions in the Reference box.

3 Click the Reference box down arrow (▼).

4 Select the function that you want to insert.

If the function is not listed, you can click More Functions.

Excel displays the Function Arguments dialog box, which prompts you for the appropriate arguments for the function, and gives you a description.

● Excel may guess which cell or range you want to use in the function, and enter it for you.

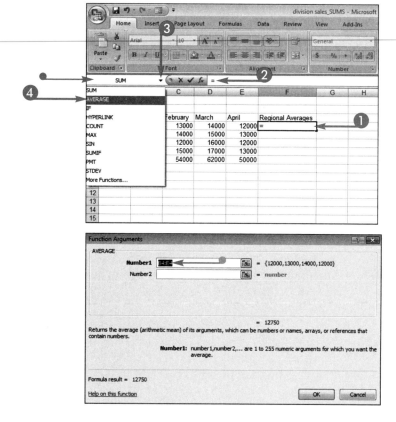

⑤ Type or select the cell or cells that you want to use for each argument.

Note: *The arguments that you must complete depend on the function that you are inserting.*

⑥ Click OK.

● The result of the function appears in the cell.

● The function for the active cell appears in the formula bar.

PART III

What is another method for entering a function?

▼ You can also the AutoSum button down arrow (Σ ▾), and then click More Functions. The Insert Function dialog box appears. Select the function and then click OK. The Function Arguments dialog box appears. Complete the arguments for the function and then click OK.

You can also explore and use the more advanced functions that are available in the Formulas tab on the Ribbon. This tab includes an entire Function Library. For more information, see the task "Using the Function Library."

How can I quickly enter the numbers that I want to use for a function?

▼ When entering numbers for a function in the Function Arguments dialog box, you can select a group of cells by clicking the range selector (▦) and then dragging over the cells to be averaged to select them in the worksheet. For more information about the Range Selector, see the task "Using the Function Library."

Can I type a function without using the Insert Function button (fx)?

▼ If you know the name of the function that you want to use, you can enter the function directly into a cell. You must start the function with an equal sign (=), enclose the arguments in parentheses (), and separate the arguments with commas (,) or a colon (:).

Using the Function Library

As you have seen, a function is a ready-to-use formula that you can use to perform a calculation in your worksheet.

Besides the basic functions in the AutoSum drop-down list, or those in More Functions, you can access numerous additional functions in the Function Library of the Formulas tab on the Ribbon.

These functions are in the following categories:

- Add-in and Automation functions
- Cube functions
- Database functions
- Date and Time functions
- Engineering functions

- Financial functions
- Information functions
- Logical functions
- Lookup and Reference functions
- Mathematics and Trigonometry functions
- Statistical functions
- Text functions

An example of using the Function Library would be calculating the payment based on a rate of interest, a principal sum, and a fixed time period. Alternatively, you could calculate the principal value, or the amount that you could borrow, based on a given payment, a rate of interest, and a fixed time period.

Using the Function Library

Access a function from the Ribbon

1 Click the Formulas tab.

2 Click the cell where you want to enter a function.

3 Click the Financial down arrow (⬇) in the Function Library group.

Excel displays a list of functions.

4 Drag the scroll bar to locate the function.

5 Click a function.

This example uses the PMT function.

- If the function is not listed, you can click More Functions in the Function Library group.

Excel displays the Function Arguments dialog box, which prompts you for the appropriate arguments for the function.

⑥ Click the range selector button (🔳) next to the argument that you want to enter.

● The Function Arguments dialog box collapses to let you select the cell or range.

⑦ Click the range or cell in the worksheet that represents the argument.

In this example, it is the rate of interest cell.

continued

Can I add functions to the Function Library?

▼ Yes. You can download or purchase add-ins to Excel for specific functions in various fields. You can also find more complex functions for OLAP databases (CUBE), statistical functions, and engineering functions by clicking More Functions in the Formulas tab of the Ribbon.

Can I create my own functions?

▼ Yes. If you have a complex calculation that you reuse frequently in Excel, you do not have to repeatedly enter a long, complex worksheet formula. Instead, you can create your own worksheet function to perform the calculation. You can then use the function to create formulas that are easier to enter and maintain.

To create your own custom functions, you must work in Microsoft Visual Basic for Applications (VBA). VBA is a programming language that is built into Excel. VBA is very flexible and can do everything that Excel formulas can do, and more. However, VBA is beyond the scope of this book.

Using the Function Library
(Continued)

The Function Library contains preset options for inserting any kind of function that you want. When you have selected the function, you need to add the arguments in the Function Argument dialog box. You can use the range selector to select cells from the worksheet or type in the data upon which the function will be performed.

The Function Arguments dialog box displays the required arguments for the selected function. For example, a simple Average function has one argument to fill in — the cells to be averaged. A more complex function might require more arguments; for example,

a PMT function requires an interest rate, number of payments, principal amount, and so on.

By clicking the range selector you minimize the Function Arguments dialog box and can select the cells which you wish to average directly from the worksheet.

You can click the range selector again to return to the Function Arguments dialog box. A more complex function might require the entry of additional arguments. When all arguments are added, you can click OK to exit the Function Arguments dialog box and set the function in the selected cell of the worksheet.

● The cell reference appears in the Function Arguments dialog box.

⑧ Click the range selector button (🔲).

The Function Arguments dialog box expands.

You can complete the rest of the arguments.

● You can divide the rate by 12 to get the monthly rate.

● You can make the payment negative to result in a positive number in the cell.

⑨ Click OK.

○ The monthly payment appears in the cell instead of the function.

Access a function from the Insert Function dialog box

1 Click the Formulas tab.

2 Select a cell where you want to insert a function.

3 Click Insert Function.

● The Insert Function dialog box opens.

4 Click 🔽 to select a category or choose All.

5 Click the function you want to use. This example uses PV (principal value).

6 Click OK.

● The Function Arguments dialog box opens.

7 When arguments are entered, click OK to set the function.

○ The principal appears in the cell.

Why did you make the additional adjustments for the payment argument?

▼ Sometimes the results from simply selecting arguments from the range selector do not bring the results that you want into the worksheet. Dividing by 12 was necessary for the monthly payment, while changing the result to a negative value was easier than changing the Cell Style for the currency value.

Can you put a function inside another function?

▼ Yes. This is referred to as a *nested function*. You might use this in a scenario with an IF statement. You can nest one function inside another using parentheses. You can enclose the arguments in parentheses ( ) to make those calculations happen first or in sequence.

Can I use names in my functions or formulas?

▼ Yes. If you know the name of the range that you want to use, you can enter it as you type a function directly into a cell. For more information, see the task "Using Cell and Range Names."

Audit
Formulas

Y ou can trace back through the *precedents*, or cells that influence a formula, or check *dependent cells*, which contain formulas that refer to other cells.

For example, if cell H10 contains the formula =D13, then cell D13 is a precedent to cell H10. However, H10 is dependent on cell D13.

As you build more complex worksheets and workbooks, the results of one formula will influence a series of results in other calculations. If there are errors in your formulas, and they are complex, you may need to relocate the source cells in order to make any adjustments.

You can use the Formula Auditing group of the Formulas tab to display lines that trace the precedents and dependents in your formulas. You can use the Trace Precedents or Trace Dependents features of the Formulas tab to see graphical representations of the cells and ranges that are responsible for the values or results of your formulas. In the case of unexpected or erroneous results, this can help you identify the source of the problem and correct it.

You can also use the Show Formulas command to show any formulas directly in their cells instead of the calculated values. This will help you locate the formulas in your worksheet. Click Show Formulas again to toggle back to having the values in the cells which are calculated by formulas.

Audit Formulas

Trace precedents

1 Click the Formulas tab.

2 Click to select the cell with the formula for which you want to trace precedents.

3 Click Trace Precedents.

● Excel draws a line to indicate the cells that contribute to the results of the formula.

4 Click Remove Arrows.

The arrows disappear.

Trace dependents

① Click the Formulas tab.

② Click to select the cell or cells for which you want to trace dependents.

③ Click Trace Dependents.

● Excel draws lines to display the cells that result from the values in those cells.

④ Click Remove Arrows.

The arrows disappear.

Can I trace precedents or dependents in another workbook?

▼ Yes. However, Excel will not automatically open other workbooks to trace dependents or precedents. In order to go into other workbooks, they must already be open when you invoke the Trace Precedents or Trace Dependents features.

How can I check the display options for precedents or dependents?

▼ Click the Office button, click Excel Options, and then click the Advanced category in the Excel Options dialog box. In the Display options for this workbook section, select the workbook that you want, and then make sure that in the For objects show section All is selected.

What other features can help me eliminate errors in my formulas?

▼ In the Formulas tab on the Ribbon, click the Error Checking down arrow (▼). You can perform an error check similar to a spell check for the entire workbook, or trace errors within your formulas back to precedent cells that may be causing unexpected results.

Using the Watch Window

You can open a Watch Window over your worksheet to track the changing values of various cells as a result of formulas and functions.

In large workbooks or worksheets, cells that you may want to track may be out of visible range. You may also just want to organize a group of cells whose values you want to track.

You can add cells to the Watch Window, and as the values of those cells are updated or changed, they are available for viewing.

You can also move the Watch Window around your screen to view other cells directly.

By using the Watch Window, you do not need to repeatedly scroll or go to different parts of your worksheet.

The Watch Window can be moved or docked. *Docked* means that it is fixed to the top, bottom, or side of the window. For example, you can dock it on the bottom of the window. The toolbar keeps track of the following properties of a cell: workbook, worksheet, name, cell, value, and formula. Keep in mind that you can only have one Watch Window for each worksheet.

Using the Watch Window

① Click the Formulas tab.

② Click Watch Window.

● The Watch Window opens.

③ Click Add Watch.

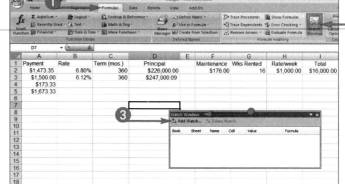

● The Add Watch window opens.

④ Type or select the cell or cells that you want to track in the Watch Window. Use the range selector button (▦) to manually select the cells.

⑤ Click Add.

⑥ When you are done adding cells, click Close (✖) to close the Add Watch dialog box.

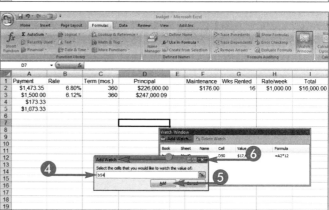

⑦ Change the value of a cell on which the watched cells are dependent.

⑧ Press Enter or click the check mark (☑).

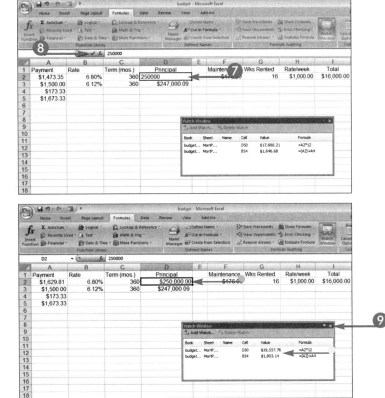

● The value returned by this function appears in the Watch Window.

The Watch Window calculates and shows the changed values of the dependent cells.

⑨ Click the Close button (☒) to close the Watch Window.

PART III

Can I select one or more cells to add them to the Watch Window?

▼ Yes. Select the cells that you want to watch. Ctrl+click to select more than one cell. Alternatively, to select all cells on a worksheet with formulas, on the Home tab, in the Editing group, click Find & Select, click Go To Special, and then click Formulas (◎ changes to ◉). Click OK. On the Formulas tab, in the Formula Auditing group, click Watch Window. Click Add Watch, use the range selector to select the cells to monitor, and then click Add.

How can I remove cells from the Watch Window?

▼ Select the item in the Watch Window that you want to remove. You can click Delete Watch, or press the Delete key.

How can I access the Watch Window from other parts of the Ribbon?

▼ You can add the Watch Window to the Quick Access toolbar. Click Quick Access toolbar More button to customize the Quick Access toolbar. Click More Commands. The Excel Options dialog box appears. Click the Choose commands from down arrow (▾) to select All Commands. Scroll down to locate the Watch Window. Click Add. Click OK to add the Watch Window to the Quick Access toolbar.

An Introduction to Charts

One of the main components of Excel is its ability to take the numerical data in your worksheet and create a chart.

Charts help to visually show the data in meaningful ways that you may not see clearly when viewing only numbers. For example, charting data as a line chart can help you to spot trends, while charting data as a pie chart helps you to see which product is a bestseller in relation to others in a set of data.

Types of Charts

Excel provides many types of charts to choose from, and one of the main decisions when creating a chart is selecting a chart that best conveys the message you want. The following table describes the most common chart types.

Excel Chart Types

Type of Chart	Example	Description
Column		Compares values from different categories.
Line		Shows changes in values over time. This is useful for showing trends.
Pie		Shows the relationship of each value to the overall total.
Bar		Similar to a column chart, except that the bars are horizontal.
Area		Shows trends, as well as the contribution of each value to the whole.
Scatter		Also known as an X/Y chart, it compares pairs of values.
Other		Additional chart types that are available include Stock, Surface, Doughnut, Bubble, and Radar.

You can see a full dialog box with all of Excel's chart types by clicking the Charts group dialog box launcher ( ) in the Insert tab on the Ribbon.

Parts of a Chart

A chart is made of different elements, each of which contributes to the overall meaning and appearance of the chart. You can customize each element as indicated, using the various tasks in this chapter. To understand how to create a chart to fit your situation, take some time to become familiar with the different parts of a chart.

A Data Marker

The individual value represented by one number from the worksheet and charted as one element in the chart. A collection of data markers makes up a data series.

B Chart Title

You can use chart titles to label the various parts of your chart, including the name of the chart and the x- and y-axis.

C Plot Area

The area on which Excel draws your chart. You can change the background color as well as the lines that Excel displays to represent your data.

D Data Series

A collection of one set of data values. For example, a data series may include sales for one particular year in your company.

E Legend

The legend contains the key to the values in the chart. You can choose whether to display the legend, as well as select its placement.

F Category Names

The names that appear along the x-, or category axis. Excel pulls these categories from the worksheet.

G Axes

Excel plots most charts using an x-axis and a y-axis — also called the horizontal and vertical axes. Excel also has chart types that include a third axis, called the z-axis. You can choose how Excel formats and labels the various axes. If you are charting two points, two axes are enough. When you need to plot three points or variables — for example, temperature, pressure, and volume — select a chart type with three axes.

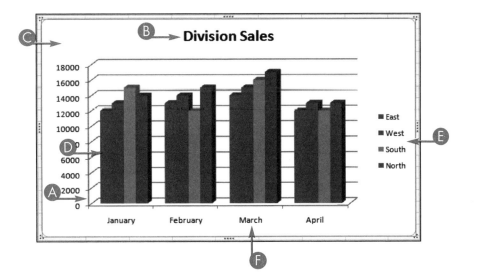

Create a Chart

You can create a chart to graphically display your worksheet data and make it easier to understand.

To create the chart, you must first organize the data for your chart into rows and columns, which you can make consecutive or non-consecutive. If you include the column or row labels in your selection, Excel uses them as titles in the chart. To learn how to enter data for your chart, see Chapter 9.

When creating a chart to plot several data values — for example, all of the divisions of a company for the four quarters of the year — you do not select the totals. Doing so would chart these values, which is not appropriate for the purpose of the chart. However, if

you want to create a pie chart and you want to compare totals of each division, then you would use only the totals for a comparison.

After you select your data, you can use the Charts group of the Insert tab on the Ribbon to create the chart. The Charts group allows you to determine the type of chart you want to create, such as a Column, Pie, or Area chart, as well as specify whether you want to plot your worksheet data by rows or columns.

You can add titles to a chart to identify the chart's subject. By default, Excel designates the x-axis title as the categories that you include in your data, and the y-axis as the unit of measure that you use in the chart. If you create a 3-D chart, Excel may allow you to add a title to the z-axis.

Create a Chart

Select the cells and create the chart

1 Click the Insert tab.

2 Select the cells that you want to display in a chart, including the row and column labels.

Note: To select a range of cells, see Chapter 11.

3 Click the type of chart that you want to create in the Charts group of the Insert tab of the Ribbon.

The options for that chart type appear.

4 Click the type of chart that you want to create.

● Excel creates the chart type that you selected.

● The Chart Tools open in the Ribbon, with the Design tab active.

5 Click the Layout tab.

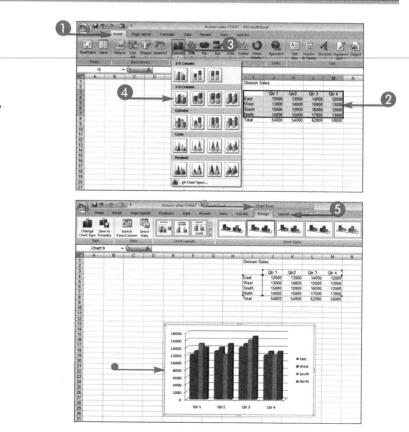

Add a chart title

6 Click Chart Title.

7 Click a title option.

This example uses Above Chart.

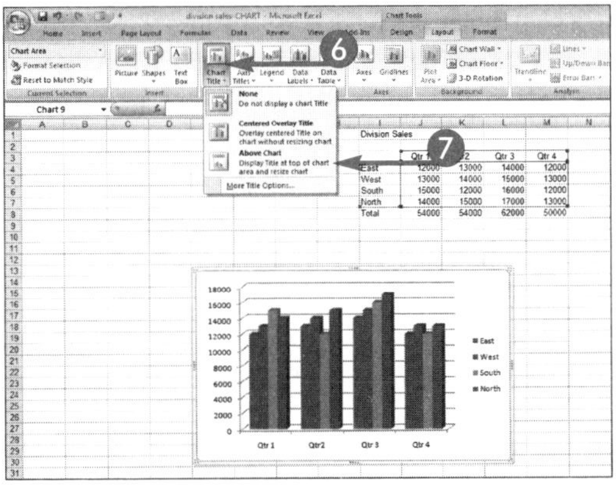

● A title placeholder opens above the chart.

8 Replace "Chart Title" with your title.

9 Click anywhere in the plot area to set the title, and continue formatting the chart.

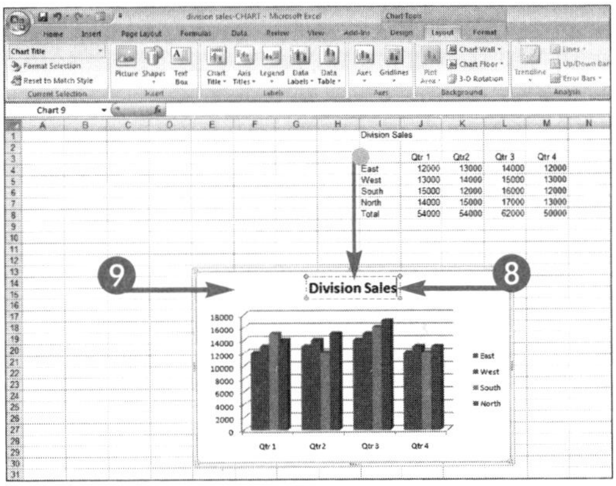

How can I get the chart to appear on its own worksheet?

▼ After you create the chart, click to select it, click the Home tab, and then click Cut. Go to the worksheet where you want the chart, and click Paste. For information on creating or renaming a worksheet, see Chapter 10. You can also select the chart, click the Design tab in Chart Tools, and then click Move Chart for more options.

Can I change the chart type after I create a chart?

▼ You can change the chart type at any time after creating a chart. For more information, see the task "Change the Chart Type."

Can I change the chart titles after I create a chart?

▼ Yes. In the completed chart, click the title that you want to change. Type the new title and then press Enter.

Is there a keyboard shortcut to quickly create a chart?

▼ Yes. You can quickly create a chart with Excel's default chart settings. Select the cells containing the data that you want to display in the chart, and then press F11. The chart appears on its own sheet in your workbook. With a newer keyboard, check that the function keys work as anticipated.

continued

Create a Chart

(Continued)

After you create your chart and add titles, Excel allows you to move or remove the legend for your chart. The *legend* is a key that identifies each data series in your chart. *Data series* are related data representing one row or column from your worksheet. When you display more than one data series in a chart, Excel uses different colors, patterns, or symbols to help you identify each data series.

Excel gives you several options for displaying the legend. You can locate the legend at the bottom,

top, right, left, or top-right corner of the chart. You can also choose to display your chart on the same worksheet as the data, or on its own sheet — called a *chart sheet*.

After you select your chart options, Excel displays the chart on your screen. Excel also displays the Chart Tools, which automatically appear in the Ribbon when you select the chart.

The handles that appear around a chart allow you to resize the chart. For information on resizing a chart, see the task "Move or Resize a Chart."

Create a Chart *(continued)*

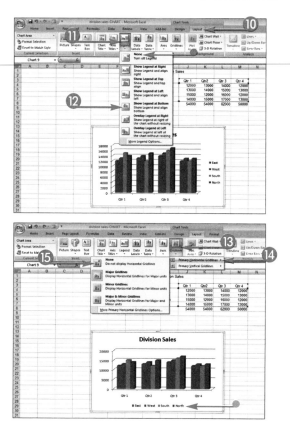

Change the legend

⑩ Click the Layout tab.

⑪ Click Legend.

⑫ Click a placement option.

This example uses Show Legend at Bottom.

● You can click None if you do not want to display a legend.

Add or remove gridlines

● The legend is moved or removed from the chart.

⑬ Click Gridlines.

⑭ Click Primary Horizontal Gridlines or Primary Vertical Gridlines.

⑮ Click to select a gridlines option.

You can choose major, minor, or no gridlines for horizontal or vertical gridlines.

This example uses None.

- Gridlines are changed or removed from the chart.

16 Click Data Table.

17 Click a data table option.

You can choose to show a data table, a data table with legend keys, or no data table.

This example shows the data table.

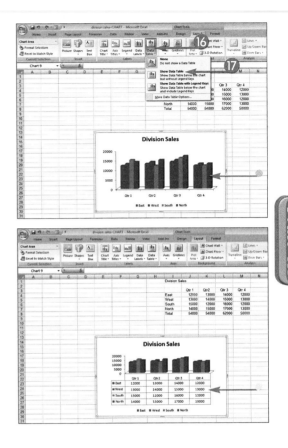

- Excel applies the options that you selected to the chart.

You can resize the chart by clicking and dragging the handles around the chart.

When you select the chart, the Chart Tools become active on the Ribbon.

What happens if I change data that is used in a chart?

▼ If you change data that is used in a chart in the underlying worksheet, Excel automatically updates the chart.

How can I format a chart?

▼ You can format each area of a chart individually. For more information, see the task "Format Chart Elements."

How do I use Data Labels?

▼ Some charts have sufficient space to include labels within or near the data series. If you want to include Data Labels, you can click the Data Labels button in the Layout tab of Chart tools and add them to the chart.

Can I add titles to the axes?

▼ Yes. You can click Axis Titles in the Labels group of the Layout tab to add primary horizontal or vertical axis titles to the chart. You can also click to make the vertical axis title read vertically.

Change the Chart Type

Y ou can change the chart type to present your data more effectively. Excel provides 11 standard chart types, and multiple configurations for column, bar, line, area, and pie charts, which are the most popular chart types. In most cases, the individual elements in the chart, such as the columns, bars, lines, areas, or pie sections, represent a data series. *Data series* are related data representing one row or column from your worksheet.

Because each chart type presents data in a specific way, your chart type depends on your data and on your preference for presenting it.

A *column chart* shows changes to data over time, or compares individual items. For example, you might compare sales of different divisions and quarters.

A *bar chart* compares individual items.

A *line chart* shows changes to data at regular intervals. For example, you might plot the yearly sales of a company to help you notice any sales trends.

An *area chart* shows the amount of change in data over time.

A *pie chart* shows the relationship of parts to a whole. For example, you might plot the total sales of each product to see how much each product contributes to the overall sales total. A pie chart can show only one data series at a time.

To learn how to create a chart, see the task "Create a Chart."

Change the Chart Type

Change the chart type

1 Click the chart.

A selection frame appears around the chart, and Excel displays the Chart Tools on the Ribbon.

To select a chart on a separate worksheet, you can click the tab containing the chart.

Note: *To create a chart, see the task "Create a Chart."*

2 Click the Insert tab.

3 Click a chart type.

The Chart Type menu appears.

4 Click the design for the chart type that you want to use.

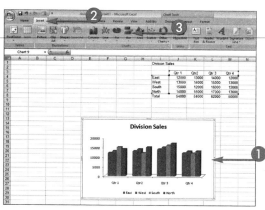

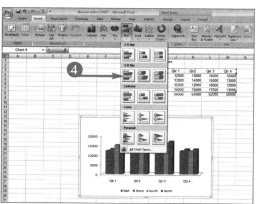

● The chart changes to the type that you selected.

Change how the data is plotted

⑤ Click the Design tab.

⑥ Click Switch Row/Column.

● Excel updates the chart to switch the data series and categories.

● You can click the Undo button (↩) to reverse the previous steps.

What is the difference between the pie and doughnut chart types?

▼ While pie and doughnut charts are both useful for showing the relationship of parts to a whole, they differ in the amount of information that they can display. A pie chart can display only one data series, but a doughnut chart can display multiple data series, with each ring of the doughnut chart representing a data series.

Can I create a different default chart type?

▼ Yes. While the Column chart is the default when you press F11, you can change this by clicking the Charts group dialog box launcher (⊡) from the Insert tab. You can then select one of the eleven chart types. Click Set as Default Chart.

Can I quickly try out different looks for my chart that may improve its appearance?

▼ Yes. Click the Design tab of the Chart Tools and click the Chart Layouts group More button. There are nine different pre-set chart layouts that you can instantly click and apply to your chart. For more information, see the tasks "Change Chart Shapes" and "Apply Chart Shape Effects."

Can I quickly change my chart type?

▼ Yes. Click the Design tab of the Chart Tools and click Change Chart Type from the Type group. The Change Chart Type dialog box appears. After selecting a chart type, click OK.

Format Chart Elements

Y ou can format each individual element that makes up a chart. This helps to enhance the appearance of each element so that the chart displays your data in the most effective manner possible.

Depending on the item you select, the options vary, and only the most common are described here. For chart titles, you can format the font, font style, font size, alignment, border, and pattern.

For data series, you can format the color and pattern, or even put an image into the shapes. For the chart axes, you can include lines and define their style, color, and weight. You can also change the scale of some types of data, for example, displaying quantities in "millions" or "thousands." For the legend, you can change the font and placement, as well as add a pattern and border.

Format Chart Elements

① Click the chart to select it.

A selection frame appears around the chart, and Excel displays the Chart Tools on the Ribbon.

② Click the Layout tab.

This example uses the Layout tab.

③ Click the down arrow (▾) to display the chart item list.

④ Click the chart item that you want to format.

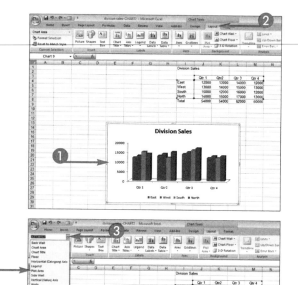

276

- Excel selects the item within the chart.

- Excel displays the item in the Current Selection group drop-down menu.

⑤ Click Format Selection.

- The Format dialog box appears for the item you selected, with formatting options for that item. The tabs and options vary, depending on what you select.

⑥ Make any changes, using the various selections to display different options.

This example adds a solid color fill.

- Excel updates the chart with your new selections.

⑦ Click Close.

What if I make a change that I do not like?

▼ If you make a formatting change that you do not like, you can undo the change by clicking the Undo button (🔄). You can also click Reset to Match Style in the Current Selection group to make the selected item conform to the overall style of the chart.

What else can I do to enhance the appearance of my chart?

▼ Probably the best thing that you can do is to simplify its appearance by removing extraneous elements. You can also click the Chart Styles More button in the Design tab of the Chart Tools to open the Chart Styles and apply pre-set designs to your chart. For more information, see Chapter 13.

How do I change the font, font size, or color of text in the chart?

▼ You can change the font elements in the same way that you would any other text in Excel. Select the text and click the Home tab. Then use the font editing tools to change the style, size, and color. See Chapter 9 for more information on changing font, font style, and font color.

Move or Resize a Chart

Y ou can move a chart to another location in your worksheet or change the size of a chart. For example, you might move a chart if it covers your data. You can also change the chart size if the chart information is too small to read.

For both moving and resizing, you use the handles that appear around the chart when you select it. Top and bottom handles allow you to change the chart height, while side handles allow you to change the chart width. Corner handles allow you to change both dimensions at the same time.

Can I move the slices in a pie chart?

▼ Yes. Click the pie chart and then click a slice. Selection handles appear around the slice. You can then drag it away from the chart.

Can I move a chart to its own chart sheet?

▼ Yes. Click the Design tab of the Chart Tools and click Move Chart in the Location group. A dialog box appears, allowing you to either move the chart to another worksheet or create a new sheet for the chart.

Move or Resize a Chart

Move a chart

1 Click to select the chart.

2 Place your cursor over an edge of the chart (⊕ changes to ✛).

3 Drag the chart to a new location.

To copy a chart, press the Ctrl key as you drag.

A rectangle indicates where the chart will move to.

4 Release the mouse, and the chart appears in the new location.

Resize a chart

1 Click to select the chart.

2 Place your cursor over a corner or edge of the chart (⊕ changes to ↖).

3 Drag the corner to a new location (↖ changes to ✛).

A rectangle indicates what the size of the chart will be.

4 Release the mouse, and the chart appears at the new size.

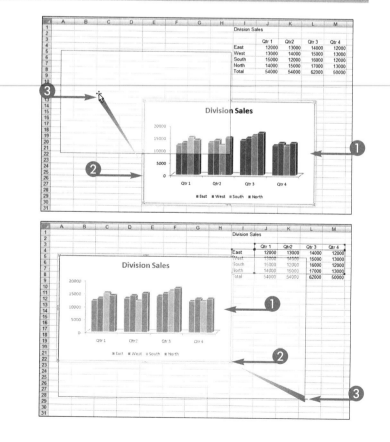

Delete a Chart

Y ou can delete a chart that you no longer need from your worksheet. You may need to delete a chart when you alter the data on your worksheet or when the chart information is no longer needed.

When you delete a chart in Excel, your data remains intact, but your chart disappears. You can retrieve a chart if you immediately use the Undo feature. If you save your workbook after you delete a chart, your deletion is permanent, and you must re-create the chart if you want to restore it. For more information on using the Undo feature, see Chapter 3. For more information on creating a chart, see the task "Create a Chart."

How do I delete a chart that is on a chart sheet?

▼ You must delete the chart sheet. Right-click the tab for the chart sheet that you want to delete. Click Delete from the menu that appears. Then click OK in the confirmation dialog box that appears.

PART III

Delete a Chart

Delete a chart

1 Click a blank area in the chart to select it.

2 Press Delete.

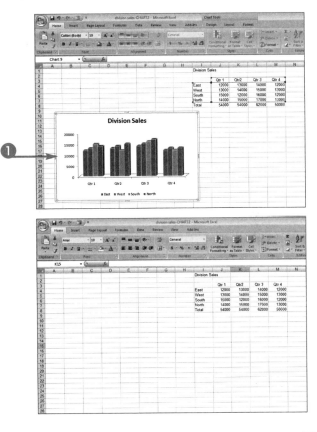

Excel deletes the chart.

Add Data to a Chart

After you create a chart, you can add a new data series to the chart rather than create a new chart. A *data series* is a group of related data representing one row or column from your worksheet. The ability to add a new data series to a chart is useful when the chart needs to be updated over time. For example, a chart containing monthly sales figures needs to be updated with a new data series each month. Excel automatically updates the legend when you add a new data series to a chart. To learn more about creating a chart, see the task "Create a Chart."

You can add a new data series to any chart type with the exception of a pie chart. This is because a pie chart displays only one data series. For more information, see the task "Change the Chart Type."

Just as you can add data, you can also delete data within a chart. You can delete data to keep your chart current. You can also delete a data series that you no longer need.

If you add or delete data and change your mind, you can undo the change using the Undo button.

Add Data to a Chart

1 Change the data in the worksheet.

2 Select the chart.

3 Click the Design tab of Chart Tools.

4 Click Select Data.

5 In the Select Data Source dialog box, click Add.

6 In the Edit Series dialog box, click the range selector (🔢) to add the series name and series values to the chart.

7 Click OK to close the Edit Series dialog box.

● The data appears in the Select Data Source dialog box.

8 Click OK to close the Select Data Source dialog box.

● The data is added to the chart.

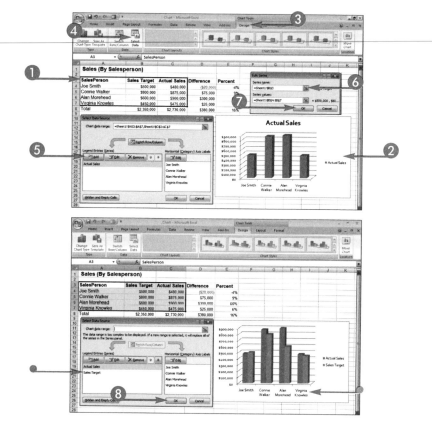

280

Print a Chart

You can print a chart with the worksheet data on its own page so that you have a hard copy of your data for a presentation or meeting.

Printing a chart with the worksheet data is useful if you want the data and the chart to appear on the same page. When you print a chart on its own worksheet, the chart expands to fill the page. The printed chart may look different from the chart on your screen. For example, you may find that the chart's legend is smaller.

If you are using a black-and-white printer to print the chart, the colors in the chart appear as shades of gray. If you have a color printer, the chart prints in the colors that you have selected.

Master It

Can I preview a chart before I print it?

▼ Yes. You preview a chart in the same way that you preview a worksheet. This allows you to see how the chart looks before you print it. Click the Office button, click Print, and then click Print Preview.

Can I print the chart from its own worksheet?

▼ Yes. Put the chart on its own worksheet and use the same steps as you would to print it on a sheet with the data. You can also click the Office button and click Print and then click Quick Print to print either the worksheet with the chart or the entire worksheet with the chart and data.

Print a Chart

Print a chart and worksheet

① Click a cell outside the chart.

② Click the Office button.

③ Click Print.

The Print dialog box opens.

● You can click the down arrow (🔽) to change the printer.

● You can also select the chart prior to printing, and click to change the selection option to print only the selected chart (⚪ changes to ◉).

④ Click OK.

Excel prints the worksheet with the chart.

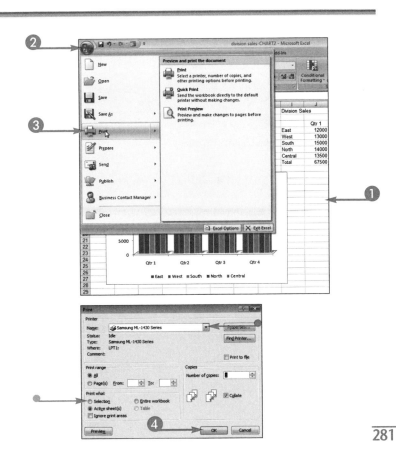

Change Chart Shapes

Y ou can change the shape of any of the graphics in your chart, particularly those that represent your data series, to make them more dramatic.

The Shapes gallery in the Format tab of the Chart Tools has a variety of shapes, including Intense, Moderate, Subtle, Outline, Colored Outline, and Colored Fill.

Depending on the shape that you select, that element in the data series will assume the shape that you apply. A live preview shows you how the shape will look as you move the mouse over a Shape Style. If you

do not like what you have applied, you can always click the Undo button to go back to before the Shape Style was changed.

You can use the Shape Fill and Shape Outline tools to manually change the colors of the shapes, either inside the borders as fills or just the borders, as outlines. If you use the Shape gallery, Excel applies a coordinated style to the selected shapes.

You can also use the Shape Fill options to put a picture inside a data series, and either stack a set of repeating pictures or tile a single picture through a shape.

Change Chart Shapes

① Click the chart to select it.

A selection frame appears around the chart, and Excel displays the Chart Tools on the Ribbon.

② Click the Format tab.

③ Click the down arrow (▼) to display the chart item list.

④ Click the chart item that you want to format.

● The item is selected within the chart.

● Excel displays the item in the Current Selection group drop-down menu.

⑤ Click the Shape Styles gallery More button.

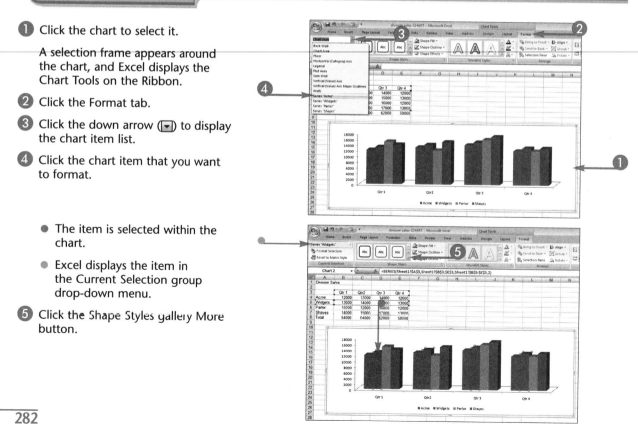

The Shape Styles gallery opens.

⑥ Move the mouse over a Shape Style to see a live preview.

The selected shapes preview the style.

⑦ Click the Shape Style that you want to apply.

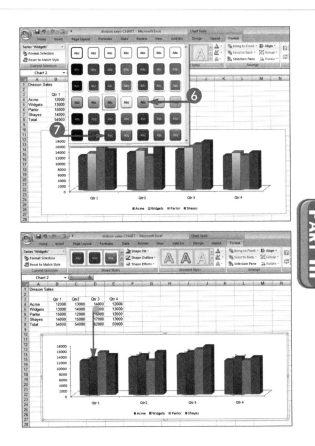

● Excel updates the chart with your Shape Style.

MASTER IT

Can I apply a Shape Style to just one part of a data series, for example, the shape representing Qtr 4?

▼ Yes. You can click any part of the data series twice. The first click selects the entire series. The second click selects only that single element. After the second click, apply your Shape Style to the single element that you selected.

How do Shape Styles differ from Chart Styles?

▼ Chart Styles apply to the entire chart, while Shape Styles apply to a single part of a chart or a series of elements. Shape Styles are in the Format tab of the Chart Tools, while Chart Styles are in the Design tab.

How do I change the shape outline color to one that is not in the Shape Styles gallery?

▼ Select the individual shape or group of shapes that you want to outline. Click the Shape Outline down arrow (▾) to display a dialog box, which allows you to customize the Outline Color or options in the way that you want.

Apply Chart Shape Effects

Depending on the type of shape and the number of shapes selected, you can choose from an entire gallery of shape effects for selected elements in your chart.

The Effects gallery has a set of pre-set effects that you can apply, as well as specific effects that will enhance the appearance of your shapes and make the chart look much more professional. The individual effects include Shadow, Reflection, Glow, Soft Edges, and Bevel.

There are also sets of 3-D Effects and 3-D Rotations that you can apply to the shapes in your chart. You

can manually set 3-D options by clicking 3-D options under the Effect pre-sets.

You can also achieve very professional effects by using the Perspective gallery under Shadow to give a sense of depth to the chart. You can fine-tune any of the effects using the set of options at the bottom of each gallery.

Not all shape effects will be available for any shape that you select; however, if you select a data series shape, there will usually be shape effects that you can apply.

Apply Chart Shape Effects

① Click in the chart to select the shapes to which you want to add effects.

● Selection handles appear around the shapes.

② Click the Format tab.

③ Click Shape Effects.

The Shape Effects menu opens.

④ Click Preset.

The Presets gallery opens.

You can see a live preview of any preset effect by moving your mouse over it.

⑤ Click the preset shape effect that you want to apply.

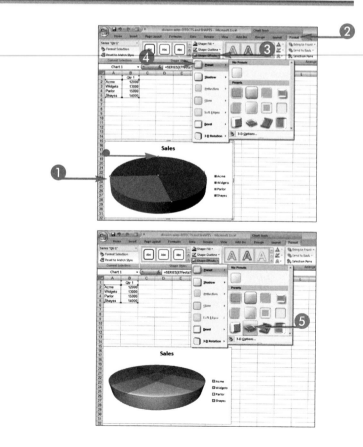

● The chart takes on the preset effect.

6 Click Shape Effects.

The Shape Effects menu opens.

7 Click a shape effect.

This example uses Shadow.

The Shadow presets appear.

8 Click a shadow option.

This example applies a shadow perspective effect.

● Excel updates the chart with your shape effects.

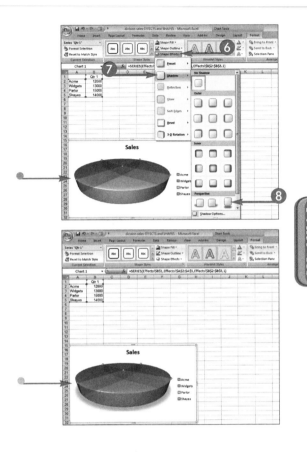

Can I apply a shape effect to just one part of a data series in a pie chart?

▼ Yes. Click to select the individual pie slice to which to apply the effect. You can make the effect more pronounced by breaking the individual piece away from the pie. You can do this by dragging the pie slice away from the rest out of the pie chart. Note that to apply a shadow effect the pie slice must be broken off from the pie chart.

Can I manually change the length and color of my shadows?

▼ Yes. Select the shape to which you want to apply the shadow effect, and click Shadow Options at the bottom of the Shadow submenu. You can use a color tool and other dialog boxes to change the appearance and size of the shadow.

I cannot seem to apply a bevel effect to the pie chart or slices, even if they are separated. Why does this happen?

▼ Different shapes will accommodate certain effects and options. Your best bet is to use trial and error to find the best effect for your shapes, and then save the file.

An Introduction to PivotTables

O ne of the main components of Excel is its ability to take the numerical data in your worksheet and make sense of it. PivotTables are a way to reorganize the information in you worksheet in different ways so that the information can help you make sense of the data.

A Shift in Perspective

While charts help to show the data in meaningful ways that you may not see clearly when viewing only the numbers, they are still limited to the way that the data is actually laid out.

Data tables have the ability to sort and filter columns of information in a useful way. However, the data remains in a fixed position within the data table. For more information, see Chapter 11.

In complex worksheets, the data may need to be moved or reorganized in order to make sense out of it. *PivotTable* means a shift in the perspective that you have on a fixed set of data, so that you can analyze it effectively from different points of view.

For example, you may have columns with headings for sales data, by salesperson, quarter, item, and region, as well as additional categories. While a data table could enable you to do some sorting and filtering within the worksheet, it would be difficult to identify which salesman sold the most of a certain product either in a certain quarter, or in a region, or both.

By reorganizing the data in a PivotTable, you can apply one or more filters, and view the data from various perspectives.

Advantages of a PivotTable

To create a PivotTable, you need to identify and confirm the range of data that you want analyzed. Excel then provides you with the tools, in the form of a grid and various drop-down menus and options, to decide exactly how you want to view the data. You can enable or drop in as many or as few parameters as you want, and each time, the data in the PivotTable changes to show you the numbers according to the criteria that you specify.

You can create a PivotTable from an existing worksheet, or use Excel's data connection tools to bring in data from an external source or database.

For example, suppose you had a set of sales data including a product, sales in a quarter, sales by person, and sales by region. In your worksheet, this would be broken down in a series of columns listing the products, the amounts sold, the names of the sales people and their region. However, the actual data would be spread throughout the various columns. While it could be sorted, filtered, or charted, you would find it difficult to determine who sold the most of which product by quarter or in which region. The PivotTable allows you to rearrange the headings and thereby answer these sorts of questions instantly and effectively.

The type of question you need answered determines the layout of your PivotTable.

Because your PivotTable can be revised instantly, you can ask different questions of the same set of data and get a different set of results.

In most cases, the data that is being compared goes in the Values box of the PivotTable. You can arrange the categories or items being compared in their own new rows and columns. This is what allows you to reorganize the original rows and columns in you worksheet.

Finally, you can also add some headings to Report Filters in your PivotTable. This lets you isolate the results; for example in the case described above, you could apply a filter by quarter, by sales person, or by region. In each case the final results would reflect only that filter, instead of the total. Removing the filter would once again show the grand totals.

Create a PivotTable

You create a PivotTable from the Insert tab of the Ribbon. By selecting a cell in your table, Excel will try to determine the range to be used in the PivotTable.

If your original worksheet is small enough, you can build your PivotTable in the same worksheet, or by default it will be placed in a new worksheet. A PivotTable placeholder shows the area for the PivotTable and a PivotTable Field List task pane will open with check boxes for fields to report.

You can select the fields by clicking check boxes. Excel will places those fields into the windows for column labels, row labels, data values, or a report filter. However, you can click and drag the labels to instantly change the look of the PivotTable.

When you rearrange the rows, columns, or values, you can see your information in new ways. You can also add a Report Filter for a field so that you can see results for only a few selected items in that field. For example, you could filter by Region, Sales Person, Quarter, or Product to see only those values for comparison, and deselect the filter to return to the grand total results.

You can use the PivotTable Tools on the Ribbon to revise the PivotTable. You can use the Options tab features to move or rearrange the PivotTable, change the field list, buttons or field headers, add formulas, or generate a PivotChart. You can use the Design tab features to apply a new PivotTable style or apply options for row headers, column headers, banded rows or banded columns. You can also create subtotals or turn totals of the values off or on.

If an arrangement of your PivotTable is particularly effective, you can name your worksheet in a way that reminds you of the parameters of the PivotTable. For more information, see the task "Rename a Worksheet" in Chapter 10.

You can also generate a chart based on the revised view of your data that is provided by a PivotTable. For more information, see the task "Create a PivotTable Chart."

PART III

Create and Use a PivotTable

Y ou can create a PivotTable to reorganize your worksheet data and make it easier to understand.

To create the PivotTable, you can let Excel guess the range of data that you want to use, or use the range selector to identify it manually.

While you will usually create a PivotTable from data in an existing worksheet, you can also connect to external data sources to reorganize your data into a PivotTable.

To help you create the PivotTable, the first step is generally to identify what is being compared, or the actual data.

For example, in a sales report, the sales data is the key numerical information that is being compared by different parameters, such as who sold what and how much, where it was sold, and when it was sold, with possible sub-categories to compare.

By checking off the criteria for comparison, you isolate only the data that you want to compare. You can change the criteria at any time, and the PivotTable refreshes to show you the new comparisons.

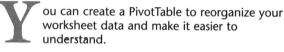

Create and Use a PivotTable

Select the cells and create the PivotTable

1. Click the Insert tab.

2. Click in the range of data that you want to analyze.

3. Click PivotTable.

   - Excel adds a dashed border around the range of data.

   The Create PivotTable dialog box opens.

   - You can use the range selector button (🔲) to change the table that is being analyzed.

   - You can accept the default option to create the PivotTable in another worksheet.

   - You can also choose to place the PivotTable in the same worksheet (◎ changes to ◉).

4. Click OK.

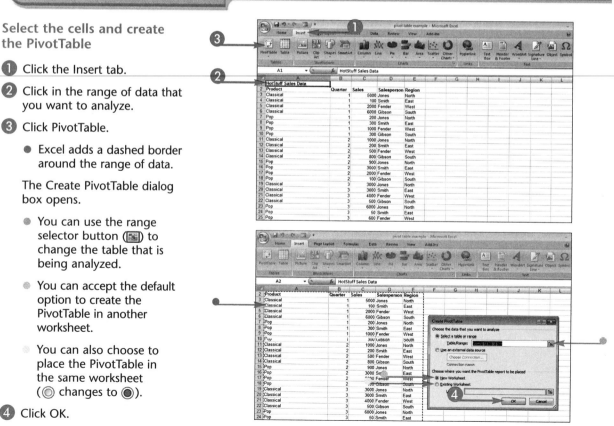

- The PivotTable placeholder is placed into a new worksheet.

- The PivotTable Field List pane opens.

- The PivotTable Tools open on the Ribbon, with the Options tab activated.

Add rows, columns, and fields

⑤ Click to choose the items that you want to compare (☐ changes to ☑).

The selected items are added to the rows and values in the PivotTable.

⑥ You can click and drag a row label to create a column to differentiate it from the other data.

Can I analyze external data in a PivotTable?

▼ You can bring in data from Access or a text database, or you can connect to a Web database. Click the Data tab and select From Other Sources or Existing Connections to bring data into Excel. You can also use the Use an external data source option and enable a connection from within the PivotTable dialog box to create a PivotTable directly from an external source.

How do I remove a parameter?

▼ Click to deactivate any field in the PivotTable and return it to the Field List. You can then drag it into another label area.

Why drag the parameter from a row to a column?

▼ Differentiating as many columns and rows as possible makes the data much easier to read and analyze.

Can I filter data in a PivotTable?

▼ Yes. You can click the filter arrow (▼) for any parameter that is placed in a row or column in a PivotTable to select or deselect which components you want to show or hide, filtering out unwanted selections. You can also drag fields into the Report Filter area, as shown in the next section of this task.

continued

Create and Use a PivotTable
(Continued)

After you create your PivotTable, Excel allows you to change the criteria or parameters for your comparisons.

You can use the Options tab in the PivotTable Tools on the Ribbon to change your view of the PivotTable. You can hide or show the field list, the buttons, and the field headers to make your task easier. In the Actions group, Clear lets you quickly clear all of the information from the PivotTable and begin activating components again. Select makes it easier to select parts of the table, for example, just the labels, just the values, or both the labels and values.

You can also create filters to enable you to further refine your data and eliminate information that you do not want to see, and to make your PivotTable less confusing.

You can rename the PivotTable from the Options group, and also display a dialog box for more options. This enables you to hide or deselect the option to show grand totals within the actual PivotTable.

You can use the field settings to determine the type of summaries that you want to appear within the table. Besides sums, these can include values such as average, maximum, minimum, and count.

Create and Use a PivotTable *(continued)*

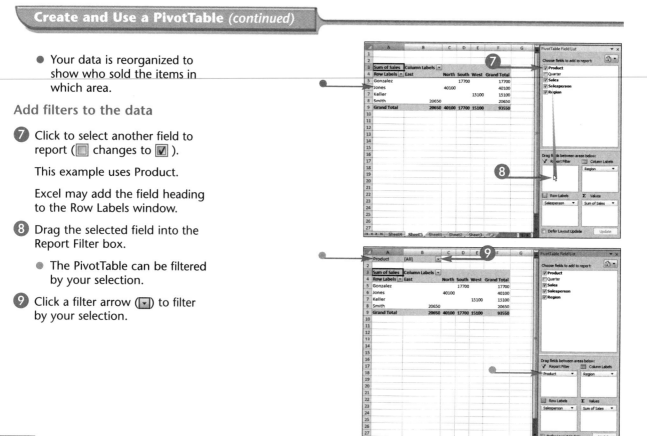

- Your data is reorganized to show who sold the items in which area.

Add filters to the data

7 Click to select another field to report (☐ changes to ☑).

This example uses Product.

Excel may add the field heading to the Row Labels window.

8 Drag the selected field into the Report Filter box.

- The PivotTable can be filtered by your selection.

9 Click a filter arrow (▼) to filter by your selection.

● The Sort dialog box opens.

⑩ Click to select a Filter category.

⑪ Click OK.

	A	B	C	D	E	F	G	H
1	Product	(All) ▼						
2	(All)							
3	Butterscotch	⑩						
4	Maple Syrup ◄		North	South	West	Grand Total		
5				17700		17700		
6			40100			40100		
7					15100	15100		
8						20650		
9			40100	17700	15100	93550		
10								
11	☐ Select Multiple Items							
12 ⑪	OK	Cancel						
13								
14								
15								
16								

● The PivotTable changes to show only the sales values for the regions filtered by your selection.

● The filter arrow (▼) indicates that the data has been sorted.

	A	B	C	D	E	F	G	H
1	Product	Maple Syrup ▼ ◄						
2								
3	Sum of Sales	Column Labels ▼						
4	Row Labels ▼	East	North	South	West	Grand Total		
5	Gonzalez			11300		11300		
6	Jones		29000			29000		
7	Keller				9500	9500		
8	Smith	13300				13300		
9	Grand Total	13300	29000	11300	9500	63100		
10								
11								
12								
13								
14								
15								
16								

Can I add more than one filter?

▼ Yes. You can place any category in the Report Filter box to use it as a filter. To remove it as a filter, you can deselect it in the Field List, or use the Filter options to enable multiple items that you want to filter by. Click to enable the selection of multiple items in the Filter Options pane. (☑ changes to ☐).

What if I want to see totals for one of my filter parameters?

▼ You can use the Field List to drag a filter parameter out of the Filters area and make it either a row or column label. Its entire set of values will then be displayed in the PivotTable.

Can I change the view of the Field List?

▼ Yes. Click the Field List down arrow (▣▼) and select a different view of the various fields. You can also change the way that they can be placed into the rows, columns, and values of the PivotTable.

Can I sort within the fields?

▼ Yes. You will find ascending or descending sort options when you click the filter arrow (▼) for any field. You can also click Sort in the PivotTable Options tab on the Ribbon to display a dialog box with manual and more extensive sort options.

Create a PivotTable Chart

With a set of data reorganized to analyze it, you can create a chart directly from a PivotTable.

You first need to select the current set of data within the PivotTable to create a PivotTable chart. It is best to omit any totals or grand totals from the selection, as those values will skew the results of the chart.

To determine which type of chart will be most appropriate for your plotted data, refer to the tasks "An Introduction to Charts" and "Change the Chart Type."

In the Options tab of the PivotTable Tools on the Ribbon, you can use PivotChart in the Tools group to

open the Chart Type dialog box and select the type of chart that you want.

Once you create your PivotTable chart, you can also change the chart type by displaying the Design tab of the PivotChart Tools on the Ribbon, and clicking Change Chart Type in the Type group.

You can also continue to revise the plotted data in the PivotTable to reflect different sets of data by row and column headers, or by adding one or more filters. You can then refresh the chart to reflect the newly added information, or create a new chart based on the revised data.

Create a PivotTable Chart

Select the data and create a PivotTable chart

1 Select the range of data that you want to chart.

Note: Do not include any grand totals or sums because they will skew the chart.

A selection frame appears around the data.

2 Click the Options tab.

3 Click PivotChart.

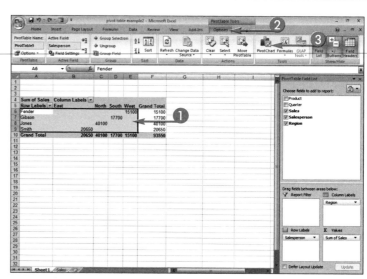

The Insert Chart dialog box opens.

4 Click the design for the chart type that you want to use.

5 Click OK.

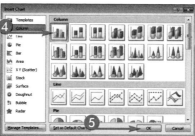

Revise the chart

- Excel creates the chart and plots the data.

- The PivotChart Filter Pane opens.

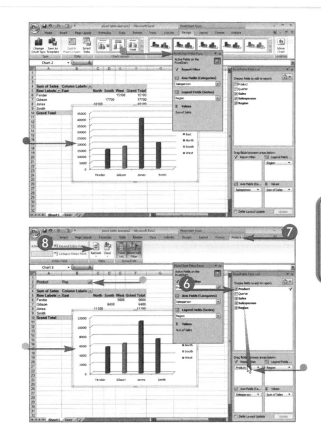

6 In the Field List, click to add a field to the PivotTable (☐ changes to ☑).

- You can click and drag to make sure that the new field is placed in the Report Filter box.

7 Click the Analyze tab.

8 Click Refresh to add the filter to the PivotTable chart.

- The revised data is reflected on the chart.

You can click the Undo button (⟲ ▾) to remove the chart and start over.

What is the best chart type for a PivotTable?

▼ You can theoretically create any of the major chart types from within a PivotTable. However, because a PivotTable is used to compare information for different criteria and then to return the relative values, a column or bar chart is the most common type of PivotTable chart.

I accidentally closed the PivotChart Filter. Can I get it back?

▼ Yes. In the Analyze tab of the PivotChart Tools, you will find buttons in the Show/Hide group to reopen the PivotChart Filter and the Field List if they become hidden. You can activate the PivotTable Tools on the Ribbon by clicking to select the PivotTable, or the PivotTable chart.

What is the quickest way to revise the Title and Axis titles in the PivotChart?

▼ Click to select the Title or Axis Title placeholders. Either drag within the placeholder to select the generic text, or, with the placeholder selected, type the new title in the Formula bar. Then either press Enter or click the check mark (☑) in the Formula bar to set the new title in place.

Add Shapes

Excel provides many ready-made shapes that you can add to enhance the appearance of your worksheet or draw attention to important information.

Excel offers several categories of shapes, including Lines, Basic Shapes, Block Arrows, Callouts, and Stars and Banners.

Each category contains individual shapes, which you can select and resize to place in the worksheet. You can later move and resize the shape to better suit your needs. You can also delete any shape that you no longer need.

After selecting the shape that you want to create, you can drag it out to a size in the worksheet. When you release the mouse to create the shape, it remains selected, allowing you to easily resize or move it. For information on moving, resizing, or deleting a graphic, see the task "Move or Resize a Graphic."

With the shape selected, the Drawing Tools open on the Ribbon. You can change the placement of the text and graphics using the Format tab of the Drawing Tools by using the Bring Forward or Send to Back options. You can also add Effects and further modify the shape using the Drawing Tools. For more information on these features, see the task "Work with Graphics and Special Effects."

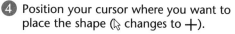

Add Shapes

① Click the Insert tab.

② Click Shapes.

The Shapes gallery appears.

③ Click the shape that you want to add.

This example uses a block arrow.

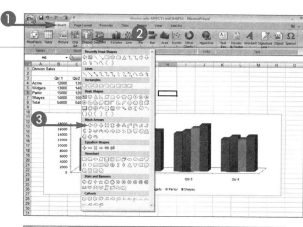

④ Position your cursor where you want to place the shape (◯ changes to +).

⑤ Click and drag the mouse until the shape is the size you want.

⑥ Release the mouse.

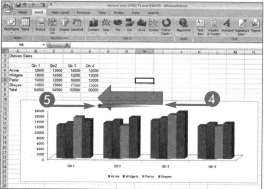

- The shape appears in the worksheet with selection handles.

- The Drawing Tools open on the Ribbon.

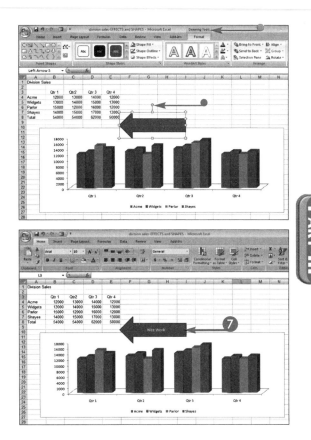

7 Type some text into the shape.

8 Click anywhere to deselect the shape and set it in the worksheet.

How can I quickly copy a shape?

▼ You can copy any shape or group of shapes by selecting them and pressing the Ctrl key as you drag out a copy or "clone" of the selected shapes. To select multiple shapes, press the Shift key as you click to select, or trace a rectangle around, a group of shapes to select them.

How do I draw a square or circle?

▼ In the Shapes gallery, click the rectangle or the oval to draw a square or a circle. Then hold down the Shift key as you draw the shape so that the rectangle is drawn as a square, and the oval is drawn as a circle.

Can I rotate the shape?

▼ Yes. With the shape selected, click the green rotate tool (⊙). The cursor (⬚) changes to a rotate cursor (↻). You can now rotate the shape at an angle by moving your mouse. When it is at the angle you want, release the mouse to set the rotation.

Can I draw my own shape?

▼ Yes. In the Insert tab, click Shapes, select the Lines category, and then click the Freeform tool (✎). When you finish drawing your shape, double-click to stop drawing.

Add a SmartArt Graphic

Excel allows you to insert fairly sophisticated diagrams into your worksheet. For example, you can include an organizational chart of your company, or flow charts of common tasks or procedures.

You can select from a gallery of pre-designed diagrams. You can then add or replace the sample text with text for your particular diagram contents.

When you insert a SmartArt graphic or diagram, the SmartArt Tools appear on the Ribbon. You can use the SmartArt Tools to select different formatting

options. For example, you can change the colors, and add text and effects. You can also use the Themes to change the look of SmartArt diagrams by applying a coordinated set of fonts, colors, and effects. For more information, see the task "Apply a Theme to a Document" in Chapter 5.

After you add a SmartArt graphic, you can move and resize it to suit your worksheet. You can also delete a diagram that you no longer need. For information on moving, resizing, or deleting a graphic, see the task "Move or Resize a Graphic."

see the task "Apply a Theme to a Document" in Chapter 5.

Add a SmartArt Graphic

1 Click the Insert tab.

2 Click SmartArt.

● The Choose a SmartArt Graphic dialog box appears.

3 Select the type of diagram that you want to insert, or stay in the All category to view all SmartArt graphics.

4 Select a SmartArt graphic.

● A description of how it can be used appears in the right panel.

5 Click OK.

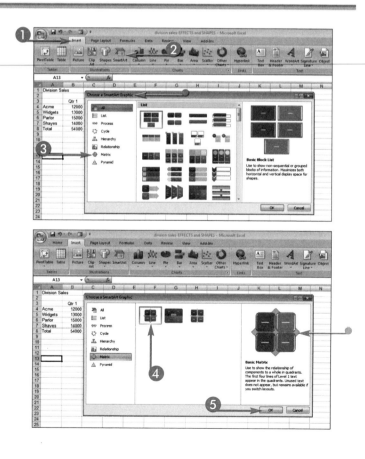

● Excel adds the diagram to your worksheet.

○ The SmartArt Tools appear on the Ribbon.

● Text placeholders appear where you can add text.

⑥ Type your text into the Type your text here panel.

● You can click the open/close arrows to close or open this panel.

⑦ Click outside the diagram box to return to the worksheet.

○ Excel sets the SmartArt graphic with your new text.

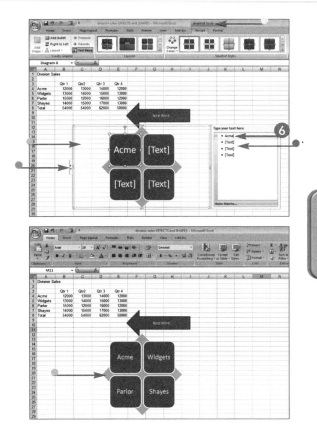

How can I best choose from the gallery of various SmartArt graphics?

▼ When you click a SmartArt graphic in the SmartArt Graphic gallery, Excel displays the appropriate usage of the selected graphic in a panel on the right of the gallery. You can use this information to determine whether you want to insert a particular SmartArt graphic.

Why do I see a more basic diagram gallery, instead of the SmartArt graphics?

▼ You are working with an older version of an Excel worksheet in Compatibility Mode. To get the full range of SmartArt graphics, save it as an Excel 2007 file. For more information, see the task "Save in Different Versions" in Chapter 2.

How do I edit text in a SmartArt graphic?

▼ Use the Type your text here panel to change the text. To edit the formatting of text that you have included as part of the SmartArt graphic, click within the SmartArt graphic and then within the particular text that you want to change. You should see the flashing insertion point. You can then make any formatting changes to the text.

Move or Resize a Graphic

Y ou can move or copy a graphic from one location in your worksheet to another. When you move a graphic, the graphic disappears from its original location in your worksheet. When you copy a graphic, the graphic appears in both the original and new locations.

You can change the size of a graphic to suit your worksheet. The resizing handles that appear when you select a graphic allow you to change the height and width of the graphic. You use the top and bottom

handles to change the height of the graphic, the side handles to change the width of the graphic, and the corner handles to change the height and width of the graphic at the same time.

To make any of these changes, you must select the graphic first. When you select the graphic, not only does the selection frame appear, but the Drawing Tools (for a shape) or the SmartArt Tools (for a SmartArt graphic) also appear automatically.

Move or Resize a Graphic

Move a graphic

① Click the graphic that you want to move (I changes to ✥).

② Drag the graphic to a new location.

As you drag, the cursor (⤶) represents the graphic.

③ Drop the graphic where you want it.

● The graphic appears in the new location.

To copy a graphic, you can hold down the Ctrl key as you perform Step 2.

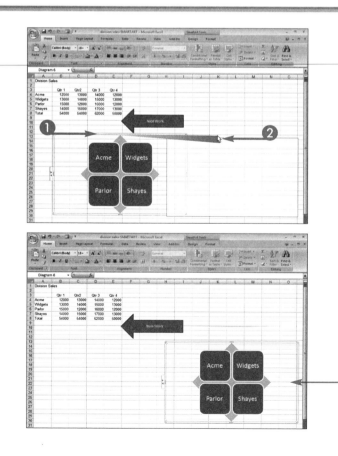

Resize a graphic

1. Click the graphic that you want to resize.

   Resizing handles appear around the graphic.

2. Position the cursor over one of the resizing handles on a corner (⬚ changes to ⬚).

3. Drag the handle until the graphic is the size you want.

   ● An outline is traced for the new size.

4. Release the handle.

   ● The graphic appears in the new size.

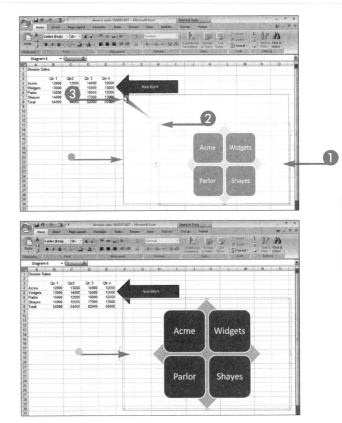

Is there an easy way to move a graphic just a little bit?

▼ Yes. You can "nudge" a selected graphic by using the arrow keys on the keyboard. Make sure that the shape or SmartArt graphic is selected, and use the right-, left-, up-, and down-arrow keys to move it just a bit at a time, or hold the key down to move the graphic more quickly.

When I click in the Matrix SmartArt graphic to select it, I just get one of the text boxes. What am I doing wrong?

▼ The SmartArt graphics are quite precise, and you can select individual elements to reformat or change them. However, to select the entire graphic as a unit, click in its area but not directly on a part of the graphic. You will see a frame around the graphic when it is entirely selected.

How can I delete a graphic?

▼ Click the graphic and press the Delete key. Doing so removes the graphic and any elements within that graphic, including the text.

Add a
Text Box

Y ou can add a text box to your worksheet or chart to display additional information.

Text boxes are useful for displaying your comments. You can also use text boxes to label, identify, or describe specific items in your worksheet or chart. The text that you type in a text box wraps to fit the width of the text box.

After you add a text box, you can move and resize the text box to suit your worksheet. You can also delete a text box that you no longer need.

In addition to text boxes, Excel offers shapes that are specifically designed to display text, such as the shapes in the Stars and Banners or Callout categories. These shapes let you neatly display additional text in your worksheet. For more information on shapes, see the task "Add Shapes."

Add a Text Box

① Click the Insert tab.

② Click Text Box.

③ Click in the worksheet where you want to add the text box.

● Excel creates a text box with selection handles and an active insertion point (|).

Note that the text box is selected for text entry and not for formatting.

● Drawing Tools open on the Ribbon.

④ Type the text that you want to appear in the text box.

You can drag a selection corner or edge to change the width of the text box.

⑤ Click the edge of the selection square around the text box.

The text box is now active for formatting.

⑥ Click the Format tab in the Drawing Tools.

You can modify the appearance of the text box with the Format options.

Can I make a text box stand out quickly and easily?

▼ Yes. With the text box selected, click the WordArt Styles group More button to open the WordArt Styles gallery. As you move the mouse over any of these styles, you can see a live preview of how it would look applied to the text box. Use the styles in the bottom panel, Applies to All Text in the Shape, to make sure that the style you select is applied to all text in the text box.

How can I change the border of a text box?

▼ You can use the Shape Outline options in the Shape Styles group of the Drawing Tools to change the color, weights, and style of the border around the text box. Select the text box and then click the Shape Outline down arrow (▼) to open the Shape Outline options.

Add a Clip Art Image

Excel includes professionally designed clip art images that you can add to your worksheet. Clip art images help to make your worksheet more interesting and entertaining. For example, you might use a clip art image as your logo or to add interest to a report.

The first time you select the Clip Art command, Excel finds the clip art that installed with Office 2007. You can add your own images by using the Organize Clips option at the bottom of the Clip Art task pane, and index and categorize your clips for future use.

After Excel categorizes your images, you can type a keyword and then search for matching images. You can find clip art images of flowers, animals, buildings, and many other types of objects. In addition to the images provided with Office, you can also purchase clip art images or find them online.

After you add a clip art image, you can move and resize the clip art image to suit your document. You can also delete a clip art image that you no longer need.

When you insert a clip art image, the Picture Tools open on the Ribbon, and you can add a border, apply picture styles, and further modify the appearance of the clip art or picture in the worksheet.

Add a Clip Art Image

1. Click the Insert tab.

2. Click Clip Art.

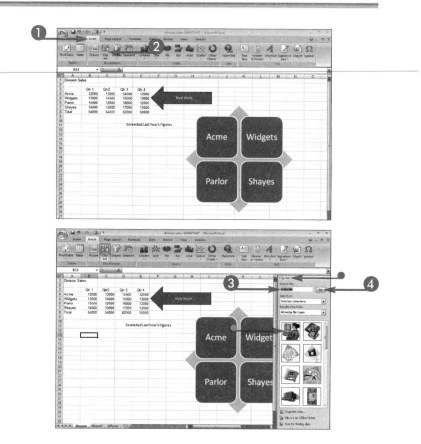

● The Clip Art task pane appears.

3. Enter a search term for the image that you want to insert.

You can limit the search to a particular folder or drive by clicking the Search in down arrow (▼) and specifying where you want to search.

To limit the search to a particular media file type, click the Results should be down arrow (▼) and click the type of file.

4. Click Go.

● Excel displays the clip art images that match your search criteria.

5 Click the Clip Art image that you want to insert into the worksheet.

● The clip art image appears in the worksheet.

The Format tab of Picture Tools becomes active on the Ribbon.

6 Click the Picture Styles More button.

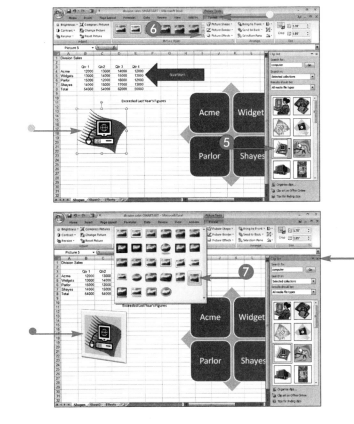

The Picture Styles gallery opens, providing a live preview of different styles for the clip art image.

7 Click to apply a style to the clip art.

● The clip art image adopts the style that you selected.

8 To close the task pane, click the Close button (⊠).

MASTER IT

Can I browse through the clip art images?

▼ Yes. To do so, click the Organize Clips link at the bottom of the Clip Art task pane. The Microsoft Clip Organizer appears with a collection list of folders on the left side of the window. Open the folder that you want to explore by clicking the plus sign next to the folder. To see the images within a particular folder, click that folder. You can insert an image from this window by right-clicking the image, selecting Copy, clicking in the document where you want to place the image, and choosing Paste from either the right-click menu or the Home tab.

Where can I find more clip art images?

▼ If you are connected to the Internet, you can visit Microsoft's Clip Gallery Live Web site to find additional clip art images. In the Clip Art task pane, click the Clip art on Office Online link and then follow the instructions on your screen.

Work with Graphics and Special Effects

Y ou can use the various formatting options in the Excel 2007 Ribbon to make any of the graphics that you inserted stand out, and to modify how they appear.

When you select a graphic, a frame appears around the graphic. At the same time, depending on what kind of graphic you selected, a corresponding tab for Design, Format, and other options becomes active on the Ribbon.

These options let you use galleries with live previews where you can apply preset options to the entire graphic or, in the case of a SmartArt graphic, apply

individual formatting options to individual shapes within the diagram.

By experimenting with the effects in the Design and Format tabs, you can add distinctive flair to various shapes and SmartArt graphics, and make your worksheet look as though it were professionally designed.

Whether you get a full range of Design options as you do with SmartArt, or more limited Formatting capability, as you do with shapes and simple graphics, depends upon the graphic that you create and select. The more sophisticated the graphic, the greater the range of effects and features that you can apply.

Work with Graphics and Special Effects

Design a SmartArt graphic

1 Click to select the SmartArt graphic.

2 Click the Design tab of the SmartArt Tools.

3 Click the SmartArt Styles More button.

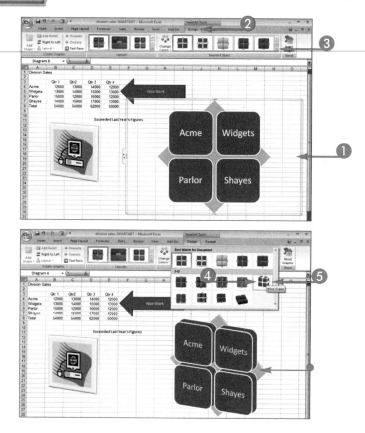

The Smart Art Styles gallery opens with Best Match for Document and 3-D sections.

4 Move your mouse over any options for a live preview.

5 Click an option to apply it to the graphic.

● Excel applies the option to the graphic.

Add effects to a SmartArt graphic

1 Click to select the SmartArt graphic.

2 Click the Format tab of the SmartArt Tools.

3 Click the Shape Effects down arrow (▼).

The Shape Effects gallery opens.

4 Choose an effect category.

You can move your mouse over any options for a live preview.

5 Click an option to apply it to the graphic.

● Excel updates the graphic with the option that you selected.

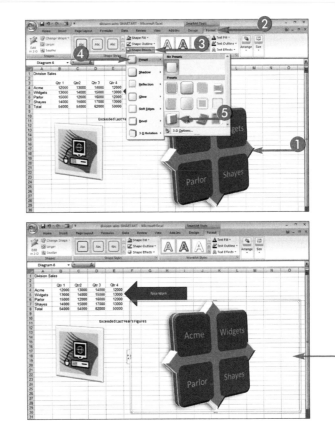

Can I use WordArt styles for SmartArt graphics?

▼ Yes. However, the WordArt styles are applied only to the text within the various shapes. In the Format tab of SmartArt Tools, click the WordArt Styles group More button. This opens the WordArt Styles gallery, where you can see a live preview of the various styles for your SmartArt graphic.

How do I change the colors in the graphic?

▼ Click the graphic to open the SmartArt Tools. In the Design tab, click the Change Colors down arrow (▼) in the SmartArt Styles group. The available colors are dependent on the theme that is applied to the worksheet. You can change the theme in the Page Layout tab of the Ribbon.

Can I change only an individual shape of a SmartArt graphic?

▼ Yes. Click the individual shape in the SmartArt graphic. Then use the Shape Styles in the Format tab of the SmartArt Tools to apply individual borders, colors, fills, and effects to the individual shape. Some options will be unavailable.

Can I cancel a change that I made to a graphic?

▼ Yes. Excel remembers your last changes. Click the Undo button (▼) on the Quick Access toolbar to immediately cancel a change that you make to a graphic.

An Introduction to Conditional Formats

One of the main components of Excel is its ability to take the numerical data in your worksheet and analyze it. *Conditional formats* are rules that you can set that can emphasize data according to criteria that are met.

For example, data displayed in a cell that is the result of a formula can be red if the result is negative, or unacceptable, or green if it is positive. Also, figures that exceed a certain total can display in bold text, or a combination of different formats, according to the rules that you set.

Create a Conditional Format

In Excel 2007 you can emphasize and highlight data in various ways, conditioned upon parameters that you set. You can access the conditional formats in Excel 2007 in the Styles group of the Home tab on the Ribbon. After selecting the range of cells to which you want to apply a conditional format, you can click Conditional Formatting to either set rules, apply preset icons, or create a new rule, clear rules, or use the rules manager.

Conditional Formatting Options

The Highlight Cells rules can set parameters that will highlight cells, with the format you determine, based upon comparisons such as greater than, less than, between, equal to, text that contains, a date that is equal to, and other similar relationships.

The other set of rules that you can use to apply conditional formats are so-called top and bottom rules. Among these are the top ten items in the selected range, or the bottom ten, or the top or bottom 10 percent, or above or below average. You can also use the More Rules option in any of these submenus to create your own rule, and the corresponding format for cells that match the rule parameters.

Beyond simple formatting and rules, the conditional formatting options in Excel 2007 can apply various types of graphics to make aspects of your data stand out.

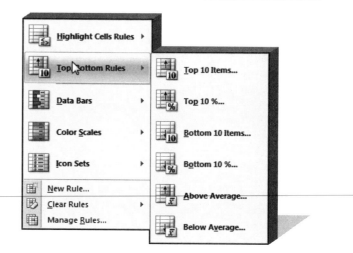

Data bars can be applied to the cells in a variety of colors that resemble a bar chart directly within the data, with the higher values having deeper color and longer bars.

Color scales apply a spectrum of colors to your data, with higher ranges of value having a different set of colors than lower values. You can use More Rules to determine colors to apply, or use one of the six preset color scales in the Conditional Formatting submenu.

Icon sets apply small coordinated symbols to reflect the relative values in your selected data. For example, directional arrows or colored traffic light icons can show the trends within your data as values move upward or downward.

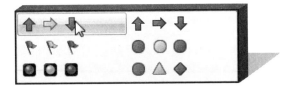

You can also see a live preview before applying a particular kind of conditional format to see if it serves your purpose before its application. You can also access the default settings for the graphics and change the rules to reflect how you want the data to be represented.

Conditional Formatting Rules

You can also create a new formatting rule for your own custom conditional format. In the New Formatting Rule dialog box, you first select a rule type from the basic categories: format based on cell values; format cells that contain predefined items; format only top and bottom ranked values; format only above or below averages that you set; format only unique or duplicate values; or use a new formula to determine which cells to format. Depending upon the rule type selected, you can go on to edit the rule description.

You can also specify maximum and minimum ranges and how they will be reflected in terms of color. For example, you can select a value type number, percent, formula, or percentile for a minimum value, or use a range selector to pick a value directly from the worksheet. Then, to reflect the minimum range of value, you can use the drop-down menu to pick a color to reflect minimum values from among your theme colors, standard colors, or more colors.

After selecting a similar set of options for the maximum values, you can see a preview of the color spectrum at the bottom of the New Formatting Rule dialog box.

You can also use the Rules Manager to view the rules that are currently in force, and apply them to other columns, rows, or ranges of data.

In the Conditional Formatting Rules Manager, you can use a drop-down menu to select and see all of the current conditional formats applied to the current selection, the worksheet, or sheets in other open Excel files. By selecting any of these rules, you can edit its parameters, delete the rule from the list, or set an option to stop applying a selected rule if its condition is either true or false.

By changing the order of rules in the Rules Manager, you also determine priorities for your rules, so that if there is a conflict between two conditions in two different rules, the one listed first is applied and will supersede the second, even if both conditions are met.

For most users, the basic conditional formats that change font color and weight, applying bold for important values, will be sufficient. Many users will also opt for the more graphically rich data bars, color scales, and icon sets, and some will create and manage their own rules.

With any conditional format applied to your data, you can very quickly zero in on the major highs and lows, or whatever parameters you have set. Because the representation is visual, it is particularly useful for presentations or if/then scenarios. You can also print a worksheet with conditional formats as a report for colleagues and associates to highlight data trends and high and low values.

Using Conditional Formats with Rules

Conditional formats allow you to visually analyze and locate the most significant trends and values in your worksheet.

To make the data in your worksheet stand out according to the values, you can apply Conditional Formatting rules.

The Highlight Cells rule let you set rules that determine how the data in your cells will be formatted according to criteria that you enter. You can make cells reflect the values by changing the color or size of the font, or attributes such as bold or italic.

Excel comes with seven built-in rules categories that you can apply, or you can create your own rules and set formats for them. For example, default rules include values over a certain amount, under a certain amount, and relative to an average.

There are also six categories of Top/Bottom rules that you can quickly apply, or revise for your own needs. Some of these include the Top Ten Values, the Bottom Ten Values, and Top or Bottom percentages.

You can also add your own custom conditional formats according to your own parameters by selecting More Rules from the Conditional Formatting menu.

Using Conditional Formats with Rules

1 Click the Home tab.

2 Select the column or row that you want to compare (⇩ changes to ↓).

3 Click Conditional Formatting.

A drop-down list appears, displaying the main conditional formatting options.

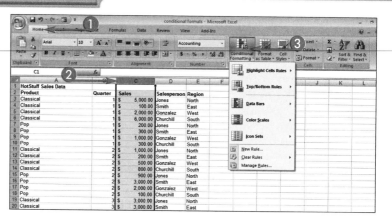

4 Click Highlight Cell Rules.

5 Click an option to compare.

This example selects the Greater Than option.

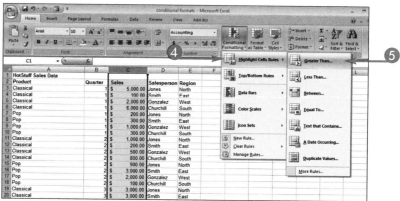

- A dialog box for the option you selected opens.

6 Enter a value to compare, or use the range selector (⊞) to pick one from the worksheet.

Note: For more information on the range selector, see Chapter 11.

- You can accept the suggested format or click the down arrow (▼) to choose another.

- Excel shows a live preview in the worksheet.

7 Click OK to set the rule and the format.

- Excel updates the column with your conditional format.

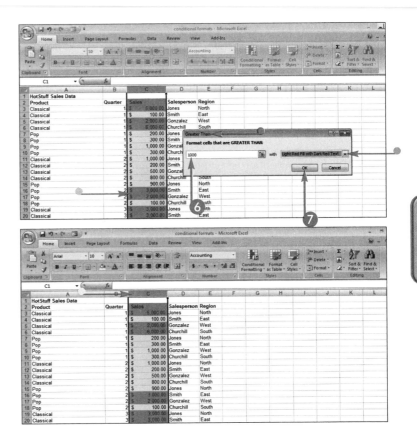

How do I clear a conditional format?

▼ The easiest way is to use the Undo button (🔄) if you have just set the format. Otherwise, select the column or row and click Conditional Formatting on the Home tab. Click Clear Rules and select to clear either the selected cells or all cells in the worksheet.

How do I change a conditional format that is already in place?

▼ Click Conditional Formatting in the Home tab. Click Manage Rules. In the Rules Manager, click to select the rule that you want to revise, and click Edit Rule. You can either change the rule parameters or click Format to change how the current parameters display.

Can I apply more than one condition?

▼ Yes. Once you have set one conditional format, you may add additional rules that highlight additional data; however, be careful about conflicts. Also, if you later apply the conditional formats with graphics, they will override the current rules and impose a different set of formats. For more information on the conditional formats with graphics, see the next task.

Using Conditional Formats with Graphics

There are several ways that conditional formats allow you to see and analyze the most significant trends and values In your worksheet.

Probably the most dramatic representation of data that you can use is the imposition of graphics on your data directly within a column, row, or range to make important values stand out.

To make the data in your worksheet stand out according to the graphics, you can apply conditional formatting data bars, color scales, or icon sets.

Each of these can give you an almost immediate representation of your data.

Data bars provide a miniature bar chart directly within the selected data that reflects the relative values.

Color scales show a spectrum of color intensity and different colors to represent the values that you have selected.

Icon sets enable you to review your data with symbols that reflect comparisons within the selected data. For example, upward trends can be shown by up arrows, and downward trends by down arrows. Traffic lights and other symbols are available to showcase your data, and you can use the More Rules feature to refine the representation of your data more specifically.

Using Conditional Formats with Graphics

① Click the Home tab.

② Select the column or row that you want to compare (⊕ changes to ↓).

③ Click Conditional Formatting.

The main conditional formatting options open.

④ Click Data Bars.

The Data Bars menu opens.

⑤ Move your mouse over a set of data bars to see a live preview in the worksheet.

⑥ Click to apply the data bars to the worksheet.

● Excel sets the data bars in the selected column.

7 Click Conditional Formatting.

The main conditional formatting options open.

8 Click Icon Sets.

The Icon Sets panel opens.

9 Move your mouse over an icon set to see a live preview in the worksheet.

10 Click to apply the icon set to the worksheet.

● Excel updates the column with your graphical conditional format.

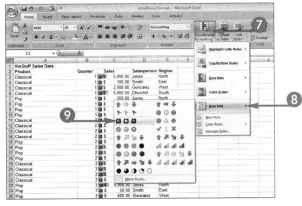

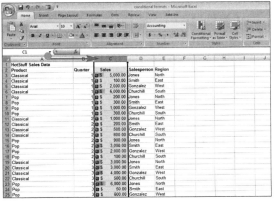

How do color scales differ from data bars and icon sets?

▼ Color scales impose a more subtle range of colors on the selected data. You can accept the color scale defaults or select the More Rules option from the Conditional Format menu to change the color scales that are applied to the data.

How do I manage conflicts between rules?

▼ Conditional formats are applied in order of precedence. To decide which rule has precedence, you move it up in the order that it appears in the Rules Manger. Click Conditional Formatting in the Home tab. From the menu that appears, click Manage Rules. In the Rules Manager, click to select the rule that you want to prevail in the conflict. Click the up arrow (⬆) or down arrow (⬇) to change the order of precedence for the selected rule in the Rules Manager hierarchy.

Can I create my rule before I select the data?

▼ Yes. While it is usually easier to create a rule based on existing data, you can create the rule parameters first and then apply them to one or more sets of data. Click Conditional Formatting in the Home tab. From the menu that appears, click New Rule. You can now use the Rules Manager to determine the precedence of the rule and the cells to which it applies.

Preview a Worksheet

You can use the Print Preview feature to see how your worksheet looks before you print it. Using the Print Preview feature can help you confirm any applied changes to options, thus saving you time and paper.

The Print Preview window indicates which page you are viewing and the total number of pages in your worksheet. If your worksheet contains more than one page, you can easily view the other pages. You can also magnify an area of a page in your worksheet to view it in more detail.

If you have a black-and-white printer, the pages in the Print Preview window display in black and white. If you have a color printer, the pages may display in color when you use the Print Preview window.

When you finish with the Print Preview feature, you can close the Print Preview window to return to your worksheet. You can also print your worksheet following the steps in the task "Print a Worksheet."

Preview a Worksheet

Display the Print Preview window

1 Click the Office button.

2 Move your mouse over Print.

3 Click Print Preview.

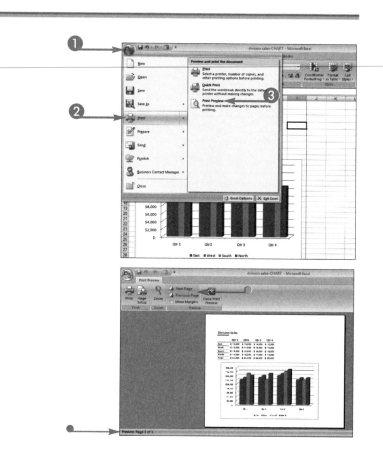

The Print Preview window appears.

● Excel indicates the current page, as well as the total number of pages in the worksheet.

● If the worksheet contains more than one page, you can click Next Page or Previous Page to view the next or previous page.

Magnify an area

④ Click Zoom.

● A magnified view of the area appears.

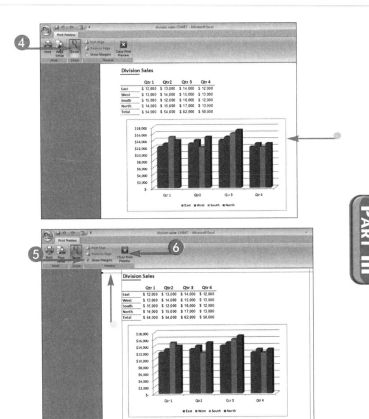

⑤ Click Show Margins (▢ changes to ☑).

Guidelines appear to show the page margins.

⑥ Click Close Print Preview to close the Print Preview window.

Excel does not display gridlines in the Print Preview window. Why not?

▼ By default, Excel does not print gridlines. To print gridlines, click Page Setup in the Print Preview window. Click the Sheet tab and then click the Gridlines option (▢ changes to ☑). Click OK. Excel displays your gridlines.

Can I change the margins in the Print Preview window?

▼ Yes. You can click Show Margins (▢ changes to ☑) to change the margins in the Print Preview window. Then click and drag the margin that you want to change to a new location.

How do I print my worksheet directly from the Print Preview window?

▼ Click Print. Excel returns to your worksheet and opens the Print dialog box. For information on printing, see the task "Print a Worksheet."

Why does the Print Preview window display only a chart from my worksheet?

▼ If you click a chart in your worksheet before you click the Print Preview command, the Print Preview window displays only the chart. To preview the worksheet, click outside the chart and then preview again.

Change Margins

You can change the margins to suit the layout of your Excel worksheet, to fit more or less data on a page, or to accommodate specialty paper. A *margin* is the amount of space between data and the top, bottom, left, or right edge of your paper. Excel automatically sets the default margins for top and bottom margins to 0.75 inch and the left and right margins to 0.7 inch.

For example, if you print on company letterhead, you may need to increase the size of the top margin. If you print on three-hole-punched paper, you may want to increase the size of the left margin.

Most printers cannot print right to the edge of a page and require that you set all margins to at least 0.25 inch. Consult your printer manual for more information on your printing capabilities.

To avoid wasting paper, consider previewing your document to ensure that your margins are correct before you print. For more information on the Preview feature, see the previous task, "Preview a Worksheet." For more information on printing your worksheet, see the task "Print a Worksheet."

Change Margins

① Click the Page Layout tab.

② Click Margins.

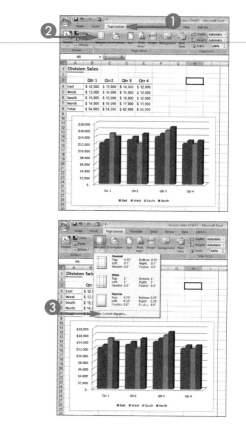

The Margin presets appear.

You can click a preset margin to apply it.

③ Click Custom Margins.

The Page Setup dialog box appears.

④ Click the Margins tab.

⑤ Type a value in the margin boxes that you want to change.

You can also click the spinner button (⊞) to incrementally change a value.

● You can click these options to center your data on the printed page (☐ changes to ☑).

⑥ Click Print Preview.

The page displays with the new margins.

You can click and drag a margin line to change margins.

The preview box reflects any changes that you make.

⑦ Click Page Setup to return to the Page Setup dialog box.

● You can click Print to print your worksheet.

⑧ Click Close Print Preview to accept the changes and return to the document.

Can I access and change settings for my printer?

▼ Yes. To view the available options for your particular printer, click Options in the Page Setup dialog box. The Properties dialog box appears for your printer. You can use this dialog box to select default options, such as the page orientation, for your printer. Make your changes and click OK to apply them.

What other margin settings can I change?

▼ You can also change the margins for the header and footer. The default header or footer margin setting is 0.3 inch. For information on adding headers and footers to your worksheet, see the task "Add a Header or Footer."

Can I make sure that certain rows or columns repeat on every page?

▼ Yes. Click Print Titles in the Page Setup group of the Page Layout tab on the Ribbon. In the Sheet tab of the Page Layout dialog box, you can set up columns or repeat at left or rows to repeat on top of each printed sheet. You can click Print or Print Preview, select more options, or click OK to exit the dialog box and set the new print options. For more information, see the task "Repeat Row or Column Headings."

What do the Center on page options do?

▼ Rather than change the margins, you can center the page to place it between the top and bottom or left and right margins. To do so, click the appropriate option (☐ changes to ☑).

Using Page Break Preview

Y ou can insert a page break when you want to start a new page at a specific place in your worksheet. A *page break* defines where one page ends and another begins.

By default, Excel automatically starts a new page by inserting a page break for you when you fill a page with data. However, you may need to insert your own page break to ensure that related data appears on the same page when you print your worksheet.

Inserting a horizontal page break above a row prints the rows below the break on a new page. Inserting a

vertical page break to the left of a column prints the columns to the right of the break on a new page.

Before you print your worksheet, you can preview all of the page breaks in the worksheet. In this view, page breaks inserted by Excel appear as dotted blue lines. Page breaks that you insert appear as solid blue lines. You can adjust the page breaks, as needed, in this view.

The page break lines do not print when you print the worksheet.

Using Page Break Preview

1 Click Page Break Preview (image).

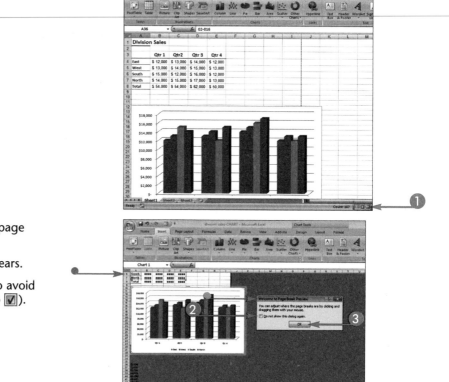

- Your worksheet appears in page break view.

- A Welcome dialog box appears.

2 Click this option if you want to avoid this dialog box (image changes to image).

3 Click OK.

- A blue indicator line appears on the screen. This line defines where one page ends and another begins.

④ You can change the page breaks by clicking the blue indicator line (↕ changes to ✛) and dragging the line.

- A gray guideline shows where the new page will break.

You can adjust the vertical break the same way by dragging the blue indicator line.

- To return to Normal view, click Normal View (▦).

- The page break appears in the worksheet as a dashed line.

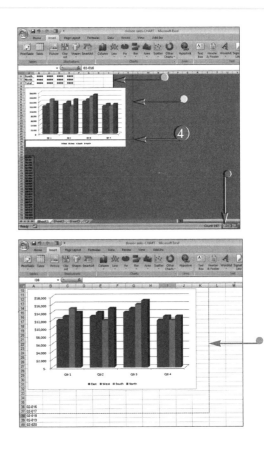

How do I remove a page break?

▼ Select a cell that is directly below or directly to the right of the page break that you want to remove. Click the Page Layout tab on the Ribbon, click Breaks in the Page Setup group, and then click Remove Page Break.

Can I remove all of the page breaks that I inserted in my worksheet at once?

▼ Yes. Click the blank area to the left of column A and above row 1 to select the entire worksheet. Click the Page Layout tab on the Ribbon, click Breaks in the Page Setup group, and then click Reset All Page Breaks.

Can I insert horizontal and vertical page breaks at the same time?

▼ Yes. Click the cell directly below and to the right of where you want the horizontal and vertical page breaks to appear. Click the Page Layout tab on the Ribbon, and click Breaks. Click Insert Page Break. Excel divides the worksheet into quadrants, with the selected cell as the top-right corner in the bottom-right quadrant. You can use this type of page break to divide a worksheet into pages both horizontally and vertically.

Fit a Worksheet to a Page or Pages

Excel allows you to reduce the size of printed data so that you can print your worksheet on a specific number of pages. This is useful when the last page of your worksheet contains a small amount of data that you want to fit on the previous page.

To change the size of printed data, you must specify how many pages you want the data to print across and down so that Excel can resize your data.

When you change the size of printed data, Excel ignores any inserted page breaks in your worksheet.

For information on page breaks, see the task "Using Page Break Preview."

Changing the size of printed data does not affect the way your worksheet appears on-screen. However, if you try to fit your worksheet on too few pages, the data may become too small to read. You may need to adjust the number of pages before Excel fits and prints your data correctly. Consider viewing your document with Print Preview before printing, as shown in the task "Preview a Worksheet." To print your worksheet, see the task "Print a Worksheet."

Fit a Worksheet to a Page or Pages

① Click the Page Layout tab.

Note: *See the task "Preview a Worksheet" to preview the results.*

② Click the Page Setup dialog box launcher (▣).

● To quickly lower the scale of the worksheet to fit the page, click the Scale spinner button (⬍) and type a lower number.

The Page Setup dialog box appears.

③ Click the Page tab.

④ Click Fit to (◉ changes to ◉).

⑤ Type the width and height of your data in pages.

⑥ Click OK.

Excel applies the new settings when you print the worksheet.

Note: *For more information on printing, see the task "Print a Worksheet."*

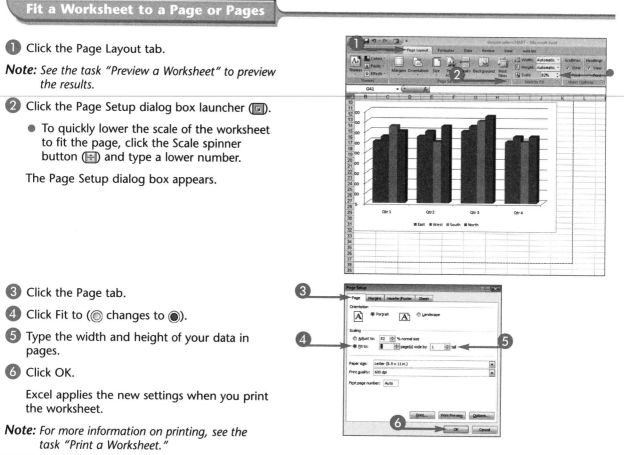

318

Repeat Row or Column Headings

I f your worksheet prints on more than one page, you can print the same row or column labels on every page.

Repeating row or column labels can help make the data in a long worksheet easier to understand. For example, repeating column labels in a worksheet containing product information can help you avoid confusing data in the "Quantity Sold" column with data in the "Quantity in Stock" column.

You need to select only one cell in each row or column of labels that you want to print on every

page. Repeating labels on printed pages does not affect the way your worksheet appears on the screen. You can use the Print Preview feature to preview how the repeated labels look when you print your worksheet. For more information, see the task "Preview a Worksheet."

Once you specify which row or column headings to repeat, you can print your worksheet. For more information, see the task "Print a Worksheet."

Repeat Row or Column Headings

1. Click the Page Layout tab.

2. Click Print Titles in the Page Setup group.

   • You can also click the Page Setup group dialog box launcher (□).

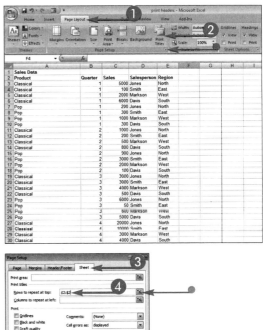

The Page Setup dialog box appears.

3. Click the Sheet tab if it is not selected.

4. Type the row or column references that you want to repeat.

   • You can also click the range selector (□) and then click the rows or columns in the worksheet.

5. Click OK.

   When you print the worksheet, Excel includes the specified rows and columns on each page.

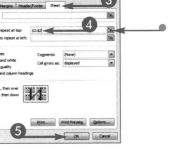

Add a Header or Footer

You can add a header or footer to display additional information on each page of your worksheet. A header or footer can contain information such as your name, the page number, and the current date.

By default, a header appears 0.3 inch from the top of a printed page, and a footer appears 0.3 inch from the bottom of a printed page. A worksheet can contain only one header and one footer. However, you can include both a header and footer on the same page.

Excel provides many header and footer elements from which you can choose. If your worksheet contains budget or financial information, you may want to choose a header that contains the word "Confidential." If you frequently update the data in your worksheet, you may want to choose a footer that includes the current date every time the worksheet is printed.

To see how a header or footer appears before you print your worksheet, you can use the Print Preview feature. For more information, see the task "Preview a Worksheet."

Add a Header or Footer

1️⃣ Click the Insert tab.

2️⃣ Click Header & Footer.

● A placeholder appears for the header.

● The Design tab of the Header & Footer Tools opens on the Ribbon.

3️⃣ Type in text for the header.

4 Scroll down through the document to the footer placeholder.

5 Enter text in the footer.

6 Click anywhere back in the worksheet to set the header and footer.

7 Click the Page Layout tab.

8 Click the Page Setup dialog box launcher (📷).

● The Page Setup dialog box appears.

9 Click the Header/Footer tab.

10 To view a list of headers that you can use, click the down arrow (▼) to display the Header or Footer drop-down list. Examples include pre-set page numbers, confidential, and file name and location.

You can click another header or footer that you want to use.

11 Click OK to close the Page Setup dialog box.

Note: To see how your header or footer appears before you print your worksheet, see the task "Print a Worksheet."

How do I remove a header or footer?

▼ Click the Insert tab on the Ribbon. Click Header & Footer. In the Design tab of the Header & Footer Tools, click Header or Footer. From the drop-down list that opens, click None.

Can I modify the text in the header or footer?

▼ Yes. You can click directly in the header or footer placeholder to select the text and revise it as you want. With the header or footer selected, you can also use the Design tab of the Header & Footer Tools on the Ribbon to add the date, time, file path, and other options to the header or footer. For additional options for pre-set headers and footers, you can click Header or Footer in the Header & Footer group of the Header & Footer Tools on the Ribbon.

How do I change where the header and footer print on the page?

▼ You can change the header or footer margins to print them further from or closer to the edge of the page. For information on changing margins, including header and footer margins, see the task "Change Margins."

Create a Custom Header or Footer

Excel includes several predefined headers and footers in the drop-down lists for headers and footers. To access these presets, you can click Header or Footer in the Header & Footer group of the Header & Footer Tools on the Ribbon. Presets are also available in the Header/Footer tab of the Page Setup dialog box, which you can open using the dialog box launcher in the Page Setup group.

If none suits your needs, you can create a custom header or footer. Custom headers and footers include three sections in which you can enter text: a left section, a center section, and a right section. You can enter text in any of the sections, as needed.

The Header & Footer Tools Design tab also includes groups for formatting text, or inserting workbook and worksheet information such as the number of pages, the name of the workbook, or the current date.

Custom footers use the default margins: a header appears 0.3 inch from the top of a printed page, and a footer appears 0.3 inch from the bottom of a printed page. A worksheet can contain only one header and one footer. However, you can include both a header and footer on the same page.

To see how a custom header or footer appears before you print your worksheet, you can use the Print Preview feature. For more information, see the task "Preview a Worksheet."

Create a Custom Header or Footer

① Scroll in the worksheet to the header or footer placeholder.

② Click to select text in the header or footer that you created.

③ Click the Home tab.

④ Use the formatting tools to change the appearance of your header and footer.

Note: *See Chapter 9 for more information on formatting the header or footer text.*

⑤ Click the Design tab of the Header & Footer Tools on the Ribbon.

⑥ Click in the right or left placeholder of the header or footer.

⑦ Click Page Number or another option in the Design tab.

● Excel adds the option as a field to the header.

⑧ Click in the worksheet to set your new header or footer.

● The header or footer appears in the worksheet in the way it will print.

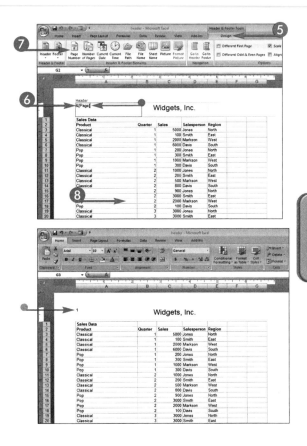

My custom header runs into the data in my worksheet. What can I do?

▼ You can increase the top or bottom margin to allow more space for a header or footer. Click the Page Layout tab of the Ribbon. Click the Page Setup dialog box launcher (▣) to display the Page Setup dialog box. Then click the Margins tab. Double-click the Top or Bottom area and type a larger number. Then click OK. For more information, see the task "Change Margins."

How do I make the header or footer read "Page 1"?

▼ Type the word **Page** and a space before the field code that Excel puts into the header and footer to include the page number.

What other elements can I include in the header or footer from the dialog box buttons?

▼ You can also include the date, time, workbook name, or worksheet name by clicking the appropriate buttons in the dialog box.

Change Page Orientation

Y ou can change the page orientation and thus the direction that a worksheet prints on a page.

Excel allows you to print worksheets using the portrait or landscape orientation. By default, Excel prints worksheets in portrait orientation. This orientation is useful for printing worksheets that have more rows than columns. When you have a worksheet with more columns than rows, you can print the worksheet in landscape orientation, which rotates the worksheet so that the data prints across the long side of a page.

Changing the page orientation only affects the displayed worksheet. It does not affect your other

worksheets or workbooks, or the way the current worksheet appears on your screen.

To make sure that your orientation change does not adversely affect the elements in your worksheet, you can use Print Preview to see how the worksheet appears when printed. For more information on Print Preview, see the task "Preview a Worksheet."

After you change your page orientation, you can print your worksheet. For more information, see the task "Print a Worksheet."

Change Page Orientation

① Click the Page Layout tab.

② Click Orientation.

③ Click Landscape.

Excel uses the new orientation.

Change Print Options

You can use the print options that Excel offers to change the way your worksheet appears on a printed page. Changing the print options for your worksheet allows you to create a printout that suits your needs.

You can select the Gridlines option to have Excel print lines around each cell in a worksheet. This can help make the data in a large worksheet easier to read.

The Black and white option prints a colored worksheet in black and white, which is useful when you have a color printer but want to print a black-and-white draft of a worksheet.

The Draft quality option helps reduce printing time because it quickly prints a rough draft of a worksheet without gridlines and most graphics.

When you click the Row and column headings option, Excel prints the row numbers and column headings in your worksheet.

Changing the print options only changes the way your worksheet appears on a printed page, and not the appearance of your worksheet on the screen.

After you select the options you want, you can print your worksheet. For more information, see the task "Print a Worksheet."

Change Print Options

1 Click the Page Layout tab.

2 Click Print Titles.

● You can also click the Page Setup dialog box launcher (▣).

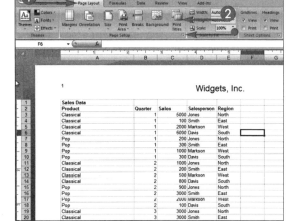

The Page Setup dialog box appears.

3 Click the Sheet tab.

4 Click each print option that you want to apply (☐ changes to ☑).

5 Click OK.

Excel applies the new settings when you print the worksheet.

Note: To print a worksheet, see the task "Print a Worksheet."

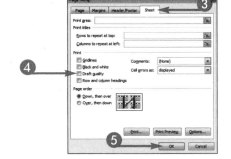

Print a Worksheet

Y ou can produce a paper copy of a worksheet that you display on your screen. This is useful when you want to present the worksheet to a colleague or refer to the worksheet when you do not have access to your computer.

If you have more than one printer installed on your computer, you can choose which printer you want to print your worksheet. Before printing, make sure that you turn on the printer and that it contains an adequate supply of paper and toner or ink.

Excel allows you to specify the part of your workbook that you want to print. You can print a selection of cells, an entire worksheet, or all of the worksheets in the workbook. To print a selection of cells, you must select the cells before you follow the steps in this task.

If the part of the workbook that you want to print contains several pages, you can specify which pages you want to print.

1 Click the Office button.

2 Move your mouse over Print.

3 Click Print.

The Print dialog box appears.

4 To select another printer, click the down arrow ($\boxed{\blacktriangledown}$) to display the Printer drop-down list.

5 Click a Print what option (◎ changes to ◉).

To print only selected cells, select the cells, perform Steps 1 to 5, and then click Selection.

5 ➤

● To print a certain page range, you can click Page(s) (◎ changes to ◉) and type the range of pages that you want to print.

6 Click OK.

Excel prints the worksheet.

6 ➤

Can I print multiple copies of a worksheet?

▼ You can print multiple copies of a worksheet, workbook, or selection of cells. In the Print dialog box, double-click the Number of copies field, and then type the number of copies that you want to print.

Can I print more than one worksheet in my workbook?

▼ Yes. Press the Ctrl key as you click the tab for each worksheet that you want to print. Then perform Steps 1 to 6 in this task, but click Active sheet(s) in Step 5 (◎ changes to ◉).

How do I print only a selected number of cells?

▼ Select the cells that you want to print. Perform Steps 2 and 3 in this task. Click the Selection option (◎ changes to ◉) in the Print dialog box and then click OK.

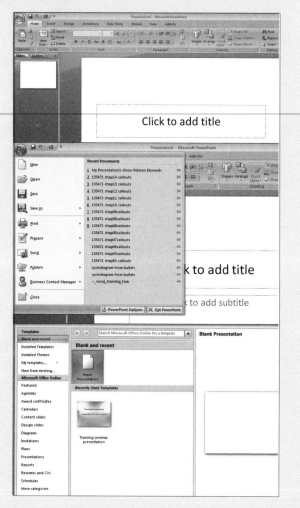

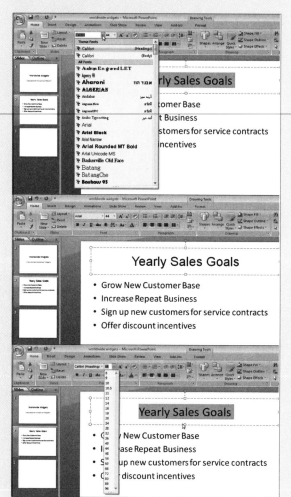

PART IV
USING POWERPOINT

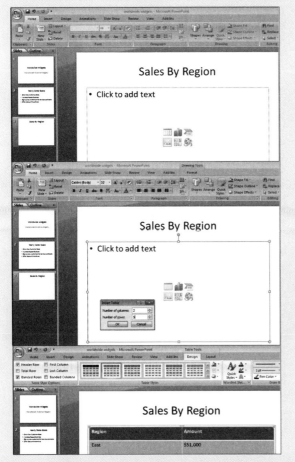

An Introduction to PowerPoint

PowerPoint helps you plan, organize, design, and deliver professional presentations. Using PowerPoint, you can use a computer screen, the Web, 35 mm slides, or overhead transparencies to deliver a presentation. Your presentation can also be projected over one or more screens to different sizes and types of audiences. PowerPoint also allows you to create handouts for the audience and speaker notes to help you when delivering the presentation.

For more information on PowerPoint, you can visit www.microsoft.com/powerpoint.

Create Presentations

PowerPoint offers several ways to create a presentation. By default, when you start the program, PowerPoint creates a blank presentation. You can start from scratch, adding the slides and formatting that suit your particular presentation needs. You can also use Installed Templates, Installed Themes, or templates from Microsoft Online to begin your own presentation. You can replace sample content in the templates with your own.

You can also edit and save PowerPoint presentations like any other Office document, which allows you to revise a slide show quickly and to customize it for a target audience without having to output actual 35 mm slides.

Creating and Editing Slides

A presentation is made up of slides, using the metaphor from the days of 35 mm slide projectors. With PowerPoint, as you build a presentation, you add the slides, selecting from various layouts. Each layout has a placeholder for text or other objects. You can add the text and objects to create the slides. You can also edit the content as needed.

When you create or edit a presentation, you can choose among several different views: Normal view for working on the slide content; Slide Sorter view for rearranging, deleting, and adding slides; and Slide Show for previewing a slide. There is also a side pane that toggles between Slide Thumbnails and Outline view for developing the content in outline format and viewing the organization.

Add Objects to Slides

Most slides contain other items besides text, and PowerPoint enables you to add several different types of objects to a slide. For example, you may want to display a table of information. You can also add a chart, which is useful for displaying trends, showing the relationship of numeric data, and illustrating other main points. Office includes a separate charting program that you access from PowerPoint to create and add charts to a slide. You can also use Office's built-in diagramming program to add diagrams such as organization charts or flow charts.

In addition to tables and charts, you can also add graphic elements to a slide, including AutoShapes, pictures, clip art images, and WordArt, which creates special text effects. You can use these elements to enhance the slide or to make a particular point. For example, you can include pictures of your products, or, in a company meeting, include pictures of your company's executives. PowerPoint also includes an assortment of SmartArt graphics to convey important ideas and messages with visual metaphors.

Enhance a Presentation

You can make a slide stand out and grab your audience's attention in several ways. You can emphasize text on a slide using common text styles including bold, italic, underline, or shadow. You can change the font, font size, or color of text. You can also use one of PowerPoint's many ready-to-use designs to give all of the slides a consistent format. You can still make changes to individual slides, but the design automatically makes key formatting changes. As another alternative, you can select from several color schemes to enhance a presentation.

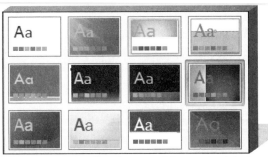

The most comprehensive set of formatting choices are PowerPoint Themes. You can change the colors, fonts, and effects associated with a theme, save a new theme, and apply a theme to a presentation to give it a distinctive look.

You can use special effects such as a chart, object, or audio clip on your slide. Animation can help emphasize important points and keep the audience's attention throughout the presentation.

You can add graphs and charts directly in PowerPoint or link to an Excel worksheet and chart. You can also add SmartArt graphics and diagrams that help you tell a story visually. You can use Shapes to call attention to individual aspects of your slides, and you can use the Shape Styles in the Format tab of the Drawing Tools on the Ribbon to add custom fills, outlines, and effects to your Shapes and SmartArt diagrams.

PowerPoint's shape effects include glows, 3D, bevels, soft edges, shadows, and reflections that can enhance your slides and give them a professional look.

You can also add pictures, sound, and movies to your slides to create a multimedia presentation. When you add one or more images to a slide, the Picture Tools can crop or recolor the picture, and PowerPoint slides support transparent image formats like GIF and PNG.

Movies and sounds can be played automatically when a slide appears or be controlled with a mouse click. You can also use tracks from an audio CD in the CD ROM or DVD drive of your computer as background music or narration for your slides. With a microphone configured in your computer, you can add narration to individual slides, which you can play during the slide show or use as part of a self-running presentation.

Fine-tune Your Presentation

After you finish the individual slides, you need to step back and consider the overall presentation.

You may want to fine-tune your presentation by checking its organizational flow and rearranging the slides so that you present your ideas in a logical order. You can also check the spelling, create a summary slide, and add transitions.

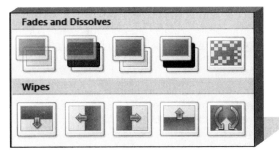

You can create and refer to speaker notes to help keep you focused as you give the presentation. You can also create handouts so that your audience has something to take with them or to refer to during the presentation.

You may also have special considerations for setting up the presentation, depending on whether you are printing the presentation, giving the presentation as a slideshow, or broadcasting the presentation over the Web.

The Slide Show tab of the Ribbon lets you prepare for the actual delivery. You can decide on how long the show should run. You can hide slides to shorten the running time, rehearse timings, and determine the screen resolutions for projecting the slide show.

PowerPoint also has other ways to prepare for your presentation. The Notes pages can be used for your own rehearsal, or as handouts with supplemental information. If you have a dual monitor output on your computer, you can use Presenter View to maintain a screen with your notes as your presentation is sent to a projector, allowing you to monitor your progress and be prepared for what is coming up next.

PART IV

Create a Blank Presentation

PowerPoint is a program that helps you plan, organize, and design professional presentations.

Each time you start PowerPoint, you see a blank presentation, with one slide. You can start building the presentation from scratch, adding slides as you need them. You create a blank presentation when you know what style, content, and formatting options you want, or when none of the design templates match your needs.

If you do not want to start from scratch, you can create a new presentation using the installed templates, installed themes, and templates on Microsoft Office Online. These options are available in the New Presentation window. For more

information, see the task "Using Online Content Presentations."

How do I get PowerPoint to appear on the first panel of the Start menu?

▼ Click Start, click All Programs, and then click Microsoft Office. Right-click Microsoft PowerPoint or any other Office program and select Pin to Start Menu. It now appears in the first panel when you click the Start button.

Create a Blank Presentation

1. Click Start.
2. Click All Programs.
3. Click Microsoft Office.
4. Click Microsoft Office PowerPoint 2007.

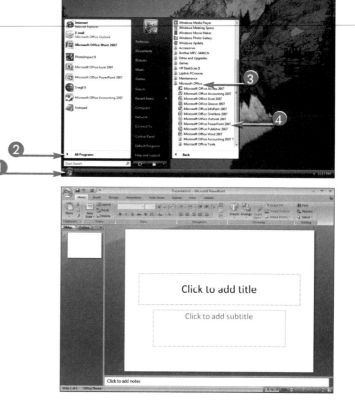

The Microsoft PowerPoint window appears.

PowerPoint creates a blank presentation.

Note: *To close the PowerPoint program, click the Close button ([×]). For more information on closing programs, see Chapter 2.*

Parts of the PowerPoint Screen

The PowerPoint screen displays several items to help you perform tasks efficiently.

A Title Bar

Displays the name of the program and the presentation. If you have not saved the presentation, you see the default name of Presentation1.

B Contextual Ribbon

Contains buttons to help you select common commands, such as Save and Print.

C Ribbon Tabs

Selecting a Ribbon tab opens up a different set of features and options.

D Outline Tab/Slides Tab

Lets you switch between Outline and Slides view.

E View Buttons

Allow you to quickly change the way the presentation displays on the screen.

F Status Bar

Provides information about the slide displayed on the screen and the current presentation.

G Notes Pane

Displays the speaker notes for the current slide.

H Slide Pane

Displays the current slide.

I Zoom Slider

Lets you zoom out of your presentation to see more cells, or zoom in for more detail.

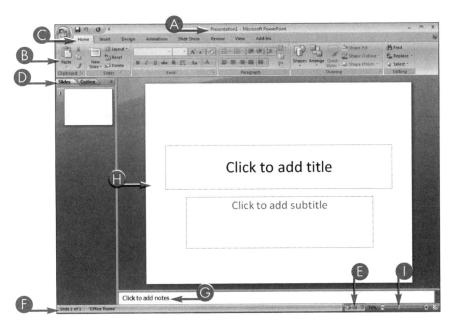

Explore the PowerPoint Ribbon

The PowerPoint 2007 Ribbon has several main components, each of which enables the user to perform specific tasks for producing professional presentations.

Clicking one of the tabs brings up a different set of related options for a particular task, and selecting a portion of a presentation brings up more contextual options.

With the Ribbon, you can work with parts of a presentation or the entire presentation to make formatting changes, reorganize sections, add references, and go through a final review process to make sure that your presentation is polished and professional.

Home
You can use the Home tab to change the fonts, paragraph, or styles of selected parts of your presentation. The Home tab also lets you copy and paste to and from the Clipboard and apply formats from one selection to another. Find and Select in the Home tab let you quickly change one word or phrase to another. The Home tab in PowerPoint also has features that let you add a new slide, change its layout, reset a layout, and delete slides. You can also add simple shapes to your slides, and arrange them from front to back or vertically and horizontally. You can change the appearance of the shapes with fills, outlines, effects, and Quick Styles.

Insert
The Insert tab lets you place important elements in your presentation to supplement the text and figures. Tables can help you organize data or text in a clear visual way that makes it easy to understand. You can also insert pictures, clip art, shapes, SmartArt, and charts to create professional-looking worksheets. The Insert tab has a Chart section that lets you create many different kinds of charts to visualize data more effectively. You can also quickly manage hyperlinks to create action settings for navigation to other slides or presentations. The Insert tab also lets you put text boxes, headers and footers, WordArt, symbols, related information, and other objects into your slides.

Design
The Design tab lets you set options for the orientation and dimensions of your slides.

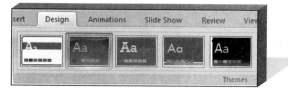

You can use, create, design, and save themes that make your slides look more professional and visually exciting. These include coordinated colors, fonts, and effects that make it more convenient to reformat the look of a set of slides or the entire presentation. You can also create backgrounds for selected slides that can include images, patterns, or color gradients.

Animations

The Animations tab lets you create and preview a set of timings for one or more slides. This enables you to have elements in the slide appear when and how you want them to, and so increase the effectiveness of your message. You can also select and apply a set of preset transition effects that create movement between slides as you present them. You can set the speed and duration of your animations and transitions, and preview them in the Animations tab. You can also determine whether slides or parts of slides advance when the speaker clicks a mouse, or automatically for a self-running presentation.

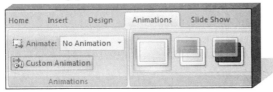

Slide Show

In the Slide Show tab you can determine how you want to play or preview your presentation as it is shown full screen on a monitor or through a projector. You can set the resolution of the show to match a monitor or projector, record narration, rehearse the animation and timings that you set in the Animation tab, and set various slides to be hidden or revealed during a given slide show. You can also create a custom show or preset group of slides from the current presentation to run in a different order. Presenter view lets you use a dual monitor configuration so that you can see your notes and present the slide show simultaneously.

Review

The Review tab lets you run spelling and grammar checks and perform a number of research functions, including translation and accessing a thesaurus. You can use the Review tab to handle markups by multiple reviewers, to protect and share a presentation, and to track changes, all in order to collaborate and edit a presentation into a final version. You can also protect your presentation in the Review tab.

View

The main presentation views are enabled in the View tab, along with the ability to show or hide rulers and gridlines, and to zoom or fit the presentation in a window. Slide, Handout, and Notes Masters are available as blueprints to help you manage and reformat those elements. Switching between windows of open presentations or viewing them on the same screen lets you work with more than one presentation at a time. The View tab also lets you manage and record macros.

Add-Ins

The Add-Ins tab is mainly for additional features created by developers and third parties. If you need to load pre-programmed code, templates, or other programs that work with PowerPoint, or to de-activate them, you can use the Add-Ins tab. Keep in mind that you may not see all of the tabs or features within any tab if you are running in Compatibility Mode (Office 97-2003).

Using Online Content Presentations

You can use the Online Content Presentations to quickly create a compete presentation.

The Online Content Presentations offer several broad categories of presentations, including Academic, Business, Health Care, Training, and others. In each case, you download a complete presentation with cues on what to add, and you can revise the presentation for your own needs.

After you select a category, you can then choose the presentation that most closely matches the goal or message of your planned presentation. You can also select from training presentations and other

presentations that you use for learning, and you can modify them for your own purposes. For example, you can modify the slides by selecting, adding, and editing the text.

Using the Online Content Presentations is a great way to get started with PowerPoint, and often to get ideas for the show that you are producing. You need a live Internet connection to download the Online Content Presentations and work with them.

Later on, you can use the templates and themes in PowerPoint to create a new blank document based on an installed design template or coordinated theme. For more information on creating a blank presentation, see Chapter 2.

Using Online Content Presentations

① Click the Office button.

② Click New.

The New Presentation window opens.

● You see options for blank, recent, and recently used presentation.

③ Click Presentations.

④ Click a category.

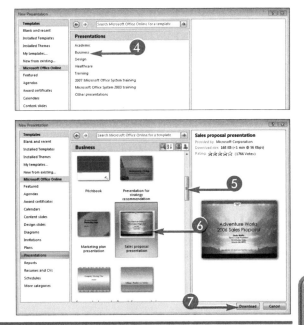

⑤ Scroll down to select a specific presentation.

⑥ Click the presentation that you want to work with.

⑦ Click Download.

A dialog box may remind you that you need to be running a genuine version of Windows.

⑧ Click Continue to receive the download.

MASTER IT

Besides the complete presentations, what is in the other online content for PowerPoint?

▼ There are individual content slides along with many different types of presentations, such as calendars, agendas, diagrams reports, and more. Most are individual slides to which you need to add similar slides with your own content for a complete presentation. Some of these have different screen sizes for different purposes, and many have unique designs and backgrounds to enhance a slide show.

How do I know whether to use a template or to start from scratch when I create a presentation?

▼ When you already have the content, you can use an installed design template or theme, which includes the formatting for the slide presentation, but not the content. You can also use templates or themes when you have content, but want some help with formatting. You can create a blank presentation and start from scratch when you know what style, content, and formatting options you want, or when none of the design templates match your needs. For more information, see the task "Create a Blank Presentation."

What is the difference between Installed Templates and Installed Themes?

▼ Because PowerPoint is so visual, the program lets you design slides in different ways. Installed Templates can contain a number of additional elements, such as shapes and pictures, to make a series of slides look exciting. Installed Themes are coordinated sets of colors, fonts, and effects that work with the elements of your slides to make them consistent. Themes do not contain additional elements but can affect the look of elements that you add. For more information, see Chapter 16.

continued

Using Online Content
Presentations *(Continued)*

When you download an Online Content Presentation, it opens in the PowerPoint Editor so that you can revise it.

Depending upon the topic of the presentation that you chose to download, you will see sample text prompting you for new ideas and content that you could use in a similar presentation.

You can modify the presentation for your own use, beginning with the techniques later in this chapter. You can also view how the slides look in Slide Sorter view and select, move, add, or delete slides. For more information, see the task "Add a Slide."

You can also practice viewing and running a final slide show with the content presentation that you downloaded and saved. When you run the presentation, it displays full screen, and you can click through the slides as you would in front of an audience. You can also connect your output to a projector to see how it would look on a larger screen.

You can save the presentation to your own computer under a new name to keep working with it. For more information, see the task "Save and Close a Document" in Chapter 2.

Using Online Content Presentations *(continued)*

A complete presentation is available in the PowerPoint Editor.

⑨ Click Slide Sorter View (⊞).

Note: *You can revise the slides in Normal view using the techniques later in this chapter.*

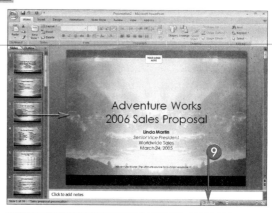

PowerPoint shows thumbnails of all of the slides in the presentation.

⑩ Click Slide Show (▤).

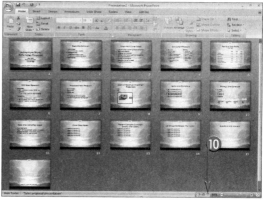

The presentation plays full screen.

You can click your mouse or use the arrow keys to advance through the slide show.

⑪ Press Esc to return to the PowerPoint Editor.

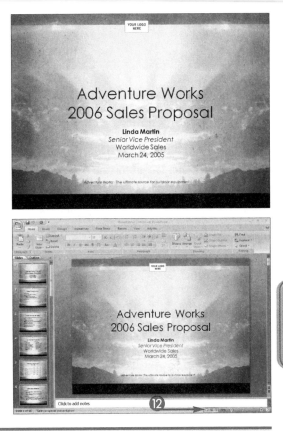

PowerPoint returns to the previous view from which you began the show.

⑫ To return to Normal view, click Normal (▭).

Why would I use Slide Sorter view instead of the slide thumbnails panel?

▼ Slide Sorter view gives you a more complete picture of your entire show, and you can zoom in and out to see greater detail and more slides. Many users find it easier to see the overall message in Slide Sorter view and to select one or more slides for formatting and other options.

Why do you call it the PowerPoint Editor?

▼ The main PowerPoint program is the Editor, which lets you create, add, and modify slides in many different ways. However, in most cases the slides are meant to be shown at full screen, either on a monitor or projector. When you click Slide Show, you leave the Editor and you lose its features but you can display your slides the way you want, and use them for speaker support or as a self-running show. You can practice and rehearse how you will present your slides.

Can I add or change the footer text on my slides later?

▼ Yes. Click the Insert tab and then click Header and Footer. For more information, see Chapter 17.

Add a Slide

Y ou can insert a new slide into your presentation to add a new topic that you want to discuss. PowerPoint inserts the new slide after the current slide on your screen.

By default, PowerPoint adds a bulleted list slide, but you can select another layout for the new slide. Using a slide layout saves you from having to arrange and position items on a slide. PowerPoint provides several slide layouts, each with certain areas for different types of content to suit the purpose of the slide. For

example, formal presentations about a company's performance would use plenty of text and financial graphics, while a 50th anniversary presentation would need more room for pictures and not nearly as much text.

If you select a slide layout that does not suit your needs, you can change the layout later. After PowerPoint adds a new slide to your presentation, you can add the items that you want to appear on the slide.

Add a Slide

Add a slide

1 Click the Home tab.

2 Display the slide that you want to appear before the new slide.

Note: *If your presentation has multiple slides, you can use the slide navigation arrows and scroll bar to display the slide.*

3 Click New Slide to add a new slide.

● PowerPoint adds a title and bulleted list slide with a content panel.

Note: *If you have used a design template, the slide uses its features.*

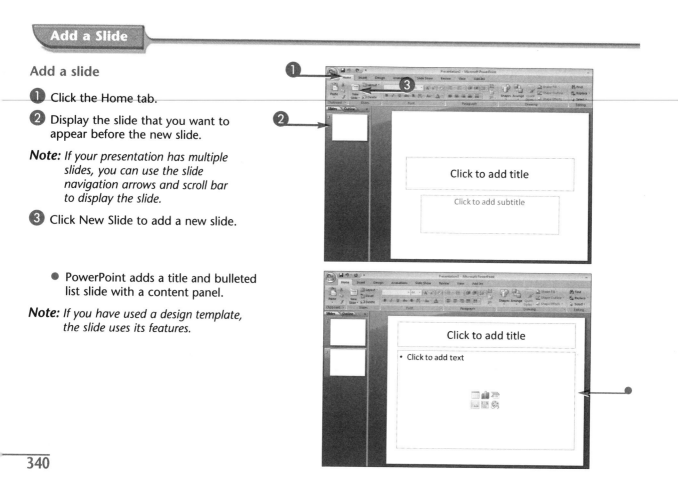

Add a slide with a different layout

1️⃣ Click the Home tab.

2️⃣ Click the New Slide down arrow (▾).

The Office Themes gallery opens.

3️⃣ Click another layout for your new slide.

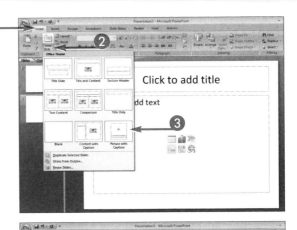

● PowerPoint creates a new slide with the selected layout.

What slide layouts are available?

▼ You can select nine types of layouts, or Office Themes, including text layouts, text and content layouts, title slides, and blank slides. For more information, see the task "Using Slide Layouts."

Can I insert a duplicate slide?

▼ Yes. Select the slide that you want to duplicate, click the New Slide down arrow (▾), and then click Duplicate Selected Slides. For a set of selected slides, select them from the slide thumbnails or go to Slide Sorter view to select them.

What is the purpose of the icons in the sample layouts?

▼ Each icon represents a placeholder for an object that you can insert in the slide. For example, the title placeholder looks like a dark bar, and chart placeholders look like mini-charts.

How do I delete a slide?

▼ The easiest way to delete a slide is to select it in the Slides panel, and either press Delete, or click Delete on the Slides group on the Home tab of the Ribbon.

Select
Text

Before changing text in a presentation, you often need to select the text with which you intend to work. For example, you must select the text that you want to move, delete, or change to a new font. PowerPoint allows you to select a single word, a bullet point, any amount of text, or an entire slide, and it highlights your selected text on your screen.

The Normal view allows you to select and work with text on all of the slides in your presentation or just the current slide. When you want to work with and select

large portions of your presentation at once, consider using Outline view. For more information on the various views in PowerPoint, see Chapter 18.

After you finish working with selected text, deselect the text. If you begin typing within selected text, PowerPoint replaces the selected text with the text you type.

PowerPoint contains text on a slide in a text placeholder or text box. You may often need to select the text box, for example, if you want to move text around on the slide.

Select Text

Select a word

1 Double-click the word that you want to select.

The word is selected.

To deselect text, click outside the selected area.

Select a bullet point

1 Click the bullet beside the point that you want to select.

That bullet point is selected.

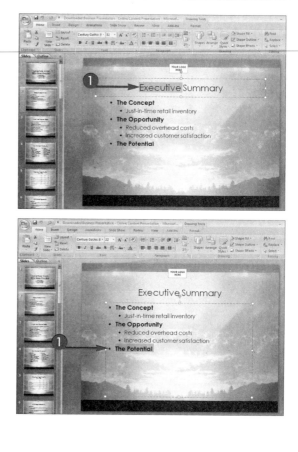

Select text

1 Position your cursor over the first word that you want to select.

2 Drag your cursor over the text that you want to select.

The text is selected.

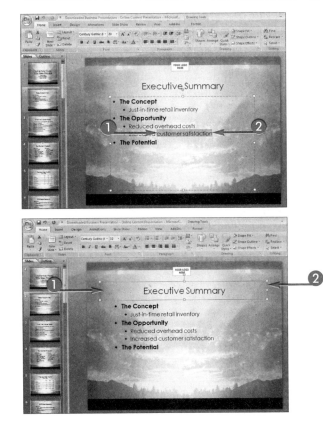

Select a text box

1 Click the text box that you want to select.

The dashed selection box makes the text box active for resizing or moving.

2 Click the edge of the text box again.

The solid selection box makes the text in the text box active for formatting.

PART IV

Can I select text using the keyboard?

▼ Yes. To select characters, press the Shift key as you press the left-arrow or right-arrow key. To select words, press Shift+Ctrl as you press the left-arrow or right-arrow key.

How do I select all of the text in my presentation?

▼ Click the text in the Outline pane and then press Ctrl+A. You can also click Edit and then click Select All.

How do I select all of the text on the current slide?

▼ Click a blank area on the slide in the Slides pane and then press Ctrl+A. PowerPoint displays a thick border around all of the selected text rather than highlighting it.

Can I select text in other views?

▼ You can select text in Outline view as you would select text in the Normal view. You cannot select text in the Slide Sorter view. For more information on the views, see Chapter 18.

Add and Edit Text

You can change the text on a PowerPoint slide very easily. When you create a new slide, PowerPoint includes text placeholders for the different text items on that particular slide. These placeholders vary, depending on the particular layout. You can replace the placeholders with your text. For more information, see the task "Using Slide Layouts."

The Online Content Presentations and other templates or files may supply sample text. You can replace the placeholders or sample text with your text.

If you have already placed text in your presentation, PowerPoint also lets you edit this text. This is useful when you need to correct a mistake, update the information on a slide, or remove text that you no longer need from your presentation. PowerPoint allows you to delete a character, word, bullet point, or entire slide. You can also add text to the existing text if you need to provide more content on a slide.

Add and Edit Text

Add text

1 Click in the text placeholder.

● The filler text disappears, and the insertion point appears in the text placeholder or text box.

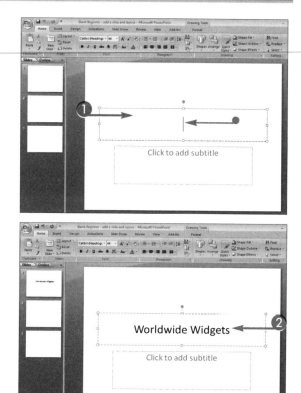

2 Type the new text.

The text is added to the slide.

3 Click outside the text placeholder to deselect it.

You can repeat Steps 1 to 3 for each text placeholder on the slide.

PowerPoint updates the slide as you continue to add new text.

Replace existing text

1 Select the text that you want to replace with new text.

Note: For information on selecting text, see the task "Select Text."

2 Type the new text.

The text that you type replaces the selected text.

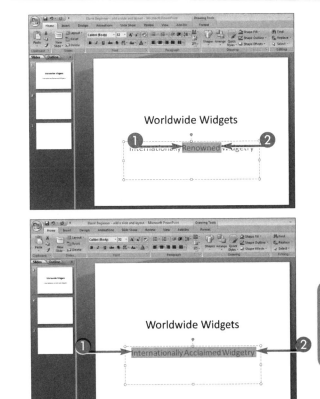

Delete text

1 Select the text that you want to delete.

2 Press Delete to remove the text.

To delete one character at a time, you can click to the right of the first character that you want to delete, and then press Backspace or Delete once for each character that you want to delete.

Why do some words in my presentation display a red underline?

▼ If PowerPoint does not recognize a word in your presentation, it considers the word misspelled and underlines the word with a red line. To spell check your presentation in order to remove the red underlines, see Chapter 18.

Can I edit text in other views?

▼ You can edit text in Outline view the same way that you edit text in Slides view. You cannot edit text in the Slide Sorter view. For more information on the views, see the task "Change Views" in Chapter 18.

What happens if I do not fill in a text placeholder?

▼ You will see the "Click to add" text in an incomplete placeholder in the PowerPoint Editor, but if you display the slide full screen, nothing appears in that area.

Can I insert a new bullet on my slide?

▼ Yes. If you forgot to include an item when you created your presentation, you can add a new point to a slide. To add an item to a bulleted list, press Enter after the last item and then type the new item.

Move or Copy Text

You can move text in your presentation to reorganize your ideas. You can also copy text from one location in your presentation to another.

When you move text, the text is removed from its original location in your presentation. For example, you most often move an entire text box, with all of the text in that area. You can also move a word, phrase, or bulleted point. For information on rearranging a slide, see Chapter 18.

Before you can move text, you must select the text or text box that you want to move. A solid line or dotted insertion point indicates the location of your text as you are moving it. When you move a text box, you see an outline of the text box as you drag it to its new location.

Copying text saves you time because you do not have to retype the text. When you copy text, the text appears in both the original and new locations.

Move or Copy Text

1. Select the text or text box that you want to move or copy.

2. To move or copy partial text, position your cursor anywhere over the selected text; to move or copy an entire text box, place your cursor on any border of the text box (◌ changes to ✛).

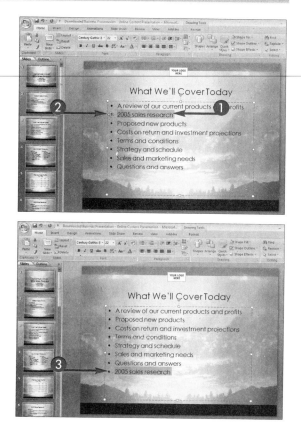

3. Drag your cursor where you want to place the text.

   To copy text, you can hold down the Ctrl key as you perform Step 3.

   PowerPoint moves or copies the text.

Resize, Add, or Delete Text Boxes

When you create a new slide, the layout determines which text boxes PowerPoint includes on a slide, as well as the size of the text box. You can also adjust the size of the text box. For example, if you need to make the text box larger, you can do so to allow for more text. If a text box is too big, you can make it smaller to make room for other items that you want to include, such as a chart or table.

You can also draw new text boxes on-screen so that you can add text to any location on the slide, regardless of the original text placeholders. For example, you may want more areas of text than the sample layouts include.

If you do not need a particular text box, you can delete it from the slide layout. PowerPoint deletes the text box and all of the text inside it.

Resize, Add, or Delete Text Boxes

Resize a text box

1 Click the text box that you want to resize.

2 Click a selection handle and drag it to resize the text box (⬚ changes to ⟷).

The text box is resized.

Add a text box

1 Click the Insert tab.

2 Click Text Box.

3 Click and drag to draw the text box (⬚ changes to +).

The text box is added.

Delete a text box

1 Click the text box.

2 Press Delete.

PowerPoint deletes the text box.

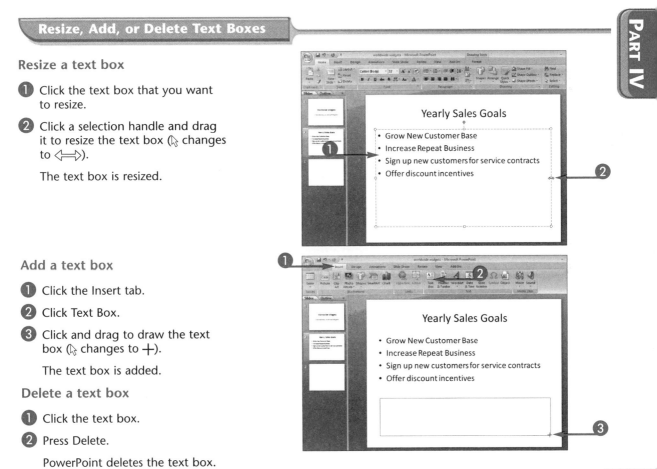

Using Slide Layouts

When you insert a new slide, PowerPoint creates it with a default title and content layout, providing one placeholder for a title and another for a set of bullets, or another type of content.

You can quickly reconfigure a slide to be one of the other eight preset content or Office Theme layouts. This makes it easier to place your text, tables, pictures, diagrams, charts, or other items in a predesigned layout that looks professional and clean.

A Title Slide layout creates a pre-designed title slide for your presentation. The Section Header layout lets you break up your presentation into topics. Title Only and Blank layouts give you the freedom to create your own

slides from scratch. Content or Picture with Caption layouts allow you to create cleanly designed slides without text clutter. Two Content and Comparison layouts give you the ability to add multiple tables, charts, diagrams, and other elements to your slides.

Once a layout is set, you can use the selection handles on the placeholders to make some areas smaller, others larger, and to move them around. To return to the last basic layout that you applied to the slide, you can click Reset in the Slides group of the Home tab of the Ribbon.

You can also use the layouts to reapply a Slide Master format or design to a slide. For more information on using Slide Masters, see Chapter 18.

Using Slide Layouts

Change a layout

1 Click the Home tab.

2 Click Layout.

The Office Theme layout gallery opens.

3 Click an alternative layout for the current slide.

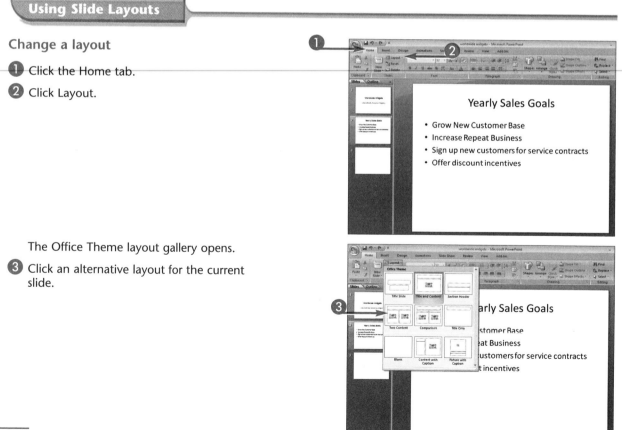

Replace existing layout

- PowerPoint creates new placeholders for content or changes the layout to the one that you selected.

④ Click Layout.

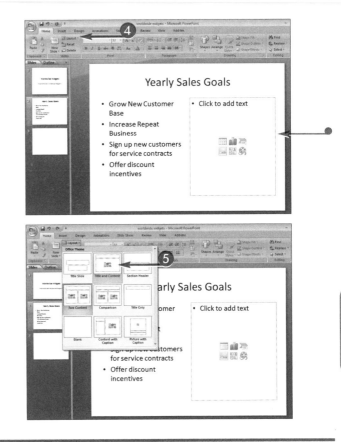

The Office Theme layout gallery opens.

⑤ Click an alternative layout for the current slide, or the original layout once again.

PowerPoint reconfigures the current slide according to the layout that you selected.

This example reapplies the original title and content layout.

Can I create my own layouts?

▼ Yes. On the View tab, in the Presentation Views group, click Slide Master. In the pane that contains the Slide Master and layouts, click a location below the Slide Master where you want to add the new layout. On the Slide Master tab, in the Edit Master group, click Insert Layout. For more information on Slide Masters, see Chapter 18.

Can I insert my own placeholders?

▼ Yes. If you add a new layout in the Slide Master, you can modify it with any combination of placeholders from a drop-down menu under Insert Placeholder. Placeholders can include text, pictures, tables, content, charts, SmartArt, media, or clip art.

Can I use my new layout in other presentations?

▼ Yes, as long as you save it as a PowerPoint Design Template and use the template for the other presentation. Click the Microsoft Office button, and then click Save As. In the File name box, type a filename, or do nothing to accept the suggested filename. In the Save as type list, click PowerPoint Template, and then click Save. When you create the new presentation, use the saved template when you begin.

Change Font Style or Font Size

Y ou can enhance the appearance of a slide by changing the design, or *font style*, of text. PowerPoint also allows you to increase or decrease the text size in your presentation. Larger text is easier to read, but smaller text enables you to fit more information on a slide.

PowerPoint provides a list of fonts from which to choose. Fonts that you used most recently appear at the top of the list, allowing you to quickly select fonts that you use often. The fonts appear in the list as they will appear in your presentation. This lets you preview a font before you select it.

You should consider your audience when choosing a font. For example, you may want to use an informal font, such as Comic Sans MS, for a presentation that you are delivering to your co-workers. A conservative font, such as Times New Roman, may be more appropriate for a presentation that you are delivering to company executives.

Using too many fonts can make your presentation difficult to read. For example, you should not use more than three different fonts in your presentation.

Change Font Style or Font Size

Change font style

1 Click the Home tab.

2 Select the text that you want to change.

3 Click the Font down arrow (▼) to display a list of the available fonts.

You can move your mouse over a font to see a live preview.

4 Click the font that you want to use.

● The text that you selected changes to the new font.

To deselect the text, you can click outside the selected area.

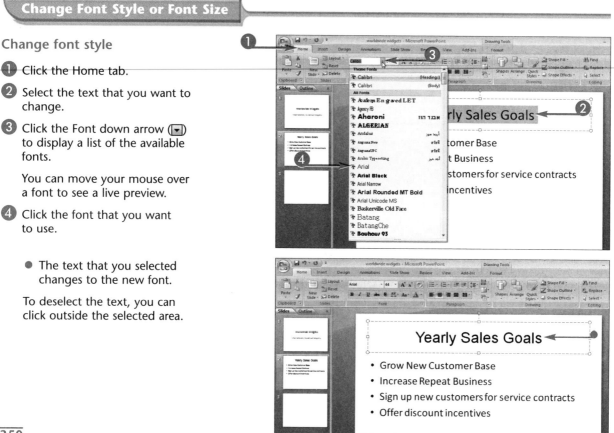

Change font size

1. Click the Home tab.

2. Select the text that you want to change.

3. Click the Font Size down arrow (▾) to display a list of the available sizes.

   You can move your mouse over a font size to see a live preview.

4. Click the size that you want to use.

   ● The selected text changes to the new size.

   To deselect the text, you can click outside the selected area.

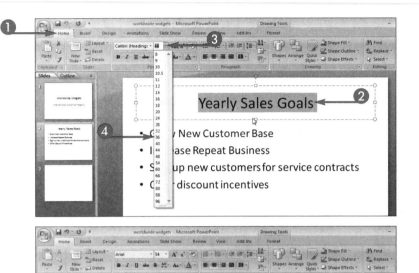

I plan to deliver my presentation on a computer screen. Which font should I use?

▼ Use a font that is easy to read on a computer screen, such as Arial, Calibri, Tahoma, or Verdana. Sans serif fonts work best for PowerPoint slide shows.

Can I replace a font throughout my presentation?

▼ You can replace a font on all of the slides in your presentation with another font. On the Home tab on the Ribbon, click the Replace down arrow (▾) in the Editing group, and select Replace Fonts. In the Replace Fonts dialog box, click the Replace down arrow (▾) and locate the font that you want to replace. Click the With down arrow (▾) and select the font that you want to use. Click Replace. PowerPoint makes the change. After the change has been made, click Close.

Is there another way to change the size of text?

▼ Yes. You can use the Increase Font Size button (A) or the Decrease Font Size button (A) in the Font group of the Home tab to change the size of text. Select the text that you want to change and then click the appropriate button until the text is the size you want. Each click increments the font to the next-larger or next-smaller size within that font.

Bold, Italicize, or Underline Text

You can use the Bold, Italic, or Underline features to change the style of text on slides in your presentation. Changing the style of text allows you to emphasize important information and enhance the appearance of slides.

You can use one feature at a time or any combination of the three features to change the style of text.

The Bold feature makes text appear darker and thicker than other text. You can bold headings and titles to make them stand out from the rest of the text on your slides.

The Italic feature slants text to the right. You may want to italicize quotations on your slides.

The Underline feature adds a line underneath text. This is useful for emphasizing important words or phrases on your slides.

You can also use the Shadow feature, which adds a three-dimensional effect to text and is useful for creating eye-catching slide titles. The Strikethrough feature can be used for different types of messages.

Avoid overusing the Bold, Italic, Underline, Shadow, and Strikethrough features, because this can make the text on your slides difficult to read and diminish the effectiveness of these features.

Bold, Italicize, or Underline Text

① Click the Home tab.

② Select the text that you want to emphasize.

③ Click one of the following buttons:

Bold (**B**)

Italic (*I*)

Underline (U)

Shadow (S)

Strikethrough (abc)

● The selected text appears in the new style.

This example adds bold, italic, and underline.

To deselect text, you can click outside the selected area.

To remove a style, you can repeat Steps 1 to 3.

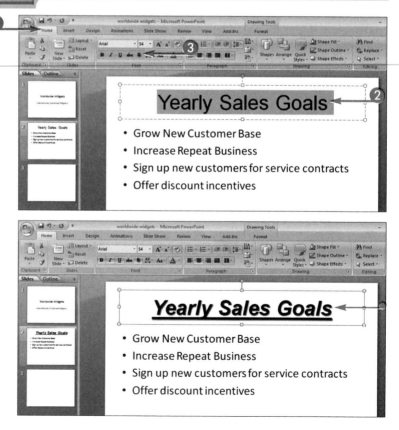

Change Text Alignment

Y ou can use the alignment buttons in the Paragraph group of the Home tab to change text alignment on a slide. Changing text alignment can make your slides easier to read and help your audience distinguish between different types of information in the presentation.

PowerPoint uses text boxes to display text on a slide. When you change the alignment of text, you change the position of the text in the text box. You can also resize, add, or delete the text box, as covered in Chapter 15.

You can use the Left Align option to line up text along the left edge of a text box. You may want to left-align the main points on a slide.

The Center Align option lets you center text between the left and right edges of a text box. This is useful for making headings and titles stand out on a slide.

You can use the Right Align option to line up text along the right edge of a text box. You may want to right-align short lists of information on a slide.

Change Text Alignment

1 Click the Home tab.

2 Select the text that you want to align differently.

3 Click one of the following buttons:

Left Align (▤)

Center (▤)

Right Align (▤)

Justify (▤)

● The text displays the new alignment.

This example left aligns the text.

To deselect text, you can click outside the selected area.

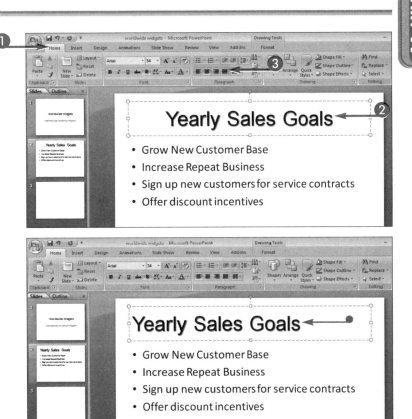

Change
Text Color

You can change the text color on a slide. This can help enhance the appearance of your text or draw attention to important information.

You can choose the text color that you want to use from a color palette. The top row of the color palette contains the ten colors that are used in the theme of the current slide. A *theme* is a set of coordinated colors for items, such as the background, text, shadows, and titles of a slide. For more information, see the task "Format a Presentation with Themes." In addition to

theme colors, you can use any of the standard colors or click to choose more colors.

Make sure that the text color that you choose works well with the background color of the slide. For example, red text on a blue background can be difficult to read.

When you change the text color in the Normal view, the text in the Slide pane displays the new color. The text in the Outline pane does not display the new color.

Change Text Color

1 Click the Home tab.

2 Select the text that you want to change to a different color.

3 Click the Font Color down arrow (▼).

The Font Color gallery opens to display Theme Colors, Standard Colors, and More Colors.

You can move your mouse over a color to see a live preview.

4 Click the color that you want to use.

● The text appears in the color that you selected.

To deselect the text, you can click outside the text area.

To once again display the text in the default color, you can repeat Steps 1 to 4, but select your original font color in Step 4.

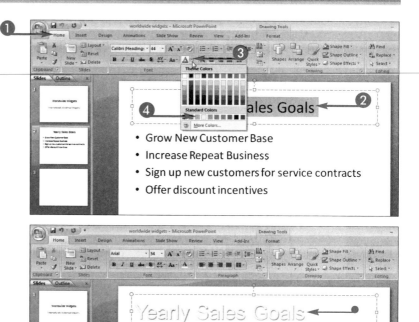

Copy Formatting

Y ou can make the text on one slide in your presentation appear exactly like the text on another slide.

You may want to copy the formatting of text to make all of the titles or important information on your slides look the same. This can help give your presentation a consistent appearance.

The Format Painter tool enables you to copy the formatting of text from one location and apply it to text somewhere else in a document. After you select text and click the Format Painter button, PowerPoint copies all formatting that is applied to that text.

MASTER IT

How can I copy the formatting to more than one selection of text?

▼ You can copy formatting to text on several slides in your presentation at once. To do so, perform the steps in this task, but double-click the Format Painter button (⟪⟫) on the Home tab on the Ribbon in Step 3. When you have finished selecting all of the text that you want to display the formatting, press Esc to stop copying the formatting.

PART IV

Copy Formatting

1 Click the Home tab.

2 Select the text that has the formatting that you want to copy.

3 Click the Format Painter button (⟪⟫).

The Format Painter button is highlighted.

Your mouse pointer (⟲) turns into a paintbrush (🖌).

4 Drag through the text that you want to change.

Release the mouse button.

● PowerPoint applies the formatting.

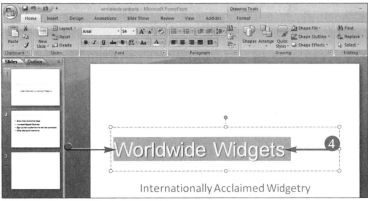

Format Bulleted and Numbered Lists

Some slide layouts include a placeholder for a bulleted list. If you have added one of these slides and created a bulleted list, you can change the appearance of the bullets on a slide. You can also change the bullets to numbers.

Bullets are useful for items that are in no particular order, such as a list of expenses. Numbers are useful for items in a specific order, such as the steps required to complete a project. You can change one, some, or all of the bullets on a slide.

PowerPoint offers several bullet styles for you to choose from, including dots, squares, and check

marks. PowerPoint also provides several number styles that you can use, including letters and Roman numerals.

You can change the color of the bullets or numbers that you select. The available colors depend on the theme of the slide. For more information, see the task "Format a Presentation with Themes."

If you want to make the bullets or numbers the same color as the default text color on the slide, you can choose the Automatic option in the main Bullets and Numbering dialog box.

Format Bulleted and Numbered Lists

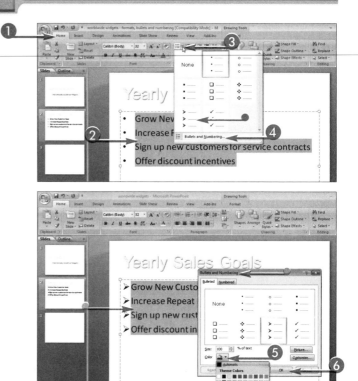

Change the bullet character

1. Click the Home tab.
2. Select the bulleted list that you want to change.
3. Click the Bullets down arrow (▤▾).

   The Bullets options gallery opens.

   You can move your mouse over the choices to see a live preview of the style.

   ● You can click the bullet style that you want to use.

4. Click Bullets and Numbering.

   ● The Bullets and Numbering dialog box appears.

5. Click the Color down arrow (▨▾) to display the color menu for the bullets.

6. Click OK.

   ● The text that you selected displays your choices.

Change the number style

1 Click the Home tab.

2 Select the list that you want to change to numbers.

3 Click the Numbering down arrow (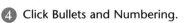).

The Numbers options gallery opens.

You can move your mouse over the choices to see a live preview of the style.

○ You can click the style that you want to use.

4 Click Bullets and Numbering.

● The Bullets and Numbering dialog box appears, with the Numbered tab open.

● You can click the Color down arrow (⬛▾) to display color options for the numbers.

5 Click OK.

○ The text that you selected displays the new style.

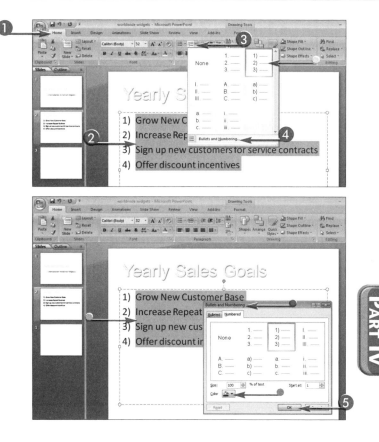

How can I quickly add bullets or numbers to text?

▼ Select the text that you want to display bullets or numbers. On the Home tab on the Ribbon, click the Bullets button (▤▾) to add bullets, or click the Numbering button (▤▾) to add numbers.

How can I add another item to a bulleted list or numbered list?

▼ You can add more items to a bulleted list or numbered list by clicking at the end of the last item in the list and pressing Enter. A new bulleted point or numbered point is added. You can then type the text for this item.

Are there more bullet styles that I can choose from?

▼ Yes. In the Bullets and Numbering dialog box, select the Bulleted tab and then click Customize. In the Symbol dialog box that appears, select the font containing the bullet style that you want to use. Click the bullet style, and then click OK.

How do I remove bullets or numbers?

▼ Select the bulleted list or numbered list, and then click the Bullets button (▤▾) or the Numbering button (▤▾).

Change the Background Style

You can select a new background style for an individual slide or for all of the slides in your presentation. Changing the background style for an individual slide is useful when you want to make an important slide stand out from the rest of the slides in your presentation. Changing the background style for all of the slides is useful when you want to keep the appearance of the presentation consistent.

Although the theme that you are using for the presentation generally determines how your slides look, you can add more versatility with a background style. In addition, you can use the Format Background options to fine-tune a background style and add other elements, such as images.

Generally, background styles offer a quick way to add a nice glow or gradient to one or more slides and increase the contrast between your font colors and the slide background. However, using too many different backgrounds can create inconsistency and make a presentation hard to follow.

Background styles work independently of the themes, design templates, and Slide Master, and applying any of these may override a Background Style. For more on using Slide Masters, see Chapter 18.

Change the Background Style

1 Select one or more slides in the Slides pane.

You can Ctrl-click to select more than one.

2 Click the Design tab.

3 Click Background Styles.

The Background Styles gallery appears.

● You can move your mouse over a style to see a live preview.

4 Click Format Background.

● The Format Background dialog box appears.

5 Click an option for the background fill.

This example selects the Picture or texture fill option (⊙ changes to ⊙).

6 Click the Texture down arrow (▣▾).

7 Select a texture to apply to the background.

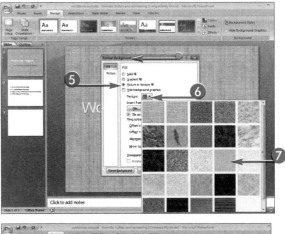

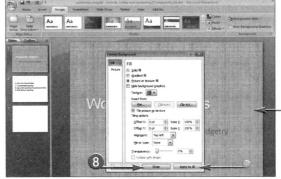

8 Click Close to apply the background style to the selected slide or slides.

● To apply the background style to all of the slides in the presentation, you can click Apply to All.

● PowerPoint applies the background style to the slides.

How can I use a picture as a background?

▼ In the Format Background dialog box, select the Picture or texture fill option (☐ changes to ☑), and click the File button. You can let the entire picture stretch over the slide, or select a Tile Picture as Texture option for a smaller image (☐ changes to ☑), so that it is repeated over the background. You can also change the alignment of the image and the space between tiles, as well as use the Transparency slider to make it more or less opaque on the slide background.

Can I create my own background styles?

▼ Unfortunately not. However, you can save a file with your background styles and then bring in other slides from other presentations. For more information, see the task "Move Slides between Presentations."

How do I undo a change?

▼ Click the Undo button (▣▾). If you cannot undo the change — perhaps because you have made other changes after applying the background style — then click Background Styles on the Background group of the Design tab and select Reset Slide Background.

Using a Design Template

You can use a design template to help create a professional-looking presentation. Design templates are useful when you know what information you want to include in your presentation, but you want to choose a design for the slides.

When you create a new presentation using a design template, PowerPoint creates one or more slides and opens the presentation in Normal view. You can add additional slides to your presentation as you need them, and PowerPoint applies the same design template to each slide that you add.

PowerPoint provides several design templates from which you can choose. Each design template conveys a specific mood and includes fonts, text colors, and a background that work well together. You can preview a design template to determine whether it is appropriate for your presentation. For additional design templates, you can go to http://template gallery.microsoft.com/templategallery/.

Using a Design Template

1 Click the Office button.

2 Click New.

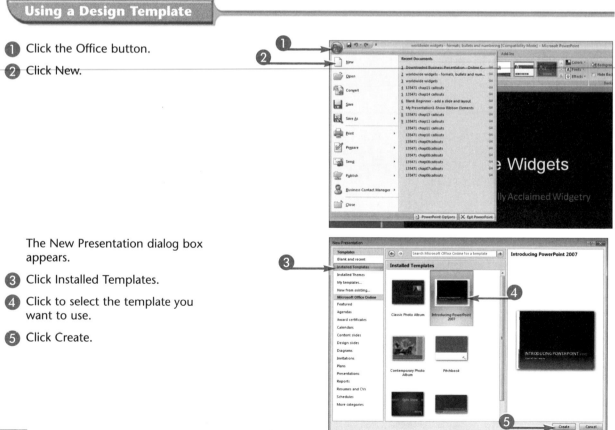

The New Presentation dialog box appears.

3 Click Installed Templates.

4 Click to select the template you want to use.

5 Click Create.

● A formatted presentation with one or more themes is created in the PowerPoint Editor.

6 Scroll down the Slides pane to see some of the other slides.

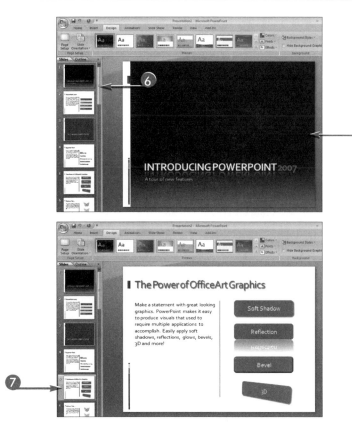

7 Click any slide in the Slide tab to view it in the Slides pane in Normal view.

8 Save the presentation under a new name.

Note: *For more information, see the task "Save and Close a Document" in Chapter 2.*

Can I create a new presentation while working in PowerPoint?	Can I move slides with their designs between presentations?	Can I change a design template later?
▼ Yes. You can use the steps in this task whether you opened a new blank presentation or you are already working in a slide show.	▼ Yes. To do this, see the task "Move Slides between Presentations." Also see the task "Work with Multiple Windows" in Chapter 2.	▼ Yes. You can change the design template for a presentation at any time. To do this, click the Design tab on the Ribbon and apply a new theme to one or more slides.

Format a Presentation with Themes

PowerPoint offers various themes that you can choose from to give the slides in your presentation a new appearance. Changing the theme of your slides can help to make your presentation more effective.

When you create a new presentation, you can base it on a design template or on a theme. If you do not like the selected template or theme, or if you start with a blank presentation, you can always change to another theme.

Each theme contains fonts, text colors, effects, and a background that work well together. If you have applied a background style, it may be modified when you later apply a theme. You can choose the theme that best suits your presentation's content and your intended audience. The theme affects only the appearance of the slides, but the slide content does not change.

The coordinate themes make dramatic changes in all of the slides to which they are applied. Themes may also vary in effect, depending upon the layout of the slide. For more information, see the task "Using Slide Layouts," in Chapter 15. In some cases, the changes may vary between the Title slide and other slides. You can go back and change elements manually, and then save them as a new theme. For more information, see the task "Save a Custom Theme."

After you change the theme, you should review your entire presentation to ensure that your slides appear the way you want.

Format a Presentation with Themes

① Display the slide that you want to change, or select multiple slides in the Slides tab.

You can Ctrl-click to select more than one slide.

② Click the Design tab.

③ Click the Themes More button.

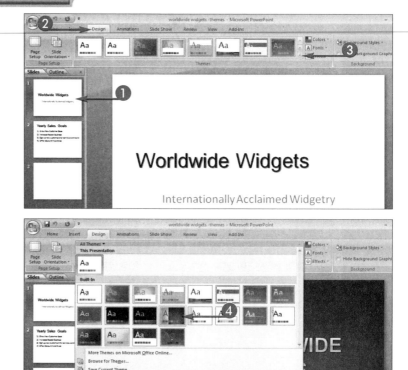

The Themes gallery displays.

You can move your mouse over a theme to see a live preview.

④ Click to apply a theme to your slide or slides.

The slides to which the theme is applied take on new, coordinated designs.

● In this example, the Slides pane shows that some designs vary by the layout of the slide.

❺ To change a theme quickly, click another theme directly in the Themes group on the Design tab.

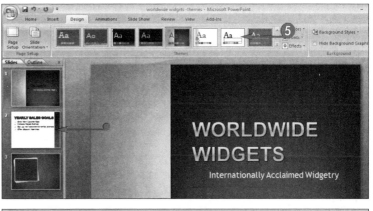

● The presentation is updated with the new theme.

Can I mix themes and background styles?

▼ Yes, but be careful. Applying a background style before a theme can lead to unexpected results, as can applying a background style on top of a theme. For best results with themes, use them over blank or simple slide designs.

Can I change the colors or fonts in the theme?

▼ Yes. You can change the effect of any theme by clicking the down arrow (▼) next to Colors, Fonts, or Effects in the Themes group of the Design tab on the Ribbon. For more information, see the task "Save a Custom Theme."

Can I have different themes for different sets of slides in the same presentation?

▼ Yes. To do so, select the slides that you want for each theme in the Slides pane before applying a theme. For more information, see the task "Move Slides between Presentations."

Can I preview how my slides will look if I print them from a black-and-white printer?

▼ Yes. You can click the buttons in the Color/Grayscale group of the View tab on the Ribbon to preview how your slides will look when printed on a black-and-white printer. Click the View tab and then select Color, Grayscale, or Pure Black and White.

Save a Custom Theme

Y ou can modify a PowerPoint theme and then save it as a custom theme to apply to other presentations and slides.

You can choose from a complete set of coordinated colors to apply over a currently selected theme. You can also select from a list of preset fonts to alter an Office theme, and choose from a variety of effects.

Depending upon the content in your slides, the new theme will have varying impact, but you can save the new custom theme to reuse it in other presentations.

Theme colors contain four text and background colors, six accent colors, and two hyperlink colors.

The colors that appear in the Colors button in the Themes group represent the current text and background colors. The set of colors that you see next to the Theme Colors name after you click the Theme Colors button represent the accent and hyperlink colors for that theme. When you change any of these colors to create your own set of theme colors, the colors that are shown in the Colors button and next to the Theme Colors name will change accordingly.

Because the theme is saved as an Office theme, you can use it in other Office documents, such as Word or Excel, to create a branded or coordinated appearance among different files for a particular project or client.

Save a Custom Theme

Change the theme

1 Display the slide that you want to change.

2 Click the Design tab.

3 Click Colors in the Themes group.

The Themes Colors gallery displays.

You can move your mouse over a Color set to see a live preview.

4 Click to apply a new Color set to your slides.

You can repeat these steps for fonts or effects.

The slides to which the changes are applied take on new, coordinated designs.

Save the theme

- Some designs vary by the layout of the slide.

- The modified theme displays in the Themes gallery.

5 Click the Themes More button.

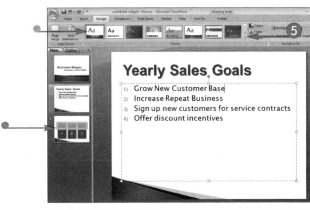

6 Click Save Current Theme.

You can give the theme a new name.

You can also save the theme as an Office theme to use in PowerPoint or other Office programs.

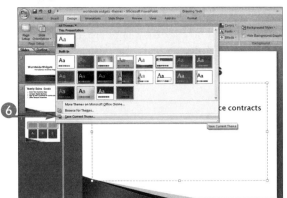

How can I locate the theme that I just saved?

▼ If you are using Vista, the easiest way is to perform the steps in the task "Using Vista Search Features" in Chapter 2. You can also browse to the default folder. For example, if you named it MyNewTheme and Professor was your username, then you would find it at C:\Users\Professor\ AppData\Roaming\Microsoft\Templates\ Document Themes\MyNewTheme.thmx.

If you have Administrator privileges, you can also save the theme directly into the Office Themes folder, at C:\Program Files\Office 12.

I have tried several of the effects, but they do not seem to work. Why is this?

▼ To see the effects, you must apply them to specific types of objects, such as shapes or elements in your diagrams or charts. For more information, see the task "Change Graphic Colors and Add Effects" in Chapter 7.

Move Slides between Presentations

O nce you have created a set of slides, you can reuse them in one of several ways.

For example, you can open the presentation or template with the set of slides and revise them. However, if you have already created a new set of slides, then you can open both presentations side by side and move slides between them.

When you move slides, by default, they take on the design of the slide directly before where they are moved. You can also click the Clipboard icon and choose to retain the original formatting in the slides.

When you open two presentations to move slides, you can use the slide thumbnails in the Slides panel, or display each presentation in Slide Sorter view.

For more information on Slide Sorter view, see the task "Using Online Content Presentations" in Chapter 15.

By default, when you drag slides between presentations, they are also copied, so that they remain in the original presentation as well as appearing in the one to which they are dragged. You can use the Cut and Paste commands if you want the slides to be removed from the original presentation.

Move Slides between Presentations

1 Open both presentations in PowerPoint.

The second presentation will replace the first one in the PowerPoint Editor.

2 Click the View tab.

3 Click Arrange All.

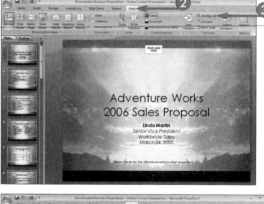

Both presentations open side by side in Normal view.

● The presentation on the left is active.

4 Click Slide Sorter view (▦).

● The active presentation displays in Slide Sorter view.

5 Click the other presentation and click Slide Sorter view (▦) so that the slides in both presentations are easy to read.

6 Click to select one or more slides in a presentation.

You can Ctrl-click for multiple slides or Shift-click for consecutive slides.

7 Drag the selected slides from one window to the other.

8 Release the mouse to drop them after a particular slide.

- The slides take on the design or theme of the slide after which they are placed.

- You can click the Clipboard icon (▣) and select Keep Source Formatting (◎ changes to ◉) to revert the slides to their original design.

How can I open the changed presentation in full screen?

▼ You can double-click the title bar of the presentation that you want to open in full screen. You can also click the View tab on the Ribbon, click Switch Windows, and then click the presentation that you want to open in full screen. The other presentation will also remain open until you manually close it.

I do not want to maintain the source formatting of the slides, but I also do not like how they look in the new theme. What can I do?

▼ You can open the presentation in Slide Sorter view, and select the slides that do not look appropriate. Use the techniques in this chapter to change their theme or give them a new background style. You may need to revise some slides individually to make them look the way you want, but the content from the old presentation will still be in the new one.

How can I use some, but not all, of the slides in different presentations?

▼ You can save a set of custom shows with different combinations for any presentation. You can also right-click any slide in Slide Sorter view and select Hide the slide; the slide will not display in full-screen presentation mode. You can also save different sets of slides with varying designs under different names for different purposes.

PART IV

Add a Table with Text

Y ou can create a table to neatly display information on a slide. Tables can help you organize information, such as a table of contents or a product price list.

Before you add a table to a slide, you should change the layout of the slide to create space for the table. You can do this by selecting a slide layout that contains a placeholder for a table. For information on adding new slides and using slide layouts, see Chapter 15.

A table is made up of rows, columns, and cells. A *row* is a horizontal line of cells. A *column* is a vertical line of

cells. A *cell* is the area where a row and column intersect.

You can enter any amount of text in a cell. When the text that you enter reaches the end of the cell, PowerPoint should automatically wrap the text to the next line in the cell. The height of the cell increases to accommodate the text that you type, and the entire row adjusts to match the cell's new height.

You can edit and format text in a table as you would any text in your presentation.

Add a Table with Text

Add a table

1 Add a new slide, selecting a layout that includes content.

Note: *For more information on how to add a new slide, see Chapter 15.*

You can also change the slide layout to one that includes a placeholder for content.

Note: *To change the slide layout, see Chapter 18.*

2 Click the Table icon (▦).

● The Insert Table dialog box appears.

3 Type the desired number of columns.

4 Type the desired number of rows.

You can also click the spinner button (▣) to increase or decrease the number of rows or columns.

5 Click OK.

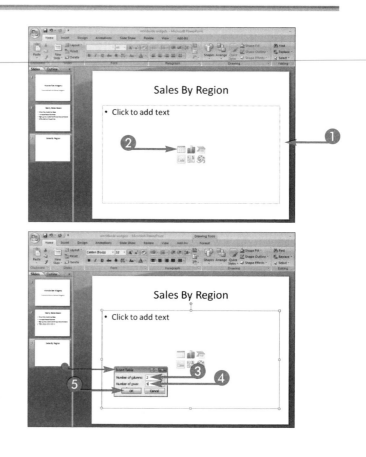

● The table is created, and the Table Tools appear on the Ribbon.

The Bullets placeholder is no longer part of the slide layout.

You can click and drag the table handles to move or resize the table.

You can use the Design or Layout tabs of the Table Tools to change the table's appearance.

Enter text in a table

6 Click the cell where you want the text to appear.

7 Type the text.

8 Repeat Steps 6 and 7 until you type all of the text in the table.

Click outside the table to set it in the slide.

Can I add a table without changing the layout of the slide?

▼ Yes. Click Table on the Insert tab on the Ribbon. Then drag your cursor over the number of rows and columns that you want the table to contain.

How do I delete the contents of cells in a table?

▼ Select the contents of the cells by dragging the mouse over the cells. Then press Delete to delete the contents of the selected cells.

Can I format the text?

▼ Yes. You can use any of the formatting buttons on the Home tab on the Ribbon to make changes to the text. For example, you may want to make the table column headings bold. You can also change the alignment of the entries within a cell using any of the alignment buttons. For more information on formatting, see Chapter 16.

Format a Table

After you add a table to a slide, you can change the width of columns and the height of rows in the table. This can help to improve the layout of your table. If you want to insert additional information into your table, you can also add a row or column to the table.

When you change the width of a column or the height of a row, PowerPoint displays a dashed line on your screen to indicate the new width or height.

You cannot change the width or height of a single cell. When you make changes to the column width or row height, all of the cells in the column or row are affected.

When you add a row, the new row appears above the selected row. When you add a column, the new column appears to the left of the selected column. After you add a row or column, the table may no longer fit on the slide. You may need to move or resize the table to make it fit on the slide.

Change column width

1 Position the cursor over the right edge of the column that you want to change (⍾ changes to ◀▮▶).

2 Click and drag the column edge to a new position.

● A dashed line shows the new position.

Change row height

1 Position the cursor over the bottom edge of the row that you want to change (⍾ changes to ⬍).

2 Click and drag the row edge to a new position.

● A dashed line shows the new position.

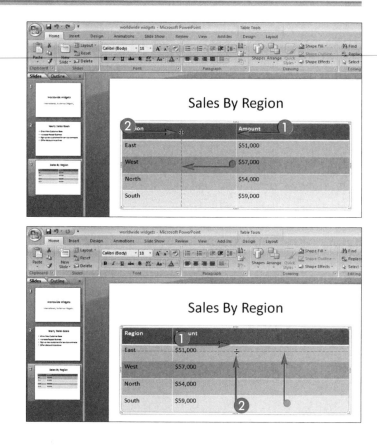

Add a row

1 Click and drag the cursor over all of the cells in the row.

2 Right-click anywhere in the row.

3 Click Insert.

4 Click Insert Rows Above.

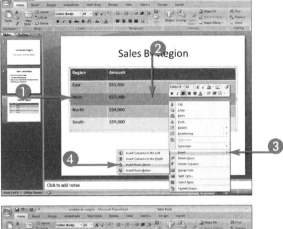

● PowerPoint adds the new row above the selected row, and all of the rows that follow shift downward.

To add a row to the bottom of a table, you can click the bottom-right cell and then press Tab.

Add a column

1 Click and drag the cursor over all of the cells in the column.

2 Right-click anywhere in the column.

3 Click Insert.

4 Click Insert Columns to the Left.

PowerPoint adds the new column to the left of the selected one.

PART IV

What other formatting changes can I make?

▼ You can use the Design tab of the Table Tools on the Ribbon to change the appearance of the table. You can select different border styles, add a fill color to selected cells, change the vertical alignment of entries in a cell, and more. If you are unsure of what a button does, place the cursor over the button to display the ScreenTip or button name.

What is the other toolbar that pops up?

▼ The Mini Toolbar enables additional formatting when you select parts of a table or other content. If you prefer not to see the Mini Toolbar, you can use the PowerPoint options in the Office button, select Popular, and disable the Mini Toolbar (☐ changes to ☑).

Can I delete an entire table from a slide?

▼ Yes. You can delete a table as you would delete any object on a slide. Click to select the table as a whole. A selection frame surrounds the table. Press the Delete key. The table disappears, and the slide layout reverts to title, bullets, and content.

Add a Chart

You can add a chart to a slide to show trends and compare data. Adding a chart is useful when a slide in your presentation contains numerical data. A chart is more visually appealing and is often easier to understand than a list of numbers.

When you add a chart to a slide, a worksheet from Microsoft Excel appears on your screen to form the datasheet for your chart, with rows, columns, and cells.

The sample data in the Excel worksheet gives you the basic structure of a chart; you replace this data with the contents of the chart that you want to create. As you enter data in the datasheet, the chart on the slide automatically changes to display the new data.

If Excel opens in full screen to obscure your PowerPoint screen, you can drag in the corners or press Alt+Tab to toggle between Excel and PowerPoint to see how the data in Excel affects the chart in PowerPoint.

Add a Chart

① Add a new slide, selecting a layout that includes content.

Note: *To add a new slide, see Chapter 15.*

You can also change the slide layout to one that includes a placeholder for content.

Note: *To change the slide layout, see Chapter 18.*

② Click the chart icon (📊).

The Insert Chart dialog box displays.

③ Select the type of chart that you want to create.

④ Click OK.

A datasheet appears in Microsoft Excel, displaying sample data to show you where to enter your information.

5 Click a cell.

6 Type your data.

To remove data from a cell and leave the cell empty, you can click the cell and then press Delete.

7 Repeat Steps 5 and 6 until you finish typing all of your data, including the labels.

As you enter data, PowerPoint updates the chart on the slide.

8 Click the Close button (⊠) to close the Excel worksheet.

You can also minimize the worksheet to change the data later.

● In PowerPoint, you the chart appears on the slide.

● The Chart Tools are active on the Ribbon to allow you to reformat the chart.

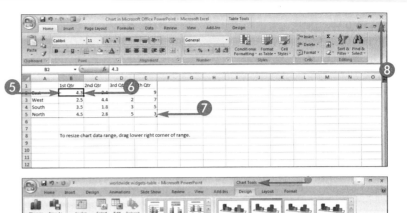

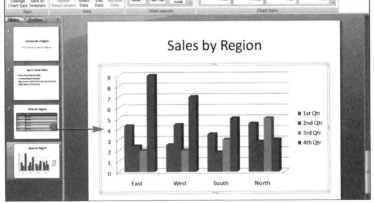

How can I change the data in the chart?

▼ You can right-click the selected chart or click the Design tab of the Chart Tools on the Ribbon, and select Edit Data.

Can I use the data from a saved Excel worksheet?

▼ Yes. You can copy and paste the data from an existing worksheet into the worksheet that becomes the datasheet for your PowerPoint chart. Alternatively, you can create the chart in Excel and then paste it into PowerPoint. For more information on Excel charts, see Chapter 12.

Can I move, resize, or delete a chart that I added?

▼ You can move, resize, or delete a chart as you would any object on a slide. Use the selection handles to drag an edge in or out, or use the crossbar move tool to drag it to a new location.

Can I add a chart from Excel?

▼ Yes. In Excel, click a blank area of the chart and then click the Copy button (🖹) on the Home tab on the Ribbon. In PowerPoint, display the slide that you want to add the chart to, and then click Paste on the Home tab on the Ribbon.

Edit or Format a Chart

You can change a chart that you added to a slide, or edit the data in the datasheet at any time to update the data that is plotted in the chart. You can also change the chart type or make other changes to the chart element. For example, you can hide or display a chart legend, or hide or display the gridlines for the chart axes.

To make changes to a chart, the chart must be active. An active chart is surrounded by a thick frame and selection handles.

The Chart Tools in PowerPoint allow you to change the chart type to suit your data. You can choose from several available chart types. The area, column, and line charts are useful for showing changes to values over time. A pie chart is ideal for showing percentages.

You can plot data by row or column. Changing the way that data is plotted determines what information appears on the x-axis.

Edit or Format a Chart

Edit a chart

1 Click to select the chart to activate it.

● The Chart Tools become active on the Ribbon.

2 Click the Design tab of the Chart Tools.

3 Click the Chart Styles More button to open a gallery of different styles.

4 Click a chart style to apply it to the chart.

● PowerPoint updates the chart.

You can use the Chart Layouts gallery in the Design tab to choose from a selection of different layouts.

Change chart type

1 Click to select the chart to activate it.

● The Chart Tools become active on the Ribbon.

2 Click the Design tab of the Chart Tools.

3 Click Change Chart Type.

The Change Chart Type dialog box opens.

4 Click the type of chart that you want to use.

5 Click OK.

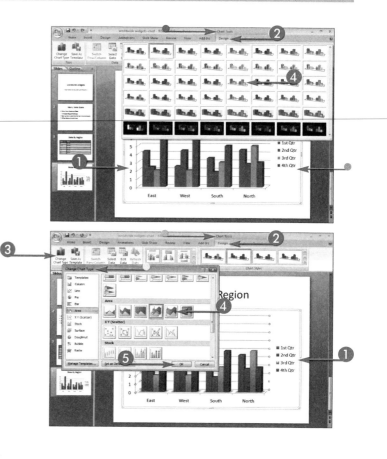

● PowerPoint updates the chart.

Change other chart options

① Click to select the chart.

● The Chart Tools become active.

② Click the Layout tab.

③ Click the Chart Area ▾.

④ Select a part of the chart to reformat.

⑤ Click Format Selection.

● The Format dialog box opens for the type of object that you selected.

⑥ You can change the element's fill, border, or other parameters.

This example changes the color of the selected chart element.

⑦ Click Close.

● PowerPoint updates your chart.

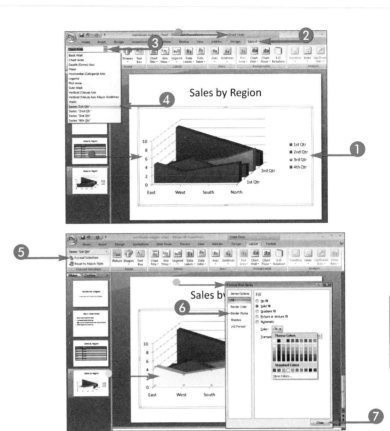

How do I move my legend or make changes to how the title appears?

▼ In the Labels and Axes groups of the Layout tab of the Chart Tools, you can find the options to add, remove, or relocate these elements. For example, to create more room for the data, you can move the legend to the bottom of the chart.

How do I add a title to a chart?

▼ From the Chart Tools on the Ribbon, select the Layout tab. Click Chart Title in the Labels group and choose the option you prefer. A Chart Title placeholder is added to the chart. You can type your title for the chart in the placeholder. You can also add a title for each axis in your chart by selecting Axis Titles from the Labels group.

Does the datasheet appear in my on-screen presentation?

▼ The datasheet does not appear in your on-screen presentation or when you print your presentation. To make the data in the datasheet part of your on-screen and printed presentation, click the Data Table option in the Layout tab of the Chart Tools. You can add a simple data table to the slide or include a data table and legend combination.

What can I do to enhance the look of the labels in the axes?

▼ You can click directly on the axis labels or select them from the Axes drop-down list in the Layout tab of the Chart Tools. You can then use the Format tab of the Chart Tools to change their appearance, including the use of WordArt styles.

Add a Clip Art Image

Y ou can add a clip art image to a slide to make your presentation more interesting and entertaining. A clip art image can illustrate a concept and help the audience to understand the information in your presentation.

Before you add a clip art image to a slide, you should change the layout of the slide to create space for the clip art image.

The Microsoft Clip Organizer contains a wide variety of images. You can scroll through the list to find a clip art image of interest. You can also search for an image by typing a keyword or phrase to match.

The Picture Tools tab on the Ribbon automatically appears on your screen when you add a clip art image to a slide. You can use the buttons on the Picture Tools tab to make changes to the clip art image. You can move or resize a clip art image that you add to a slide. You can also delete a clip art image that you no longer need. Just select the object and press Delete.

Add a Clip Art Image

1 Click the Home tab.

2 Click New Slide to add a new slide.

Note: To add a new slide, see Chapter 15.

3 Click the Layout down arrow (▼) to include text with the clip art image.

Note: To change the slide layout, see Chapter 18.

4 Click a layout with content options.

This example uses the Two Content layout.

● The slide layout reflects the layout you chose in Step 4.

You can type in bullet text in the first panel.

5 In the other content panel, click the Clip Art icon (▦).

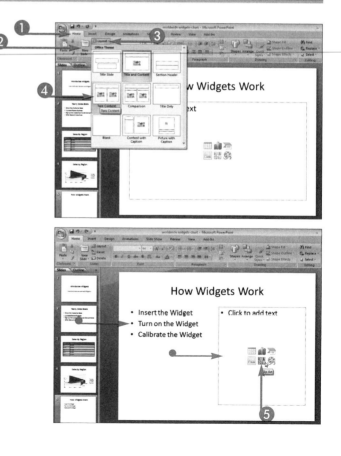

● The Clip Art task pane appears.

6 Enter a search term to look for the clip art images that you want.

7 Click Go to search for images.

You can scroll through the gallery or search again.

8 Click an image to place it in the slide.

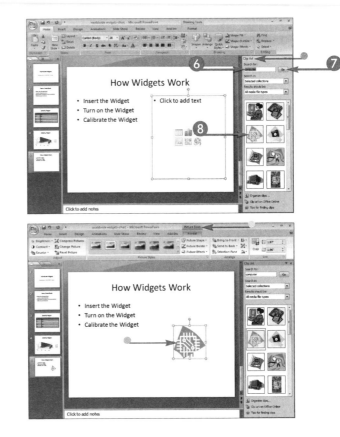

● PowerPoint adds the clip art image and selects it in the slide.

○ The Picture Tools open on the Ribbon.

Can I have the same clip art image appear on each slide in my presentation?

▼ Yes. You can add a clip art image or any other object to the Slide Master to have the image appear on each slide in your presentation. For information on the Slide Master, see Chapter 18.

How can I quickly find all clip art images that loaded with Office?

▼ Leave the Search for field blank before clicking Go. You can also find more clip art on Office online by clicking the link in the task pane.

Can I add a clip art image without changing the layout of my slide?

▼ Yes. Click the Insert Clip Art icon (🖼) in the original layout to insert your clip art. Then add any other elements to the rest of the slide, or use a text box to insert text.

What is the difference between using clip art images and pictures?

▼ When you use clip art, you access Microsoft's Clip Organizer, which is a catalog of images on your computer. When you add a picture, you need to know the location of the image file on your computer to bring it into your slide.

PART IV

Add a Picture

Y ou can add a picture that is stored on your computer to a slide in your presentation. Adding a picture is useful if, for example, you want to display your company logo or a picture of your products.

PowerPoint allows you to use several popular graphics file formats, including Enhanced Metafile (.emf), Graphics Interchange Format (.gif), JPEG (.jpg), Portable Network Graphics (.png), Windows Bitmap (.bmp), and Windows Metafile (.wmf).

By default, PowerPoint opens the My Pictures folder in Windows XP, or the Pictures folder in Vista, but you

can change to any other folder or drive on your computer. You can use the Places bar to quickly locate the picture in a folder that you frequently use.

The Picture Tools automatically appear on the Ribbon when you add a picture to a slide. You can use the Picture Tools to change the appearance of the picture.

You can crop, move, and resize a picture to suit your slide, or add Picture effects. You can also delete a picture that you no longer need. Just select the picture and press Delete.

Add a Picture

1 Display the slide to which you want to add a picture.

2 Click the Insert tab.

3 Click Picture.

The Insert Picture dialog box appears.

You can select another location for the file.

4 Click the picture that you want to add.

5 Click Insert.

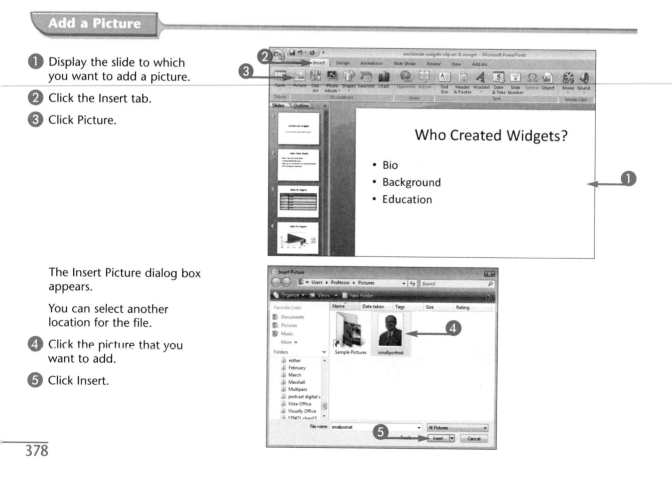

- The picture appears in the slide.

- The Picture Tools appear on the Ribbon.

You can click and drag the selection handles around the picture to resize it or drag the picture itself to move it.

- You can click a button on the Adjust group of the Picture Tools to edit the picture.

6 Click the Picture Styles More button.

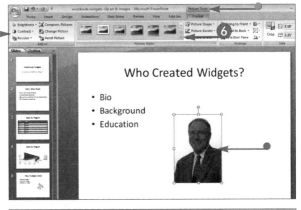

The Picture Styles gallery opens.

You can move your mouse over any style to see a live preview of the style applied to the picture.

7 Click a picture style to change its appearance in the slide.

- PowerPoint changes the picture in the slide.

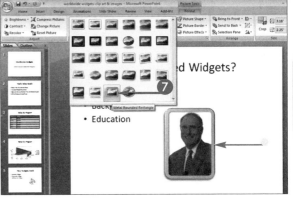

The picture that I added covers text on my slide. How can I move the picture behind the text?

▼ You can change the order of objects on the slide. Click the picture to select it and right-click its border. You can choose Send to Back to move the picture behind another object or text. With the picture selected, and the Picture Tools open, you can also choose Bring to Front or Send to Back in the Arrange group of the Format tab to move it ahead of other objects.

Can I have the same picture appear on each slide in my presentation?

▼ Yes. You can add a picture to the Slide Master to have the picture appear on each slide in your presentation. For information on the Slide Master, see Chapter 18.

How can the buttons on the Picture Tools tab help me change the appearance of a picture?

▼ You can use Contrast in the Adjust group to change the contrast of a picture. You can use Brightness to change the brightness of a picture. Compress Pictures lets you compress the current picture, or all pictures in the presentation, to make the file size smaller; however, this reduces the quality of your output to a printer. Crop in the Size group allows you to trim the edges of a picture.

Add a Shape

Y ou can add simple shapes to the slides in your presentation. Adding shapes can help emphasize important information on your slides.

PowerPoint offers several categories of shapes from which you can choose. For example, in the Basic Shapes category, you can find rectangles, ovals, and triangles. In the Block Arrows category, you can find straight, bent, and curved arrows. The Stars and Banners category includes stars and ribbons. The

Callouts category contains shapes that you can use to add captions. You can use entries from the Action buttons to help your audience navigate through a presentation, especially if you broadcast the presentation, or present through a kiosk.

When you add a shape to a slide, PowerPoint lets you specify its location and size. You can later move and resize the shape to suit your slide. You can also delete a shape that you no longer need. Just select the shape and press Delete.

Add a Shape

1 Display the slide to which you want to add a shape.

2 Click the Home tab.

3 Click Shapes.

Note: *Shapes are also accessible from the Insert tab on the Ribbon.*

4 Click the shape that you want to add.

5 Position your mouse where you want to begin drawing the shape.

6 Drag the mouse until the shape is the size you want ($\mathbb{Q}$ changes to $+$).

7 Release the mouse button.

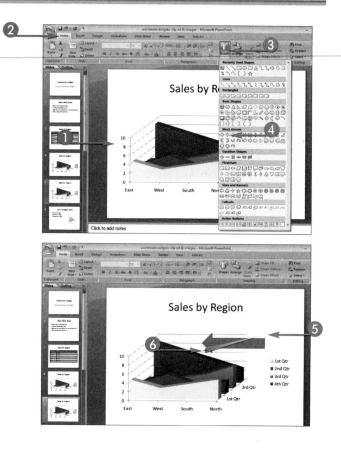

- The shape appears on the slide. Selection handles appear around the shape, so that you can resize or move the shape.

- Drawing Tools appear on the Ribbon.

8 If applicable, type a caption to add text to the shape.

You can drag the shape, resize it, or twist the green rotate tool to rotate it.

9 Click Quick Styles.

10 Move your mouse over a style to see a live preview of the shape with the new style.

11 Click to apply the shape style.

- PowerPoint adds the shape to the slide.

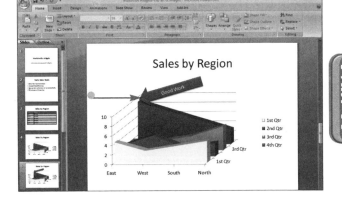

MASTER IT

How else can I change the appearance of a shape?	**Can I add a texture to a shape?**	**Can I change a shape to another shape?**
▼ You can use the Format tab of the Drawing Tools. You can apply Word Art Styles to the text, or change the shape properties by clicking Shape Fill for the interior, Shape Outline for the border, and Shape Effects for more artistic options.	▼ Yes. PowerPoint offers several textures, such as marble and canvas, which you can use to enhance a shape. Click the shape that you want to change. Click the Format tab of the Drawing Tools. Click Shape Fill in the Drawing group. Click Texture and click the texture that you want to use.	▼ Yes. Click the Edit Shape button (⌗) in the Insert Shapes group of the Format tab of the Drawing Tools and select Change Shape. You can change the selected shape into another type of shape.

Add WordArt Styles

You can use the WordArt feature to add text effects to your slides. A text effect can help enhance the appearance of a title or draw attention to an important point in your presentation.

If changing the font, size, and color of text does not allow you to achieve the look you want, you can add a text effect that skews, rotates, shadows, or stretches the text. You can also make text appear three-dimensional.

When you select a text box, PowerPoint automatically displays the Drawing Tools on the Ribbon. You can

click the Format tab of the Drawing Tools to reveal the WordArt styles.

The WordArt styles can be applied to captions for shapes, or to the text in a selected text box. To make sure that they are applied uniformly to all of the text, it is best to drag through the text to select it.

You can also move and resize a text effect to suit your slide, or delete a text effect that you no longer need. Just select the text box and press Delete.

Add WordArt Styles

① Select the text box to which you want to add the text effect.

● The Drawing Tools open on the Ribbon.

② Drag through the text to select it completely.

③ Click the WordArt Styles More button.

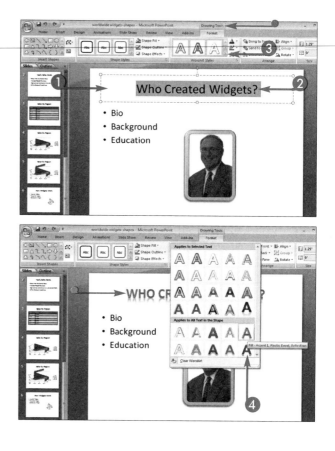

The WordArt Styles gallery appears.

You can move your mouse over any style to see a live preview.

④ Click the type of text effect that you want to add.

● PowerPoint applies the WordArt style to the text.

⑤ Click the Text Effects button ().

⑥ Select a text effect.

This example selects a Shadow.

PowerPoint provides a live preview of the effect.

⑦ Click to add the text effect to the selected text.

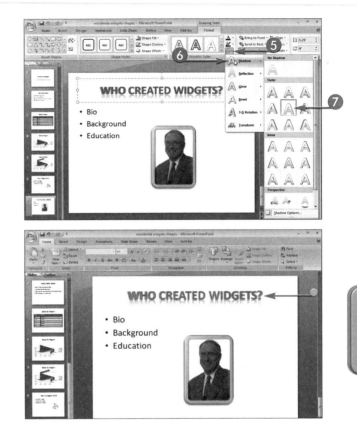

⑧ Click outside the WordArt object.

● PowerPoint adds the effects to the selected text.

Can I add WordArt styles and effects to bullets?

▼ Yes. Select an individual bullet or set of bullets and follow the steps in this task to add text effects or WordArt styles to the bullets.

How do I edit WordArt text?

▼ You can edit the text to which you applied WordArt styles or text effects the same as normal text. Place your cursor within the text, delete the text that you do not want, and type in new text. As long as you are within the text that you formatted, the new text will assume the same styles.

How can I change the color of a text effect?

▼ Select the entire set of text by dragging through it and then click the Text Fill button (▲) in the WordArt Styles group. This allows you to maintain the same effects that you added, but change the underlying color of the actual text.

What is the green handle on the text box used for?

▼ You can use the green handle to drag the text box and change its rotation. Simply click this handle and drag until the text box is rotated to the degree that you want.

Add or Edit a Header or Footer

You can display additional information at the bottom of every slide in your presentation, and the top or bottom in your notes and handouts. Text that appears at the top of the page is called a *header*, while text that appears at the bottom of the page is called a *footer*. They are useful when you want the audience to keep certain information in mind during your presentation, such as the name of your company or the occasion for the presentation.

You can display the date and time, a page or slide number, or other text in the footer on every slide in your presentation. You can display the same items and

header text on notes and handouts by clicking that tab in the Header and Footer options dialog box.

You can have the date and time update automatically each time you open your presentation. You can also display a fixed date and time, such as the date the presentation was created. If you choose to update the date and time automatically, PowerPoint gives you several options as to how the date and time will appear, such as 15-July-2008 3:59 PM. In the Header and Footer dialog box you can see a preview of how the header and footer appear on the slide.

Add or Edit a Header or Footer

Add a footer to a slide

1 Click the Insert tab.

2 Click Header & Footer.

The Header and Footer dialog box appears.

Each item that is selected in the Include on slide section appears on all of the slides in the presentation.

3 To select a date format, click to select the Date and Time option (☐ changes to ☑).

4 Click to select whether you want the date to automatically update or remain fixed (◉ changes to ◉).

● If you click Update automatically, then you can click the down arrow (▼) and select a format.

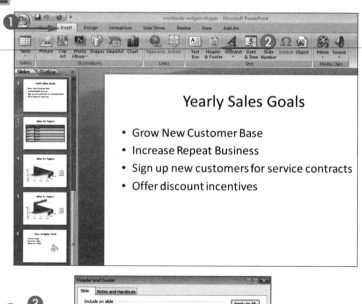

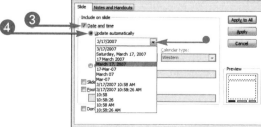

5 To include footer text, click to select the Footer option (☐ changes to ☑) and type the footer text.

6 Click Apply to All to apply the changes to the entire presentation. You can click Apply to apply the changes to only the current slide.

● Your footer appears on the slide.

Add a header or footer to notes and handouts

1 Perform Steps 1 and 2 of the previous section, but click the Notes and Handouts tab in the Header and Footer dialog box.

2 Add a header or footer.

3 Click Apply to All.

A header or footer is added to your notes and handouts pages.

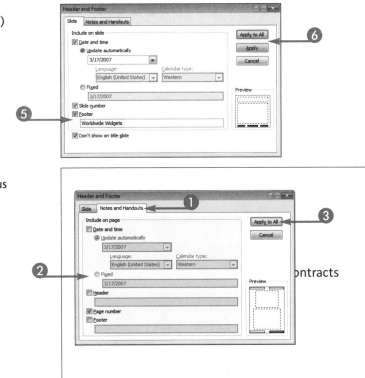

How can I create a header?

▼ Follow the steps to create a footer. When the footer is applied, open the Slide Master and drag any footer placeholder anywhere on the slide that you want. If you want a header, place it at the top. For more information on Slide Masters, see Chapter 18.

Can I start numbering the slides in my presentation at a number other than 1?

▼ Yes. Click the Design tab on the Ribbon and then select Page Setup. Click the spinner button (⬍) or type the number that you want to display on the first slide of the presentation. Click OK.

Can I change the appearance and position of text in a header or footer?

▼ You can change the appearance and position of text in a header or footer on your slides, speaker notes, and handouts. Click the View tab on the Ribbon, select Master, and then choose the appropriate Slide Master. For more information on the Slide Master, see Chapter 18.

Convert Bullets to SmartArt Graphics

I n PowerPoint 2007, you can quickly and easily convert ordinary bullets into much more expressive, visually powerful SmartArt diagrams. After all, slide after slide of bulleted text can give your audience a glazed-over expression.

Using SmartArt graphics effectively can enable you to tell your story visually, which is really what sets PowerPoint apart from the other Office programs as a communication tool.

You can select from many different types of SmartArt shapes, which are broken down into categories that include List, Process, Cycle, Hierarchy, Relationship, Matrix, and Pyramid in the SmartArt gallery. The

intended meaning of your bullets will help you choose the most appropriate SmartArt diagram.

Before converting your bullets, you can open the SmartArt gallery in the Insert tab on the Ribbon to decide which diagram to use. Alternatively, before selecting a SmartArt diagram from your bullets, you can open the gallery by choosing to see More SmartArt Graphics.

The Smart Art gallery contains helpful hints to guide you in your selection of a SmartArt diagram. Just click any SmartArt graphic in the gallery for a brief description of the kind of message that it can be used for.

Convert Bullets to SmartArt Graphics

① Click and drag through your bullets to select them.

② Right-click the selected bullets.

The Context Menu opens.

③ Click Convert to SmartArt.

● You can select one of the diagrams that appear in the pop-up gallery.

④ Click More SmartArt Graphics.

The Choose a SmartArt Graphic dialog box opens.

⑤ Choose an appropriate category for your bullets.

This example chooses List.

The List SmartArt diagrams appear.

⑥ Choose a SmartArt list.

● A preview and description appears in the right panel.

⑦ Click OK.

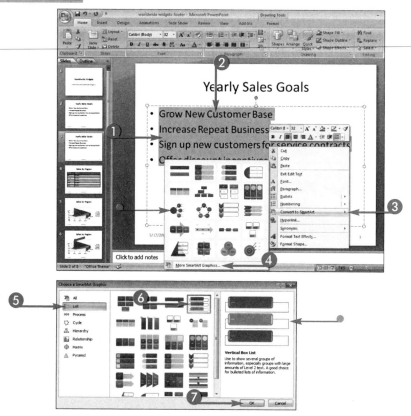

- PowerPoint places the SmartArt graphic in your slide.

- The SmartArt Tools open on the Ribbon.

You can select any placeholder to revise the text.

8 If it has not opened by default, click the Open Your Text Panel arrow pointing left.

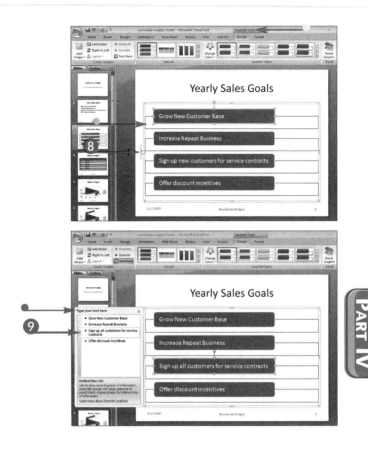

- The Type your text here panel opens.

9 Make the changes you want to the text in the SmartArt graphic.

Click outside the SmartArt graphic to set it in the slide.

Can I use a SmartArt graphic without starting with bullets?

▼ Yes. You can click the SmartArt icon (▣) in any slide layout and follow the same steps. Use the Type your text here panel to enter your text. You can also use the SmartArt Graphic button in the Insert tab of the Ribbon to insert a SmartArt graphic.

Can I change the fills of the components of the SmartArt graphic?

▼ Yes. You can select any individual part of the graphic and use the Shape Fill button of the Drawing Tools of the Home tab. You can also use the SmartArt Graphic Tools. For more information, see the task "Add Special Effects to Graphics."

How do I add more content to a slide with a SmartArt graphic?

▼ Use the Home tab on the Ribbon and change the layout of the slide to accommodate two content panels. For more information, see the task "Using Slide Layouts" in Chapter 15.

PART IV

Add Special Effects to Graphics

Y ou can use the various formatting options in the PowerPoint 2007 Ribbon to make any of the graphics that you inserted stand out by modifying how they appear.

When you select a graphic, a frame appears around it. At the same time, depending on what kind of graphic is selected, a corresponding tab for Design or Format, as well as other options, becomes active on the Ribbon.

These options enable you to use galleries with live previews to apply preset options to the entire graphic, or, in the case of a SmartArt graphic, to apply individual formatting options to individual shapes within the diagram.

By experimenting with the effects in the Design and Format tabs, you can add distinctive flair to various shapes and SmartArt graphics, and make your worksheet look as though it were created by a professional designer.

Whether you get a full range of Design options (as you do with SmartArt), or more limited formatting capability (as you do with shapes and simple graphics), depends upon the graphic that you create and select. The more sophisticated the graphic, the greater the range of effects and features that you can apply.

Add Special Effects to Graphics

Design a SmartArt graphic

1 Select the entire SmartArt graphic.

2 Click the Design tab of the SmartArt Tools.

3 Click the SmartArt Styles More button.

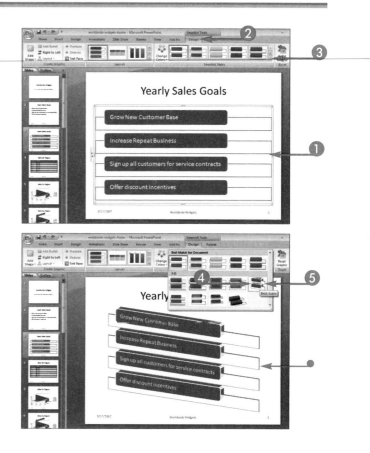

The Smart Art Styles gallery opens, displaying Best Match for Document and 3-D Options galleries.

4 Move your mouse over any options to see a live preview.

5 Click an option to apply it to the graphic.

● PowerPoint applies the effect.

Add effects to a SmartArt graphic

① Select the entire SmartArt graphic.

② Click the Format tab of the SmartArt Tools.

③ Click Shape Effects.

The Shape Effects gallery opens.

④ Select a shape effect.

⑤ Move your mouse over any options to see a live preview.

⑥ Click an option to apply it to the graphic.

● PowerPoint updates the graphic with the options that you selected.

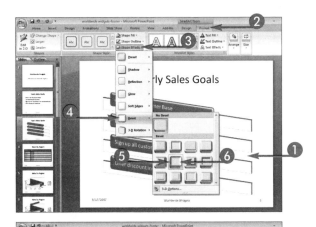

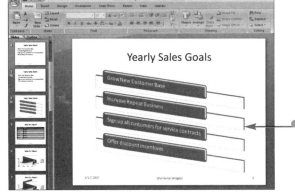

Can I use WordArt styles for SmartArt graphics?

▼ Yes. However, the WordArt styles will be applied only to the text within the various shapes. In the Format tab of the SmartArt Tools, you can click the WordArt Styles More button to open the WordArt Styles gallery and see a live preview of the various styles for your SmartArt graphic.

How do I change the colors in the graphic?

▼ Click the graphic to open the SmartArt Tools, and in the Design tab, click the Change Colors down arrow (▾) in the SmartArt Styles group. The available colors depend on the theme that is applied to the worksheet. You can change the theme in the Page Layout tab on the Ribbon.

Can I change only an individual panel of a SmartArt graphic?

▼ Yes. Click the individual shape in the SmartArt graphic. Then use the shape styles in the Format tab of the SmartArt Tools to apply individual borders, colors, fills, and effects to the individual shape. Some options will be unavailable.

Can I cancel a change that I made to a graphic?

▼ Yes. PowerPoint remembers your last changes. Click the Undo button (🔄) on the Quick Access toolbar to immediately cancel a change that you made to a graphic.

Animate Slide Objects

You can add movement to the text or any selected object on your slides, including the title or the bullets. By controlling the entrance of text or other objects, you can emphasize key points as you move through the presentation, and maintain the interest of your audience.

By giving your text or other object an entrance, the object being animated receives a moment of attention during the presentation. In addition, by not displaying all of the text at once, you do not distract the audience by having them read all of your text as you speak.

You can animate the bullets all together, or break them up to accommodate the entrance of other

objects in your slides. To break up the bullets and animate other objects, see the task "Using Custom Animation."

The Animations tab on the Ribbon gives you quick access to the most commonly used entrance effects in PowerPoint. When you select a text box or the title placeholder, you can quickly apply one of these entrance effects.

When you select a set of bullets, the Animations button in the Animations tab on the Ribbon also lets you determine whether the bullets will be divided into sub-bullets, or whether sub-bullets will accompany their parent bullets as they enter the slide.

Animate Slide Objects

Animate the title

1. Click the Title placeholder to select it.
2. Click the Animations tab.
3. Click the Animate down arrow (⏷).

   The Animate drop-down list opens.

   You can move your mouse over an effect to preview it.

4. Click an effect to apply it to the title placeholder.

   PowerPoint applies the animation.

Animate the bullets

1. Click the bullet placeholder to select it.
2. Click the Animations tab.
3. Click the Animate down arrow (⏷).

   The Animate drop-down list opens to display bullet options.

4. Click an effect to apply it to the bullets and sub-bullets placeholder.

   PowerPoint applies the animation.

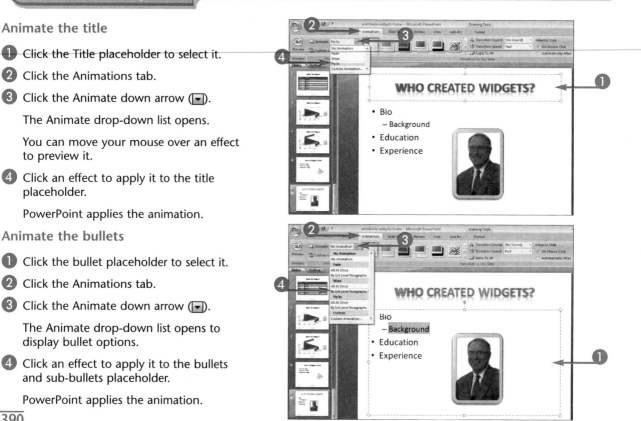

Animate an object and preview the slide

① Click an object to select it.

② Click the Animations tab.

③ Click the Animate down arrow (▾).

The Animate drop-down list opens to display bullet options.

You can move your mouse over an effect to preview it.

④ Click an effect to apply it to the picture placeholder.

⑤ Click Slide Show (▣) or press Shift+F5.

Preview animation

PowerPoint opens the slide in full screen.

You can click through the effects to have the objects enter in the order that you added them.

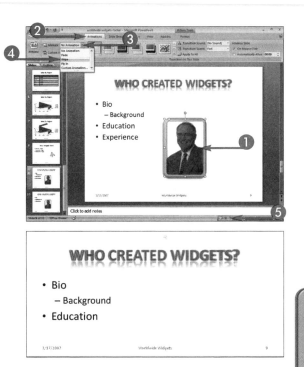

<table>
<tr><td>

How can I have an animated object appear automatically during a slide show instead of waiting for a mouse click?

▼ You can click the animated object that you want to have automatically appear. Click the Animations tab and click Custom Animation. In the Custom Animation task pane, display the Start drop-down list and select when to play the animation.

How do I change the order of animations on a slide?

▼ Click the animated object for which you want to change the order. Click the Animations tab and click Custom Animation. In the Custom Animation task pane, click the object that you want to move. Click the up (▲) or down (▼) re-order buttons to move the object up or down in the animation order.

</td><td>

How do I turn off an animation?

▼ Click the animated object from which you want to remove the animation. Click the Animations tab and then click Custom Animation. Select the animation that you want to remove, and then click the Remove button.

Are those the only animations that are available?

▼ No. There are many more animation effects available. As you use these other effects, they appear in the Animations drop-down list in the Animation tab on the Ribbon.

</td></tr>
</table>

Using Custom Animation

Custom Animation is a task pane that you can use to fine-tune existing animations or add new ones. You can add an entrance effect to any selected object in your slide, or coordinate their appearance using mouse clicks, automatic timings, or combinations of both.

PowerPoint offers several animation categories that each contain different effects. For example, you can select from entrance effects, emphasis effects, exit effects, or motion paths. Each of these categories offers its own set of animations; the available animation effects depend on the object that you select. In addition to the effect, you can select when the animation starts, its properties (such as direction), and its speed.

You can preview an effect to see the animation. If you add more than one effect to a slide, PowerPoint displays the effects in the order in which you added them to the slide. You can use the Up and Down arrows in the Order List to decide which items appear in the slide, in which sequence.

You can also break up bullets and see an Advanced Timeline to intersperse your bullets with other entrance effects.

To display an animated object during a slide show, you must click the slide that contains the object. The click sequence depends upon the choices that you made in the Custom Animation task pane. For information on viewing a slide show, see Chapter 18.

Using Custom Animation

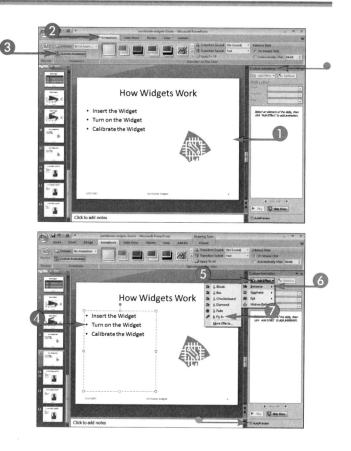

① Display the slide that you want to animate.

② Click the Animations tab.

③ Click Custom Animation.

● The Custom Animation task pane opens.

④ Select the bullet placeholder.

⑤ Click Add Effect.

⑥ Click Entrance.

⑦ Click to apply an entrance effect.

You can click More Effects to see more choices.

● If the AutoPreview option at the bottom of the Custom Animation task pane is checked, then you see a preview of the selected animation.

- PowerPoint adds the Bullet Entrance effect to the task pane. Numbers are added to the bullets to indicate the order of their entrance.

⑧ Select another object in the slide.

⑨ Click Add Effect.

⑩ Click Entrance.

⑪ Click to apply an entrance effect.

You can click More Effects to see more choices.

- If the AutoPreview option at the bottom of the Custom Animation task pane is checked, then you see a preview of the selected animation.

● PowerPoint animates the slides with the selected entrance effects. The next number appears by the object to indicate the order of its entrance.

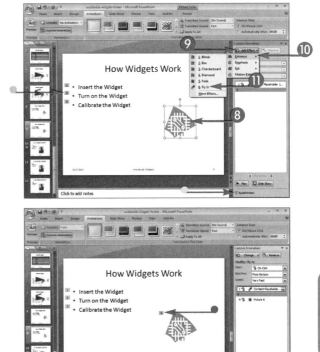

Can I animate charts and diagrams?

▼ Yes. Click Add Effect, and then click Entrance for a chart or SmartArt Graphic. Select Effect Options. Depending upon the object, you will see a tab for Chart or SmartArt Animation. Depending upon the type of chart or graphic, you can animate data series, categories, or parts of the diagram sequentially.

Can I animate a table?

▼ You can animate the appearance of the entire table with an entrance effect, but you cannot break up the table. The best way to animate a table is to break it up into several slides using the Insert Duplicate Slide option in the Home tab. Then delete the unwanted portions of the table in each consecutive slide to build it over the series.

Can I add emphasis to bullets?

▼ Yes. After giving the bullets an entrance effect, select them again and add an emphasis effect. You can make them expand, change the font in various ways — including the style and color — or apply other effects.

continued

Using Custom
Animation *(Continued)*

The Custom Animation task pane gives you a great deal of additional control over the entrance and other effects in your slides. After adding a few entrance effects, you can open the Advanced Timeline to make the entrances of various objects coordinate in the way you want.

With a set of bullets, you can break them up into individual chunks so that you can move other entrance effects between them. You can time entrances together, control them with clicks, or make them come in automatically with a previous animation. You can also change the direction or speed of animations, and determine exactly when they begin.

Besides entrance and emphasis effects, you can use an exit effect to take an object off a slide before, or even just as, another object enters. You can use Motion Path Animations to move objects around, and even to create a Custom Motion Path for any object to move around the slide.

Working with the Custom Animation feature can become fairly complex, and you may want to turn off the AutoPreview option to work more quickly. You can then play the slide when you have added your animations to make sure that the timings and sequence are what you had in mind.

Using Custom Animation *(continued)*

⑫ Click the Expand Bullets arrow (▼) of the Bullet animation to expand the bullets.

⑬ Click the down arrow (▼) for the bullets.

⑭ From the drop-down list, click Show Advanced Timeline.

- The Advanced Timeline opens to let you fine-tune the timings.

- The bullets are broken up into individual components.

⑮ Select the entrance animation effect for an object.

⑯ Click the Start down arrow (▼).

⑰ Select a Start option.

This example uses With Previous.

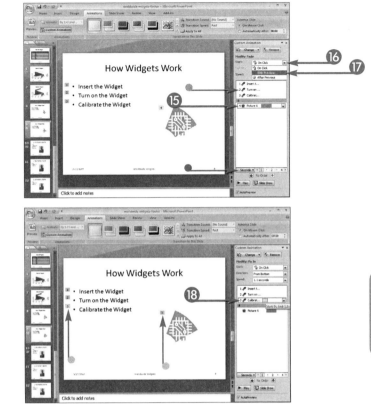

- Both objects share the number 3 in the slide to indicate their entrance together.

⑱ Drag the beginning and end points of the two animation effects so that one begins as the other ends.

PowerPoint animates the slides with the entrance effects coordinated.

Can I add sound to an animation?

▼ Yes. Click the down arrow (▼) for its effect and then click Effect Options. In the Effect tab, you can select the option to add sound to accompany the animation effect.

How do I make an exit effect work directly with the entrance of another object?

▼ Set the exit effect to start on a click. Set the entrance effect directly after it, and select With Previous. Use the Advanced Timeline to drag the entrance to begin just as the exit ends.

Is there an easy way to make all of the animations automatic?

▼ Yes. Click the Slide Show tab on the Ribbon and click Rehearse Timings. The slide show will begin in full screen, and you can click through the show as you would normally. At the end, you can save the timings with the show; the timings that you clicked will happen automatically. However, be careful: If you want to be able to click through your show on other occasions, save the original, manually advanced version first under a different name.

PART IV

Change Views

PowerPoint offers several ways to display your presentation on-screen. You can choose the view that best suits your needs. Each view displays the same presentation; if you make changes to a slide in one view, the other views also display the changes.

Normal view displays all of the text in your presentation, the current slide, and the speaker notes for the current slide. Normal view has two tabs: Slides and Outline. Using the Slides tab, you can work with all of the parts of your presentation in a single screen.

The Outline tab in Normal view displays all of the text in your presentation, a miniature version of the current slide, and the speaker notes for the current slide. This view is useful for developing the content and organization of your presentation. You can also hide the slide content and display just the titles in this view.

Slide Sorter view displays a miniature version of each slide to provide an overview of your entire presentation. This view is useful for adding, deleting, and reorganizing slides. To learn how to change the slide order, see the task "Rearrange Slides."

Change Views

Normal view

① Click the Normal View button (▣).

② Click the Slides tab.

- This area displays miniature versions of each of the slides.

- This area displays the current slide and the speaker notes for the slide.

View the Outline pane in Normal view

① Click the Outline tab.

- This area displays all of the text in the presentation.

- This area displays the current slide and the speaker notes for the slide.

You can resize the slide area or the notes panel by dragging the border between them up or down.

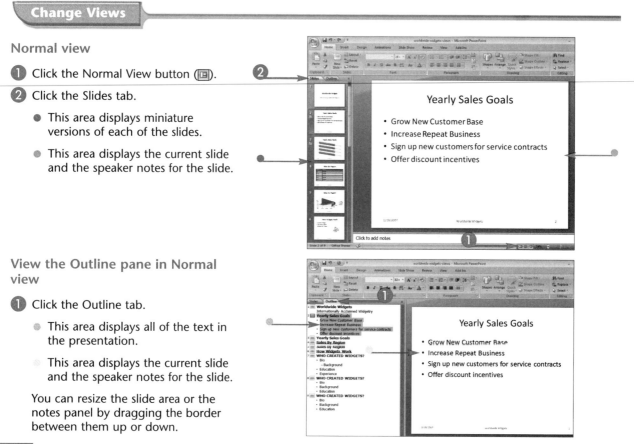

② To show only the slide titles, double-click the slide icon (▣).

The text for each slide is hidden, and only the titles appear.

You can double-click the slide icon (▣) again to redisplay all of the text.

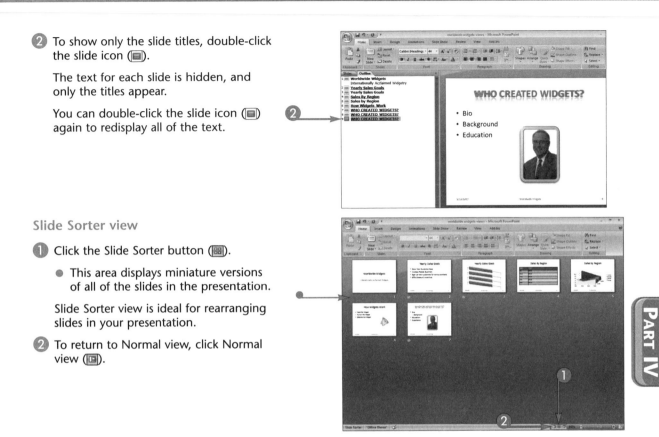

Slide Sorter view

① Click the Slide Sorter button (▦).

● This area displays miniature versions of all of the slides in the presentation.

Slide Sorter view is ideal for rearranging slides in your presentation.

② To return to Normal view, click Normal view (▣).

Does PowerPoint offer any other views?

▼ Yes. PowerPoint also offers the Notes Page view. This view displays the current slide and the speaker notes for the current slide. To display your presentation in the Notes Page view, select View and then click Notes Page.

What do I use the Slide Show button for?

▼ The Slide Show button (▣) allows you to view a slide show of your presentation on your screen. For information on viewing a slide show, see the task "Preview a Slide Show."

Can I change the size of an area of the screen in the Normal view?

▼ Yes. In the Normal view, PowerPoint divides its screen into panes. You can change the size of a pane to display more of the pane. Position your mouse over the vertical or horizontal bar that separates the panes, and then drag the bar to resize the pane.

Is there an easy way to fit my slide on the screen?

▼ Yes. If you have zoomed in or out too much or increased the size of a panel, you can click the Fit Slide to Current Window icon (▣) next to the zoom slider to quickly fit your slide into the current window.

Browse a Presentation

Your computer screen may not be able to display your entire presentation at once. You can browse through the presentation to view the text or slides that PowerPoint does not display on your screen. In the Slides and Outline panes, you can use the scroll bar to scroll up or down through all of the text in your presentation.

When you are browsing from slide to slide, the status bar displays the number of the current slide and the total number of slides in the presentation.

To quickly browse through your presentation, you can drag the scroll box along the scroll bar. When you drag the scroll box, PowerPoint displays a yellow box containing the number and the title of the slide that appears on your screen.

You can also display the previous or next slide in your presentation.

In Normal view, you can browse through the contents of the outlined slides using the scroll bar in the Outline pane.

Browse a Presentation

Using Normal view

1 Click the arrow to scroll up one slide.

2 Click the arrow to scroll down one slide.

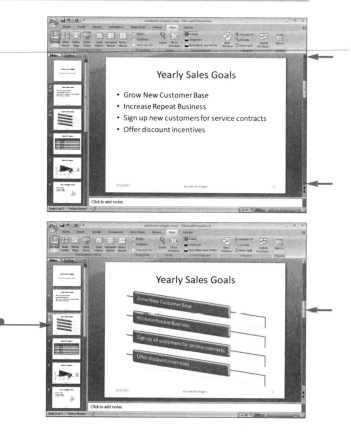

3 To quickly scroll through the presentation, drag the scroll box along the scroll bar.

The location of the scroll box indicates which part of the presentation you are viewing.

● The currently displayed slide also appears highlighted in the Slides pane.

View the Outline pane in Normal view

1. Click the arrow to scroll up one slide.

2. Click the arrow to scroll down one slide.

   PowerPoint scrolls up or down through the slides.

   - The currently displayed slide also appears highlighted in the Outline pane.

View previous or next slide

1. Click the double arrow to view the previous slide.

2. Click the double arrow to view the next slide.

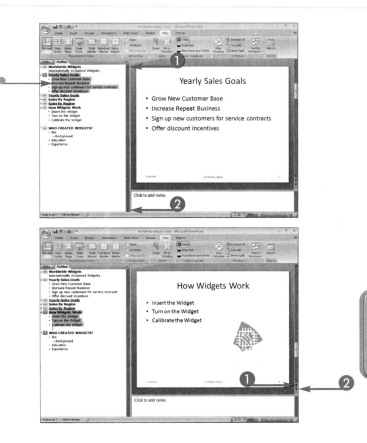

How can I browse through the speaker notes in my presentation?

▼ In the Normal view, you can click the up or down arrows in the Notes pane, located at the bottom of the window, to display the speaker notes for the current slide. You can also change the size of the Notes pane, or the other panes, by dragging the border of the pane.

How do I use a wheeled mouse to browse through my presentation?

▼ Moving the wheel between the left and right mouse buttons up or down lets you quickly browse through your presentation. The Microsoft IntelliMouse is a popular wheeled mouse that lets you move through documents using the wheel.

How can I use my keyboard to browse through my presentation?

▼ In the Outline pane of Normal view, you can press the up- or down-arrow keys to browse through your presentation one line at a time. In Normal view with a slide displayed, you can press the Page Up or Page Down key to browse through your presentation one slide at a time. You can also press the Home key to move to the first slide, or the End key to move to the last slide.

Using the Slide Master

You can use the Slide Master to simultaneously change the appearance of all of the slides in your presentation. Using the Slide Master helps you apply a consistent style to your presentation.

The Slide Master contains a placeholder for the title, bullet points, date, footer text, and slide number on each slide in your presentation. You can format the sample text in a placeholder to format text on all of your slides. Formatting text on the Slide Master does not affect text that you previously formatted on individual slides.

You can add an object to the Slide Master — such as a clip art image, picture, or chart — that you want to appear on all of your slides. You can move, resize, or delete items on the Slide Master as you would any object in your presentation. For example, you can change the placement of the text boxes or other slide objects. In essence, the Slide Master is the blueprint for all slides based on that Slide Master.

After changing the Slide Master, review your entire presentation to make sure that text and objects do not look out of place.

Using the Slide Master

① Click the View tab.

② Click Slide Master.

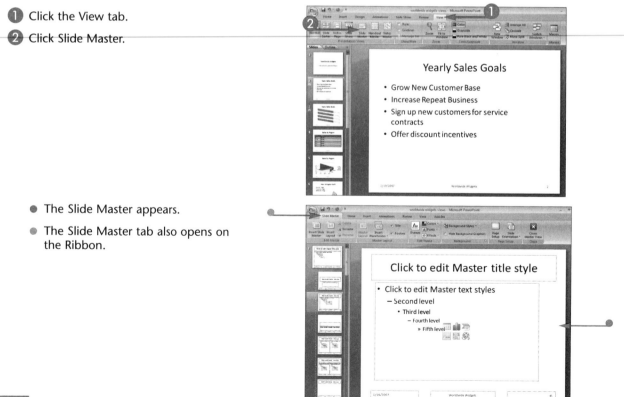

● The Slide Master appears.

● The Slide Master tab also opens on the Ribbon.

③ Click the title area and make any formatting changes.

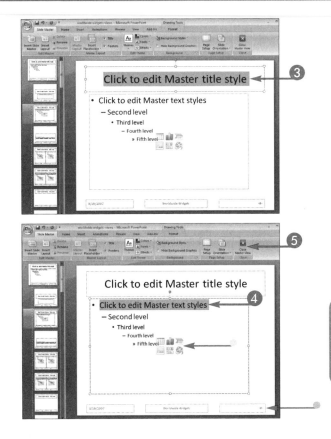

④ Click the text area and make any formatting changes.

● You can make formatting changes to the date area, footer text area, or number area.

You can add objects that you want to appear on all slides to the Slide Master, such as pictures or company logos.

Note: *See Chapter 17 for more information on adding objects to your slides.*

⑤ Click Close Master View.

All slides in the presentation are updated to reflect the changes that you made to the Slide Master.

Are there other masters available?

▼ Yes. The Handout Master allows you to change the appearance of handouts. The Notes Master allows you to change the appearance of speaker notes. To use one of these masters, click the View tab on the Ribbon, click Slide Master, and then select the master that you want to use.

Can I have more than one Slide Master?

▼ Yes. In the Slide Master tab, click Insert Slide Master. This provides you with an entirely new set of masters that you can modify. To apply the new master, open the slide in Normal view and change its layout. The new masters will be in the bottom Custom Design panel of the Slide Layouts. For more information, see the task "Using Slide Layouts" in Chapter 15.

Can I add a new placeholder or restore a placeholder that I accidentally deleted from the Slide Master?

▼ Yes. Click Insert Placeholder in the Master Layout group of the Slide Master tab and select the type of placeholder that you want to add.

How do I delete something that I added to the Slide Master?

▼ Click the main Slide Master or a layout to which you added the object. Select the object and press Delete.

Rearrange Slides

You can change the order of the slides in your presentation. This is useful when you have finished creating your presentation and realize that you want to present the slides in a different order.

The Slide Sorter view displays a miniature version of each slide so that you can see a general overview of your presentation. This view allows you to easily reorder your slides. For more information on the different views, see the task "Change Views."

A slide number appears below each slide in your presentation. When you move a slide, PowerPoint automatically renumbers the slides for you. These slide numbers do not appear in the presentation; they simply help you to keep track of the number and order of slides.

You can move one slide or several slides at once. To move several slides at once, you must first select the slides that you want to move. PowerPoint displays a line to indicate the new location of the slides in the presentation.

Rearrange Slides

① Click the Slide Sorter View button (▦) to change to the Slide Sorter view.

② Click to select the slide that you want to move.

To select multiple slides, press the Ctrl key as you click each slide. To select several slides that are next to each other, click the first slide and then press the Shift key while clicking the last slide.

③ Drag the slide to a new location (⟍ changes to ⟍).

● A line shows where the slide will appear.

④ Release the mouse.

● The slide appears in the new location.

You can also move a slide in the Slides panel.

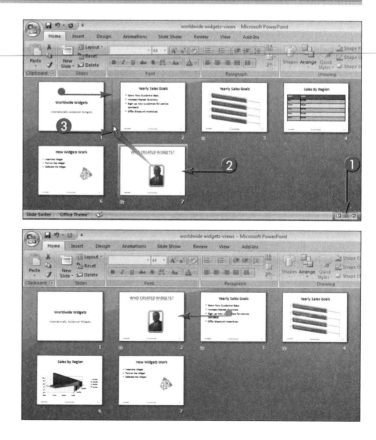

Delete a Slide

Y ou can remove a slide that you no longer need in your presentation. This is useful when you are reviewing your presentation and realize that a slide contains incorrect or outdated information.

The Slide Sorter view displays a miniature version of each slide in your presentation. This view allows you to easily see the slide that you want to delete. For more information on different views, see the task "Change Views."

You can delete one slide or several slides at once. To delete several slides at once, you must first select the slides that you want to delete.

When you delete a slide, PowerPoint automatically renumbers the remaining slides in your presentation for you.

PowerPoint remembers the last changes that you made to your presentation. If you change your mind after deleting a slide, you can use the Undo feature to immediately cancel the deletion.

Delete a Slide

1 Click Slide Sorter View button (▦) to change to the Slide Sorter view.

2 Click the slide that you want to delete.

To select multiple slides, press the Ctrl key as you click each slide. To select several slides that are next to each other, click the first slide and then press the Shift key while clicking the last slide.

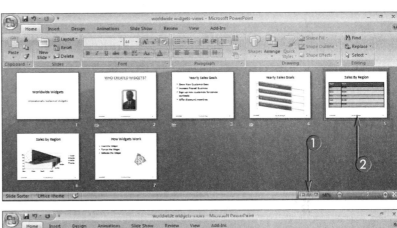

3 Press Delete.

● PowerPoint deletes the slide or slides.

You can also delete a slide in the Slides panel.

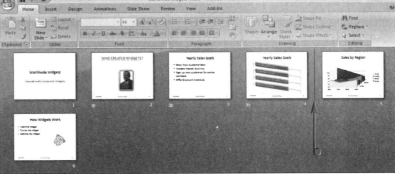

Hide a Slide

You can hide a slide in your presentation so that the slide does not display when you deliver the presentation.

Hiding a slide is useful when a slide in your presentation contains supporting information that you do not want to include unless the audience requires clarification. For example, you may not want to show your audience a slide containing sensitive financial information unless they ask to see the information.

Hiding a slide can also help you prepare for questions from the audience. You can create slides that answer common questions and then display the slides only when necessary.

When you hide a slide in your presentation, a symbol appears through the number for the slide in the Slide Sorter view.

If you want to present the information on a hidden slide during a slide show, you can easily display the hidden slide. For information on viewing a slide show, see the task "Preview a Slide Show."

Hide a Slide

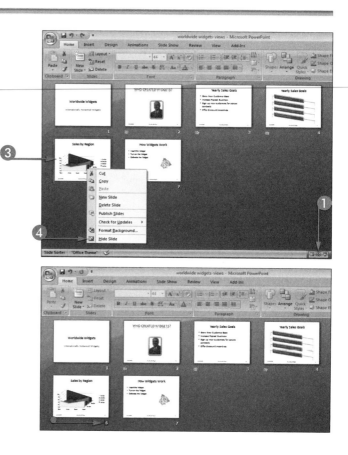

1. Click the Slide Sorter View button (▦) to change to Slide Sorter view.

2. Click to select the slides you want to hide.

3. Right-click the selected slides.

   The right-click submenu opens.

4. Click Hide Slide.

● A slash symbol appears through the slide number.

To unhide the slide, repeat Steps 1 to 4.

To display a hidden slide during a slide show, you can press the H key when viewing the slide before the hidden slide.

Hidden slides appear faded in the Slides panel.

Using the Selection Pane

Y ou can get a quick overview of all of the objects in a slide, including the placeholders for headers and footers. You can also change the layers of the slide on which the objects appear, which determines which objects they overlap or obscure. The Selection pane also lets you temporarily hide objects in your slide to work with the slide more efficiently.

Items that you hide on one slide still appear on the others.

By using the Selection pane, you can quickly locate any item that you want to select and reformat.

You can also locate selected items in a slide by selecting one object and then pressing Tab to toggle through all of the objects. However, using the Selection pane gives you a quick overview of all of your objects as well as more control, because you can hide certain objects to continue to work with others.

When you select an object in the Selection pane, the Drawing Tools open on the Ribbon, allowing you quick access to editing tools for the item that you have selected.

Using the Selection Pane

1 In Normal view, click the Home tab.

2 Click Select.

3 Click Selection Pane.

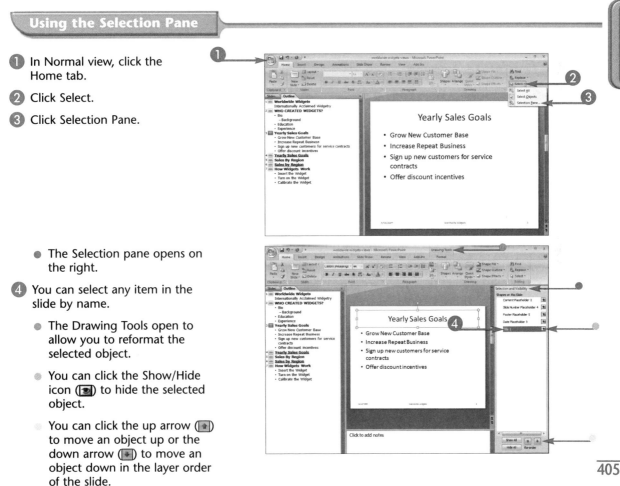

● The Selection pane opens on the right.

4 You can select any item in the slide by name.

● The Drawing Tools open to allow you to reformat the selected object.

● You can click the Show/Hide icon (📷) to hide the selected object.

● You can click the up arrow (🔼) to move an object up or the down arrow (🔽) to move an object down in the layer order of the slide.

405

Add Slide Transitions

You can use effects called *transitions* to help you move from one slide to the next. A transition determines how one slide is removed and the next slide is presented on the screen.

Using transitions can help you introduce each slide during an on-screen slide show. They also add interesting visual effects to your presentation, and signal to the audience that new information is appearing.

PowerPoint offers many slide transitions for you to choose from, including Blinds Vertical, in which the slides appear on the screen like vertical blinds on a window; Checkerboard Across, in which the slide

appears in a checkerboard pattern; and Dissolve, in which the slide fades away on the screen.

You can preview a slide transition to determine whether it is appropriate for your presentation. You can also add Random transitions to your slides if you do not want to spend time on each slide to determine a different option.

You can set the speed of a slide transition to slow, medium, or fast.

You can add a transition to one slide or to your entire presentation. PowerPoint displays the transition when you rehearse or present your slide show.

Add Slide Transitions

① Click the Slide Sorter View button (⊞) to change to Slide Sorter view.

② Select the slides to which you want to add a transition.

To select all slides, you can press Ctrl+A.

③ Click the Animations tab.

④ Click the Transition to This Slide More button.

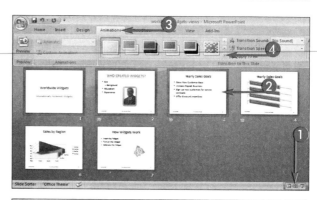

The Slide Transition gallery appears.

⑤ Scroll through the list of transitions.

⑥ Click the transition that you want to use.

You can see a live preview of the transitions for each of the selected slides.

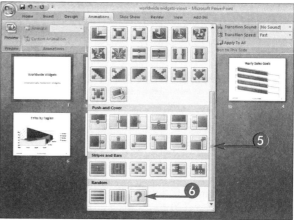

7 To change the speed of the transition, click the Transition Speed down arrow (▾) and click the speed that you want to use.

8 To add the transition to every slide in the presentation, click Apply to All.

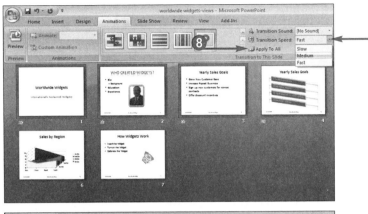

● PowerPoint adds the transitions to the selected slides, and indicates them with a star.

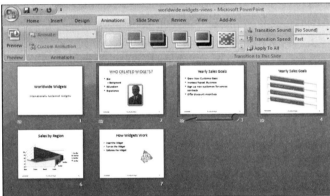

How do I select when to advance to the next slide?

▼ The default setting is to move to the next slide when you click the mouse. However, you can select to display the next slide after a certain interval. Click Automatically After in the Advance slide area of the Animations tab (☐ changes to ☑). Then type the number of seconds or minutes to wait.

How do I remove a transition?

▼ Click the slide from which you want to remove a transition. Perform Steps 2 to 6 in this task, but select No Transition in Step 6.

How do I add a sound to a transition?

▼ With the slide displayed, in the Animation tab on the Ribbon, click the Transition Sound down arrow (▾) and then select the sound that you want to use.

Can I have a transition sound continue playing?

▼ You can have a transition sound continue playing until PowerPoint displays a slide with a new sound. In the Animation tab on the Ribbon, click the Transition Sound down arrow (▾) and, after selecting the sound, click the Loop until next sound option at the bottom of the drop-down list.

Rehearse a Slide Show

You can rehearse your slide show and have PowerPoint record the amount of time that you spend on each slide. Timing your slide show can help you decide whether you need to add or remove information.

While you rehearse your slide show, PowerPoint displays the time that you spend on the current slide and the total time for the slide show. If you make a mistake while rehearsing and you want to begin a slide again, you do not have to restart the entire rehearsal. You can restart the timer for the current slide as many times as necessary.

When you finish rehearsing your slide show, PowerPoint displays the total time for the slide show. You can choose to record the time that you spend on each slide.

If you record the timings for each slide, these timings appear below each slide in the Slide Sorter view. PowerPoint uses the timings to advance your slides automatically during a slide show. To maintain your original manual timings, click the Slide Show tab on the Ribbon and click to select the Use Rehearsed Timings option.

Rehearse a Slide Show

① Click the Slide Show tab.

② Click Rehearse Timings to rehearse the slide show.

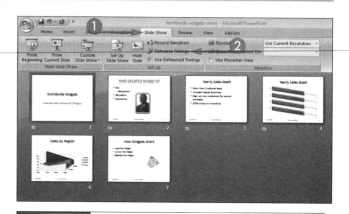

The first slide in the slide show appears.

● The Rehearsal toolbar displays the time spent on the current slide and the total time spent on the slide show.

③ When you finish rehearsing the current slide, click the mouse button to display the next slide.

● If you make a mistake and want to reset the timer for the current slide, you can click the Pause button (▮▮).

Yearly Sales Goals

• Grow New Customer Base

• Increase Repeat Business

• Sign up new customers for service contracts

• Offer discount incentives

4 View each slide until you finish rehearsing the slide show.

● PowerPoint displays the total time for the slide show.

5 To record the time that you spent on each slide and use the timings when you later view the slide show, click Yes.

● The time that you spent on each slide appears below the slides.

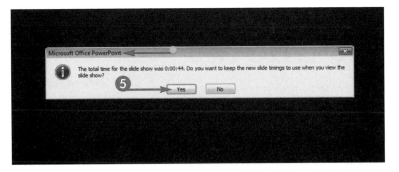

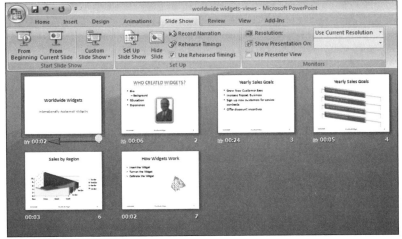

Can I change the timing for a slide after rehearsing my slide show?

▼ Yes. If you do not like the timing that you recorded for a slide, you can change the timing for the slide. Click the slide and then click the Slide Sorter View button (⊞). In the Animations tab, in the Automatically After text field, drag the cursor over the current timing and type the new timing.

I do not want to use my timings to advance my slides automatically during a slide show. How can I advance my slides manually?

▼ From the Slide Show tab, click to deselect the Use Rehearsed Timings option (☑ changes to ☐).

Can I see my timings as I present the show?

▼ Yes. Your presentation laptop or notebook must be configured for dual monitor support. You can then use Presenter view by enabling it in the Slide Show tab of the Ribbon (☐ changes to ☑). You can then show the presentation on a projector while maintaining a view of speaker notes and timings on your local laptop monitor.

PART IV

Set Up a Slide Show

Y ou can specify how you want to present a slide show on a computer. You can deliver a slide show in one of three ways: a slide show can be presented by a speaker, browsed by an individual, or set up to run at a kiosk. Kiosks are often found at shopping malls and trade shows.

You can set up your slide show to display all of the slides in your presentation or only a specific range of slides. During a slide show, the slides can be advanced manually or automatically. If you choose to advance slides manually, you must perform an action, such as

clicking the mouse, to move to the next slide. If you choose to advance slides automatically, you must set timings for your slides. To set timings for your slides, see the task "Rehearse a Slide Show."

You can have your slide show run continuously until you press Esc. This is useful if your slide show runs at a kiosk. If your presentation contains animations, you can choose not to include these effects in your slide show. For more information on animation, see Chapter 17.

Set Up a Slide Show

① Click the Slide Show tab.

② Click Set Up Slide Show.

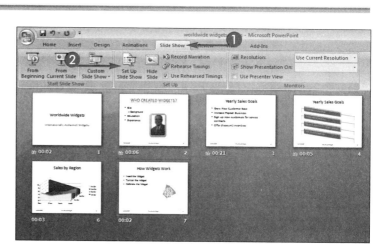

The Set Up Show dialog box appears.

③ Click an option to specify how you want to deliver the slide show (☐ changes to ☑).

● To run the slide show continuously until you press Esc, you can click here (☐ changes to ☑).

● To run the slide show without voice narration or slide animation, you can click here (☐ changes to ☑).

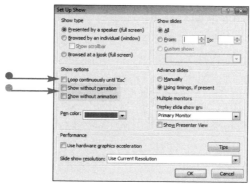

④ Click an option to specify which slides you want to present in the slide show (◎ changes to ◉).

● If you select the From option in Step 4, you can type the starting and ending slide numbers.

⑤ Click an option to specify whether you want to advance the slides manually or automatically using timings that you have set (◎ changes to ◉).

⑥ Click OK.

The slide show is set up with these selections.

Can I add tools to help an individual who is viewing the slide show?

▼ Yes. If you select the Browsed by an individual option (☐ changes to ☑) in the Set Up Show dialog box, you can display a scroll bar during the slide show that lets an individual easily move through the slide show.

Can I use multiple monitors to present my slide show?

▼ Yes. If you use multiple monitors, the audience can view the slide show on one monitor while you view the outline, speaker notes, and slides on another. In the Set Up Show dialog box, click the Display slide show on down arrow (▼) and then click a monitor.

What does the Pen color option do?

▼ To select the color of pen that is used to draw on the slides, click the Pen color down arrow (▼) and select the color that you want to use. For more information about drawing on slides, see the task "Preview a Slide Show."

What are the performance options?

▼ You can use available hardware graphics acceleration by clicking the Use hardware graphics option (☐ changes to ☑) in the Set Up Show dialog box. You can also select a resolution for the slide show by clicking the Slide show resolution down arrow (▼) and selecting a resolution.

Preview a Slide Show

Y ou can view a slide show of your presentation on a computer screen. A slide show displays one slide at a time using the entire screen.

If you create your presentation for on-screen viewing, a slide show allows you to preview how your slides look and to rehearse the pace of your presentation.

Any objects or enhancements that you added to your slides, including clip art, animations, or transitions, appear during the slide show.

You can display the next slide or return to the previous slide while viewing a slide show. You can also end the slide show at any time.

PowerPoint allows you to draw on the slides during a slide show. This is useful if you want to add a check mark beside an important point or circle a key word on a slide. If a slide becomes cluttered with drawings, you can erase all of the drawings. The drawings that you add during a slide show are temporary and do not appear on the slides when the slide show is over, unless you choose to save them from the option window when ending the slide show.

Preview a Slide Show

Preview the slide show

1 Click the Slide Show tab.

2 Click From Beginning.

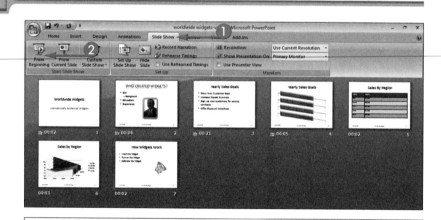

The first slide fills the screen.

3 Click the current slide or press the spacebar to view the next slide.

To return to the previous slide, press Backspace.

● You can click these buttons for Slide Show options. The main menu button displays a menu with commands for ending the show, adding notes, and so on.

Clicking the right arrow advances the slide show; the left arrow goes back one slide. The pen button opens the pen and arrow options.

Yearly Sales Goals

• Grow New Customer Base
• Increase Repeat Business
• Sign up new customers for service contracts
• Offer discount incentives

3/19/2007   Worldwide Widgets   2

Draw on a slide

① Right-click the slide on which you want to draw.

② Click Pointer Options.

③ Click a pen.

PowerPoint activates the pen.

④ Position your mouse where you want to start drawing on the slide.

⑤ Drag your mouse to draw on the slide.

To erase all of the drawings on the slide, press the E key.

Note: *When drawing on a slide, you cannot click directly in the slide to display the next slide. To once again use a mouse click to move through slides, right-click the slide, click Pointer Options, click Arrow Options, and then click Automatic.*

Sales By Region

Region	Amount
East	$51,000
Central	$56,000
West	$57,000
North	$54,000
South	$59,000

Sales By Region

Region	Amount
East	$51,000
Central	$56,000
West	$57,000
North	$54,000
South	$59,000

Can I run another program during a slide show?

▼ Yes. Open the program before beginning the slide show. Then, with the slide show in progress, click Alt+Tab to see icons for all open programs. Keep clicking Tab with Alt depressed until the program you want is highlighted. Release both keys to open the desired program full screen. Repeat the process and select the icon for the slide show to return to full screen view of the presentation. You can also use an Action button to run another program or open a file. For more about Action buttons, see *Teach Yourself VISUALLY PowerPoint 2007* (Wiley, 2007).

Can I get rid of the pop-up menu?

▼ Yes. Right-click the slide during the presentation, click Pointer Options, click Arrow Options, and then select Hidden. You can also disable the popup toolbar by opening the PowerPoint options from the Office button, and selecting Advanced. In the Slide Show section, deselect the Show Popup Toolbar option (☑ changes to ☐).

How can I pause or end a slide show?

▼ Press the B key to pause the slide show and blank the screen. Press the B key again to resume the slide show. To end a slide show, either press Esc or right-click any slide and click End Show.

What other methods do I have for presenting a slide show?

▼ If you have a microphone and camera, you can present online or record a presentation for broadcasting later with Live Meeting. You can learn more about Live Meeting in Chapter 29 or at Office online.

Create
Speaker Notes

You can create speaker notes that contain copies of your slides with all of the points you want to discuss. You can use these notes as a guide when delivering your presentation.

Although you can create speaker notes in all four views, Normal and Notes Page views provide the easiest way for you to do so. Normal view provides a notes pane where you can enter speaker notes while creating your slides. This lets you record your ideas while working on your presentation.

The Notes Page view is useful for editing and formatting your speaker notes. Each notes page includes a small version of a slide and a text area. You can magnify the text area to make it easier to see the text. You can edit and format text in the text area as you would any text in the presentation.

When you finish creating your speaker notes, you can print the notes pages so that you have a paper copy of your notes to refer to while delivering your presentation. For information on printing a presentation, see the task "Print a Presentation."

Create Speaker Notes

Using Normal view

1 Display the slide for which you want to create speaker notes.

2 Click the note pane area.

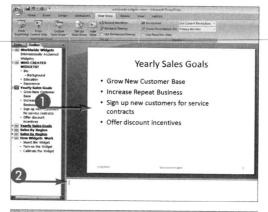

3 Type the points that you want to discuss when you display the slide during the presentation.

If you type more than one line of text, you can use the scroll bar to browse through the text.

4 When you are finished adding notes, click in the slide to exit the note page area.

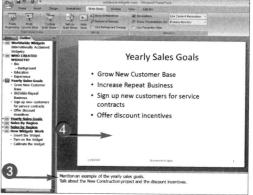

Using Notes Page view

1. Display the slide for which you want to create speaker notes.

2. Click the View tab.

3. Click Notes Page to display the presentation in the Notes Page view.

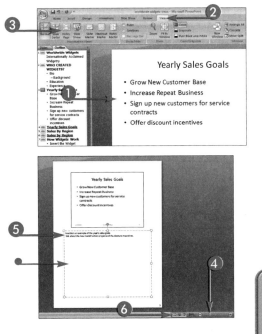

- The notes page for the current slide appears on the screen.

4. Increase the Zoom level so that you can more easily type and format the text.

5. Type and format the speaker notes as you would any text in the presentation.

6. When you finish reviewing the notes pages, click the Normal View button (⬛) to return to Normal view.

Can I increase the height of the Notes pane in Normal view?

▼ Yes. Position your mouse over the horizontal bar above the notes pane and then drag the bar up.

Can I type speaker notes in other views?

▼ You can type speaker notes only for the displayed slide in the notes pane of Normal view. You can also click the View tab on the Ribbon and then click Notes Page in the Presentation View group. Enter your notes for the slides you want.

I have notes for my own preparation and others for the audience. How can I keep them from seeing my prep notes in the handouts?

▼ Save two versions of the presentation: one for handout notes for your audience and the other for your own preparation notes.

How can I display speaker notes on my screen during a slide show?

▼ You will need to have dual monitor support for the presentation laptop. You must also use the Presenter view so that your notes are on the laptop screen and the presentation is sent to a projector. Enable Presenter view in the Slide Show tab on the Ribbon (⬜ changes to ☑). During a full-screen presentation, you can have your notes available on the laptop monitor and the presentation displayed on a projector screen.

Check Spelling

Before printing or presenting your presentation, you should be sure that it does not contain spelling errors. A misspelled word can mar an otherwise perfect presentation, creating an impression of carelessness. PowerPoint's spell check feature can help you check for spelling errors.

The spell check feature compares every word in your presentation to words in its dictionary. If the word is not found in the dictionary, PowerPoint flags it. However, a flagged word does not always indicate a misspelled word; the word is just not in Office's dictionary. For each flagged word, PowerPoint usually offers suggestions for correcting the errors in your document. You can accept one of these suggestions, edit the word, ignore the misspelling, or add the word to the dictionary.

Even after using the spell check feature, you should still proofread your presentation. PowerPoint only recognizes spelling errors, not usage errors. For example, to, two, and too all have different meanings and uses. If they are spelled correctly, PowerPoint does not flag them, even if you use them incorrectly, as in, "I went too the grocery store."

Check Spelling

① Click the Review tab.

② Click Spelling to start the spell check.

If you only want to check a word or a sentence, then you can select the word or sentence first.

The Spelling dialog box appears.

● This area displays the first misspelled word.

● This area displays suggestions for correcting the text.

③ Click to select one of the suggestions, or type your own replacement word in the Change to text box, and click Change.

To add the flagged word to the PowerPoint dictionary, you can click Add.

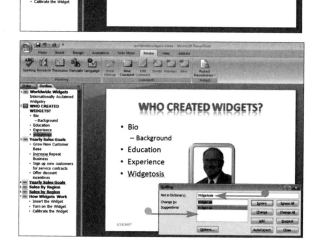

The spell check moves to the next incorrect word.

④ Click the appropriate correction button.

You can click Change to correct only this error, or Change All to correct this flagged word throughout the document.

If the word is spelled correctly, you can click Ignore to skip this occurrence, or Ignore All to ignore all occurrences.

⑤ Continue making changes until the spell check is complete.

• A dialog box appears, telling you that the presentation's spelling has been checked.

⑥ Click OK to close the dialog box.

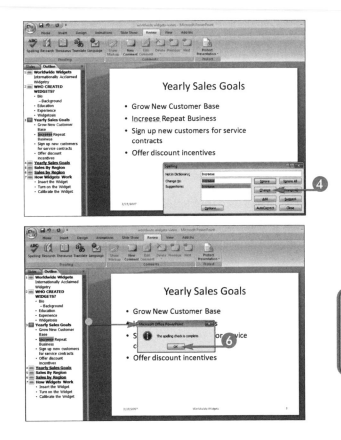

What are AutoCorrect options?

▼ AutoCorrect options are changes that PowerPoint makes automatically. For example, if you type two initial capitals in a word, PowerPoint fixes this error. You can review the changes that PowerPoint makes by clicking the Office button, clicking PowerPoint Options, clicking Proofing, and then clicking AutoCorrect.

You can turn off any option by deselecting its check box (☑ changes to ☐) in the AutoCorrect dialog box. Keep in mind that Word automatically replaces some misspelled words with the correct spelling, and some characters such as (c) with a symbol (©). You can scroll through the list of AutoCorrect entries to see which changes are made.

How can I stop PowerPoint from flagging words that are spelled correctly, such as my company name?

▼ PowerPoint considers any words that do not exist in its dictionary to be misspelled. You can add a word to the dictionary so that PowerPoint recognizes the word during future spell checks. When the word is flagged, click the Add button.

If you want to have PowerPoint automatically correct the word, you can create an AutoCorrect entry by clicking AutoCorrect in the Spelling dialog box.

Set Up a Presentation for Printing

You can change the setup of your presentation before printing it. PowerPoint allows you to specify how you want to output your presentation, such as on paper, 35mm slides, or overheads.

You can choose the *orientation* that you want to use when printing your presentation. Orientation refers to the way information is printed on a page. The orientation that you select for the slides affects every slide in your presentation. Portrait orientation prints information across the short side of a page. Landscape orientation prints information across the long side of a page and is the standard orientation for slides.

You can also choose the orientation that you want to use for speaker notes, handouts, and the outline of your presentation. Portrait is the standard orientation for speaker notes, handouts, and the outline.

After you set up your presentation for printing, PowerPoint adjusts the presentation to reflect the new settings.

Set Up a Presentation for Printing

1 Click the Design tab.

2 Click Page Setup.

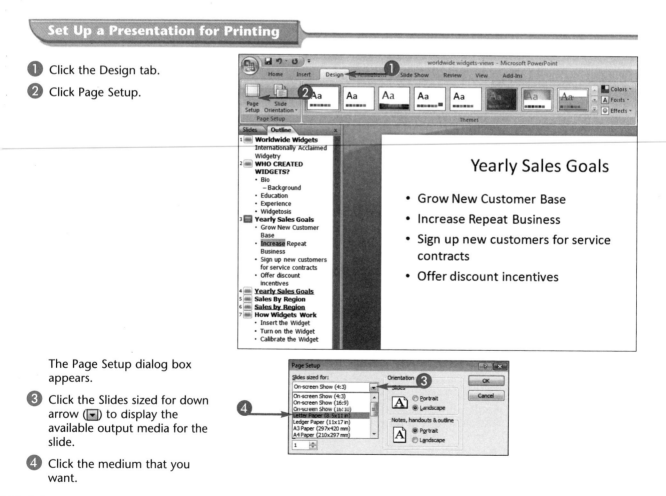

The Page Setup dialog box appears.

3 Click the Slides sized for down arrow (⏷) to display the available output media for the slide.

4 Click the medium that you want.

⑤ Type a new width and height, or accept the default, for the output size.

Page Setup

Slides sized for:
Letter Paper (8.5x11 in)

Orientation
Slides
○ Portrait
◉ Landscape

Width:
10 Inches

Height:
7.5 Inches

Number slides from:
1

Notes, handouts & outline
◉ Portrait
○ Landscape

OK   Cancel

⑥ Click the orientation that you want to use for the slides (○ changes to ◉).

⑦ Click the orientation that you want to use for speaker notes, handouts, and the outline of the presentation (○ changes to ◉).

⑧ Click OK.

The presentation is set up for printing with the options that you selected.

Page Setup

Slides sized for:
Letter Paper (8.5x11 in)

Orientation
Slides
⑥ ○ Portrait
◉ Landscape

Width:
10 Inches

Height:
7.5 Inches

Number slides from:
1

Notes, handouts & outline
⑦ ◉ Portrait
○ Landscape

⑧ OK   Cancel

Should I review my presentation after setting it up for printing?

▼ Yes. You should review your presentation after changing the output or orientation of slides to ensure that the information on your slides still appears the way you want.

The layout of information on my slides does not suit the new orientation. What can I do?

▼ You can move and resize text placeholders and objects on the Slide Master to better suit the new orientation of the slides. Click the View tab on the Ribbon, and then click Slide Master. For more information, see the task "Using the Slide Master."

Can I start numbering the slides in my presentation at a number other than one?

▼ Yes. Changing the numbering of slides is useful if your presentation is part of a larger presentation. In the Page Setup dialog box, double-click the Number slides from text field and then type the number that you want to use for the first slide of the presentation.

Print a Presentation

You can produce a paper copy of your presentation. PowerPoint lets you specify the part of the presentation that you want to print, such as slides or handouts. When printing handouts, you can choose the number of slides that you want to appear on each printed page.

You can print every slide in your presentation, the current slide, or a series of slides.

PowerPoint offers several options for changing the appearance of your printed presentation. The Grayscale option improves the appearance of color slides printed on a black-and-white printer. The Pure

Black and White option eliminates shades of gray and prints in black and white.

The Include Animations option prints slides as they appear when animated. The Scale to fit paper option adjusts the size of slides to fill a printed page. The Frame slides option adds a border around your slides, handouts, and Notes pages. The Print hidden slides option prints slides that you have hidden. This option is available only if your presentation includes hidden slides.

For information on animating slides, see Chapter 17. For information on hiding slides, see the task "Hide a Slide."

Print a Presentation

Print slides

1 Click the Office button.

2 Click Print.

You can also move your mouse over Print and then click Print in the submenu.

The Print dialog box appears.

3 Click an option from this area to print all slides, the current slide, the selected slides, or a range of slides (◎ changes to ◉).

● If you select Slides, you can type the range that you want to print.

4 Click the Print what down arrow (▾) to select any other print options.

5 Click OK.

PowerPoint prints the presentation.

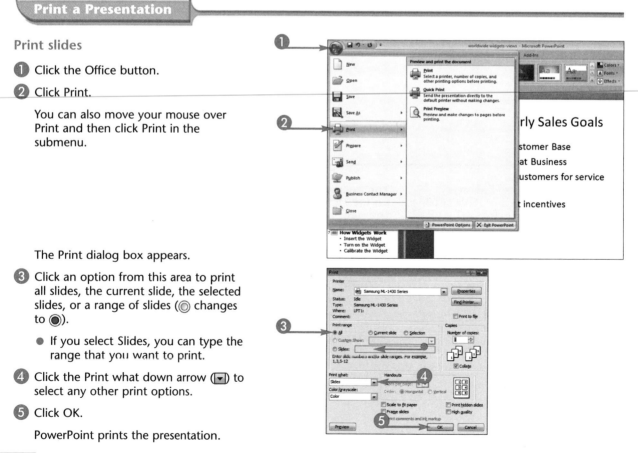

Print audience handouts

1. Perform Steps 1 and 2 in the "Print slides" section.

2. Click the Print what down arrow (▼) to display printing options.

3. Click Handouts.

4. Type the number of slides that you want to print on each page.

   ● You can click Preview to view a preview of the handouts.

5. Click OK.

   PowerPoint prints the handouts.

How do I print notes or an outline?

▼ To print notes, click the Print what down arrow (▼) and select Notes Pages. Select Outline View to print an outline.

Why did only part of my outline print?

▼ Your outline prints as it appears in the Outline pane. If you have hidden text, double-click the Slide icon (▣) to display all of the text. For information on hiding slide text, see the task "Hide a Slide."

How do I produce 35 mm slides?

▼ You can send your presentation to a service bureau to create 35mm slides through an online upload, on a disk or CD, or using a flash drive.

Can I preview how my slides will look when printed from a black-and-white printer?

▼ Yes. In the View tab on the Ribbon, click Grayscale or Pure Black and White. To return to color, click Color.

Can I print more than one copy?

▼ Yes. In the Print dialog box, double-click the Number of copies text field and type the number of copies that you want to print.

PART IV

Present with a Projector

The easiest way to present with a projector is have the projector take over for the laptop or notebook monitor or simply show exactly what it is showing.

If you have a dual monitor capability on the notebook or laptop from which you are presenting, you can also enable Presenter view in the Slide Show tab on the Ribbon. This enables you to view your speaker notes on your laptop monitor while the actual presentation is sent to the projector.

Generally, turning on the projector puts the projector into standby mode. A second button turns it on completely. In either case, turning on the projector and then the laptop generally causes the laptop to synchronize with the projector as a monitor, and to

place a copy of the notebook monitor image on the projector and have it projected to a screen.

Sometimes you need to press the correct Function (F) key on the laptop to toggle between three modes: laptop monitor, external monitor (projector), and both. In this case, you want both. On many laptops this is the F5 or F7 key; check your laptop documentation.

With older projectors, it is occasionally necessary to lower the resolution of the notebook graphics card output to make the projector capable of synchronizing with the laptop. You can do this in the Control Panel of Windows XP or Windows Vista, or by right-clicking the desktop. You should only have to perform these steps if you are having a problem with the projector. Most newer projectors are easy to set up.

Present with a Projector

① Right-click the desktop.

② Click Personalize.

In Windows XP, you can right-click the desktop and click Properties.

The Appearance and Personalization window appears.

③ Click Display Settings.

In Windows XP, you can click the Display Settings tab.

The Display Settings dialog box appears.

4 In the display settings for the primary monitor, move the slider down to a resolution of 800 x 600.

5 Click Advanced Settings.

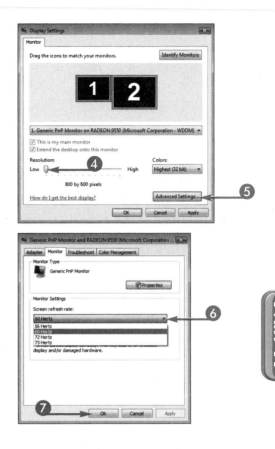

A dialog box appears, where you can specify advanced settings for the monitor.

6 Click the Screen refresh rate down arrow (🔽) and select 60 Hertz.

7 Click OK.

8 Click the function key on the laptop that resynchronizes with the projector.

If necessary, you can restart the laptop or notebook with the new display settings.

I have a newer projector (XGA) and a high-performance notebook. Why is there no image on the projector?

▼ Check your notebook or laptop documentation and make sure that you have attempted to press the F5 or F7 key on the Function keyboard to toggle between output modes.

My projector image is distorted. What can I do?

▼ More projectors now have a menu for adjusting the image and fixing distortion with automatic keystoning. *Keystoning* is the adjustment for an image that has one edge displayed out of proportion with the other. Try to locate this feature and enable it. Also, you can use the remote or turn the projector lens carefully to focus the image.

My projected image is stuck while the image on the monitor works fine. Why is this?

▼ You have inadvertently pressed the Freeze button on the projector remote. Press the Freeze button again to unfreeze the image.

When I open PowerPoint, the audience sees all of my slides. How do I make sure that this does not happen?

▼ Use the projector remote to blank the screen or put something in front of the lens while you open PowerPoint. You can also right-click the icon representing your presentation and select Show. The presentation goes directly into the full-screen slide show without opening the PowerPoint Editor.

PART IV

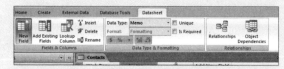

PART V
USING ACCESS

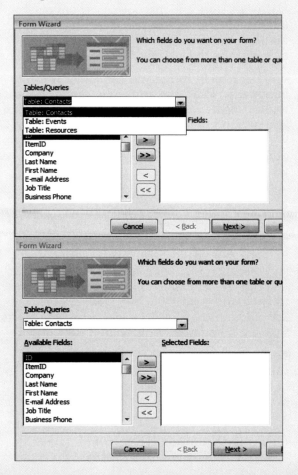

An Introduction to Access

Access is a database program that enables you to store and manage large collections of information. Access provides you with all of the tools that you need to create an efficient and effective database. Databases are useful for finding specific data in a large collection of information, and you can perform calculations on the information contained in a database. For more information on Access, you can visit the Microsoft Web site at www.microsoft.com/access.

Database Uses

Many people use *databases* to store and organize personal information, such as addresses, music and video collections, recipes, or a wine list — much more efficient than using sheets of paper or index cards. Companies use databases to store information such as mailing lists, billing information, client orders, expenses, inventory, and payroll. A database can help a company effectively manage information that it must constantly review, update, and analyze.

Access 2007 comes with a set of database templates that you can modify for your own use and a comprehensive sample database called Northwind Traders.

Types of Databases

Flat file databases store information in one large table, and often contain duplicate information. Although easy to set up, a flat file database is not flexible or efficient for storing large amounts of information.

Relational databases store information in separate tables, and enable you to use relationships to bring together information from different tables. This type of database is powerful and flexible, and it effectively stores large amounts of information. A relational database is faster and easier to maintain than a flat file database.

Access uses a relational model for its databases. Therefore, you can link a customer database to an order database, and link the order database to a product database. Each database is separate, but by linking information, you can keep track of orders, inventory, and client billing.

Database Benefits

Databases store and manage collections of information related to a particular subject or purpose. You can efficiently add, update, view, and organize the information stored in a database.

Another benefit is that you can instantly locate information in a database. For example, you can find all clients with the last name Smith. You can also perform more advanced searches, such as finding all clients who live in California and who purchased more than $100 worth of supplies last year.

The local and online database templates in Access 2007 can help you create a database to track assets, contacts, events, marketing projects, and other projects. You can also use these databases to manage a sales pipeline, work with students, and manage tasks. For each of these endeavors, you can create a table to hold your data, forms to enter and display the information, queries to ask questions of your data, and generate reports that can be printed or distributed electronically.

Additional benefits include performing calculations on the information in a database to help you make quick, accurate, and informed decisions.

Parts of a Database

A ccess databases consist of objects such as tables, queries, forms, reports, macros, and modules.

Tables

A table is a collection of related information about a specific topic. You can have one or more tables in a database. A table consists of fields and records. A field is a specific category of information in a table, such as clients' first names. A record is a collection of information about one thing, such as the name and address of one client.

Queries

Queries enable you to find information of interest in a database. When you create a query, you ask Access to find information that meets the criteria, or conditions, that you specify. For example, you can create a query to find all items that cost less than $100.

Forms

Forms provide a quick way to view, enter, and modify information in a database by presenting information in an easy-to-use format. A form clearly shows you where to enter or modify information. Forms usually display information from one record at a time so that you can concentrate on that particular record rather than the entire set of records.

Reports

Reports are professional-looking documents that summarize data from your database. You can perform calculations, such as averages or totals, in a report to summarize information. For example, you could create a report that displays the total sales for each product. Reports can be in different formats, such as screen output, printed documents, or Web pages.

Macros

A macro saves you time by combining a series of actions into a single action. Macros are ideal for tasks that you perform frequently. For example, you can create a macro that calculates and prints daily sales figures. Instead of having to perform each action individually, you can have a macro automatically perform all of the actions for you.

Modules

Modules are programs created in a programming language called Visual Basic for Applications (VBA). Modules enable you to efficiently control a database. Access also includes Class modules that enable you to define custom methods and options called properties for forms and reports.

Plan a Database

Take time to properly design a database. Good database design ensures that you can perform tasks efficiently and accurately. As you add information and objects to a database, the database becomes larger and more complex. A properly designed database is easier to modify and work with as it grows. Good planning can also make it easier for other users to work with a database that you create.

Determine the Purpose of the Database
Decide what you want the database to do and how you plan to use the information. You can consult others concerning their expectations if you intend to use the database with a group of people. This can help you determine what information you need to include to make the database complete.

With a table created hold your data, Access 2007 provides a set of field templates that you can add to contain your data.

Determine the Tables that You Need
Gather all of the information that you want to store in the database and then divide the information into separate tables. A table should contain related information about one subject only. The same information should not appear in more than one table in a database. You can work more efficiently and reduce errors if you need to update information in only one location. You can also link tables together to combine information or show relationships among data in different tables.

Determine the Fields that You Need
In each table, you should consider which fields you plan to include. Each field should relate directly to the subject of the table. When adding fields, make sure to break down information into its smallest parts. For example, break down names into two fields called First Name and Last Name. Doing so provides more flexibility in sorting and using the information.

Do not include fields that you can get from other tables or calculations. For example, if you have a total field and a sales tax percentage field, you can calculate the sales tax by multiplying the total by the sales tax percentage. Tables with many fields increase the time that the database takes to process information.

Determine the Relationships between Tables
A relationship tells Access how to bring together related information stored in separate tables. You can use the primary key to form a relationship between tables. Access defines a *primary key* as one or more fields that uniquely identify each record in a table. For example, the primary key for a table of employees could be the Social Security number for each employee. You can learn more about primary keys in Chapter 21.

Start
Access

Y ou can start Access to create a new database or work with an existing database. Each time you start Access, the Getting Started window appears. This window enables you to create a blank database or use a template to create a database. In the right panel, a list of recently created and saved databases also appears.

When you click to select a template, you are prompted to give the template a new name and to save it to the default folder, My Documents in Windows XP or Documents in Vista. You can also create a link to a Windows SharePoint Services site. For more about SharePoint Services, see Chapter 29.

What other ways can I start Access?

▼ You can also start Access from a shortcut icon placed on the desktop. To create this icon, open the program folder that contains Access. Then, with the right mouse button, click and drag the program icon to the desktop. Release the right mouse button and, from the shortcut menu that appears, select Create Shortcut(s) Here.

Start Access

① Click Start.

② Click All Programs.

③ Click Microsoft Office.

④ Click Microsoft Office Access 2007.

The Microsoft Access window appears.

The Getting Started window appears each time you start Access, enabling you to create a new blank database, create a database from a template, or open an existing database.

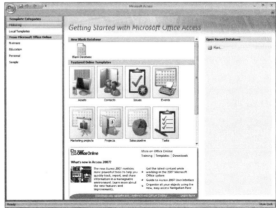

PART V

Create a Blank Database

I f you want to design your own database, you can create a blank database.

Each time you start Access, a New File task pane appears, enabling you to create a blank database or use a template to create a simple database. You can use a blank database when you have experience using Access and know exactly which fields you want to include, or when you want to create a complex database.

To store the database as a file on your computer, you must give the database a name. Access assigns a

default name to each database that you create, based on the template that you have chosen. In the case of a blank database the default is Database 1. You can give the database a more descriptive name to help you recognize it later.

Access automatically stores the database in the My Documents folder, but you can specify another location. In Vista this folder is named Documents.

Access displays the blank database on your screen. The database does not yet contain any objects, such as forms, reports, or tables.

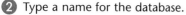

Create a Blank Database

① Click Blank Database.

Note: See Chapter 1 to learn how to open the Getting Started window.

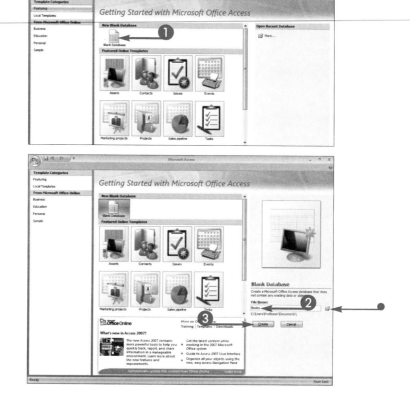

The Blank Database task pane appears.

② Type a name for the database.

- You can click the More icon (🖼) to change the location where Access stores your database.

③ Click Create.

Access creates a blank database with a new blank table.

● The Datasheet tab opens on the Ribbon.

④ Click New Field.

● The Field Templates task pane opens for the new blank table.

You can now add other objects, such as tables and reports, to the database.

⑤ To close this window, click the Close button (ⓧ).

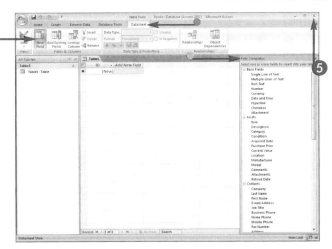

To reopen your database, start Access again.

○ Your new database is listed in the Open Recent Database task pane.

● You can also find your most recently used databases by clicking the More icon (📄) and browsing to their locations.

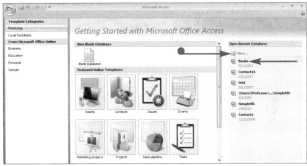

When I reopened my named blank database, the empty table was missing. What should I do?

▼ Although you saved the database, you did not enter any information into the table and you did not save the new table. You can follow the steps to create a table in Chapter 20. You can also find more information in the task "Rename or Delete an Object."

Can I create a blank database while working in Access?

▼ Yes. Click the Office button and select New to display the Getting Started window. Then follow the steps in this task.

I got a security warning when my database opened. Is that normal?

▼ Yes. Click the Options button in the security warning. In the dialog box that appears, click the Enable this Content option (☐ changes to ☑).

How do I create a new folder to store my database?

▼ When you click the More icon (📄) to choose a location for your new database, the File New Database dialog box opens. Click the Create New Folder button. Type a name for the folder and then press Enter.

Create a Database Using a Template

The Getting Started window lets you create a database quickly and efficiently by providing ready to use database templates. To display available templates, click Local Templates in the Getting Started window. From the Local Templates window, you can then select the type of database that you want to create.

Access offers ten database templates, including Assets, Contacts, Marketing Projects, and Tasks databases. You can choose the database that best suits the type of information that you want to store. Northwind Traders 2007 is a sophisticated database sample that you can open and explore to practice and learn more.

Microsoft Office Online offers four more categories of database templates: Business, Education, Personal, and Sample. For additional templates, you can visit http://office.microsoft.com.

When you open a database from a template, some database objects, such as tables and forms, are already created for you in the database. You can explore these objects by opening the Navigation pane. For more information about the Navigation pane, see the task "Using the Navigation Pane."

Create a Database Using a Template

1. Start Access and open the Getting Started window.

Note: See Chapter 1 to learn how to start Access.

2. Click Local Templates.

   The Local Templates window appears.

3. Select the type of template that you want to use.

   Access names the database for the template.

4. Type a new name for the database, or accept the template name.

   ● You can click the More icon (🔳) to change the database location.

   ● You can select this option to place your database directly on a SharePoint Services site (🔳 changes to ✅).

5. Click Create.

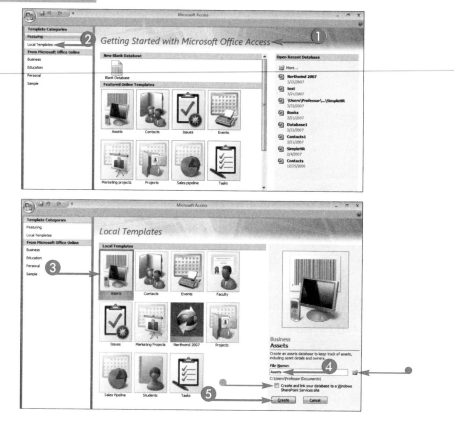

A new database is created, based on the template.

● A table with fields is created as part of the template.

⑥ Click Options.

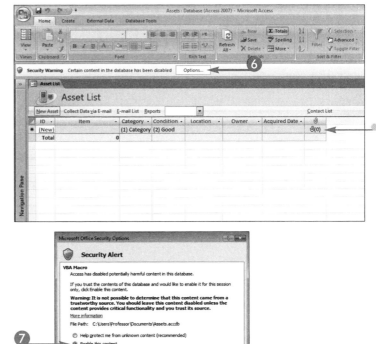

A Security Alert appears.

⑦ Click to select the Enable this content option (◉ changes to ◉).

⑧ Click OK.

The Security Alert closes.

How can I start the Database Templates feature while working in Access?

▼ Click the Office button and click New to display the Getting Started window. Then follow the steps in this task. When you create a new database, Access closes any currently open databases.

How can I use a SharePoint Services site?

▼ SharePoint Services sites are part of Windows Server solutions for local and wide area networks that enable collaboration. For more information about using a SharePoint Services site, see Chapter 29.

Explore the Contextual Ribbon

The Access Ribbon has five main components, each of which enables the user to perform specific tasks for producing professional documents.

Clicking one of the tabs brings up a different set of related options for a particular task, and selecting a portion of a document brings up more contextual options.

With the Ribbon, you can work with parts of a document or the entire document to make formatting changes, reorganize sections, add references, and go through a final review process to make sure that your document is polished and professional.

Keep in mind that you may not see all of the tabs, or all of the features within a tab, if you are running in Compatibility Mode (Office 97-2003).

Home

You can use the Home tab to change the appearance of parts of a database such as a table. In the Views group, you can also toggle between Design and Datasheet view for a table, or open the various views for other database objects.

The Home tab lets you change formatting. You can change fonts and font size or add bold, italic, or underline to selected text in your database. You can also copy and paste, and apply formats from one selection to another. The Home tab also lets you work with individual records, perform sort and filter operations, and find and replace text.

Create

The Create tab lets you create new tables from templates, from SharePoint lists or directly in design mode. The Create tab also lets you create and design forms to enter data into tables, and create and manage reports for accumulating information. In the Create tab, you can use the Query Wizard or design queries to sort, filter, and otherwise extract information from your tables. You can also use the Macro feature in the Create tab to create macros that you can attach to buttons and other objects.

External Data

In the External Data tab, you can manage data tasks for importing and exporting information from other Access databases, Excel spreadsheets, SharePoint lists, and other data sources. You can also collect data from e-mail, and manage e-mail replies with data. If you are connected to a SharePoint server, you can manage your SharePoint lists from the External Data tab.

Database Tools

The Database Tools tab lets you run macros and access the VBA editor. The Database Tools show existing relationships between tables and help you create new ones, along with showing object dependencies. The Analyze group lets you document and analyze the performance of the database, as well as analyze individual tables. The Move Data group provides options to move information to an SQL or other Access database. In the Database Tools tab, you can also add encryption with a password, create switchboards that introduce the database, and manage add-ins.

Datasheet

The Datasheet tab is active when you are working on a table to add and manage fields, create a lookup entry from another table, and insert or rename fields and columns. The Datasheet tab allows you to assign a data type to a field, and also view and manage relationships and dependencies.

Using the Navigation Pane

Y ou can use the Navigation pane to organize or reorganize your database objects in a way that makes sense to you.

In a larger and more complex database, using the filters in the Navigation pane allows you to locate and work with specific objects by their category, type, created date, and modified date.

By choosing to organize your Navigation pane by object type, you can quickly differentiate your tables, forms, queries, and reports.

You can close the Navigation pane if you need more space to work in the Access window.

How do I reopen the Navigation pane?

▼ You can click the reverse double arrow to reopen the Navigation pane when it is closed. The words *Navigation Pane* appear vertically in the panel when it is closed.

I am just getting started and do not have any objects in my database. How can I see a complete Navigation pane?

▼ Follow the steps in the tasks "Start Access" and "Create a Database Using a Template." You can choose to open a new database based on the Northwind 2007 sample. It contains many different objects in the Navigation pane, including tables, forms, reports, and queries.

Using the Navigation Pane

● The Navigation pane is open with the database window.

You can click double arrow (<<) to close the Navigation pane.

You can click double arrow (>>) to collapse the Navigation pane.

① Click the Expand down arrow (▼) to display the Navigation pane options.

② Click Object Type.

The objects in your database are reorganized by tables, forms, queries, reports, macros, and modules (if any).

PART V

Parts of the Database Window

Y ou can use the Database window to view and work with all of the objects in a database. Each type of object in the Database window displays a different icon. When the Database window is hidden, you can press the F11 key to bring the

Database window in front of all other open windows in Access.

The Database window enables you to quickly open an object in the database to perform a task, such as adding a record to a table or changing a form.

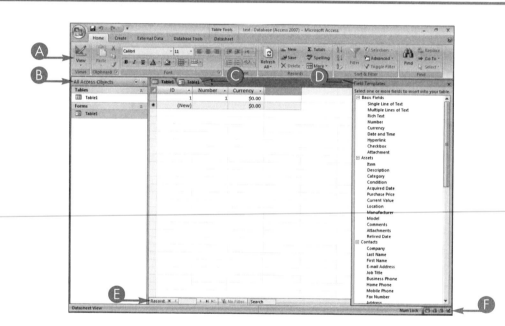

Ⓐ Ribbon

This area opens a set of contextual tabs that enable the tasks described in the task "Explore the Contextual Ribbon."

Ⓑ Navigation Pane

This area displays the types of objects in the database, including tables, forms, queries, reports, macros, and modules (if any). When you double-click an object, it opens in the main database window with an object tab.

Ⓒ Object Tabs

Tabs represent the objects that are opened from the Navigation pane for further revision.

Ⓓ Field Templates

This task pane appears when you click to add a new field to a table. It lets you automatically add a specific field and data type to a table.

Ⓔ Status Bar

Located at the bottom of the database window, the status bar provides navigation through database objects, along with filter and search features.

Ⓕ Views

These are buttons that let you alternate between Data Sheet, PivotTable, PivotChart, and Design view for tables. Forms have three views: Form view, Layout view, and Design view. Reports have the same views as forms, along with Print Preview.

Rename or Delete an Object

To meet the needs of your constantly changing database, you can change the names of the objects in your database to better identify them. You can also delete objects that you no longer need. Before you can delete a table with a relationship to another table, you must first delete the relationship. If you delete or rename items, some queries, reports, and macros may not function properly. For more information on relationships, see Chapter 21.

I tried to rename a table in my Navigation pane and I got an error message telling me to close it. How do I do that?

▼ When an object such as a table, form, or report is open in the database window, it has a tab at the top of the window. Right-click the tab and click Close to remove the tab and close the object. You can then rename or delete the object.

Rename or Delete an Object

Rename an object

1 Right-click the object name that you want to change.

This example uses Table1 on the Navigation pane.

2 Click Rename.

The object name is highlighted.

3 Type a new object name.

4 Press Enter.

• Access renames the object.

Delete an object

1 Click the object that you want to delete on the Navigation pane.

2 Click the Home tab.

3 Click Delete.

• A dialog box appears, confirming the deletion.

4 Click Yes.

Access permanently deletes the object.

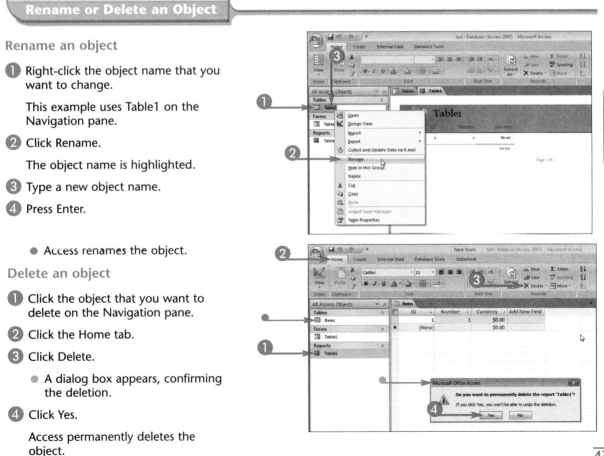

Open and Save a Database

Y ou can open an existing database and display it on your screen. After you open a database, you can review and make changes to it.

Databases can be located on your computer, on someone else's computer, or on a server on your network. In many offices, databases are kept on a central computer so that office staff can work with the data. This is common for customer contact information, product inventory, or financial applications.

You can have only one database open at a time. Access closes a database that displays on your screen when you open another database.

When you create a database, you assign it a name and then save it. After that, you do not need to resave the database. Access saves data in tables each time you add a record. However, you do need to save other objects, such as forms, reports, and queries. Saving these objects is covered in the chapters on each object type.

Open and Save a Database

1 Click the Office button.

2 Click Open.

● You can click any recent documents that are shown in the right panel to open the databases.

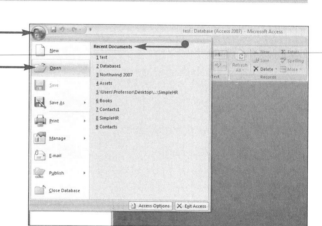

The Open dialog box appears.

You can scroll through the list for the current folder, or click another location for your file.

3 Click the database that you want to open.

4 Click Open.

Access opens the database.

⑤ You can click the Options button to enable all content in the database.

⑥ You can click the open double arrow (⏩) to open the Navigation pane.

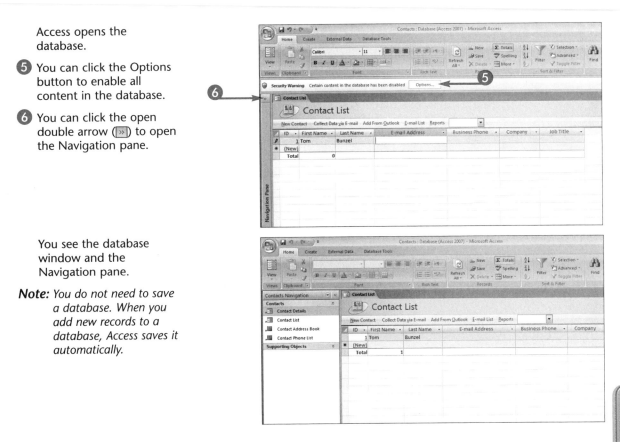

You see the database window and the Navigation pane.

Note: *You do not need to save a database. When you add new records to a database, Access saves it automatically.*

MASTER IT

Can I prevent other people on a network from opening a database?

▼ Yes. If you save the database on a network, other people can open it even while you are using it. To prevent others from opening the database while you are working on it, click the Office button and click Open. In the Open dialog box, click the Open down arrow (🔽) and then click Open Exclusive. Now you have exclusive access to the file. No one else can open or modify it.

Why do some sample databases require that I reinsert the Office disc before the database will load?

▼ The database templates may not have been installed along with Access. This is the case if you attempt to open one of the sample databases and a message box appears, prompting you to install the database. Click Yes to install the sample database. A dialog box appears, asking you to insert the Office installation disc. Insert the Office installation disc and click OK.

Create
a Table

A table in a database stores a collection of information about a specific topic, such as a list of client addresses. You can create a table in Datasheet view to store new information in rows and columns.

A table consists of fields and field names. A *field* is a specific category of information in a table. A *field name* identifies the information in a field. You can use up to 64 characters to name a field.

A *record* is a collection of information — a set of completed fields — about one person, place, or thing in a table.

When you save a table, you give the table a name. You can use up to 64 characters to name a table. You should use a descriptive name so that you can easily identify the table and its purpose or contents.

By default, in the first field created in your table, Access automatically sets a primary key as a field named ID. A *primary key* is one or more fields that uniquely identify each record in a table. Each table that you create should have a primary key. Later on, you can change the field that is the primary key from ID to another field that you create in which each record is unique.

Create a Table

1 Click the Create tab.

2 Click Table.

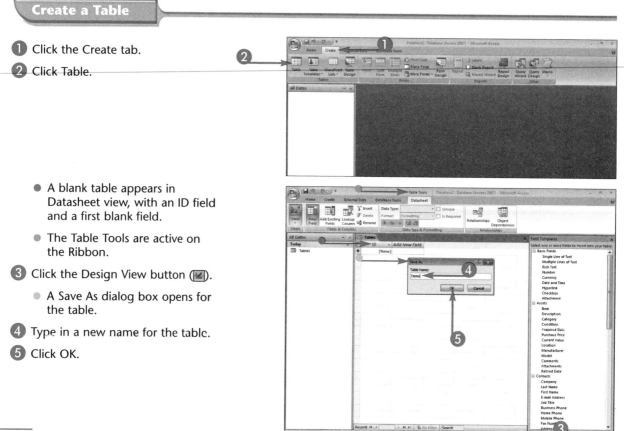

- A blank table appears in Datasheet view, with an ID field and a first blank field.

- The Table Tools are active on the Ribbon.

3 Click the Design View button (⊞).

- A Save As dialog box opens for the table.

4 Type in a new name for the table.

5 Click OK.

The table opens in Design view.

- The Design tab of Table Tools is active on the Ribbon.

- The first default ID field is identified as the primary key.

6 Click the Datasheet View button (▦).

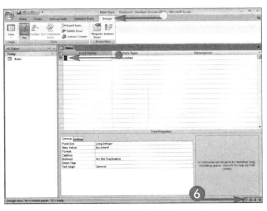

The table opens in Datasheet view.

- The Field Templates panel opens.

- You can click to change to Design view (▨).

Is there another way to create a table?

▼ Yes. You can create a table in Design view. In the Create tab, click Table Design in the **Tables** group. Design view gives you more control over the structure of the table and the type of information that each field will contain. When you open a new table in Design view, a tab with a default name (Table2) opens in the Database window. For information on working in Design view, see Chapter 21.

Can I use a table that I created in another database?

▼ Yes. You can import a table from another database, which saves you from having to create a new table. Click the External Data tab in the Ribbon to display the Import group. You can click to import a table from another Access database, Excel, a SharePoint List, a text or XML format, and more.

Can I set a different primary key later?

▼ Yes. You can set the primary key at any time. See Chapter 21 for details on setting a primary key.

Create a Table Using Templates

The Table templates help you to quickly create a table that suits your needs. There are five template categories to choose from: Contacts, Tasks, Issues, Events, and Assets.

Each of these templates automatically includes a few default fields when you create the table. You can scroll along the bottom of the Database window to see all of the default field headings.

The new table opens in Datasheet view, with the Field templates accessible. There are specific field templates available for each of the table templates, or you can add field templates from any other category.

With the new table open in Datasheet view, you can close the tab to rename the table in the Navigation pane, or click the Design View button; you are then prompted to keep the default name or rename the table.

Create a Table Using Templates

1 Click the Create tab.

2 Click Table Templates.

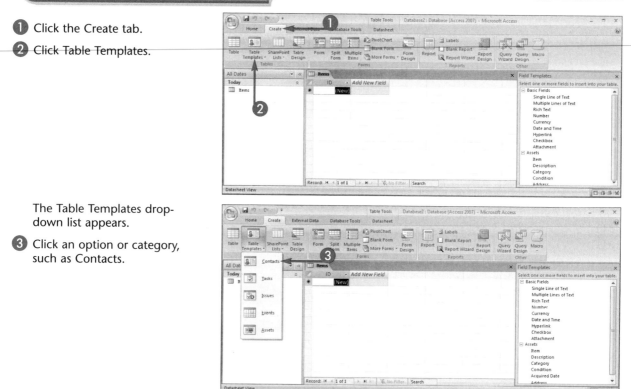

The Table Templates drop-down list appears.

3 Click an option or category, such as Contacts.

- A new table opens in Datasheet view, based on the chosen template.

- The Table Tools are active on the Ribbon.

4 Scroll along the bottom of the window to see all of the fields that were created by the template.

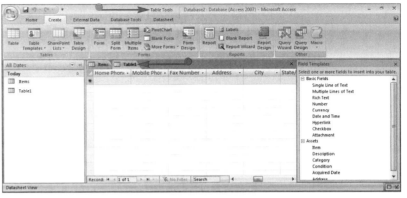

5 Right-click the tab for the table.

6 Click Save.

- The Save As dialog box opens.

You can rename the table in the Table Name text field.

7 Click OK.

- The table that you created with the template is saved and renamed, and appears in the Navigation pane.

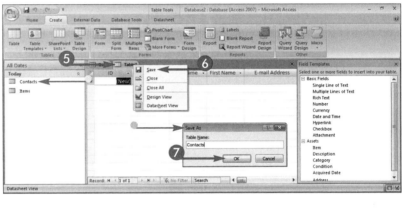

How can I quickly delete any unwanted fields that were created by the template?

▼ You can right-click a field and select Delete Column. Alternatively, click to switch to Design view (🗔). Then click to select the row that represents the field, and press the Delete key.

Can I close the Field Templates panel to see more of the datasheet?

▼ Yes. You can click the Close button (🗵) to close the Field Templates panel and expand your Datasheet view. To reopen the Field Templates panel, click the Datasheet tab on the Ribbon and click New Field in the Fields & Columns group. The Field Templates panel reappears.

How can I quickly rename a default field?

▼ Right-click the field name and click Rename Column. A black highlight appears over the current name, and you can type in a new name. Although you can rename the field, the data type represented by the field remains the same. For more information, see the task "Understanding Data Types."

PART V

Add Fields from Templates

The Table templates automatically create a table with a set of fields, based on the template that you chose.

You can quickly add other fields to your table from any of the other templates, Basic fields, and Project fields, by using the Field Templates panel.

With the table created, the Table Tools are active on the Ribbon. You can click the Datasheet tab of the Table Tools and then click New Field to toggle between opening and closing the Field Templates panel.

To add a field from the Field templates, click to select the column to the left of where you want to add the field.

When you double-click the field name in the Field Templates panel, that field is added to the table.

You can click the Design View button to modify the new field and its properties. For more information on changing the properties of a field, see the task "Display Field Properties" in Chapter 21.

If you need to undo the addition of a new field, the Undo button in the Quick Access toolbar will not work. You need to right-click the field name and choose Delete Column. If you want to move the field in Datasheet view, you must delete the column first and then add the field in a new location from the Field Templates panel. Keep in mind that you can lose important data if you delete a column. To temporarily save a column, you can copy it to the Clipboard before you delete it.

Add Fields from Templates

① Click the Datasheet tab of the Table Tools.

● You can click New Field to open the Field Templates panel.

② Scroll through the fields to locate the field that you want to add.

③ Click to select the field column to the left of the one that you want to add.

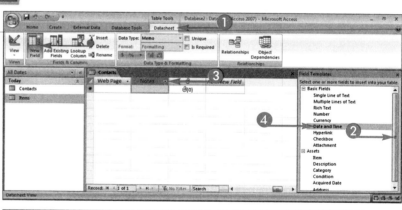

④ Double-click the name of the field that you want to add.

● The field that you chose is added to the table.

This example adds a date and time field, and a calendar icon (🗓️) also appears.

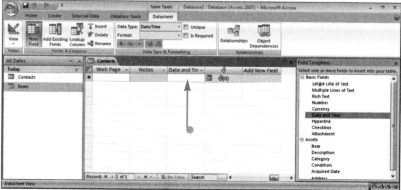

- You can drag to expand the column to accommodate the name (♀ changes to ╬).

The new field is ready for you to enter data.

Note: *To enter data into the table, see the task "Add or Delete Records."*

PART V

Which field should I use as the primary key?

▼ You should use a field that holds a unique value for each record. For example, in a table that stores data related to inventory, you could use the Part Number field as the primary key, because each product has its own unique catalog or stock number.

What is the little pop-up that appeared in the task?

▼ In this task, a Date and Time field is added. The pop-up is a calendar (🗓) that you can use to quickly add a date to a record. The pop-up appears when you click in the empty field to add your data.

How do I delete a table?

▼ Before you delete a table, make sure that the table does not contain information that you will need in the future and is not used by any other objects in your database, such as a form or report. Locate the table that you want to delete in the Navigation pane, select the table, right-click it, and choose Delete. You can also click to select the table and then press the Delete key.

Enter Data in a Table

Y ou can enter data into a table in Access in much the same way as you enter data into a worksheet in Excel. That is, you enter data into a *cell*, which is the intersection of a column and row.

The field names that you typed when you created the table are the column headings, and they help to identify what contents you need to enter into each cell. For more information on creating a table, see the task "Create a Table."

Access adds a new row to the table each time you enter another record, and so you can enter as many records as you need. Access automatically saves each record that you enter.

When you finish entering the records for a table, you can close the table. The name of the table appears in the Database window as long as the table is selected in the Navigation pane.

To enter large amounts of data, you may want to use a form. For more information on forms, see Chapter 22.

Enter Data in a Table

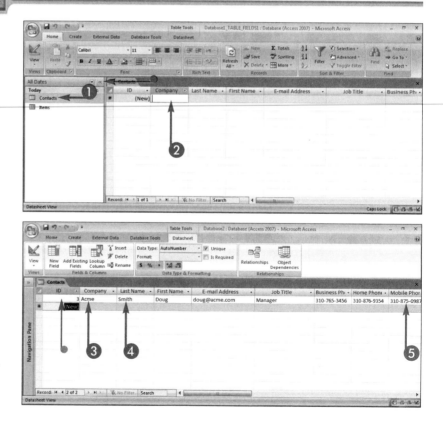

① Double-click the table in the Navigation pane to open it in the Database window.

Note: Access creates a default ID primary key field when it creates the table.

② Click the first empty cell in the row.

● You can click the close panel arrow (《) to close the Navigation pane and create more space for fields.

③ Type the data for each field.

④ Press Tab or Enter to move from field to field.

⑤ At the end of each record, press Enter to add a new record.

● The record is added.

Access automatically saves your data after you enter the data in a cell.

⑥ Repeats Steps 2 to 5 until you have added all of the records that you need.

7 Right-click the tab for the table.

8 Click Close.

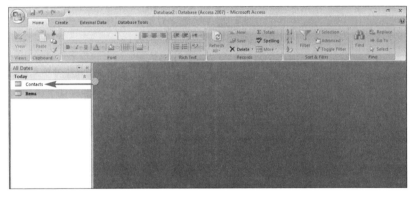

● The name of the table appears in the Navigation pane.

What are the symbols that appear in the fields?

▼ The asterisk icon (⁎) indicates where you can enter data for a new record. The pencil icon (🖉) indicates the record that you are editing. The drop-down arrow (▾) allows you to sort a column. For more information, see the task "Sort Records" in Chapter 23.

Is there an easier way to enter records into the datasheet?

▼ Yes. Forms are the preferred way to streamline data entry. See Chapter 22 for information on creating a data form.

What are the controls for at the bottom of the Database window?

▼ When you have entered a lot of records, these controls help you to move through them. For more information, see the task "Move through Records."

Understanding Data Types

Each database field accepts a specific type of data. If you use a template to create a table, the template determines the proper data types, depending on the data field content. If you set up a table by entering data, the data types are all set to match the type of entry that you make in that field. When adding records, you should enter the appropriate data type into the field. Chapter 21 explains how you can change the data type.

Text
This data type accepts entries up to 255 characters long that include any combination of text and numbers, such as an address. Use this data type for numbers that you do not want to use in calculations, such as phone numbers or ZIP codes.

Memo
This data type accepts entries up to 64,000 characters long that include any combination of text and numbers. This data type is useful for notes or lengthy descriptions.

Number
This data type accepts only numbers. These numbers can be used in calculations.

Date/Time
This data type accepts only dates and times. You can enter dates as 6/18/03 or Jun-18-03, and you can enter times as 6:25AM, 6:25:55, or 18:25.

Currency
This data type accepts only monetary values. It accepts up to 15 numbers to the left of the decimal point and 4 numbers to the right of it. The Currency data type automatically displays data as currency. For example, if you type 3428, the data appears as $3,428.00.

AutoNumber
This data type automatically numbers each record for you. The AutoNumber data type automatically assigns a unique number in a sequential or random order to each record in a table.

Yes/No
This data type accepts only one of two values — for example, Yes/No, True/False, or On/Off.

OLE Object
This data type accepts OLE objects. An *OLE object* is an item created in another program, such as a document created in Word or a chart created in Excel. OLE objects can also include sounds and pictures. The Attachments field is a more user-friendly way to add these types of files.

Hyperlink
This data type accepts hyperlinks. You can select a hyperlink to jump to another document on an intranet, on a Web page, or on the World Wide Web. You can enter a Web site address, such as www.wiley.com.

Attachment
You can use attachments to store multiple files in a field, and you can even store various types of files in that field. For example, in a Contacts database, you can attach one or more pictures, as well as biographical information, to the record for each contact.

Lookup Wizard
The Lookup Wizard lets you connect fields or results in another table to the field in the current table.

Open a Table

You can open a table and display its contents on your screen, so that you can review and make changes to the table.

You can open a table in Datasheet or Design view. Datasheet view displays all of the records in a table so that you can enter, edit, and review records. If you are adding records to a table, you do not need to save the table; the table is saved each time you add or edit a record.

Design view displays the structure of a table. You can change settings in Design view to specify the kind of data that you want to enter in each field of a table. For more information on Design view, see Chapter 21.

When you finish working in Design view, you need to save the changes that you made; unlike Datasheet view, changes are not automatically saved in Design view.

Open a Table

1 If it is closed, open the Navigation pane by clicking open panel arrow (⟫) or by pressing the F11 key.

2 Double-click the table that you want to open.

The table appears.

● The Table Tools are active on the Ribbon.

3 Make any editing changes or add any records.

Note: *To edit table data, see the task "Edit Data." To add records, see the task "Add or Delete Records."*

4 When you finish reviewing the table, right-click its tab.

5 Click Close.

The table is saved and closed.

Add or Delete Records

Y ou can add a new record to insert additional information into your table. Access automatically saves each new record that you add to a table.

You can use the blank row at the bottom of a table to add a record. You cannot add a record to the middle of a table. If you want to change the order of the records, you can sort the records. See Chapter 23 for more information on sorting records.

In your AutoNumber or primary key field, Access automatically enters a number for each record that you add.

In addition to adding records, you can also delete records that you no longer need. For example, you can delete a record containing information on a company that you no longer use.

When you delete a record, you may also want to delete any related records in other tables. For example, if you delete a company from your supplier table, you may also want to delete records from your product table that contain information about the products that the company supplies.

Add or Delete Records

Add a record

1 Open the Datasheet view (📧) in the Database window.

2 Click the first available new blank record in the field after the ID field.

The insertion point moves into the field.

3 Type the data for this field.

4 Press Tab and type the data for the next field.

5 Repeat Steps 3 and 4 to complete the record.

The record is entered in the table.

Delete a record

① Click to the left of the record that you want to delete.

● The record is selected.

② Click the Home tab.

③ Click Delete.

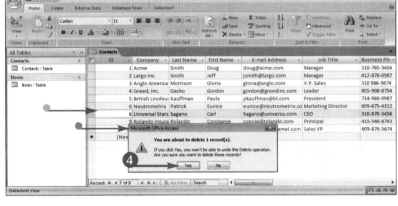

● A warning dialog box prompts you to confirm the deletion.

④ Click Yes.

● The record is deleted from the table.

Is there a faster way to enter data into cells in a new record?

▼ Yes. You can copy the data from the cell above the current cell. To do so, press Ctrl+' (apostrophe). To insert the current date, press Ctrl+; (semicolon).

Can I use a form to add a record?

▼ Yes. You can use a form to add a record to a table. See Chapter 22 for information on creating and using data forms.

How do I delete several records at once?

▼ Select the records that you want to delete by dragging through the row selector for these records. In the Home tab, click the Delete button. Confirm the deletion by clicking Yes. Keep in mind that you cannot delete noncontiguous records.

Can I undo a record deletion?

▼ No. As a result, you must be sure that you want to delete a record. If you delete a record accidentally, you have to re-create the record. To remind you of the consequences, Access displays a dialog box asking you to confirm the deletion.

PART V

Move through Records

Y ou can easily move through the records in your table when reviewing or editing information.

When editing records, you can change the location of the insertion point in your table. The insertion point must be located in the cell that you want to edit. Access provides buttons that allow you to instantly move the insertion point to the first, last, previous, or next record. You can also move from field to field within a record.

If your table contains a large amount of information, your computer screen may not be able to display all of the fields and records at once. You can use the scroll bars to view the fields and records that are not displayed. You can scroll one field or record at a time. You can also quickly scroll to any field or record in your table. The scroll bars do not appear if all of the fields and records are displayed on your screen.

Keep in mind that, although scrolling allows you to see the rest of the table, it does not move the insertion point.

Move through Records

Click to select a cell

1 Click the cell that you want to contain the insertion point.

● This area displays the number of the record containing the insertion point and the total number of records in the table.

Use the record buttons

1 To quickly move to another record, click one of the following buttons:

First Record (⏮)

Previous Record (◀)

Next Record (▶)

Last Record (⏭)

New Record (▶*)

● A different record displays, depending on the button that you press.

Scroll through fields

1 To quickly scroll to any field, drag the scroll box along the scroll bar until the field that you want to view appears.

Search records

1 To locate a record, you can begin to type its contents in the Search box.

● As you type letters, the first relevant record is highlighted in the Datasheet view.

How do I use my keyboard to move through fields and records?

▼ Press the Tab key to move to the next field in the current record. Press the up- or down-arrow key to move up or down one record. Press the Page Up or Page Down key to move up or down one screen of records.

How can I quickly sort and filter records?

▼ You can click the down arrow (▼) in any field label to open the sort window. You can sort the records in ascending or descending order (A to Z or Z to A). You can also deselect any records that you want to hide (☑ changes to ☐), or apply one of several text filters or number filters, depending upon the data type of the field. For more information on filters, see Chapter 23.

Select Data

Before performing many tasks in a table, you must select the data with which you want to work. For example, you must select data that you want to move or copy.

Selected data appears highlighted on your screen, which makes the selected data stand out from the rest of the data in your table.

You can select the part of the table with which you want to work — for example, a field, record, cell, or

data in a cell. Selecting a field or record is useful when you need to delete the field or record from your table. Selecting one cell, or data in a cell, is useful when you are editing data in your table.

You can select multiple fields, records, or cells to perform the same task on all of the fields, records, or cells at once. This saves you from having to perform the same task again and again.

Select a field

1️⃣ Position the mouse over the name of the field that you want to select.

2️⃣ Click the field name.

The column and all of its contents are selected.

To select multiple fields, position the mouse over the name of the first field. Then click and drag until you highlight all of the fields that you want to select.

Select a record

1️⃣ Click the area to the left of the record that you want to select.

That record is selected.

To select multiple records, position the mouse over the area to the left of the first record. Then click and drag until you highlight all of the records that you want to select.

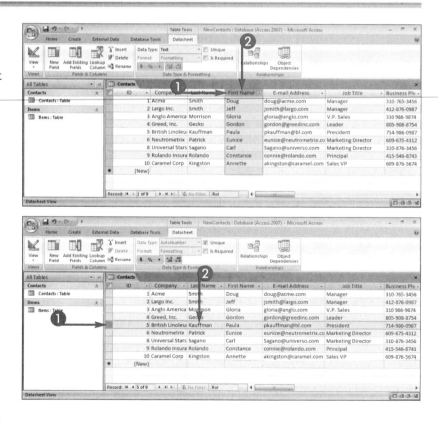

Select a cell

1. Position the mouse over the left edge of the cell that you want to select.

2. Click that edge to select the cell.

   That cell is now selected.

   To select multiple cells, position the mouse over the left edge of the first cell. Then click and drag until you highlight all of the cells that you want to select.

Select data in a cell

1. Position the mouse pointer over the data (⇩ changes to 〕).

2. Click and drag until you highlight all of the data that you want to select.

   The data is now selected.

How do I deselect data?

▼ To deselect data, click anywhere in the table.

How do I select all of the records in a table?

▼ To select all of the records in a table, click the blank area to the left of the field names. You can also press Ctrl+A to select all of the records in a table.

Is there a fast way to select a word in a cell?

▼ Yes. To quickly select a word, double-click the word.

How can I quickly select a large group of cells?

▼ To quickly select a large group of cells, click the first cell in the group that you want to select, and then scroll to the end of the group. Hold down the Shift key as you click the last cell in the group. Access highlights all of the cells between the first and last cell that you select.

Edit
Data

Y ou can quickly replace all of the data in a cell with new data. After you enter data into your table, you can change the data to correct a mistake or update the data.

The flashing insertion point in a cell indicates where Access will remove or add data. When you remove data using the Backspace key, Access removes the character to the left of the insertion point. When you insert data, Access adds the characters that you type at the location of the insertion point.

As you edit data, Access displays symbols to the left of the records. The arrow icon indicates the current

record. The pencil icon indicates the record that you are editing. The asterisk icon indicates where you can enter data for a new record.

If you make a mistake while editing data, you can use the Undo feature to immediately undo your most recent change.

You do not have to save the changes that you make. When you move from the field that you are editing to another field, Access automatically saves your changes.

Edit Data

Change data

1 Click the location in the cell where you want to change the data (⟨ changes to ⌶).

A flashing insertion point appears in the cell.

You can press the left- or right-arrow key to move the insertion point to where you want to remove or add characters.

2 Type or edit your data.

● To remove the character to the left of the insertion point, press the Backspace key.

To insert data where the insertion point flashes on your screen, type the data.

3 Press Enter.

The record is now updated.

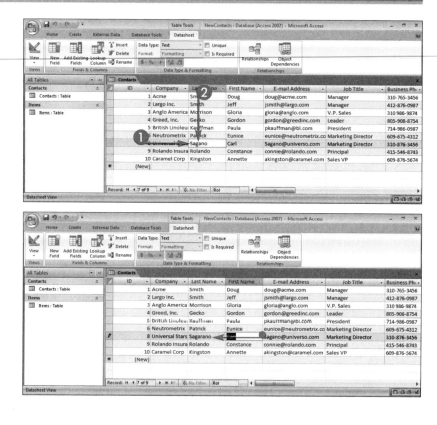

Replace all data in a cell

1 Double-click the contents of the cell that you want to replace.

The entire contents of the cell are highlighted.

2 Type the new data.

3 Press Enter.

• The new data replaces the original data.

• To undo the change, click the Undo button (⟲).

Note: *You can only undo the last edit that you made.*

How can I quickly find data that I want to edit?

▼ Click a cell in the field containing the data that you want to find. Click Find on the Home tab. The Find and Replace dialog box opens with the Find tab active. Type the data that you want to find, and then click the Find Next button.

Can I check my table for spelling errors?

▼ Yes. You can find and correct all of the spelling errors in a table. Click the Spelling button in the Records group of the Home tab to start the spell check. To spell check a single field or record, select the field or record before you begin.

Can I copy data in a table?

▼ Yes. Copying data is useful when you want several records in a table to display the same information. After you edit the data in one record, you can copy the data to other records. Select the data that you want to copy, and then click the Copy button (📋) in the Home tab. Click the location where you want to place the data, and then click Paste on the Home tab.

Zoom Into a Cell

You can zoom into any cell in a table, which can make the contents of the cell easier to review and edit.

Zooming into a cell is useful when the columns in your table are not wide enough to display the entire contents of a cell. For example, a cell may contain a long address or a long description that Access cannot completely display.

When you zoom into a cell, Access displays the contents of the cell in the Zoom dialog box. You can edit the contents of the cell directly in the Zoom dialog box.

If you plan to enter a large amount of data into a cell, you can also zoom into an empty cell, which lets you easily view all of the data that you are typing into the cell at once.

Zoom Into a Cell

① Click the cell containing the data that you want to review and edit.

② Press the Shift key as you press the F2 key.

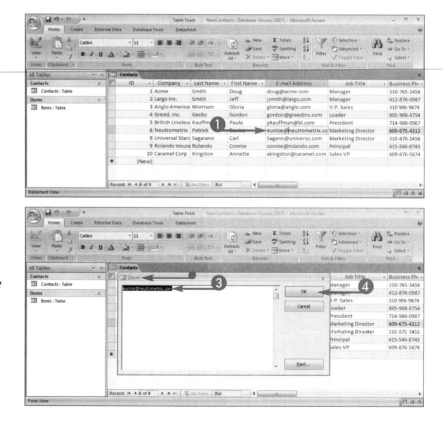

● The Zoom dialog box appears.

③ Review or edit the data.

Note: For more information about editing table contents, see the task "Edit Data."

④ Click OK.

The table displays any changes that you made to the data.

Change Column Width

You can change the width of a column in your table, which lets you view data that is too long to display in the column. Reducing the width of a column allows you to display more fields on your screen at once.

You can have Access automatically adjust the width of a column to fit the longest item in the column.

After you change the width of a column, you must save the table to have Access save the new column width.

MASTER IT

How do I change the height of the rows?

▼ To change the height of rows in your table, position the mouse over the bottom edge of the row that you want to change. You can then drag the row edge either up or down. When you change the height of a row, all of the rows in the table automatically change to the new height. You cannot change the height of a single row.

Change Column Width

① To change the width of a column, position the mouse over the right edge of the column heading (⟨⟩ changes to ╋).

② Click and drag the column edge until the line displays the column width that you want.

The column displays the new width.

③ Click the Save button (💾).

To change a column width to fit the longest item in the column, you can double-click the right edge of the column heading.

Hide a Field

Y ou can temporarily hide a field in your table to reduce the amount of data displayed on your screen. This can help you to work with specific data and can make your table easier to read.

Hiding a field enables you to review only fields of interest. For example, if you want to browse through the names and telephone numbers of all of your clients, you can hide the fields that display all other information.

When you hide a field, Access does not delete the field. The data in the hidden field remains intact.

Hide a Field

① Click the name of the field that you want to hide.

The field is selected.

② Right-click the field.

③ Click Hide Columns.

● The field disappears from the table, and remaining columns shift to the left.

Freeze a Field

Y ou can freeze a field to make it remain on your screen at all times. Freezing a field enables you to keep important data displayed on your screen as you move through a large table. For example, you can freeze a field containing the names of your clients so that the names remain on your screen while you scroll through the rest of the data for the clients.

You can unfreeze a field at any time. With the column selected, right-click it and select Unfreeze All Columns. You can also hide or freeze more than one field at a time. To hide or freeze multiple fields, you must first select the fields that you want to hide or freeze. You can then hide or freeze the fields as you would hide or freeze a single field.

Freeze a Field

① Click the name of the field that you want to freeze.

The field is selected.

② Right-click the field.

③ Click Freeze Columns.

④ Click any cell in the table to deselect the field.

● Access moves the field to the left side of the table and frames it.

● You can use this scroll bar to move through the fields to the right of the dark vertical line.

The frozen field remains displayed on-screen, regardless of how far you scroll.

Embed Attachment Files in Fields

Besides creating fields that hold the various other data types, you can also use attachments to store several files in a single field, and you can even store multiple types of files in that field. For example, in a contacts database, you can now attach one or more supporting documents, such as a resume, to the record for each contact. In the same field, you can also attach a photo of each contact, or any other file on your computer.

Attachments only work in the Access 2007 file format; to add attachments to files created in earlier versions, these files must first be converted to the 2007 format. For more information, see the task "Save in Different Versions" in Chapter 2.

You can automatically create an Attachment field by opening a table from a template. You can also add an Attachment field from the Basic section of the Field Templates panel. For more information, see the tasks "Create a Table Using Templates" and "Add Fields from Templates."

You can attach a maximum of 2GB of data (the maximum size for an Access database). Individual files cannot exceed 256MB in size.

You can use the Attachments dialog box to add, edit, and manage attachments. You can open the dialog box directly from the Attachment field in a table by double-clicking the field. If you want to manage attachments from a form or view attachments from a report, you must add the attachment control to the form or report. See Chapter 22 for information on forms and Chapter 24 for more about reports.

Embed Attachment Files in Fields

① In Datasheet view (📄), scroll to the Attachment field (📎).

② Double-click the record to which you want to add attachments.

  ● The Attachments dialog box opens.

③ Click Add.

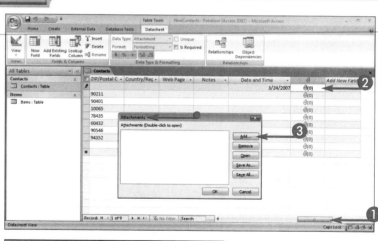

The Choose File dialog box opens.

④ Scroll through and locate the file or files that you want to attach.

⑤ Select the files that you want to attach.

You can select multiple files by pressing the Ctrl key while you select them.

⑥ Click Open.

- The Choose File dialog box closes, and the Attachments dialog box shows the attachments.

7 Click OK.

- The record in the Attachment field shows two attachments.

How can I open the attachments from the database?

▼ Repeat Steps 1 and 2 in this task. When the Attachments dialog box opens, select the attachment that you want to view, and click Open. The file opens in the program that is registered for that file type. To save your changes permanently, return to Access and, in the Attachments dialog box, click OK.

A message similar to the following appears: "Changes to the attachment were saved to your hard drive in a temporary file. Would you like to save updates to the database?" Click Yes to save your changes.

Can I save attachments elsewhere?

▼ Yes. When you open the attachment in its native program, you can use Save As from the Office button. The Save As dialog box opens, and you can save the attachment to another location. However, to maintain the current version of the attachment in Access, you must also save it in the temporary folder (its default location) or reattach it to the field from its new location.

Switch between Datasheet and Design Views

You can view a table in Datasheet view or Design view. Each view allows you to perform different tasks, and Access allows you to quickly switch between the two views.

Datasheet view displays all of the records in a table. You can enter, edit, and review records in this view. Working in this view is covered in Chapter 20.

Design view displays the structure of a table. You can use this view when you want to make changes to the structure, layout, and design of the table.

You can change the data type and field property settings in this view. The data type determines the type of information that you can enter in a field, such as text, numbers, or dates. Specifying a data type helps to ensure that you enter the correct information in a field.

The field properties are a set of characteristics that provide additional control over the information that you can enter in a field. For example, you can specify the maximum number of characters that a field accepts.

Switch between Datasheet and Design Views

In this example, the table appears in Datasheet view (▦).

1 Click the Design View button (▨).

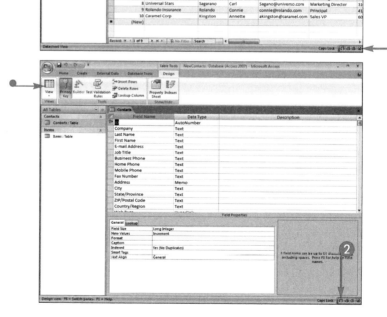

The table appears in Design view.

● The View button in the Views group of the Design tab on the Ribbon changes to the Datasheet button.

Note: *The View button in the Views group of the Design tab on the Ribbon toggles between Design and Datasheet view. You can click the View down arrow (▾) to choose these views as well as the PivotTable or PivotChart views.*

2 Click to switch to Datasheet view (▦).

Rearrange Fields

Y ou can change the order of fields to better organize the information in your table. For example, in a table that stores employee names and phone numbers, you may want to move the field containing work phone numbers so that it is in front of the field containing home phone numbers.

Rearranging the fields in a table does not affect how the fields display in other objects in the database, such as a form. Rearranging fields in Datasheet view also does not affect the arrangement of fields in Design view.

A thick line indicates the new location of the field that you are moving. If you move a field to an area of your table that is not displayed on the screen, Access scrolls through the table to show you the new location of the field.

After you change the order of fields in your table, you must save the table to keep the new arrangement of fields.

Rearrange Fields

1 In Design view, click to the left of the name of the field that you want to move.

Note: See the task "Switch between Datasheet and Design Views" to switch to Design view.

Access highlights the field.

2 Position the mouse over the field selector and then click and drag the selector to the new location.

A thick line shows the field's new location.

3 Release the mouse.

● The field appears in the new location.

4 Click the Save button (📄) to save your change.

Access saves the table design.

Note: The field's new location is also shown in Datasheet view.

Display Field Properties

Each field in a table has properties that you can display. The field properties are a set of characteristics that provide additional control over the kind of information that you can type in a field. For example, the Field Size property tells Access the maximum number of characters that a field can contain. You can display these properties to see the settings that affect data entry and the table display.

The properties that are available for a field depend on the type of data that the field contains. For example,

the Field Size property is available for a field containing text, but is not available for a field containing currency. The Decimal Places property is available for a field containing currency, but is not available for a field containing text.

You can display the available properties for any field in your table.

If you use a field in other objects in the database, such as a form or report, the other objects also use the same field properties.

Display Field Properties

1 Change to Design view.

Note: *See the task "Switch between Datasheet and Design Views" to switch views.*

● This area displays the field name and data type for each field in the table.

A frame appears around the current field.

● This area displays the properties for the current field.

2 To display the properties for another field, click the field name.

● This area displays the properties for the new field that you selected.

Add a Field Description

You can add a description to a field to identify the type of information the field contains. You can use up to 255 characters, including spaces, to describe a field.

Adding a description to a field can help you determine what kind of information you should enter in the field. For example, if a field has an abbreviated field name such as CNum, you can add a description such as "This field contains customer numbers" to help you enter information in the field.

After you add a description to a field, you must save the table to have Access save the description.

When you display your table in Datasheet view, you can click anywhere in the field to display the description that you added. The description appears on the status bar at the bottom of your screen.

If you use the field in another object in the database, such as a form, the other object displays the description when you are working with the field.

Add a Field Description

1. Click the description area for the field to which you want to add a description.

2. Type the description.

3. Click the Save button ().

4. Click to display the table in Datasheet view ().

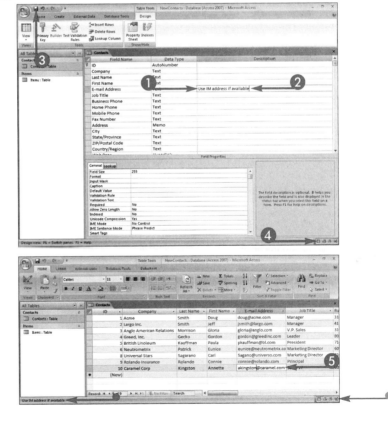

5. Click anywhere in the field to which you added the description.

● The description for the field appears in this area.

● You can click to return to Design view ().

PART V

Change the Data Type

You can change the type of data that you can enter in a field. You should first consider what type of data you want to be able to enter in the field. Access does not accept entries that do not match the data type that you specify. This helps to prevent errors when entering data. For example, you cannot enter text in a field with the Number data type.

Determine whether you want to be able to perform calculations using the data in the field. Access can calculate numbers in a Number or Currency field, but it cannot calculate numbers in a Text field.

The ability to sort records is also a consideration. Some data types, such as Memo, Hyperlink, and OLE Object, cannot be sorted.

If you change the data type for a field, Access may delete data in the field. Access displays a warning message before deleting any data. You can click OK to confirm the change or keep the original data type.

For more information on available data types, see Chapter 20.

Change the Data Type

① Display the table in Design view.

Note: See the task "Switch between Datasheet and Design Views" to switch views.

② Click the Data Type area for the field that you want to change.

A drop-down arrow (▼) appears.

③ Click the down arrow (▼) to display a list of data types.

④ Click the appropriate data type.

● The field changes to the new data type, and the properties that are available for the field may change.

⑤ Click the Save button (🖫).

Access saves the table design.

Rename a Field

Y ou can give a field a different name to more accurately describe the contents of the field, which can help prevent confusion between two similar fields in a table.

If you rename a field that is used in other objects in the database, such as a form or report, Access automatically changes the references in the database to ensure that the objects can access the information in the renamed field.

You can use up to 64 characters to name a field. You cannot use periods (.), exclamation points (!), or brackets ([ ]) in the name of the field. You should also avoid including spaces when you rename a field if you plan to enter the field name in an expression for a calculation. A field name that contains spaces is more likely to be entered incorrectly than one without spaces. For more information on using expressions in calculations, see Chapter 23.

Rename a Field

1 In Design view, double-click the field name that you want to change.

Access highlights the field name.

2 Type a new field name.

3 Press Enter.

● The field displays the new name.

Change the Field Size

You can change the field size of a text or number field to specify the maximum size of data that you can enter into the field.

You can change the maximum number of characters that a text field accepts. You can specify a field size of up to 255 characters for all fields except Memo, which you can make much larger.

You can change the number field to specify the size and type of numbers that you can type into the field. Most field size options allow you to enter whole numbers only. If you want to be able to enter decimal

numbers, such as 1.234, you can select up to 15 decimal places. When you add decimal places, you also increase the size of the field. Some number field types automatically include decimal numbers.

Access processes smaller field sizes more quickly than larger ones. Using smaller field sizes can help speed up tasks, such as searching for data in a field. This can also reduce the amount of space required to store a table on your computer. If a table contains thousands of records, reducing the size of a text field by one or two characters may save a considerable amount of drive space.

Change the Field Size

Change text field size

1. Click the field in which you want to accept a maximum number of characters.

   • This area displays the maximum number of characters that you can currently type in the field.

2. Double-click the number.

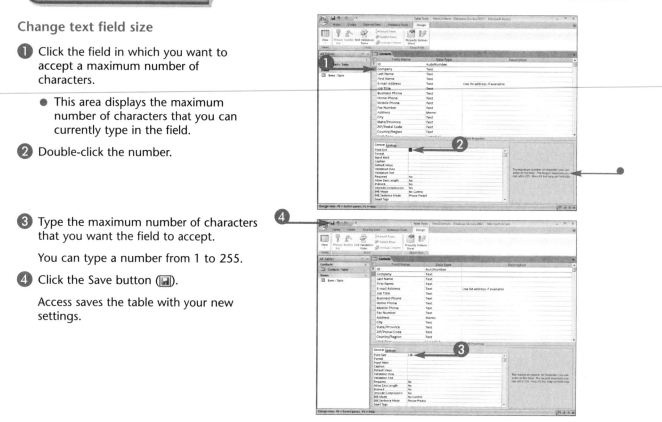

3. Type the maximum number of characters that you want the field to accept.

   You can type a number from 1 to 255.

4. Click the Save button (🖫).

   Access saves the table with your new settings.

Change number field type

① Click the field in which you want to accept only a certain type of numbering format.

② Click in the area beside Format.

③ Click the down arrow (🔽) to display a list of options.

④ Click the type of number format that you want the field to accept.

● Access sets the new format.

⑤ Click the SmartTag bolt icon (🔷); you can then also change any existing fields.

⑥ Click the Save button (💾).

Access saves the table with your new settings.

What are the minimum and maximum ranges for number fields?

Setting	Number Size
Byte	Between 0 and 255
Integer	Between –32,768 and 32,767
Long Integer	Between –2,147,483,648 and 2,147,483,647

Can I change the size of a field that already contains data?

▼ Yes. If you reduce the size of a text field containing data, Access shortens any data that is longer than the new field size. If you reduce the size of a number field containing data, Access may change or delete data that is larger than the new field size. Access displays a warning message before changing any data.

Can I change the field size that Access automatically uses for new text or number fields?

▼ Yes. Click the Office button and then click Access Options. The Access Options dialog box opens. Click the Object Designers tab. To change the size of text fields, click the Default Text field size spinner button (🔼) or type a new value. To change the size of number fields, click the Default Number field size down arrow (🔽) and choose a different option. Then click OK.

PART V

Select a Data Format

You can select a format to customize the way information appears in a field. When you select a format, you only change the way Access displays information on the screen. The values in the field do not change.

You can select a format for Number, Date/Time, Currency, AutoNumber, and Yes/No fields. Access does not provide formats for Text, Memo, OLE Object, or Hyperlink fields.

In a Number field, you can choose to display numbers in a format such as 1234.00 or $1,234.00. If you want

a number to display decimal places, you may also need to change the field size. For more information, see the task "Change the Field Size."

In a Date/Time field, you can choose to display a date as Tuesday, July 15, 2008 or 7/15/08. A Yes/No field can display values such as True/False, Yes/No, or On/Off.

After you select a format, Access automatically changes any data that you enter in the field to the new format. For example, if you type 3456, Access automatically displays the data as $3,456.00 if you chose the Currency format.

Select a Data Format

1. Click the field in which you want to use a new format.

2. Click the area beside Format.

3. Click the down arrow (▾) to display a list of formats.

   If you are asked to save the table, click Yes.

4. Click the format that you want to use.

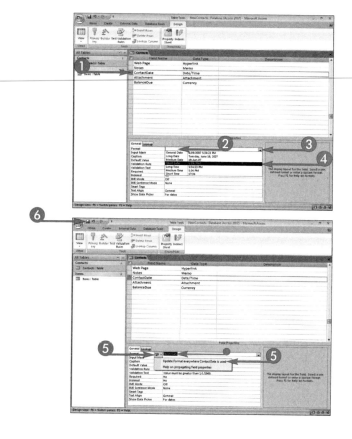

● Access displays the format in the Format property box.

5. Click the SmartTag bolt icon (⚡); you can then also change any existing fields.

6. Click the Save button (💾).

   Access updates the field with the new format.

Change the Number of Decimal Places

Y ou can specify how many decimal places Access uses to display numbers in a field. Some numbers, such as prices, require only two decimal places. Numbers used in scientific calculations may require more decimal places.

You can choose to display between 0 and 15 decimal places after the decimal point.

Changing the number of decimal places only affects how a number displays on the screen, not how a number is stored or used in calculations. For example, if you change the number of decimal

places to 1, the number 2.3456 displays as 2.3. However, Access stores and performs calculations using the number 2.3456.

If the Format property of a field is blank or set to General Number, then changing the number of decimal places does not affect the field. For information on selecting a format, see the task "Select a Data Format."

You may also need to change the field size so that the field can display numbers with decimal places. For information on changing the field size, see the task "Change the Field Size."

Change the Number of Decimal Places

① Click the field in which you want to display a specific number of decimal places.

② Click the area beside Decimal Places.

③ Click the down arrow (▼) to display a list of decimal place options.

④ Click the number of decimal places that you want to use.

● The number that you choose appears in the Decimal Places property box.

⑤ Click the Save button (▣).

Access updates the table design.

Add or Delete a Field

Y ou can add a field to a table when you want the table to include an additional category of information. For example, you may want to add a field for e-mail addresses to a table that contains client information.

If you no longer need a field, you can delete the field from your table. Deleting a field permanently deletes all of the data in the field. Deleting unneeded fields makes your database smaller and may speed up the searches that you perform.

Before you delete a field, make sure that the field is not used in any other objects in the database, such as forms, queries, or reports. If you delete a field that is used in another object, Access cannot find all of the data for the object.

When you add or delete a field, Access automatically saves the changes for you.

Add or Delete a Field

Add a field

1. In Design view, click in the last row of the table in the Field Name column.

  - You can also right-click the field selector box and choose Insert Rows.

2. Type the field name and press Tab.

3. Type a data type, or choose one from the list, and press Tab.

Note: For more information on data types, see the task "Change the Data Type."

  - You can type a description here.

4. Make any changes to the field properties.

Note: For more information about changing field properties, see the other tasks in this chapter.

5. Click the Save button (📄).

  Access adds the new blank field to the table.

Delete a field

① In Design view, click the row containing the field that you want to delete.

② Click the Home tab.

③ Click Delete.

● A warning dialog box appears, asking you to confirm the deletion.

④ Click Yes to permanently delete the field and the data within it.

The field disappears from the table.

Do I have to insert my field at the end of the table as the last field?

▼ No. You can insert a new row into the Design view table and then add the field in that location. You can also move fields in Design view. For more information, see the task "Rearrange Fields."

Can I add a field in Datasheet view?

▼ Yes. Select the column where you want to insert the new field. Right-click and choose Insert Column. The field is assigned a generic name, such as Field3. Double-click the field name and type a more descriptive name. Then press Enter. You can also use the Add Field column at the end of the fields in Datasheet view.

After I delete a field from a table, can I undo the change?

▼ No. You cannot use the Undo feature (⟲ ▾) to reverse the results of deleting a field. If you have deleted a field from your table that you want back, you must add the field and all of the deleted data again.

Why does Access prevent me from deleting a field?

▼ The field may be part of a relationship. You must delete the relationship before you can delete the field. To delete a relationship, see the task "Define Relationships between Tables."

Add a Caption

You can create a caption for a field when you want the heading for the field to be longer and more descriptive than the field name allows. Adding a caption can help you recognize the field more easily when you are entering or reviewing data in your table. For example, the caption Home Phone Number is much easier to understand than the field name HPhone.

The caption appears as the heading for the field instead of the field name. A caption can be up to

2,048 characters in length, including letters, numbers, and spaces.

After adding a caption to a field, any forms, reports, or queries that you create that use the field, display the caption instead of the field name. Any forms or reports that you created before adding the caption continue to display the field name.

Add a Caption

1 Click the field in which you want to display a caption.

2 Click the area beside Caption.

3 Type the text for the caption.

4 Click the Save button (⊞).

5 Click Datasheet View (⊞).

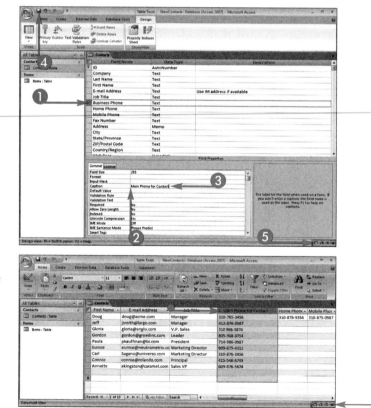

The caption replaces the field name.

Note: *You may need to adjust the width of the column to display the entire caption name. For information on changing column width, see Chapter 20.*

● You can click to return to Design view (⊠).

Add a Default Value

You can specify a value that you want to appear automatically in a field each time you add a new record, which saves you from having to type the same data over and over again.

For example, a table containing the addresses of your clients may contain a field for the country in which each client lives. If the majority of your clients live in the United States, you can set United States as the default value for the field. This can save you a

considerable amount of time if the table contains a large number of records.

You do not have to accept the default value for each new record that you add to your table; you can enter another value in the field.

Setting a default value does not affect the existing data in a field. To change existing data to the default value, click a cell containing data that you want to change, and then press Ctrl+Alt+spacebar.

Add a Default Value

1 Click the field in which you want to have a default value.

2 Click the area beside Default Value.

3 Type the text or number for the default value.

Access automatically adds quotation marks for text fields.

4 Click the Save button (📄).

5 Click Datasheet View (🔳).

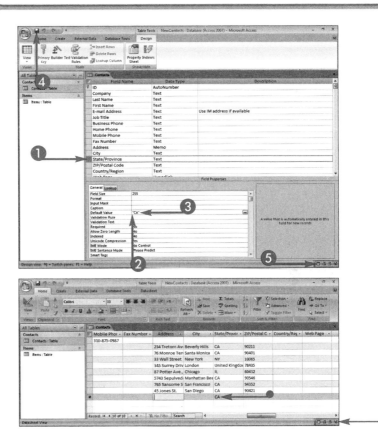

● The default value automatically appears in the field each time you add a new record.

You can accept the default value or type another value.

The new default value does not affect existing data in a field.

● You can click to return to Design view (🔲).

Require
an Entry

To avoid leaving out important information, you can specify that a field must contain data for each record. For example, in a table that stores customer information, you can specify that a user must type data in the Telephone Number field.

After you specify that a field must contain data, Access can verify whether the field contains data for all of the existing records in the table. When you add a new record in the table, an error message appears if you do not type data in the field.

You can also specify that a field requiring data may accept *zero-length strings*. A zero-length string indicates that no data exists for the field. For example, if you set the Fax Number field to require data, but one of your clients does not have a fax machine, then you need to enter a zero-length string in the field.

To enter a zero-length string in a cell, you can type "" in the cell. When you enter a zero-length string, the cell in the table appears empty.

Require an Entry

Specify a required field

1 Click the field in which you want to require an entry.

2 Click the area beside Required.

3 Click the down arrow (▾).

4 Click Yes to specify that the field must contain data.

Specify a zero-length string

5 Click the area beside Allow Zero Length.

6 Click the down arrow (▾).

7 Click Yes to specify that the field can accept a zero-length string.

8 Click the Save button (💾).

● A warning dialog box appears, asking if you want to check whether the field contains data for all existing records.

⑨ Click Yes to check the field or No to avoid checking the fields.

If you click Yes, Access checks the current data. If the contents do not meet the requirements, you see an error message allowing you to fix the field content.

● The field now requires an entry. If you try to skip making an entry, a warning dialog box appears.

⑩ Click OK to clear the error message. Then type an entry or enter a zero value ("").

What is the difference between a null value and a zero-length string?

▼ A null value indicates that you do not know the information for the field. If the field is not set to require data, you can enter a null value by pressing Enter, which leaves the cell blank and allows you to move to the next field. A zero-length string indicates that no data exists for the field.

I set a field in my table to require data and accept zero-length strings. Are these properties also used in my forms?

▼ Yes. Properties that you specify for a table also apply to forms that use data from the table. Make sure that you set the properties for a table before creating a form based on the table.

Why do I not see the entry for Allow Zero Length in the Design property boxes?

▼ You can set the zero length for only Text, Memo, and Hyperlink fields, not Numeric or Date/Time fields. You can require entries for these fields, but they cannot accept zero-length entries.

Add a Validation Rule

You can add a validation rule to a field to help reduce errors when entering data. A field that uses a validation rule can accept only data that meets certain requirements.

Access automatically sets rules based on the data type of the field. For example, you cannot type text in a field that has a Number data type. You can use a validation rule to set more specific rules. For example, you can type **<50** so that users do not type a value greater than 50 in the field.

Access displays an error message if the data that you type does not meet the requirements of the field. You can specify the error message that you want Access to display. The error message can contain up to 255 characters. If you do not specify an error message, Access displays a standard error message.

When you add a validation rule, you can check to see if the existing data in the field meets the requirements of the new rule. Access notifies you if any existing data violates the new rule.

Add a Validation Rule

1 Click the field in which you want to accept only certain values.

2 Click the ellipses (⌷⌷⌷) beside Validation Rule.

The Expression Builder dialog box opens.

3 Type the validation rule that limits the data that you can type into the field.

4 Click OK.

5 Type the error message that you want to appear in the Validation Text field.

6 Click the Save button (💾).

● A dialog box appears to warn you of a rule change.

7 Click Yes to check the existing data and No if you do not want to check the existing data.

If you click Yes, Access tells you whether the current data violates the new rule.

● When you type data that does not meet the field requirements, the error message that you typed in Step 5 appears.

8 To clear an error message, click OK and then type an entry that is within the specified validation rules.

What types of validation rules can I use?

▼ Examples of validation rules include the following:

<1000	Entry must be less than 1000
<M	Entry must begin with M or a letter after M
<>0	Entry cannot be zero
Between 100 and 200	Entry must be between 100 and 200
USA or	Entry must be USA
Canada	or Canada
Like "????"	Entry must have four characters
Like "##"	Entry must have two numbers

How do I build the expression?

▼ You build the expression by clicking the appropriate operators to make the comparison and by typing any text or values against which to compare the entry.

What type of error message should I create?

▼ You should create an error message that explains exactly why the data violates the validation rule. For example, the error message, "You must enter a number between 0 and 9," is more informative than the message, "Data Rejected."

Create a
Yes/No Field

Y ou can create a field that accepts only one of two values, such as Yes or No. Creating a Yes/No field is useful when a field in your table requires a simple answer. For example, a table that stores product information could contain a Yes/No field that indicates whether a product has been discontinued.

You can choose one of three available formats for a Yes/No field — Yes/No, True/False, or On/Off.

Access offers three ways to display data in a Yes/No field. The Check Box option displays a check box to indicate a value, such as Yes or No. The Text Box option displays a text value, such as "Yes" or "No." The Combo Box option displays a text value, such as "Yes" or "No," and allows you to select the value that you want from a drop-down list.

When you display your table in Datasheet view, the Yes/No field displays the options that you selected.

Create a Yes/No Field

① Click the Data Type area for the field in which you want to make a Yes/No field.

② Click the down arrow (🔽) to display a list of data types.

③ Click Yes/No.

④ Click the area beside Format.

⑤ Click the down arrow (🔽) to display a list of formats.

⑥ Click the format that you want to use.

7 To change the way that data appears in the field, click the Lookup tab.

8 Click the area beside Display Control.

9 Click the Save button (🔽) and click the display option that you want to use.

10 Click the Save button (🖫).

11 Click to display the table in Datasheet view (🖩).

● This area displays the Yes/No field.

● In this example, a check box appears for each record in the field. You can click the check box to indicate Yes or No.

● You can click to return to Design view (🖉).

Master It

When would I use the True/False format?

▼ The True/False format is often used to determine whether an action is required. For example, you can use a True/False format to indicate whether you should send mailings, such as newsletters, to a client.

How can I speed up the entry of data in a Yes/No field?

▼ By default, Access displays the No value in Yes/No fields. If most of your records require a Yes value, you can change the default value to Yes. For more information, see the task "Add a Default Value."

In Datasheet view, why does the Combo Box drop-down list not display any values?

▼ You must specify the values that you want the drop-down list to display. In Design view, click the Lookup tab and then click the area beside Row Source Type. Click the the down arrow (🔽) that appears and then select Value List. Click the area beside Row Source and then type the values that you want to display in the drop-down list, separated by a semicolon. For example, you could type **Yes;No**.

Create a Lookup Column

Y ou can create a list of values, called a *lookup column*, from which you can choose when entering information in a field. This can save you time because you do not have to type the values for each record.

Creating a lookup column is very useful if you repeatedly enter the same values in a field. For example, if you always use one of three methods to ship your orders, you can create a lookup column that displays the three shipping methods, such as US Mail, UPS Ground, or Express.

You can enter the values that you want to appear in the lookup column using the Lookup Wizard, or you can specify a table to use for the values.

The Lookup Wizard displays the name of the field that offers the lookup column. If you want the field to display a different field name, you can enter a new name.

Create a Lookup Column

1 Click the Data Type area for the field in which you want to use a lookup column.

2 Click the down arrow (▼) to display a list of data types.

3 Click Lookup Wizard.

The Lookup Wizard appears.

4 To type the values that you want the lookup column to offer, click the I will type in the values that I want option (◉ changes to ◉).

5 Click Next.

You can click Cancel at any time if you decide to not use the wizard.

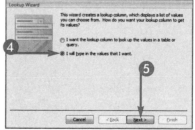

6. Type the number of columns and press Tab.

   You move to the first entry in the column.

7. Type the first value that you want to appear in the lookup column and press Tab.

8. Repeat Step 7 until you complete the lookup list.

9. Click Next.

10. To change the field name, type a new name.

11. Click Finish to create the lookup column.

12. Click the Save button (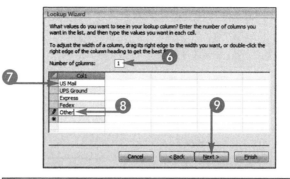) to save the table.

    Access creates the lookup column.

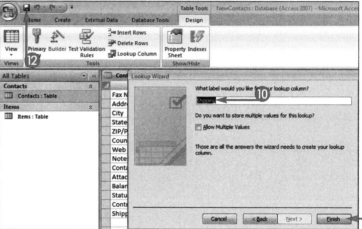

How can I ensure that users enter a value only from the lookup column?

▼ You can have Access display an error message when a user enters a value that is not displayed in the lookup column. In Design view, click the field that offers the lookup column, click the Lookup tab, and then click the area beside Limit To List. Click the down arrow (⏷) that appears and then select Yes.

Can I change the values in an existing lookup column?

▼ Yes. In Design view, click the field that offers the lookup column and then click the Lookup tab. The area beside Row Source displays the values that currently appear in the lookup column. You can delete, edit, or add values in this area. You must use a semicolon (;) to separate the values.

Can I create a lookup column that uses values from a table or query in my database?

▼ Yes. In the Lookup Wizard, choose the I want the lookup column to look up the values in a table or query option (◉ changes to ◉). For more information on queries, see Chapter 23.

PART V

Using a Lookup Column to Enter Data

When users display your table in Datasheet view, they can display the lookup column and select the value that they want to enter in the field. Entering information by selecting a value from a lookup column can help prevent errors such as spelling mistakes. Using a lookup column can also ensure that users enter the correct type of information in a field.

You can tell which fields have a lookup column because a drop-down arrow appears next to the field when you move to that field to enter data. You can display and then select the data for the field from the list.

If a lookup column does not display the value that you want to use, you can type a different value in the field. To hide a lookup column that you displayed without selecting a value, you can click outside the lookup column. Then you can type in any entry that you want, as long as the value list does not have the Limit To List attribute set to Yes.

For information on creating a lookup column, see the task "Create a Lookup Column."

Using a Lookup Column to Enter Data

1 Display the table in Datasheet view (▣).

Note: *See the task "Switch between Datasheet and Design Views" to switch views.*

2 Click a cell in the field that offers the lookup column.

3 Click the down arrow (▾) to display the lookup column.

4 Click the value that you want to enter.

● Access enters the value that you selected from the lookup column.

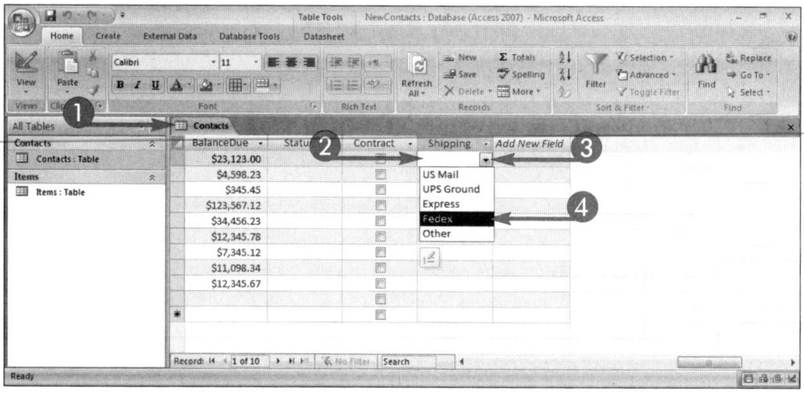

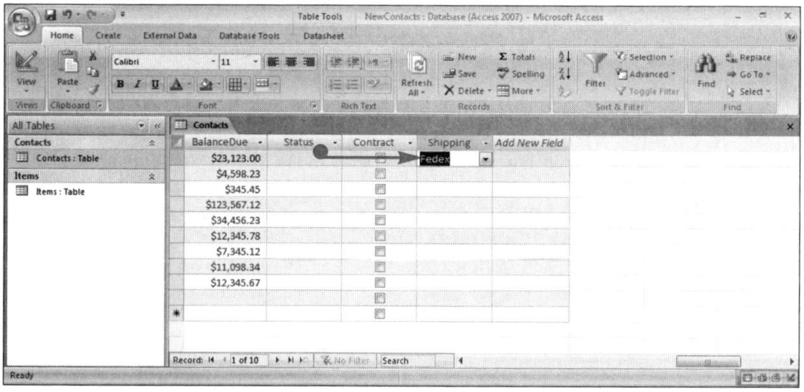

Create an Index

You can create an index for a field to speed up searching and sorting of information in the field. Access uses the index to find the location of information.

You can index the fields that you frequently search. For example, in a table containing client information, you can index the Last Name field because you are likely to search for a client using the last name.

You can specify whether the field that you want to index can contain duplicates. The Yes (Duplicates OK) option allows you to enter the same data in

more than one cell in a field. The Yes (No Duplicates) option does not allow you to enter the same data in more than one cell in a field. Use the first option if the field may contain duplicates, such as a last name that may be duplicated within the database table. Use the second option if you enter unique values in this field, such as Social Security numbers.

The primary key, which uniquely identifies each record in a table, is automatically indexed. The index for the primary key is automatically set to Yes (No Duplicates).

Create an Index

① In Design view, click the field that you want to index.

② In the Field Properties area, click the area beside Indexed.

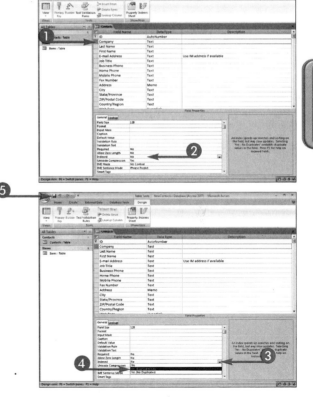

③ Click the down arrow (▼).

④ Click an option to specify whether you want to create an index for the field.

⑤ Click the Save button (📄).

Access creates the index for the table.

Set the Primary Key

A *primary key* is one or more fields that uniquely identify each record in a table. Each table in a database should have a primary key. You should not change the primary key in a table that has a relationship with another table in the database.

There are three types of primary keys that you can create — AutoNumber, single-field, and multiple-field.

The AutoNumber primary key field automatically assigns a unique number to each record that you add. When you create a table, Access can create an AutoNumber primary key field for you.

A single-field primary key is a field that contains a unique value for each record, such as a Social Security number.

A multiple-field primary key consists of two or more fields that together make up a unique value for each record.

Access does not allow you to enter the same value in the primary key field more than once. If you create a primary key for a field that already contains data, Access displays a warning message if the field contains duplicate values or an empty cell.

Set the Primary Key

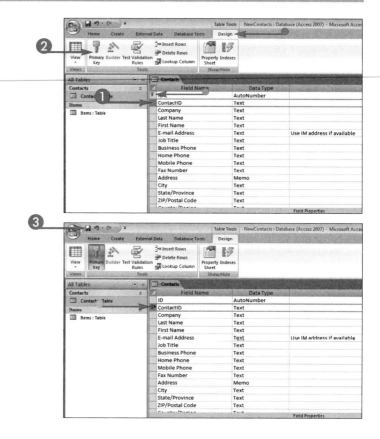

- With your table open in Design view, the Design tab of Table tools is active on the Ribbon.

- The field that is currently set as the primary key displays a key icon.

1 To set another field as the primary key, click the area to the left of the field.

Note: *To set more than one field as the primary key, press the Ctrl key as you click the area to the left of each field.*

2 Click Primary Key to set the field as the primary key.

- A key icon appears beside the field.

3 Click the Save button ( ).

The new primary key is set.

Display a Subdatasheet

When viewing the records in a table, you can display a subdatasheet to view and edit related data from another table.

Access displays subdatasheets only for tables that have a relationship. You can also set relationships yourself. For more information, see the task "Define Relationships between Tables."

A plus sign appears beside each record that has related data. You can click the plus sign to display

the related data in a subdatasheet. For example, a table containing customer information may be related to a table containing product orders. When viewing the customer table, you can click the plus sign beside the record for a customer. A subdatasheet appears, displaying information about the products that the customer has ordered.

When you finish viewing and editing the data in a subdatasheet, you can hide the subdatasheet to remove it from your screen.

Display a Subdatasheet

- When records in a table relate to data in another table, a plus sign (⊞) appears beside each record.

① Click the plus sign (⊞) beside a record to display the related data from the other table.

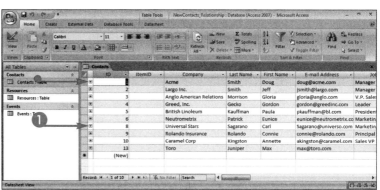

- The related data from the other table appears. You can review and edit the data.

② To once again hide the related data, click the minus sign (⊟) beside the record.

Access hides the related data.

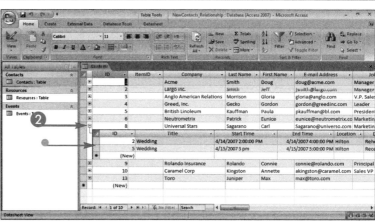

Define Relationships between Tables

You can create relationships between tables to bring together related information. Relationships between tables are essential for creating a form, report, or query that uses information from more than one table in a database.

For example, one table in the database may contain the names and addresses of your clients, while the other table may contain the events that you have managed for these clients. After you define a relationship between the two tables, you can create a query to have Access display client names and their current orders.

The Relationships window shows the relationships that exist between the tables in your database. You can add tables to this window.

You establish a relationship by identifying matching fields in two tables. The fields do not need to have the same name, but they must use the same data type and contain the same kind of information. You usually relate the primary key in one table to a matching field in the other table. For more information on primary keys, see the task "Set the Primary Key."

Define Relationships between Tables

① Click the Database Tools tab.

② Click Relationships.

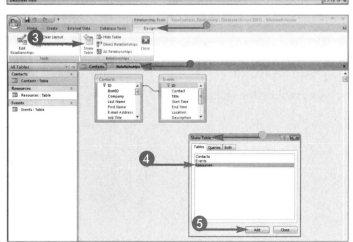

● The Relationships tab opens in the Database window.

Note: This example shows an existing relationship, indicated by the connector line between the two tables. This task adds another relationship.

● The Design tab opens on the Ribbon.

③ Click Show Table.

○ The Show Table dialog box opens.

④ Click a table that you want to add to the Relationships window.

⑤ Click Add.

● The tables are added to the Relationships window.

⑥ Repeat Steps 3 to 5 for each table that you want to add.

⑦ Click Close.

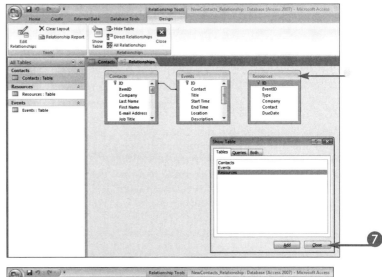

● The Relationships window displays a box for each table. Each box displays the fields for one table.

● The primary key in each table displays the key icon (🔑).

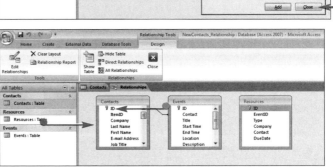

Why do I see the Relationships window instead of the Show Table dialog box?

▼ If any relationships exist between the tables in the database, a box for each table appears in the window. If you use the Database templates to create your database and add related fields, Access automatically creates relationships between tables.

How do I remove a table from the Relationships window?

▼ Right-click the box for the table that you want to remove, and then click Hide Table. This table and any relationships defined for the table are removed from the Relationships window, but not from the database.

How can I view the relationships for just one table?

▼ Click Clear Layout in the Tools group of the Design tab to remove all of the tables from the Relationships window. Click Yes in the dialog box that appears, and then perform Steps 3 to 5 in this task to add a table to the Relationships window. Right-click the table and click Show Direct to view the relationships for the table.

How can I quickly display all of the relationships in the database?

▼ To view all of the relationships in the database, click All Relationships in the Relationships group on the Design tab.

PART V

continued

Define Relationships between Tables *(Continued)*

The type of relationship that Access creates between two tables depends on the fields that you use to create the relationship.

If only one field in the relationship is a primary key, Access creates a one-to-many relationship. In this type of relationship, each record in a table relates to one or more records in the other table. For example, if one table stores the names of clients and the other table stores orders, the one-to-many relationship allows each client to have more than one order. This is the most common type of relationship.

If both fields in the relationship are primary keys, Access creates a one-to-one relationship. In this type of relationship, each record in a table relates to just one record in the other table. For example, if one table stores available rental cars and the other table stores the dates that the cars are reserved, the one-to-one relationship allows each car to have only one reserve date.

Define Relationships between Tables *(continued)*

⑧ Position the mouse over the field that you want to use to form a relationship with another table.

⑨ Click and drag the field (⍉ changes to ⍉) over the matching field in the second table until a small box appears. Release the mouse.

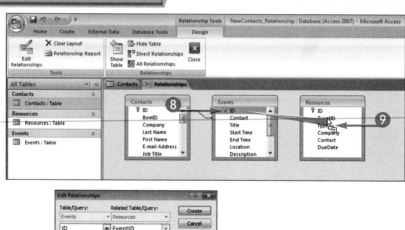

The Edit Relationships dialog box appears.

● This area displays the names of the tables between which you are creating a relationship, and the names of the matching fields.

● This area displays the relationship type.

⑩ To enforce referential integrity between the tables, click this option (☐ changes to ☑).

⑪ To have Access automatically update related fields or delete related records, click each option that you want to use (☐ changes to ☑)

⑫ Click Create to establish the relationship.

The Edit Relationships window closes.

● A line connects the fields in the two tables to show the relationship.

⑬ Click the Save button (🖫).

The table relationships are established.

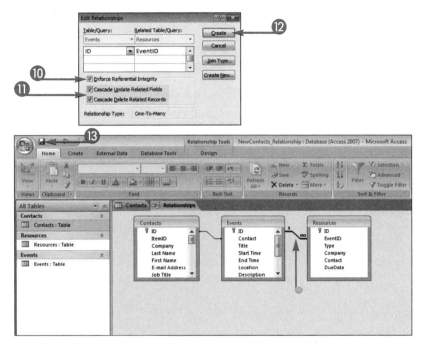

What is referential integrity?

▼ Referential integrity is a set of rules that prevent you from changing or deleting a record if matching records exist in a related table. Access provides two options in the Edit Relationships dialog box that let you override the rules of referential integrity but still protect data from accidental changes or deletions. Check the Cascade Update Related Fields option (☐ changes to ☑) to allow Access to update matching data in all related records when you change the data in the primary key. Check the Cascade Delete Related Records option (☐ changes to ☑) to allow Access to delete matching 0 records in related tables when you delete a record.

Can I change the referential integrity options later?

▼ Yes. To redisplay the Edit Relationships dialog box so that you can change these options, double-click the line representing the relationship that you want to change.

How do I delete a relationship?

▼ In the Relationships window, right-click the line representing the relationship that you want to delete, and then press Delete.

Why is the line showing the second relationship thicker than the first?

▼ This task adds options to the relationship in the Edit Relationships window, including enforcing referential integrity (☐ changes to ☑) in Steps 10. The thicker connector line indicates a relationship with added options.

PART V

Create a Form Using a Wizard

A form presents information from a database table in an attractive format, and so you may find that a form is easier to work with than a table. You can use a form to add, edit, and delete information in a table. You can also create a form for queries.

The Form Wizard helps you to create a form that suits your needs. The wizard asks you a series of questions and then sets up a form based on your answers.

To start, the Form Wizard allows you to select the table or query containing the fields that you want to include in the form.

After you create a table, you can select the fields that you want to include from a list in the table. A form can include all or only some fields in a table.

Create a Form Using a Wizard

① Click the Create tab.

② Click More Forms.

A drop-down menu opens.

③ Click Form Wizard.

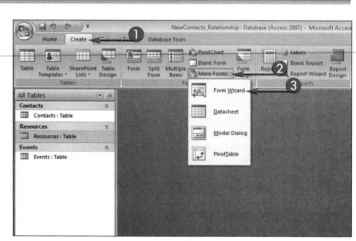

The Form Wizard appears.

④ Click the Tables/Queries down arrow (▼).

⑤ Click the table or query that you want to use.

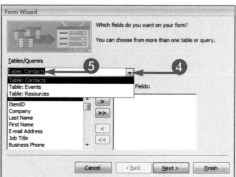

6 Double-click each field that you want to include in the form.

- To add all of the fields at once, you can click the double arrow (>>).

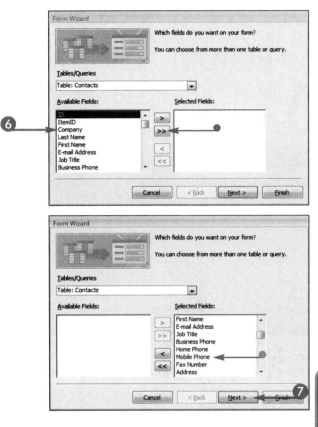

- Each field that you select appears in this area.

7 Click Next to continue.

You can click Cancel at any time if you decide not to use the Form Wizard.

Can I create a form that uses fields from more than one table?

▼ Yes. Perform Steps 1 to 7 in this task to select the fields that you want to include from one table. Then repeat Steps 1 to 7 until you have all of the tables and fields that you want to include. To use more than one table, relationships must exist between the tables. For information on defining relationships between tables, see Chapter 21.

How do I remove a field that I accidentally added?

▼ To remove a field, double-click the field in the Selected Fields list. To remove all of the fields at once, click the double arrow (<<).

In what order do the fields that I select appear in the form?

▼ The fields appear in the form in the order that you select them. You can rearrange the fields after you create the form. For more information, see the task "Add a Field to a Form."

Can I change the appearance of the form that I created with the Form Wizard?

▼ Yes. In the following tasks in this chapter, you will open forms in Design view and change how they look and work.

PART V

continued

Create a Form Using a Wizard

(Continued)

After you select all of the fields for your table, you can select which layout you prefer for the form. The layout of a form determines the arrangement of information on the form.

The *Columnar* layout displays one record at a time and lines up information in a column. The *Tabular* layout displays multiple records and presents information in rows and columns. The *Datasheet* layout displays multiple records and is similar to the Datasheet view for tables. The *Justified* layout displays one record at a

time and aligns information along both the left and right sides of a form.

You can apply a style to the form, such as Blends, International, or Stone. Most styles use colors and patterns to enhance the form's appearance.

After you select a layout for your form, Access requires that you name the form. The name, which appears at the top of the form and in the Forms area of the Navigation pane, can contain up to 64 characters.

Create a Form Using a Wizard *(continued)*

8 Click the layout that you want to use for the form (◎ changes to ◉).

● This area displays a sample of the layout that you selected.

9 Click Next to continue.

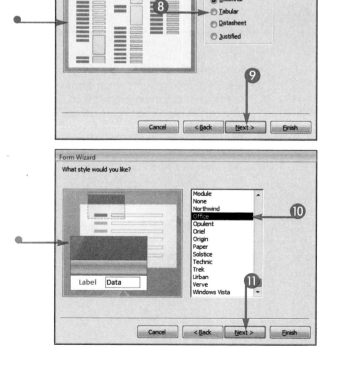

10 Click the style that you want to use for the form.

● This area displays a sample of the style that you selected.

11 Click Next to continue.

You can click Back at any time to return to a previous step and change your answers.

12 Type a name, or accept the default name, for the form.

13 Click an option to review the form (◎ changes to ◉).

You can either open and edit the form, or choose to modify its layout and appearance.

14 Click Finish to create the form.

● The form appears, displaying the field names that you selected and the first record.

● Any attachment is also shown.

Note: For more information about attachments, see the task "Embed Attachment Files in Fields" in Chapter 20.

● The form is added to the Navigation pane.

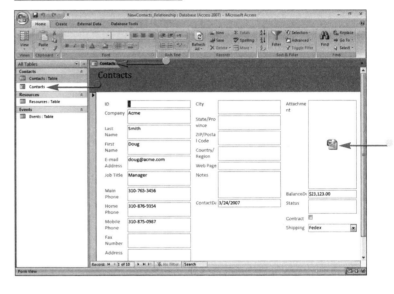

Is there a faster way to create a form?

▼ Yes. You can use Form in the Forms group of the Create tab to quickly create a new form, based on a table that you select in the Navigation pane. You can add fields from the Field List that opens when the form is created, and then revise the form in Design view. You can also click Blank Form in the Forms group to open a blank form with the Field List, or click Form Design in the Forms group to begin a form in Design view.

How do I rename an existing form?

▼ In the Navigation pane, right-click the form that you want to rename. From the menu that appears, select Rename. Type a new name for the form and then press Enter.

Can I change the style of an existing form?

▼ Yes. You can use the AutoFormat feature to change the style at another time. To do so, display the form that you want to change in Design view and then click the Arrange tab of the Form Design Tools that are active on the Ribbon. Click AutoFormat to open a gallery of pre-set formats and select the style that you want to use. Alternatively, click the AutoFormat Wizard to return to the styles options of the Form Wizard and choose another style. For more information on the AutoFormat feature, see the task "AutoFormat a Form."

Open a Form

Y ou can open a form and display its contents on your screen to review and make changes to the form.

When you double-click a form, you can open it in Form view. Form view usually displays one record at a time in an organized and attractive format. This view is useful for entering, editing, and reviewing records. You can also delete records that you no longer need from this view.

You can open a form in Design view, where you can see the structure of a form. This view also allows you

to customize the appearance of a form to make the form easier to use. You can use this view to change the contents of a form   that is, which fields from the underlying database table are included.

When you finish working with a form, you can close the form to remove it from your screen.

You can find information on changing the form design in several tasks in this chapter, including "Add a Field to a Form," "AutoFormat a Form," and "Change a Form Control."

Open a Form

Open a form in Form view

1 Locate the form (⊞) in the Navigation pane.

Note: For more information on viewing database objects, see the task "Using the Navigation Pane" in Chapter 19.

2 Double-click the form that you want to open.

● The form opens in Form view.

You can make changes to the records.

Note: To add or delete a record, see the task "Add or Delete Records" in Chapter 20.

3 When you finish using the form, click the Close button (⊠) to close the form.

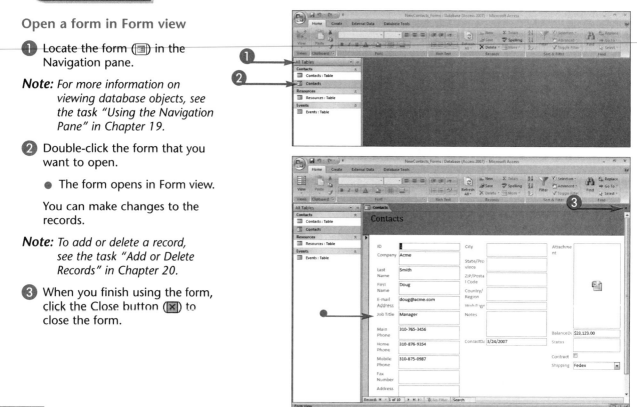

Open a form in Design view

1 Locate the form (▦) in the Navigation pane.

2 Right-click the form.

3 Click Design View.

- Access opens the form in Design view.

- The Form Design Tools are active on the Ribbon.

4 Make changes to the form design.

Note: For more information about form design, see later tasks in this chapter, beginning with the task "AutoFormat a Form."

5 Click the Save button (▤) to save the new form design.

6 When you finish working with the form, click the Close button (✖).

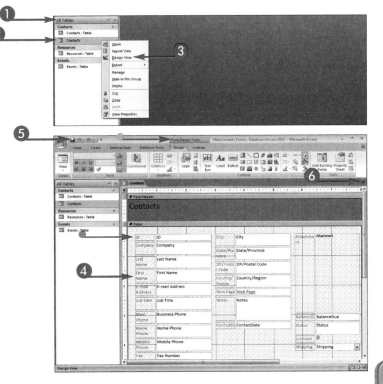

PART V

When do I need to save the form?

▼ Unlike changes made to records, design changes are not automatically saved. If you open a form in Design view and make changes, click the Save button (▤) to save the form. If you close the form in Design view without saving, you are prompted to save it.

Can I delete an entire record from a form?

▼ Yes. With the record on display in the form, you can click the Delete down arrow (▾) in the Records group of the Home tab on the Ribbon and select Delete Record. Access asks you to confirm that the record is to be deleted. Click Yes. Access deletes the record from the form and from the table on which the form is based.

What other layouts can I use for forms?

▼ Datasheet view displays all of the records in rows and columns. Each row displays the information for one record. The field names appear directly above the first record. You can enter, edit, and review records in this view.

Can I change from one view to another after I open a form?

▼ Yes. You can change views using the View buttons in the bottom-right corner of the screen:

Form View (▤)
Layout View (▣)
Design View (▨)

Alternatively, you can toggle through the views by clicking Views in the Forms group on the Create tab on the Ribbon.

Move through Records with a Form

You can use the navigation tools of the Form view to easily move through the records in a form to review or edit information.

Any changes that you make to the information in a form also appear in the tables that you use to create the form.

Access displays the number of the current record and the total number of records in the form. It also displays buttons that you can use to move through the records. You can quickly move to the first, last, previous, or next record. If you know the number of the record that you want to view, you can quickly move to that record.

Can I use the keyboard to quickly move through records?

▼ Yes. Press the Page Up key to move to the previous record. Press the Page Down key to move to the next record. Press Ctrl+up arrow key to move to the first record, or press Ctrl+down arrow key to move to the last record.

Move through Records with a Form

Using form buttons

① Click to move through your records.

First Record (⏮)

Previous Record (◀)

Next Record (▶)

Last Record (⏭).

Access moves to the appropriate record.

● You can view the number of the current record and the total number of records here.

Go to a specific record

① Click and drag over the current record number.

② Type the number of the record to which you want to go.

③ Press Enter.

● Access displays the record.

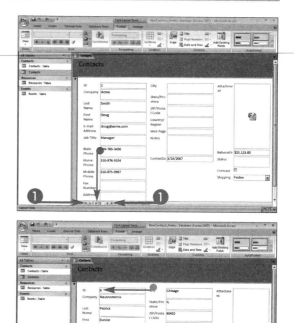

Edit Data Using a Form

Access enables you to edit the data in a form using the Form view, which lets you correct a mistake or update the data in a record.

You can insert new data in a cell. The flashing insertion point in a cell indicates where Access inserts new data. You can also delete all or part of the data that you no longer need from a cell.

Access remembers the changes that you make to a record. If you make a mistake while editing data in a cell, you can use the Undo feature to immediately reverse the changes in the current cell.

You do not have to save the changes that you make. When you move from the record to edit another record, Access automatically saves your changes.

I changed a record by mistake. How do I change it back?

▼ If you move your mouse to another cell and then click the Undo button ( ), Access reverts your record to its original state. If you are still in the cell, press Esc; the previous data reappears.

Edit Data Using a Form

Insert data

1 Click the Form View button ().

● You can also click View in the Home tab to toggle to Form view.

2 Click the location in the cell where you want to insert data.

A flashing insertion point appears in the cell.

You can press the left- or right-arrow key to move the insertion point, or drag through the data to select it all.

3 Type the data that you want to insert.

4 Press Tab to move to the next field, or click in another field.

Access adds the data.

Delete data

1 Click and drag over the data that you want to delete.

2 Press Delete.

Access deletes the data.

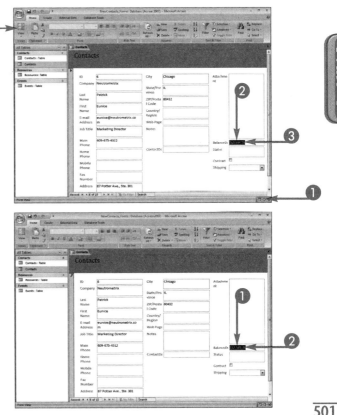

Add a Record

Y ou can use a form to add a record to the table. The new record is added to the table that you used to create the form. For example, you may want to add information about a new client.

Access checks to make sure that the data that you enter in each field is valid for the specified data type and field properties. If an entry is invalid, Access notifies you before you move to the next field or record. For example, Access alerts you if you try to enter text in a Number field.

To delete a record, you can click the Delete down arrow in the Records group of the Home tab on the Ribbon and select Delete Record. Access asks you confirm that the record is to be deleted. Click Yes. Access deletes the record from the form and from the table on which the form is based.

Add a Record

① Click the New Record button (▶*) to add a record.

- Alternatively, click New in the Records group of the Home tab.

- A blank form appears.

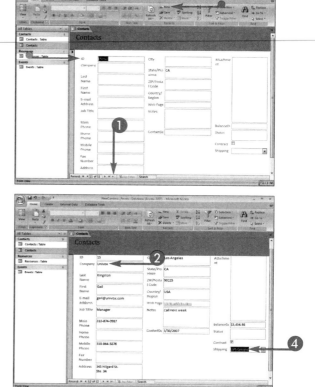

② Type the data for the first field.

③ Press Tab.

④ Repeat Steps 2 and 3 until you finish typing all of the data for the record.

Access adds the record.

Access automatically saves each new record.

Add a Field to a Form

I f you neglected to add a field from the table when you created a form, you can add the field. For example, you may want to add a telephone number field to a form that displays client addresses.

Before you can add a field to a form, you must display the form in Design view. You can add a field from the table that you used to create the form.

Access uses labels and text boxes to display information on a form. When you add a field,

Access adds a label and its corresponding text box for you.

Access automatically uses the correct data type and field properties for a field that you add to a form. For example, if you add a field that has the Yes/No data type with the Check Box option, Access adds a check box to the form instead of a text box.

You may need to resize a form to make room for a field that you add. For information on resizing a form, see the task "Change a Form Control."

Add a Field to a Form

1 Open the form that you want to change in Design view.

Note: To open a form in Design view, see the task "Open a Form."

● The Form Design Tools are active on the Ribbon.

2 Click the Design tab of the Form Design Tools.

3 Click Add Existing Fields.

● A list of fields displays from the table that you used to create the form.

4 Double-click the field that you want to add.

Access adds the label and corresponding text box for the field to the form.

● You can click and drag to move the new field (◌ changes to ✛).

5 Click the Save button (🖫) to save the form.

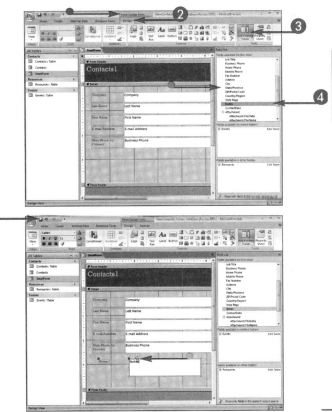

PART V

AutoFormat a Form

Y ou can choose to AutoFormat your form to instantly change the overall look of the form. AutoFormatting changes the background and text colors of a form.

Before you can AutoFormat your form, you must display the form in Design view. You might consider using the same AutoFormatting for all of the forms in your database to give the database a more consistent appearance.

You can choose from a gallery of AutoFormats, including Blends, Industrial, International, and Stone. Each one changes the background color and the color of the form controls. Each AutoFormat also uses different font choices for the form controls.

You can also use the AutoFormat Wizard option in the AutoFormat gallery. In the Form Wizard that opens, you can choose a style for the form by name and see a preview. For a less colorful but functional form, select None.

AutoFormat a Form

1 Open the form that you want to change in Design view.

Note: To open a form in Design view, see the task "Open a Form."

2 Click the Arrange tab in the Form Design Tools on the Ribbon.

3 Click AutoFormat.

The AutoFormat gallery appears.

4 Click an option to apply it to the form.

- The form displays the new format in Design view.

5 Click Form View (📧).

- The Form view displays the new format where you can enter information.

What is the easiest way to realign the fields in my form?

▼ Click to switch to Layout view (📧). It is a cleaner view of the form, where you can easily move and resize fields, and realign the controls. You can use Layout view to review the form information and make changes to its appearance, but not to change information in records.

I want to work on the form in Design view, but many of the options in the Arrange tab are grayed out. What should I do?

▼ In order for some of the options to be active, you first need to select one or more controls on the form, so that you can apply the options to them.

Change a Form Control

A *control* is an item on a form, such as a label, that displays a field name or a text box that shows data from a field. You can move, resize, or delete a control to make the form easier to use.

You can change the location of a control on a form. You can also move a label and its corresponding text box, either together or individually.

You can change the size of a control. Larger controls allow you to display longer entries. For example, you may want to resize a text box that displays long Web page addresses.

When you move or resize a control, Access automatically aligns the control with the dots on the form, also known as the grid, which enables you to neatly arrange controls on the form.

You can delete a control that you no longer want on a form. Access allows you to delete just a label or a label and its corresponding text box.

Before you close a form, make sure that you save the changes that you made to the form. If you forget, Access reminds you to save them.

Change a Form Control

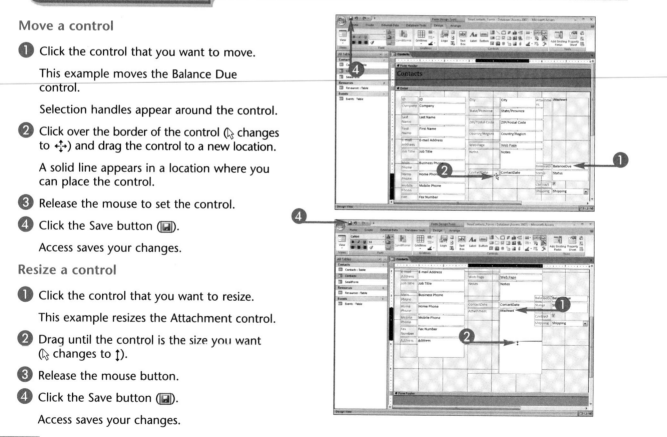

Move a control

① Click the control that you want to move.

This example moves the Balance Due control.

Selection handles appear around the control.

② Click over the border of the control (changes to ✛) and drag the control to a new location.

A solid line appears in a location where you can place the control.

③ Release the mouse to set the control.

④ Click the Save button ().

Access saves your changes.

Resize a control

① Click the control that you want to resize.

This example resizes the Attachment control.

② Drag until the control is the size you want (changes to ↕).

③ Release the mouse button.

④ Click the Save button ().

Access saves your changes.

Delete a control

1 Click the control that you want to delete.

This example deletes the Status control.

Selection handles appear around the control.

You can click a label to delete only the label, or click a text box to delete the label and the corresponding text box.

2 Press Delete.

● Access deletes the control.

3 Click the Save button (🖫).

Access saves your changes.

Can I resize an entire form?

▼ Yes. Resizing a form is useful when you want to increase the space available for moving and resizing controls. Click and drag over an edge of the form until the form is the size that you want.

If I delete a field from a form, is it deleted from the table? Is the data deleted?

▼ No. The field is not deleted from the table, only from the form. The data is also unaffected in the table.

How do I move, resize, or delete several controls at once?

▼ To select multiple controls, hold down the Shift key as you click each control. If they are close together, you can drag a box around the controls to select them all. They will be framed with a solid line when selected.

Can I undo a change?

▼ Yes. You can undo a change by clicking the Undo button (🔄) on the Quick Access toolbar.

PART V

Change the Appearance of Form Controls

Y ou can change the font, size, style, and alignment of text in a control to customize the appearance of a form. You must display the form in Design view before you can format the text in a control. This activates the Form Design Tools on the Ribbon so that you can use the Design tab to make your changes.

Access provides a list of fonts from which you can choose. The fonts appear in the list as they will appear in the control, which enables you to preview a font before you select it.

You can increase or decrease the size of text in a control, which Access measures in points. There are 72 points in an inch.

You can use the Bold, Italic, and Underline features to change the style of text in a control. This can help you to emphasize important information on a form.

Access automatically aligns text to the left, and numbers to the right, in a control. You can choose to align data to the left, to the right, or in the center of a control.

After you make changes to the form design, you must save the form to apply all of your changes.

Change the Appearance of Form Controls

Change the font

1. In Design view, select the controls that display the text that you want to change.

   The Form Design Tools are active on the Ribbon.

   Note: To open your form in Design view, see the task "Open a Form."

2. Click the Font down arrow (▼).

3. Click a font.

   ● The font changes.

Change the font size

4. Click the Font down arrow (▼).

5. Click the size that you want to use.

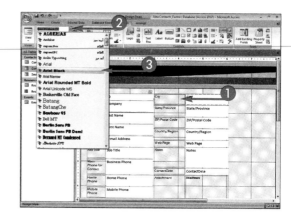

● Access changes the font size.

Change the font style

6 Click one of the following buttons:

Bold (**B**)

Italic (*I*)

Underline (U̲)

This example uses italic.

● Access changes the font style.

Change alignment

7 Click one of the following buttons:

Align Text Left (▤)

Center (▤)

Align Text Right (▤)

● Access changes the alignment.

8 Click the Save button (▤).

Access saves all changes to the form.

My formatted text no longer fully displays in the control. Why not?

▼ Changing the font or size of the text may make the text too large to fully display in the control. To display all of the text, you can resize the control. For more information on how to move and resize controls, see the task "Change a Form Control."

How can I preview the form?

▼ To check the appearance of the form as you make changes, click the Form View button (▤) to see how the form will look. To change back to Design view, click the Design View button (▤).

Can I format several controls at once?

▼ Yes. To select multiple controls, hold down the Shift key as you click each control. Usually, you want to maintain a consistent appearance for the controls. You can save time by selecting all of the controls that you want to change and then making the change. You can also select all of the controls in a vertical column by moving your mouse over the top of the column (⇧ changes to ↓) and clicking to select all of the controls vertically.

Change Form Control Colors and Gridlines

You can change the background, text, and border colors of a control on a form. You can also change the width of a control's border.

Changing the background and text colors of a control can help draw attention to important information on a form. Access provides several background and text colors from which to choose. You can change the color and width of a control's border to make the control stand out.

Before formatting a control, you must display the form in Design view. This activates the Form Design Tools

on the Ribbon, so that you can use the Design tab to make your changes.

When you change the colors and borders, make sure that your text remains legible and that the colors do not clash. Also remember that if you are printing a form using a black-and-white printer, any colors that you add to the text, background, or border of a control appear as shades of gray.

Before you close a form, you must save the changes that you made to the controls, or Access does not apply them.

Change Form Control Colors and Gridlines

Change background color

① In Design view, select a control.

② Click the Fill Color button down arrow (⬛▾).

Access displays a list of colors.

③ Click a background color.

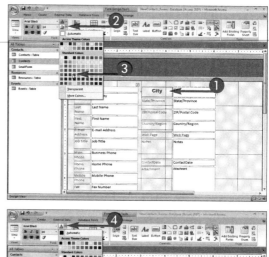

● Access changes the background color.

Change text color

④ Click the Font Color button down arrow (⬛▾).

Access displays a list of colors.

⑤ Click the text color that you want to use.

● Access changes the text color.

Change gridline color

6 Move your mouse over the top of the column (⥁ changes to ↓) and click to select the controls.

This example changes the controls vertically.

7 Click the Border Color button down arrow (⬚·).

Access displays a list of colors.

8 Click the border color that you want to use.

● Access changes the border color.

Change the gridlines

9 Click Gridlines.

A list of gridlines appears.

10 Click the gridlines that you want to use.

● Access applies the gridlines to the form.

11 Click the Save button (🖫).

Access saves all changes to the form.

Is there another way to enhance the appearance of a control?

▼ Yes. You can make a control appear raised, sunken, or shadowed. Click the controls that you want to enhance. Right-click the selected controls and choose Special Effect. From the menu that opens, select the effect that you want to apply to the selected controls.

How can I quickly change the line width in the gridlines?

▼ After selecting the controls and setting the gridlines, you can click the Line Style button down arrow (▤·) to change the line style for the applied gridlines. You can click the Line Width button down arrow (▤·) to change the line width. Both are in the Gridlines group of the Design tab of Form Design Tools.

How do I apply the same formatting options to another control on the form?

▼ To save time, you can copy the formatting — not just the borders and colors, but also the font changes and alignment. Select the control with the formatting that you want to copy, click the Format Painter button on the Home tab (🖊), and then click the control to which you want to copy the formatting.

Using Conditional Formats

Conditional formats allow you to visually analyze and locate the most significant trends and values in a form.

To make the data in your forms stand out according to the values, you can apply Conditional Formatting Rules.

The Conditional Format dialog box lets you set rules that determine how the data in your cells will be formatted according to criteria that you enter.

Access lets you create a first criterion with resulting formats in the Conditional Formatting dialog box, but you can add additional conditions with different formats.

For example, you can have one condition for a balance due of over a certain amount, and another condition for balances below a different amount.

Conditions that you can set include equal to or not equal to, greater than, less than, greater than or equal to, and less than or equal to.

In each case, when the record is accessed within the form, the condition is met, and the format displays in the control.

Besides the value of a field, you can also set a condition based on an expression, or whether the field has focus — meaning that it has been selected.

Using Conditional Formats

Change background color

1. In Design view, select a control that you want to format based on a value.

2. Click the Design tab in the Form Design Tools.

3. Click Conditional.

   The Conditional Formatting dialog box opens.

4. Click the Condition down arrow (⏷).

   Access displays a list of criteria.

5. Click the criterion that you want to use.

6. Enter the amount to which the condition applies.

7. Select an effect, such as bold text or a background color, if the condition is met.

   ● A preview of the format is shown.

8. Click OK.

You return to Design view.

9 Click to change to Form view (🔲).

10 Open a record in which the condition is met.

Note: *To find a record in which the condition is met, see the task "Move through Records with a Form."*

• The field is formatted with the options that you selected.

Do I have to be in Design view to apply a conditional format?

▼ No. You can also select a control and format it by conditions in Layout view (🔲).

How can I delete a condition without changing others that I have added?

▼ Click Delete in the Conditional Formatting dialog box. The conditions that you have set are listed by number. Select the number of the condition that you want to delete (🔲 changes to ☑). When you click OK, only the selected conditions are deleted.

Can I quickly disable a condition temporarily?

▼ Yes. When you open the Conditional Formatting dialog box, the enabled button (🔲) is active for each condition. Click the button for any condition to temporarily disable it. You can enable the condition in the same way when you want the formatting to be applied again.

Find Data

You can search for records that contain specific data. You can also search for data in tables, queries, and forms.

By default, Access performs a search of the current table. To perform a more advanced search, you can create a query.

You can specify how you want Access to search for data in a field. The Any Part of Field option allows you to find data anywhere in a field. For example, a search for smith finds Smithson and Macsmith. The Whole Field option allows you to find data that is exactly the same as the data that you specify. For example, a search for smith finds Smith but not Smithson. You can also choose the Start of Field option to find data only at the beginning of a field. For example, a search for smith finds Smithson but not Macsmith.

After you start the search, Access finds and highlights the first instance of the data. You can continue the search to find the next instance of the data.

For more information about queries, see the later tasks in this chapter on creating queries.

Find Data

① Click the Home tab.

② Click anywhere in the table containing the data that you want to find.

③ Click the Find button.

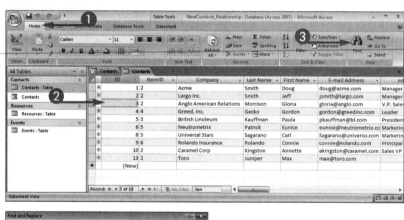

The Find and Replace dialog box appears.

④ Type the data that you want to find.

⑤ Click the Look In down arrow (▼) and select the entire table to search. Make any other changes to the search options.

⑥ Click Find Next to start the search.

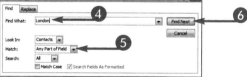

● Access highlights the data in the first matching record that it finds.

● You may need to scroll through the table or move the Find and Replace dialog box to see the match. To move a dialog box, you can drag its title bar.

7 Click Find Next to find the next matching record.

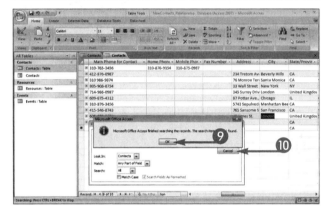

8 Repeat Step 7 until a dialog box appears, telling you that the search item is not found, which means that the search is complete.

9 Click OK.

10 To close the Find and Replace dialog box, click Cancel.

How do I specify a search direction?

▼ In the Find and Replace dialog box, click the Search down arrow (⏷) and click either Up or Down to search above or below the current record.

How can I have Access replace the data that I find with new data?

▼ Perform Steps 1 to 4 in this task and then click the Replace tab. In the Replace With text field, type the new data. Click Find Next. To replace the data that Access finds with the new data, click Replace. To ignore the data and continue with the search, click Find Next.

Can I find data that matches the case of the data that I specify?

▼ Yes. You can have Access find only data with exactly matching uppercase and lowercase letters. In the Find and Replace dialog box, click the Match Case option (☐ changes to ☑).

What is the difference between the Find button and the Search box?

▼ They both offer ways to locate information in a table. However, the Search box in the navigation tools instantly locates items as you type them in, but you cannot use it to replace text or fine-tune the search. For more information, see the task "Move through Records" in Chapter 20.

PART V

Sort Records

Y ou can change the order of records in a table, query, or form to help you find, organize, and analyze data.

You can sort by one or more fields. Sorting by more than one field can help you to refine the sort. For example, if several of your clients have the same last name, you can sort by the last name field and the first name field. When you sort by multiple fields, you must place the fields side-by-side and in the order that you

want to perform the sort. Access sorts the records in the far-left field first.

You can sort records In ascending or descending order. Sorting in ascending order displays text in alphabetical order from A to Z, and displays numbers from smallest to largest. The opposite occurs when you sort text or numbers in descending order.

When you save the table, query, or form, Access saves the sort order that you specified.

Sort Records

Sort by one field

① Click anywhere in the field that you want to use to sort the records.

② Click the field name down arrow (▾).

The Sort menu opens.

③ Click Sort A to Z (🔼) or Sort Z to A (🔽).

Note: In a numeric field, options to sort smallest to largest and sort largest to smallest appear.

● The records appear in the new order.

In this example, the records are sorted by last name in ascending order.

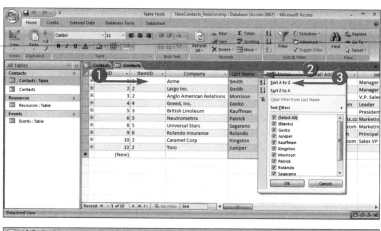

Sort by two fields

① Click the Home tab.

Make sure that the fields that you want to use to sort the records are side-by-side and in the order that you want to perform the sort.

② Position the mouse over the name of the first field that you want to use to sort the records, and then drag the mouse until you highlight the second field.

③ Click Sort Ascending (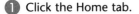) or Sort Descending ().

Note: In a numeric field, options to sort smallest to largest and sort largest to smallest appear.

● The records appear in the new order.

In this example, the records are sorted by company and then by last name.

How do I rearrange the fields in a table?

▼ You may need to rearrange the fields when sorting records by two fields. Click the name of the field that you want to move. Position the mouse over the field name and then drag the field to a new location. A thick black line shows where the field will be placed.

How do I remove a sort from my records?

▼ If you no longer want to display your records in the sort order that you specified, you can return your records to the primary key order at any time. Click the Home tab on the Ribbon and then click the Clear All Sorts button (). Your table is resorted by the primary key.

How do I exclude an item from being sorted?

▼ Select the record in the field that you want to include or exclude from the sort. In the Home tab on the Ribbon, click Advanced in the Sort & Filter group. From the drop-down menu, select the type of sort or filter that you want to perform.

PART V

Filter Data

You can filter records in a table, form, or query to display only specific records. Filtering data can help you to review and analyze information in your database by temporarily hiding information that is not currently of interest. For example, in a table that stores client addresses, you can filter out clients who do not live in Indiana.

When you filter by selection, you select data and have Access display only the records that contain the same data.

When you filter by input, you enter data or criteria and have Access display only the records that contain matching data or data that meets the entered criteria. Filtering by input is useful when you want to specify exact data or find records within a specific range.

Filtering data does not change how Access stores the records in the database.

You can add, delete, or edit records when you are viewing filtered records. Changes that you make to filtered data are updated in the table.

Filter Data

Filter by selection

1 Click the Home tab.

2 Click a field that contains the data that you want to use to filter the records.

3 Click Selection.

Access displays choices for the filter.

4 Click to filter the records that contain the matching data.

- Matching records display, and all other records are hidden. A filtered funnel icon indicates the field has been filtered.

- The word *Filtered* appears in this area to indicate that you are looking at filtered records.

5 Click Toggle Filter to once again display all of the records.

Access removes the filter and displays all records.

Filter by input

1. Right-click the field that you want to use to filter the records.

2. In the drop-down list that appears, select a criterion by which to filter.

   - Access displays the records that contain the matching data. All other records are hidden. A filtered funnel icon indicates the field has been filtered.

   - The word *Filtered* appears in this area to indicate that you are looking at filtered records.

3. Click Toggle Filter to once again display all of the records.

   Access removes the filter and displays all records.

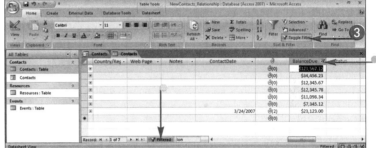

MASTER IT

Can I use a filter to hide records that contain specific data?	How can I use more criteria to filter data?	Can I filter records that have already been filtered?
▼ Yes. Click the data that you do not want to display. Click Selection in the Sort & Filter group of the Datasheet tab, click Filter, and then click Filter Excluding Selection.	▼ When filtering by input, you can use additional criteria to define which records Access displays. In the drop-down menu that appears when you right-click a criterion, select Number Filters and type an amount. For example, you would type **<$5,000** to display records with amounts less than $5,000. For more information, see the task "Examples of Criteria."	▼ Yes. You can continue to narrow the records by filtering them again and again, until you see the records you want to view. When you perform multiple filters, you cannot back up one filter. When you remove the filter, all of the records are displayed.

Filter Data by Form

You can use the Filter by Form feature to perform powerful searches of a table, form, or query in a database. Filtering records allows you to quickly find and display records of interest.

When you filter by form, you can specify the criteria that records must meet in order to display. For example, you can have Access find clients who have outstanding balances of more than $5,000.

You can specify multiple criteria to filter records. Access displays only records that meet all of the criteria that you specify. For example, you can have Access find clients in London who have outstanding balances of more than $5,000. For more information on search criteria, see the task "Examples of Criteria."

When you save a table, form, or query, the last filter that you performed is also saved. You can quickly apply the same filter again later.

Filter Data by Form

① Click the Home tab.

② Click Advanced.

Filter options appear.

③ Click Filter by Form.

The Filter by Form window appears.

④ Click the down arrow (▼) in the first field that you want to use to filter the records.

⑤ Select the first item by which you want to filter.

520

● You can scroll across the fields to locate another field.

⑥ Click in another field and use a second field to filter the records.

⑦ Type the data or criteria to specify which records you want to find.

⑧ Click Toggle Filter to filter the records.

● Access displays only the records containing the data that you specified.

● The word *Filtered* appears in this area to indicate that you are looking at filtered records.

⑨ Click Toggle Filter to once again display all of the records.

Access removes the filter and displays all records.

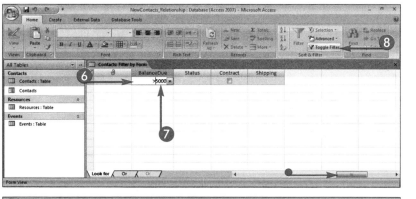

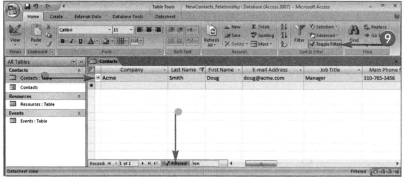

MASTER IT

How can I quickly enter the data that I want to use to filter records?

▼ Click the field that you want to use to filter records. To display a list of the values in the field, click the field name down arrow (▾). A drop-down list of the values appears, each with a ☑. You can click to change ☑ to ☐ for each value that you want to exclude from the filter of the records. Click OK; only the checked records are shown and filtered.

What types of criteria can I use?

▼ You can use the typical comparison operators, such as = (equal to), < (less than), and > (greater than). For more information on search criteria, see the task "Examples of Criteria."

Can I display records that meet one of several criteria that I specified?

▼ Yes. You can use the Or tab when filtering by form to display records that meet at least one of the criteria. For example, you can find clients with the first name Bill or William. Perform Steps 1 to 5 in this task to enter the first criterion that you want the records to meet. Click the Or tab in the bottom-left corner of the Filter by Form window and then enter the second criteria. Click Toggle Filter to filter the records.

Create a Query Using the Simple Query Wizard

query is similar to asking a question of the database and getting a response. The response that you get is a set of records, much like a filter. With a query, you have a great deal more control. You can perform calculations on the data, use more than one table, and save queries.

You can use the Simple Query Wizard to gather information from one or more tables in a database. The wizard asks you a series of questions and then sets up a query based on your answers. The Simple Query Wizard is useful when you want to perform simple calculations in a query, such as finding the sum of fields within a table.

The Simple Query Wizard allows you to choose the table containing the fields that you want to include in the query. After you choose a table, you can select the fields that you want to include. A query can include all or only some of the fields in a table.

You can select fields from multiple tables if they are related. For information on relationships between tables, see Chapter 21.

Create a Query Using the Simple Query Wizard

1 Click the Create tab.

2 Click Query Wizard in the Other group.

● The New Query window opens.

3 Click Simple Query Wizard.

4 Click OK.

The Simple Query Wizard appears.

5 Click the Tables/Queries down arrow ( ).

6 Click the table containing the fields that you want to use.

You can also select a previously saved query on which to base the new query.

● This area displays the fields from the table that you selected.

⑦ Double-click each field that you want to include in the query.

To add all of the fields at once, you can click the double arrow (⯈⯈).

● Each field that you selected appears in this area.

If needed, you can add fields from other tables by performing Steps 1 to 8 for each table.

⑧ Click Next.

You can click Cancel at any time if you decide not to use the wizard.

Can I use other wizards to create a query?

▼ Yes. Click the Create tab on the Ribbon. Click Query Wizard in the Other group. In the New Query window, the Crosstab Query Wizard allows you to create a query that groups related information together and displays summarized information. The Find Duplicates Query Wizard allows you to find records that contain the same values to avoid duplication. The Find Unmatched Query Wizard allows you to compare two tables to find records in one table that do not have related records in the other table.

Why should I use a wizard instead of creating my own query?

▼ Using a wizard is a fast way to create a basic query. If you want to plan and set up your own query, you can create a query in Design view. For more information, see the task "Create a Query in Design View."

Can I remove fields that I have added to the query by mistake?

▼ Yes. You can remove a field by double-clicking the field in the Selected Fields list in the Simple Query Wizard dialog box.

continued

523

Create a Query Using the Simple Query Wizard *(Continued)*

If the fields that you selected for a query contain information that can be calculated, you can choose to display all of the records or a summary of the records as part of the query results.

You can calculate values in a query to summarize information. The Sum option adds values. The Avg option calculates the average value. The Min and Max options find the smallest or largest value.

When you calculate values in a query, Access groups related records together. For example, in a query that

contains an Employee Name field and a Products Sold field, Access groups together the records for each employee to find the total number of products that each employee sold.

You can have Access count the number of records used in each group to perform a calculation. The count appears as a field in the query results.

To finish creating a query, you must name the query. Choose a descriptive name that can help you to recognize the query in the future.

Create a Query Using the Simple Query Wizard *(continued)*

⑨ Click to select how you want to display the information in the query results (◎ changes to ◉).

If you selected Detail, skip to Step 15.

If this question window does not appear, skip to Step 16.

⑩ If you selected Summary, click Summary Options to select how you want to summarize the information.

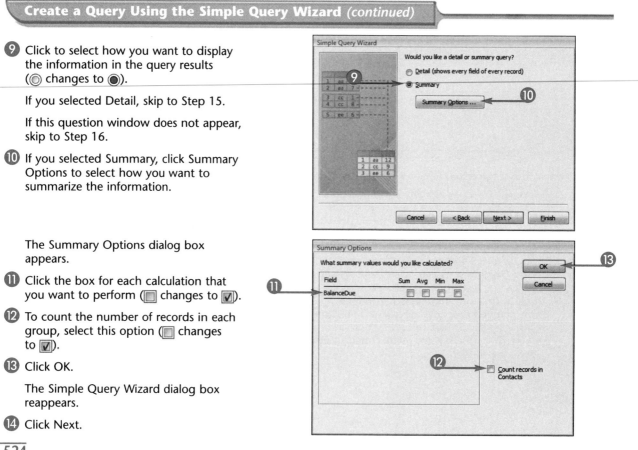

The Summary Options dialog box appears.

⑪ Click the box for each calculation that you want to perform (☐ changes to ☑).

⑫ To count the number of records in each group, select this option (☐ changes to ☑).

⑬ Click OK.

The Simple Query Wizard dialog box reappears.

⑭ Click Next.

⑮ Type a name for the query, or accept the default.

⑯ Click Finish to create the query.

● The results of the query appear.

⑰ Click the Save button (🖫) to save the query.

⑱ When you finish working with the query, you can click the Close button (✕).

How can I make changes to a query that I created using the Simple Query Wizard?

▼ You can use Design view to make changes to any query that you create. You can sort records, add and remove fields, and more. For more information, see the task "Change the Query View."

Why does another dialog box appear, asking me how I would like to group dates in my query?

▼ It may appear if one of the fields in your query stores dates. You can choose to group the dates in your query by the individual date, day, month, quarter, or year.

Why did Access not summarize my information properly in the query?

▼ Make sure that you include only the fields that you need to create the query. Also, make sure that you select the field by which you want to group the records first. Access groups records starting with the first field, and then considers the data in each of the following fields.

Create a Query in Design View

Design view allows you to plan and set up your own query. If you cannot find a wizard that matches your query needs, you can build one from scratch. You can also build a query using Design view if you need to create a complex query that finds results based on multiple criteria.

To start, select each table that contains information that you want to use in a query. To perform a query on more than one table, the tables that you select must be related.

The tables that you use in the query appear in the top half of the Select Query window.

The bottom half of the window displays a grid, called the *design grid,* where you can specify the information that you want the query to display. You can use this grid to select the field, sort order, and criteria. You can type the criteria to match. For information on entering criteria, see the task "Set Criteria."

Create a Query in Design View

① Click the Create tab.

② Click Query Design.

The Select Query window opens and names the new query Query1 on the top tab.

● The Show Table dialog box appears with the Tables tab active.

● This area lists all of the tables in the database.

③ Click a table that contains information that you want to use in the query.

④ Click Add to add the table to the query.

- A box appears in the Select Query window, displaying the fields for the table that you selected.

5 Repeat Steps 3 and 4 for each table that you want to use in the query.

- Additional boxes appear.

6 Click Close to hide the Show Table dialog box.

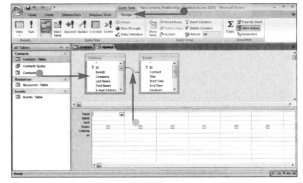

- The Design tab of Query Tools opens on the Ribbon.

- Each box in this area displays the fields for one table.

- If the tables that you selected are related, Access displays a line joining the related fields.

Note: *For more information on defining relationships, see the task "Define Relationships between Tables" in Chapter 21.*

How do I add another table to a query?

▼ Click Show Table in the Design tab of the Query Tools on the Ribbon to redisplay the Show Table dialog box. Double-click the table that you want to add to the query and then click Close.

How do I remove a table from a query?

▼ In the Select Query window, click the box displaying the fields for the table that you want to remove, and then press Delete. Access removes the table from the query, but not from the database.

Can I use an existing query to create a new query?

▼ Yes. This is useful if you want to refine an existing query to produce fewer records. In the Show Table dialog box, click the Queries tab and then double-click the name of the query that you want to use. Click Close and then perform Steps 7 to 9 in the next part of this task to create the new query.

PART V

continued

Create a Query in Design View
(Continued)

After you select the fields that you want to include, you can choose to hide a field. Hiding a field is useful when you need to use a field to find information in the database but do not want the field to appear in the results of the query.

When you run a query, Access displays the results of the query in Datasheet view. If you change the information when the query displays in Datasheet view, the table that supplies the information for the query also changes.

If you want to run a query later, you must save the query. When you save a query, you save only the conditions that you specified. You do not save the information gathered by the query. This allows you to view the most current information each time you run the query.

You can give the query a name. Make sure that you use a descriptive name that allows you to distinguish the query from the other queries in the database.

Create a Query in Design View *(continued)*

● The bottom part of the window displays areas for selecting the fields to include and for entering criteria.

⑦ Double-click a field that you want to include in the query.

⑧ Repeat Step 7 for each field that you want to include.

● Each field displaying a check mark (☑) appears in the results of the query.

If you do not want a field to appear in the results of the query, deselect the Show check box for the field (☑ changes to ▢).

When all of the fields are added, the query is complete. You can now run the query to see the results.

⑨ Click Run in the Design tab of the Query Tools to run the query.

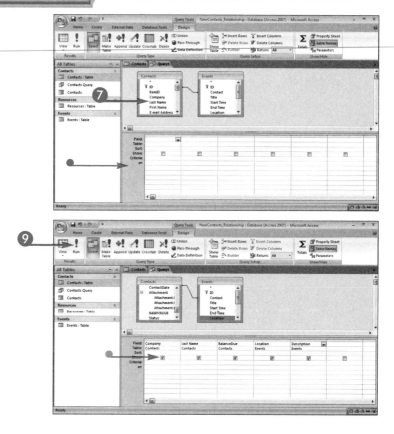

● The results of the query appear in Datasheet view.

Save the query

❶ Click the Save button (🖫) to save the query so that you can run the query again later.

● The Save As dialog box appears.

❷ Type a name for the query.

❸ Click OK.

Access saves the query.

How do I remove a field that I included in a query?

▼ Move your mouse to the top of the field (🗘 changes to ↓), and then click to select the field. Press the Delete key to remove the field from the query.

How do I quickly include all of the fields from a table in a query?

▼ In the Select Query window, double-click the title bar of the box displaying the fields for the table to select them all. Position your mouse over the selected fields and then drag the fields to the first empty column in the design grid.

Can I clear a query and start over?

▼ If you make mistakes while selecting fields for a query, you can start over by clearing the design grid. Move to the top of the first field (🗘 changes to ↓), and then click to select the field. Drag across the grid to select all fields. Press the Delete key to remove the field from the query.

Can I change the order of fields in a query?

▼ Yes. Rearranging fields in a query affects the order in which the fields appear in the results. In the design grid, position your mouse over the top of the field that you want to move (🗘 changes to ↓), and then click to select the field. Position your mouse directly above the selected field, and drag the field to a new location.

Open a Query

You can open a query to display the results of the query or change the design of the query. You can open a query in Datasheet or Design view.

When you open a query in Datasheet view, Access runs the query and displays the results. This view is similar to Datasheet view for tables but it displays only the information that meets the criteria or conditions of the query.

In Design view, you can make changes to the structure of a query. You can use this view to tell Access what data you want to find, where to find the data, and how you want to display the results.

When you have finished working with a query, you can close the query to remove it from your screen. A dialog box appears if you have not saved changes that you made to the query.

Open a Query

① Locate queries in the Navigation pane.

Note: For more information, see the task "Using the Navigation Pane" in Chapter 19.

② Double-click the query (⊡) that you want to open.

Double-clicking runs a query. To view a query, you can select it and then click Design view (⊠).

● Access opens the query.

③ When you finish viewing the query, click the Close button (⊠) to close the query.

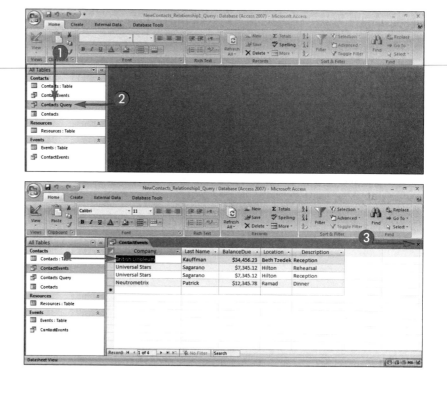

Change the Query View

There are several ways that you can view a query. Each view allows you to perform different tasks.

Design view allows you to plan your query. You can use this view to tell Access what data you want to find, where Access can find the data, and how you want to display the results.

Datasheet view allows you to review the results of a query. The field names appear across the top of the window. Each row shows the information for a record that meets the criteria or conditions that you specify.

SQL view displays the SQL statement for the current query. *Structured Query Language (SQL)* is a language specifically designed for working with databases. When you create a query, Access creates the SQL statement that describes your query. You do not need to use this view to use Access.

You can also use the PivotTable and PivotChart views to change the view of the query to reorganize the layout of the fields and records. These views function similar to Excel PivotTables (see Chapter 12) and are beyond the scope of this book.

Change the Query View

In this example, the query appears in Datasheet view.

1. Click the Home tab.

2. Click the View down arrow (▼).

3. Click to select another view that you want to use.

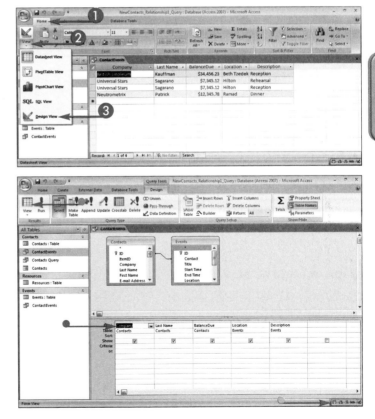

- The query appears in the view that you selected.

This example shows Design view.

- You can click View to toggle back to Datasheet view.

- You can also click the various View buttons in the lower-right corner of the Access window.

PART V

Set Criteria

Y ou can use criteria to find specific records in a database. *Criteria* are conditions that identify which records you want to find. To set criteria, you need to display the query in Design view. You can enter a single criterion; for example, type **IN** in the State field to find all clients in Indiana.

You also can use multiple criteria. Using the OR condition allows you to find records that meet at least one of the criteria that you specify. For example, you can find clients in Indiana or Texas. You can use the OR condition with one or more fields.

Using the AND condition allows you to find records that meet all of the criteria that you specify. You can use the AND condition with one or more fields. For example, you can find clients in London or Chicago whose outstanding balance is over a certain amount. This task includes both OR and AND conditions.

You can combine criteria. For example, you can enter criteria for more than one field. Access displays only records that match all of the criteria that you enter.

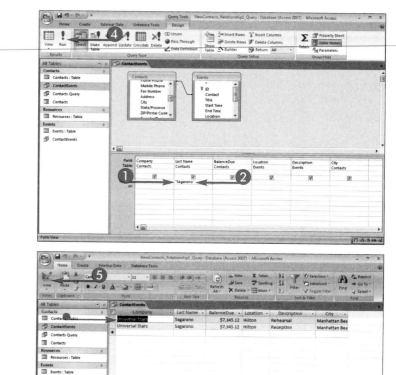

Set Criteria

Using simple criteria

1. In Design view, click the Criteria area for the field that you want to use to find specific records.

2. Type the criteria.

3. Press Enter.

   Access may add quotation marks (" ") or number signs (#) to the criteria that you type.

4. Click Run to run the query.

• The results of the query appear.

In this example, Access finds records for the last name Sagarano.

5. To return to Design view, click View.

Using multiple criteria

① In Design view, type the first criterion in the appropriate field.

You can click the Criteria area for the second field and then type the second criterion.

② To have Access match all records that must meet more than one criterion (AND condition), click in the second field and type the criterion.

In this example, the query will display all balances over $10,000 from London.

③ Click Run.

● The results of the query display.

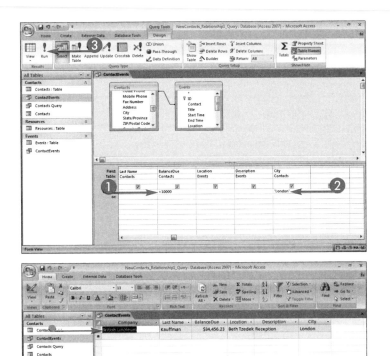

Can I have Access display only a portion of the records in the results?

▼ Yes. When you know there will be many records in the results of a query, you can have Access display only the top or bottom values in the results. Click the Sort area for the field for which you want to show the top or bottom values. Click the down arrow (▼) that appears. Select Ascending to display the bottom values, or Descending to display the top values. In the Query Setup group of the Design tab, click (▼) for Return: All and then select the values that you want to display when the query is run.

How do I use the AND condition in one field?

▼ In the Criteria area for the field, enter both criteria separated by the word *AND*. For example, to find records that contain invoice numbers between 100 and 150, type >**100 AND** <**150** in the Criteria area of the Invoice Number field.

Should I save the query?

▼ Yes. You should save the query if you want to use it again. To do this, click the Save button (🖫).

Examples
of Criteria

Exact Matches

=100	Finds the number 100
=California	Finds California
=1/5/08	Finds the date 5-Jan-08

Less Than

<100	Finds numbers less than 100
<N	Finds text starting with the letters A to M
<1/5/08	Finds dates before 5-Jan-08

Less than or equal to

<=100	Finds numbers less than or equal to 100
<=N	Finds text starting with the letters A to N
<=1/5/08	Finds dates on or before 5-Jan-08

Greater than

>100	Finds numbers greater than 100
>N	Finds text starting with the letters O to Z
>1/5/08	Finds dates after 5-Jan-08

Greater than or equal to

>=100	Finds numbers greater than or equal to 100
>=N	Finds text starting with the letters N to Z
>=1/5/08	Finds dates on or after 5-Jan-08

Not equal to

<>100	Finds numbers not equal to 100
<> California	Finds text not equal to California
<>1/5/08	Finds dates not on 5-Jan-08

Empty Fields

Is Null	Finds records that do not contain data in the field
Is Not Null	Finds records that do contain data in the field

Find List of Items

In (100,101)	Finds the numbers 100 and 101
In (California, CA)	Finds California and CA
In (#1/5/08#,#1/6/08#)	Finds the dates 5-Jan-08 and 6-Jan-08

Between...and...

Between 100 and 200	Finds numbers from 100 to 200
Between A and D	Finds text starting with the letters A to D
Between 1/5/08 and 1/15/08	Finds dates on and between 5-Jan-08 and 15-Jan-08

Wildcards

The asterisk (*) wildcard represents one or more characters. The question mark (?) wildcard represents a single wildcard.

Like Br	Finds text starting with Br, such as Brenda or Brown
Like ar	Finds text containing ar, such as Arnold or Mark
Like Terr?	Find five letters starting with Terr, such as Terri or Terry

Sort Query Results

Y ou can sort the results of a query to better organize the results. This can help you to find information of interest more quickly.

The results of a query can be sorted in ascending or descending order. Sorting in ascending order sorts text in alphabetical order from A to Z and sorts numbers from smallest to largest. When you sort in descending order, the opposite occurs.

You can choose not to sort the results of a query. If you do not sort the results, Access displays the results in the order that they are found.

You can sort by one or more fields. When you sort by more than one field, you must place the fields in the order in which you want to perform the sort. Access sorts the records in the far-left field first.

You cannot sort a field that has a Hyperlink, Memo, OLE Object, or Attachment data type.

Sort Query Results

1 In Design view, click the Sort area for the field that you want to use to sort the results of the query.

2 Click the field down arrow (⏷).

3 Click to select how you want to sort the data.

4 Click Run to run the query.

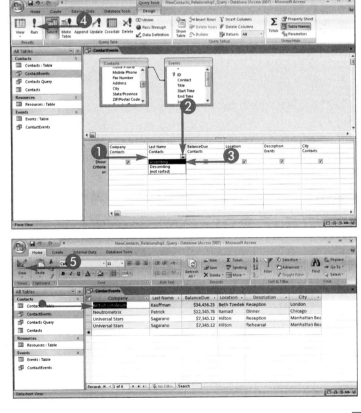

● The records appear in the new order.

In this example, the call records are sorted in ascending order by last name.

5 To return to Design view, click View.

Perform Calculations

You can perform calculations on records in a database. You can then review and analyze the results.

In a blank field, you can type a name for the field that displays the results of the calculation, followed by an expression. An *expression* tells Access which items to use in the calculation. An expression also contains operators that tell Access to multiply (*), add (+), subtract (–), divide (/), or raise values to a power (^).

To enter a field name in an expression, type the field name in square brackets. For example, you would type **[Quantity]*[Cost]** to multiply the Quantity field by the Cost field. Make sure that you type the field names exactly.

If the same field name is found in more than one table, you must type the table name in square brackets followed by a period (.), and the field name in square brackets. For example, you would type **[Products].[Quantity]** to ensure that Access uses the Quantity field in the Products table.

The results of a calculation are not stored in the database. If you run the query again, Access uses the most current data in the database tables to perform the calculation.

1 Display the query that you want to change in Design view.

Note: For more information, see the task "Open a Query."

2 Click the Field area in the first empty column.

3 Type a name for the field that will display the results of the calculation, followed by a colon (:).

4 Press the spacebar to leave a blank space.

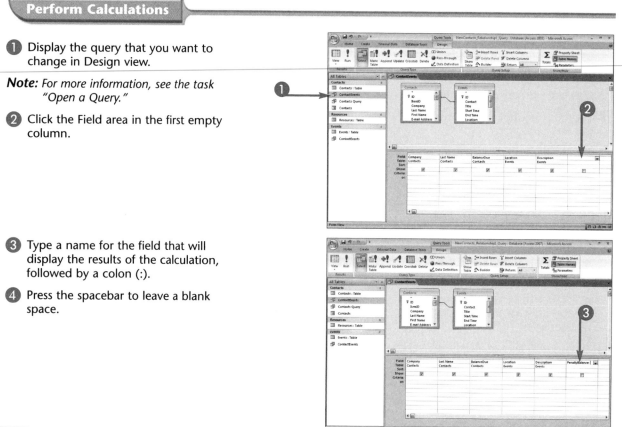

⑤ Type an expression that describes the calculation that you want to perform.

In this example, the expression is PenaltyBalance: [BalanceDue] * 1.15, which represents a penalty.

⑥ Click Run to run the query.

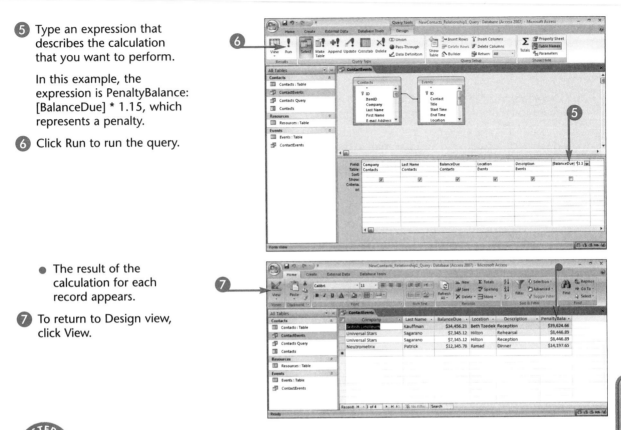

● The result of the calculation for each record appears.

⑦ To return to Design view, click View.

Can I change the format of calculated information?

▼ Yes. In Design view, right-click anywhere in the calculated field. Click Properties. The Properties tab opens. In the General tab, click the down arrow (▾) that appears in the format that you want to change, and then select the format that you want to use. You can also specify the number of decimal places to display for numeric fields.

How can I display an entire expression?

▼ An expression that you type may be too long to fit in the Field area. To display the entire expression, click the cell containing the expression, and then press Shift+F2. The Zoom dialog box appears, displaying the entire expression.

What types of expressions can I use?

▼ Here are some examples of expressions that you can use.

Inventory Value	[Price]*[Quantity]
Total Price	[Cost]+[Profit]
New Price	[Price]–[Discount]
Item Cost	[Price of Case]/[Items]

Summarize Data

Y ou can summarize the information in a database to help you analyze the information.

You can divide records into groups and summarize the information for each group. For example, you can summarize information grouped by date to determine the number of orders for each day.

To group records, you must display the Total row. The words *Group By* automatically appear in each field in the Total row. You can leave the words *Group By* in the field that you want Access to use to group the records.

In the other field, you can specify the calculation that you want to perform on the group to summarize the information.

Access provides several calculations that you can perform. The Sum option adds the values. The Avg option calculates the average value. You can use the Min or Max option to find the smallest or largest value. The Count option calculates the number of values, excluding empty records. You can use the StDev (standard deviation) or Var (variance) option to perform statistical functions. You can use the First or Last option to find the value of the first or last record.

Summarize Data

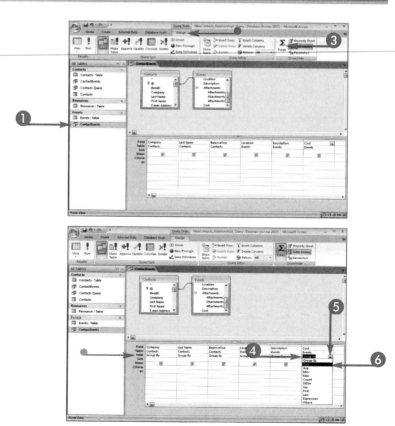

1 Create a query that includes the field that you want to use to group the records, and the field that you want to summarize.

2 Display the query in Design view.

● The Design tab of the Query Tools is open on the Ribbon.

3 Click Totals to display the Total row.

● The Total row appears.

You can repeat Step 3 at any time to remove the Total row.

4 Click the Total area for the field that you want to summarize.

5 Click the field down arrow (▼) to display a list of calculations that you can perform on the field.

6 Click the calculation that you want to perform.

- The summary calculation is set up.

7 Click Run to run the query.

- The results of the calculations appear.

In this example, Access calculates the balance due by client.

8 To save the query, click the Save button ( ) and type a query name.

Can I use more than one field to group records?

▼ Yes. You can group records using more than one field. For example, you can use the Company and Product fields to group the records, and the Quantity Ordered field to summarize the data. This lets you display the total amount of each product purchased by each company. Access groups records using fields from left to right. In Design view, place each field in the order that you want to group the records.

Do I have to use more than one table in a query?

▼ No. You can create a query based on one table, as shown in this example.

Can I limit the records that appear in the results?

▼ Yes. You can summarize all of the records in a query but show only some of the records in the results. For example, you may want to display only the companies who had outstanding balances of more than $10,000. In the Criteria area of the field that you are summarizing, type the criteria that you want to limit the records that show in the results. For more information on search criteria, see the task "Examples of Criteria."

Connect an InfoPath Web Form

You can use Microsoft InfoPath to create forms that will work directly with your Access database to enter information and also to perform queries.

While this book does not cover InfoPath in detail, it is easy to connect your InfoPath form directly to a table or query that you create in Access. The underlying database file can be local, or on a network or a SharePoint site. For more information about SharePoint, see Chapter 29.

InfoPath forms are similar to those created directly in Access. The difference is that anyone can open an InfoPath form whether or not they have Access, and connect to the database table to enter and revise data,

if they have permission. For more information about forms, see Chapter 22.

An InfoPath form can also be accessed over the Internet in a Web browser, allowing users all over the world with the proper permission to see or even add or edit records in an Access database.

By using the XML capability of InfoPath, you can allow users to connect to all kinds of XML databases using a standard Web browser.

To connect your InfoPath Web form to an Access table, you open the program and go through a simple template. The fields from your database will be available in InfoPath, allowing you to design a form based on the Access table.

Connect an InfoPath Web Form

1. Click Start.
2. Click All Programs.
3. Click Microsoft Office.
4. Click Microsoft Office InfoPath 2007.

The Getting Started Window appears.

5. Click Design a Form Template.

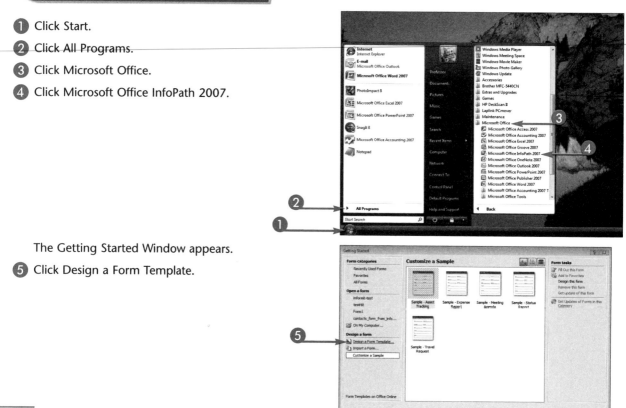

The Design a Form Template dialog box appears.

6 Click to select Database.

7 Click OK.

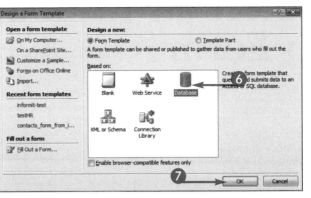

The Data Connection Wizard appears.

8 Click Select Database.

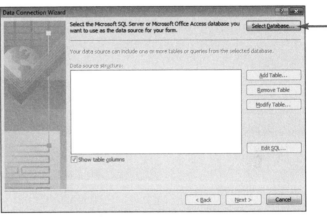

Can I use an Access form on the Internet?

▼ No. That is the purpose of using InfoPath. Access used to have Data Access Pages that you could post online, but InfoPath is designed to add security and publishing capability to Access, as well as to connect with other data sources.

Can I connect to more than one table using the Data Connection Wizard?

▼ Yes. You can create a form based on one table, one query, or multiple tables and queries by clicking Add Table in the Data Connection Wizard.

Can I use InfoPath to fill out a form?

▼ Yes. InfoPath forms can be designed in InfoPath to connect to Access and for other data sources. InfoPath users can also fill out a form using InfoPath by clicking File and then Fill out a form; they can also press Ctrl+Q.

continued

Connect an InfoPath Web Form *(Continued)*

O nce you open InfoPath, you can connect directly to a local database or to one on a SharePoint server.

A system administrator can help you publish your forms so that other users can access them with permission through the Internet or a local network.

InfoPath has two main parts: filling out forms and designing form templates. Once you create a form

template connected to a database, users with permission can use the form to query a table or add or review information in the table.

Once you connect to a data source, you can use InfoPath to design or redesign a form template. You can also change your view to load and fill out an existing form that is already connected to a data source.

Connect an InfoPath Web Form *(continued)*

The Select Data Source dialog box appears.

● You can scroll through your folders to locate your saved Access database.

⑨ Click to select the database.

Note: *For more information, see the task "Open a Document" in Chapter 2.*

⑩ Click Open.

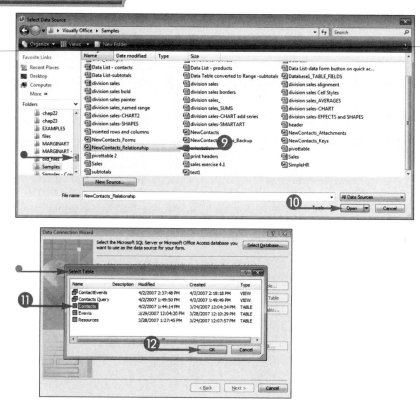

● The Select Table dialog box appears.

⑪ Click the table or query to which you want to connect your form.

⑫ Click OK.

● The Data Connection Wizard shows the data source structure.

⑬ Click Next and then click Finish to complete the database wizard connection.

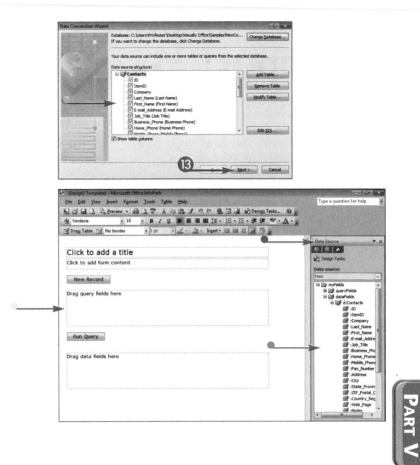

● Your form template opens in InfoPath.

● The Data Source task pane shows your table.

● You can click the plus sign (⊞) next to the table to reveal individual fields to add to your form template.

When your form is completed and published, users can view and query the Access database using the InfoPath Web form.

Do I have to open the Data Connection Wizard each time I start InfoPath?

▼ No. Once you connect, save, and publish a form, the connection is established. You can also save an existing connection to keep working with the same database as a data connection file.

Can I create a form based on a template?

▼ Yes. You can open a form template through the Forms on Office Online link, located in the Design a Form Template dialog box, to see examples of other InfoPath forms. You can also click Customize a Sample and choose from samples including Asset Tracking, Expense Report, Meeting Agenda, Status Report, and Travel Request forms.

Can I use other Office programs to create a form to use in InfoPath?

▼ Yes. In the Design a Form Template window, you can click the Import link and open XML-based forms created in Word or Excel.

PART V

Create a Report Using the Report Wizard

Y ou can use the Report Wizard to help you create a professionally designed report that summarizes the data from a table or a query. The Report Wizard asks you a series of questions and then creates a report based on your answers.

You can choose the table or query that contains the fields you want to include in the report. After you choose a table, you can select the fields you want to include. For example, in a report that displays monthly

sales, you may want to select the Date, Customer, Sales Rep, and Order Total fields. A report can include all or only some of the fields in a table.

The Report Wizard can help you organize the data in the report by grouping related data together. If you choose to group related data together, Access automatically places the data in the appropriate sections in the report. For example, you can group data by the Date field to have Access place all the sales for the same month together.

Create a Report Using the Report Wizard

1 Click the Create tab.

2 Click Report Wizard.

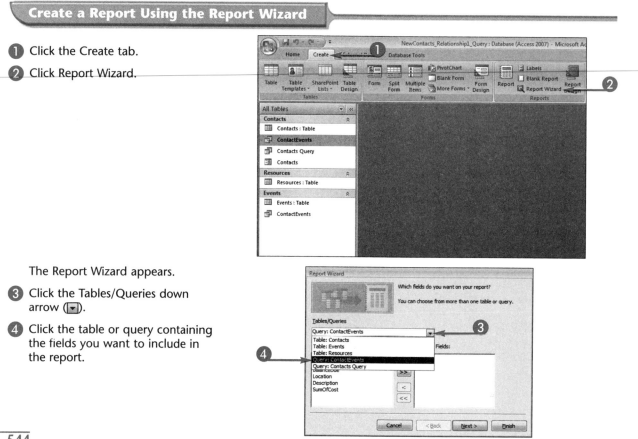

The Report Wizard appears.

3 Click the Tables/Queries down arrow ( ).

4 Click the table or query containing the fields you want to include in the report.

● Fields display from the table or query you selected.

5 Double-click each field you want to include in the report.

To add all the fields at once, you can click the double arrow (⟩⟩).

● Each field you select appears in this area.

6 Click Next.

You can click Cancel at any time if you decide not to use the Report Wizard.

● Access asks whether you want to group related data.

7 Double-click the field you want to use to group the data.

● This area displays how Access will group the data.

8 Click Next.

Can I specify how I want Access to group data in my report?

▼ Yes. After you select the field you want to use to group data, click the Grouping Options button. The Group Intervals window opens. Click the Grouping intervals down arrow (▾) and click how you want to group the data. The available options depend on the type of field you selected.

How do I remove a field I added by accident?

▼ To remove a field, double-click the field in the Selected Fields list. To remove all fields, click the double arrow (⟨⟨).

Can I create a report based on more than one table?

▼ Yes. Relationships must exist between the tables you use, or you can use a query that contains links between tables. For information on table relationships, see Chapter 21. To create the report, perform Steps 1 to 5 in this task and then repeat Steps 3 to 5 until you have chosen all of the tables and fields you want to include. Click Next. If you are prompted to select how to view data, click the fields below the question until the preview area displays the view you want. Finally, perform Steps 6 to 25 to finish the report.

continued

PART V

Create a Report Using the Report Wizard *(Continued)*

You can sort the records in a report to better organize the records. The Report Wizard lets you select the fields you want to use to sort the records. For example, you can alphabetically sort records by the Last Name field. If the same data appears more than once in the field, you can sort by a second field, such as First Name.

You can sort records in ascending or descending order. When you sort in ascending order, text is sorted from A to Z and numbers are sorted from 1 to 9. When you sort in descending order, the opposite occurs.

You can perform calculations to summarize the data in a report. When you perform calculations, you can have Access display all the records and the calculated summary for each group of records or just the calculated summaries in the report.

You can also choose to display the percentage of the total that each group represents. For example, in a database that stores sales information, you can calculate the percentage of total sales for each region.

Create a Report Using the Report Wizard *(continued)*

Access asks how you want to sort reports.

⑨ Click the first field's down arrow (▼).

⑩ Click the field you want to use to sort the records.

⑪ Click Ascending or Descending until the list appears the way you want to sort the records.

Note: *Ascending is the default. With a field selected for Ascending, the Descending option becomes available.*

The wizard sets up the sort field.

⑫ To sort by a second field, repeat Steps 9 to 11 for the second field.

⑬ To show calculations in the report, click Summary Options.

If the Summary Options button does not appear, skip to Step 18.

The Summary Options dialog box appears.

⓮ Click the box for each calculation you want to perform (☐ changes to ☑).

⓯ Click to show either all the records and summary information or just the summary (◉ changes to ◉).

⓰ Click this option to display the percentage of the total that each group represents (☐ changes to ☑).

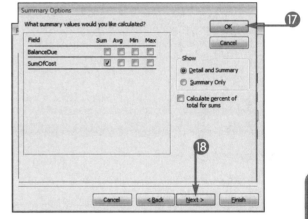

The summary options are set.

⓱ Click OK.

You are returned to the Report Wizard.

⓲ Click Next.

You can click Back at any time to return to a previous step and change your answers.

Why does the Summary Options button not appear?

▼ The Summary Options button does not appear if you do not include any fields that store numbers in the report or if you do not choose to group related data together in your report. For information on grouping related data, see the preceding pages of this task.

What calculations can I perform on the data in my report?

▼ Access offers several calculations that you can perform. The Sum option adds values. The Avg option calculates the average value. The Min and Max options find the smallest or largest value, respectively.

Is there a faster way to create a report?

▼ Yes. You can use an AutoReport to quickly create a report based on one table in your database. Select the table or query in the Navigation pane. In the Database window, click Report in the Reports group on the Create tab. A new report based on the table opens in the database window and is named for the table or query. It opens in Layout view. You can revise it using Design view (▨) and the Report Layout Tools which are available on the Ribbon. You can also click Blank Report in the Reports group on the Create tab. A blank report opens. You can use the options available in the Field List task pane and from the Report Layout Tools on the Ribbon.

PART V

continued

Create a Report Using the Report Wizard *(Continued)*

Y ou can choose from among several layouts for a report. The layout you choose determines the arrangement of data in the report.

The available layouts depend on the options you previously selected for the report. If you chose to group related data, Access makes the Stepped, Block, Outline, and Align Left layouts available. If you chose not to group related data, Access makes the Columnar, Tabular, and Justified layouts available.

You can specify the page orientation of the printed report. The portrait orientation prints data across the

short side of a page. The landscape orientation prints data across the long side of a page.

You can choose a style for the report, such as Casual, Corporate, or Formal. Most styles use colors and patterns to enhance the appearance of a report.

The Report Wizard asks you to name your report. The name you select appears in the Reports area of the Database window.

The report appears in a window on your screen. If the report consists of more than one page, you can move through the pages in the report.

Create a Report Using the Report Wizard *(continued)*

Layout options appear.

⑲ Click the layout you want to use for the report (◎ changes to ◉).

The available layouts depend on the options you selected for the report.

● This area displays a sample of the layout you selected.

⑳ Click the page orientation you want to use (◎ changes to ◉).

㉑ Click Next.

㉒ Click the style you want to use for the report.

● This area displays a sample of the style you selected.

㉓ Click Next.

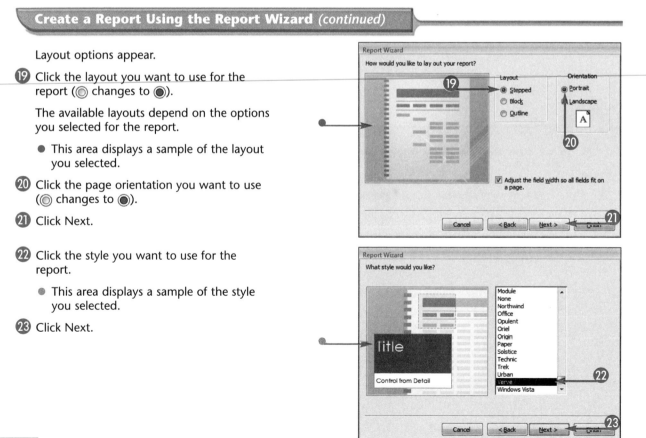

Access asks you to name your report.

㉔ Type a name for the report.

㉕ Click Finish to create the report.

● Access displays the report.

You can use the scroll bars to scroll through the report.

㉖ When you are finished viewing the report, click the Close button (⊠).

How do I print a report?

▼ When the report appears on your screen, click the Office button and click Print to print the report.

When viewing my report, how can I display an entire page or other pages on-screen?

▼ You can drag the Zoom slider (🔳) in the lower-right corner of the window to display the entire page on your screen. You can also use the scroll buttons at the bottom to display other pages. For more information on changing the magnification of a page, see the task "Preview a Report."

Can I later change the style of a report?

▼ Yes. With the report open in Design view, the Report Design Tools display on the Ribbon. Click the Arrange tab and click AutoFormat. A gallery of formats opens, where you can select the style you want to use.

I changed data in a table I used to create a report. How do I update the report?

▼ When you close and reopen the report, Access automatically gathers the most current data from the table. Access also updates the date that displays in the report.

Open a Report

Y ou can open a report to display its contents and to review its information.

You can open a report in Report, Print Preview, Layout, or Design view. Print Preview view allows you to see how a report will look when you print it. Design view allows you to change the design of a report, make formatting changes, or rearrange the report items. Report view lets you make minor text changes, and Layout view lets you quickly and easily change how the report looks.

When you open a report, Access gathers the most current data from the table or query used to create the report. If the table or query contains a large amount of data, it may take a few moments for the report to appear on your screen.

When you finish working with a report, you can close the report to remove it from your screen. A dialog box appears if you have not saved changes that you made to the design of the report, such as changing the font or size of text. You can choose to save the report or cancel the changes.

Open a Report

① Locate the reports icons () in the Navigation pane.

② Double-click the report you want to open.

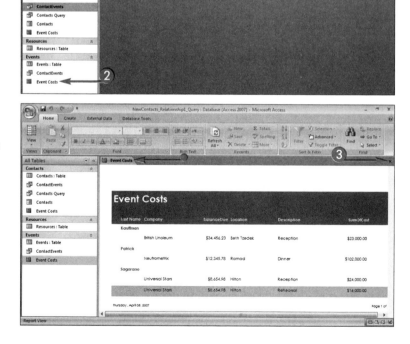

● The report appears.

③ When you finish reviewing the report, click the Close button (⊠) to close it.

Change the Report View

Y ou can view a report in four ways. Each view allows you to perform a different task.

Report view is the view that shows you the data in the report without any formatting. You can scroll through the report and see the information without the distraction of formatting.

Print Preview view allows you to display all the pages in the report and see how each page will print.

Layout view allows you to quickly view and change the layout and style of a report.

Design view allows you to change the layout and design of a report. Design view displays a grid of small, evenly spaced dots to help you line up the items in a report. This view displays information in several sections, such as the report header and page footer sections.

Change the Report View

1 Click the View down arrow ( ).

2 Click the view you want to use.

This example uses Design view.

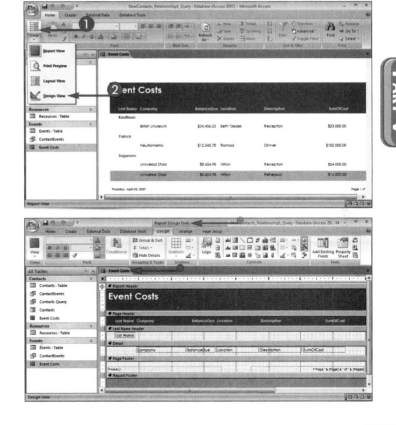

● The report appears in the view you selected.

● The Report Design Tools open on the Ribbon.

Preview a Report

Y ou can use the Print Preview feature to see how your tables, queries, forms, and reports will look when you print them. Using the Print Preview feature can help you confirm that the printed pages will appear the way you want.

The Print Preview window indicates which page you are currently viewing. If an report contains more than one page, you can easily view the other pages.

You can magnify an area of a page. This allows you to view the area in more detail. When you magnify a page, Access displays scroll bars that you can use to move through the information on the page.

You can have Access display several pages in the Print Preview window at once. This gives you an overall view of the pages in an report.

When you have finished using the Print Preview feature, you can close the Print Preview window to return to the Database window.

Preview a Report

① Open the report by double-clicking its name in the Navigation pane.

Note: For more information, see the task "Open a Report."

The Report window appears.

② In the Home tab, click the View down arrow (▼).

③ Click Print Preview.

- The Print Preview tab appears on the Ribbon.

- You can click one of these buttons to view the other pages:

First Page (⏮)

Previous Page (◀)

Next Page (▶)

Last Page (⏭)

You can position the mouse (🔍) over the area of the page you want to magnify.

④ Click the mouse (🔍) to magnify the area.

⑤ Click Two Pages to display two pages.

⑥ Click Portrait to change the orientation.

The preview displays the selected number of pages and the orientation.

⑦ Click the Close button (✕) to close the Print Preview window.

Can I preview an report at different magnification levels?

▼ Yes. You can drag the Zoom slider (🔲) in the lower-right corner of the window to display the entire page on your screen. You can also use the scroll buttons at the bottom to display other pages. By default, Access displays an report in the Fit zoom setting, which uses the magnification level that displays all of the currently displayed pages.

Can I print directly from the Print Preview window?

▼ Yes. To print an report directly from the Print Preview window, click Print in the Print group of the Print Preview tab on the Ribbon.

In the Print Preview window, I can tell that I have more fields than will fit on a page. Any ideas on what I can do?

▼ Click Landscape in the Page Layout group of Print Preview to have your report print in Landscape orientation.

How do I preview only one page of an report after displaying multiple pages?

▼ To preview one page of an report, click One Page in the Zoom group of the Print Preview tab on the Ribbon.

Print Data from a Database

You can produce a paper copy of a table, query, form, or report. A paper copy is often referred to as *hard copy*.

Before printing, make sure your printer is turned on and contains an adequate supply of paper and ink or toner.

You can choose the information you want to print. For example, you can print all the records, specific pages, or specific records. Printing only specific records saves you from printing information you do not want to review. To print only specific records, you must select the records before you begin.

If the current printer settings suit your needs, you can use the Print button to quickly print all the records without displaying the Print dialog box.

When you print a table or query, Access prints the title, date, and page number on each page. This information can help you organize the printed data.

Print Data from a Database

Print database records

1 Open the table that contains the records you want to print.

If you want to print only some records, select only those records.

2 Click the Office button.

3 Click Print.

The Print dialog box appears.

4 If you selected records following Step 1, click the Selected Record(s) option. To print all records, click All (○ changes to ●).

5 Click OK.

Access prints the records.

Print a report or form

1 Open the report or form you want to print.

2 Click the Office button.

3 Click Print.

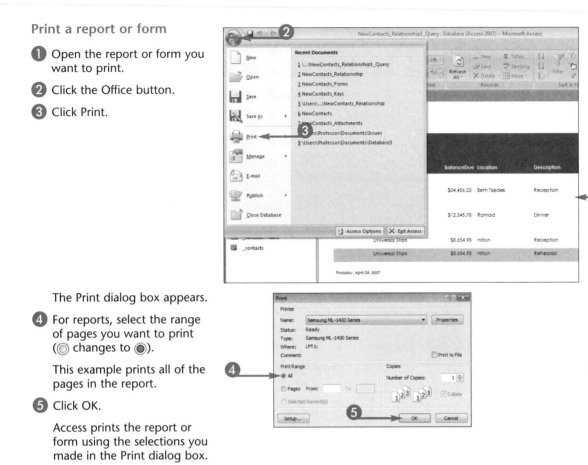

The Print dialog box appears.

4 For reports, select the range of pages you want to print (◉ changes to ◉).

This example prints all of the pages in the report.

5 Click OK.

Access prints the report or form using the selections you made in the Print dialog box.

Can I specify the printer I want to use to print information?

▼ If you have more than one printer installed, you can select the printer you want to use. For example, you may want to use your color printer to print forms and a black-and-white printer to print tables. In the Print dialog box, click the Name down arrow (▼) and then select the printer you want to use.

Can I print multiple copies?

▼ Yes. In the Print dialog box, double-click the Number of Copies field and then type the number of copies to print.

How do I change the page margins?

▼ Click the Setup button in the Print dialog box. In the Page Setup dialog box, click the Margins tab and then type the margins you want to use for the top, bottom, left, and right. The default margin setting is one inch. Click OK to confirm your new margins.

An Introduction to Interactive Design Modes

You can use the interactive design modes, or Layout views, for both reports and forms. This allows you to quickly modify the way your report or form will print or appear on-screen.

When you click the View down arrow for either a report or a form, you can select the Layout view.

You can also click the Layout View button at the bottom of either the Form or Report window to switch to Form or Report Layout view.

Report Layout View

In Report Layout view, you can quickly move fields and widen or narrow their labels. When you open Report Layout view, the Report Layout Tools become active on the Ribbon and allow you to work with three additional tabs: Format, Arrange, and Page Setup.

In the Format tab, you can change the look of elements in the report or apply an AutoFormat from the gallery.

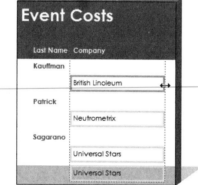

In the Format tab of the Report Layout view, you can also change the appearance of the text in your fields and labels, and add conditional formatting to a report. See the task "Using Conditional Formatting in Controls" in Chapter 22 for information about conditional formats in forms Conditional formats work similarly in reports.

In the Arrange tab, you can use the Control Layout group to quickly revise the entire layout of the report, change margins, and reposition items in the report. You can also change the order of how the user can tab through the fields. By clicking a control and then clicking Property Sheet in the Tools group of the Arrange tab, you can open the Property Sheet task pane to change the properties of the selected item.

In the Page Setup tab, you can change margins and page sizes to accommodate your printer. You can also click Columns, Page Setup, or the dialog box launcher to open the Page Setup dialog box. There, you can make more precise revisions for print options, page setup, and columns in their respective tabs.

Form Layout View

In Form Layout view, you can also quickly move fields or records, or widen or narrow their labels or fields. When you open Form Layout view, the Form Layout Tools become active on the Ribbon and allow you to work with two additional tabs: Format and Arrange.

In the Format tab, you can change the look of elements in the report or apply an AutoFormat from the gallery. For more information, see the task "AutoFormat a Form" in Chapter 22.

In the Format tab of the Form Layout view, you can also change the appearance of the text in your fields and labels.

In the Arrange tab, you can use the Control Layout group to quickly revise the layout of different fields in the form, change margins, and reposition items in the form. You can also change the order of how the user can tab through the fields. By clicking a control and then clicking Property Sheet in the Tools group of the Arrange tab, you can open the Property Sheet task pane to change the properties of a selected item or control. You can also add conditional formats to any field in the form for which they are appropriate. For more information, see the task "Using Conditional Formats" in Chapter 22.

Layout view is the most intuitive view to use for report or form modification, and you can use it for nearly all the changes that you would want to make to a report in Access.

In the Form Layout Tools on the Ribbon for Form Layout view, you have most of the formatting features of Design view, along with the Field List task pane, the gridlines options, and the AutoFormat gallery in the Format tab. In the Arrange tab, you can change the layout of the controls along with their margins. Even with both of these tabs active, the form is still as functional as it is in Forms view; you can still move through the records using the navigation tools and add or revise records in the table on which the form is based. See the tasks "Move through Records with a Form" and "Add a Record" in Chapter 22.

In Report Layout view, a report is actually running, and so you can see your data much as it will appear when printed. However, you can also make changes to the report design in this view. Because you can see the data while you are modifying the report, it is a very useful view for setting column widths, adding grouping levels, or performing almost any other task that affects the appearance and readability of the report.

The report you see in Layout view does not look exactly the same as the printed report. For example, there are no page breaks in Layout view. Also, if you have used the Page Setup feature to format your report with columns, the columns do not display in Layout view. However, Layout view gives you a very close approximation of the printed report. If you want to see how the report will look when printed, use Print Preview.

Certain tasks cannot be performed in Layout views for either reports or forms; for these tasks, switch to Design view. In certain situations, Access displays a message telling you that you must switch to Design view to make a particular change. For example, adding new controls to a form such as combo boxes, list boxes, and option buttons must be done in Design view for both forms and reports.

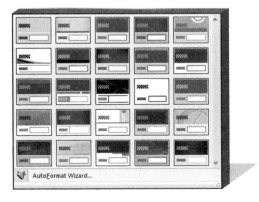

PART V

Create Mailing Labels Using the Label Wizard

You can create a mailing label for every person in a database table. You can use labels for addressing envelopes and packages, labeling file folders, and creating name tags.

The fastest way to create mailing labels is to use the Access Label Wizard. The Label Wizard asks you a series of questions and then creates labels based on your answers.

You can choose the table that contains the names and addresses you want to appear on the labels.

You can use two types of labels — sheet feed and continuous. Sheet-feed labels are individual sheets of labels. Continuous labels are connected sheets of labels, with holes punched along each side.

You can select the label size you want to use. Check your label packaging to determine which label size to select.

The wizard allows you to change the appearance of the text that appears on the labels. You can choose various fonts, sizes, weights, and colors. The text appearance that you choose affects all of the text on every label.

Create Mailing Labels Using the Label Wizard

① Select the table that has the information for the labels in the Navigation pane.

② Click the Create tab.

③ Click Labels.

The Label Wizard appears.

④ Click the Filter by manufacturer down arrow (▼) to select the manufacturer of the label size you want to use.

You can click Cancel at any time if you decide not to use the Label Wizard.

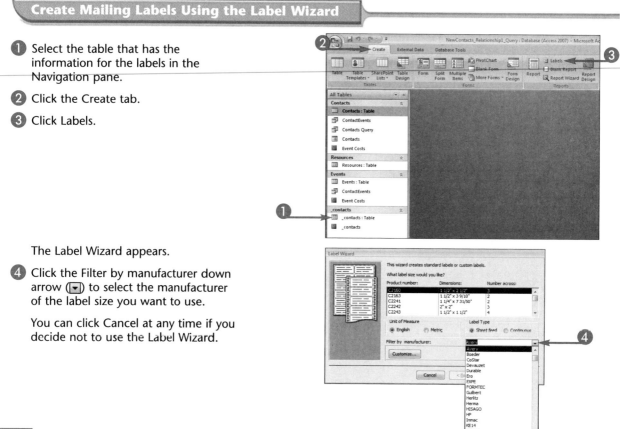

⑤ Scroll to locate the label size you want to use.

⑥ Click to select the correct label size.

⑦ Click Next.

You can click Cancel at any time if you decide not to use the Label Wizard.

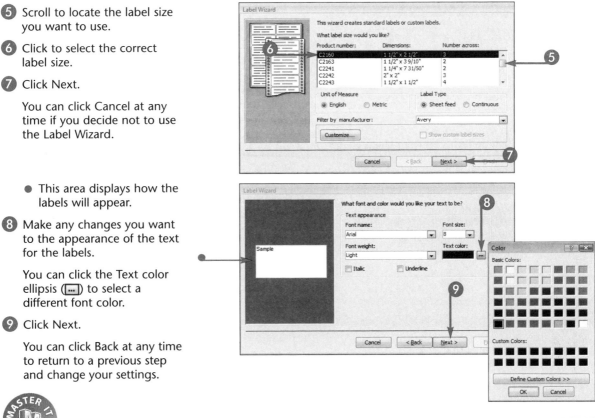

● This area displays how the labels will appear.

⑧ Make any changes you want to the appearance of the text for the labels.

You can click the Text color ellipsis (⋯) to select a different font color.

⑨ Click Next.

You can click Back at any time to return to a previous step and change your settings.

There are no fields available in the Label Wizard. How can I fix this?

▼ Before you begin, make sure that the table that you select has the proper fields. Also, make sure that you select a table and not a form or report as the basis for your labels.

How do I specify a custom label size in the Label Wizard?

▼ Click Customize and then click New. A dialog box appears, displaying sample labels and areas where you can enter measurements for your labels. Type in the measurements you want to use and then click OK.

How do I change the text appearance options in the Label Wizard?

▼ You can click the down arrow (▾) in the Font name, Font size, or Font weight fields to display a list of options. You can then select the option you want to use. Click the Text color ellipsis (⋯) to display a list of colors and then click the color you want to use. To italicize or underline text, click the appropriate option (☐ changes to ☑).

continued

PART V

Create Mailing Labels Using the Label Wizard *(Continued)*

Y ou can select the fields you want to appear on the labels. You do not have to select all of the fields from the table.

The fields you select should appear in the Label Wizard in the order and location that you want them to print on the labels. Make sure that you add spaces or commas where needed, such as a space between the first and last name, or a comma between the city and state.

You can specify how you want to sort the labels. Sorting the labels determines the order in which

Access arranges the labels on a printed sheet. For example, you may want to sort mailing labels by ZIP code: Mass mailings can receive a discount if the pieces are in ZIP Code order.

You can type a name for the labels. Access stores the labels as a report that you can open as you would any report. For more information, see the task "Open a Report."

The labels appear on your screen as they will look when you print them. This allows you to preview the labels before you print them.

Create Mailing Labels Using the Label Wizard *(continued)*

⑩ Double-click each field that you want to appear on the labels.

- Each field that you select appears in this area.

Note: *The fields should appear the same way that you want them to print on the labels. Make sure that you add spaces and commas where needed.*

⑪ Click Next.

⑫ To sort the labels, double-click the field by which you want to sort.

- The field you select appears in this area.

⑬ Click Next.

560

⑭ Type a name for the labels.

⑮ Click Finish to create the labels.

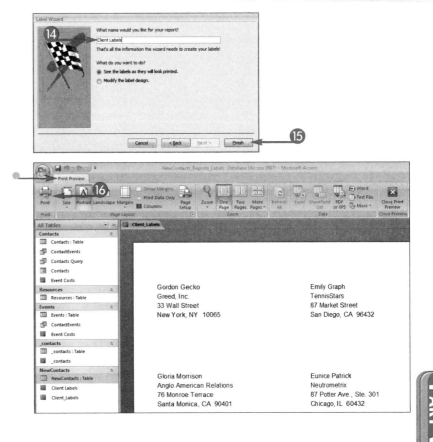

● A Print Preview window opens, displaying a personalized label for each item in the table.

⑯ To print the labels, insert the blank labels into your printer and then click Print.

Can I sort the labels by more than one field?

▼ Yes. If the first field that you are using to sort the labels contains matching data, you can sort by a second field. In the Label Wizard, double-click the first field by which you want to sort and then double-click the second field by which you want to sort.

How do I edit labels I created?

▼ You must change the data in the table you used to create the labels. Changes that you make in the table automatically appear in the labels.

What if I see a mistake when I am previewing the labels?

▼ You can start over and create new mailing labels, being sure to make the appropriate changes to the label format. You can also edit the label report design, inserting spaces and punctuation as needed. To edit a report design, open the report and then click the Design View button (▣). Make any changes to the layout and then click the Save button (▣).

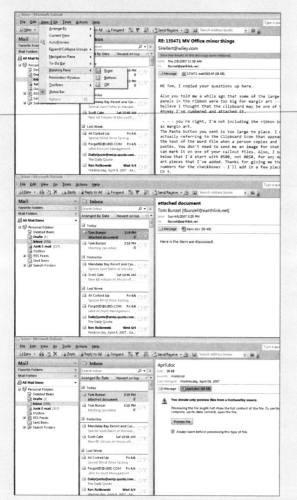

27

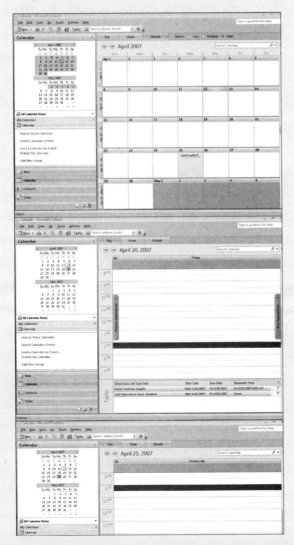

An Introduction to Outlook

Outlook is an e-mail and personal information manager. The program includes tools for sending, receiving, and managing e-mail messages, and includes components for keeping track of people, appointments, and to-do lists.

For more information on Outlook, you can visit www.microsoft.com/outlook.

Electronic Mail

The main purpose of Outlook is to handle your electronic mail, or e-mail. If you have an Internet connection or a network e-mail system, you can send e-mail to others. To use your connection, you must set up Outlook to dial in or establish the network connection to your e-mail account. For this procedure, you enter specific information about your system, including information about the mail server, your username, and your password. Outlook includes a wizard that prompts you for this information and then sets up an account.

Because everyone has a unique system, the setup steps are not provided in this chapter. Check with your network Administrator or your e-mail provider for the exact information and steps that you need to follow to set up your e-mail account.

After you set up Outlook to handle e-mail, you can send and receive e-mail. You can delete, print, forward, and respond to messages. You can even attach files and open files that are attached to a message.

E-mail has many benefits, including cost, convenience, and speed. Your message is sent instantaneously, and you can send messages at any time you choose. You can also preview attached files directly in Outlook. For more information on sending and handling e-mail, see Chapter 26.

Appointments, Contacts, and To-Do Lists

In addition to handling e-mail, you can also use Outlook and its various components to schedule appointments and other events on the Calendar; to keep track of friends, employees, business clients, and other contacts using Contacts; to keep a to-do list of tasks; and to record notes or other journal entries.

Each of these parts of Outlook have their own separate folders and views, which you can configure for the way that you work. For example, you can view your calendar by day, week, or month, and you can see your contacts in a phone list or as a group of business cards.

All of the parts of Outlook are integrated so that you can send an e-mail out from Contacts or send your Calendar as an e-mail message. Outlook tasks and e-mail also coordinate with parts of OneNote. For more information on these features of Outlook, see Chapter 27. For more about OneNote, see Chapter 28.

Outlook 2007 with Business Contact Manager is only included with Office Small Business 2007 and Office Professional 2007. Business Contact Manager is not covered in this book.

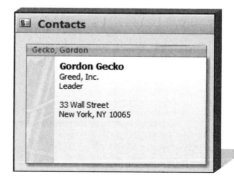

Start Outlook

You can start Outlook to access a wide range of e-mail features. When you start the program, you see the Outlook window, which is divided into two areas. The area on the left side of the window contains the Outlook Navigation pane. The Outlook Navigation pane displays icons for the different features of Outlook. The area on the right side of the window displays the current feature.

You can use Outlook's features to manage many different types of information. The *Inbox* lets you send and receive e-mail messages. The *Calendar*

helps you keep track of your appointments. You can use *Contacts* to store information about people with whom you correspond. *Tasks* allows you to create a list of items that you want to accomplish. *Notes* lets you create brief reminder notes. *Deleted Items* stores items that you have deleted.

The first time you start Outlook, a wizard appears, allowing you to set up Outlook on your computer. Follow the instructions on your screen to set up Outlook, referring to the previous task, "An Introduction to Outlook."

Start Outlook

① Click Start.

② Click All Programs.

③ Click Microsoft Office.

④ Click Microsoft Office Outlook 2007.

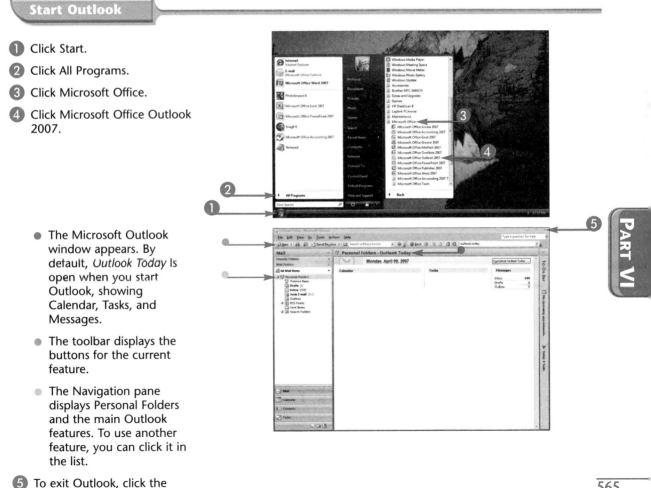

● The Microsoft Outlook window appears. By default, *Outlook Today* Is open when you start Outlook, showing Calendar, Tasks, and Messages.

● The toolbar displays the buttons for the current feature.

● The Navigation pane displays Personal Folders and the main Outlook features. To use another feature, you can click it in the list.

⑤ To exit Outlook, click the Close button (⊠).

PART VI

Using the Outlook
To-Do Bar

Outlook has two main ways to quickly see your important information.

The Outlook To-Do Bar lets you see all of your important tasks, activities, and appointments whenever you need to, without closing another window. With the To-Do Bar, you can quickly access important information by opening it in Normal view. By keeping the To-Do Bar minimized, on the right side of the screen, it is always available as a quick pop-up tool.

Like the Outlook To-Do Bar, Outlook Today also provides you with a summary of important information. By default, Outlook Today is selected as the default feature when you start Outlook. However, Outlook Today disappears whenever you open Mail, Calendar, Contacts, or another Outlook feature.

Can I close or reopen Outlook Today?

▼ Yes. Click Personal Folders (📁) in the Navigation pane to return to Outlook Today. You can click the Customize Outlook Today button to open the Customize Outlook Today window, and select, for example, not to use Outlook Today on startup (☑ changes to ☐). You change other options before clicking Save Changes. You can also open Outlook directly through E-mail on the Start menu.

Using the Outlook To-Do Bar

① Click View.

② Click To-Do Bar.

③ Click Normal.

● The To-Do Bar opens to its full size.

You can see your calendar, upcoming appointments, and tasks.

④ Click Close To-Do Bar double arrow (≫) to minimize the To-Do Bar on the right side of the screen.

When minimized, the To-Do Bar still shows the number of appointments and tasks.

You can quickly reopen the To-Do Bar by clicking the Open To-Do Bar double arrow (≪).

Using the Navigation Pane

Y ou can change what appears in the main Outlook window quickly and easily from the Navigation pane.

You can keep the Navigation pane fully open to see your personal folders, including e-mail, or minimize it and still have access to different parts of Outlook.

Besides the folder list, the Navigation pane can quickly access the Mail, Calendar, Contacts, and Tasks features. Clicking any of these items in the Navigation pane opens them in the main window of Outlook, and contextual options display in the Navigation pane.

You can also access the Notes feature by clicking the Notes icon at the bottom of the Navigation pane. To open the Journal feature, click Go on the main menu and select Journal.

Can I change the way the Navigation pane displays information?

▼ Yes. Click the down arrow (⏷) at the bottom of the Navigation pane to add or remove buttons from the Navigation pane. You can click the Shortcuts button (⧉) to reopen the Personal Folders list.

Using the Navigation Pane

① Click Mail in the Navigation pane to display your Personal Folders.

② Click the Inbox in the Navigation pane.

● You can click the double arrow (≫) to minimize the To-Do Bar for more space. The To-Do Bar is open or closed depending upon how you last closed Outlook.

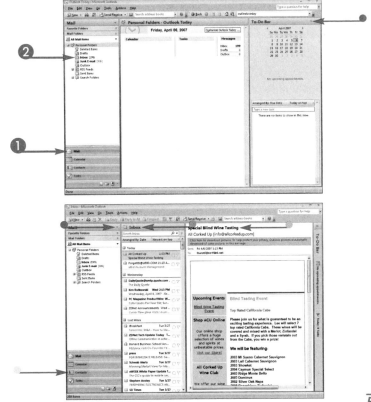

● Outlook opens your e-mail Inbox.

● By default, Outlook opens a Reading pane.

● You can instantly open the other parts of Outlook — Calendar, Contacts, and Tasks — by clicking them in the bottom of the Navigation pane.

● You can minimize the Navigation pane by clicking the double arrow (≪).

PART VI

Read
Messages

Outlook allows you to exchange electronic mail, or e-mail, with friends, family members, colleagues, and clients. When you receive new e-mail messages, Outlook stores the messages that you receive in the Inbox. You can use the Inbox to open the messages and read their contents.

In the folder list of the Navigation pane, the Inbox appears bold and indicates the number of new messages in parentheses when you have new mail. If you have Outlook open and you receive new e-mail, an envelope icon also appears in the Windows system tray in the taskbar.

Each unread message displays a closed envelope and appears in bold type. After you read a message, Outlook displays an open envelope and uses regular type. For each e-mail you receive, Outlook displays the author, subject, and date.

If you choose to use Outlook Today, Outlook also displays the number of new messages in bold next to the Inbox under the Messages section. You can also open your Inbox directly from Outlook Today by clicking the Messages link.

Read Messages

① Click Mail.

② Click Inbox to view the messages you have received.

The number in parentheses beside the Inbox indicates the number of unread messages.

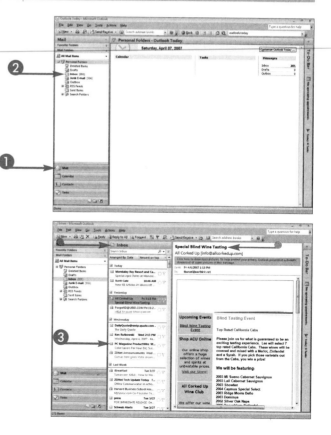

- The Inbox displays your messages. Unread messages display a closed envelope (⊠) and appear in bold. Read messages display an open envelope (⊡).

- The Reading pane displays the contents of the current message.

③ Double-click the message you want to read.

Outlook displays the message in its own window.

● The Ribbon contains buttons for working with the message.

④ Click the scroll buttons or drag the slider to scroll through the message.

④

⑤ To display other messages, click one of these buttons:

Display the next message (⬇)

Display the previous message (⬆)

⑥ When you are finished reading the message, click the Close button (✕).

Outlook returns you to the Inbox.

⑤   ⑥

How do I check for new messages?

▼ When you connect to your e-mail provider, that server (computer) downloads your messages to your computer. To check for new messages immediately, click the Send/Receive button.

How can I turn off the Reading pane?

▼ Click View on the Outlook main menu. Click Reading Pane and choose to place it on the right (default) or at the bottom, or to turn it off.

Does Outlook automatically check for new messages?

▼ If you are connected to your e-mail server, Outlook checks for new messages at regular intervals. To change how often Outlook checks for messages, click Tools, click Options, and then click the Mail Setup tab in the Options window. Click the Send/Receive button. Be sure that the Include this group in send/receive option is checked for when Outlook is online (☐ changes to ☑). In the minutes area beside the Schedule, there is an automatic send/receive every [xx] minutes option. Click the spinner button (⬆) to set an interval or double-click the number and then type the number of minutes you want to use. Click Close and then click OK.

Create a New Message

You can create and send an e-mail message to exchange ideas or request information.

Outlook allows you to send a message to more than one person. To send a message, you must know the e-mail address of each person who you want to receive the message. You can type the address of each recipient in the To area. You can also select it from an address list. For more information on the address list, see the task "Select a Name from the Address Book."

You can also type an address in the Cc, or *carbon copy*, field to send a copy of the message to a person who is

not directly involved in the subject of the e-mail, but who may find the message of interest.

When you create a message, be sure to type a subject that helps the reader quickly identify the contents of your message.

Outlook stores messages that you have sent or are planning to send in three mail folders. The *Drafts* folder stores incomplete, unsent messages. The *Outbox* folder stores messages that you have not yet sent. The *Sent Items* folder stores sent messages.

Create a New Message

1 Click Inbox.

2 Click New.

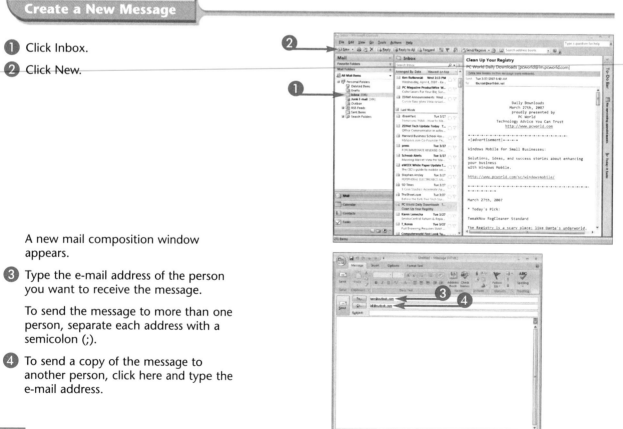

A new mail composition window appears.

3 Type the e-mail address of the person you want to receive the message.

To send the message to more than one person, separate each address with a semicolon (;).

4 To send a copy of the message to another person, click here and type the e-mail address.

5 Click this area and then type the subject of the message.

6 Click this area and then type the message.

Note: *To format the appearance of the text, see Chapter 26.*

7 Click Send.

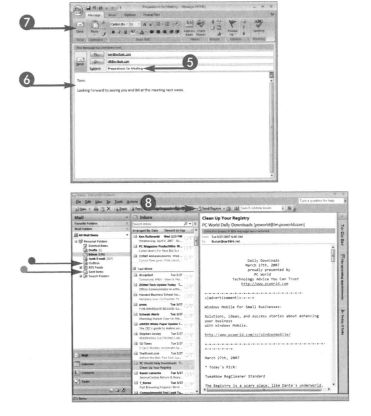

● Outlook places the message in the Outbox and sends it at the next send/receive interval.

8 To send the message right now, click Send/Receive.

● In addition to sending the message, Outlook stores a copy of the message in the Sent Items folder.

Can I correct spelling errors in my message?

▼ Yes. To find and correct spelling errors in a message, click Spelling in the Proofing group of the Message tab to start the spell check.

How can I prevent Outlook from saving my messages in the Sent Items folder?

▼ In the Outlook window, click Tools, click Options, and then click the Preferences tab in the Options window. Click E-mail Options and uncheck the Save copies of messages in Sent Items folder option (☑ changes to ☐). Then click OK.

Can I add a priority to my message?

▼ Yes. You can change the priority of the message, flagging it as high or low priority. The default is regular priority. Specify the importance on the Message tab: select the High icon (❗) to assign a high priority, or select the Low icon (⬇) to assign a low priority.

Select a Name from the Address Book

Whenen creating a message, you can select the name of the recipient from an Address Book. Your Contacts list is generally your main Address Book, but you can have others.

Using an Address Book makes it easy to send a message without having to remember the recipient's e-mail address. It also reduces the possibility that your e-mail service cannot deliver your e-mail due to a typing mistake in the address.

You can use an Address Book to send a message to more than one person. You can specify whether the

recipients receive the original message or a carbon copy, or Cc, of the message. You can use the Cc option if your recipient is not directly involved in the e-mail, but may find the message of interest. Outlook also lets you send a blind carbon copy, or Bcc, which lets you send a copy of the message to a person without anyone else knowing that the person received the message.

You must list the address of your recipients in the Address Book before you can select their names. See Chapter 27 for information on adding contacts to an Address Book.

Select a Name from the Address Book

① Click Inbox.

② Click New.

An untitled message appears.

③ Click the To button to select a name from the Address Book.

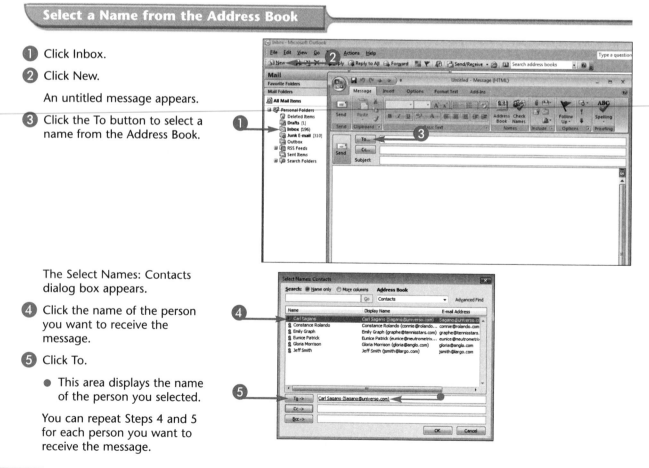

The Select Names: Contacts dialog box appears.

④ Click the name of the person you want to receive the message.

⑤ Click To.

● This area displays the name of the person you selected.

You can repeat Steps 4 and 5 for each person you want to receive the message.

● You can also use Steps 4 and 5 to send copies to recipients in the Cc and Bcc fields.

Note: Bcc stands for blind carbon copy. Recipients in the To or Cc fields will not see recipients in the Bcc field.

6 Click OK.

This area displays the name of each person you selected from the Address Book.

7 Type a subject.

8 Type the message.

9 Click Send to send the message.

● Outlook places the message in the Outbox and sends it at the next send/receive interval.

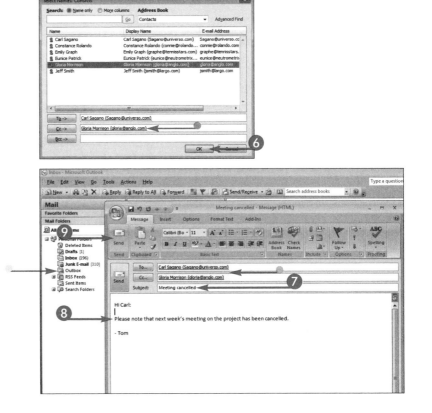

How can I quickly select a group of people from my Address Book?

▼ You can create a distribution list. Click the Address Book button (📖) in the Outlook toolbar for the Inbox. When the Address Book opens, click File, click New Entry, and then click New Distribution List. The Distribution List window opens, with a Ribbon tab. In the Members group, click Add New to type in new members, or click Select Members from the Address Book. Create the distribution list and save it with Save & Close. When you send a message, select the saved distribution list name as the recipient; Outlook sends the message to each person on the list.

What is the format for an e-mail address?

▼ The format for an e-mail address is *username@servername.ext*. The *username* is the person's assigned username, and the *servername* is the name of that person's server or domain. The extension indicates the type of server. For example, lgodiva@aol.com is an example of an e-mail address, where the server name is America Online.

Attach a File to a Message

Y ou can attach a file to a message you are sending. Attaching a file is useful when you want to include additional information with a message. To learn how to send a message, see the task "Create a New Message."

Outlook allows you to attach many different types of files to a message, including images, documents, videos, sound recordings, and program files.

To attach a file, you must select the drive and folder where the file is located. Outlook lists the attached file in the message header.

While Outlook does not restrict the number of attachments you can send with a message, the size of your file may prevent you from sending it. Many e-mail servers on the Internet do not transfer large messages properly, if at all. Also, some mail recipients or their e-mail providers may block file attachments over a certain size. When sending e-mail messages over the Internet, you should keep the total size of attachments to less than 150KB, unless your recipient has a fast connection, or the receiving mailbox can take larger attachments.

The recipient of your message must have the necessary hardware and software installed on his computer to display or play the file that you attached.

Attach a File to a Message

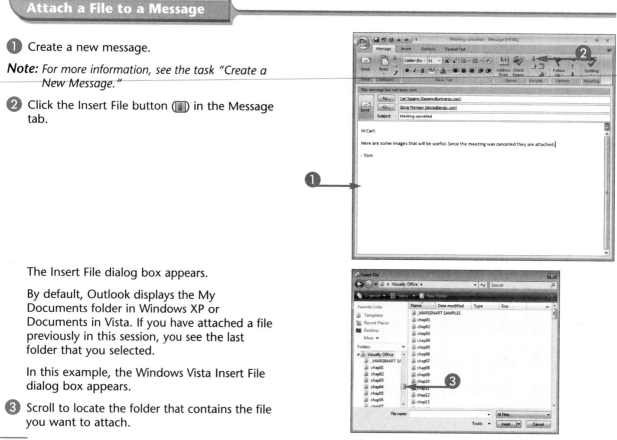

1 Create a new message.

Note: *For more information, see the task "Create a New Message."*

2 Click the Insert File button (📎) in the Message tab.

The Insert File dialog box appears.

By default, Outlook displays the My Documents folder in Windows XP or Documents in Vista. If you have attached a file previously in this session, you see the last folder that you selected.

In this example, the Windows Vista Insert File dialog box appears.

3 Scroll to locate the folder that contains the file you want to attach.

④ Click the name of the file or files that you want to attach to the message.

You can press Ctrl and click to select more than one file at a time to add them to your message.

⑤ Click Insert.

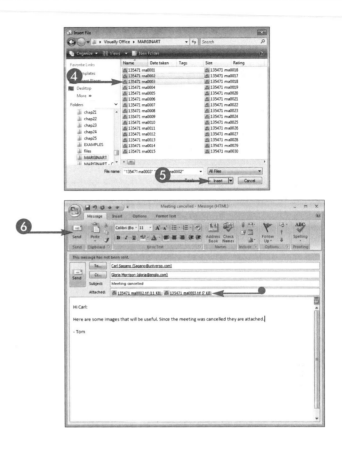

● Outlook adds an Attached field to the message header and lists your file or files.

⑥ Click Send.

Outlook sends your message with the attachments.

How do I remove a file I attached to a message?

▼ Right-click the icon or name of the file and then click Remove.

How can I send large files?

▼ Some mail servers have limits on file sizes that you can send as attachments. If you need to send large files, you can compress them before sending. You can do so using a compressed folder, which is a Windows feature. You can also use a compression program such as WinZip. You can find other available compression programs on the Internet.

Why is it taking so long to send the message?

▼ Outlook sends a simple text message quickly, but depending on the file size, a message with an attachment may take more time to send. You can display the status of the send/receive operation by clicking the status bar message that says Send/Receive Status and then clicking Details. To close the Outlook Send/Receive Progress dialog box, click the Close button (⊠). Your antivirus program may also be taking time to scan the message.

Open and Save Attachments

When you receive a message with an attached file, you can open or save the file. Messages with an attached file display a paper clip icon in the message list.

When you select an attached file that you want to view, Outlook asks if you want to open the file or save it on your computer.

What happens when you open the file depends on the file type. If the file is a graphic file or document, that file or document appears on-screen. If the file attachment is a program, Windows runs the program.

Some files, such as program files, may contain viruses. If you open and run a file that contains a virus, the virus could damage information on your computer. You should only open files sent by people you trust, and even then, scan the attachment with a virus scan program before opening it.

If you receive an attachment that you want to save, you can save it to your hard drive or a floppy disk.

Open and Save Attachments

Open attachments

1. Open a message with an attached file.

- The attachment or attachments are listed here.

2. Click the attachment for Preview options.

- A preview warning appears in the message area.

3. Double-click the file you want to open.

You can also click Preview file to view the file directly in the message area. For more information, see the task "Preview Messages and Attachments."

Depending on the attachment type, Outlook may automatically open the attachment for you, or display a dialog box containing information about the attachment.

4. Click OK.

- The appropriate program opens and displays the file on-screen.

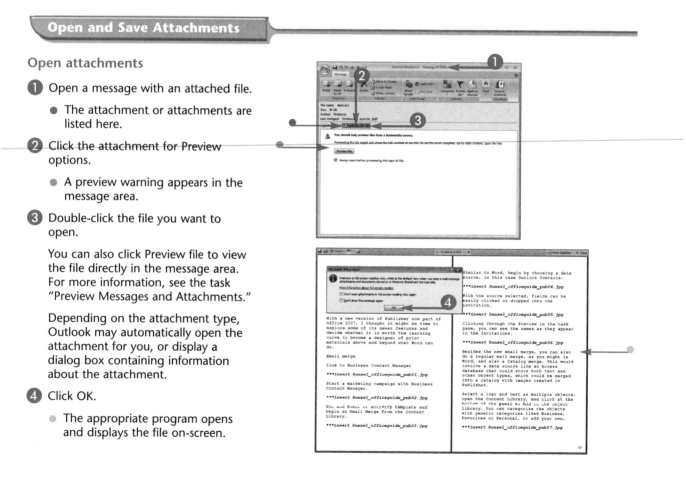

Save attachments

1 Right-click the attachment in the e-mail message.

2 Click Save As.

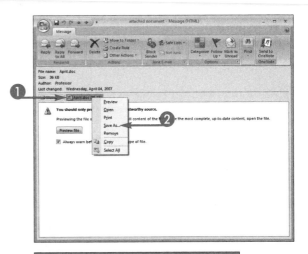

The Save Attachment dialog box opens.

3 Click a drive and folder where you want to store the file.

4 You can change the filename if you want to make it more descriptive.

5 Click Save.

Outlook saves the file to the location that you specified.

How can I check an attached file for viruses before opening the file?

▼ Many anti-virus programs scan the attachment when it is being downloaded. If you do not have one installed, then when Outlook asks if you want to open or save the attached file; save the file to a folder on your computer. You can then use an anti-virus program to check the file for viruses before opening it.

If I do not save the attachment, can I open it again?

▼ Yes. Outlook stores the attachment with the e-mail message, and you can open it again by displaying the message. If you want to keep the attachment, save it to your hard drive. You can then delete the message permanently and still have the attachment available. For information on deleting messages, see Chapter 26.

I see an error message when I try to open a file. What is wrong?

▼ Each type of file is associated with one or more programs, which can be used to open or run that file. If you do not have the appropriate programs and attempt to open the file, Windows prompts you to select the program to use to open the file. Click the appropriate program and click OK. If you do not have the appropriate program, you cannot open the file.

PART VI

Reply to or Forward a Message

You can reply to a message to answer a question, express an opinion, or supply additional information.

You can send a reply to just the person who sent the message or to the sender and everyone else who received the original message.

When you reply to a message, a new window appears, displaying the names of the recipients and the subject of the message to which you are replying. The reply includes a copy of the original message, which Outlook calls *quoting*. Including a copy of the original

message helps the reader identify the message to which you are replying. To save the reader time, you can delete all parts of the original message that do not directly relate to your reply.

You can also forward a message to another person. When you forward a message, you can add your own comments to the original message.

Outlook stores a copy of each message you send in the Sent Items folder. For information on the mail folders, see Chapter 26.

Reply to or Forward a Message

Reply to a message

1 Double-click to open the message to which you want to reply in the Inbox.

Note: *For more information, see the task "Read Messages."*

2 Click a reply option.

The Reply button replies to the sender of the original message.

The Reply to All button replies to the original sender and to everyone who received the original message.

A window appears, displaying a copy of the original message.

● Outlook fills in the e-mail address and subject for you.

3 Type your reply.

4 Click Send to send the reply.

Outlook places the message in the Outbox and then sends it at the next send/receive interval.

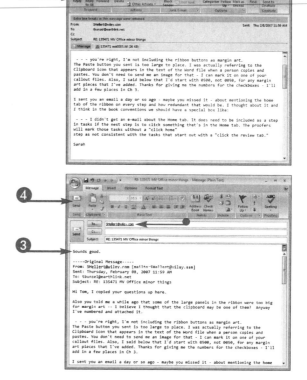

Forward a message

1 Double-click to open the message that you want to forward in the Inbox.

Note: For more information, see the task "Read Messages."

2 Click Forward.

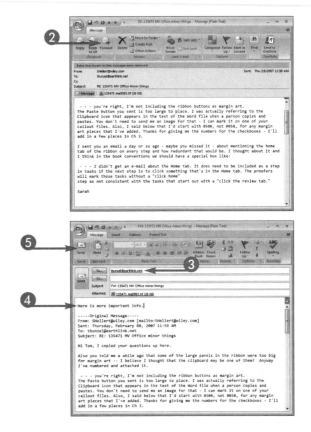

A window appears, displaying the message that you are forwarding.

3 Type the e-mail address of the recipient or recipients who you want to receive the message.

4 Type any comments that you want to make about the message.

5 Click Send.

Outlook places the message in the Outbox and sends it at the next send/receive interval.

Are there two Send buttons when I reply to a message?

▼ Yes. One button is in the Ribbon, and the other is in the message. You can use either button.

Can I respond to more than one person?

▼ Yes. When you reply, the recipient's name is used as the address, but you can also add other recipients to the To or Cc fields. Either type their addresses or use the Address Book to add them to the message.

How do I forward multiple messages?

▼ Press Ctrl as you click each message that you want to forward. Then perform Steps 2 to 5 in the step section, Forward a Message. If you forward more than one message at a time, Outlook sends the messages as attachments in a new e-mail.

Can I prevent Outlook from including a copy of the original message in my replies?

▼ Yes. Choose the Tools menu and then click Options. The Options window opens. Click the Preferences tab and then click the E-mail Options button. In the E-mail Options dialog box, click the When replying to a message down arrow (▼) and select Do not include original message. Then click OK.

Preview Messages and Attachments

Y ou can display the Reading pane to preview any e-mail messages, or even their attachments, without opening the e-mail or the attachment.

By default, the Reading pane appears on the right side of the Outlook window when you click Mail or Inbox.

You can turn off the Reading pane or move it to the bottom by clicking View, then selecting Reading Pane, and then selecting the appropriate option.

To make more room, you may need to minimize or close the Outlook To-Do Bar. For more information, see the task "Using the Outlook To-Do Bar."

When you click a message in the Inbox, if the Reading pane is available, the message is previewed directly in the Reading pane.

If the message has an attachment, clicking the attachment opens a Preview option in the Reading pane, along with a warning.

If you are confident that the attachment is not a threat, click the Preview file button to view the attachment in the Reading pane. Just like opening an attachment, the appropriate program must be loaded on your computer to enable you to preview the attachment. For example, if the program is Microsoft Word, the Word Full Screen Reading view will open. For an image, the registered image-viewing or image-editing program will preview the image in the Reading pane.

Preview Messages and Attachments

① Click View.

② Click Reading Pane.

③ Click a viewing selection.

You can choose to view the Reading pane on the right or at the bottom of the window, or you can choose to turn it off.

This example keeps the Reading pane on the right.

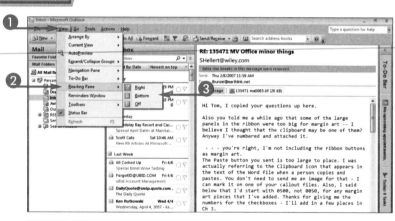

④ Click the message in the Inbox.

Outlook previews the body of the message in the Reading pane.

If the message contains images, you can right-click the warning and enable the pictures in order to download and view them in the Reading pane.

⑤ Click the attachment.

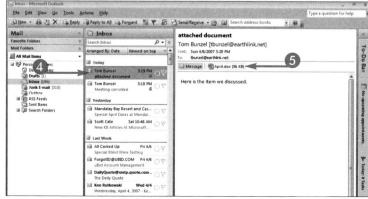

The attachment warning appears with a Preview file button.

6 Click the Preview file button.

● You can turn off the warning for other attachments (☑ changes to ☐).

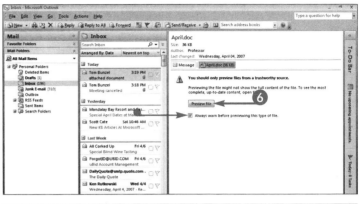

● Outlook previews the attachment using the appropriate program in the Reading pane.

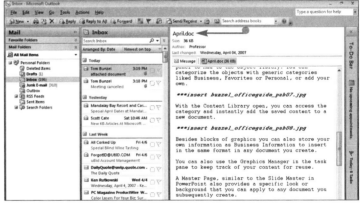

Can I mark items as read once they are previewed?

▼ Yes. On the Tools menu, click Options, and then click the Other tab in the Options window. Click Reading Pane. Select the options you want. One option is to mark items in the Reading pane as read.

Can I remove the header information from the Reading pane?

▼ Yes. On the View menu, click Arrange By, and then click Custom. The Customize View: Messages window opens. Click Other Settings. Under Reading pane, select the Hide header information check box (☐ changes to ☑).

Is there a way to preview items without having to click them?

▼ Yes. On the View menu, click AutoPreview. A brief preview of all messages appears with them in the Inbox. You can AutoPreview only the first three lines of unread messages. On the View menu, click Current View, and then click Customize Current View. Click Other Settings, and then click Preview unread items.

Open E-mail Folders

Outlook includes several e-mail folders so that you can keep your messages organized. You can view any of these folders to review and work with the messages that are stored in them.

The *Inbox* folder contains messages you have received. This includes both read and unread messages. Messages that you have not read appear in bold.

The *Outbox* folder stores messages you have created but not yet sent. You can click the Send/Receive button to send these messages. Otherwise, Outlook sends them during the next send/receive interval.

The *Drafts* folder contains messages you have created, and want to save to send at a later time. By default,

Outlook saves messages every three minutes as you create them.

When you delete a message, Outlook does not actually delete it, but simply moves the message to the *Deleted Items* folder. You must delete the message from the Deleted Items folder or empty the entire folder to permanently remove the message.

The *Sent Items* folder contains a copy of all messages you have sent.

You can also create your own folders to organize your work. For more information, see the task "Create a New Mail Folder."

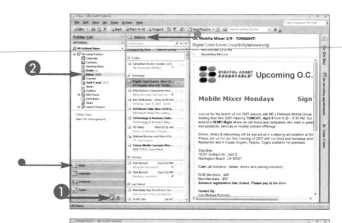

Open E-mail Folders

1 Click the Folder List button (▣).

● You can also click Mail to see a list of mail folders only.

2 Click the desired folder in the Folder List.

This example shows the Inbox.

● Outlook highlights the selected folder and displays its contents.

3 To view deleted items, click the Deleted Items folder.

● You see all of the messages and other Outlook items, such as contacts, notes, and tasks, that you have deleted.

④ To view messages that have been sent, click the Sent Items folder.

● You see copies of all messages you have sent, including replies and forwarded messages.

⑤ To view messages that you have created, but not sent, click the Drafts folder.

● You see messages that you have created, but not sent.

How can I prevent Outlook from saving my messages in the Sent Items folder?

▼ In the Microsoft Outlook window, click Tools, click Options, and then click the Preferences tab. Click the E-mail Options button and uncheck the Save copies of messages in Sent Items folder option (☑ changes to ☐). Then click OK.

How do I empty the Deleted Items folder?

▼ Click the Tools menu and then select Empty "Deleted Items" Folder. Click Yes to confirm that you want to permanently delete all items.

Can I change the width of the columns?

▼ Yes. You can change the width of the Folder List column, the preview pane, or the panes for the message list. To do so, click the border of the pane and drag to resize.

Print a Previewed Message

Y ou can produce a paper copy of a message. A printed message is useful when you need a reference copy of the message. For example, you might print directions to a meeting to take with you, or a message might include phone numbers or other information for which you need a paper copy.

Outlook prints the date and time the message was sent on the first page of the message. The page number appears at the bottom of each page of the printed message. If the message includes replies and responses, all of the messages are printed.

If you use the Print dialog box, you can select which printer to use, the print style, whether attachments are printed, and the number of copies to print.

You can also print the message by opening it in a new window. Click the Office button and then click Print to print an opened message. The same print dialog box opens. For more information, see the task "Read Messages" in Chapter 25.

Print a Previewed Message

1 Click the message you want to print.

● The message opens in the Reading pane.

2 Click File.

3 Click Print.

Note: *If you do not need to preview the message, you can click it in the Inbox and click the Print button (📷) on the Outlook toolbar to print it.*

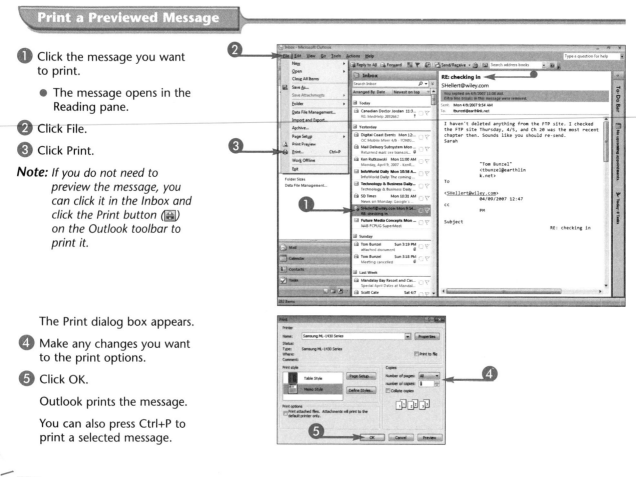

The Print dialog box appears.

4 Make any changes you want to the print options.

5 Click OK.

Outlook prints the message.

You can also press Ctrl+P to print a selected message.

Delete a Message

Y ou can delete a message you no longer need. Deleting messages prevents your mail folders from becoming cluttered with unneeded messages.

You can delete a message from an open message window or from the Inbox. When you delete a message, Outlook places the deleted message in the Deleted Items folder. You can view the contents of the Deleted Items folder by clicking the folder in the Folder List. For more information, see the task "Open E-mail Folders."

To restore a message, move it from the Deleted Items folder to another folder. For more information, see the task "Move a Message."

Can I permanently delete selected messages?

▼ Yes. Open the Deleted Items folder and then select the messages you want to permanently delete. Click the Delete button (☒). When a dialog box appears, asking whether you really want to delete the item, confirm the deletion by clicking Yes. You can completely delete a message and bypass the Delete Messages folder by selecting the message and pressing Shift+Del.

Delete a Message

1 Click the message in the Inbox.

2 Click the Delete button (☒).

Outlook deletes the message.

You can also right-click a message and choose Delete from the menu that appears.

You can click Delete in the Action group on the Ribbon of an opened message to delete it.

Note: For more information, see the task "Read Messages" in Chapter 25.

3 In the Folder List, click the Deleted Items folder.

● Outlook places the deleted message in the Deleted Items folder.

You can permanently delete the message from the Deleted Items folder by clicking Tools and then clicking Empty Deleted Items Folder.

You can delete all items at once in the Deleted Items folder by right-clicking the folder and then clicking Empty Deleted Items Folder.

Create a New Mail Folder

Over time, you may find that your folders become cluttered with e-mail messages. To keep your e-mail correspondence organized, you can create mail folders.

For example, you may want to set up one folder for personal correspondence and another for business correspondence. If you receive a lot of jokes, you may want to set up a folder for jokes that you want to save. If you subscribe to mailing lists, you may want to store these e-mail messages in their own separate folder.

You can also *nest* folders, by creating folders inside folders. For example, under business correspondence, you can set up folders for specific clients or for correspondence regarding specific projects.

You can set up as many folders as needed. You can then move messages from one folder to another to keep them organized. For information on moving a message from one folder to another, see the task "Move a Message." You can also create rules to directly route your mail to new folders. For more information, see the task "Sort Messages Using Rules."

Create a New Mail Folder

① Click Personal Folders to select the main folder.

● The Outlook Today panel opens.

② Click the New down arrow (▼).

③ Click Folder.

The Create New Folder dialog box appears.

④ Type a name for the new folder.

● You can click the Personal Folders plus sign (⊞) to open the other folders. You can then click one of the other folders in which you want to nest the new folder.

⑤ Click OK.

Outlook adds the folder to your Personal Folders.

Move a Message

To keep your e-mail correspondence organized, you can create mail folders and move messages to the appropriate folder. For example, you can set up folders named Personal and Business and move messages to them from your Inbox. This way, you save your messages, but your Inbox is not cluttered with read messages.

You may also want to move messages from one of Outlook's default folders. For example, if you delete a message by mistake, you can move it from the Deleted Items folder to another folder. For information on creating folders, see the task "Create a New Mail Folder."

Is there another way to move messages?

▼ Yes. You can click and drag the message from the message list to the appropriate folder. You can also use a shortcut menu for working with messages. To display the shortcut menu, right-click the message and then select the command you want. For example, right-click a message and then click Move to Folder.

Move a Message

1 Click the message you want to move.

2 Click Edit.

3 Click Move to Folder.

You can also click the Move to Folder button (📁) on the Standard Outlook toolbar.

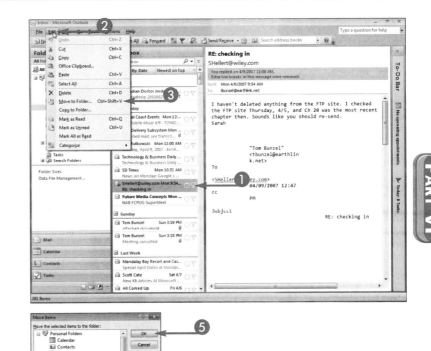

The Move Items dialog box appears.

4 Click the folder in which you want to place the selected message.

5 Click OK.

Outlook moves the message to the selected folder.

PART VI

Archive
Messages

To periodically make a backup copy of the messages in your folder, you can archive them. *Archiving* messages copies them to a special mail archive file and removes the archived items from the original folders. Archiving offers several advantages over manually moving or copying messages. You can set up a schedule so that you are reminded to archive, and you can archive several folders at once. You can specify a date so that any items older than that date are archived. You can also name the archive file and choose a folder location for it.

When you use AutoArchive, you select which folders are archived, and Outlook archives the selected folder and any subfolders.

How do I view archived messages?

▼ When you archive the messages, Outlook creates a file with the .pst extension. You can open this file if you need to access archived messages. To open an archive file, click File, click Open, and then click Outlook Data File. Go to the folder that contains your file, select the file, and then click OK.

Archive Messages

1 Click File.

2 Click Archive.

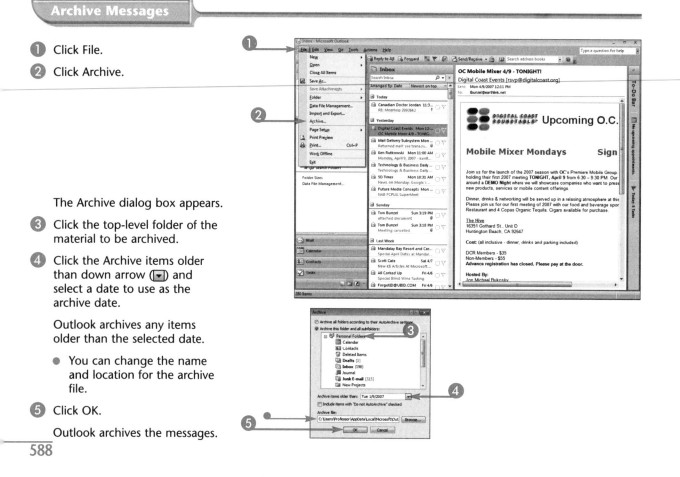

The Archive dialog box appears.

3 Click the top-level folder of the material to be archived.

4 Click the Archive items older than down arrow (▼) and select a date to use as the archive date.

Outlook archives any items older than the selected date.

● You can change the name and location for the archive file.

5 Click OK.

Outlook archives the messages.

Format a Message

When you create a mail message, you can select the format for the message. You can select HTML (the same format as Web pages), Rich Text (text that allows formatting), and Plain Text (text that contains no formatting).

If you select HTML or Rich Text, the formatting tools become available, and you can use these tools to make formatting changes to the text.

The formatting options for message text are similar to the formatting options in other Office programs. You can change the font, font size, font style, and font color. You can also add bullets, indent text, or change the text alignment.

Keep in mind a couple of points about formatting. First, do not overdo the formatting. Too many changes not only distract from your message, but also make the message file size larger, which takes longer to download on your recipient's computer. Second, some e-mail programs can handle only certain e-mail formats. If you send a message to someone and she has trouble reading or opening the message, try a plain-text message without any formatting.

Because Outlook uses Microsoft Word to create e-mail by default, you can use many of the features in Chapter 4 to format the text, including Quick Styles.

Format a Message

① Create a new message.

Note: *To create a new message, see Chapter 25.*

② Click the Options tab on the New Message Ribbon.

③ Click the format type you want to use.

④ Select the text you want to format.

⑤ Click the Format Text tab on the New Message Ribbon.

⑥ Click the Quick Styles down arrow (▼) to make formatting changes.

⑦ Click a style.

● Outlook formats the selected text.

⑧ Click Send.

Outlook sends the formatted message.

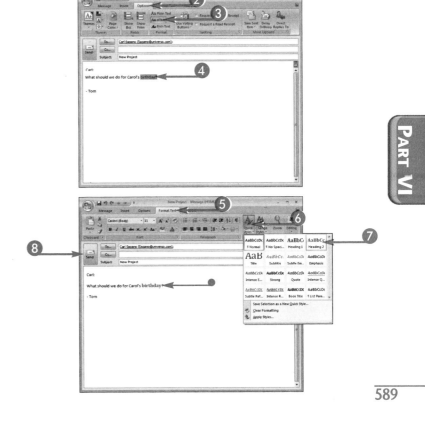

Sort or Find Messages

Messages are usually sorted in descending order by the date they were received, but you can select a different sort order so that you can more easily find messages.

You can sort by the name of the people who sent the messages, the subjects of the messages, or retain the default option for the dates the messages were received. You can also sort messages in ascending or descending order. You can sort not only the messages in the Inbox, but in any folder.

If you cannot find a message by sorting, you can also use Outlook's Find command to search for a message. You can search in any folders in Outlook. By default, Outlook searches all text in each message in a selected folder for the text you enter.

When the search is complete, Outlook displays the matching messages. You can then open, move, or delete these messages as needed.

Sort or Find Messages

Sort messages

① Click the folder with the messages you want to sort.

② Click View.

③ Click Arrange By.

The sort method menu appears.

④ Click a sort method.

This example uses Subject.

- Outlook sorts your messages using the selected method.

- The sort order is indicated in the heading with a triangle icon ( ) and the text *A on top*.

Find messages

1 Click the folder that you want to search.

The folder name appears at the top of the Search panel, followed by the text, *(Search in).*

2 Click in the Search field.

● The Search field becomes active (yellow).

3 Begin typing your search term.

○ Outlook searches the selected folder and displays any matching messages.

● In the Deleted Items folder, items you deleted from Contacts or other folders may also appear in the search.

The wrong folder is selected. How can I select another folder?

▼ By default, Outlook selects the current folder to search in and displays this folder name next to Search. If the wrong folder is selected, select the correct folder and use the search panel again to conduct another search. You can also click the Search down arrow (▼) and select other locations, including All of Outlook.

Outlook found too many matches. How can I better refine the search?

▼ If you use a common word or phrase, you may receive too many matches. Try searching for a unique word or phrase, or try using the advanced options.

What other options can I use for searching?

▼ Click the Advanced Search double arrow (▼) in the Search panel to display the advanced search options. Depending upon the folder, you will see a form with additional search parameters, such as From, Body, Subject, and To. You can also click the Search down arrow (▼) for additional criteria to narrow down your search.

Sort Messages Using Rules

You can use Outlook to sort your incoming e-mail automatically using its powerful Rules feature. Rules allow you to take action on e-mail messages, depending on whom they are from, the message content, or priority.

When you use rules, you can have Outlook automatically move messages into a particular folder; keep a copy in your Inbox and put a copy into another folder; or even delete messages that meet certain criteria.

For example, your boss may always flag his messages as High Priority, even if the message is about the company softball game and is sent to everyone. With rules, you can separate the messages your boss sent just to you from those sent to everyone. This keeps messages from your boss to you in your Inbox, while putting the softball notices into the General Work folder. Your Inbox remains less cluttered, and you can read the softball e-mail at your leisure.

Sort Messages Using Rules

① Click Tools.

② Click Rules and Alerts.

● The Rules and Alerts dialog box appears.

③ Click New Rule.

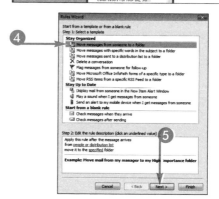

The Rules Wizard appears.

④ Click the Move messages from someone to a folder option.

⑤ Click Next.

6️⃣ Click the From people or distribution list option (☐ changes to ☑).

You can also select other conditions here if you want.

7️⃣ Click People or distribution list.

The Address Book appears.

8️⃣ Click an address.

9️⃣ Click From.

Outlook adds the address to the list.

🔟 Click OK.

What kinds of actions can Outlook perform on messages?

▼ Outlook can do more than just move messages to folders. It can change a message's priority, display a notification window when a message arrives, play a sound, or even send a page or text message to a pager or cell phone. A complete discussion of Outlook's rules is beyond this book, but you can find more information by using the Office Help files. Press F1 to read the Help files.

How many conditions can I use?

▼ In the Rules Wizard, you can select as many conditions as you want. However, it is best to keep your rules as simple as possible, using as few conditions as possible. This makes it easier to create rules, and helps you later if you want to edit, delete, or troubleshoot a rule.

Is there a way to modify a rule's conditions?

▼ Yes. After you have created a rule, you can modify it. In the Rules and Alert dialog box click the rule you want to edit, and then click Change Rule. You can click Edit Rule or one of the pre-set rule changes. You can also click any of the underlined conditions and edit them directly.

continued

Sort Messages Using Rules *(Continued)*

Rules are most effective when you use them together with a well-ordered folder system. You could have only three or four folders for all of your e-mail, but over time this would be as effective as using only your Inbox to store messages. Instead, Outlook can become a powerful organizer and information manager when you build folders and use message rules that match your work needs.

For example, you may have several projects that you work on. You can create a project folder, and within that folder have subfolders for different groups

working on the project: one for software development, one for testing, one for software documentation, one for customer contacts, and one for project management. After you set up the folders, you can create rules that route e-mail and information from particular users or groups to the appropriate folder.

Then, when you need to find information quickly, you can look in a particular folder rather than manually browsing or using the Find feature to locate the appropriate e-mail.

Sort Messages Using Rules *(continued)*

The Rules Wizard reappears.

⑪ Click the Specified link to move an e-mail message to a specified folder.

Note: *If you need to create a new folder, see the task "Create a New Mail Folder."*

A new Rules and Alerts dialog box appears.

⑫ Click a folder.

⑬ Click OK.

The Rules and Alerts dialog box closes.

● Your selections appear in the Conditions window of the Rules Wizard.

⑭ Click Finish.

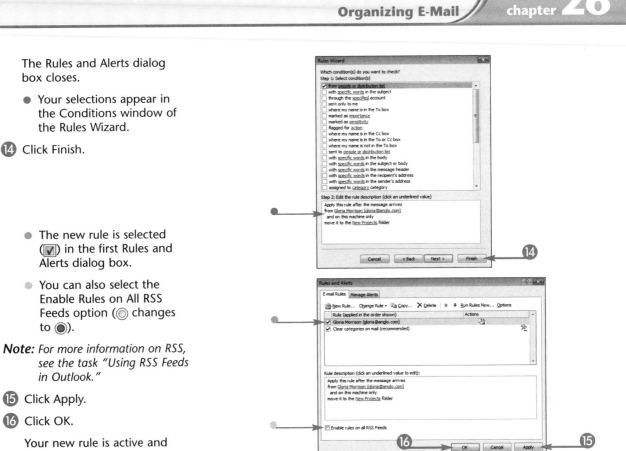

● The new rule is selected (☑) in the first Rules and Alerts dialog box.

● You can also select the Enable Rules on All RSS Feeds option (◉ changes to ◉).

Note: *For more information on RSS, see the task "Using RSS Feeds in Outlook."*

⑮ Click Apply.

⑯ Click OK.

Your new rule is active and routes messages using your conditions.

Can I test the rule?

▼ Yes. In Step 16, instead of clicking OK, click Run Rules Now. A dialog box appears, showing you a list of active and inactive rules — active rules display a ☑, and inactive rules display a ☐. Click the rules you want to run (☐ changes to ☑), and then click Run Rules Now. The selected rules run on the appropriate folder.

Why is my e-mail not being processed by my rules into the correct folder?

▼ Rules are processed in order, from top to bottom. Use the Move Up and Move Down buttons (⬆ and ⬇) in the E-mail Rules tab of the Rules and Alerts dialog box to change the rule processing order.

How do I turn off a rule?

▼ Open the Rule Wizard, click the rule you want to turn off (☑ changes to ☐), and click OK. The rule remains inactive until you turn it on again.

Can I delete a rule?

▼ You can delete rules you no longer need. In the Rules and Alert dialog box, click the rule you want to delete and click Delete. A dialog box asks if you want to delete the selected rule. When you click Yes, the rule is deleted from the Rules Wizard.

Using the Spam Filter

U nsolicited commercial e-mail, or *spam*, consists of messages that are sent to millions of addresses at once. They are typically messages that you did not ask for (unsolicited), advertise a product or adult-content Web site (commercial), and were sent to you because the sender obtained your e-mail address. Spam typically has headings such as "MAKE MONEY FAST!!!" or contains adult language to lure you to a pornographic Web site.

These messages are annoying and waste your time. In addition, spam often contains code or malicious bugs

that can reveal information about you to others. Because spam is a nuisance and a threat, Outlook contains a spam filter that moves spam into its own folder where it can be ignored or deleted.

In addition to using the filter, safe surfing helps you avoid spam. Do not enter your e-mail address on any Web page unless it is a business with a privacy policy in place, such as eTrust. Do not post your e-mail address on a Web page or message board. Also, do not heedlessly forward joke or humor e-mails with your e-mail address within the message.

Using the Spam Filter

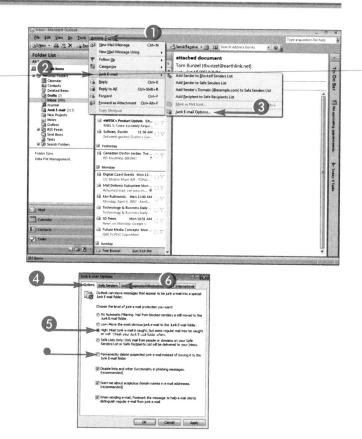

1 Click Actions.

2 Click Junk E-mail.

3 Click Junk E-mail Options.

The Junk E-mail Options dialog box appears.

4 Click the Options tab.

5 Click the level of spam filtering you want (◎ changes to ◉).

● Check this box if you want to permanently delete spam (☐ changes to ☑).

Note: *Be careful with automatic deletion — spam filters can make errors and filter out messages you want to receive. The default setting filters messages to the Junk E-mail folder. You can review that folder before deleting its contents to avoid problems.*

6 Click the Safe Senders tab.

7 Click Add.

The Add address or domain dialog box appears.

8 Type the e-mail address or Internet domain that you want to trust.

9 Click OK.

Outlook adds the address to the Safe Senders list.

10 Click the Blocked Senders tab.

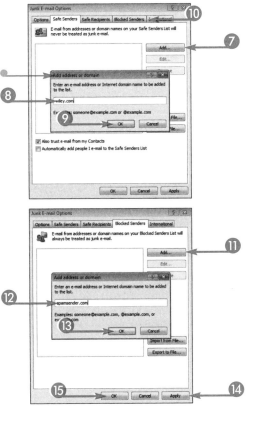

11 Click Add.

The Add address or domain dialog box appears.

12 Type the e-mail address or Internet domain that you want to always treat as junk mail.

13 Click OK.

Outlook adds the address to the Blocked Senders list.

14 Click Apply.

15 Click OK.

The Junk E-mail Options dialog box closes.

Will the spam filter catch all spam?

▼ Because spammers keep changing tactics, it is difficult to catch all spam that may be sent to you. It is also possible that a legitimate e-mail sent by a friend becomes categorized as spam. Because of this, it is worth your time to check the folder where you put your spam once a week to make sure that legitimate e-mail was not put there by mistake.

Can I add particular message senders to the spam filter?

▼ You can add spammers to the list by right-clicking the particular message you want to filter, clicking Junk E-mail, and then clicking Add Sender to Junk Senders List. The sender's e-mail address is added to the appropriate list.

Can I stop spam by replying to it or clicking the "unsubscribe" links in an e-mail?

▼ Do not reply to any spam or click any link that asks you to unsubscribe. Those are tricks that spammers use to see if they reached a legitimate e-mail address, and when you reply, they know they reached a legitimate target.

PART VI

Using RSS Feeds in Outlook

Really Simple Syndication, or RSS, is a way to have Web content delivered directly to your computer without having to look for it in your Web browser.

Many large content providers, such as Microsoft and the Los Angeles Times, create RSS *feeds* that you can subscribe to as you would a magazine. However, unlike a physical magazine, an RSS feed delivers new Web content to your computer.

Outlook 2007 is an RSS *aggregator*; this means that it lets you manage and view your RSS feeds directly in

your Navigation pane and main window. You can click a subscribed feed to see the daily (or otherwise regularly delivered) content in your Reading pane. You can also click a link within the preview in the Reading pane to read the entire page.

Internet Explorer 7 has an RSS icon that alerts you when there are feeds on a page. When you click the RSS icon in a page, it takes you to a subscription link. You can also insert an RSS Web link, generally to an XML page, directly in Outlook.

Using RSS Feeds in Outlook

Subscribe to RSS

1 Open a Web page with RSS links (⬚) in your Web browser.

- Internet Explorer 7 alerts you to links on a Web page.

2 Click the RSS link or the RSS icon (⬚).

The RSS Subscription page appears.

3 Click the Subscribe to this feed link.

- A subscription dialog box opens.

4 Click Subscribe.

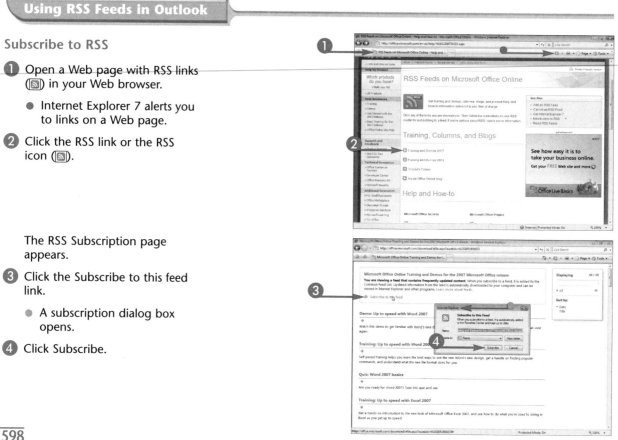

Using RSS feeds in Outlook

1 In Outlook 2007, click the RSS Feeds folder plus sign (⊞).

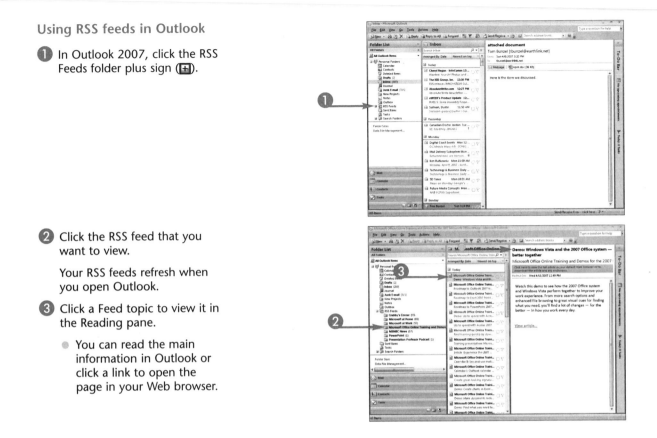

2 Click the RSS feed that you want to view.

Your RSS feeds refresh when you open Outlook.

3 Click a Feed topic to view it in the Reading pane.

● You can read the main information in Outlook or click a link to open the page in your Web browser.

What if there is no Subscribe link?

▼ Click the RSS icon (🔊) to open the link page. In the Web browser address window, copy the URL of the RSS subscription page to your Clipboard. In Outlook, right-click the RSS Feeds link in the Navigation pane. From the drop-down menu, click Add a New RSS Feed. In the New RSS Feed window, right-click and paste the copied URL or link into the form, and click Add. The RSS feed is handled by Outlook.

How can I find more RSS feeds?

▼ You can click the RSS Feeds link in the Navigation pane. In the Reading pane, there is a comprehensive description of RSS as well as a catalog of featured RSS sources, including Featured Feeds and Microsoft Office-related feeds.

How do I delete an RSS feed I no longer want?

▼ Right-click the feed in the Outlook Navigation pane and click Delete "(name of the feed)."

View the Calendar

The Outlook Calendar window offers you an easy way to quickly view all of your appointments. By default, the Calendar displays the appointments you have scheduled for the current day. However, you can easily display the appointments for another day.

The Calendar window also displays all the days in the current month and the next month. Today's date displays a red outline, and days with appointments appear in bold. Clicking any day brings up the appointments for that day.

You can flip through all the months in the Calendar to view past or future appointments. Viewing past appointments is useful when you have to report the amount of time you spent working on a particular project.

The Calendar also displays a list of tasks you created using the Tasks feature. For information on the Tasks feature, see the task "Create a Task List."

By default, the Calendar displays your appointments in the Month view. You can change the view to display your appointments in the Day or Week view.

View the Calendar

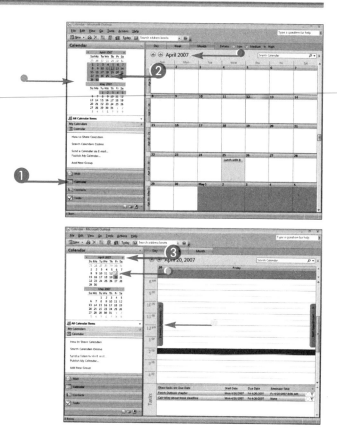

① Click Calendar to display the Calendar window.

● This area displays the appointments for the month.

● This area displays the current and subsequent months. Days with appointments are shown in bold.

② To display the appointments for another day, click that day.

Outlook highlights the day you select on the Calendar, and displays the scheduled activities for that day in the appointment list.

● The current day displays a red outline.

● You can use the Next and Previous Appointment tabs to navigate to items in the Calendar. These tabs do not appear if no such appointments exist.

Note: *For more information, see the task "Create New Appointments."*

③ To display the days in the previous or next month, click the Next Month or Previous Month buttons (◀ or ▶).

Change the Calendar view

1 Click a button to change the view of the Calendar.

Day

Week

Month

Back ()

Forward ()

● Outlook displays the view that you selected.

This example shows a five-day week view, the default.

● You can show either the work week or the full week (○ changes to ●).

Why is the Calendar displaying the wrong date for today?

▼ Outlook uses the date and time set in your computer to determine today's date. Your computer's clock may be set incorrectly. Use the Date/Time Control Panel in Windows to change the date.

Are other views available in the Calendar?

▼ Yes. The Calendar also offers the Active Appointments, Events, Annual Events, Recurring Appointments, and By Category views. To change to one of these views, choose the View menu and select Current View. Then select the view that you want to use. For more about creating appointments, see the task "Create New Appointments."

How do I quickly display today's appointments?

▼ You can click Today in the Outlook toolbar at any time to display today's appointments.

How do I add holidays to the Calendar?

▼ Click the Tools menu and select Options. In the Options window, click the Calendar Options button. Click the Add Holidays button and then select the country for the holidays you want to add. Click OK. Outlook adds the holidays to the Calendar. Click OK three more times to close the message box and the two dialog boxes.

Create New Appointments

Y ou can use the Calendar to keep track of your appointments. An appointment can be an activity such as going to the dentist, attending a meeting, or having lunch with a prospective client.

The Calendar allows you to enter information about each appointment you want to schedule. You can enter a subject for an appointment. The subject is the description of an appointment that appears in the Calendar. You can also enter the location for an appointment and add comments about the appointment.

When you enter a start date, end date, or time for an appointment, you can type text such as "next Tuesday," "tomorrow," or "noon" instead of typing a date or time. If an appointment will last an entire day, you can make the appointment an all-day event. Outlook displays an all-day event just below the date in the Calendar. You can still schedule other appointments after scheduling an all-day event.

As a reminder, Outlook plays a brief sound and displays a dialog box 15 minutes before a scheduled appointment.

Create New Appointments

1 Click Calendar.

2 Click New.

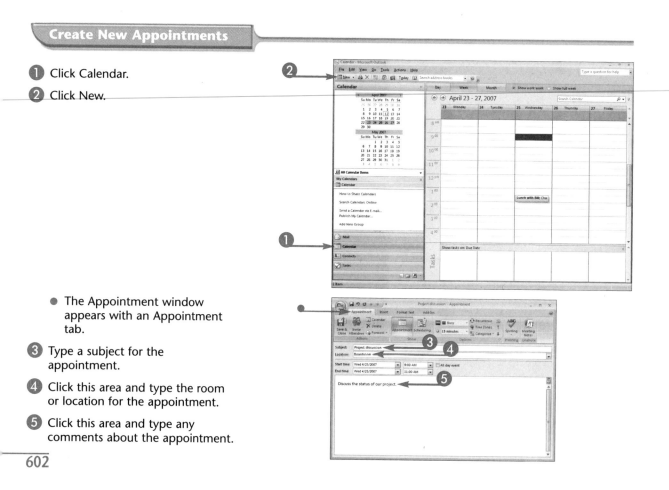

● The Appointment window appears with an Appointment tab.

3 Type a subject for the appointment.

4 Click this area and type the room or location for the appointment.

5 Click this area and type any comments about the appointment.

6 To change the date, type the date or click the down arrow (▼) and select the appropriate date.

7 Type the start time and end time or click the down arrow (▼) and select the appropriate times.

● To make the appointment an all-day event, select the All day event check box (☐ changes to ☑).

8 Click Save & Close to save the information.

● To view the appointment, you can click the date for which it is scheduled.

The appointment appears in the Calendar.

Can I schedule a recurring appointment?

▼ Yes. In the Appointment tab, click Recurrence. In the Appointment Recurrence dialog box, specify the information about the recurring appointment, including the start and end time, duration, and recurrence pattern. Select when to start and end the recurring appointment. You can easily schedule your weekly staff meetings or quarterly company meetings this way.

How do I delete an appointment?

▼ You can delete an appointment that has been canceled or that you no longer want to keep. Click to select the appointment and then click the Delete button (☒) in the Outlook menu. You can also open an appointment and click Delete in the Actions group of the Appointment tab.

How can I quickly schedule an appointment?

▼ In the Day, Week, or Month view, click the time slot area to select the time for the appointment. Type a subject for the appointment and then press Enter. In the Month view, you can only select the day; to schedule the appointment more specifically, double-click it to open it.

PART VI

Print a Calendar

If you use your Calendar on a daily basis, you end up with meetings, notes, tasks, and appointments that help you keep track of where you need to be and what you need to get done. It can be tricky to remember all of the details: Was the meeting with the boss at 3:00 p.m., or 3:30 p.m.? Was it in the big conference room or her office?

You can print your Calendar so that you have hard copy to take with you to meetings, to off-site events, or to any situation where you do not have access to

your computer. That way, you have a listing of your important meetings, tasks, and notes that can help you plan your day and make arrangements for new meetings or follow-up appointments.

Outlook gives you several different Calendar styles that help you keep track of information, much like a paper personal organizer. You can print out a daily, weekly, or monthly Calendar, and keep track of your meetings and appointments without fumbling with a personal organizer.

Print a Calendar

1 Switch to the Calendar if it is not already open.

2 Click File.

3 Click Print.

You can also press Ctrl+P to display the Print dialog box.

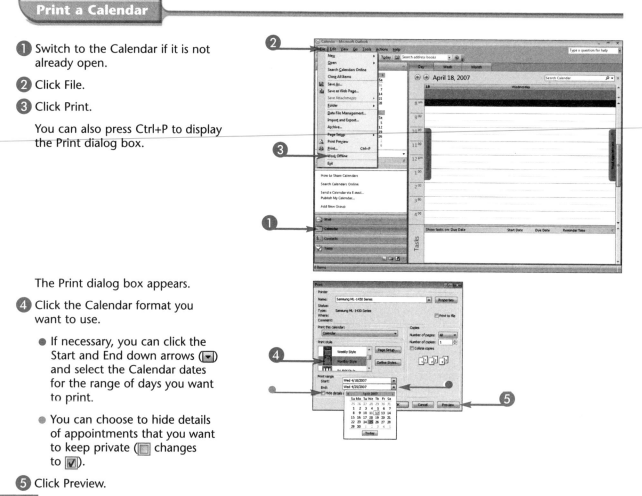

The Print dialog box appears.

4 Click the Calendar format you want to use.

- If necessary, you can click the Start and End down arrows (⏷) and select the Calendar dates for the range of days you want to print.

- You can choose to hide details of appointments that you want to keep private (☐ changes to ☑).

5 Click Preview.

The Print Preview window appears.

Depending on the Calendar format, your Calendar, tasks, and notes appear.

6 Click Print.

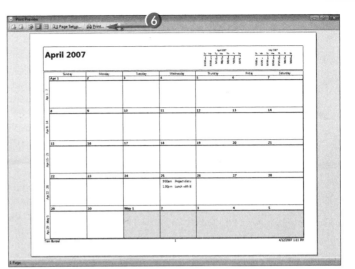

The Print dialog box reappears.

7 Click OK.

Outlook prints your Calendar.

If you do not want to print a Calendar, you can click Cancel.

What do the different Calendar styles look like?

▼ There are six basic Calendar styles you can print: Daily, Weekly, Monthly, Tri-fold, Memo, and Calendar Details. Each style shows different amounts of information that may be useful to you. For example, the daily style shows the daily appointments, the current month, and the next month as mini-calendars, task pad items that are due or overdue, and your notes for the day. You can preview what each style looks like, or modify the details. Click a print style in the Print dialog box and click the Preview button. A full-size preview of your Calendar appears.

Can I change my printed Calendar's appearance?

▼ You can change many settings for the Calendar style you want to use. Click a Calendar style and then click the Page Setup button. The Page Setup dialog box appears, where you can change the fonts, layout, and range of the appointment times. You can adjust margins, paper alignment, or paper sizes by clicking the Paper tab. You can add custom headers and footers by clicking the Header/Footer tab. You can also click the Define Styles button in the Print dialog box to fine-tune your print output for each style you select.

Share a Calendar

Outlook 2007 allows you to e-mail or publish your Calendar so that you can share it with others.

To publish your Calendar, you need to be on an Exchange Server network or you must create an Office Online account. Exchange Server is beyond the scope of this book.

You can register for a free Office Online account and share your Calendar directly from Outlook. After registering, you will be able to publish your Calendar online and send other users links to the Calendar to allow them to view it; if they have permission, you can also allow them to add items to your online Calendar.

When you e-mail your Calendar, you can specify the Calendar you want to e-mail, as well as the date range, and the amount of detail that you want to share with others. You can let others know the dates on which you are available for appointments.

A Calendar Snapshot is sent in an e-mail message in the iCalendar format. It is a static Calendar that can be updated only after the Calendar owner sends a new Calendar Snapshot. There are two ways in which you can view the Calendar information in a Calendar Snapshot: in the message body or as an additional Calendar in Calendar view in Outlook.

You can add a new Calendar with specific items by opening the Calendar window, clicking New, and selecting Calendar.

Share a Calendar

E-mail a Calendar

1 Click Calendar.

The Calendar appears.

2 Click Send a Calendar via E-mail.

The Send a Calendar via E-mail dialog box appears.

- You can click the Calendar the down arrow (▼) to choose a Calendar if you have created other calendars.

- You can click the Date Range down arrow (▼) to choose a date range.

- You can click the Detail down arrow (▼) to choose a level of detail.

3 Click OK.

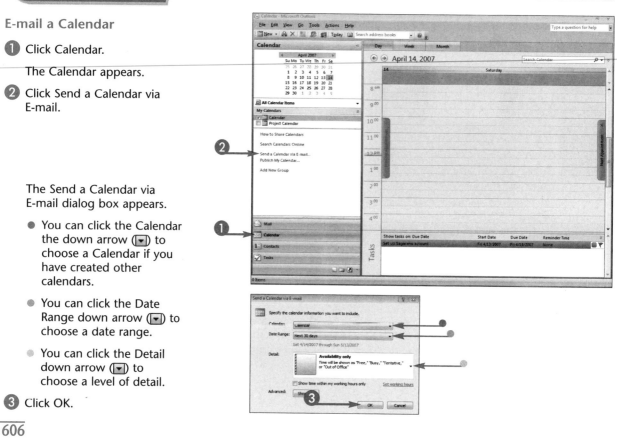

Outlook creates an e-mail message with your Calendar.

Note: For more information about sending a message, see Chapter 25.

④ Type the recipient's e-mail address or click To to add it from the Address Book.

Note: See the task "Select a Name from the Address Book" in Chapter 25.

⑤ Type a message with the Calendar.

⑥ Click Send.

Publish a Calendar

① Click Calendar.

The Calendar appears.

② Click Publish My Calendar.

Note: If you have not registered for Office Online, the Office Online Registration window opens. Follow the steps to register.

● The Publish Calendar to Microsoft Office Online dialog box appears.

③ Choose with whom you want to share your Calendar (◎ changes to ◉).

④ Click OK.

Your Calendar is published on Office Online.

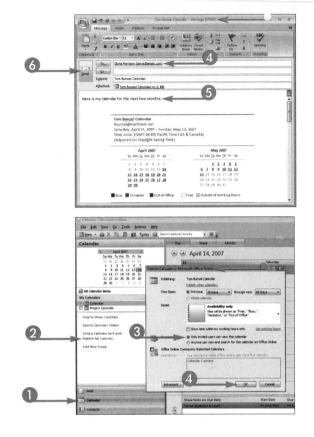

How do I create a new Calendar?

▼ Click Calendar in the Navigation pane to open your Calendar. Click the New down arrow (▾) and choose Calendar. Name the new Calendar and click OK. Both your default and new Calendar appear in the Navigation pane. Click to change ☐ to ☑ to enable your new Calendar. You can display either or both Calendars by clicking the appropriate check box.

Can I format how the shared Calendar will look?

▼ Yes. In the both the Send a Calendar via E-mail and Publish Calendar to Microsoft Office Online dialog boxes, click the Detail down arrow (▾) and select Show Full Details. Under Advanced, click Show. You can select the option to show details for private items or add attachments (☐ changes to ☑). You can click the down arrow (▾) to select the option to show the Calendar as a daily schedule or list of events.

PART VI

Add
Contacts

O utlook has a personal information manager, or contacts list, where you can keep detailed information about your friends, family members, colleagues, and clients.

When you add a contact to the list, Outlook provides spaces for you to enter information about the contact. You can enter the contact's full name, job title, company name, and address. You can also enter the contact's business phone, home phone, business fax, and mobile phone numbers.

You can include the contact's e-mail address. This information is necessary if you intend to use the

Address Book/Contact List when creating e-mail messages. You can also enter the contact's Web page address and notes about the contact.

You can add information such as directions to his house or the names of his children. You can update or add additional information to a contact in your list at any time.

You do not need to fill in all of the spaces provided; you can use only the ones that are useful to you now, and add to the other fields when that information becomes useful.

Add Contacts

1 Click Contacts.

 • The Contacts pane appears with a list of contacts in your contact list.

2 Click New.

The Contact window appears with a Contact tab.

3 Click an area and type the contact's name, job title, and company name.

4 Click this area and type the contact's business, home, business fax, or mobile phone numbers.

5 Click this area and type the contact's address.

6 Click this area and type the contact's e-mail address.

 • You can click this area and type the contact's Web page address.

Repeat these steps for other information you want to add.

⑦ Click Categorize to select a category for the contact.

You can rename the category before closing the Category dialog box.

Note: *For more information on categories, see the task "Organize Contacts with Categories."*

⑧ Click Save & Close to save the information for the contact.

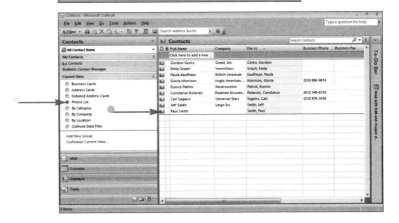

● The contact appears in the contact list.

● To change the view of the Contacts pane, click a different view in the Current View pane (◎ changes to ◉).

This example uses the Phone List view.

To change the information for a contact, you can double-click the contact to redisplay the Contact window.

Why did the Check Address dialog box appear after I entered an address?

▼ If the address you entered is incomplete, the Check Address dialog box appears to help you complete it.

Can I view a list of e-mail messages that I have exchanged with a contact?

▼ Yes. In the Contact tab on the Ribbon, click the Activities button. This displays a summary of Outlook items, such as e-mail messages and tasks that relate to the contact.

Can I sort contacts by categories?

▼ Yes. Click the By Category option in the Current View pane in the Navigation pane (◎ changes to ◉). You can also right-click the header row and choose Customize Current View. In the dialog box, click Fields and add or delete any fields you want in the phone list view.

Can I display a map showing a contact's address?

▼ If a contact's address is in the United States, you can view a map for her address. In the Ribbon of the person's Contact window, in the Communicate group, click the Map button (🔲). If you have an active Internet connection, your Web browser opens and displays the map.

Organize Contacts with Categories

Outlook 2007 has a color-coded list of category pre-sets that you can assign to contacts. When you enter a new contact, the Contact tab in the Contact window contains a Categorize button in the Options group.

When you click the Categorize button, you can use the color codes, or assign your own names to a particular color. For example, you can categorize by orange and rename the category as *Close Friends*, or categorize by red and rename it as *Hot Prospects*. When you save the contact with a category, the color band and the new name display in the Contact window.

When you return to the main Contacts view, you can then sort or arrange them by category. This allows you to instantly find, identify, and follow up with contacts that are important in different areas of your life.

There are other ways to view your contacts. Like a paper address book, the default contact list displays buttons that you can use to browse through contacts alphabetically.

You can use any of the Current View options to see your contacts in different ways. You can also customize any Current view or create your own view if none of the pre-sets fit your needs.

Organize Contacts with Categories

Add a category to Contacts

1. Open a Contact window.

2. Click Categorize.

3. Choose a color.

   This example uses the Red Category.

Customize the category

The Rename Category dialog box appears.

4. Click the Name text field and add a description.

5. Click Yes to rename the Red category.

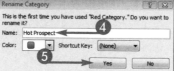

- A red band identifies the contact as a member of the Red category, now named *Hot Prospect*.

6 Click Save & Close.

- Your contacts appear in your selected view.

7 Click the By Category option (◎ changes to ◉).

- Your contacts are sorted by category.

Can I assign more than one category to a contact?

▼ Yes. When you assign a second category, both color bands appear in the Contact window, and the contact appears in both categories when you select the By Category option (◎ changes to ◉) in the Current View pane.

How do I print the information for a contact?

▼ In the contact list, click the contact whose information you want to print; then click the Office button and click Print. In the Print range area, click the Only Selected Items option (☐ changes to ☑). Select a print style and then click OK.

Can I quickly change or add categories for a contact?

▼ Yes. When you select the By Category option from the Current View pane, you can click and drag any contact with no category or a given category into the area for another category. The contact remains in that category grouping, and the category is added to its contact record. You can also select the contact in the list and choose a category from the Category button (▦) on the Outlook toolbar.

Can I manage my categories?

▼ Yes. When you add a category to a contact through the Ribbon in Step 3, click All Categories. A dialog box enables you to manage and rename your categories.

PART VI

Create a
Task List

The Tasks feature of Outlook allows you to create an electronic to-do list of personal and work-related tasks that you want to accomplish. A *task* is a duty or errand that you want to keep track of until it is complete.

When you create a new task, you should enter a descriptive subject to help you recognize the task later, such as "submit marketing report" or "book airline reservations." The subject appears in your task list.

You can also specify a due date for a task. The due date appears in your task list and helps remind you of upcoming deadlines.

Outlook allows you to specify the status and priority of a task. Setting the status of a task can help you monitor your progress. Assigning a priority can help you organize your tasks and budget your time. You can also add comments to a task to record details about the task.

Tasks can also reflect the color-coded categories that are applied to contacts. For more information, see the task "Organize Contacts with Categories."

Create a Task List

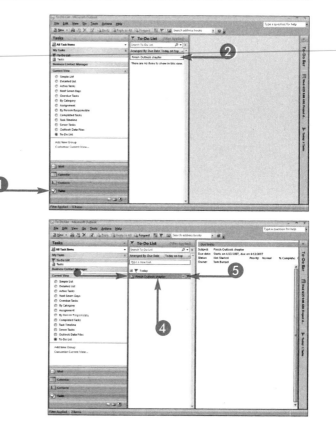

1 Click Tasks in the Navigation pane to open the To-Do List.

The To-Do List window appears.

2 Click in the New Task pane and enter a task.

3 Press Enter.

● The task is entered with today's date.

4 Click the task to see its details in the Reading pane.

5 Double-click the task to open it.

The task opens in a Task window with a Task tab displaying additional features.

6 Click the Status down arrow (▼) and select a status for the task.

7 Click the Priority down arrow (▼) and select a priority for the task.

8 Click the Due date down arrow (▼) to change the due date.

9 Click this area and type any comments about the task.

10 Click Save & Close to save the changes.

The task appears in the task list.

● Additional details appear in the Reading pane.

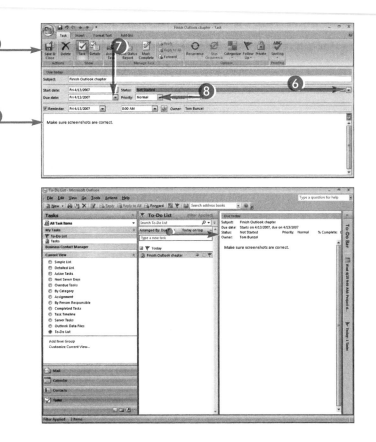

How do I edit a task?

▼ To change the information for a task, double-click the task to redisplay the Task window. Make any changes and click OK.

Can I create a recurring task?

▼ Yes. Open the Task by double-clicking it in the To-Do List or create a new task. Click Recurrence in the Options group in the Task tab. In the Task Recurrence dialog box, click the Daily, Weekly, Monthly, or Yearly option to specify the frequency of the task. The available options vary, depending on your selection. Select the options you want to use to specify when the task occurs. Then click OK.

I clicked the Task flag icon, and it disappeared. What happened?

▼ When you create a task, it goes into the To-Do List. When you click the flag icon (▼) in the To-Do List, it tells Outlook that the task is completed. You can see it crossed out if you click Tasks under My Tasks in the Navigation pane. If you click the flag icon (▼) in the Task window, you can set a different due date for follow-up.

Can I have Outlook remind me of a task?

▼ Yes. In the Task window, select the Reminder check box (☐ changes to ☑). Then set the date and time for the reminder in the appropriate areas. Outlook displays a Reminder dialog box on your screen at the time you specify.

Manage a Task List

Y ou can sort the tasks in your To-Do List by subject or due date to help you find tasks of interest. You can sort tasks in ascending or descending order or by color-coded categories. For more on categories, see the task "Organize Contacts with Categories."

After you accomplish a task, you can click its flag icon in the To-Do List to mark the task as complete. When you open the Tasks List, Outlook draws a line through each completed task. This allows you to see which

tasks are outstanding and which tasks are complete. You can delete a task you no longer want to display in your Tasks List.

By default, Outlook displays your Tasks List in the To-Do List view. You can change the view of your tasks: Outlook offers several views. The Detailed List view displays details about each task, including the priority. The Active Tasks view displays only tasks that are incomplete. The Next Seven Days view displays tasks that are due in the next week. The Task Timeline view lets you see your tasks extended out over time.

Manage a Task List

Sort the To-Do List

① Click Tasks to open the To-Do List.

② Click the Arranged By panel for a list of sorting options.

- A small triangle icon (▲) appears in the heading of the column, indicating the order in which the items are sorted. You can click the triangle again to sort the tasks in the opposite order. This example uses Due Date. The triangle toggles between Today on Top and Later on Top.

③ Click a sort option.

- Outlook sorts your tasks.

Mark a task as complete

① Click Tasks to open the Tasks List.

② In the Tasks List, click the check box next to the completed task (☐ changes to ☑).

- Outlook marks the task as complete and draws a line through it.

- You can sort the Tasks List by Due Date, Subject, or Flag.

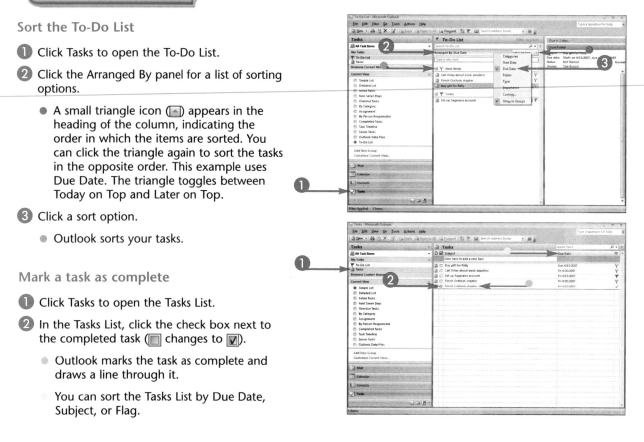

Delete a task

1 Click the task you want to delete.

2 Click the Delete button (⊠).

Outlook removes the task from the Tasks List.

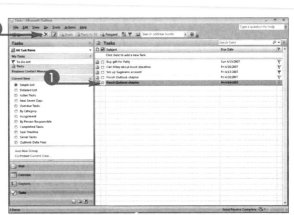

Change the view of tasks

1 Click the way you want to view the tasks (◎ changes to ◉).

● Outlook displays the tasks in the selected view. This example shows the Timeline view.

Can I restore a task that I have deleted?

▼ When you delete a task, Outlook places the task in the Deleted Items folder. To restore a task, click to open the Folder List (▣) and click the Deleted Items icon in the Folder List. The Deleted Items folder opens; you can click and drag the task you want to restore to the Tasks icon in the Folder List.

How do I display comments in my To-Do List?

▼ If you entered comments about a task, you can display the comments in your To-Do List. When you click the task in the To-Do List, the comments appear in the details in the Reading pane.

Can I see my tasks while I am sending or reading my e-mail?

▼ Yes. Your tasks and Calendar items are available whenever you are in Outlook. Simply click the To-Do Bar on the right side of the screen, or click the double arrow (≪).

Keep Personal Notes

U sing Outlook, you can create electronic notes that are similar to paper sticky notes that are often used in offices.

Notes are useful for storing small pieces of information such as reminders, questions, ideas, and anything else you would record on note paper. Notes are often used to store information on a temporary basis.

When you create a note, Outlook records and saves the current date and time at the bottom of the note.

This information helps you keep track of your notes and identify notes that are outdated.

You can open a note to read or edit the contents of the note. When you make changes to the contents of a note, the changes are automatically saved.

You can delete a note that you no longer need. Deleting old notes reduces the number of notes on your screen and makes it easier to see new or important notes.

Keep Personal Notes

1 Click the Notes button (▣) in the Navigation pane.

● The Notes pane appears.

● The Notes toolbar contains buttons for creating and working with notes.

2 Click New.

● A small window appears where you can type the note. The bottom of the window displays the current date and time.

3 Type the text for the note.

④ Click the Notes options button ()
to open the Note options.

The Note options display.

  You can categorize the note by
  using Outlook colors.

⑤ When you finish, click the Close
button (▣) to close the note.

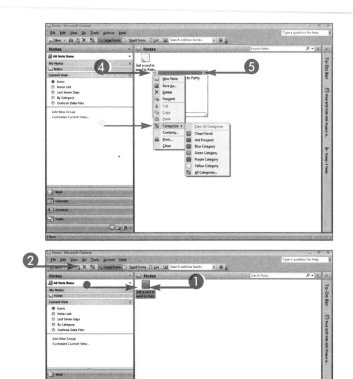

● The note appears on the screen.

To open the note to display its
contents, you can double-click the
note.

Delete a note

① Click the note you want to delete.

② Click the Delete button (✕).

Outlook deletes the note.

Can I change the size of a note?

▼ Yes. Display the contents
of the note. Position the
mouse over the bottom-
right corner of the note
window and then drag
the corner until the note
displays at the size you
want.

Can I put a note on my desktop?

▼ Yes. You can drag a note
to your desktop if you
reduce the size of the
Outlook screen. The note
remains available and
active, even if Outlook is
closed.

Can I locate a specific word or phrase in my notes?

▼ Yes. Click in the Search
Notes field at the top of
the Notes screen and type
the word or phrase you
want to locate. Outlook
lists the notes that contain
the word or phrase you
specified. You can double-
click a note to display its
contents.

PART VI

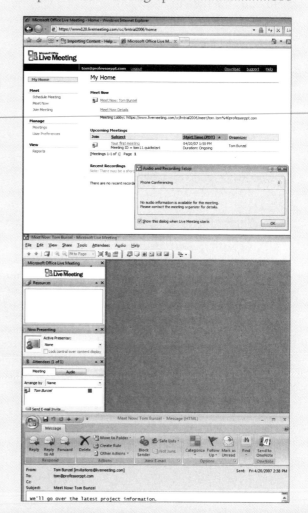

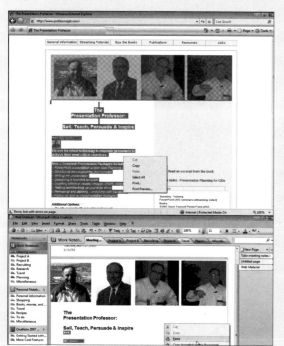

A

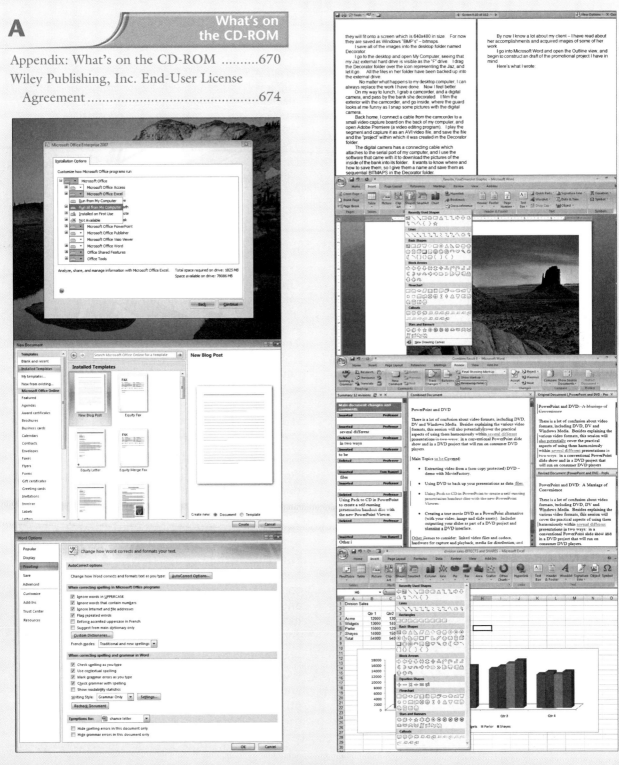

An Introduction to OneNote

OneNote is a program that lets you manage and organize large and minute amounts of information. While it was originally conceived mainly for tablet PC users, OneNote has proven to be a valuable part of Office for anyone who needs to create, organize, and retrieve different types of information.

For business users, OneNote is a great way to take notes during meetings or to prepare for meetings in advance. By categorizing items in sections, pages, and subpages, you can quickly locate important items and maintain order among many different projects. In addition, you can maintain your personal items in a separate OneNote Notebook with its own distinct sections.

OneNote also includes a pre-set Notebook about itself, with many tips on how to use it more effectively.

Types of Notes

OneNote lets you create notes for virtually any reason you can think of. For meetings, you can create notes that anticipate a meeting, including an agenda or items that you need to cover. During a meeting, you can use OneNote to take down important information and place it in different organized areas for subsequent retrieval. After a meeting, you can use OneNote to review important items or follow up on matters that need attention.

In an educational setting, you can use OneNote in the classroom to take notes, and also in the library or online for research. You can easily copy and paste Web pages into OneNote; they will include images along with the link to the Web page.

OneNote can also help in project planning. You can devote OneNote pages to a project and group them together, or you can even create an entire Notebook for a large, complex project. In either case, you can keep the information relating to the project organized, and easily find important facts and snippets of information once you have entered them in OneNote.

In your personal life, you can use OneNote to plan special events or travel, including maps, to-do lists, reservations, e-mail addresses, and any other useful information.

If you set up a microphone with your OneNote computer, you can also record audio directly into OneNote pages while being able to catalog the information with page and section tabs.

Note Benefits

There are many different types of written notes, but they may become lost or misplaced. OneNote information is always available in the program, and it can be kept organized in exactly the way that you specify. You can also easily search for information stored in OneNote, or use the flag feature to keep important information summarized.

You can organize important items using bullet or numbered lists, and highlight items on your OneNote pages to make them stand out.

OneNote also integrates well with other applications. Internet Explorer 7 has a Send to OneNote feature in the Web browser. Outlook has the same feature for e-mail. In addition, you can easily copy and paste almost anything from any program into a OneNote page to keep it catalogued and organized.

From OneNote you can quickly send a page directly to someone else using e-mail, or to Word. This lets you easily and seamlessly share your OneNote information and also use it in other important documents.

Start
OneNote

Y ou can start OneNote from the Start button of Windows XP or Vista.

When OneNote opens, its organizational structure is fairly intuitive. On the left side of the screen is a panel with three pre-set Notebooks. You have a Work Notebook, with pre-set project, planning, and travel sections. There is a Personal Notebook already set up, with various types of personal information sections, including travel, cooking, and so on. There is also a Notebook to get you started with the program, along with a summary of interesting features.

You can probably begin using OneNote without learning much about it. As you click a page tab, it provides a blank area in which you can enter

information, along with a header for quickly naming the page.

Pages automatically appear in the Unfiled Notes section whenever you use OneNote to create a screen clipping or a side note. They also appear whenever you use the Send to OneNote command in programs such as Internet Explorer and Outlook 2007.

Can I permanently delete selected sections or pages?

▼ Yes. If you find some of the Notebook pre-sets annoying or confusing, you can right-click a section tab at the top or a page tab on the right, and quickly delete them.

Start OneNote

① Click Start.

② Click All Programs.

③ Click Microsoft Office.

④ Click Microsoft Office OneNote 2007.

The OneNote window opens.

● OneNote displays a set of pre-set Notebooks in the left panel.

● You can click the Open/Close Notebooks double arrow to open or minimize the Notebook panel.

● OneNote displays section tabs for the selected Notebook at the top of the window.

● OneNote displays the pages for the currently selected section on the right side of the screen.

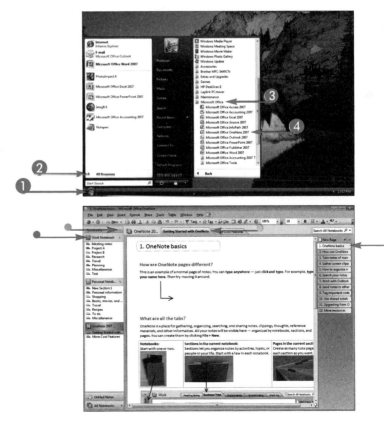

PART VII

Create a
New Section

A *section* is the main component of a OneNote Notebook. By maintaining, adding, and revising your sections you can keep your notes organized and find information quickly.

OneNote 2007 comes with three pre-set Notebooks: Work, Personal, and OneNote 2007 Guide. You can easily create a new section in any of these Notebooks, or first create a new Notebook and then add the section to it. Each Notebook section is represented by a tab at the top of the OneNote window, making navigation between sections very easy.

To create a new section in OneNote, you must first select the Notebook for the new section in the Navigation Pane. You can then add a new section, which becomes the last tab in the Notebook. You can move the new section to any position in the Notebook after it has been created.

For example, in your Work Notebook you can create a new section called *Recruiting*. You can then move that tab between any other tabs in the same Notebook, or even to another Notebook.

Create a New Section

① Click the Notebook in which you want to add a new section.

② Right-click a tab in that Notebook.

③ Click New Section.

● The new section is added to the Notebook with its name highlighted.

④ Type a name for the new tab.

⑤ Press Enter.

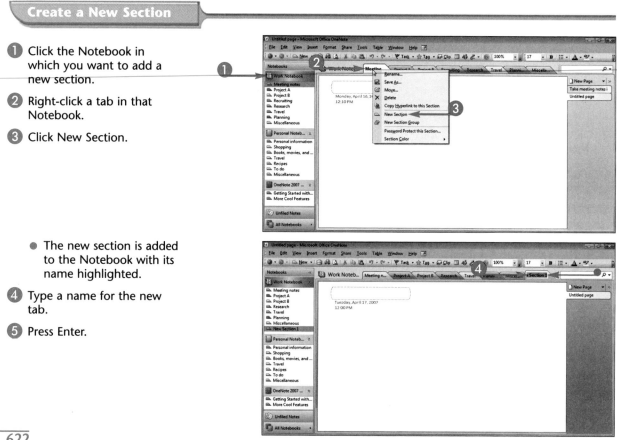

● OneNote creates a new section in the Notebook with the newly named tab.

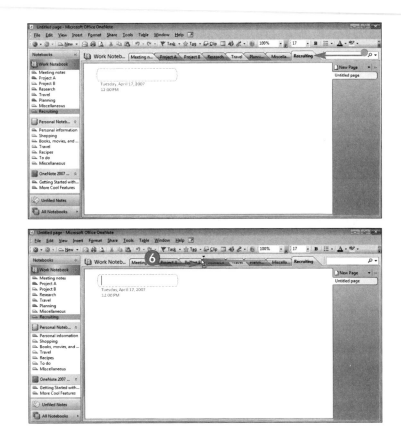

⑥ Place your cursor over the new tab and drag it to where you want it in the Notebook (ᐟ₃ changes to ᐟ₃).

The section is moved to a new tabbed position in the notebook.

How can I create a new Notebook?

▼ Click File, click New, and then select Notebook. The New Notebook Wizard guides you through choosing a template for a new Notebook that will be added to the Navigation Pane. For more information on the New Notebook Wizard, see the task "Share Notes."

Can I change the tab color of the section?

▼ Yes. Right-click the tab for the section and select New Section Color. A drop-down menu of colors opens. You can select a new color for the section from the drop-down list.

I have created a new section, but then I noticed that there is already a section that I can use. How do I delete the new section?

▼ Right-click the section tab and select Delete. When the message box appears, click Yes to delete the section.

Add a New Page

Pages are the individual components of OneNote sections that contain your actual notes. When you click a section tab to select that section, the pages already in the section appear on the right side of the OneNote window.

You can select any page to continue adding notes to that page. You can select an untitled page to give it a new *header* or title, and then add your notes. You can also click the New Page button to add a new blank, untitled page with which to work. Pages can also be grouped if they contain related information, or you can add a subpage to an existing page to allow it to hold related information with its own heading or title.

Subpages remain connected to their main pages if you move them.

In OneNote 2007, many of the existing sections in the Work and Personal Notebooks already contain template pages. For example, the Travel section of the Work Notebook has pages named for Hotel Information, Sightseeing, and Trip. If you click to access one of these pages, you can take advantage of the formatting and tables to add your own information. You can also click in the header to revise it, or revise the time and date stamp for the page; however, if you sort pages by time and date, the original time remains the basis for sorting the page.

Add a New Page

Using an untitled page

1. Click the tab for the section where you want to use an untitled page.

2. Click the Untitled page tab.

3. Click in the header of the untitled page.

4. Type a new name for the page in the header.

5. Press Enter.

   ● The Page tab now displays the name for reference.

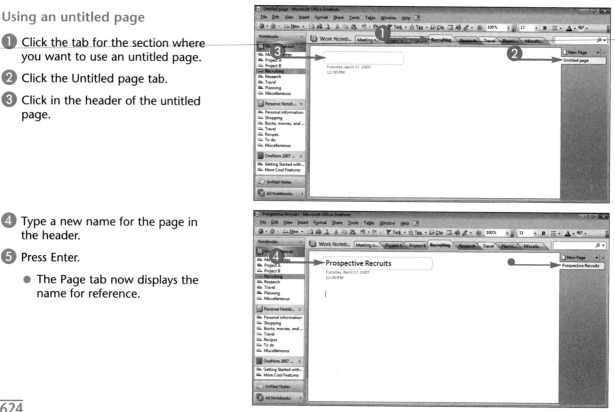

Create a new page

1 Click New Page.

- A new Untitled page is created.

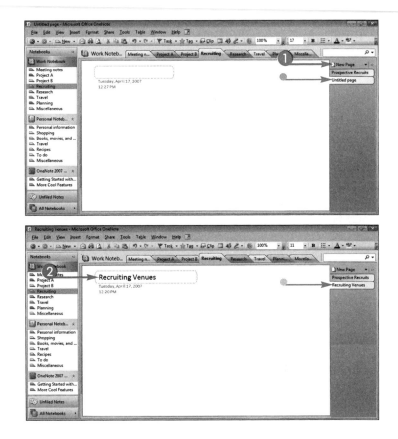

2 Type a new name for the page in the header.

3 Press Enter.

- The Page tab displays the new name for reference.

How can I create a subpage?

▼ Click the New Page down arrow (▼) and select SubPage. An untitled subpage is created, and is connected to the currently active page.

How can I copy a page with content that I want to reuse?

▼ Right-click the page you want to copy and select Copy. Click to select the page after which you want to place the content of the new page. Right-click its tab and select Paste.

Can I undo the creation of a new page?

▼ Yes. Press Ctrl+Z or click the Undo button (ↄ) to undo the creation of a new page.

Work with Pages

You can use OneNote pages to hold all kinds of information, including typed text objects; "ink," written in freehand using a tablet PC or similar tool; and graphics, such as pictures or clip-art images. These pages can also contain highlighting, background objects, sounds, videos, screen captures, Office documents and links to the documents, and Web content.

The most basic entry would be a text entry that you type into a OneNote page. Each time you finish typing an entry and click elsewhere, the completed entry is stored as a unit or note in a text placeholder. You can freely move these individual units around the OneNote page. To add to a unit, click inside it where you want to add information, and begin typing.

Each text placeholder expands as you type. You can later drag the border to resize the text placeholder, or add hard returns within it to add more information.

To move information from one text placeholder to another, you can drag through the text, cut or copy it, and then paste it, or simply drag the selected text into another text placeholder where you would prefer it to be.

Work with Pages

① Click anywhere in the OneNote page.

② Type your note.

● A placeholder surrounds your note.

③ Click elsewhere on the page.

④ Type another note.

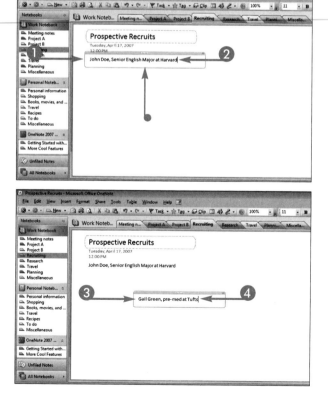

⑤ Place your cursor over the top border of a note (🔾 changes to ✛).

⑥ Drag the note anywhere else on the page and release the mouse.

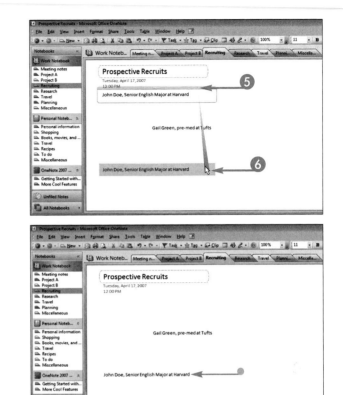

● The note is repositioned on the page.

Can I resize the header placeholder?	Can I change how information displays in the Time and Date Stamp?	Are there alignment tools to line up your notes?
▼ Yes. The header accommodates text as you enter it, but only some of the text will appear on the tab that identifies the page. If you would like to add lines to the header, press Shift+Enter to create additional lines.	▼ Yes. The Time and Date Stamp in OneNote reflects the format that is set in the version of Windows you are using. You can use the Control Panel to change how it displays. In Windows XP and Vista (change to Classic View), double-click the Regional and Language Options in the Control Panel and click the Customize button.	▼ Not at this time.

Note a
Web Page

Because so much information is available on the Internet, it is natural that you will want to use material in Web pages in your OneNote notes. You can easily select parts of a page from your Web browser, and copy the material to the Clipboard.

When you paste the material from the Clipboard into a OneNote page, it appears within a placeholder in the page. In addition, the URL or hyperlink to the original Web page is maintained, so that you can click to return to that site.

I noticed the Internet Explorer Send to OneNote feature. How does it work?

▼ When you click Send to OneNote from the Page menu in Internet Explorer, the entire Web page is sent to the Unfiled Notes section in the OneNote Notebooks panel. You can then drag that page directly into any section of any Notebook.

Note a Web Page

1. In your Web browser, drag through a Web page to select the material you want.

2. Right-click and select Copy.

3. Click the tab of a OneNote page to open it.

4. Right-click and select Paste.

   The page with pictures is pasted into OneNote.

   ● The Web link URL is also added to the note.

Find Text

As you gather and compile new information in OneNote, you may forget exactly where certain content is located. OneNote has a very robust search capability that allows you to quickly search for and locate any text you have added to a note.

By default, OneNote searches all of your Notebooks for a block of text in the search field. However, you can narrow your search down to a Notebook, a section, or to a section group.

When the search is completed, you can progress through the pages where the search term has been located; each instance is highlighted within the OneNote pages.

You can also click View List to open a task pane with synopses of all instances of the term that you can scroll through and select to go to that page.

How do I narrow the search?

▼ Type your term in the search field and click the search button down arrow (🔎). Select one of these search parameters: This Section, This Section Group, This Notebook, or All Notebooks (default).

Find Text

1 Type a term into the search field.

2 Click the Search button (🔎).

● A search compilation opens with the first instance in the window and the term highlighted.

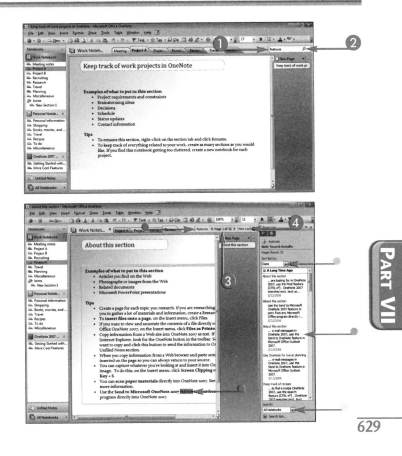

3 Click to go to the next (◀) or previous (▶) search term.

4 Click View List for more information.

● The Page List task pane opens. You can scroll through the descriptions and click a link to open the page.

● You can click the Sort list by down arrow (▼) to change the sort options.

● You can click the Search down arrow (▼) to change the Search options.

629

Change Font Style or Font Size

Y̲ou can enhance the appearance of your page by changing the appearance, or font, of text. By default, OneNote uses the Calibri font, but you can apply another font to draw attention to headings or emphasize important data in your page. OneNote fonts display in the list as they appear in your page so that you preview a font before you select it.

Most fonts in the list display either the TT icon or a printer icon. The TT icon indicates that the font is a TrueType font, which means that the font prints

exactly as it appears on your screen. The printer icon, indicating a printer font, means that the font may print differently from how it appears on your screen.

In addition to changing the font, you can also increase or decrease the size of text in your page. By default, OneNote uses a text size of 11 points (72 points make an inch). Larger text is easier to read, but smaller text allows you to fit more information on your screen and on a printed page.

Change Font Style or Font Size

Change font style

① Click the placeholder for the text you want to reformat.

The text is selected.

② Click the Font down arrow (▼).

③ Click the font you want to use.

● OneNote displays the text in the selected font.

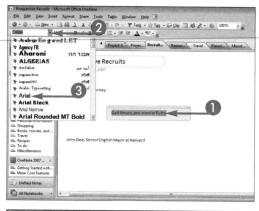

Change font size

1 Click the placeholder for the text you want to reformat.

The text is selected.

2 Click the Font Size down arrow (⏷).

3 Click the size you want to use.

You can also type a font size in the text box.

● OneNote displays the text in the selected size.

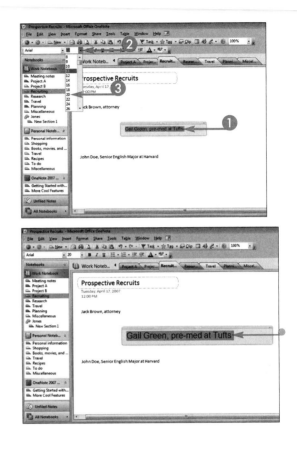

I do not see the Font drop-down list in my Formatting toolbar. What should I do?

▼ By default, OneNote 2007 combines the Standard and Formatting toolbars. Grab the toolbar handle (⌖ changes to ✛) and drag the formatting toolbar to its own row, as shown in this task. You can also click Tools and then click Customize. When the Customize window opens, click Options and select the Show Standard and Formatting toolbars on two rows option (☐ changes to ☑).

Can I only reformat a portion of the text in a placeholder?

▼ Yes. Select only the text you want to reformat by dragging through it before applying a font style or a font size.

Can I change the default font and font size?

▼ Yes. Click Tools, click Options, and then select Editing in the Options window. You will find down arrows (⏷) to change the default font style, font size, and text color for all new entries in OneNote.

Bold, Italicize, or Underline Text

You can use the Bold, Italic, and Underline features to emphasize and enhance the style of text in your page. You can apply one or all of these features quickly using the appropriate buttons on the Formatting toolbar.

The Bold feature makes the selected text appear darker and thicker than other text in your page. You can use the Bold feature to emphasize row and column headings or other important information.

The Italic feature slants the selected text to the right. You may want to italicize notes or explanations that you add to your page.

The Underline feature adds a line underneath the selected text. You can underline text to emphasize specific text in your page, such as subtotals and totals.

Bold, Italicize, or Underline Text

1 Select the placeholder containing the text you want to change.

2 Click one or more of the following buttons:

Bold (**B**)

Italic (*I*)

Underline (<u>U</u>)

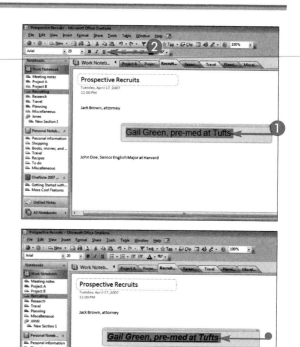

The text displays in the style you selected.

● You can remove a style by repeating Steps 1 and 2.

Change Text Color

Y ou can add a variety of text colors to your pages to make certain text stand out.

You can change the color of text in a page to draw attention to titles or other important information in your page.

When adding color to your text, make sure that you choose background page colors and text colors that work well together. For example, red text on a pink background may be difficult to read.

How can I quickly change the color of all of the text in my page?

▼ You can hold down the Ctrl key and select multiple placeholders to apply a new font color to them, or press Ctrl+A to select all placeholders in your page.

Change Text Color

1 Select the text you want to change.

2 Click the Font Color down arrow (🔺▾).

3 Click the color you want to use.

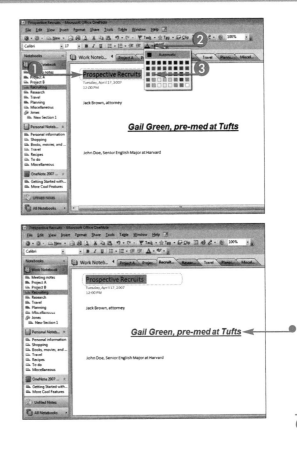

● The text changes to the new color.

To remove a color from text, you can perform Steps 1 to 3, except click Automatic in Step 3.

Indent
Text

You can apply an indent to move text away from the left edge of a placeholder or margin. When you indent text, OneNote moves the text over the default amount of space. You can continue to indent by pressing the Increase Indent button, or reverse it with the Decrease Indent button.

To use the Increase or Decrease Indent buttons, you first need to select the text that you want to indent. The best way to do this is to drag your cursor through the text until it is highlighted and then release the left mouse button.

Increasing the indent of a portion of text decreases its hierarchical importance within OneNote's outline format. Decreasing the indent and bringing the text closer to the left margin makes it of relatively higher importance.

If the text to be indented is bulleted, you can also click the last bullet in the sequence. The set of bullets is highlighted, allowing you to increase or decrease the indent.

If either the Increase or Decrease Indent buttons are inactive, make sure you have selected the text you want to indent.

Indent Text

① Place your cursor before the text to be indented.

② Click an indent option:

  Increase Indent (▣)

  Decrease Indent (▣)

● OneNote indents the entries.

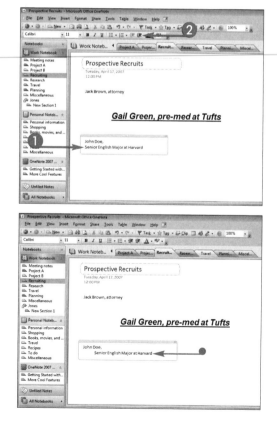

Add Numbers or Bullets

You can begin each item in a list with a bullet. Bullets can help make the list easier to read. You use bullets for items in no particular order, such as items in a shopping list or agenda, and key points in a document.

You can also use a numbered list to place items in order or in a hierarchy. If you drag items in a numbered list to a new part of the list, the items automatically renumber to reflect their new position in the list. To select the items for a list, drag through them with the cursor. If the placeholder contains only items that you want to list, you can also select the entire placeholder before applying the number or bullet format.

Can I use sub-bullets or numbers?

▼ Yes. If you press Enter to add another item to a bullet or numbered list, another main bullet or number appears. Press Tab to make it a sub-bullet or sub-number. In the case of a sub-number, outlining rules apply; a letter is assigned to the next level, and then a number for the following level.

Add Numbers or Bullets

Add bullets

1 Select the text to which you want to add bullets.

2 Click the Bullets button (☰▾).

● The text is arranged in a bullet list.

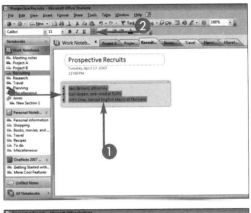

Add a numbered list

1 Select the text to which you want to add numbers.

2 Click the Numbering button (☰▾).

● The text is arranged in a numbered list.

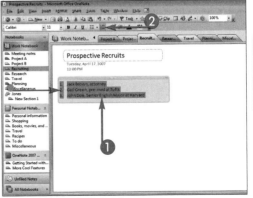

Using Tags for Organization

A *tag* is a reminder or addition that you can associate with a note to enable you to follow up or locate the item more quickly. You can create a new note directly from a tag, or select a note and apply a tag from the Standard toolbar.

OneNote 2007 comes with dozens of predefined tags that you can use. After you create a note with a tag, you can use the Tags Summary task pane to quickly locate your tagged items and work with them.

From the Tags Summary task pane, you can group your tags by name or type, section, title, date, or note text. You can also filter your search by Notebooks, sections, groups, or spans of time. You can generate a Summary Page of tagged items that you can print and refer to in order to work with different items or projects. You can also customize any of the existing tags, or use the Customize Tags task pane to create personal tags for your own use.

Using Tags for Organization

1 Click the page where you want a tag.

2 Click the Tag down arrow (▼).

The Tag drop-down list opens.

3 Click a tag that you want to create.

This example uses To Do (☑).

● A new To Do tag is created.

4 Type an entry for the new tag.

5 Select another item to tag.

6 Click the Tag down arrow (▼).

The tag drop-down list opens.

7 Click a tag that you want to create.

This example uses Question (?).

636

- OneNote applies a Question tag to the selected item.

⑧ Click the Tag down arrow (▼).

The Tag drop-down list opens.

⑨ Click Show All Tagged Notes.

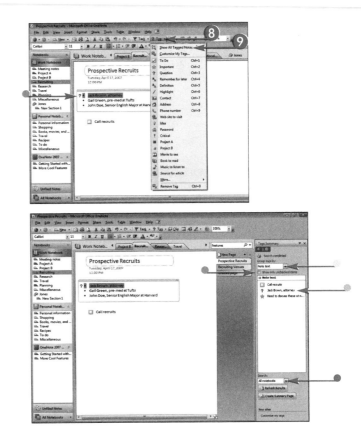

- The Tags Summary task pane opens. All of your tags appear in the task pane.

- You can click Group tags by down arrow (▼) to group tags.

- You can click the Search down arrow (▼) to limit the search.

- You can click this option to limit the search to unchecked items (▢ changes to ☑).

How do I mark a tag as complete, or remove the tag?

▼ Click the To Do tag (▢ changes to ☑). It is now marked as checked or complete. Right-click any tag and select Remove. The tag is now removed.

How do I create a Summary Page?

▼ Set your search parameters in the Tags Summary task pane and click the Create Summary Page button. OneNote creates a new page in the same section named Note text, which you can rename and use for future reference.

How do I customize or create tags?

▼ Click the Tag down arrow (▼) and choose More. An additional set of predefined tags becomes available for your use. You can also click the Tags Summary down arrow (▼) at the top of the Tags Summary task pane and choose Customize My Tags. A new task pane lets you add, remove, or modify existing tags. Click the Add button to name and create your own custom tag.

Add an
Outlook Task

OneNote 2007 is tightly integrated with Outlook 2007, which enables you to manage and create tasks directly from a OneNote page. You can create a new task in OneNote, or select an existing note and add a task to it. In either case, you can then select the task and choose to open it in Outlook to redefine the start and due dates, or otherwise change its contents. Outlook opens the task so that you can add information and then save and close the task. See Chapter 27 for more information on Outlook tasks.

The tasks in Outlook contain a link back to the OneNote page and task that you created originally. This allows you to integrate your items in OneNote directly with the tasks in Outlook, and maintain a coordinated Calendar of items.

From OneNote, you can also mark a task as complete, or delete it entirely, and the results also update in Outlook.

You can add an Outlook task in OneNote from the Insert command on the OneNote main menu or by using the Task down arrow on the Standard toolbar in OneNote.

Add an Outlook Task

① Click the page where you want to add a task.

② Click the Task down arrow (⯆).

The Task drop-down list opens.

③ Click a task that you want to create.

This example uses Next Week.

● A new task is created.

④ Type an entry for the new task.

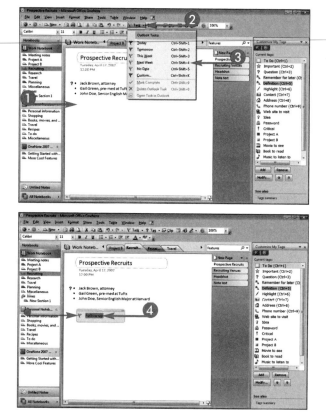

⑤ Select the task in OneNote.

⑥ Click the Task down arrow (▼).

The Task drop-down list opens.

⑦ Click Open Task in Outlook.

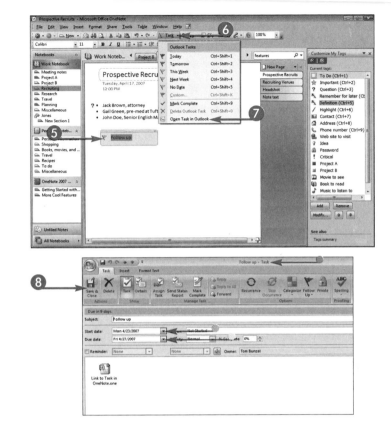

● The task opens in Outlook.

● You can click Start date down arrow (▼) to change the start date.

● You can click the Due date down arrow (▼) to change the due date.

⑧ Click Save & Close.

The final task is saved in both Outlook and OneNote.

Why are some task flags dimmed?

▼ Shared tasks involve synchronizing information between OneNote and Outlook. Dimmed flags are for tasks that are due later on and require longer to synchronize.

Why did Outlook not open with the task?

▼ Sometimes you need to start Outlook for the task to open. Occasionally the task will be open, but it displays beneath the OneNote window. You can press Alt+Tab to toggle between programs and manually open the task if necessary.

What is the difference between tasks and tags?

▼ Both tasks and tags let you organize and locate your notes. Tasks allow you to use your Outlook Calendar to remind you of items in OneNote. Tags allow you to mark items in OneNote that you can quickly locate using the Tags Summary task pane or by creating a summary page. For more information, see the task "Using Tags for Organization."

PART VII

Add a Picture

You are not limited to text in OneNote. For example, you can insert a Web page into a OneNote page. You can also directly insert many other file types. As another example, you may want to insert a picture of a prospective employee in a recruiting page. OneNote lets you insert a picture from a file or directly from a scanner or digital camera. After you have placed the image, you can move the picture anywhere in the page, or resize the picture to suit your needs.

You can insert a picture into a OneNote page from any folder on your computer, as long as you know

where it is located. When you download a picture from a scanner or camera, it is generally saved as a file in My Pictures in My Documents (Windows XP) or in Pictures (Windows Vista).

In order to acquire a picture directly from a scanner or digital camera, the peripheral must be set up on your computer. A scanner typically uses a utility program to enable direct import. A digital camera may appear as a hard drive in Windows, enabling you to directly download an image into OneNote.

Add a Picture

1 Click Insert.

2 Click Pictures.

3 Click From Files.

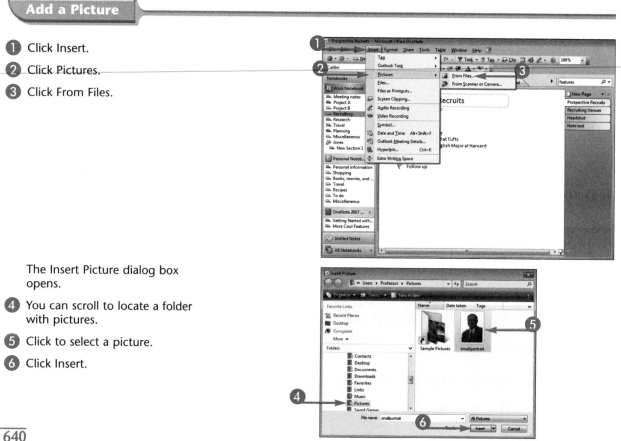

The Insert Picture dialog box opens.

4 You can scroll to locate a folder with pictures.

5 Click to select a picture.

6 Click Insert.

The picture is inserted into the page.

⑦ Click to select the picture.

● You can drag the picture move icon (⊞) to move the picture around the page.

● You can use the selection handles to resize the picture.

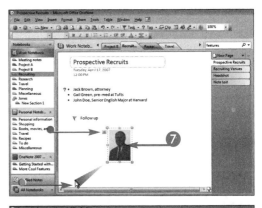

The picture is now part of the OneNote page.

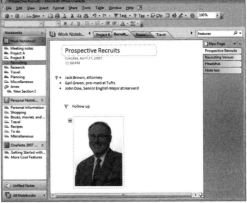

Can I search for pictures?

▼ Yes. There are a number of ways to make pictures searchable in OneNote. To use text search, add a text note describing the picture with a picture caption. For more on adding a note, see the task "Work with Pages." You can also add either a tag or an Outlook task, or both, to a selected picture. For more information, see the tasks "Using Tags for Organization" and "Add an Outlook Task."

Can I scan text into OneNote?

▼ No. The Insert Picture from Scanner or Camera command does not directly support optical character recognition (OCR), and so you would need a third-party program to do this. However, you can right-click a picture that contains text and select Copy Text from Picture. You can then click in a page and paste the text, which may or may not be accurately copied but which you can now edit or revise in OneNote.

Using the All Notebooks Window

OneNote can become fairly complex as you continue to add sections and pages to existing Notebooks, or even create your own new Notebooks for specific projects or other uses.

While you can use the main OneNote window to view the various tabs for sections and pages, sometimes a title will be obscured. Also, if you add many pages to a section, some of the tabs may not be visible without scrolling through the window. The *All Notebooks* feature of OneNote 2007 allows you to see your entire OneNote installation in one window by Notebook and sections. All of your color-coded tabs are visible in the window, and you can move or drag and drop sections from one Notebook to another.

You can also create a hyperlink from a section and paste it into any page, providing quick links between different parts of your Notebooks.

By using the All Notebooks window, you can quickly add sections or section groups to a Notebook while you see the big picture. You can also password-protect specific sections of your Notebook, or change the tab colors from the All Notebooks window.

① Click All Notebooks.

● The All Notebooks window opens.

② Click a section.

● The first complete page of that section opens.

③ Click All Notebooks.

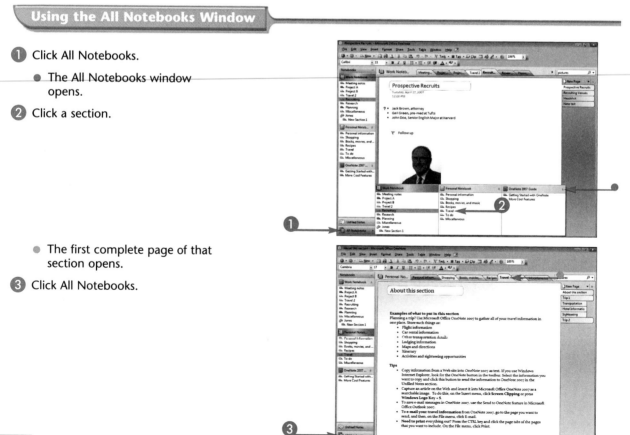

The All Notebooks window opens.

4 You can click and drag a section to another Notebook (⊕ changes to ⊕).

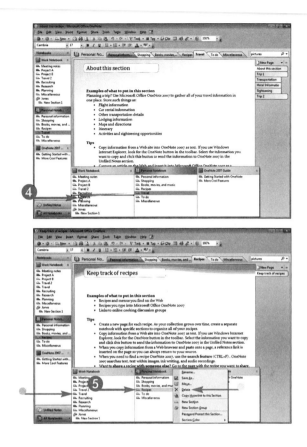

● The section appears in the other Notebook.

5 Right-click a section.

○ Options open for deleting, moving, renaming, recoloring, or password-protecting a section.

How do I hyperlink to a section or page?

▼ Right-click a section tab in All Notebooks; you can also right-click a section tab or page tab directly from within OneNote. Click Copy Hyperlink to this Section. Go to a page where you want to create a link to that section. Click Edit and then click Paste (or press Ctrl+V). A link is created that takes you from that page to the other section.

Can I save a OneNote section in another file format?

▼ Yes. When you right-click a section tab, you can select Save As. Click the Save as type down arrow (▼) to display the various formats, including XML, XPS, PDF, Microsoft Word, and a OneNote package. You can also click the Page Range option (◎ changes to ◉) to save selected pages, the current section, or the current Notebook.

PART VII

Protect and Back Up Your Notebook

As you accumulate information in OneNote and organize it into various sections and pages, the data becomes extremely valuable. It is important to know the location of your Notebooks in order to back them up to other media, and also to be able to move them to other computers.

OneNote has an automatic backup system that saves the latest versions of your Notebooks under your username; it saves them in the AppData section by default, but you can change this location. You can also determine how often OneNote automatically backs up

your data, manually run a backup, or just back up the changed pages.

In addition, OneNote's main Notebook files, as well as your unfiled notes, are saved in the OneNote Notebooks folder in My Documents in Windows XP, or the Documents folder in Windows Vista. By moving that folder to a flash drive or burning it to CD or DVD, you can create a set of backup files that you can reopen from another OneNote installation. However, you should be aware that you will not be able to open OneNote 2007 files with earlier versions of OneNote.

① Click Tools.

② Click Options.

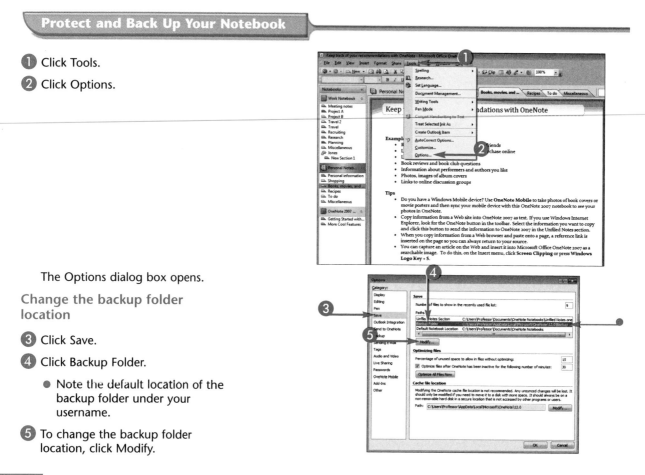

The Options dialog box opens.

Change the backup folder location

③ Click Save.

④ Click Backup Folder.

- Note the default location of the backup folder under your username.

⑤ To change the backup folder location, click Modify.

The Select Folder dialog box appears.

6 Click a folder location for your backup.

This example uses the desktop.

7 Click Select to close the Select Folder dialog box.

Back up your Notebook

8 In the Options dialog box, click Backup.

9 Click a backup option.

● You can click here to immediately back up all Notebooks.

● You can click here to immediately back up changed files.

○ You can click the down arrow (▾) to change the frequency of automatic backups.

10 Click OK.

Your Notebook is backed up to the selected location.

How do restore a backup to OneNote?

▼ Click File, and then click Open Backup. OneNote locates the backup folder and shows you the various Notebook folders. Double-click any folder to open a specific section.

How do I keep my OneNote files small enough for a flash drive?

▼ As long as your OneNote files are mainly text and links to Web pages, they are not very large and should be easy to move. If you paste a lot of images into your OneNote pages, the file sizes can increase dramatically. To keep sizes small, use hyperlinks whenever possible; right-click and choose Insert Hyperlink instead of pasting material directly into OneNote.

Can I open a OneNote section or Notebook files from another folder or drive?

▼ Yes. Click File and then click Open in OneNote and browse to the folder or drive. You can open an entire Notebook or just a specific section from any folder or location. You can also open files from previous versions of OneNote, but you cannot open OneNote 2007 files with a previous version.

Share Notes

Y ou can use OneNote to brainstorm as a group in meetings, use the Notebook pages as a whiteboard with annotations, or set up shared Notebooks in which everyone can view, add, and edit information. OneNote offers the ability to store and maintain shared Notebooks on a network server or file share, where multiple users can simultaneously access shared notes and contribute to them on an ongoing basis.

Taking notes as a group is a collaborative process, and OneNote lets everyone access a shared set of notes at once. It automatically synchronizes everyone's changes to the Notebook. The result is a Notebook that is maintained as up-to-date and that keeps everyone informed of changes.

The New Notebook Wizard guides you through the steps for setting up a shared Notebook. You need to have a network location that you and your team members can access. You can also create the Notebook on a file share on your computer.

When multiple users access a shared Notebook, OneNote can continually synchronize the changes that are made. OneNote also maintains a separate offline copy of the notes on each user's computer. That way, participants can edit notes locally even when they are disconnected from the network. The next time they connect to the shared Notebook, OneNote automatically merges their changes.

Share Notes

① Click File.

② Click New.

③ Click Notebook.

● The New Notebook Wizard opens.

④ Type a name.

● You can click the Color button down arrow (⬚▾) to change the color of the Notebook tab.

⑤ In the From Template list, click the type of Notebook you want to create.

This example uses Shared Notebook – Group Project.

⑥ Click Next.

⑦ Select an option for who will use the Notebook and how she will use it (◎ changes to ◉).

⑧ Click Next.

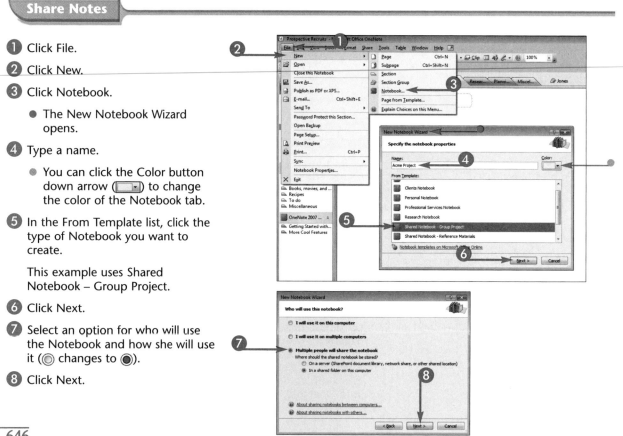

9 Confirm the path and location of the Notebook.

● You can select this option to create an e-mail with a link to the Notebook (🔲 changes to ✅).

10 Click Create.

OneNote creates a new Notebook that users can share if they have access to your network.

● A Share command is added to the OneNote menu.

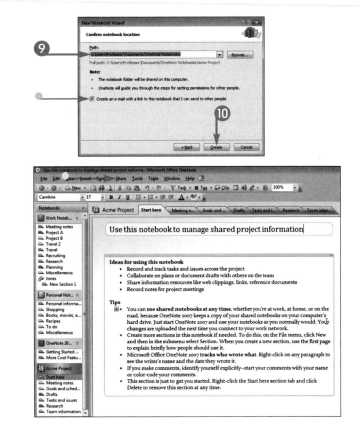

How do I send an e-mail link to the shared Notebook after it has been created?

▼ With a shared Notebook, a Share command appears on the main menu. Click the Share command and choose Send Shared Notebook Link to Others.

Can I share an existing Notebook?

▼ Yes. If you have already shared another Notebook, you can use the Share command to select Create Shared Notebook for another Notebook. If you have not already shared another Notebook, you need to close the Notebook that you want to share, and exit OneNote. Then, depending upon your network, you can share the folder containing your Notebook on the network. To locate or reset the location of your Notebooks, see the task "Protect and Back Up Your Notebook."

PART VII

Start a OneNote Shared Session

I f your computer is connected to the Internet or a network, you can conduct shared note-taking sessions with other OneNote users. Shared sessions make it possible for all participants to view and edit each other's notes in real time.

During a shared session, you can share one or more specific sections or pages in a Notebook. Typed text, highlights, and handwritten digital ink are all viewed as though you are watching a participant work on his own computer. You can use a telephone conversation or instant messaging during a shared session to convey additional information and determine who is adding comments or editing notes.

As a OneNote user, you can either start a new shared session or join an existing session as a participant. If you initiate a shared session, you can select the section that you want to share and then invite the participants.

When you invite others to a shared session, an e-mail message is automatically created that contains the invitation to the session, the IP address of the session host's computer, and the password for the session, if one is needed. After you review the message, you can send it to the participants.

Start a OneNote Shared Session

1 Press Ctrl+F1 to open the OneNote task pane.

2 Click the down arrow (▼) in the task pane selector.

3 Click Start Live Session.

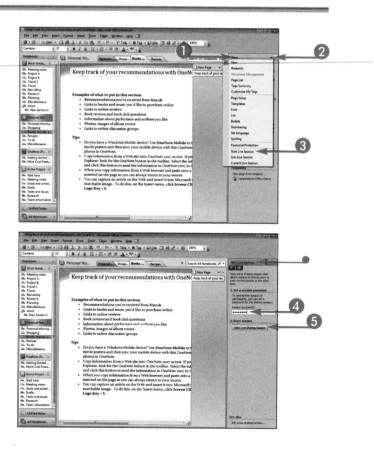

● The Start Live Session task pane opens.

4 Type a password if you want to protect the session. Protecting the session is not mandatory.

5 Click Start Live Sharing Session.

Note: *A warning message appears that the section will be shared and asks if you want to continue. Click OK.*

The Current Live Session task pane opens.

● Current participants are shown here.

● You can click here to invite participants; an e-mail message opens, displaying session information.

Note: For more information on sending Outlook e-mail, see Chapter 25.

You can click Shared Address Information to view the IP address to manually invite others.

⑥ Click Go to Live Shared Section to begin the session.

Users who have OneNote and have joined the Live Session will see your OneNote page in their OneNote window.

Join a live session

① Click the task pane down arrow (⏷) and select Join Live Session

② Type the live sharing session address here.

③ Type a session password.

④ Click Join Session.

You will see the host's OneNote page in your OneNote window.

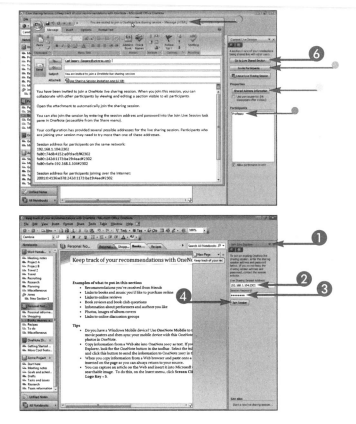

PART VII

An Introduction to Live Meeting

Live Meeting is a collaboration tool that lets you meet with your colleagues, customers, and associates using an Internet connection. A conferencing tool like Live Meeting allows you to reduce costs by avoiding travel, and to increase productivity by conducting meetings online instead of going to a venue where all participants are physically present. In this way, meetings can be convened on short notice, and participants can attend from all over the world without getting on an airplane or booking a hotel room. Productivity is increased because the entire team can participate in a meeting directly. Live Meeting allows for more participation than a SharePoint Web site, conference call, or an e-mail routed among team members. From the Live Meeting home page you can schedule future meetings, meet now (immediately), or join a meeting in progress. You can also manage upcoming meetings by inviting participants and planning resources.

Using PowerPoint with Live Meeting

By using your PowerPoint slides in a Live Meeting session, you can present over the Internet and use a conventional phone line with conferencing capability for the audio portion of the presentation.

With the Whiteboard or the Annotation features on a PowerPoint slide, you can also collaborate and brainstorm with Live Meeting. Office documents can be shared, viewed, and edited during a Live Meeting session, and decisions can be made without the limitations of being in the same place. When a PowerPoint slide show is shown in Live Meeting, the Live Meeting interface is minimized into a bar on the left side of the screen. The PowerPoint window and slides are available for all meeting attendees to see.

Share Control and Mark Up

While one participant may start a Live Meeting session, control can be shared among others. This can be useful for software demonstrations or simply to encourage participation among meeting attendees. In addition, different users can present with different tools; a financial expert might use PivotTables in Excel after a marketing director shows a PowerPoint slide show.

Live Meeting Interactivity

Live Meeting's Question Manager also encourages participation, by letting any presenter view and respond to inquiries by other attendees. Key features include Real-Time Polls, Mood Indicator, Chat, Annotations, Whiteboard, Text Slide, and Web Slide.

For example, a facilitator or speaker running a whiteboard during a Live Meeting conference can draw up concepts on the fly for attendees to see. With a transfer of control, others can mark up the diagrams or other drawings.

Distribute Meeting Content

At the conclusion of a Live Meeting conference, all meeting documents, including changes and annotations, can be saved and distributed to participants. You can make these documents available at a SharePoint Web site or distribute them via e-mail.

A video recording of the conference can also be archived for future review. Attendees or even those who missed the meeting can be directed to a Web page where they can download a movie of the conference, including audio, or watch the video of the conference directly in a Web page.

Start a Conference or Meeting

After you download Live Meeting, you can access a Web page that shows you the currently scheduled meetings and allows you to schedule other meetings and invite other participants.

You can also start Live Meeting conferences from Microsoft Office programs including Outlook, Word, Excel, and PowerPoint. You can also schedule conferences from within the Outlook Calendar, and send out invitations using Outlook e-mail. Please note that you need to load an add-in to work with these applications. With the Live Meeting Add-in Pack, you can perform conferencing tasks directly from Microsoft Office Outlook, Word, Excel, PowerPoint, Project, Visio, as well as from Windows Messenger, MSN Messenger, and Office Communicator 2005. This download is available at Office Online or www.microsoft.com/downloads/details.aspx ?FamilyId=D1984810-117A-45FF-BFEC-2756C6111097&displaylang=en.

Live Meeting conferences are particularly well suited for help-desk, human resources, and training applications. These applications allow control to be transferred from the expert to the novice and back again, along with commentary, over a telephone line. For marketing and sales, you can conduct meetings quickly without traveling to address important concerns and to finalize documents. You can share any application, including a PowerPoint slide show.

Some telephone services allow you to control audio conference calls directly from Live Meeting. This enables you to dial out directly to participants, mute and unmute participant phone lines, eject participants, and lock the meeting.

As an alternative to audio conferencing, Internet Audio Broadcast in the Professional Edition enables presenters to stream audio over the Internet. This allows participants to listen to the broadcast using their computer speakers.

Test Drive Live Meeting

A great way to learn Live Meeting and see if it works for you is to download a free limited time trial version. From your user Web page, begin a meeting and invite some associates to see one of your PowerPoint presentations, or share another Office document.

You can download Live Meeting from www.office.microsoft.com in two versions, the Standard Edition and Professional Edition. The main difference is that the Professional version includes application and desktop sharing features, along with remote assistance and control. This makes it more appropriate for human resources and training applications. The Professional version also includes the option to create an Internet Audio Broadcast. There are also some features in the Professional version that enhance registration, invitation, and branding procedures, and include personal Address Books.

The current version of Live Meeting is 2005. Live Meeting has various pricing and licensing plans, with different licensing options to choose from. These options depend on the number of online meetings you expect to conduct, as well as the number of participants who you anticipate.

Start a Live Meeting Conference

When you register an account with Live Meeting, you receive a username, a password, and a URL or Web location to log in to your meetings in an e-mail message. You can open your Web browser to your Live Meeting home page by logging in with your username and password. From your Live Meeting My Home page, you can schedule meetings, join a meeting, or choose to Meet Now. You can initiate a new meeting to share a PowerPoint presentation, discuss a project using shared documents, or poll participants on their opinions on various matters.

When you first sign up for Live Meeting, there is a meeting already available for you to participate. This can give you a quick overview of the features of the conferencing program.

When you schedule a new meeting in the future, you can invite participants and then open the meeting at the scheduled time. When you choose to Meet Now, you can invite your participants directly from within the Live Meeting interface. Your attendees receive an e-mail that provides them with the meeting location (online Web address), a Meeting Key, and their role in the meeting.

Even if you are not the original presenter in a Live Meeting conference, you can be granted control and the ability to share an application.

When you enter a Live Meeting, you can see the names of the presenter and any attendees who have joined the meeting. You can also use the Audio menu to set up or distribute information about the conference-call audio portion of the event.

Start a Live Meeting Conference

① Log on to Live Meeting.

Live Meeting opens in your Web browser.

Note: *You may be prompted to allow Live Meeting to install software or controls. Answer yes to any such prompts.*

- You can click this link to view an instructional demonstration meeting.

② Click Meet Now.

- Live Meeting tells you whether audio information is available.

③ Click OK.

The Live Meeting window opens.

④ Click Send E-mail Invite.

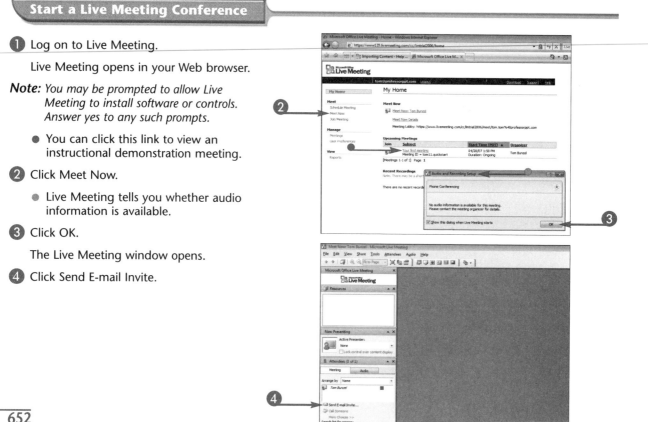

The Send Email Invite dialog box opens.

5 Type the attendees' e-mail addresses, each separated by a semicolon.

6 Type the presenters' e-mail addresses, separated by a semicolon.

7 Type a message about the meeting.

8 Click Send Message.

 • Live Meeting confirms that it has sent invitations.

9 Click OK to close the prompt.

E-mail recipients receive a meeting invitation.

Join the meeting

1 Your participants should review the user information in their e-mail message.

2 Your participants can click this link to join the meeting.

Participants are prompted to download software. Live Meeting loads, and participants can join the meeting to which they were invited.

Can I invite participants from a meeting that is already in progress?

 ▼ Yes. In the Live Meeting program, you can always click the Attendees section and reopen the Send E-mail Invite dialog box.

How do I use my Outlook contact to send invitations?

 ▼ You need to load the Live Meeting add-in for Outlook. This is included in the Live Meeting 2005 Add-in Pack, which includes add-ins for other Office programs. After downloading and installing the Add-in pack, you can use the Live Meeting toolbar in Outlook to identify individual meeting participants as attendees or presenters. You can then send separate invitations for attendees and for presenters. The Add-in pack is available at www.microsoft.com/downloads/details.aspx?FamilyId=D198481 0-117A-45FF-BFEC-2756C6111097& displaylang=en.

PART VII

Present PowerPoint in Live Meeting

Running a PowerPoint slide show in Live Meeting is a great way to include important information and visuals. Because you are not physically present in a meeting room when you use Live Meeting, using resources like PowerPoint gives your attendees something to view as they participate and can enhance their comprehension of your intended message.

The left side of the Live Meeting window shows any resources that are currently available. These resources may include a PowerPoint slide show, a document for review, a Whiteboard, a poll, or a snapshot. You can have a PowerPoint slide show already open when the meeting begins, or load it into the Resources panel at any time.

The Share menu lets you determine which applications or files you want to show to other participants in the Live Meeting window by sharing your desktop or main view.

When you enable sharing for the PowerPoint file, unless it is already displaying full screen, you can see it in the PowerPoint Editor with the Live Meeting window minimized into a toolbar on the left side of the screen. This screen setup allows you to make changes in a presentation that you are working on with your colleagues. Alternatively, you can actually present from within Live Meeting by showing the PowerPoint file in full screen, and using the annotation tools and hyperlink capabilities of PowerPoint in your Live Meeting conference. For more information about using PowerPoint as an editor and in full screen, see the task "Preview a Slide Show" in Chapter 18.

Present PowerPoint in Live Meeting

The presenter appears in the Meeting tab of Live Meeting.

Note: For more information on beginning a meeting, see the task "Start a Live Meeting Conference."

① Click Share.

② Click Share Document to Edit.

You can also select Share Document to View or Share Application.

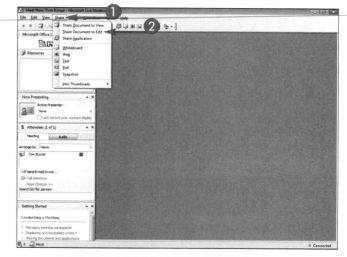

The Open dialog box appears.

③ Scroll to locate the PowerPoint file you want.

④ Click to select the presentation.

⑤ Click Open.

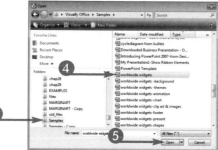

The presentation opens in PowerPoint.

- The Live Meeting window is minimized.

Live Meeting participants can now see what is in your main window.

6 Click the Slide Show button () to start the presentation.

- To return to Live Meeting, you can click the End Application Sharing and Return to Console arrow (⬅).

Your presentation displays in full screen to all attendees in the Live Meeting window. You can narrate the presentation through the audio portion of the conference.

7 Press Esc.

You return to PowerPoint in Live Meeting.

To end PowerPoint sharing and return to the Live Meeting window, you can click the End Application Sharing and Return to Console arrow (⬅).

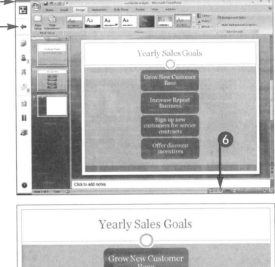

Can I show the shared application in the window in full screen?

▼ Yes. You can click the Full Screen button (🔲) to show the entire application on your monitor. You will no longer see the Resources panel on the left side of the screen. Press Esc to return to the menu and toolbar view.

Can I print the contents of the window?

▼ Yes. You can click File and choose to print the contents in PDF format. You can also click the Snapshot Frame button (🔲) to take a snapshot of the window. Resize the frame over the portion of the screen that you want to capture, right-click the frame, and choose Take Snapshot. A picture of the screen is saved as an image and is placed into the Live Meeting Resources panel.

Can I save the resources used in the conference?

▼ Yes. You can click Tools and select Manage Resources. The Manage Meeting Resources window opens. Click the resource you want to save to select it and click the Save button (🔲) to save it. Any resource that has been used in the session, including Whiteboard annotations can be saved as a file.

Poll in Live Meeting

Live Meeting can replace a real-time conference in a physical location because of its interactive features. These include the Whiteboard, chat, and questions and answers over the conference line. You can also poll the audience. Polls are particularly useful when evaluating the success of a meeting as it is going on and making adjustments, as well as connecting with your participants. Because you cannot see your audience, using a poll to get feedback and learn about your audience's reactions is a great way to make a Live Meeting conference more like a face-to-face meeting.

The presenter can create polling questions before the session, or even during a Live Meeting conference. When the polling questions display, participants can choose from multiple-choice responses, and the results can appear in real time. Alternatively, the results can be hidden by the presenter until later in the presentation, and then revealed. You can have up to seven possible responses to a polling slide or panel. You can easily alternate between showing a polling slide, returning to a PowerPoint slide show, or sharing any other resources with your audience.

Poll in Live Meeting

The presenter appears in the Meeting tab of Live Meeting.

Note: *For more information on beginning a meeting, see the task "Start a Live Meeting Conference."*

① Click Share.

② Click Poll.

The Create Poll Slide dialog box opens.

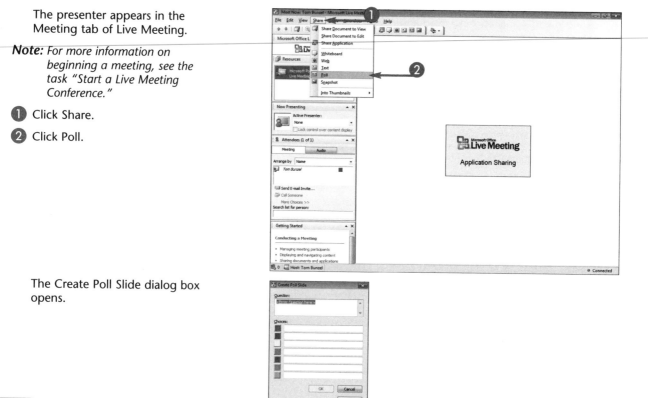

③ Type a question for attendees.

④ Type multiple-choice responses.

⑤ Click OK.

The poll is presented to attendees.

You can see results instantly as attendees vote.

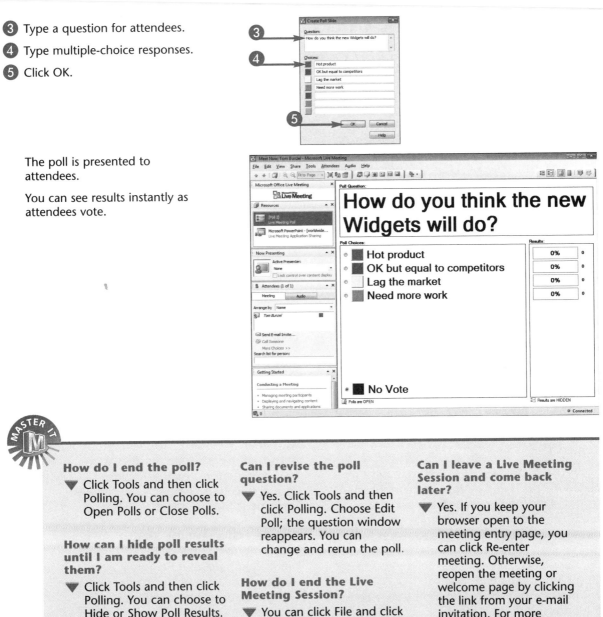

How do I end the poll?

▼ Click Tools and then click Polling. You can choose to Open Polls or Close Polls.

How can I hide poll results until I am ready to reveal them?

▼ Click Tools and then click Polling. You can choose to Hide or Show Poll Results.

Can I revise the poll question?

▼ Yes. Click Tools and then click Polling. Choose Edit Poll; the question window reappears. You can change and rerun the poll.

How do I end the Live Meeting Session?

▼ You can click File and click either Exit or Exit and End Session. If you click Exit the meeting continues for the other invited participants. If you Exit and End Session, the meeting itself is closed down.

Can I leave a Live Meeting Session and come back later?

▼ Yes. If you keep your browser open to the meeting entry page, you can click Re-enter meeting. Otherwise, reopen the meeting or welcome page by clicking the link from your e-mail invitation. For more information on beginning a meeting, see the task "Start a Live Meeting Conference."

PART VII

An Introduction to SharePoint Workspaces

Because the Web provides virtual real estate, SharePoint workspaces provide you with a central location, accessible by Web browser, where you can work and collaborate with others. A component of Windows Server 2003, Windows SharePoint Services allows you to share documents, manage discussion threads and calendars, run a blog or wiki, assign and supervise tasks, make announcements, and interact with other team members in your business or organization.

Using SharePoint Workspaces

You can use either the templates already available on SharePoint services to create Web pages for a group to read and review, or share your actual Office documents. A SharePoint site can serve a small or large group, or you can create subgroups within the site, each with different functions and responsibilities. You can assign new users to groups and also determine their permissions to view or actually edit SharePoint documents.

With SharePoint, you can create a single place to share and manage all of your team information, such as calendars, tasks, and lists. You can also better manage your document creation, review document versions, and check in and check out documents.

You can use templates, Web Parts, (small applications that work in your Web browser; for example, a customized expense report), views, and custom lists to easily customize your workspaces. You can also keep teams up to date by using alerts, discussion boards, surveys, and announcements. You can keep teams connected through integration with Microsoft Live Communications Server, Microsoft Live Meeting, and Microsoft Office Outlook.

Connect to a SharePoint Site

You can access your team workspace directly from any Web browser and from other Office programs, such as Word. When you connect to a SharePoint site through your Web browser, you must first log in. Then you can navigate through the site as you would any other Web site. If you have permission, you can use the templates to add pages to the site, or upload files to the various pages and libraries.

You can assign tasks or let others know the status of projects, participate in a group calendar or team discussions, and take advantage of resources that other team members have put on the site.

As a team member with permission, you can also connect to a SharePoint site through an Office program. If you click the Publish option in the Office button, for example, you can create or access a Document Workspace directly through the program. A task pane opens on the right side of the document window in your Office application. This task pane allows you to interact with your workspace. You can check out documents, participate in discussions, manage tasks and perform team functions directly within your application task pane by using the Document Management features.

Create a SharePoint Site

You can build a SharePoint workspace or Web site using SharePoint Designer 2007, which has replaced Microsoft Front Page as a Web-site creation and maintenance tool.

You can also add components to a SharePoint site using the Web tools and browser. You can create document libraries, conference areas, client or associate contact lists, and many other resources directly in the Web site. These resources can then be accessed and used by users who have permission to enter the SharePoint site.

You can also use the Publish options within the Office button of your Office applications to send documents to a shared workspace. If you have permission and access, you can download files from a SharePoint site.

When you create a SharePoint site, you can begin to populate it with various templates. In addition, you can continue to create a library, list, or Web page and refine these elements to help you to develop the SharePoint site. You can also administer the site directly through the Web browser.

The Site Home Page
The Site Home page is your starting point for adding announcements or events that can be viewed and participated in by users with access to the site. The left panel of the Home Page allows you to access the shared documents area of the site, and lists of events and tasks, including a site calendar. It also allows you to access discussion areas or forums where members can manage projects and collaborate on team activities.

Depending upon the purpose of your SharePoint site, you can add links to your home page to the SharePoint site. You can also link to other important parts of the Internet, such as your company intranet or to other pages in the SharePoint site itself.

Set Up Groups
As an administrator, you can set up user groups with various roles and permissions, including visitor, members, and owners.

On the site home page, you can click the Site Actions menu, click Site Settings, and then click People and Groups. To see all of the users who have been added directly to the site or inherited from the parent site, click All People.

The People and Groups: All Groups page displays your current groups and allows you to add and manage more.

To view all of the SharePoint groups that are available on the site, click Groups. Depending upon permissions, a user may be able to add other users and groups to the site. In the People and Groups area, you can invite new members to the site and grant them permissions to either view or check out and edit documents. You can also create groups of users who can have their own area of the site with a calendar, discussion area, and lists and libraries.

A SharePoint site can be a subsite of a "parent" site; for example, the head office might set up a main site. The head office IT department would provide administrators the information required to set up sites for branch offices. In some cases, the branch office site can inherit some groups from the parent site, or the branch office can just set up its own groups.

Portal Sites
SharePoint sites are scalable; that is, they can work for a small organization or be used by large enterprises to disseminate news and information across many offices in many continents.

Logging in to a portal site might be the first thing any worker does. She might see industry news from the main site while also seeing shared documents from her local site. Tasks might be shown in part of the home page along with calendar listings and a tracker of where colleagues might be at any given time.

A large portal site might also support a blog, wiki, or RSS subscriptions that keep workers updated with the latest information. For more on RSS, see the task "Using RSS Feeds in Outlook" in Chapter 26. You could set up an RSS feed that lets users know in Outlook when a particular type of information is available. They can read an introduction in Outlook and then click a link to take them to the page in the local SharePoint site or the main office portal.

Using Files in SharePoint

Y ou can work with files in SharePoint by uploading them to the SharePoint site. You can then allow other users with permission to download them and then return them to the site.

You can create a document workspace, either from the SharePoint site or within your Office 2007 applications. For example, you can use the Publish option under the Office button to create a document workspace from within Word, Excel, or PowerPoint. The first time you create a document workspace, you need to know the Web connection or location of the Web site, and have your username and password available.

The document workspace is available within a task pane in the Office application. From the document workspace, you can check its status, add new members to the workspace, add or manage tasks, access the documents, or add or manage links from the workspace.

If you prefer, you can also manage your documents and upload and check out documents directly from the SharePoint site through your Web browser. You can create a workspace in the site using your Web browser so that you can manage the documents or files, assign and manage tasks, and add announcements for your team.

Using a document workspace

1. Click the Office button in Word, Excel, or PowerPoint.

2. Click Publish.

3. Click Create Document Workspace.

   - The Document Management task pane opens.

4. Type a workspace name.

5. Type the URL or location.

6. Click Create.

   - The connection dialog box opens.

7. Type your username.

8. Type your password.

9. Click OK.

   - Your SharePoint site opens in the Document Management task pane.

   - You can also click to open the site in the Web browser.

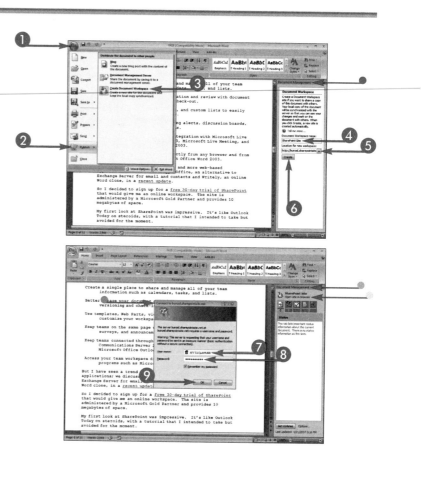

10 Click the Documents button in the workspace task pane.

- You can display or access documents in your workspace.

Upload to the SharePoint site

1 Click Shared Documents.

- The Shared Documents window opens.

2 Click the Upload down arrow (▾).

3 Click Upload Document.

An Explorer window opens so that you can select the document to upload.

4 You can upload one or multiple documents to the SharePoint Shared Documents area.

- Your uploaded document appears in the Shared Documents window.

I could not connect to the document workspace. What should I do?

▼ Make sure that you can access the site through Internet Explorer. Click Tools and then click Internet Options. In the Internet Options dialog box that opens, click the Security tab. Click a security zone — Local intranet, Trusted sites, or Restricted sites. Then click Sites. The Web site should appear in the Add this Web site to the zone field. Click Add. If the site is not a secure site, which would be indicated by HTTPS:, clear the Require server verification (HTTPS:) for all sites in this zone check box (☑ changes to ☐). Click Close.

When should I use the document workspace and when should I upload files?

▼ It depends upon the purpose of the site and how it is configured. You can design your own workflow or work with your IT department or network administrator to determine the best strategy.

If I upload my document into SharePoint, is it automatically in a workspace?

▼ No. You need to click the document in the Shared Documents window and click Actions to choose to create a workspace for the document. The uploaded document will then be in a workspace that includes Shared Documents, Tasks, and Announcements.

Using a PowerPoint Slide Library

Office SharePoint Server 2007 provides specialized libraries for storing individual PowerPoint slides. These PowerPoint Slide Libraries enable users to easily repurpose existing content and build presentations from existing slide sets, reducing the need to recreate content.

Users can publish presentations to a PowerPoint Slide Library directly from Office PowerPoint 2007. For presentations that include slides from PowerPoint slide libraries, Office PowerPoint 2007 checks to see whether those slides have changed, notifies the user if they have, and replaces them with the updated version.

For example, an art department in your company may have created a set of branded templates for use in accounting, finance, sales, and other branches of the company. By making these templates available in the slide library, PowerPoint users can use these for a new presentation, and maintain a consistent look. For more information, see the task "Using a Design Template" in Chapter 16.

A proficient PowerPoint user may create a set of diagrams with custom animation to describe processes within the company. By publishing these slides to the SharePoint slide library, other users through the company can reuse these slides with their timings in their own presentations. For more information, see the task "Using Custom Animation" in Chapter 17.

Using a PowerPoint Slide Library

Publish to the SharePoint slide library

1. Open the PowerPoint file with the slides you want to publish.

2. Click the Office button.

3. Click Publish.

4. Click Publish Slides.

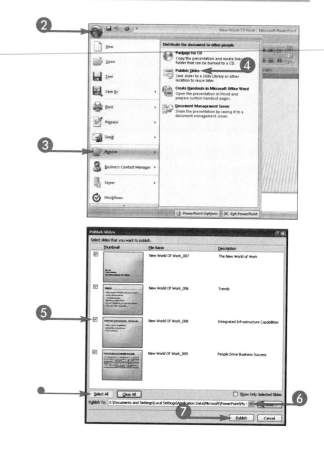

The Publish Slides dialog box opens.

5. Click to select individual slides (☐ changes to ☑).

- You can also click Select All to choose all slides.

6. Click the drop-down arrow (⊡) here and select the slide library.

7. Click Publish.

The slides are published to your SharePoint slide library.

Access the SharePoint slide library

1 Open an existing presentation or create a new presentation.

Note: See Chapter 15 for more information about creating a presentation in PowerPoint.

2 Click the Home tab.

3 Click New Slide.

The Office Theme menu opens.

4 Click Reuse Slides.

● The Reuse Slides task pane opens.

5 Click Open a Slide Library.

● The slide library appears, enabling you to add slides from the library.

● You can keep the original slide format by clicking the Keep source formatting option (☐ changes to ✓).

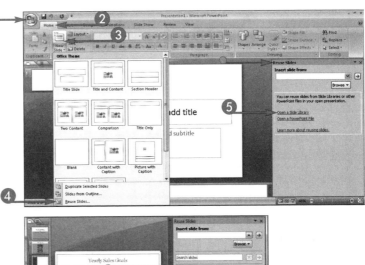

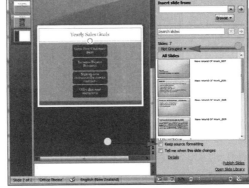

When I upload a PowerPoint file to the SharePoint site, I just see an icon for the file, not thumbnails. What am I doing wrong?

▼ To make the slide library available, you may need to enable it under the Site Features on the home page. Click the Actions down arrow (▼), click Site Settings, and then click Site Features. After clicking Site Features, the Site Features window opens. Make sure that Slide Library is activated. Then return to the home page, click the Actions down arrow (▼), and choose Create. You should now have Slide Libraries as an item to be created under the Libraries column. Select Slide Libraries and click Create.

Can I use the library for templates?

▼ Yes. A good use of the library is to distribute templates for consistency. When you insert the slide from the library, enable the Keep source formatting option (☐ changes to ✓). This adds the master and design for the slide to the existing presentation. You can then apply this design to other slides in the presentation. For more information on how to format a presentation, see Chapter 16.

How can I reuse SmartArt or charts from the slide library?

▼ When you insert a SmartArt diagram or chart, you can revise the text for the diagram or change the data for the chart to serve your own purposes. For more information on SmartArt diagrams and charts, see Chapter 17.

PART VII

663

Using a Team Discussion

Another way that a SharePoint site can facilitate interaction among team members or co-workers is the Team Discussion feature. Discussions are *threads* of messages posted by team members to which others reply. The easiest way to use a discussion is to post a message about an item and then send e-mail alerts to team members who are accountable for that item so that they can respond to the message created in the discussion area. For example, you can post a message about the status of a project and have team members from offices around the world respond to the message.

You can also take various actions with respect to discussion items. For example, you can connect to Outlook to synchronize and make them available offline, export them to a spreadsheet, open them with Access to maintain them in a database, syndicate items so that an RSS aggregator can subscribe to them, or receive e-mail notifications when items change or responses are posted.

When you post a new discussion item or respond to a posted item, you type your text into a window similar to a word processor. However, the toolbar gives you the opportunity to add elements that can display in a Web browser. Besides text, your item can include hyperlinks, pictures, and HTML, along with various formatting features such as bold, underline, and font elements. You can also attach a file to your discussion item.

Using a Team Discussion

① From the SharePoint home page, click Team Discussion.

Note: Your administrator will provide you with user ID and password to access the site home page.

The Team Discussion page opens.

● Active discussions are listed by subject.

② Click the down arrow (▼) for an item to see the options.

③ Click View Item.

● The discussion item opens for your review.

④ Click Reply.

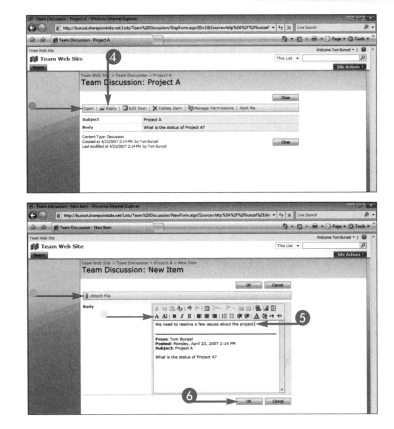

The reply pane opens with a text editing toolbar.

⑤ Type your response to the item.

● You can attach a file to the response.

● You can use the toolbar to format the response.

⑥ Click OK.

Your response is added to the discussion item and is visible to appropriate team members.

Can I change the view of the discussion area?

▼ Yes. To change the way the discussions are listed, click the View down arrow (▾) at the far right of the Team Discussion page and choose Modify. A Modify Discussion Page window opens, allowing you to activate other columns by which to sort and view your discussion area. From this window, you can also click the Settings down arrow (▾) to add columns and different views, as well as change how the list of discussion items displays.

Can I make someone accountable for a discussion item?

▼ Yes. You can link the discussion item to a task, and use a task in the Lists portion of the site to assign the task with a start time and due date.

How can I find a discussion item that may have been posted somewhere else on the site?

▼ You can use the search panel in the SharePoint site to locate an item by key words or phrases.

PART VII

An Introduction to Groove Workspaces

Groove is another tool that Microsoft has added to Microsoft Office that lets you collaborate with other team members. While there is a Groove Server available, the basic premise of Groove is that you establish a workspace online and invite others to participate. The number of members depends upon the number of licenses you purchase. You can invite other members to your workspace by e-mail, using Outlook or any e-mail client.

Collaborate in Groove Workspace

The key to Groove, in contrast to SharePoint, is the availability of other users directly in the workspace. You can see who is available online, and who is currently offline, which allows users to communicate instantly. You can also set alerts to let you know when someone has logged in to the workspace, so that Groove is not just a Web location, but rather an active area where you can communicate as though you were in the same room. In the workspace you can see exactly who is working on what project, even if they are doing it across the globe.

For example, if you see that a colleague has logged in to the workspace and is online, you can get immediate feedback on a document by uploading the file. You can use the chat and messaging capability of Groove to communicate directly with anyone in the workspace. When your colleague has made changes to the file, you can open it from the Groove workspace, review the changes, and continue a discussion about the changes using chat.

When you have reviewed your colleague's suggested changes to the document, you can chat about the document changes or the project as a whole. You can set up meetings and invite others to the workspace, or add items relating to the document or project to the workspace calendar.

Even when you are not connected to a network, you can continue working in the Groove workspace. When a network connection is reestablished, the files you revised and all of your other work, such as comments in discussion areas, is automatically synchronized with other workspace members.

The Groove Workspace

The Groove workspace consists of an optional Launch bar and expanded window. The window includes a calendar that floats above your desktop.

Share Documents

The key element of Groove is that it can be used as a centralized repository of documents that team members share. You can manage the files in the workspace through an interface that is similar to Windows Explorer. The files you are working on are loaded into Groove and are visible to anyone with permission to use them. You can also run Groove as a full-screen application, where the Launch bar and main window combine.

Discussion Area

Like SharePoint's Discussion area, Groove has a discussion feature that allows members to post topics to which other members can respond. You can attach files to a discussion item and filter and sort discussion topics by category. A discussion thread is a record of various peoples' input that you can save and refer to to remind everyone of their respective contributions to a project or concept.

The Groove workspace has a number of additional features, including alerts in real time to users who are logged on and through e-mail, a sketchpad where members can brainstorm, forms tools to track issues, and connections to SharePoint sites.

Conduct Meetings

You can conduct a meeting in real time within the Groove workspace. You can post an agenda, invite attendees, share files, assign actions, and generate minutes for others to refer to after the meeting is complete.

In the Meetings tab of the workspace, you can set up meetings which other users can attend. You can invite others to the meeting, set an agenda, generate minutes, and distribute action items, all from within Groove. All of those with access to the workspace can see the meeting on the calendar and participate.

Groove stores workspaces and the data they contain right on your computer, not on a central server. You can access and update the information in your workspaces whether or not you are connected to the network. Each time you alter a document — for example, if you update a file, respond to a discussion, or post some text in the chat area — Groove automatically sends your changes (and only the changes) to all of the members of your workspace. If you are offline when you make the changes, Groove sends them the next time that you connect. If your team members are not connected, then they receive the changes when they connect.

Keep Up-to-Date Document Versions

Because Groove synchronization operates constantly in the background, it is best to run Groove while your computer is connected to your corporate network or the Internet, or to connect as often as possible. This helps to ensure that you have the most current versions, and that your team members are also up to date. Just as you keep your e-mail up and running all day to monitor incoming messages, you should keep Groove open to monitor workspace activity.

Manage Roles and Permissions

In the Properties window of the workspace, the Manager can manage the roles of other users. Any user can be set up as a Manager, Participant, or a Guest.

A Manager generally has all permissions. She can invite or uninvite other users, add tools to the workspace, delete a tool from the workspace, and cancel all outstanding invitations.

A Participant may have all or none of these permissions depending upon which items are allowed by the Manager.

A Guest generally has the fewest permissions, but the guest role allows the participation of users for temporary periods. For example, a guest can be invited to participate in one meeting or to contribute ideas on a particular project or file. When the guest has completed his association with the workspace, he can be uninvited, which frees up a user license that can be granted to another guest.

Explore Vista Meeting Space

Meeting Space is a feature of some versions of the Windows Vista operating system that lets you conduct quick ad hoc meetings with anyone connected to your network. For example, if you are in a wireless zone, you can quickly make the meeting visible to anyone who is in the zone or connected to your local area network, or LAN. You can also invite specific individuals to participate as long as they have Windows Vista.

In many ways, Meeting Space is a "lite" version of Live Meeting. You can invite participants, share a desktop or an application, present and view PowerPoint presentations, and distribute handouts to users who are logged on to a wireless network or LAN.

The easiest way to share a PowerPoint slide show is to open it prior to joining the meeting. You can then click to share an application, and choose PowerPoint from the options window.

In most cases, you will be in the same location as other participants, and so you should not need an audio conference line to narrate your presentation. Meeting Space is not meant for international conferences, but rather for less formal situations where file sharing and collaboration would enhance communication.

Meeting Space is part of a Microsoft initiative called "People Near Me" for peer-to-peer networking, which will likely find its way into many Office-related and other applications.

Explore Vista Meeting Space

① Click Start, All Programs, and then Windows Meeting Space.

Note: *The first time you use Windows Meeting Space, a Setup box appears. After you click Yes to continue setting up Windows Meeting Space, a People Near Me dialog box appears, showing others who are connected to your network. After you click OK, the Windows Meeting Space opens.*

● The Windows Meeting Space window opens.

● You can click here to join an ongoing meeting. Meeting Space prompts you for your password.

● Other meetings on the network are shown here.

② Click Start a New Meeting.

The Start a New Meeting pane appears.

③ Type a name for the meeting.

④ Type a password.

⑤ Click the arrow (⊙) to start the meeting.

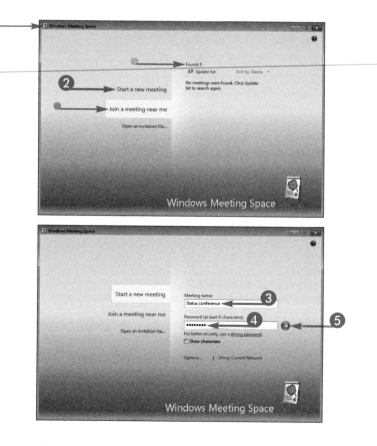

The meeting pane opens.

○ You can invite other people who are connected to the network.

● You can create handouts.

● You can see who else is attending the meeting.

⑥ Click here to share an open application such as a PowerPoint slide show.

○ Your PowerPoint slide show opens in the Meeting Space window.

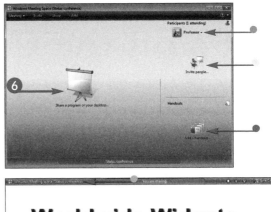

Worldwide Widgets

Internationally Acclaimed Widgetry

How do I make the meeting visible or invisible?

▼ When you begin the meeting and choose your password, click Options. Under Options, you can determine whether the meeting is fully visible or whether participants need a password to attend.

How do I create handouts?

▼ Click the Handouts link in the meeting to upload a document as a handout. From the meeting menu, click Add and an Explorer window opens. Select the files you want and click Open. All of the handouts are copied to each participant's computer. One participant at a time can make changes, which are reflected on each participant's copy, but the original handout remains unchanged.

How do I invite others?

▼ There are three ways to invite someone. First, you can send an e-mail invitation as covered in these steps. Second, you can select names in the Invite people dialog box. To open the Invite people dialog box, in a meeting click Invite People, and the dialog box opens. In it, select the check box beside the name of each person you want to invite (☑ changes to ☐), and then click Send invitations. Third, you can create an invitation file. In the Invite people dialog box, click Invite others, click Create an invitation file, and save the file. Distribute the file by e-mail or by providing it on removable media, such as a flash drive.

How do I share my desktop?

▼ Click Share from the Meeting menu. This displays a list of programs that are currently running. When you select a program, it opens full screen (or in a window that you resize) on the desktop and is visible to everyone in the meeting.

Appendix:
What's on the CD-ROM

This appendix provides you with information on the contents of the CD-ROM that accompanies this book. For the latest and greatest information, please refer to the ReadMe file located at the root of the CD-ROM. Here is what you will find:

- System Requirements
- Using the CD ROM
- What's on the CD-ROM
- Troubleshooting

System Requirements

To use this CD-ROM and the related programs, you need at least the basic version of the Microsoft Office 2007 suite. These are the hardware and software requirements for using the suite and the programs on the CD-ROM:

- **Computer and processor:** 500 megahertz (MHz) processor or higher
- **Memory:** 256 megabytes (MB) of RAM or higher
- **Hard drive:** 1.5 gigabytes (GB); a portion of this disk space will be freed after installation if the original download package is removed from the hard drive.
- **Drive:** CD or DVD drive
- **Display:** 1024×768 or higher resolution monitor
- **Operating System:** Microsoft Windows Vista; Microsoft Windows XP with Service Pack (SP) 2, Windows Server 2003 with SP1; or later operating system.

Using the CD-ROM

To install the items from the CD-ROM to your hard drive, follow these steps:

1. Insert the CD-ROM into your computer's CD drive. The license agreement appears.

   Note to Windows users: The interface does not launch if you have autorun disabled. In that case, for Windows XP, click Start and then click Run. For Windows Vista, click Start, click All Programs, click Accessories, and then click Run. In the dialog box that appears, type **D:\Start.exe**. Replace D with the proper letter if your CD drive uses a different letter. If you do not know the letter, see how your CD drive is listed under My Computer in Windows XP, or Computer in Windows Vista. Click OK.

2. Read through the license agreement and then click the Accept button if you want to use the CD-ROM.

   The CD-ROM interface appears. The interface allows you to install the programs and run the demos with just one or two mouse clicks.

What's on the CD-ROM

The following sections provide a summary of the software and other materials that you will find on the CD-ROM.

Author-created materials

All author-created materials from the book, including code listings and samples, are on the CD-ROM in the folder named Samples.

These sample files are in the file format of the applications that created them and are named for the tasks or features that they were used to create.

Applications

The following applications are on the CD-ROM:

Anagram

Enables you to copy blocks of text, including e-mail or schedules. Automatically opens the appropriate part of Outlook and pastes the data into the appropriate area, either as contact information or as an appointment. See www.getanagram.com for more information.

MeetingSense

An add-in for Outlook that provides organization and accountability for all types of meetings by using the Outlook data in a more efficient interface. See www.yonsoftware.com for more information.

PFC (Plays for Certain)

A video conversion program that ensures that your video plays in PowerPoint. See www.playsforcertain.com/index.htm for more information.

PowerFrameworks

Visual metaphors and diagrams that enhance the impact of PowerPoint slides. See www.powerframeworks.com for more information.

TechSmith Camtasia and SnagIT

Excellent screen capture utilities for training and for turning PowerPoint presentations into video. See www.techsmith.com for more information.

continued

Appendix: What's on the CD-ROM *(Continued)*

Xcelsius CX Now

A free version of the award-winning dashboard program that turns Excel data into Interactive Flash files for PowerPoint or Web pages. See www.businessobjects.com/jump/cxnow for more information.

Shareware programs are fully functional, trial versions of copyrighted programs. If you like particular programs, register with their authors for a nominal fee and receive licenses, enhanced versions, and technical support.

Freeware programs are copyrighted games, applications, and utilities that are free for personal use. Unlike shareware, these programs do not require a fee or provide technical support.

GNU software is governed by its own license, which is included inside the folder of the GNU product. See the GNU license for more details.

Trial, demo, or evaluation versions are usually limited either by time or functionality (such as being unable to save projects). Some trial versions are very sensitive to system date changes. If you alter your computer's date, the programs "time out" and are no longer functional.

Troubleshooting

If you have difficulty installing or using any of the materials on the companion CD-ROM, try the following solutions:

- **Turn off any anti-virus software that you may have running.** Installers sometimes mimic virus activity and can make your computer incorrectly believe that it is being infected by a virus. (Be sure to turn the anti-virus software back on later.)

- **Close all running programs.** The more programs you are running, the less memory is available to other programs. Installers also typically update files and programs; if you keep other programs running, installation may not work properly.

- **Reference the ReadMe file.** Please refer to the ReadMe file located at the root of the CD-ROM for the latest product information at the time of publication.

Customer Care

If you have trouble with the CD-ROM, please call the Wiley Product Technical Support phone number at (800) 762-2974. Outside the United States, call 1(317) 572-3994. You can also contact Wiley Product Technical Support at http://support.wiley.com. John Wiley & Sons will provide technical support only for installation and other general quality control items. For technical support on the applications themselves, consult the program's vendor or author.

To place additional orders or to request information about other Wiley products, please call (877) 762-2974.

Wiley Publishing, Inc. End-User License Agreement

READ THIS. You should carefully read these terms and conditions before opening the software packet(s) included with *Master VISUALLY Microsoft Office 2007* ("Book"). This is a license agreement ("Agreement") between you and Wiley Publishing, Inc. ("WPI"). By opening the accompanying software packet(s), you acknowledge that you have read and accept the following terms and conditions. If you do not agree and do not want to be bound by such terms and conditions, promptly return the Book and the unopened software packet(s) to the place you obtained them from for a full refund.

1. **License Grant.** WPI grants to you (either an individual or entity) a nonexclusive license to use one copy of the enclosed software program(s) (collectively, the "Software") solely for your own personal or business purposes on a single computer (whether a standard computer or a workstation component of a multi-user network). The Software is in use on a computer when it is loaded into temporary memory (RAM) or installed into permanent memory (hard disc, CD-ROM, or other storage device). WPI reserves all rights not expressly granted herein.

2. **Ownership.** WPI is the owner of all right, title, and interest, including copyright, in and to the compilation of the Software recorded on the disc(s) or CD-ROM ("Software Media"). Copyright to the individual programs recorded on the Software Media is owned by the author, or other authorized copyright owner of each program. Ownership of the Software and all proprietary rights relating thereto remain with WPI and its licensers.

3. **Restrictions on Use and Transfer.**

   (a) You may only (i) make one copy of the Software for backup or archival purposes, or (ii) transfer the Software to a single hard disc, provided that you keep the original for backup or archival purposes. You may not (i) rent or lease the Software, (ii) copy or reproduce the Software through a LAN or other network system or through any computer subscriber system or bulletin-board system, or (iii) modify, adapt, or create derivative works based on the Software.

   (b) You may not reverse engineer, decompile, or disassemble the Software. You may transfer the Software and user documentation on a permanent basis, provided that the transferee agrees to accept the terms and conditions of this Agreement and you retain no copies. If the Software is an update or has been updated, any transfer must include the most recent update and all prior versions.

4. **Restrictions on Use of Individual Programs.** You must follow the individual requirements and restrictions detailed for each individual program in the appendix of this Book. These limitations are also contained in the individual license agreements recorded on the Software Media. These limitations may include a requirement that after using the program for a specified period of time, the user must pay a registration fee or discontinue use. By opening the Software packet(s), you will be agreeing to abide by the licenses and restrictions for these individual programs that are detailed in the appendix and on the Software Media. None of the material on this Software Media or listed in this Book may ever be redistributed, in original or modified form, for commercial purposes.

5. **Limited Warranty.**

   (a) WPI warrants that the Software and Software Media are free from defects in materials and workmanship under normal use for a period of sixty (60) days from the date of purchase of this Book. If WPI receives notification within the warranty period of defects in materials or workmanship, WPI will replace the defective Software Media.

(b) WPI AND THE AUTHOR OF THE BOOK DISCLAIM ALL OTHER WARRANTIES, EXPRESS OR IMPLIED, INCLUDING WITHOUT LIMITATION IMPLIED WARRANTIES OF MERCHANTABILITY AND FITNESS FOR A PARTICULAR PURPOSE, WITH RESPECT TO THE SOFTWARE, THE PROGRAMS, THE SOURCE CODE CONTAINED THEREIN, AND/OR THE TECHNIQUES DESCRIBED IN THIS BOOK. WPI DOES NOT WARRANT THAT THE FUNCTIONS CONTAINED IN THE SOFTWARE WILL MEET YOUR REQUIREMENTS OR THAT THE OPERATION OF THE SOFTWARE WILL BE ERROR FREE.

(c) This limited warranty gives you specific legal rights, and you may have other rights that vary from jurisdiction to jurisdiction.

6. **Remedies.**

   (a) WPI's entire liability and your exclusive remedy for defects in materials and workmanship shall be limited to replacement of the Software Media, which may be returned to WPI with a copy of your receipt at the following address: Software Media Fulfillment Department, Attn.: *Master VISUALLY Microsoft Office 2007*, Wiley Publishing, Inc., 10475 Crosspoint Blvd., Indianapolis, IN 46256, or call 1-800-762-2974. Please allow four to six weeks for delivery. This Limited Warranty is void if failure of the Software Media has resulted from accident, abuse or misapplication. Any replacement Software Media will be warranted for the remainder of the original warranty period or thirty (30) days, whichever is longer.

   (b) In no event shall WPI or the author be liable for any damages whatsoever (including without limitation damages for loss of business profits, business interruption, loss of business information, or any other pecuniary loss) arising from the use of or inability to use the Book or the Software, even if WPI has been advised of the possibility of such damages.

   (c) Because some jurisdictions do not allow the exclusion or limitation of liability for consequential or incidental damages, the above limitation or exclusion may not apply to you.

7. **U.S. Government Restricted Rights.** Use, duplication, or disclosure of the Software for or on behalf of the United States of America, its agencies and/or instrumentalities (the "U.S. Government") is subject to restrictions as stated in paragraph (c)(1)(ii) of the Rights in Technical Data and Computer Software clause of DFARS 252.227-7013, or subparagraphs (c) (1) and (2) of the Commercial Computer Software - Restricted Rights clause at FAR 52.227-19, and in similar clauses in the NASA FAR supplement, as applicable.

8. **General.** This Agreement constitutes the entire understanding of the parties and revokes and supersedes all prior agreements, oral or written, between them and may not be modified or amended except in a writing signed by both parties hereto that specifically refers to this Agreement. This Agreement shall take precedence over any other documents that may be in conflict herewith. If any one or more provisions contained in this Agreement are held by any court or tribunal to be invalid, illegal, or otherwise unenforceable, each and every other provision shall remain in full force and effect.

PART VII

A

absolute reference, 257

Access. *See also* databases
- contextual ribbon, 29, 434
- Database window, 436
- design modes, 556–557
- Navigation Pane, 435
- overview, 426
- starting, 429

accessing SharePoint slide library, 663

Add-Ins tab
- Excel, 189
- PowerPoint, 335
- Word, 39

Address Book, 572–573

aligning
- database form control, 508
- text
  - Excel, 206–207
  - PowerPoint, 353
  - Word, 70–71, 98

All Notebooks window, 642–643

Anagram, 671

animating PowerPoint slides, 390–391

Animations tab, 335

appointments, 564, 602–603

archiving e-mail messages, 588

attachments
- database, 448, 462–463
- e-mail, 574–577, 580–581

audience handouts, 421

auditing Excel formulas, 264–265

author-created materials, 671

AutoComplete, Excel, 235

AutoCorrect, Word, 54–55

AutoFormat, database form, 504–505

AutoNumber, as data type, 448

AutoSum, 252–253

B

back up, OneNote, 644–645

background
- conditional formats and, 512
- database form control and, 510
- PowerPoint presentation, 358–359

bold text
- Excel, 196
- OneNote, 632
- PowerPoint, 352
- Word, 66

borders
- Excel, 208–209
- of table in Word, 128–129

browsing PowerPoint presentation, 398–399

Building Blocks Organizer, 114–117

bullets
- animating, 390
- converting, to SmartArt, 386–387
- for OneNote lists, 635
- PowerPoint
  - formatting, 356–357
  - selecting, 342
- Word, 78–79

C

calculation of database query, 536–537

calendar, 600–601, 604–607

Camtasia, 671

caption, for database field, 476

categories, of contacts, 610–611

CD-ROM, 670–675

cell range, Excel
- naming, 236
- selecting, 238–239
- subtotals in, 248–249

centering Excel data, 206–207

chart shapes, changing, 282–283

INDEX

D

continued

INDEX

BONUS CONTENT INDEX

You can master all kinds of topics visually, including these.

All designed for visual learners—just like you!

Read Less–Learn More®

MASTER VISUALLY *Step Up to Success—Visually*

Macromedia **Dreamweaver 8 and Flash 8**

ISBN-10: 0-471-77618-1
ISBN-13: 978-0-471-77618-5

Microsoft® **Windows Vista**

ISBN-10: 0-470-04577-9
ISBN-13: 978-0-470-04577-0

3ds Max® 8

ISBN-10: 0-7645-7992-4
ISBN-13: 978-0-7645-7992-9

Read Less–Learn More®

Visual™

There's a Visual book for every learning level...

Simplified®

The place to start if you're new to computers. Full color.

- Computers
- Creating Web Pages
- Mac OS
- Office
- Windows

Teach Yourself VISUALLY™

Get beginning to intermediate-level training in a variety of topics. Full color.

- Access
- Bridge
- Chess
- Computers
- Crocheting
- Digital Photography
- Dog training
- Dreamweaver
- Excel
- Flash
- Golf
- Guitar
- Handspinning
- HTML
- Jewelry Making & Beading
- Knitting
- Mac OS
- Office
- Photoshop
- Photoshop Elements
- Piano
- Poker
- PowerPoint
- Quilting
- Scrapbooking
- Sewing
- Windows
- Wireless Networking
- Word

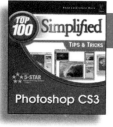

Top 100 Simplified® Tips & Tricks

Tips and techniques to take your skills beyond the basics. Full color.

- Digital Photography
- eBay
- Excel
- Google
- Internet
- Mac OS
- Office
- Photoshop
- Photoshop Elements
- PowerPoint
- Windows

...all designed for visual learners—just like you!

Master VISUALLY

Your complete visual reference. Two-color interior.

- 3ds Max
- Creating Web Pages
- Dreamweaver and Flash
- Excel
- Excel VBA Programming
- iPod and iTunes
- Mac OS
- Office
- Optimizing PC Performance
- Photoshop Elements
- QuickBooks
- Quicken
- Windows
- Windows Mobile
- Windows Server

Visual Blueprint™

Where to go for professional-level programming instruction. Two-color interior.

- Ajax
- ASP.NET 2.0
- Excel Data Analysis
- Excel Pivot Tables
- Excel Programming
- HTML
- JavaScript
- Mambo
- PHP & MySQL
- SEO
- Vista Sidebar
- Visual Basic
- XML

Visual Encyclopedia™

Your A to Z reference of tools and techniques. Full color.

- Dreamweaver
- Excel
- Mac OS
- Photoshop
- Windows

Visual Quick Tips

Shortcuts, tricks, and techniques for getting more done in less time. Full color.

- Crochet
- Digital Photography
- Excel
- iPod & iTunes
- Knitting
- MySpace
- Office
- PowerPoint
- Windows
- Wireless Networking

Visual®
An Imprint of **WILEY**
Now you know.